SIR MAX HASTINGS is the author of twenty-four books, many of them about war. He was educated at Charterhouse and University College, Oxford, which he quit after a year to become a journalist. Thereafter he reported for newspapers and BBC TV from sixty-four countries and eleven conflicts, notably the 1973 Arab-Israeli War, Vietnam and the 1982 Battle for the Falklands. Between 1986 and 2002 he was editor-in-chief of the *Daily Telegraph*, then editor of the *Evening Standard*. He has won many prizes both for journalism and for his books, most recently the 2012 Chicago Pritzker Library's literary award for his contribution to military history, and the RUSI's Westminster Medal for his international best-seller *All Hell Let Loose*. He has two grown-up children, Charlotte and Harry, and lives with his wife Penny in West Berkshire, where they garden enthusiastically.

From the reviews of *Catastrophe*:

'Hastings is a brilliant guide to that strange, febrile twilight before Europe plunged into darkness. Writing in pungent prose suffused with irony and underpinned by a strong sense of moral outrage, *Catastrophe* is a frontal assault on what Hastings calls the "poets' view" of the First World War. Hastings is crisp, and definitive on the balance of guilt ... Scholarly and fluent, relating with equal verve the attitudes and experiences of crowned heads and peasants ... for anyone wanting to understand how that ghastly, much-misunderstood conflict came about, there could be no better place to start than this fine book'   BEN MACINTYRE, *The Times*

'Magisterial'   *Independent on Sunday*, Books of the Year

'Hastings is rightly regarded as Britain's most accomplished military historian ... Hugely entertaining'
                DOMINIC SANDBROOK, *Sunday Times*, Books of the Year

'Does the world need another book on that dismal year? Absolutely, if it's by Hastings ... Readers accustomed to Hastings' vivid battle descriptions, incisive anecdotes from all participants, and shrewd, often unsettling opinions will not be disappointed. Among the plethora of brilliant accounts of this period, this is one of the best'   *Kirkus*

'Authoritative and immensely readable'   *Prospect*

'If you're going to read only one history of World War I, the chances are this is going to be it. Hastings is blistering about the incompetence of the commanders-in-chief on all sides. However it's Hastings' depiction of the cost of the war on the soldiers and their families that really gives *Catastrophe* its power'   JOHN PRESTON, *Daily Mail*, Books of the Year

'This excellent chronicle of World War I's first months dispels some popular myths'   *New York Times*

'Writing with marvelous cogency and trenchancy ... a valuable contribution'   PIERS BRENDON, *Independent*

'Invites consideration as the best in his distinguished career, combining a perceptive analysis of the Great War's beginnings with a vivid account of the period from August to September of the titular year'
                                                      Publishers Weekly

'Admirable in its scope and vividly told'   *Independent on Sunday*

'Truly a masterpiece. What [Hastings] does, in the same absorbing style that we enjoyed in *All Hell Let Loose*, is to explain how the Great Powers got into it, and he does so with commendable clarity ... The extent of his research is truly impressive ... a book that is as enjoyable to read as it is important historically'   *Country Life*

By the same author

REPORTAGE
America 1968: The Fire this Time
Ulster 1969: The Struggle for Civil Rights in Northern Ireland
The Battle for the Falklands (with Simon Jenkins)

BIOGRAPHY
Montrose: The King's Champion
Yoni: Hero of Entebbe

AUTOBIOGRAPHY
Did You Really Shoot the Television?
Going to the Wars
Editor

MILITARY HISTORY
Bomber Command
The Battle of Britain (with Len Deighton)
Das Reich
Overlord: D-Day and the Battle for Normandy
Victory in Europe
The Korean War
Warriors: Extraordinary Tales from the Battlefield
Armageddon: The Battle for Germany 1944–45
Nemesis: The Battle for Japan 1944–45
Finest Years: Churchill as Warlord 1940–45
All Hell Let Loose: The World at War 1939–45

COUNTRYSIDE WRITING
Outside Days
Scattered Shots
Country Fair

ANTHOLOGY (EDITED)
The Oxford Book of Military Anecdotes

MAX HASTINGS
CATASTROPHE
EUROPE GOES TO WAR 1914

WILLIAM
COLLINS

William Collins
An imprint of HarperCollins*Publishers*
77–85 Fulham Palace Road,
Hammersmith, London W6 8JB
www.harpercollins.co.uk

This William Collins paperback edition published 2014

1

Copyright © Max Hastings 2013

Max Hastings asserts the moral right to
be identified as the author of this work

A catalogue record for this book is
available from the British Library

ISBN 978-0-00-751974-3

Typeset in Minion by G&M Designs Limited,
Raunds, Northamptonshire
Printed and bound in Great Britain by
Clays Ltd, St Ives plc

MIX
Paper from
responsible sources
FSC® C007454

FSC™ is a non-profit international organisation established to promote
the responsible management of the world's forests. Products carrying the
FSC label are independently certified to assure consumers that they come
from forests that are managed to meet the social, economic and
ecological needs of present and future generations,
and other controlled sources.

Find out more about HarperCollins and the environment at
www.harpercollins.co.uk/green

For

PENNY

who does the real work

Contents

List of Illustrations   xiii
List of Maps   xvii
Introduction   xxi
1914 Chronology   xxvii
The Organisation of Armies in 1914   xxix
Prologue: SARAJEVO   xxxi

1   'A Feeling that Events are in the Air'   1
   1 CHANGE AND DECAY   1
   2 BATTLE PLANS   25

2   The Descent to War   41
   1 THE AUSTRIANS THREATEN   41
   2 THE RUSSIANS REACT   54
   3 THE GERMANS MARCH   75
   4 THE BRITISH DECIDE   85

3   'The Superb Spectacle of the World Bursting Into Flames'   103
   1 MIGRATIONS   103
   2 PASSIONS   110
   3 DEPARTURES   126

4   Disaster on the Drina   138

5   Death with Flags and Trumpets   159
   1 THE EXECUTION OF PLAN XVII   159
   2 'GERMAN BEASTLINESS'   187
   3 LANREZAC ENCOUNTERS SCHLIEFFEN   194

6 The British Fight   200
   1 MONS   200
   2 LE CATEAU: 'WHERE THE FUN COMES IN,   219
   I DON'T KNOW'

7 The Retreat   239

8 Tannenberg: 'Alas, How Many Thousands   259
   Lie There Bleeding!'

9 The Hour of Joffre   286
   1 PARIS AT BAY   286
   2 SIR JOHN DESPAIRS   290
   3 SEEDS OF HOPE   298

10 The Nemesis of Moltke   313
   1 THE MARNE   313
   2 'STALEMATE IN OUR FAVOUR'   342

11 'Poor Devils, They Fought Their Ships Like Men'   356

12 Three Armies in Poland   386

13 'Did You Ever Dance With Him?'   411
   1 HOME FRONTS   411
   2 NEWS AND ABUSE   434

14 Open Country, Open Sky   442
   1 CHURCHILL'S ADVENTURE   442
   2 'INVENTIONS OF THE DEVIL'   455

15 Ypres: 'Something that was Completely Hopeless'   463

16 'War Becomes the Scourge of Mankind'   497
   1 POLAND   497
   2 THE SERBS' LAST TRIUMPH   509

17 Mudlife   515

18 Silent Night, Holy Night   541

   Acknowledgements   565
   Notes and References   567
   Bibliography   595
   Index   605

Illustrations

Author's note: Images of the campaigns of 1914 are rare. Those professing to portray combat are often posed or faked, and many contemporary captions are wilfully or accidentally inaccurate. The pictures in this book have been chosen with these realities in mind, to give the most vivid possible impression of what the battlefields looked like, while recognising that few can be appropriately placed and dated, and some predate the war.

Kaiser Wilhelm II (Popperfoto/Getty Images)

Poincaré and the Tsar, St Petersburg, July 1914 (© Interfoto/Alamy)

Asquith and Lloyd George (Private collection)

Pasic (Imagno/Getty Images); Berchtold (akg/Imagno); Sazonov (© RA/ Lebrecht Music & Arts); Grey (Hulton Archive/Getty Images); Churchill (Hulton Archive/Getty Images); Bethmann Hollweg (DPA/ Press Association Images)

Russians solicit divine assistance (Mirrorpix)

Moltke (The Granger Collection/Topfoto); Ludendorff (Hulton Archive/ Getty Images); Hindenburg (Hulton Archive/Getty Images); Kitchener (Hulton Archive/Getty Images); Lanrezac (Mary Evans/Epic/Tallandier)

Conrad (© Ullsteinbild/Topfoto); Joffre (© Roger Viollet/Topfoto); French (© Roger Viollet/Topfoto); Haig (© Roger Viollet/Topfoto); Falkenhayn (Hulton Archive/Getty Images); Franchet d'Espèrey (DeAgostini/Getty Images)

Russians in Galicia (Mirrorpix)

Serbian troops advance (© Robert Hunt Library/Mary Evans)

Putnik (© The Art Archive/Alamy)

Potiorek (Getty Images)

Corporal Egon Kisch (© IMAGNO/Lebrecht)

Austrian troops conduct a mass execution of Serbian civilians (© Robert Hunt Library/Mary Evans)

An Austrian siege piece (Photo12/Ann Ronan Picture Library)

Kluck (akg-images)

Bülow (© INTERFOTO/Alamy)

French troops, before the deluge (© Roger-Viollet/Topfoto)

Belgians in action (Underwood Archives/Getty Images)

The legendary French *soixante-quinzes* (Roger-Viollet/Rex Features)

Smith-Dorrien (Mirropix)

Wilson, Foch and Huguet (Hulton Archive/Getty Images)

Murray (Universal History Archive/UIG/The Bridgeman Art Library)

Germans advance (RA/Lebrecht Music & Arts)

Frenchmen display offensive spirit (Mirrorpix)

Austro-Hungarian cavalry in Galicia (© Robert Hunt Library/Mary
    Evans)

The British deploy on their first battlefield (© IWM (Q 53319))

British troops await the enemy

Samsonov (DeAgostini/GettyImages)

Russians under attack

Russian prisoners after Tannenberg (© Robert Hunt Library/Mary
    Evans)

Rennenkampf (RIA Novosti)

Fortunino Matania's painting of L Battery's action at Néry (© David
    Cohen Fine Art/Mary Evans Picture Library)

The Middlesex under fire (R.C. Money. LC GS 1126. Reproduced with
    the permission of Leeds University Library)

A Suffolk girl at the handle of a Lowestoft tram (© IWM (Q 31032)

Russian soldiers in bivouac (David King Collection)

A Russian field hospital (David King Collection)

The Western Front, winter 1914 (© SZ Photo/Scherl/The Bridgeman Art
    Library)

Dorothie Feilding (Warwickshire County Record Office collections:
    CR2017/F246/326); Edouard Cœurdevey (Personal archives of Jean
    Cœurdevey); Jacques Rivière (All rights reserved. Private collection);
    Richard Hentsch (bpk/Studio Niermann/Emil Bieber); Paul Lintier
    (From *Avec une batterie de 75. Le Tube 1233. Souvenirs d'un chef de
    pièce (1915–1916)* by Paul Lintier, Paris 1917); Vladimir Littauer
    (From *Russian Hussar* by Vladimir S. Littauer, J.A. Allen & Co.,
    London, 1965); Constantin Schneider (Constantin Schneider als
    Oberleutnant; Foto: Privatbesitz; Reproduktion: Salzburger
    Landesarchiv; aus: Veröffentlichungen der Kommission für Neuere

Geschichte Österreichs, Bd. 95, Wien [u.a.] Böhlau, 2003); Lionel
Tennyson (Tennyson Research Centre, Lincolnshire County Council);
Venetia Stanley (© Illustrated London News Ltd/Mary Evans); Louis
Spears (Patrick Aylmer); Helene Schweida and Wilhelm Kaisen (State
Archive of Bremen); Louis Barthas (From *Les Carnets de guerre de
Louis Barthas, tonnelier, 1914–1918* © Editions de la Découverte. Paris.
English edition to be published in 2013 by Yale University Press);
François Mayer (© IWM Q 111149)
A family flees a battlefield (Mirrorpix)
British soldiers in Belgium, winter 1914 (K.W. Brewster/The Liddle
Collection/Leeds University Library. Photograph LC GS 0195)

*While every effort has been made to trace the copyright holders of photo-
graphs, in some cases this has not proved possible. The author and publishers
would welcome any information that would enable such omissions to be
rectified in future editions.*

Maps

Author's note: The movements of the vast armies in 1914 were so complex that it is almost impossible to depict them cartographically in detail. In these maps I have striven for clarity for non-specialist readers, for instance by omitting divisional numbers except where essential. They are generally based upon the maps in Arthur Banks's *A Military Atlas of the First World War* (Heinemann, 1975).

Rival concentrations on the Western Front, August 1914   130

Serbia, 1914   144

Frontier battles in Lorraine, 10–28 August 1914   173

The German advance through Belgium, August 1914   196–7

The Battle of Mons, 23 August 1914   207

The British at Le Cateau, 26 August 1914   232

The allied retirement, 23 August–6 September 1914   244

A View of the Eastern Front   262

The Russian advance into East Prussia   267

The Battle of Tannenberg, 24–29 August 1914:
   the pre-battle situation   277

The Battle of Tannenberg: the final act   279

German advance, 17 August–5 September 1914   299

The Battle of the Marne, 5–6 September 1914   317

The Battle of the Marne, 7–8 September 1914   323

The Battle of the Marne, 9 September 1914   333

The German armies in retreat towards the Aisne   344

The Galician theatre   390

The allied withdrawal to the Yser–Lys position,
  9–15 October 1914   452–3

The First Battle of Ypres: the first moves   470

The First Battle of Ypres: final positions   492

Approximate positions on the Eastern and
  Western Fronts, December 1914   544

As commandant of the British Army's staff college in 1910, Brigadier-General Henry Wilson asserted the likelihood of a European war, and argued that Britain's only prudent option was to ally itself with France against the Germans. A student ventured to argue, saying that only 'inconceivable stupidity on the part of statesmen' could precipitate a general conflagration. This provoked Wilson's derision: 'Haw! Haw! Haw!!! Inconceivable stupidity is just what you're going to get.'

'We are readying ourselves to enter a long tunnel full of blood and darkness' ANDRÉ GIDE, 28 July 1914

A bantering Russian foreign ministry official said to the British military attaché on 16 August: 'You soldiers ought to be very pleased that we have arranged such a nice war for you.' The officer answered: 'We must wait and see whether it will be such a nice war after all.'

Introduction

Winston Churchill wrote afterwards: 'No part of the Great War compares in interest with its opening. The measured, silent drawing together of gigantic forces, the uncertainty of their movements and positions, the number of unknown and unknowable facts made the first collision a drama never surpassed. Nor was there any other period in the War when the general battle was waged on so great a scale, when the slaughter was so swift or the stakes so high. Moreover, in the beginning our faculties of wonder, horror and excitement had not been cauterized and deadened by the furnace fires of years.' All this was so, though few of Churchill's fellow participants in those vast events embraced them with such eager appetite.

In our own twenty-first century, the popular vision of the war is dominated by images of trenches, mud, wire and poets. It is widely supposed that the first day of the 1916 Battle of the Somme was the bloodiest of the entire conflict. This is not so. In August 1914 the French army, advancing under brilliant sunshine across a virgin pastoral landscape, in dense masses clad in blue overcoats and red trousers, led by officers riding chargers, with colours flying and bands playing, fought battles utterly unlike those that came later, and at even more terrible daily cost. Though French losses are disputed, the best estimates suggest that they suffered well over a million casualties* in 1914's five months of war, including 329,000 dead. One soldier whose company entered its first battle with eighty-two men had just three left alive and unwounded by the end of August.

The Germans suffered 800,000 casualties in the same period, including three times as many dead as during the entire Franco-Prussian War. This also represented a higher rate of loss than at any later period of the war. The British in August fought two actions, at Mons and Le Cateau, which entered their national legend. In October their small force was plunged into the

* The term 'casualties' signifies soldiers killed, missing, wounded or captured.

three-week nightmare of the First Battle of Ypres. The line was narrowly held, with a larger French and Belgian contribution than chauvinists acknowledge, but much of the old British Army reposes forever in the region's cemeteries: four times as many soldiers of the King perished in 1914 as during the three years of the Boer War. Meanwhile in the East, within weeks of abandoning their harvest fields, shops and lathes, newly mobilised Russian, Austrian and German soldiers met in huge clashes; tiny Serbia inflicted a succession of defeats on the Austrians which left the Hapsburg Empire reeling, having by Christmas suffered 1.27 million casualties at Serb and Russian hands, amounting to one in three of its soldiers mobilised.

Many books about 1914 confine themselves either to describing the political and diplomatic maelstrom from which the armies flooded forth in August, or to providing a military narrative. I have attempted to draw together these strands, to offer readers some answers, at least, to the enormous question: 'What happened to Europe in 1914?' Early chapters describe how the war began. Thereafter, I have traced what followed on the battlefields and behind them until, as winter closed in, the struggle lapsed into stalemate, and attained the military character that it retained, in large measure, until the last phase in 1918. Christmas 1914 is an arbitrary point of closure, but I would cite Winston Churchill's remarks above, arguing that the opening phase of the conflict had a unique character which justifies examining it in isolation. My concluding chapter offers some wider reflections.

The outbreak has been justly described as the most complex series of happenings in history, much more difficult to comprehend and explain than the Russian Revolution, the onset of World War II or the Cuban missile crisis. This part of the story is inevitably that of the statesmen and generals who willed it, of the rival manoeuvres of the Triple Alliance – Germany and Austria-Hungary with Italy as a non-playing member – against the Triple Entente of Russia, France and Britain.

In today's Britain, there is a widespread belief that the war was so horrendous that the merits of the rival belligerents' causes scarcely matter – the *Blackadder* take on history, if you like. This seems mistaken, even if one does not entirely share Cicero's view that the causes of events are more important than the events themselves. That wise historian Kenneth O. Morgan, neither a conservative nor a revisionist, delivered a 1996 lecture about the cultural legacy of the twentieth century's two global disasters, in which he argued that 'the history of the First World War was hijacked in the 1920s by the critics'. Foremost among these was Maynard Keynes, an impassioned German sympathiser who castigated the supposed injustice and folly of the 1919 Versailles Treaty, without offering a moment's speculation about what sort of peace Europe would have had if a victorious *Kaiserreich* and its allies had been making it. The contrast is striking, and wildly overdone, between the revulsion of the British people following World War I, and their triumphalism after 1945. I am among those who reject the notion that the conflict of 1914–18 belonged to a different moral order from that of 1939–45. If Britain had stood aside while the Central Powers prevailed on the continent, its interests would have been directly threatened by a Germany whose appetite for dominance would assuredly have been enlarged by victory.

The seventeenth-century diarist John Aubrey wrote: 'About 1647, I went to see Parson Stump out of curiosity to see his Manuscripts, whereof I had seen some in my childhood; but by that time they were lost and disperst; his sons were gunners and souldiers, and scoured their gunnes with them.' All historians face such disappointments, but the contrary phenomenon also afflicts students of 1914: there is an embarrassment of material in many languages, and much of it is suspect or downright corrupt. Almost all the leading actors in varying degree falsified the record about their own roles; much archival material was destroyed, not merely by carelessness but often because it was deemed injurious to the reputations of nations or individuals. From 1919 onwards Germany's leaders, in pursuit of political advantage, strove to shape a record that might exonerate their country from war guilt, systematically eliminating embarrassing evidence. Some Serbs, Russians and Frenchmen did likewise.

Moreover, because so many statesmen and soldiers changed their minds several times during the years preceding 1914, their public and private words can be deployed to support a wide range of alternative judgements about their convictions and intentions. An academic once described oceanography as 'a creative activity undertaken by individuals who are … gratifying their own curiosity. They are trying to find meaningful patterns in the research data, their own as well as other people's, and far more frequently than one might suppose, the interpretation is frankly speculative.' The same is true about the study of history in general, and that of 1914 in particular.

Scholarly argument about responsibility for the war has raged through decades and several distinct phases. A view gained acceptance in the 1920s and thereafter, influenced by a widespread belief that the 1919 Versailles Treaty imposed unduly harsh terms upon Germany, that all the European powers shared blame. Then Luigi Albertini's seminal work *The Origins of the War of 1914* appeared in Italy in 1942 and in Britain in 1953, laying the foundations for many subsequent studies, especially in its emphasis on German responsibility. In 1961 Fritz Fischer published another ground-breaking book, *Germany's War Aims in the First World War*, arguing that the *Kaiserreich* must bear the burden of guilt, because documentary evidence showed the country's leadership bent upon launching a European war before Russia's accelerating development and armament precipitated a seismic shift in strategic advantage.

At first, Fischer's compatriots responded with outrage. They were members of the generation which reluctantly accepted a necessity to shoulder responsibility for the Second World War; now, here was Fischer insisting that his own nation should also bear the guilt for the First. It was too much, and his academic brethren fell upon him. The bitterness of Germany's 'Fischer controversy' has never been matched by any comparable historical debate in Britain or the United States. When the dust settled, however, a remarkable consensus emerged that, with nuanced reservations, Fischer was right.

But in the past three decades, different aspects of his thesis have been energetically challenged by writers on both sides of the Atlantic. Among the most impressive contributions was that of Georges-Henri Soutou, in his 1989 work *L'Or et le sang*. Soutou did not address the causes of the conflict, but instead the rival war aims of the allies and the Central Powers, convincingly showing that rather than entering the conflict with a coherent plan for world domination, the Germans made up their objectives as they went along. Some other historians have ploughed more contentious furrows. Sean McMeekin wrote in 2011: 'The war of 1914 was Russia's war even more than it was Germany's.' Samuel Williamson told a March 2012 seminar at Washington's Wilson Center that the theory of explicit German guilt is no longer tenable. Niall Ferguson places a heavy responsibility on British foreign secretary Sir Edward Grey. Christopher Clark argues that Austria was entitled to exact military retribution for the murder of the Archduke Franz Ferdinand upon Serbia, which was effectively a rogue state. Meanwhile John Rohl, magisterial historian of the Kaiser and his court, remains unwavering in his view that there was 'crucial evidence of intentionality on Germany's part'.

No matter – for the moment – which of these theses seems convincing or otherwise: suffice it to say there is no danger that controversy about 1914 will ever be stilled. Many alternative interpretations are possible, and all are speculative. The early twenty-first century has produced a plethora of fresh theories and imaginative reassessments of the July crisis, but remarkably little relevant and persuasive new documentary material. There is not and never will be a 'definitive' interpretation of the coming of war: each writer can only offer a personal view. While I make plain my own conclusions, I have done my best to rehearse contrary evidence, to assist readers in making up their own minds.

Contemporary witnesses were as awed as are their twenty-first-century descendants by the immensity of what befell Europe in August 1914 and through the months and years that followed. Lt. Edward Louis Spears, British liaison officer with the French Fifth Army, reflected long afterwards: 'When an ocean liner goes down, all on board, great and small alike, struggle with equal futility and for about the same time, against elements so overwhelming that any difference there may be in the strength or ability of the swimmers is insignificant compared to the forces against which they are pitted, and which will engulf them all within a few minutes of each other.'

Once the nations became locked in strife I have emphasised the testimony of humble folk – soldiers, sailors, civilians – who became its victims. Although famous men and familiar events are depicted here, any book written a century on should aspire to introduce some new guests to the party, which helps to explain my focus on the Serbian and Galician fronts, little known to Western readers.

One difficulty in describing vast events that unfolded simultaneously on battlefields many hundreds of miles apart is to decide how to present them. I have chosen to address theatres in succession, accepting some injury to chronology. This means readers need to recall – for instance – that Tannenberg was fought even as the French and British armies were falling back to the Marne. But coherence seems best served by avoiding precipitate dashes from one front to another. As in some of my earlier books, I have striven to omit military detail, divisional and regimental numbers and suchlike. Human experience is what most readily engages the imagination of a twenty-first-century readership. But to understand the evolution of the early campaigns of World War I, it is essential to know that every commander dreaded 'having his flank turned', because the outer edges and rear of an army are its most vulnerable aspects. Much that happened to soldiers in the autumn of 1914, alike in France, Belgium, Galicia, East Prussia and Serbia, derived from the efforts of generals either to attack an open flank, or to escape becoming the victim of such a manoeuvre.

Hew Strachan, in the first volume of his masterly history of World War I, addressed events in Africa and the Pacific, to remind us that this became indeed a global struggle. I decided that a similar canvas would burst through the frame of my own work. This is therefore a portrait of Europe's tragedy, which heaven knows was vast and terrible enough. In the interests of clarity, I have imposed some arbitrary stylistic forms. St Petersburg changed its name to Petrograd on 19 August 1914, but I have retained throughout the old – and modern – name. Serbia was commonly spelt 'Servia' in contemporary newspapers and documents, but I have used the former, even in quotations. Hapsburg citizens and soldiers are here often described as Austrians rather than properly as Austro-Hungarians, save in a political context. After the first mention of an individual whose full name is 'von', as in von Kluck, the honorific is omitted. Place-names are standardised so that, for instance, Mulhouse loses its German designation as Mülhausen.

Though I have written many books about warfare, and especially about the Second World War, this is my first full-length work about its forerunner. My own engagement with the period began in 1963, when as a callow school-leaver in my 'gap year', I was employed as an assistant researcher on BBC TV's epic twenty-six part series *The Great War* at a salary of £10 a week, at least £9 more than I was worth. Programme writers included John Terraine, Correlli Barnett and Alistair Horne. I interviewed and corresponded with many veterans of the conflict, then merely entering old age, and explored both the published literature and archive documents. I embraced that youthful experience as one of the happiest and most rewarding of my life, and some of the fruits of my 1963–64 labours have proved useful for this book.

My generation of students eagerly devoured Barbara Tuchman's 1962 best-seller *August 1914*. It came as a shock, a few years later, to hear an academic historian dismiss her book as 'hopelessly unscholarly'. It remains nonetheless a dazzling essay in narrative history, which retains the unembarrassed affection of many admirers, including myself, in whom it contributed significantly to stimulating a passion for the past. Those days will exercise an undying fascination for mankind: they witnessed the last fatal flourishes of the old crowned and cockaded Europe, followed by the birth of a terrible new world in arms.

MAX HASTINGS
Chilton Foliat, Berkshire
June 2013

1914 Chronology

28 June	Archduke Franz Ferdinand assassinated in Sarajevo
23 July	Austria-Hungary's ultimatum delivered to Serbia
28 July	Austria-Hungary declares war on Serbia
29 July	Austrians bombard Belgrade
31 July	Russia mobilises,* German ultimatums dispatched to Paris and St Petersburg
1 August	Germany and France mobilise
3 August	Germany declares war on France
4 August	Germany invades Belgium, Britain declares war on Germany
8 August	French briefly occupy Mulhouse in Alsace
13 August	Austrians invade Serbia, French launch major thrusts into Alsace and Lorraine
15 August	First Russo-Austrian clashes in Galicia
16 August	Last fort of Liège falls to the Germans
20 August	Serbs inflict defeat on Austrians at Mount Cer
20 August	Brussels falls
20 August	French repulsed at Morhange
20 August	Germans defeated at Gumbinnen in East Prussia
22 August	France loses 27,000 men killed in one day of the abortive 'Battles of the Frontiers'
21–23 August	Battle of Charleroi
23 August	British Expeditionary Force fights first action at Mons
24–29 August	Battle of Tannenberg

* Mobilisation dates are confusing, because in all cases preliminary military measures had been adopted earlier, and in most cases heads of state signed the formal decrees after troops began to move.

26 August	BEF fights at Le Cateau
28 August	Battle of Heligoland Bight
29 August	Battle of Guise
2 September	Austrian fortress of Lemberg falls to the Russians
6 September	France launches Marne counter-offensive
7 September	Austrians renew invasion of Serbia
9 September	Germans begin retreat to the Aisne
9 September	Battle of the Masurian Lakes
23 September	Japan declares war on Germany
9 October	Antwerp falls
10 October	Austrian fortress of Przemyśl falls to the Russians
12 October	Flanders campaign begins, climaxing in three-week First Battle of Ypres
29 October	Ottoman Empire enters the war on the side of the Central Powers
18–24 November	Battle of Łódź, ending in German withdrawal
2 December	Belgrade falls
15 December	Austrian army in Galicia driven back to the Carpathians
17 December	Austrians once more expelled from Serbia

The Organisation of Armies in 1914

The structure of each belligerent's forces and the size of their sub-units varied, but it may be helpful to offer readers a very rough crib:

An ARMY might be composed of anything from two to five CORPS (each usually commanded by a lieutenant-general). A corps comprised two or three infantry DIVISIONS (commanded by major-generals), each with an establishment of 15–20,000 men – cavalry divisions averaged about one-third of that strength – together with support, engineer and logistics units, and usually some heavy artillery. A British division might consist of three BRIGADES (commanded by brigadier-generals), all with their own guns – so-called field artillery – ideally in the proportion of at least one battery for each infantry battalion. Some continental armies placed regiments of two or three battalions directly under divisional command. A British infantry brigade, meanwhile, usually consisted of four BATTALIONS, initially about 1,000 strong apiece, commanded by lieutenant-colonels. A battalion had four rifle COMPANIES of two hundred men, each led by a major or captain, together with a support echelon – machine-guns, transport, supply and suchlike. A company had four rifle PLATOONS commanded by lieutenants, with forty men apiece. Cavalry regiments, each of four to six hundred men, were instead divided into squadrons and troops. All these 'establishment' strengths diminished fast under the stress of battle.

Prologue

SARAJEVO

The quirky little melodrama that unfolded in Bosnia on 28 June 1914 played the same role in the history of the world as might a wasp sting on a chronically ailing man who is maddened into abandoning a sickbed to devote his waning days to destroying the nest. Rather than providing an authentic 'cause' for the First World War, the murder of the Archduke Franz Ferdinand of Austria-Hungary was exploited to justify unleashing forces already in play. It is merely a trifling irony of history that a teenage terrorist killed a man who, alone among the leaders of the Hapsburg Empire, would probably have used his influence to try to prevent a cataclysm. But the events of that torrid day in Sarajevo exercise a fascination for posterity which must be indulged by any chronicler of 1914.

Franz Ferdinand was not much loved by anyone save his wife. A corpulent fifty-year-old, one of the Hapsburg Empire's seventy archdukes, he became heir to the throne after his cousin Crown Prince Rudolf shot himself and his mistress at Mayerling in 1889. The Emperor Franz Joseph resented his nephew; others considered him an arrogant and opinionated martinet. Franz Ferdinand's ruling passion was shooting: he accounted for some 250,000 wild creatures to his own gun, before ending his days in Gavrilo Princip's threadbare little gamebag.

In 1900 the Archduke conferred his affections on a Bohemian aristocrat, Sophie Chotek. She was intelligent and assertive: at army manoeuvres she once scolded the presiding officers for the imprecision of their men's marching. But lack of royal blood rendered her in the eyes of the imperial court ineligible to become empress. The monarch insisted that their marriage, when he grudgingly consented to it, should be morganatic. This placed them beyond the social pale of most of Austria's haughty aristocracy. Though Franz Ferdinand and Sophie were blissfully happy with each other, their lives were marred by the petty humiliations heaped upon her, as an unroyal royal appendage. Franz Ferdinand named a favourite walk at his Bohemian castle of Konopiště '*Oberer Kreuzweg*' – 'the upper Stations of the Cross'. At court functions, he followed the Emperor in precedence – but without his wife; he nursed a loathing for the lord chamberlain, Alfred Prince Montenuovo, who orchestrated such insults.

Franz Ferdinand's status as heir apparent nonetheless ensured that he and his wife entertained generals, politicians and foreign grandees. On 13 June 1914, Germany's Kaiser visited them at Konopiště, accompanied by Grand-Admiral Alfred von Tirpitz, a rose-fancier who was keen to see the castle's famous borders. Wilhelm II was prone to social mishaps: on this occasion his dachshunds, Wadl and Hexl, disgraced themselves by killing one of Franz Ferdinand's exotic pheasants. The Kaiser and the Archduke appear to have discussed trivia, rather than European or Balkan politics.

Next day, Sunday the 14th, Austria's foreign minister and most important politician, Count Leopold Berchtold, visited Konopiště with his wife. The Berchtolds were fabulously rich, and lived the smart life to the full. They were enthusiastic racehorse-owners, and that spring one of their yearling fillies had won the prized Con Amore handicap at Freudenau. Nandine, the Countess, was a childhood friend of Sophie Hohenburg. The visitors arrived at the castle for breakfast, spent the day looking at the garden and paintings, of which the Count was considered a connoisseur, then caught an evening train back to Vienna, never to meet their hosts again.

The Archduke's political and social views were conservative and vigorously expressed. After attending Edward VII's 1910 funeral in London, he wrote home deploring the boorishness of most of his fellow sovereigns, and the alleged impertinence of some politicians present, notable among them ex-US president Theodore Roosevelt. It is sometimes suggested that Franz Ferdinand was an intelligent man. Even if this was so, like so many royal personages into modern times, he was corrupted by position, which empowered him to express opinions unenlightened even by contemporary standards.

He loathed Hungarians, telling the Kaiser: 'the so-called noble, gentlemanly Magyar is a most infamous, anti-dynastic, lying, unreliable fellow'. He regarded southern Slavs as sub-humans, referring to the Serbians as 'those pigs'. He hankered after recovering Lombardy and Venetia, lost to Italy in his lifetime, for the Hapsburg Empire. Visiting Russia in 1891, Franz Ferdinand declared that its autocracy offered 'an admirable model'.

Tsar Nicholas II recoiled from Franz Ferdinand's intemperance, especially on racial matters. Both the Archduke and his wife were strongly Catholic, favouring Jesuits and professing hostility towards Freemasons, Jews and liberals. Such was Sophie's religious fervour that in 1901 she led two hundred fashionable women on a Catholic march through Vienna.

The Archduke nonetheless cherished one prudent conviction: while many Austrians, notably including army chief of staff Gen. Conrad von Hötzendorf, detested Russia and welcomed the prospect of a battlefield showdown with the Tsar, Franz Ferdinand dissented. He was determined, he said repeatedly, to avoid a clash of arms. Desiring a 'concord of emperors', he wrote: 'I shall never lead a war against Russia. I shall make sacrifices to avoid it. A war between Austria and Russia would end either with the overthrow of the Romanovs or with the overthrow of the Habsburgs – or perhaps the overthrow of both.' He once wrote to Berchtold: 'Excellency! Don't let yourself be influenced by Conrad – ever! Not an iota of support for any of his yappings at the Emperor! Naturally he wants every possible war, every kind of hooray! rashness that will conquer Serbia and God knows what else … Through war he wants to make up for the mess that's his responsibility at least in part. Therefore: let's not play Balkan warriors ourselves. Let's not stoop to this hooliganism. Let's stay aloof and watch the scum bash in each other's skulls. It'd be unforgivable, insane, to start something that would pit us against Russia.'

Franz Ferdinand, although as prone as Kaiser Wilhelm to outbursts of violent rhetoric, was a less reckless actor. Had the Archduke been alive when the decisive confrontation with Russia came, it is likely that his influence would have been wielded to avert war. As it was he was dead, because he insisted upon making an official visit to one of the most turbulent and perilous regions his uncle ruled. Every European monarchy shared a belief that ownership of large territories – empire – was a critical measure of virility and grandeur. While the colonies of Britain and France lay far away across oceans, those of the Hapsburgs and Romanovs were next door. Hungarian coins bore an abbreviation of the inscription 'Francis Joseph by the Grace of God Emperor of Austria and Hungary, Croatia, Slavonia, Dalmatia, Apostolic King'. In 1908 Austria-Hungary annexed Bosnia and Herzegovina, rousing Russian fury. The twin provinces, former Ottoman possessions with mingled Serb and Muslim populations, had been Austrian-occupied since 1878, under a mandate conceded by the Congress of Berlin, but most Bosnians bitterly resented their subjection.

In 1913, a foreign diplomat exclaimed despairingly of the Austro-Hungarians: 'Never have I seen people so determined to work against their own interests!' It was an extraordinary folly, for an empire already groaning under the weight of its own contradictions and the frustrations of its oppressed minorities, wilfully to seize Bosnia-Herzegovina. But Franz Joseph still smarted beneath the humiliations of losing his northern Italian dominions soon after he inherited the throne, and of suffering military defeat by Prussia in 1866. The acquisition of new colonies in the Balkans seemed to offer a measure of compensation, as well as frustrating Serbia's ambitions to incorporate them in a pan-Slav state.

Given the febrile mood in the provinces, it was rash to advertise the schedule for Franz Ferdinand's visit to Bosnia as early as March. This prompted one of many groups of violent dissidents, the Young Bosnians, a secret society for students of peasant origins, to seize the opportunity to kill him. They reached this resolution perhaps on their own initiative, or perhaps at the behest of puppet-masters in Belgrade: in the absence of concrete evidence, either view is tenable. One of their number was nineteen-year-old Gavrilo Princip. Like many figures who have played such a role in history, Princip spent his short life striving to induce people to overcome their instinct to dismiss him because of his slight stature and colourless personality. In 1912, he volunteered to fight for Serbia in the First Balkan War, only to be rejected as too small. At his first interrogation after achieving notoriety in June 1914, he explained himself by saying, 'Wherever I went, people took me for a weakling.'

In May, Princip and two fellow conspirators travelled to Belgrade. The city was capital of a young and volatile country, fully independent from the Ottoman Empire only since 1879, a constitutional monarchy that was heart and soul of the pan-Slav movement. Princip knew Serbia well, having lived there for two years. The 'Young Bosnians' were provided with four Browning semi-automatic pistols and six bombs by Maj. Vojin Tankosić of *Ujedinjenje ili Smrt*, a terrorist movement nicknamed 'the Black Hand', derived from German and Italian secret societies.

The group was led by the thirty-six-year-old head of military intelligence Col. Dragutin Dimitrijević, familiarly known as 'Apis', after the Egyptian bull god. He was the principal personality in one of three factions engaged in a struggle for Serbian domestic mastery. The other two elements were led respectively by Alexander, the Prince Regent – who hated the colonel because he refused to defer to the royal family – and

Nikola Pašić, the prime minister. Apis looked the part of a revolutionary fanatic: pale, bald, heavy, enigmatic – like 'a giant Mongolian', in the words of a diplomat. He never married, devoting his life to the movement which boasted a hooded initiation ritual and a seal engraved with a skull-and-crossbones flag, a dagger, a bomb and poison. Murder was his business: he had been prominent among a group of young army officers who conducted the 1903 butchery of King Alexander of Serbia and Queen Draga in their own palace bedroom.

The Black Hand's influence pervaded many Serbian institutions, notably including its army. Pašić, a sixty-nine-year-old of venerable appearance with his white hair and beard, was an inveterate enemy of Apis, some of whose associates in 1913 discussed murdering him. The prime minister and many of his colleagues regarded the colonel as a threat to his country's stability and even existence; internal affairs minister Milan Protić spoke of the Black Hand to a visitor on 14 June as 'a menace to democracy'. But in a society riven by competing interests, the civilian government lacked authority to remove or imprison Apis, who was protected by the patronage of the army chief of staff.

Beyond guns, bombs and cyanide suicide capsules, there is no hard evidence about what further support or direction Princip and his comrades received in Belgrade. The assassins went to their graves denying Serbia's official complicity. It seems overwhelmingly probable that the Black Hand incited and instructed the Young Bosnians for the archducal murder; but all that is certain is that its agents provided them with means to commit terrorist acts in Hapsburg territory. Princip conducted pistol practice in a Belgrade park, then on 27 May enjoyed a farewell dinner with his two co-conspirators, Trifko Grabež and Nedeljko Čabrinović, before starting what became an eight-day journey to Sarajevo. Part of Princip's and Grabež's route was covered on foot across open country, assisted by a frontier officer instructed by the Black Hand. Yet if Apis was wholly committed to the assassination plot, it is puzzling that the embryo assassin had to pawn his overcoat for a few dinars shortly before leaving Belgrade, to pay his expenses.

Who else knew what? Russia's ambassador in Belgrade was a fanatical pan-Slavist and friend of the Black Hand, Nikolai Hartwig; it is possible that he was party to the plot. But claims that St Petersburg had prior knowledge of the assassination are unsupported by a shred of evidence, and are hard to credit. The Russian government was strongly hostile to Austria-Hungary because of its persecution of its Slav minorities, but the

Tsar and his ministers had no plausible reason to want Franz Ferdinand dead.

The Bosnian peasant who guided Princip and Grabež back into Hapsburg territory – their other partner, Čabrinović, travelled independently – was a Serbian government informer, who passed word about their movements, and about the bombs and pistols in their luggage, to the Interior Ministry in Belgrade. His report, which the prime minister read and summarised in his own hand, made no mention of a plot against Franz Ferdinand. Pašić commissioned an investigation, and gave orders that the movement of weapons from Serbia into Bosnia should be stopped; but he went no further. A Serbian minister later claimed that Pašić told the cabinet at the end of May or the beginning of June that some assassins were on their way to Sarajevo to kill Franz Ferdinand. Whether or not this is true – no minutes were taken of cabinet meetings – Pašić appears to have instructed Serbia's envoy in Vienna to pass on to the Austrian authorities only a vague general warning, perhaps because he was unwilling to provide the Hapsburgs with a fresh and extremely serious grievance against his country.

Serbians played something of the same violent role on the margin of the Hapsburg Empire as did Irish factions in the affairs of Britain at several periods of the twentieth century, though the latter proved more resilient. Chronic Serb brutality towards their own minorities, especially Muslims, was a poor advertisement for the state. Some historians believe that its rulers were so intimately involved in terrorism, and explicitly in the conspiracy against Franz Ferdinand, that the country should be considered a rogue state. This view, once again, relies upon circumstantial evidence and speculation. Given the hostility between Apis and Pašić, it seems unlikely that they would have forged a common front to encompass the death of the Archduke.

Even without forewarning from Belgrade, the Austrian authorities had the strongest reasons to anticipate violent protest or some murderous attempt against Franz Ferdinand, who himself fully recognised the danger. Leaving his estate at Chlumetz on 23 June, he and his wife were obliged to begin their trip to Bosnia in a first-class compartment of the Vienna express, because the axles of his automobile were overheating. He said crossly: 'Our journey starts with an extremely promising omen. Here our car burns, and down there they will throw bombs at us.' The pre-1914 era was characterised by endemic acts of terrorism, especially in the Balkans, which were the butt of condescending British humour: a *Punch* joke had one anarchist asking another: 'What time is it by your bomb?' Saki penned a black-comic short story about an outrage – 'The Easter Egg'. Both Joseph Conrad and Henry James wrote novels about terrorists.

For the Hapsburgs, such matters were commonplaces. Franz Joseph's semi-estranged wife, the Empress Elisabeth, had been stabbed to death by an Italian anarchist while boarding a steamer at Geneva in 1898. Ten years later in Lemberg, a twenty-year-old Ukrainian student assassinated the governor of Galicia, Count Potocki, crying out, 'This is your punishment for our sufferings.' The judge at the trial of a Croat who shot at another Hapsburg grandee asked the terrorist, who had been born in Wisconsin, if he thought killing people was justified. The man replied: 'In this case it is. It is the general opinion in America, and behind me are 500,000 American Croats. I am not the last among them … These actions against the lives of dignitaries are our only weapon.' On 3 June 1908 Bogdan Žerajić, a young Bosnian, intended to shoot the Emperor in Mostar, but relented at the last moment. Instead he travelled to Sarajevo, fired several times at Gen. Marijan Varešanin, then – wrongly supposing that he had killed him – shot himself with his last bullet. It was later alleged, though never proven, that the Black Hand had provided the revolver. The Austrian police sawed off the terrorist's head for preservation in their black museum.

In June 1912 a schoolboy shot at the governor of Croatia in Zagreb, missing his target but wounding a member of the imperial administration. In March 1914 the vicar-general of Transylvania was killed by a time-bomb sent through the post by Romanians. Yet Franz Ferdinand was capable of seeing the funny side of the threat: while watching military manoeuvres one day, his staff succumbed to panic when a dishevelled figure suddenly sprang from a bush clutching a large black object. The Archduke laughed heartily: 'Oh, let him shoot me. That's his job – he's a court photographer. Let him make a living!'

There was nothing comic, however, about the obvious threat in Bosnia. The Austrian police had detected and frustrated several previous conspiracies. Gavrilo Princip was known to be associated with 'anti-state activities'. Yet when he registered himself in Sarajevo as a new visitor, nothing was done to monitor his activities. Gen. Oskar Potiorek, governor of Bosnia, was responsible for security for the royal visit. The chief of his political department warned about the threat from the Young Bosnians, but Potiorek mocked the man 'for having a fear of children'. Officials were later said to have devoted more energy to discussing dinner menus, and the correct temperature at which to serve the wines, than to the guest of honour's safety. Official negligence alone gave Princip and his friends their chance.

On the evening of 27 June, though Franz Ferdinand and Sophie were not scheduled to enter Sarajevo until next day, on an impulse they drove into the town, an exotic half-oriental community of some 42,000 people, to visit craft shops, including a carpet stall, watched by a crowd that included Princip. The couple thoroughly enjoyed themselves. In the spa town of Ilidže later that evening Dr Josip Sunarić, a prominent member of the Bosnian parliament who had urged cancelling the visit, was presented to the Duchess. She reproached him, saying, 'My dear Dr Sunarić, you are wrong after all. Things do not always turn out the way you say they will. Wherever we have been everyone, down to the last Serb, has greeted us with such great friendliness, politeness and true warmth, that we are very happy with our visit.' Sunarić answered, 'Your Highness, I pray to God that when I have the honour of meeting you again tomorrow night, you can repeat those words. A great burden will be lifted from me.'

That night a banquet was held for the Archduke at Ilidže's Hotel Bosna: guests were served *potage régence, soufflés délicieux, blanquette de truite à la gelée*, chicken, lamb, beef, *crème aux ananas en surprise*, cheese, ice cream and bon-bons. They drank Madeira, Tokay and Bosnian Žilavka. Next morning before leaving for Sarajevo, Franz Ferdinand sent a telegram to his elder son Max, congratulating the boy on his exam results at Schotten Academy. He and Sophie adored their children: he was never happier than when sharing their toys in the playroom at Konopiště. This was the couple's fourteenth wedding anniversary, and also a date pregnant with painful significance for Serbs – the anniversary of their 1389 defeat by the Ottomans at Kosovo.

The Archduke set forth in the dress uniform of a cavalry general – sky-blue tunic, gold collar with three silver stars, black trousers with a red stripe, surmounted by a helmet with green peacock feathers. Sophie, a buxom, stately figure, wore a white picture hat with a veil, a long white silk dress with red and white fabric roses tucked into a red sash, an ermine stole on her shoulders. Late on the morning of the 28th, in accordance with the published schedule, the archducal motorcade left Sarajevo station. Seven Young Bosnian killers had deployed themselves to cover each of three river bridges, one of which Franz Ferdinand was sure to cross.

The royal automobiles passed through what the Catholic archbishop later described as 'a regular avenue of assassins'. Shortly before reaching its first scheduled stop, a bomb thrown by Nedeljko Čabrinović, a printer, struck Franz Ferdinand's car, but bounced off the folded hood before it exploded, wounding two of the archducal suite. Čabrinović was seized and led away after making a half-hearted attempt to kill himself. He declared proudly, 'I am a Serbian hero.' Most of the other conspirators failed to use their weapons, later making assorted excuses for loss of nerve. The Archduke drove on to the town hall, where he displayed understandable exasperation when obliged to listen patiently to a pre-scripted speech of welcome. As the party re-entered their vehicles, he said he wished to visit the officers injured by Čabrinović's bomb. At the entry to Franz Joseph Street Gen. Potiorek, in the front seat of the archducal motor, expostulated: the driver was going the wrong way. The car stopped. It had no reverse gear, and thus had to be pushed backwards onto the Appel Quay, immediately alongside the spot where Princip stood.

The young man drew and raised his pistol, then fired twice. Another conspirator, Mihajlo Pucará, kicked a detective who saw what was happening and sought to intervene. Sophie and Franz Ferdinand were both hit from a range of a few feet. She immediately slumped in death, while he muttered, 'Sophie, Sophie, don't die – stay alive for our children.' Those were his last words: he expired soon after 11 a.m. Princip was seized by the crowd. Pucará, a strikingly handsome young man who had rejected an offered role at Belgrade's National Theatre in favour of a career in terrorism, grappled with an officer who tried to attack Princip with his sabre. Another young man, Ferdinand Behr, also did his best to save the assassin from retribution.

The plot to kill the Archduke was absurdly amateurish, and succeeded only because of the failure of the Austrian authorities to adopt elementary precautions in a hostile environment. This in turn raises the question: did the killing really represent the best effort of Apis, the arch-conspirator, or merely an almost casual, anarchic sideswipe at Hapsburg rule? No conclusive answer is possible, but the investigating judge at Sarajevo District Court, Leo Pfeffer, thought on his first glimpse of Princip that 'it was difficult to imagine that so frail-looking an individual could have committed so serious a deed'. The young assassin was at pains to explain that he had not intended to kill the Duchess as well as the Archduke: 'a bullet does not go precisely where one wishes'. Indeed, it is astonishing that even at close range Princip's pistol killed two people with two shots – handgun wounds are frequently non-fatal.

In the first forty-eight hours after the killings, more than two hundred leading Serbs in Bosnia were arrested and taken to join Princip and

Čabrinović in the military prison. Several peasants were hanged out of hand. Within days all the conspirators were in custody except a Muslim carpenter, Mehmed Mehmedbašić, who escaped to Montenegro. By the end of July 5,000 Serbs had been jailed, of whom about 150 were hanged when hostilities subsequently began. Auxiliaries of the Austrian Schutzkorps militia exacted summary vengeance from many more Muslims and Croats. At the trial which began in October, Princip, Čabrinović and Grabež were sentenced to twenty years' imprisonment – as minors, they escaped capital punishment. Three others received jail terms, while five were hanged on 3 February 1915, and four more accessories received terms from three years to life. Nine of the accused were freed, including some peasants whom Princip said he had forced to help him.

Word of the deaths of the Archduke and his wife swept across the Empire that day, and thereafter across Europe. At Vienna's Aspern airfield, the band was playing a new tune, 'The Airmen's March', in the midst of a flying display when at 3 p.m. the proceedings were abruptly terminated on receiving the tidings from Sarajevo. The Emperor Franz Joseph was at Ischl when his adjutant-general Graf von Paar brought him news of the murders. He received it with no visible emotion, but decided to eat his dinner alone.

The Kaiser was attending Kiel Regatta. A launch approached the royal yacht, which Wilhelm attempted to wave away. Instead it closed in, carrying Georg von Müller, chief of the Kaiser's naval cabinet. The admiral placed a note in his cigarette case and threw it up to the *Hohenzollern*'s deck, where a sailor caught it and carried it to the Emperor. Wilhelm took the case, read its message, turned pale and murmured: 'Everything has to start again!' The Kaiser was among the few men in Europe who personally liked Franz Ferdinand; he had lavished emotional capital on their relationship, and was genuinely grieved by his passing. He gave orders to abandon the regatta. Rear-Admiral Albert Hopman, chief of the Imperial Naval Office's central staff, was also at Kiel, just leaving a lunch at which the British ambassador had been a fellow guest, when he heard a report that Franz Ferdinand had 'died suddenly'. At nightfall, having learned the exact circumstances, he wrote of 'a dreadful act of which the political consequences are incalculable'.

But most of Europe received the news with equanimity, because acts of terrorism were so familiar. In St Petersburg, British correspondent Arthur Ransome's Russian friends dismissed the assassinations as 'a characteristic bit of Balkan savagery', as did most people in London. In Paris another journalist, Raymond Recouly of *Le Figaro*, recorded a general view that 'the crisis in progress would soon recede into the category of Balkan squabbles, such as recurred every fifteen or twenty years, and were sorted out among the Balkan peoples themselves, without any of the great powers needing to become entangled'. President Raymond Poincaré was at Longchamps races, where reports of the shots in Sarajevo did not impede his enjoyment of the running of the Grand Prix. Two days later in a Prussian school, twelve-year-old Elfriede Kuhr and her classmates peered at newspaper photographs of the assassin and his victim. 'Princip is better-looking than that fat pig Franz Ferdinand,' she observed mischievously, though her classmates deplored her flippancy.

The Archduke's funeral service, in the stifling heat of the Hofburgpfarrkirch, lasted just fifteen minutes, following which Franz Joseph resumed his cure at Ischl. The old Emperor made little pretence of sorrow about his nephew's death, though he was full of rage about its manner. Most of his subjects shared his sentiments, or lack of them. On 29 June in Vienna, Professor Josef Redlich noted in his diary: 'there is no sense of grief in the town. Music has been playing everywhere.' The London *Times* reported the funeral on 1 July in terms measured to the point of somnolence. Its Vienna correspondent asserted that 'so far as the press is concerned, there is a remarkable absence of any inclination that revenge should be taken upon the Serbs of the Monarchy as a whole for the misdeeds of what is believed to be a small minority … With regard to Serbia also the utterances of the press are on the whole remarkably restrained.'

Foreign observers expressed surprise that Viennese mourning for the heir to the imperial throne was perfunctory and patently insincere. It was thus ironic that the Hapsburg government scarcely hesitated before taking a decision to exploit the assassinations as a justification for invading Serbia, even at the cost of provoking an armed collision with Russia. And Princip had killed the one man in the Empire committed to avert this.

1

'A Feeling that Events are in the Air'

1 CHANGE AND DECAY

One day in 1895, a young British army officer lunched in London with the old statesman Sir William Harcourt. After a conversation in which the guest took, by his own account, none too modest a share, Lt. Winston Churchill – for it was he – asked Harcourt eagerly, 'What will happen then?' His host replied with inimitably Victorian complacency: 'My dear Winston, the experiences of a long life have convinced me that nothing ever happens.' Sepia-tinted photographs exercise a fascination for modern generations, enhanced by the serenity which long plate exposures imposed upon their subjects. We cherish images of old Europe during the last years before war: aristocrats attired in coronets and ball gowns, white ties and tails; Balkan peasants in pantaloons and fezzes; haughty, doomed royal family groups.

Young men with moustaches, smoking pipes, clad in the inevitable straw hats, poling punts occupied by reclining girls with bobbed hair and high collars, suggest an idyll before the storm. In polite circles even language was tightly corseted: the words 'damn' and 'bloody' were impermissible, and more extreme epithets were unusual between men and women save in the most intimate circumstances. 'Decent' was an adjective of high praise, 'rotter' a noun of profound condemnation. Fifty years later British writer and war veteran Reginald Pound asserted: 'The sardonic objectivity of our latter-day school of historians can neither penetrate nor dissipate the golden haze of that singular time. For all its rampant injustices, its soaring unearned incomes, its abounding wretchedness, its drunkenness galore, the people knew a kind of untainted happiness that has since gone from the world.'

Yet even though Pound was there and we were not, it is hard to accept his view. Only a man or woman who chose to be blind to the extraordinary happenings in the world could suppose the early years of the twentieth century an era of tranquillity, still less contentment. Rather, they hosted a ferment of passions and frustrations, scientific and industrial novelties, irreconcilable political ambitions, which caused many of the era's principals to recognise that the old order could not hold. To be sure, dukes were still attended by footmen wearing white hair-powder; smart households were accustomed to eat dinners of ten or twelve courses; on the continent duelling was not quite extinct. But it was plain that these things were coming to an end, that the future would be arbitrated by the will of the masses or those skilled in manipulating it, not by the whims of the traditional ruling caste, even if those who held power strove to postpone the deluge.

It is a conceit of our own times to suppose that we are obliged to live, and national leaderships to make decisions, amid unprecedentedly rapid change. Yet between 1900 and 1914, technological, social and political advances swept Europe and America on a scale unknown in any such previous timespan, the blink of an eye in human experience. Einstein promulgated his special theory of relativity. Marie Curie isolated radium and Leo Baekeland invented Bakelite, the first synthetic polymer. Telephones, gramophones, motor vehicles, cinema performances and electrified homes became commonplace among affluent people in the world's richer societies. Mass-circulation newspapers soared to unprecedented social influence and political power.

In 1903 man first achieved powered flight; five years later, Ferdinand Count Zeppelin lyricised the mission to secure unrestricted passage across the skies, an increasingly plausible prospect: 'Only therewith can the divine ancient command be fulfilled ... [that] creation should be subjugated by mankind.' At sea, following the 1906 launch of the Royal Navy's *Dreadnought*, all capital ships lacking its heavy ordnance mounted in power-driven turrets became obsolete, unfit to join a fleet line of battle. The range at which squadrons expected to exchange fire, a few thousand yards when admirals were cadets, now stretched to tens of miles. Submarines were recognised as potent weapons. Ashore, while the American Civil War and not the First World War was the first great conflict of the industrial age, in the interval between the two the technology of destruction made dramatic advances: machine-guns achieved reliability and efficiency, artillery increased its killing power. It was realised that barbed wire could be employed to check the movements of soldiers as effectively as those of beasts. Much speculation about the future character of war was nonetheless mistaken. An anonymous 1908 article in the German publication *Militär-Wochenblatt* asserted that the 1904–05 Russo-Japanese experience in Manchuria 'proved that even well-defended fortifications and entrenchments can be taken, even across open ground, by courage and cunning exploitation of terrain ... The concept of states waging war to the point of absolute exhaustion is beyond the European cultural experience.'

Socialism became a major force in every continental state, while Liberalism entered historic decline. The revolt of women against statutory subjection emerged as a significant issue, especially in Britain. Across Europe real wages rose almost 50 per cent between 1890 and 1912, child mortality declined and nutrition greatly improved. But despite such advances – or, in accordance with de Tocqueville's view that misery becomes less acceptable when no longer absolute, because of them – tens of millions of workers recoiled from the inequalities of society. Industries in Russia, France, Germany and Britain were convulsed by strikes, sometimes violent, which spread alarm and even terror among the ruling classes. In 1905 Russia experienced its first major revolution. Germany displaced France and Russia as the British Empire's most plausible enemy. Britain, which had been the world's first industrialised nation, saw its share of global manufacturing fall from one-third in 1870 to one-seventh in 1913.

All this took place within a similar modest timescale to that dividing us today from the 2001 terrorist assaults on the United States. Social historian and politician Charles Masterman mused in 1909 about his uncertainty 'whether civilization is about to blossom into flowers, or wither in a tangle of dead leaves and faded gold ... whether we are about to plunge into a new period of tumult and upheaval or whether a door is to be suddenly opened, revealing unimaginable glories'. Austrian writer Carl von Lang wrote early in 1914: 'There is a feeling that events are in the air; all that is unpredictable is their timing. Perhaps we shall see several more years of peace, but it is equally possible that overnight some tremendous upheaval will happen.'

It is unsurprising that the wing-collared statesmen of Europe found it difficult to adjust their thinking and conduct to the new age into which they were so abruptly thrust, to the acceleration of communication which transformed human affairs, and to an increase of military destructive power which few understood. Horse-and-carriage diplomacy, like governance by crowned heads selected by accident of birth, proved wholly inadequate to address a crisis of the electric age. Winston Churchill wrote in

1930: 'Scarcely anything material or established which I was brought up to believe was permanent or vital has lasted. Everything I was sure or taught to be sure was impossible, has happened.'

Between 1815 and 1870 Russia, Prussia, Austria and France carried about equal weight on the world stage, behind Britain. Thereafter the new Germany powered ahead, becoming recognised as by far the most successful continental nation, world leader in almost every industrial sphere from pharmaceuticals to automobile technology, and a social pioneer in promoting health insurance and old-age pensions. Some British jingos allowed the vastness of their empire to delude them about the primacy of their own little country, but economists coolly measured its eclipse by America and Germany as both manufacturer and trader, with France ranking fourth. All the major nations acknowledged as a proper ambition the maximisation of their own greatness and territorial possessions. Only Britain and France favoured maintenance of the status quo abroad, because their own imperial ambitions were sated.

Others chafed. In May 1912 Lt. Col. Alick Russell, the British military attaché in Berlin, expressed concern about the febrile mood he identified. There was, he thought, 'an uncomfortable feeling in German hearts that the army of the Fatherland is gaining a reputation for being unwilling to fight, an intense irritation at what is considered French arrogance and the apparently inevitable hostility of ourselves'. Put together, he suggested, 'we obtain a sum of national sentiment, which might on occasion turn the scale, when the issue of peace or war was hanging in the balance'. Russell's concern about German volatility, sometimes trending towards hysteria, was reflected in all his dispatches, and increased during the two years that followed.

Contrary to the belief of their neighbours, however, many German people had no enthusiasm for war. The country was approaching a constitutional crisis. The Social Democratic Party which dominated the Reichstag – the German socialist movement was the largest in the world – was deeply hostile to militarism. Early in 1914, the British naval attaché reported with some surprise that Reichstag navy debates were sparsely attended; only between twenty and fifty members turned up, who gossiped incessantly during speeches. The industrial working class was profoundly alienated from a government composed of conservative ministers appointed for their personal acceptability to the Kaiser.

But Germany, if no longer an absolutist state on the Russian model, remained more of a militarised autocracy than a democracy. Its most powerful institution was the army, and its crowned head loved to surround himself with soldiers. On 18 October 1913, Kaiser Wilhelm II decreed large-scale celebrations for the centenary of the victory at Leipzig, the 'Battle of the Nations' against Bonaparte. Following royal example, German department stores surrendered generous floorspace to commemorative dioramas. The marketplace was lavishly endowed with militaristically-tinted products. A harmonica named '*Wandervogel*', in honour of an Austro-German youth hiking movement of that name, was sold in a military postal service box. A best-selling harp was inscribed with the words: '*Durch Kampf zum Sieg*' – 'Through Battle to Victory'. Gertrud Schädla, a twenty-seven-year-old teacher living in a small town near Bremen, described in her May 1914 diary a fund-raising event for the Red Cross: 'I am quite interested in this – how could I not be, having three brothers liable to military call-up? More than that, I have recognised the critical nature of its work since I read a life of Florence Nightingale, and because I know from Paul Rohrbach's interesting book *German World Policies* how grave and how constant is the threat of war facing us.'

Wilhelm II presided over an empire unified only in his lifetime, which had achieved immense economic strength, but remained prey to insecurities which its ruler personified. He had no real thirst for blood, but a taste for panoply and posturing, a craving for martial success; he displayed many of the characteristics of a uniformed version of Kenneth Grahame's Mr Toad. Visitors remarked the notably homoerotic atmosphere at court, where the Kaiser greeted male intimates such as the Duke of Württemberg with a kiss on the lips. In the first decade of the century, the court and army were convulsed by a series of homosexual scandals almost as traumatic as was the Dreyfus Affair for France. In 1908, Dietrich Graf von Hülsen-Haeseler, chief of the Kaiser's military secretariat, died of a heart attack while performing an after-dinner *pas seul* dressed in a ballet tutu before a Black Forest shooting-lodge audience which included the Emperor himself.

And while Wilhelm's intimate circle displayed a taste for the grotesque, he himself pursued enthusiasms with tireless lack of judgement; most of his contemporaries, including the statesmen of Europe, thought him mildly unhinged, and this was probably clinically the case. Christopher Clark has written: 'He was an extreme exemplar of that Edwardian social category, the club bore who is forever explaining some pet project to the man in the next chair. Small wonder that the prospect of being buttonholed by the Kaiser over lunch or dinner, when escape was impossible, struck fear into the hearts of so many European royals.' Rear-Admiral

Albert Hopman, a shrewd and iconoclastic naval officer, wrote of the Kaiser in May 1914: 'He is vanity itself, sacrificing everything to his own moods and childish amusements, and nobody checks him in doing so. I ask myself how people with blood rather than water in their veins can bear to be around him.' Hopman described to his diary a strange dream on the night of 18 June 1914: 'I stood in front of a castle ... There I saw the old, broken-down Kaiser Wilhelm [I], talking to some people while holding a sabre stuck in its scabbard. I walked towards him, supported him, and led him into the castle. As I did so he said to me: "You must draw the sword ... My grandson [Wilhelm II] is too feeble [to do so]."'

All Europe's monarchs were wild cards in the doom game played out in 1914, but Wilhelm was the wildest of all. Bismarck's legacy to his country was a dysfunctional polity in which the will of the German people, expressed in the composition of the Reichstag, was trumped by the powers of the Emperor, his appointed ministers and the army's chief of staff. Jonathan Steinberg describes the era inaugurated by Wilhelm's dismissal of his chancellor in 1890, soon after assuming the throne: 'Bismarck ... left a system which only he – a very abnormal person – could govern and then only if he had as superior a normal Kaiser. [Thereafter] neither condition obtained, and the system slithered into the sycophancy, intrigue and bluster that made the Kaiser's Germany a danger to its neighbours.' Max Weber, who was born into that era, wrote similarly of Bismarck: 'He left a nation *totally without political education ... totally bereft of political will*. It had grown accustomed *to submit patiently* and fatalistically to whatever was decided for it in the name of monarchical government.'* Democratic influence was strongest on domestic financial matters, weakest on foreign policy, which was deeply secretive, conducted by ministers who were the Kaiser's personal appointees, heedless of the balance of representation in the Reichstag, with variable but critical influence from the army.

The Hohenzollerns got everything wrong socially. The Crown Prince returned from a 1913 fox-hunting tour of England convinced – quite mistakenly – of Germany's popularity with that country's ruling class. His father, with his withered arm and obsession with the minutiae of military uniforms and regulations, was a brittle personality whose yearning for respect caused him to intersperse blandishments and threats in ill-judged succession. Wilhelm once demanded of the imperialist Cecil Rhodes:

---

* Emphases in original.

'Now tell me, Rhodes, why is it that I am not popular in England? What can I do to make myself popular?' Rhodes answered: 'Suppose you just try doing nothing.' The Kaiser hesitated, then exploded into heavy laughter. It was beyond his powers to heed such advice. In 1908 Wilhelm scrawled a marginal note on a dispatch from his ambassador in London: 'If they want a war, they may start it, we are not afraid of it!'

In the years before 1914 European allegiances were not set in stone: they wavered, flickered, shifted. The French entered the new century with a possible invasion of England docketed in their war scenarios, and in 1905 the British still had contingency plans to fight France. They believed for a time that Russia might abandon the Triple Entente and join the Triple Alliance. In 1912 Austria's Count Berchtold indeed dallied with a rapprochement with St Petersburg, though this foundered over irreconcilable differences about the Balkans. The following year, Germany offered loans to Serbia. Many of the first generation of Rhodes Scholars at Oxford were young Germans, whose presence reflected British respect, even reverence, for their nation's culture. And industry: until 1911, Vickers collaborated with Krupp on the design and manufacture of shell fuses.

Though the Anglo-German 'naval race' grievously impaired bilateral relations, Chancellor Theobald Bethmann Hollweg and Lord Chancellor Richard Haldane made fumbling efforts to improve them, the former by seeking an assurance of British neutrality in the event of a continental war. Bethmann paid a domestic price for such advances, becoming mistrusted by fanatical German nationalists as an alleged anglophile. Meanwhile the Kaiser's brother Prince Heinrich of Prussia, during a January 1914 conversation in Berlin with British naval attaché Captain Wilfred Henderson, remarked in idiosyncratic English readily comprehensible at any London dining table, that 'other large European maritime nations are not white men'. This comment, which placed alike beyond the pale Russians, Italians, Austro-Hungarians and Frenchmen, won Henderson's warm approbation. Reporting the royal remarks to the Admiralty, he wrote: 'I could not help feeling that His Royal Highness had voiced in a peculiarly British way a view that is very prevalent in our own Service.'

These words were thought sufficiently embarrassing to be expunged from a volume of such diplomatic reports published a generation later. But the Prince's theme was pursued on an evening when German and British naval officers dined together, and the only toast offered was that of 'the two white nations'. At the 1914 Kiel Regatta, some German sailors swore eternal friendship to their visiting counterparts of the Royal Navy. The commander of *Pommern* told officers of the cruiser *Southampton*: 'We try and mould ourselves in the traditions of your navy, and when I see in the papers that the possibility of war between our two nations must be considered, I read it with horror – to us such a war would be a civil war.' Grand-Admiral Tirpitz employed an English governess for his daughters, who completed their education at Cheltenham Ladies' College.

Yet if Germany admired Britain, it also sought to challenge her, most conspicuously through the creation of a fleet capable of engaging the Royal Navy – this was overwhelmingly the Kaiser's personal commitment, strongly opposed by the chancellor and the army – and more fundamentally by rejecting the continental balance of power, so dear to British hearts. At Kiel in 1914, Vice-Admiral Sir George Warrender sought to flatter Tirpitz. The Englishman said: 'You are the most famous man in Europe.' Tirpitz answered: 'I have never heard that before.' Warrender added: 'At least in England.' The admiral growled: 'You in England always think that I am the bogey of England.' So Tirpitz was, and so too was the Kaiser. However Germany dressed matters up, its leaders aspired to secure a dominance in the management of Europe which no British government would concede, and thereafter they proposed to reach out across the oceans of the world.

Lord Haldane told Prince Lichnowsky, in the German ambassador's words: 'England, if we attacked France, would unconditionally spring to France's aid, for England could not allow the balance of power to be disturbed.' Lichnowsky was not taken seriously in Berlin, partly because of his enthusiasm for things English. His hosts did not reciprocate. British prime minister Herbert Asquith wrote of the Lichnowskys to his confidante Venetia Stanley: 'rather trying guests. They have neither of them any manners, and he is loquacious and inquisitive about trifles.'

Haldane's warning, transmitted to Berlin by the ambassador, was contemptuously dismissed. Gen. Helmuth von Moltke, Germany's chief of staff, thought the British Army an imperial gendarmerie of little consequence, and the Royal Navy irrelevant in a continental clash of soldiers. The Kaiser scrawled on the ambassador's report his own view that the British concept of a balance of power was an 'idiocy' which would make England 'eternally into our enemy'. He wrote to Franz Ferdinand of Austria, describing Haldane's remarks as 'full of poison and hatred and envy of the good development of our mutual alliance and our two countries [Germany and Austria]'. Several British academics warned of the prevalence of opinion in German universities about the inevitability of a historic struggle between the Kaiser's people and their own, identified as ascendant Rome and doomed Carthage.

Germany and the Dual Monarchy of Austria-Hungary were twin pillars of the Triple Alliance, of which Italy was a third member, upon whose attendance in the event of war nobody relied. For much of the previous century, the Ottoman Empire had been known as 'the sick man of Europe', its might and territories shrivelling. It had now been supplanted in that predicament by the Hapsburg Empire, whose dissolution in the face of its own contradictions and disaffected minorities was a focus of constant speculation in chancelleries and newspapers, not least in Germany. But the rulers of the Hohenzollern Empire elevated preservation of their tottering ally to a key objective of foreign policy. The Kaiser and his advisers shackled themselves to the Hapsburgs, not least because the beneficiaries of Austria-Hungary's dissolution would be their chosen enemies: Russia and its Balkan clients. The Kaiser delivered frequent denunciations of 'Slavdom' and Russia's alleged leadership of a front against 'Germandom'. On 10 December 1912 he told the Swiss ambassador in Berlin: 'we will not leave Austria in the lurch: if diplomacy fails we shall have to fight this racial war'.

The Hapsburg Empire embraced fifty million people of eleven nationalities, occupying the territories of modern Austria, Slovakia, the Czech Republic, Hungary, Croatia, Bosnia-Herzegovina, parts of Poland and north-east Italy. Franz Joseph was a weary old man of eighty-three, who had occupied his throne since 1848, and created the Dual Monarchy in 1867. For twenty-eight years he had enjoyed an intimacy with the actress Katharina Schratt. He wrote to her as 'My Dear Good Friend'; she replied to 'Your Imperial and Royal Majesty, my Most August Lord'. She was fifty-one in 1914, and they had long since settled into a pleasant domesticity. At Ischl, his summer residence, the Emperor rambled alone to her house, Villa Felicitas, where he would sometimes arrive at 7 a.m. after sending a note: 'Please leave the small door unlocked.'

Having spent some years of his youth as a soldier, even seeing a little action, the Emperor almost invariably affected military uniform; he perceived his army as the unifying force of the empire. Its officer corps was dominated by noblemen, most of whom combined conceit with incompetence. Franz Joseph's reign was symbolised by his insistence, when a young monarch, upon holding military exercises on a parade ground sheeted in ice, which caused many horses to slip and fall, killing two of their riders. On a larger scale, this was how he continued to rule, seeking to defy inexorable social, political and economic forces. Norman Stone has categorised the Hapsburg monarchy as 'a system of institutionalised escapism'. Its capital harboured as much poverty and unemployment as any European city, and more despair than most: in 1913 almost 1,500 Viennese attempted suicide, and more than half succeeded. As for popular consent, one writer has observed of the Austrian parliament: 'It was less a legislature than a cacophony. But since it was a Viennese cacophony, it shrilled and jangled with a certain flair.' In March 1914 the racket grew too loud for Franz Joseph: he prorogued the Reichsrat in the face of relentless clashes between its Czech and German members. He and his ministers thereafter ruled by decree.

Austria-Hungary was a predominantly rural society, but Vienna was toasted as one of the most cultured and cosmopolitan capitals on earth, beloved of Franz Lehár and Thomas Mann. Lenin thought it 'a mighty, beautiful and vivacious city'. Irving Berlin's 'Alexander's Ragtime Band' was sung there in English, and in 1913 it played host to the world premiere of Bernard Shaw's *Pygmalion*. It is an oddity of history that in the same year Stalin, Trotsky, Tito and Hitler alike lived for some months in Vienna. The great American boxer Jack Johnson was star turn of that winter's season at the Apollo Theatre. Among a host of popular cafés, the Landtmann was the favourite of Sigmund Freud. The city represented a global pinnacle of snobbery: bowing, scraping and even hand-kissing shopkeepers flattered their middle-class customers by adding an aristocratic 'von' to their names, and addressing them as 'Your Grace'. Domestic servants were subject to almost feudal routines: employment law entitled housemaids to only seven hours off a fortnight, every alternate Sunday. Aristocratic Viennese had a New Year custom of pouring gobbets of molten lead into buckets of iced champagne, then trying to predict the future by the shapes into which they hardened.

Austrian aristocratic social life was the most ritualised in Europe, dominated by appearances in the boxes of the Parquet Circle at the Court Theatre and Court Opera, and weekly At Homes. Every smart Viennese knew that Sunday was the afternoon of Princess Croy; Monday, of Countess Haugwitz; Tuesday, Countess Berchtold; Wednesday, Countess Buquoy. Countess Sternberg organised weekend ski outings at the Semmering Alp; Countess Larisch presided at bridge parties; Pauline, Princess Metternich, was alleged to entertain so many Jewish bankers that she received sneers as '*Notre Dame de Zion*'. Vienna boasted one of the largest and most influential Jewish communities in Europe, and formidable anti-Semitism to go with it.

Though the Germans condescended politically and militarily to the Austrians, they were prone to spasms of social inadequacy when meeting Hapsburg grandees on their home turf. Wickham Steed, the long-serving *Times* correspondent, wrote of Vienna: 'The combination of stateliness and homeliness, of colour and light, the comparative absence of architectural monstrosities and the Italian influence everywhere apparent, contribute, together with the grace and beauty of the women, the polite friendliness of the inhabitants and the broad, warm accent of their speech, to charm the eye and ear of every travelled visitor.' But Steed found Viennese vanity 'insufferable'; he perceived 'a general atmosphere of unreality', and complained that the city lacked a soul.

The Austrians cultivated relationships with Germany, Turkey and Greece in efforts to frustrate Serbian ambitions to create a pan-Slav state, a Yugoslavia, embracing several million Hapsburg subjects. In the years before 1914, the Empire also grew accustomed to employing military threats as a routine extension of its diplomacy. Its generals regarded war with reckless insouciance, as a mere tool for the advancement of national interests rather than as a passport to Hades. As Hapsburg minorities became ever more alienated, imperial repression became increasingly heavy-handed. Vienna fostered divisions between its subject Muslims, Serbs and Croats. Most minorities were denied political rights, while being liable to punitive taxation. Vienna might waltz, but there was little grace or mercy about anything else in Franz Joseph's dominions. The best that might be said was that its neighbours behaved no better.

The leaders of Russia shared with the Kaiser's court a belief that the two empires were fated to participate in a historic struggle between Germanism and Slavdom. Germans made no secret of their contempt for the Russians, and subjected them to constant snubs. Meanwhile the Tsar's subjects were resentful of German cultural and industrial superiority. The two nations' most conspicuous point of friction and threatened collision was Turkey. They circled the ailing Ottoman Empire as predators, each bent upon securing choice portions of its carcass. Control of the Dardanelles entrance to the Black Sea, through which 37 per cent of Russian exports passed, was an especially critical issue. Weak Ottoman supervision was just acceptable in St Petersburg. German dominance was not, yet this was a key objective of the Kaiser's foreign policy. The Young Turks who seized power in Constantinople in 1908 welcomed German aid, and especially military advisers, in their drive to modernise the country. As for Berlin's view, when Gen. Liman von Sanders departed to command the Constantinople garrison in 1913, Wilhelm urged him: 'create for me a new strong army which obeys my orders'.

Liman's appointment to Turkey provoked consternation in St Petersburg. The president of the Duma urged Nicholas II to act boldly to wrest the Dardanelles from the Ottomans before the Germans did so: 'the Straits must become ours. A war will be joyfully welcomed, and will raise the government's prestige.' At a December 1913 Russian Council of Ministers meeting, the navy and war ministers were questioned about the readiness of their services to fight, and answered that 'Russia was perfectly prepared for a duel with Germany, not to speak of one with Austria.' The following February, Russian military intelligence passed to the government a German secret memorandum which shocked St Petersburg: it emphasised Berlin's commitment to controlling the Dardanelles, and to securing for the Kaiser's officers command of the straits' gun batteries. It seems extravagant to suggest, as do some historians, that the Russians wished to start a war in 1914 to gain the Black Sea approaches. But they were almost certainly willing to fight to stop the Germans getting them.

Russia boomed in the last years before Armageddon, to the dismay of its German and Austrian enemies. After 1917, its new Bolshevik rulers forged a myth of Tsarist industrial failure. In reality, the Russian economy had become the fourth largest in the world, growing at almost 10 per cent annually. The country's 1913 national income was almost as large as that of Britain, 171 per cent of France's, 83.5 per cent of Germany's, albeit distributed among a much larger population – the Tsar ruled two hundred million people to the Kaiser's sixty-five million. Russia had the largest agricultural production in Europe, growing as much grain as Britain, France and Germany combined. After several good harvests, the state's revenues were soaring. In 1910, European Russia had only one-tenth the railway density of Britain or Germany, but thereafter this increased rapidly, funded by French loans. Russian production of iron, steel, coal and cotton goods matched that of France, though still lagging far behind Germany's and Britain's.

Most Russians were conspicuously better off than they had been at the end of the previous century: per-capita incomes rose 56 per cent between 1898 and 1913. With an expansion of schools, literacy doubled in the same period, to something near 40 per cent, while infant mortality and the over-all death rate fell steeply. There was a growing business class, though this had little influence on government, still dominated by the landowning aristocracy. Russian high life exercised a fascination for Western Europeans. That genteel British magazine *The Lady* portrayed Nicholas II's empire in romantic and even gushing terms: 'this vast country with its great cities and arid steppes and extremes of riches and poverty, captures the imagination. Not a few Englishmen and Englishwomen have succumbed to its fascinations and made it their home, and English people, generally speaking, are liked and welcomed by Russians. One learns that the girls of the richer classes are brought up very carefully. They are kept under strict control in the nursery and the schoolroom, live a simple, healthy life, are well taught several languages including English and French ... with the result that they are well-educated, interesting, graceful, and have a pleasing, reposeful manner.'

It was certainly true that Europe's other royal and noble fraternities mingled on easy terms with their Russian counterparts, who were as much at home in Paris, Biarritz and London as in St Petersburg. But the Tsarist regime, and the supremely hedonistic aristocracy behind it, faced acute domestic tensions. Whatever the Hapsburg Empire's difficulties in managing its ethnic minorities, the Romanov Empire's were worse: enforced Russification, especially of language, was bitterly resisted in Finland, Poland, the Baltic states and Muslim regions of the Caucasus. Moreover Russia faced massive turmoil created by disaffected industrial workers. In 1910 the country suffered just 222 stoppages, all attributed by the police to economic rather than political factors. By 1913 this tally had swelled to 2,404 strikes, 1,034 of them branded as political; in the following year there were 3,534, of which 2,565 were deemed political. Baron Nikolai Wrangel observed presciently: 'We are on the verge of events, the like of which the world has not seen since the time of the barbarian invasions. Soon everything that constitutes our lives will strike the world as useless. A period of barbarism is about to begin and it will last for decades.'

Nicholas II was a sensitive man, more rational than the Kaiser if no more intelligent. Having seen the 1905 Russo-Japanese war – which Wilhelm incited him to fight – provoke a revolution at home, the Tsar understood that a general European conflict would be disastrous for most, if not all, of the participants. But he cherished a naïve faith in the common interests of the emperors' trade union, supposing that he and Wilhelm enjoyed a personal understanding, and were alike committed to peace. He was contradictorily influenced, however, by Russia's recent humiliations – in 1905 by Japan's forces, in 1908 by Austrian diplomacy when the

Hapsburgs summarily annexed Bosnia-Herzegovina. The latter especially rankled. In January 1914 the Tsar sternly declared to former French foreign minister Théophile Delcassé: 'We shall not let ourselves be trampled upon.'

A conscientious ruler, Nicholas saw all foreign dispatches and telegrams; many military intelligence reports bear his personal mark. But his imagination was limited: he existed in an almost divine seclusion from his people, served by ministers of varying degrees of incompetence, committed to sustaining authoritarian rule. An assured paternalist, on rural visits he was deluded about the monarchy's popularity by glimpses of cheering peasantry, with whom he never seriously engaged. He believed that revolutionary and even reformist sentiment was confined to Jews, students, landless peasants and some industrial workers. The Kaiser would not have dared to act as arbitrarily as did the Tsar in scorning the will of the people: when the Duma voted against funding four battleships for the Baltic Fleet, Nicholas shrugged and ordered that they should be built anyway. Even the views of the 215-member State Council, dominated by the nobility and landowners, carried limited weight.

If no European government displayed much cohesion in 1914, Nicholas II's administration was conspicuously ramshackle. Lord Lansdowne observed caustically of the ruler's weak character: 'the only way to deal with the Tsar is to be the last to leave his room'. Nicholas's most important political counsellor was Sergei Sazonov, the foreign minister. Fifty-three years old and a member of the minor nobility, he had travelled widely in Europe, serving in Russia's London embassy, where he developed a morbid suspiciousness about British designs. He had now led the foreign ministry for four years. His department – known for its location as the Choristers' Bridge, just as its French counterpart was the Quai d'Orsay – spoke scarcely at all to the Ministry of War or to its chief, Vladimir Sukhomlinov; meanwhile the latter knew almost nothing about international affairs.

Russian statesmen were divided between easterners and westerners. Some favoured a new emphasis on Russian Asia and exploitation of its mineral resources. The diplomat Baron Rosen urged the Tsar that his empire had no interests in Europe save its borders, and certainly none worth a war. But Rosen was mocked by other royal advisers as 'not a proper Russian'. Nicholas's personal respect and even sympathy for Germany caused him to direct most of his emotional hostility towards Austria-Hungary. Though not committed to pan-Slavism, he was determined to assert the legitimacy of Russian influence in the Balkans. It remains a focus of keen dispute how far such an assumption was morally or politically justifiable.

Russia's intelligentsia as a matter of course detested and despised the imperial regime. Captain Langlois, a French expert on the Tsarist Empire, wrote in 1913 that 'Russian youth, unfortunately supported or even incited by its teachers, adopted anti-military and even anti-patriotic sentiments which we can scarcely imagine.' When war came, the cynicism of the educated class was evidenced by its many sons who evaded military service. Russian literature produced no Kipling to sing the praises of empire. Lack of self-belief, coupled to nationalistic aggressiveness, has always been a prominent contradiction in the Russian character. Nicholas's thoughtful subjects were conscious of their country's repeated failures in wars – against the British, French, Turks, Japanese. The last represented the first occasion in modern history when a European nation was defeated by an Asiatic one, which worsened the humiliation. In 1876 the foreign minister Prince Gorchakov told a colleague gloomily: 'we are a great, powerless country'. In 1909 Gen. A.A. Kireyev lamented in his diary, 'we have become a second-rate power'; he believed that imperial unity and moral cohesion were collapsing. When Russia acquiesced in Austria's annexation of Bosnia-Herzegovina, he exclaimed bitterly: 'Shame! Shame! It would be better to die!'

France's new relationship with Russia began in 1894, when the two governments signed a military convention; it derived from a belief that neither nation could alone aspire to climb into the ring against Germany, which posed a common threat, and that only such an alliance could offer security against the Kaiser's expansionist ambitions. Thereafter, the French advanced large loans to St Petersburg, chiefly to fund the building of strategic railways. France had many cultural ties with Russia, symbolised by Diaghilev's Ballets Russes, the toast of Paris. The close military relationship known as the Dual Entente evolved progressively: in 1901, the Russians agreed with the French that their army would engage the Germans eighteen days after any declaration of war. France's cash funded a big rearmament programme; Russians even aspired to create a first-class navy by 1930.

The Tsar's peacetime army was Europe's largest – 1.42 million men, potentially rising to five million on mobilisation. But could they fight? Many foreigners were sceptical. After attending Russian manoeuvres, the British military attaché wrote: 'we saw much martial spectacle, but very

little serious training for modern war'. France's Gen. Joseph Joffre, invited
to inspect Nicholas's forces in August 1913, agreed. He found some of the
Tsar's advisers, the war minister among them, frankly hostile to their
country's French alliance. The Russian army was burdened with weak
leaders and chronic factionalism; one historian has written that it retained
'some of the characteristics of a dynastic bodyguard'. Its ethos was defined
by brutal discipline rather than skill or motivation, though its commanders persuaded themselves that their men would fight better in a Slav cause
than they had done against Japan in 1904–05.

Russians were proud of their role in helping to free much of the Balkans
from Ottoman rule, and determined not to see this supplanted by Austrian
or German hegemony. The semi-official St Petersburg newspaper *Novoe
Vremya* wrote in June 1908 that it was impossible 'without ceasing to be
Russian' to allow Germanic cultural domination of southern and eastern
Europe. In 1913 the British minister in Belgrade, G.H. Barclay, wrote that
'Serbia is, practically speaking, a Russian province.' This was an exaggeration, because Serb leaders were intensely self-willed, but St Petersburg
made plain that the country was under its protection. Russian security
guarantees to Serbia proved as fatal to European peace as was German
support for Austria – with the important difference that the former were
defensive, the latter aggressive. But at the very least, Russia was irresponsible in failing to insist upon a halt to Serbian subversion in the Hapsburg
Empire as the price for its military backing.

The south Slavs lived in four different states – the Hapsburg Empire,
Serbia, Montenegro and Bulgaria – under eight different systems of
government. Their impassioned nationalism imposed a dreadful blood
forfeit: about 16 per cent of the entire population, almost two million
men, women and children, perished violently in the six years of struggle
that preceded Armistice Day 1918. Serbia fought two Balkan wars, in 1912
and 1913, to increase its size and power by seizing loose fragments of the
Ottoman Empire. In 1912 the Russian foreign minister declared that a
Serb–Bulgarian triumph over the Turks would be the worst outcome of
the First Balkan War, because it would empower the local states to turn
their aggressive instincts from Islamism, against Germanism: 'In this event
one … must prepare for a great and decisive general European war.' Yet the
Serbs and Bulgarians indeed triumphed in that conflict; a subsequent
Serb–Romanian victory in the Second Balkan War – a squabble over the
spoils of the First – made matters worse. Serbia doubled its territory by

incorporating Macedonia and Kosovo. Serbians burst with pride, ambition and over-confidence. Wars seemed to work well for them.

In June 1914 the Russian minister in Belgrade, the dedicated pan-Slavist Nikolai Hartwig, was believed actively to desire an armed clash between Serbia and Austria, though St Petersburg almost certainly did not. The Russian ambassador in Constantinople complained that Hartwig, a former newspaper columnist, 'shows the activity of an irresponsible journalist'. Serbia was a young country wrested from the Ottoman Empire only in 1878, which now clung to the south-eastern frontier of the Hapsburg Empire like some malevolent growth. Western statesmen regarded the place with impatience and suspicion. Its self-assertiveness, its popular catchphrase 'Where a Serb dwells, there is Serbia,' destabilised the Balkans. Europe's chancelleries were irritated by its 'little Serbia', proud-victim culture. Serbs treated their own minority subjects, especially Muslims, with conspicuous and often murderous brutality. Every continental power recognised that the Serbs could achieve their ambition to enfold in their own polity two million brethren still under Hapsburg rule only at the cost of bringing down Franz Joseph's empire.

Just four and a half million Serbs occupied 87,300 square kilometres of rich rural regions and barren mountains, a smaller country than Romania or Greece. Four-fifths of them lived off the land, and the country retained an exotic oriental legacy from its long subjection to the Ottomans. Such industries as it had were agriculturally based – flour and sawmills, sugar refineries, tobacco. 'Within little more than two days' rail from [London],' wrote an enthusiastic pre-war British traveller, 'there lies an undeveloped country of extraordinary fertility and potential wealth, possessing a history more wonderful than any fairy tale, and a race of heroes and patriots who may one day set Europe by the ears … I know no country which can offer so general an impression of beauty, so decided an aroma of the Middle Ages. The whole atmosphere is that of a thrilling romance. Conversation is larded with accounts of hairbreadth 'scapes and deeds of chivalry … Every stranger is welcome, and an Englishman more than any.'

Others saw Serbia in much less roseate hues: the country exemplified the Balkan tradition of domestic violence, regime change by murder. On the night of 11 June 1903, a group of young Serb officers fell upon the tyrannical King Alexander and his hated Queen Draga by candlelight in the private apartments of their palace: the bodies were later found in the garden, riddled with bullets and mutilated. Among the assassins was

Dragutin Dimitrijević, who became the 'Apis' of the Sarajevo conspiracy: he was wounded in a clash with the royal guards, which earned him the status of a national hero. When King Peter returned from a long exile in Switzerland to take the throne of a notional constitutional monarchy, Serbia continued to seethe with factionalism. Peter had two sons: the elder, Djordje, educated in Russia, was a violent playboy who was forced to relinquish his claim to the throne after a 1908 scandal in which he kicked his butler to death. His brother Alexander, who became the royal heir, was suspected of attempting to poison Djordje. The Serb royal family provided no template for peaceful co-existence, and the army wielded as much power as that of a modern African statelet.

Though Serbia was a rural society, it boasted a dynamic economy and a Western-educated intellectual class. One of the latter's aspiring sophisticates enthused to a foreign visitor: 'I am so fond of this country. It is so pastoral, don't you think? I am always reminded of Beethoven's Pastoral Symphony.' He whistled a few bars abstractedly. 'No, I made a mistake. That is the Third, isn't it?' Centuries of Ottoman dominance had bequeathed an exotic Eastern cultural legacy. American correspondent John Reed wrote:

> All sorts of people hung about the stations, men turbaned and fezzed and capped with conical hats of brown fur, men in Turkish trousers, or in long shirts and tights of creamy homespun linen, their leather vests richly worked in colored wheels and flowers, or in suits of heavy brown wool ornamented with patterns of black braid, high red sashes wound round and round their waists, leather sandals sewed to a circular spout on the toe and bound to the calf with leather ribbons wound to the knees; women with the Turkish yashmak and bloomers, or in leather and woollen jackets embroidered in bright colors, waists of the rare silk they weave in the village, embroidered linen underskirts, black aprons worked in flowers, heavy overskirts woven in vivid bars of color and caught up behind, and yellow or white silk kerchiefs on their heads.

In cafés, men drank Turkish coffee and ate *kaymak* cheese-butter. Every Sunday in village squares peasants gathered to dance – different dances for marriages, christenings, and even for each party at elections. They sang songs that were often political: 'If you will pay my taxes for me, then I will vote for you!' This was the nation that was the focus of intense Austrian anxiety and hostility, matched by Russian protectiveness. Whatever view is adopted about Serbia's role in the crisis of 1914, it is hard to make a case that its people were martyred innocents.

In western Europe, Balkan violence was so familiar that new manifestations aroused only weary disdain. In Paris in June 1914, the general European situation was thought less dangerous than it had been in 1905 and 1911, when acute tensions between the Triple Alliance and the Triple Entente were defused by diplomacy. Raymond Poincaré, fifty-three years old, was a former conservative prime minister who was elected president in 1913, and made his office for the first time executive rather than ceremonial. Though he became the first holder of the post since 1870 to dine at the Germans' Paris embassy, he loathed and feared the Kaiser's nation, and caused support for Russia to become the central pillar of French foreign policy. Few responsible historians suggest that the French desired a European war in 1914, but to a remarkable degree Poincaré relinquished his country's independence of judgement about participating in such an event. The Germans were the historic enemies of his people. Their war plan was known to demand an immediate assault on France, before addressing Russia. Poincaré believed, perhaps not wrongly, that the Entente powers must hang together, or Germany would hang them separately.

France had recovered brilliantly from defeat by Prussia in 1870. Bismarck's annexation of the twin French provinces of Alsace and Lorraine as a strategic buffer zone west of the Rhine remained a grievance, but was no longer a bleeding wound in the national consciousness. The French Empire was prospering, despite chronic discontent among its Muslim subjects, especially in North Africa. The army's prestige had been appallingly damaged by its senior officers' decade-long parade of brutality, snobbery, stupidity and anti-Semitism in the Dreyfus case, but it was now recognised – though not by the Kaiser – as one of the most formidable fighting forces in Europe. France's surging fortunes and commitment to innovation were symbolised by the first telephone boxes, railway electrification, the birth of Michelin maps. The brothers Lumière pioneered the development of cinema. Transport was being mechanised, with Paris becoming the fourth world city to acquire a metro, soon transporting four hundred million passengers a year. It was acknowledged as the cultural capital of the world, home to the avant-garde and the finest painters on earth.

The Third Republic was known as the '*république des paysans*'; though social inequality persisted, the influence of the landowning class was weaker than in any other European nation. French social welfare was evolving, with a voluntary pensions scheme, accident-insurance law, improved public health. France's middle class wielded more political power than that of any other European nation: Poincaré was the son of a civil servant, and himself a lawyer; former and future prime minister Georges Clemenceau was a doctor and the son of another. Insofar as the aristocracy played a part in any profession, it was the army, though it is noteworthy that the origins of France's principal soldiers of 1914–18, Joseph Joffre, Ferdinand Foch and Philippe Pétain, were alike modest. The influence of the Church was fast diminishing among the peasantry and the industrial masses; its residual power rested with the aristocracy and the bourgeoisie. The nation was becoming more socially enlightened: though Article 213 of the *Code Napoléon* still decreed that a wife owed legal obedience to her husband, a modest but growing number of women entered the legal or medical professions, foremost among them Marie Curie, who won two Nobel Prizes.

Rural conditions remained primitive, with peasants living in close proximity to their animals. Foreigners sneered that French standards of hygiene were low: most people had only one bath a week, and humbler middle-class men kept up appearances with false collars and cuffs. The French were more tolerant of brothels than any other nation in Europe, though there was some dispute about whether this reflected enlightenment or depravity. Alcoholism was a serious problem, worsened by rising prosperity: the average Frenchman consumed 162 litres of wine a year; some miners assuaged the harshness of their labours by drinking up to six litres a day. The country had half a million bars – one for every eighty-two people. Mothers were known to put wine in their babies' bottles, and doctors frequently prescribed it for illness, even in children. Alcohol and masculinity were deemed inseparable. To drink beer or water was unpatriotic.

French politicians were obsessed with the need to counter Germany's demographic advantage. Between 1890 and 1896, the years when many of those who would fight the First World War were born, Kaiser Wilhelm's people produced more than twice as many children as the Republic; the 1907 census showed France's population at just thirty-nine million, meaning that there were three Germans for every two Frenchmen. French working mothers received paid maternity leave, with a cash bonus to those who breast-fed. Health standards had risen impressively since the beginning of the twentieth century, when one in ten new French military recruits stood less than five feet one inch tall, but many bourgeois families chose to defy their priests and restrict themselves to one child. Poincaré presented his 1913 three-year compulsory military service law as an essential defensive measure. By heroic endeavours, France had restored itself to the status of a great power. But almost no one, including its own people, supposed its unaided military strength the equal of Germany's – which was why it had sought the alliance with Russia.

The British, last-comer to create a third pillar of the Entente, ruled the largest empire the world had ever seen, and remained its foremost financial power, but discerning contemporaries understood that their dominance was waning. At home, vast new wealth was being generated, but social and political divisions had become acute. Britain's five million most prosperous inhabitants shared an annual income of £830 million, while the remaining thirty-eight millions made do with the balance, £880 million. The journalist George Dangerfield looked back at Britain's condition in the Edwardian and post-Edwardian era from the perspective of 1935 in his milestone work *The Strange Death of Liberal England*:

> The new financier, the new plutocrat, had little of that sense of responsibility which once had sanctioned the power of England's landed classes. He was a purely international figure, or so it seemed, and money was his language ... Where did the money come from? Nobody seemed to care. It was there to be spent, and to be spent in the most ostentatious manner possible; for its new masters set the fashion ... Society in the last pre-war years grew wildly plutocratic; the middle classes became more complacent and dependent; only the workers seemed to be deprived of their share in prosperity ... The middle classes ... looked upon the producers of England with a jaundiced, a fearful and vindictive gaze.

In 1926 C.E. Montague took much the same view of the pre-1914 period in *Rough Justice*, an autobiographical novel: 'The English world that he loved, and believed in, seemed now to be failing, and failing first at the top ... The old riders seemed to be falling out with their horses – fearing them, not going near them if they could help it, shirking the old job of understanding their wants and sharing their slow, friendly thoughts ... The only rights of captaincy that the old ruling class had ever possessed were drawn from the strength of its members' love and knowledge of tenants, labourers, servants, private soldiers and sailors, their own lifelong comrades in the rural economy, in sport, in the rearing of children and in the chivalries of war and adventure.' This was sentimental tosh, but reflected the fact that the aristocracy and the Conservative Party fought tooth and nail to resist the Liberals' 1909 introduction of basic social reforms.

Government and its bureaucracies scarcely impinged on most people's lives, for good or ill. It was possible to travel abroad without a passport, and freely to exchange unlimited sums of currency. A foreigner could take up residence in Britain without any process of official consent. Though since gaining office in 1905 the Liberals had doubled expenditure on social services, the £200 million raised by all forms of taxation in 1913–14 amounted to less than 8 per cent of national income. The school-leaving age was thirteen; at seventy a British citizen became eligible for a meagre pension, and in 1911 Lloyd George had created a primitive insurance scheme to protect the sick and unemployed.

Nonetheless, a decade into the new century the British worker was poorer in real terms than he had been in 1900, and disaffected in consequence. There were constant disputes and stoppages, especially in the coal industry. In 1910 seamen and dockers struck to demand a minimum wage and better working conditions; there was also a transport strike. Women workers in a Bermondsey confectionery factory, paid between seven and nine shillings a week – young girls got three shillings – won increases of one to four shillings a week after downing tools. In 1911, over ten million working days were lost to strikes – compare this with 2011's figure of 1.4 million days. Militancy derived not from trade union leaders, many of whom became as frightened as employers, but from the shop floor. A despairing union secretary told an industrial arbitrator that he could not understand what had come over the country: 'Everyone seems to have lost their heads.'

The hand of the state was most visible in its use of military power to suppress working-class revolt. In 1910 troops were deployed against rioters at the Rhondda Valley coal pits: Hussars and Lancashire Fusiliers were sent to Tonypandy. Winston Churchill as home secretary dispatched a cavalry column to cow London's East End, home to thousands of striking dockers. During a rail strike, the Mayor of Chesterfield urged troops to fire on a mob wrecking the town's station; the officer in command prudently refused to give the order.

Coal owners were the least sympathetic representatives of contemporary capitalism: in 1912 they summarily rejected union demands that men should be paid five shillings a shift, boys two shillings – what became known as 'the five and two'. This at a time when the London wine merchants Berry Bros charged ninety-six shillings a dozen for Veuve Clicquot champagne, sixty shillings a dozen for 1898 Nuits Saint-Georges. That year, over thirty-eight million working days were lost to strikes. Nor was it hard to understand workers' grievances: in October 1913 an explosion at Senghenydd colliery, caused by criminal management safety negligence, cost 439 lives. In the Commons tears ran down the face of Herbert Asquith, the prime minister, as he appealed to striking workers to return to the pits. Asquith's wife Margot, a raffish creature of indifferent judgement but forceful personality, sought to negotiate privately with the miners' leader to resolve the dispute. When he refused, she wrote crossly: 'I don't see why anyone should know we have met.' Between 1910 and 1914, trade union membership rose from 2.37 million to almost four million. In the seven months before the outbreak of war, British industry was hit by 937 strikes.

Yet at least as grave as industrial warfare was the Ulster crisis. Between 1912 and 1914 this created a real prospect of civil war within the United Kingdom. Home Rule for Ireland was the price Asquith had agreed to pay for the support of Irish MPs in passing his bitterly divisive 1909 budget, seed of the Welfare State. Thereafter the Protestants of Ulster, determined to resist becoming a minority in a Catholic-ruled society, armed themselves. Their rejection of the Home Rule legislation then passing through Parliament won the support of the Conservative Party and its leaders, even unto preparing violent resistance to its implementation. Much of the aristocracy owned Irish property, which spawned a special sense of outrage against Asquith.

In March 1914, some army officers made explicit their refusal to participate in coercion of the Ulster rebels through the so-called 'Curragh Mutiny', which precipitated the resignation of the Chief of the Imperial General Staff, Field-Marshal Sir John French, and the secretary for war, Col. Jack Seely. The latter, in a moment of madness, told the commander-in-chief that officers who did not wish to serve in Ulster could 'disappear'. Maj. Gen. Sir Henry Wilson, director of military operations at the War Office, wrote triumphantly in his diary: 'we soldiers beat Asquith and his vile tricks'. The prime minister temporarily took on the war portfolio himself.

The Liberals whom Asquith led formed one of the most talented administrations in British history, dominated in 1914 by such figures as Lloyd George, Chancellor of the Exchequer; Winston Churchill, First Lord of the Admiralty; Richard Haldane, a former reforming war minister, now

Lord Chancellor. The prime minister himself was a survivor of an earlier era, old enough to have seen, as a boy of twelve in 1864, the bodies of five murderers dangling from the gallows outside Newgate, their heads concealed by white hoods. A lawyer of modest middle-class origins, 'a Roman reserve was always natural to Asquith', in the words of his biographer. 'He fought against any expression of his stronger feelings.' George Dangerfield went further, asserting that Asquith lacked imagination and passion; that, for all his high intelligence, he failed convincingly to address any of the great crises which overtook Britain during his years of office: 'He was ingenious but not subtle, he could improvise quite brilliantly on somebody else's theme. He was moderately imperialist, moderately progressive, moderately humorous, and being the most fastidious of Liberal politicians, only moderately evasive.' If this judgement was cynical, it is plain that by August 1914 Asquith was a tired old man.

British politics had become savage in temper and often irresponsible in conduct. Lord Halsbury, a veteran Conservative lawyer, denounced 'government by a cabinet controlled by rank socialists'. A Tory MP hurled a rule book at Winston Churchill in the Commons library, striking him in the face. Before the great Ulster struggle, rival party leaders were often seen in the same drawing room, but now they and their respective followers were socially estranged. When Margot Asquith wrote to protest at being excluded from Lord Curzon's May ball, attended by the King and Queen, Curzon replied haughtily that it would be 'impolitic to invite, even to a social gathering, the wife and daughter of the head of a Government to which the majority of my friends are inflexibly opposed'.

The Scottish-Canadian Bonar Law had succeeded Arthur Balfour as Tory standard-bearer in November 1911, and played the Ulster 'Orange card' as a cynical gambit against the Liberals. On 28 November 1913, the leader of 'His Majesty's Loyal Opposition' publicly appealed to the British Army not to enforce Home Rule in northern Ireland. This was a staggering piece of constitutional impropriety, which nonetheless commanded the support of his party and most of the aristocracy, while not provoking the censure of the King. Prominent among the Unionists was the lawyer Sir Edward Carson, courtroom nemesis of Oscar Wilde and aptly characterised as 'an intelligent fanatic'. Captain James Craig, leader of the rebellious Ulstermen, wrote: 'There is a spirit spreading abroad which I can testify to from my personal knowledge, that Germany and the German Emperor would be preferable to the rule of John Redmond [and his Irish Home Rulers].'

Field-Marshal Lord Roberts, Britain's most famous old soldier, publicly applauded the April 1914 shipment of guns to the Protestant rebels, and declared that any attempt to coerce Ulster would be 'the ruin of the army'. Thousands of openly armed men paraded in Belfast, addressed by Carson, Craig and that most incendiary of Conservatives, F.E. Smith. And all the while the British government did – nothing. In southern Ireland, militant nationalists took their cue from Carson and his success in defying Parliament: they set about procuring their own weapons. The British Army proved much less indulgent to nationalist militancy than to the Ulstermen's excesses. On Sunday, 26 July 1914 at Bachelor's Walk in Dublin, troops fired on unarmed civilians – admittedly in the aftermath of a gun-running episode – killing three and injuring thirty-eight.

If the British Empire was viewed around the world as rich and powerful, the Asquith government was seen as chronically weak. It was conspicuously failing to quell violent industrial action or the Ulster madness. It seemed unable effectively to address even the suffragette movement, whose clamorous campaign for votes for women had become deafening. Militants were smashing windows all over London; using acid to burn slogans on golf club greens; hunger-striking in prison. In June 1913 Emily Davison was killed after being struck by the King's horse at the Derby. In the first seven months of 1914, 107 buildings were set on fire by suffragettes.

Asquith's critics ignored an obvious point: no man could have contained or suppressed the huge social and political forces shaking Britain. George Dangerfield wrote: 'Very few prime ministers in history have been afflicted by so many plagues and in so short a space of time.' The prominent Irish Home Ruler John Dillon told Wilfrid Scawen Blunt: 'the country is menaced with revolution'. Domestic strife made a powerful impression on opinion abroad: a great democracy was seen to be sinking into decadence and decay. Britain's allies, France and Russia, were dismayed. Its prospective enemies, notably in Germany, found it hard to imagine that a country convulsed in such a fashion – with even its little army riven by faction – could threaten their continental power and ambitions.

2 BATTLE PLANS

Many Europeans anticipated with varying degrees of enthusiasm that their two rival alliances would sooner or later come to blows. Far from being regarded as unthinkable, continental war was viewed as a highly plausible, and by no means intolerable, outcome of international tensions. Europe had twenty million regular soldiers and reservists, and each nation developed plans for every contingency in which they might be deployed. All the prospective belligerents proposed to attack. The British Army's 1909 Field Service Regulations, largely drafted by Sir Douglas Haig, asserted: 'Decisive success in battle can be gained only by a vigorous offensive.' In February 1914, Russian military intelligence passed to its government two German memoranda, discussing the need to prepare public opinion for a two-front war. The Triple Alliance's third party, Italy, was notionally committed to fight alongside Germany and Austria, which meant that the French must allocate troops not only to meet the Germans, but also to defend their south-eastern frontier. All the European powers remained nonetheless uncertain what Italy would do in the event of a war, as were Italians themselves. What seemed plain was that the Rome government would eventually offer support to whichever power promised to indulge its ambitions for territorial aggrandisement.

In Germany, chief of staff Helmuth von Moltke inherited in 1906 from his predecessor, Alfred Graf von Schlieffen, a scheme for a massive sweeping advance through northern France, around Paris, to smash the French army before turning on Russia. For the past century, Schlieffen's vision has lain at the heart of all debate about whether Germany might have won the war in 1914. The confidence of the nation's leadership that it could successfully launch a general European conflict rested entirely upon the Schlieffen concept, or more exactly Moltke's modification of it.

The Kaiser liked to pretend that he ruled Germany, and occasionally he did so; his appointed chancellor, the liberal-conservative Bethmann Hollweg, exercised varying influence, while striving to manage an increasingly hostile Reichstag. But the most powerful single figure in the Wilhelmine Empire was Moltke, controlling the most formidable military machine in Europe. He was an unexpected general, a Christian Scientist who played the cello and was prey to deep melancholy – '*der traurige Julius*' – 'sad Julius'. Conspicuous in his life were devotion to his wife and a fascination with the afterlife, spiritualism and the occult, which she encouraged. Moltke believed that he occupied the most honourable position on earth. He and the army answered to no politician, only to the Kaiser.

The Great General Staff, which operated under his direction, was Germany's most respected institution. It consisted of 625 officers, who worked in a building on Berlin's Königsplatz in which Moltke and his family occupied a flat. Security was tight: there were no secretaries or clerks; staff officers drafted all documents. Once the cleaners left each morning, no women save Eliza Moltke and her maid entered the building. Each year when a new mobilisation plan was prepared, copies of the redundant version were meticulously destroyed. The Staff's output owed little to technology: it owned no automobiles; even the influential Railway Department had only one typewriter; urgent telephone calls were made from a single box in a corridor. There was no canteen, and most officers brought in packed lunches to eat at their desks during working days of twelve to fourteen hours. Every member of the General Staff was taught to think of himself as one among a hallowed elite, subject to social rules which were meticulously observed: no man – for instance – might enter a bar frequented by socialists.

Moltke himself sought to convey an impression of personal strength that would soon prove to have been illusory, but which exercised a critical influence on the advance to war. A highly intelligent and cultured man, he rose through a close association with the Kaiser, which began when he served as adjutant to his uncle, 'the great Moltke', victor over France in 1870–71. Wilhelm found the hero's nephew congenial, and clung to a conviction that the old man's genius must have passed to the next generation. But the decision to appoint Helmuth chief of staff was controversial, indeed to some shocking. One of Moltke's former military instructors wrote: 'This man could be disastrous.' Wilhelm's choice plainly derived from their personal relationship: he found the general an agreeable companion with a pleasing bedside manner, that essential requirement for courtiers through the ages. Moltke had shown himself a competent officer without offering – or having much opportunity to display – evidence of military genius.

It was ironic that after 1890 the elder Moltke argued that Europe's fate should thenceforth be decided diplomatically rather than on the battlefield: he thought the usefulness of war to Germany was exhausted. But from 1906 onwards, his much less gifted nephew professed to think that Schlieffen's concept of a grand envelopment offered the prospect of securing German dominance of Europe. Moltke told Austrian chief of staff Conrad von Hötzendorf in February 1913: 'Austria's fate will not be definitively decided along the Bug but rather along the Seine.' He became imbued with faith that new technologies – balloons and motor vehicles – would empower highly centralised battlefield control of Germany's armies by himself. Some other senior officers were much more sceptical. Karl von Einem, especially, warned about the difficulties of directing the

movements of almost three million men, and the likely operational limitations of unfit and ill-trained reservists; he anticipated in a fashion that
proved prescient a progressive loss of momentum during the proposed
epic dash across France.

Moltke, however, remained if not an enthusiast, at least a consistent
fatalist about the inevitability of war with Russia and France. In October
1912, by then sixty-four, he said: 'If war is coming, I hope it will come
soon, before I am too old to cope with things satisfactorily.' He told the
Kaiser he was confident a decisive campaign could be swiftly won, and
restated this advice early in the 1914 July crisis. The huge enigma about
the chief of staff was that all the while, he nursed private doubts and fears
which would burst forth in the most dramatic fashion when conflict came.
The rational part of his nature told him that a great clash between great
powers must be protracted and hard, not swift and easy. He once told the
Kaiser: 'the next war will be a national war. It will not be settled by one
decisive battle but will be a long wearisome struggle with an enemy who
will not be overcome until his whole national force is broken … a war
which will utterly exhaust our own people even if we are victorious.'

Yet his own conduct in the years before 1914 belied such prudent
caution. He acquiesced in the prospect of a grand European collision with
a steadiness that prevailed when others – Bethmann and the Kaiser –
sometimes faltered. Germany's highest commander succumbed to a
disease common among senior soldiers of many nationalities and eras: he
wished to demonstrate to his government and people that their vastly
expensive armed forces could fulfil their fantasies. Moltke famously, or
notoriously, characterised himself to Prince von Bülow: 'I do not lack
personal courage, but I lack the power of rapid decision; I am too reflec-
tive, too scrupulous, or, if you like, too conscientious for such a post. I lack
the capacity for risking all on a single throw.' Yet, in contradiction of such
a profession of self-knowledge, he yearned to show himself worthy of a
responsibility for which most of his peers thought him unfit, by achieving
a triumph for his country. This required an awesomely fast mobilisation
and concentration of forces; the deployment of a small holding force to
check the Russians, while the nation's overwhelming strength conquered
France in a campaign of forty days, before turning East.

Austria-Hungary's plans were more flexible, indeed chaotic, because
the Empire could not be sure whether it would be fighting Serbia alone –
as it hoped – or contesting a second front on its Galician border with
Russian Poland. Many bizarre figures jostled for attention on the European

stage in 1914, but Conrad Hötzendorf was notable among them. Churchill described him as a 'dark, small, frail, thin officer with piercing and expressive eyes set in the face of an ascetic'. It is hard to imagine a man less suited to his role: an epic incompetent, he was also an extreme imperialist, wanting the Hapsburgs to dominate the Adriatic, the eastern Mediterranean, the Balkans and North Africa. He perfectly fulfilled the elder Moltke's dictum about the most dangerous kind of officer, by being both stupid and intensely energetic. His wife had died a decade earlier, and he shared a home with his mother. He had lately fallen in love with Virginie von Reininghaus, a brewery magnate's wife, who became his obsession. He convinced himself that if he could lead Austria to a great military victory, he could surf a wave of personal glory to persuade his Gina to divorce her husband and marry him. He wrote to her of his hope for a 'war from which I could return crowned with success that would allow me to break through all the barriers between us ... and claim you as my own dearest wife'.

Since 1906 Conrad had been demanding military action against Serbia. In the seventeen months between 1 January 1913 and 1 June 1914, the chief of staff urged war on his government twenty-six times. He wrote to Moltke on St Valentine's Day 1914, asserting the urgency of Austria's need to 'break the ring that once again threatens to enclose us'. For Conrad, and indeed for Berchtold, the Archduke's death offered a heaven-sent excuse for war, rather than a justification for it. After witnessing the shrinkage of the Ottoman Empire, humbled by young and assertive Balkan nations during the regional conflicts of the preceding three years, Conrad believed that Sarajevo offered Austria its last chance to escape the same fate, by destroying the threat of assertive Slavdom embodied by Serbia. He said: 'Such an ancient monarchy and such an ancient army [as those of the Hapsburgs] cannot perish ingloriously.'

Berchtold, Austria's foreign minister, characterised Conrad's policy in July 1914 as 'war, war, war'. Wishing to expunge the shame of Austria's 1866 defeat by Prussia, the general deplored 'this foul peace which drags on and on'. So powerful was his craving for military collision that he gave scarcely a thought to its practical aspects. For years Austria's army had lagged behind those of its neighbours, gathering mould. Parliament resisted the higher taxes that would have been required by bigger budgets, and the navy consumed much of the available cash. Though Austrian industry developed good weapons – especially heavy artillery and the M95 rifle – the army remained too poor to buy them in adequate numbers.

There were many disaffected people among the hotchpotch of ethnic minorities that made up the Empire. According to 1911 figures, among every thousand Austro-Hungarian soldiers, there were an average of 267 Germans, 233 Hungarians, 135 Czechs, eighty-five Poles, eighty-one Ukrainians, sixty-seven Croatians and Serbs, fifty-four Romanians, thirty-eight Slovaks, twenty-six Slovenes and fourteen Italians. Of the officer corps, by contrast, 76.1 per cent were Germans, 10.7 per cent Hungarians and 5.2 per cent Czechs. In proportion to population, Germans had three times their rightful number of officers, Hungarians half, Slavs about one-tenth. The Austrian army was thus run on colonial lines, with many Slav riflemen led into battle by Germans, rather as British officers led their Indian Army. Of all the European powers, Austria was least fit to justify its pretensions on the battlefield. Conrad simply assumed that, if Russia intervened in Serbia's interest, the Germans would take the strain.

Vienna had been urged by Berlin to adopt harsh policies towards the Serbs. As early as 1912, Wilhelm and Moltke assured Franz Ferdinand and Conrad that they 'could fully count on Germany's support in all circumstances' – what some historians have called 'the first blank cheque'. Nor did Berlin make any secret of its commitment: on 28 November the secretary of state, Alfred von Kiderlen-Waechter, told the Reichstag: 'If Austria is forced, for whatever reason, to fight for its position as a Great Power, then we must stand by her side.' Bethmann Hollweg echoed this message on 2 December, saying that if the Austrians were attacked by Russia for asserting their legitimate interests in the Balkans, 'then we would fight for the maintenance of our own position in Europe, in defence of our own future and security'.

A meeting of the Kaiser and his warlords – Bethmann and foreign minister Gottlieb von Jagow were absent – which took place at the Royal Palace on 8 December 1912 has been the focus of intense attention throughout the three generations since it was revealed. Wilhelm and Germany's principal generals and admirals debated Haldane's reported insistence upon Britain's commitment to preserving a continental balance of power. Though no minutes were taken, immediately afterwards Georg Müller, chief of Wilhelm's naval cabinet, recorded in his diary that Moltke said: 'War the sooner the better.' The admiral added on his own account: 'he does not draw the logical conclusion from this, which is to present Russia or France or both with an ultimatum which would unleash the war with right on our side'.

Three other sources confirm Müller's account, including that of Saxony's military plenipotentiary in Berlin, who wrote on the 11th to his state's minister of war: 'His Excellency von Moltke wants war ... His Excellency von Tirpitz on the other hand would prefer if it came in a year's time when the [Kiel] canal and the Heligoland submarine base would be ready.' Following the 8 December meeting, Germany's leaders agreed that there should be a press campaign to prepare the nation to fight Russia, though this did not happen. Müller wrote to Bethmann to inform him of the meeting's conclusions. Even if a cautious view is taken of the 1912 War Council's significance, rejecting the darkest 'Fischer' thesis that Germany thereafter directed policy towards precipitating a general European conflict, the record of subsequent German conduct shows Berlin strikingly untroubled by the prospect of such an outcome. The nation's leaders were confident they could prevail, so long as a clash came before Russian re-armament was completed in 1916. Müller felt obliged to inform the Kaiser that some senior officers were so convinced war was imminent that they had transferred their personal holdings of cash and shares into gold.

Bethmann at times thereafter seemed to waver. For instance, he said in June 1913: 'I have had enough of war and bellicose talk and of eternal armaments. It is high time that the great nations settle down and pursue peaceful work. Otherwise it will certainly come to an explosion, which no one wants and which will hurt everyone.' Yet the chancellor played a prominent role in strengthening Germany's war machine. In conversation with Field-Marshal Wilhelm von der Goltz, he told the old soldier and military intellectual that he could secure the Reichstag's support for any amount of military funding. Goltz responded that in that case the army had better hurry to present its shopping list. Yes, said the chancellor, but if you ask for a lot of money you will need to be seen to use it soon – to strike. Goltz warmly agreed. Then Bethmann added, in a characteristic moment of hesitation: 'But even Bismarck avoided a preventive war in the year [18]75.' He was very conscious that the Iron Chancellor, towards the end of his life, had urged that Germany should stop fighting. Goltz said scornfully that it was easy for Bismarck to take that line, after winning three earlier wars. Bethmann became a prime mover in pushing through parliament the huge 1913 Army Bill, which dramatically increased the nation's military strength.

Meanwhile, Moltke was only the foremost of Germany's leading soldiers who, during the nineteen months between the December 1912 War Council and the August 1914 outbreak of war, displayed a keen appetite for a European showdown. In May of the latter year, army quartermaster-general Gen. Count Georg von Waldersee wrote a memorandum which expressed optimism about Germany's immediate strategic prospects, coupled to gloom about the longer term: 'Germany has no reason to expect to be attacked in the near future, but … it not only has no reason whatever to avoid a conflict, but also, more than that, the chances of achieving a speedy victory in a major European war are today still very favourable for Germany and for the Triple Alliance as well. Soon, however, this will no longer be the case.' There is vastly more documentary evidence to support the case that German leaders were willing for war in 1914 than exists to sustain any of the alternative scenarios proposed in recent years.

The Triple Entente had in common with the Triple Alliance the fact that only two of its parties were firmly committed to fight together. It represented an expression of goodwill and possible – but by no means assured – military collaboration: something more than that between France and Russia, something less on the part of Britain. The Russians always knew that they must fight any war from the exposed salient of Poland, vulnerable in the north and west to Germany, in the south to the Hapsburg Empire. The race to deploy forces following mobilisation was in the Russians' eyes a race to save Poland; their first priority was to secure its borders.

Back in 1900 they had made a decision to launch simultaneous offensives against the Germans in East Prussia, against the Austrians in Galicia. Though they wavered about this in 1905, by 1912 they had renewed the commitment, and sustained it thereafter: they were much attracted to the notion of conquering Hapsburg Galicia, and thus acquiring a strong new mountain frontier on the Carpathians. They had two alternative schemes. The first, 'Plan G', covered the unlikely contingency that Germany deployed the bulk of its army in the East. The second, implemented in 1914, was 'Plan A'. This required two armies to drive into East Prussia as a preliminary to an invasion of Germany proper. Meanwhile a further three armies were to launch the main thrust against the Austrians, driving them back to the Carpathians.

France proposed to implement against Germany its 'Plan XVII'. This had been refined by Joffre, but was far less detailed than Moltke's arrangements. Where Schlieffen sketched a design for a grand invasion of France, the French General Staff merely schemed operations against the German army, though these assumed a subsequent advance into the Kaiser's realm.

Plan XVII principally addressed the logistics for concentrating forces behind the frontier, and contained no timetable for operations, nor commitment to explicit territorial objectives. Much more important than the plan were the ethos and doctrine promoted with messianic fervour by the chief of staff. 'The French Army,' declared its 1913 Regulations, the work of Joffre, 'returning to its traditions, henceforth knows no law but the offensive.' Berlin's best source in Paris, 'Agent 17', an Austrian *boulevardier* named Baron Schluga von Tastenfeld who acquired much of his information by mingling at the grand salons, informed Moltke – correctly – that Joffre was likely to make his main effort in the Ardennes, at the centre of the front.

France's chief of staff was a technician, not an intellectual. Always a grave figure, he had acquired in childhood the nickname '*le père Joffre*' – 'Papa Joffre'. German intelligence characterised him as hard-working and responsible, but judged him too slow and heavy to respond effectively to such a spectacular initiative as the Schlieffen envelopment. French politicians, however, approved of Joffre because – unlike many of his peers – he was devoid of personal political ambitions. They also found him refreshingly direct. Legend held that Joseph Caillaux, France's leader during the Agadir crisis, asked the chief of staff, then newly appointed: 'General, they say Napoleon waged war only if he thought he had a 70–30 chance of winning. Have we a 70–30 chance?' Joffre answered tersely: '*Non, monsieur le premier ministre*.'

Whether or not the chief of staff indeed took such a cautious view in 1911, he had since become more confident. Joffre believed that, in partnership with the Russians, the French army now possessed the strength, and above all the spirit, to vanquish the Germans. He made a misjudgement common to all Europe's soldiers in 1914, based upon an exaggerated belief in the power of human courage. The French called it '*cran*' – guts – and '*élan vital*'. Training emphasised the overriding importance of the will to win. The French army equipped itself with large numbers of its superb *soixante-quinze* – a 75mm quick-firing field gun – but neglected howitzers and heavy artillery, which it considered irrelevant to its offensive doctrine. Events would demonstrate that 75s and *cran* did not constitute an effective system for making war, but in the summer of 1914 Joffre and most of his colleagues supposed that they did.

As for French appraisals of German intentions, the intelligence officers of the Deuxième Bureau importantly underestimated the overall strength of the German army, because they did not anticipate that Moltke would deploy his reserve formations alongside his regular ones; they also thought he would send twenty-two divisions to face the Russians, whereas in reality he committed only eleven. They correctly predicted that the Germans would attempt an envelopment, but because of their misjudgement of enemy strength, they greatly mistook its geographical scope. They supposed that the Germans would come through only a corner of Belgium, instead of sweeping across the entire country. Joffre calculated that German concentrations in the north and south must make Moltke's centre weak, and vulnerable to a French thrust. In this he was quite mistaken.

Both sides' commanders grossly underrated their opponents. Elaborate rival plans for mobilisation and deployment were not the cause of conflict in 1914, but the Great Powers might have been much less willing for war had their soldiers recognised the fundamental weakness of their offensive doctrine. All the nations' assessments were critically influenced by Japanese successes in attack in 1905, against Russian machine-guns. They concluded that this experience demonstrated that if the spirit was sufficiently exalted, it could prevail against modern technology.

Enthusiastic British patriots, in the early summer of 1914, were looking forward to a commemoration the following June of the centenary of the Battle of Waterloo: they proposed to make the occasion a celebration of the fact that for a hundred years no British army had shed blood in western Europe. Nonetheless, cautious contingency plans were in place to do so again. The British and French armies had begun staff talks in 1906, and Britain signed an agreement with Russia the following year. The Russians, however, saw reason to question their new friend's good faith when in 1912 a British shipyard began building for the Turks two battleships, which represented a mortal threat to the Tsar's dominance of the Black Sea. Challenged by St Petersburg, the Foreign Office responded blithely that it could not interfere with private commercial contracts. A British naval mission was meanwhile aiding the Turkish fleet, at the same time as Liman von Sanders trained the Turkish army.

Once in 1908 when Bethmann Hollweg was dining with Lloyd George, Germany's chancellor became strident, waving his arms as he denounced the 'iron ring' enemies were forging around his nation: 'England is embracing France. She is making friends with Russia. But it is not that you love each other; it is that you hate Germany!' Bethmann was wrong. Britain's adherence to the Entente was prompted much less by enthusiasm for embracing Russia and France as allies or partners against the Kaiser than by a desire to diminish the number of Britain's enemies. It was increasingly understood, at least in Whitehall, that the vast empire of which the British people were so proud threatened to become an economic and strategic burden rather than a source of wealth. Russian power in central Asia, and the Great Game which derived from it, demanded much effort and expenditure to counter. Britain's 1898 confrontation with France over Fashoda on the Upper Nile had reawakened visceral jealousies and enmities. What evolved during the first decade of the twentieth century was less a triple entente to which Britain was a committed partner, than two parallel processes of détente.

Sazonov, in St Petersburg, knew how badly his country and France needed Britain. He wrote on 31 December 1913: 'Both powers [France and Russia] are scarcely capable of dealing Germany a mortal blow even in the event of success on the battlefield, which is always uncertain. But a struggle in which England took part might be fatal for Germany.' Thus the foreign minister was infuriated by London's 'vacillating and self-effacing policy', which he considered a critical impediment to deterrence. But British enthusiasm for Russia remained tepid. It was a source of embarrassment to many doughty democrats that their country should be associated with an absolutist autocracy, and worse still with its Balkan clients. In Paris near the climax of the July 1914 crisis, Raymond Recouly of *Le Figaro* met Sir Francis Bertie, the British ambassador, as he was about to enter the Quai d'Orsay. The Englishman, nicknamed 'the Bull' by colleagues, wrung his hands about Europe's condition, then said: 'Do you trust the Russians? We don't, above half!' He added: 'I would say pretty much the same of the Serbs. That is why our country is not going to feel comfortable about entering a quarrel in which the Serbs and Russians are involved.' Moreover, many British people, especially the elderly, were less than enthusiastic about entering any conflict on the same side as France. Lord Rosebery said crossly in 1904 when his Conservative colleagues welcomed the Entente: 'You are all wrong. It means war with Germany in the end!' Old Lady Londesborough, Wellington's great-niece, told Osbert Sitwell in 1914: 'It's not the Germans but the French I'm frightened of!'

Such mistrust was reciprocal. A prime motive for President Poincaré's determination to cling close to Russia as a military ally was his fear that Britain would not be there beside the French army on the day. While France and Russia had signed a bilateral treaty and were committed to support each other against attack, Britain was party to no such intimate pact, instead merely to expressions of good intentions, and army and naval staff talks. The first discussions of a possible expeditionary force to France took place in December 1908. Thereafter, a sub-committee meeting of the Committee of Imperial Defence on 23 August 1911, attended by Asquith and Churchill, addressed at length the contingency that Britain would be obliged to intervene in the event of a European war. One modern historian has suggested that this gathering 'set the course for a military confrontation between Britain and Germany'. That seems a wild exaggeration: no one knew better than Asquith how reluctant might be his own party, and Parliament, to endorse participation in a European conflict.

The prime minister wrote sternly after the CID meeting that 'all questions of policy have been & must be reserved for the decision of the Cabinet, & it is quite outside the function of military or naval officers to prejudge such questions'. The contemporary view of an exasperated senior British staff officer – Henry Wilson – was that 'there was still no definite agreement with France to come in with her, nothing but a very grudging authorisation by our Gov to the General Staff on the theory of eventual co-operation'. This seems about right. The head of the Foreign Office, Sir Arthur Nicolson, reminded the foreign secretary in August 1914 that 'you have over and over again promised M. Cambon [the French ambassador] that if Germany was the aggressor you would stand by France'. Grey replied in a manner that justified every French prejudice about Anglo-Saxon duplicity: 'Yes, but he has nothing in writing.'

One recent chronicler of this period suggests that Asquith's ministers and generals engaged in 'enthusiastic planning for war' following the 1911 meeting. Precautionary steps were certainly taken and plans made from that year onwards – for instance, earmarking Oxford University's Examination Schools for use as a hospital. But it seems impossible justly to characterise these measures as enthusiastic. What was extraordinary about all British policy-making during the evolution of the Entente, reflected in attitudes struck at the 1911 CID meeting, was that the government acknowledged possible participation in a continental war, while proposing to contribute an absurdly small army to fulfilling such a purpose. Winston Churchill wrote later that as a young cavalry officer in the 1890s, he and his kind were so conscious of the insignificance of the British Army by comparison with its continental counterparts that 'no Jingo lieutenant or fire-eating staff officer … even in his most sanguine moments, would have believed that our little Army would again be sent to Europe'. Fifteen years on, while Haldane had reformed the army's structure, it remained tiny by continental standards. The 1913 Army Estimates made no mention whatsoever of a possible British ground role in a European conflict. The putative Expeditionary Force was given that designation because nobody knew where abroad it might be deployed – conceivably in India, Africa, the Middle East.

Here was a manifestation of a huge, historic British folly, repeated over many centuries including the twenty-first: the adoption of gesture strategy, committing small forces as an earnest of good intentions, heedless of their gross inadequacy for the military purpose at hand. Since 1907, Lord Northcliffe had been campaigning for conscription in his *Daily Mail*, to create a British army of a size to match the Empire's greatness, but his crusade roused little support. The most grievous charge against the Asquith government, and explicitly against the foreign secretary Sir Edward Grey, is that they pursued policies which sensibly acknowledged a likelihood that Britain would be unable to remain neutral in the event of a general European war, because German hegemony on the continent would represent an intolerable outcome, but they declined to take appropriate practical measures to participate in such a struggle.

Grey is usually depicted as a gentle, civilised figure who lamented the coming of war in 1914 with unaccustomed eloquence, and wrote fine books on birdwatching and fly-fishing. A widower of fifty-two, his personal affairs were less arid than most of his contemporaries assumed. He conducted a lively love life, albeit much more discreetly than his colleague Lloyd George; Grey's most recent biographer identifies two illegitimate children. Some of his contemporaries disdained him. Sir Eyre Crowe, a Foreign Office official who was admittedly prone to intemperance, called Grey 'a futile, useless, weak fool'. The foreign secretary's accustomed taciturnity caused Lloyd George, for one, to conclude that there was less to him than met the eye; that his economy with words reflected not strength of character, but debility. Grey spoke no foreign languages, and disliked Abroad. Although a highly intelligent man, he was also a narrow one, subject to violent mood swings.

Yet from 1905 to 1916 he ran Britain's foreign policy as a private bailiwick. Lloyd George wrote: 'During the eight years that preceded the war, the Cabinet devoted a ridiculously small percentage of its time to a consideration of foreign affairs.' The Asquith government's attitude to such matters, and to the other European powers, reflected an epic moral conceit, manifested in a condescension which especially upset the Germans. The French ambassador in London, Paul Cambon, observed sardonically that nothing gave greater pleasure to an Englishman than to discover that the interests of England matched those of mankind at large: 'and where such a confluence does not exist, he does his best to create it'. At a dinner party where several members of the government were present, Lord Northcliffe asserted contemptuously that Britain's newspaper editors were better informed about foreign affairs than any cabinet minister. The chancellor said of the foreign secretary: 'Sir Edward Grey belongs to the class which, through heredity and tradition, expects to find a place on the magisterial bench to sit in judgement upon and above their fellow men, before they ever have any opportunity to make themselves acquainted with the tasks and trials of mankind.'

This was a characteristically nasty jibe, but Henry Wilson wrote after his own 1911 conversations with ministers about conflict scenarios that he was not impressed by 'the grasp of the situation possessed by Grey and Haldane [then secretary for war], Grey being much the most ignorant & careless of the two, he not only had no idea of what war means but he struck me as not wanting to know ... an ignorant, vain & weak man quite unfit to be the Foreign Minister of any country larger than Portugal'. Bernard Shaw hated Grey as 'a Junker from his topmost hair to the tips of his toes ... [with] a personal taste for mendacity', a charge that related to a brutal British response to a 1906 Egyptian village dispute about officers' pigeon-shooting rights.

If this was Shavian hyperbole, Grey's secret diplomacy was certainly high-handed – as was all British conduct of foreign affairs in that era. In August 1904 Lord Percy, for the then-Conservative government, responded with patrician magnificence to a Commons question about the newly concluded Anglo-French Agreement: 'Speculation and conjecture as to the existence or non-existence of secret clauses in international treaties is a public privilege, the maintenance of which depends upon official reticence.' But Asquith wrote to Grey on 5 September 1911, warning about the perils of the dialogue the foreign secretary had authorised between the British and French general staffs: 'My dear Grey, Conversations such as that between Gen. Joffre and Col. Fairholme seem to me rather dangerous; especially the part which refers to possible British assistance. The French ought not to be encouraged, in present circumstances, to make their plans on any assumptions of this kind. Yours always, H.H.A.'

Yet amid the prime minister's huge difficulties at home, by default he allowed Grey almost a free hand abroad. The foreign secretary felt able to give assurances to France about likely British support in the event of war, without reference to the full cabinet or the House of Commons, in a manner incompatible with modern or even contemporary notions of democratic governance, and arguably unmatched until the far less defensible 1956 Anglo-French collusion to invade Egypt. Grey acted in secrecy because he knew he could secure no parliamentary mandate. During the July crisis, his personal willingness for Britain to fight beside France ran well ahead of that of most of his government colleagues or the public.

But it is hard to sustain the argument that Grey thus bears a large responsibility for war because of his failure either to speak frankly to the British people during the last years of peace, or explicitly to warn Berlin that Britain would not remain neutral. The Germans, in pursuing their course in 1914, had discounted British intervention and were unimpressed by the potential involvement of an army they despised. They were undeterred by the economic perils posed by Britain's absolute dominance of the world's merchant shipping and capability for imposing a blockade, because they intended to win quickly. It is unlikely that any course of action adopted by Asquith's government could have averted a European war in 1914, though another foreign secretary might have adopted a different view about British participation.

The planned British Expeditionary Force was well-equipped for its size, but its inadequate mass reflected reluctance to spend big money on soldiers when the Royal Navy was absorbing a quarter of state expenditure. Henry Wilson, as director of military operations between 1910 and 1914, spoke of 'our funny little army', and said contemptuously that there was no military problem on the continent to which the appropriate British answer was a mere six divisions. But these were all the government would stand for, and its policy reflected popular sentiment. Sailors were what the British loved and cherished; by contrast both the regular and the Territorial forces were under-recruited, with enthusiasm for military service especially low among country-dwellers and the Welsh.

Wilson played a critical role in promoting a military relationship with France much closer than most British soldiers wanted, or the cabinet knew. A brilliantly fluent speaker, of erratic and often reckless convictions, he failed the military academy entrance exams five times. He was a long-time advocate of conscription, describing the part-time volunteers of the Territorial Force as 'the best & most patriotic men in England because they are trying to do something'. In 1910, as commandant of the Staff College, he asserted the likelihood of a European war, and argued that Britain's only prudent option was to ally itself with France against the Germans. A student ventured to disagree, saying that only 'inconceivable stupidity on the part of statesmen' could precipitate a general conflagration. This provoked Wilson's derision: 'Haw! Haw! Haw!!! Inconceivable stupidity is just what you're going to get.' Lord Esher wrote later that Wilson returned his pupils to their formations 'with a sense of [war's] cataclysmic imminence'. Wilson was described by the prime minister to Venetia Stanley as 'that poisonous tho' clever ruffian', which seems about right. He was a shameless intriguer who meddled in everything, including offering support to the Ulster Protestants' threatened rebellion. But it was almost entirely his doing that the British Army had plans prepared to send a force to the continent – what was known as the 'W.F.' or 'With France' scheme.

In 1911, Wilson secured Grey's agreement that he should liaise with Britain's railway companies about a schedule for moving units to the ports in the event of war, and appropriate timetables were drawn up. At the end of July that year, Lloyd George made a speech at the Mansion House, placing Britain firmly beside France in any dispute with Germany, and Wilson became the foremost British instrument in preparing to implement such a commitment. In 1913 he visited France seven times, and in conversations with Joffre and his staff promised 150,000 men for the thirteenth day after mobilisation, to concentrate between Arras–Saint-Quentin and Cambrai ready for operations. This was fanciful, but a senior British officer thus created a military convention. Wilson argued that, though a BEF would be small, its moral contribution could be critical. He grossly underestimated prospective German strength. But, though then still only a brigadier-general, he exercised an extraordinary influence towards persuading Asquith to contemplate, though emphatically not to confirm, a continental military commitment. This seems to reflect a sense of statesmanlike prudence, rather than any taste for warmongering.

Meanwhile, at 1914 Anglo-Russian naval staff talks the British discussed providing support for a Russian landing in Pomerania. This was the sort of war-gaming all armed forces indulge in, but when news of it was leaked to Berlin by a Russian diplomat, German paranoia about the Entente was intensified. Unfortunately, the Pomeranian scheme lacked plausibility. The Royal Navy's preparation for Armageddon focused chiefly upon a blockade of which the diplomatic complications had been inadequately considered. Like all British war planning, it was limited in scale and incoherent in substance, lacking the political impetus to make it anything more. The continental nations expected to clash in arms sooner or later, which helped to ensure that they did so. The offshore islanders, however, thought it more plausible that they would soon be fighting each other.

2

The Descent to War

If the Hapsburg Empire witnessed little sincere mourning for Franz Ferdinand following his assassination, Austrian rage towards its perpetrators was manifest. Joven Avakumović, a well-known Serbian lawyer and liberal opposition politician, was being shown his room at the Tyrolean hotel where he and his family were starting a holiday when the porter handed him a newspaper announcing the murders in Sarajevo. Gravely, Avakumović told his wife and daughter that these tidings were bound to have important implications for their own country. That evening after dinner, in the lounge he listened to the speculations of fellow guests, who insisted Serbia was involved in the killings, and must be called to account: 'I noticed especially one well-dressed, well-mannered man who spoke very harshly, and sat with three others at the next table to our own. He declared loudly: "Serbia is guilty; she must be punished," and the other three affirmed: "That is right!" I ... later learnt from the porter that the man was a foreign ministry official.'

In Vienna, the Sarajevo assassins were first branded 'Bosniacs', then simply 'Serbs'. Violent anti-Serbian demonstrations took place across the empire. In Sarajevo the Serb-owned Hotel Europa was wrecked, together with a Serb school; the German consul wrote that the city was living through 'its own St Bartholomew's Eve'. In Vienna on 30 June, a crowd of some two hundred students demonstrated in front of the Serbian embassy. They yelled: 'Down with Serbia! Long live Austria! Hail the Hapsburgs!' and burnt the hated flag. Such scenes were repeated through the days that followed.

The Austrian *chargé* in Belgrade, Wilhelm von Stork, reported angrily to Vienna on 30 June: 'There is exultation in the streets and cafés on account of our tragedy, and it is described as the finger of God and a justified punishment for everything bad Austria-Hungary has ever done to Serbia.' The Serbian opposition press, with stunning indifference to its country's interests and reputation, applauded the Archduke's killing. When student Jovan Dinić hurried to Belgrade's main square to discuss the news with friends, he was surprised to find them holding forth not in shocked whispers, but in strident exultation. A famously bright young aspiring lawyer proclaimed that Austrian military manoeuvres in Bosnia had been an intolerable provocation and a direct threat to all Serbs; that the Serbs of Bosnia would now 'leap through fire' alongside the Serbian nation. Misunderstandings intensified rancour: on that same 30 June, the Montenegrin border town of Metalka was bedecked with flags, causing the outraged Austrians to suppose that their neighbours were celebrating Franz Ferdinand's murder. Only a week later did they learn that Metalka had been marking the birthday of Montenegro's Crown Prince. Austria embraced such petty fantasy provocations alongside the large and real one of the archducal murder.

Participants in all conflicts with more than two belligerents have different motivations for deciding to fight, and this was emphatically true in 1914. The decision-making of seven governments was influenced by widely diverse ambitions and fears. Though struggles ensued in many parts of the world, and especially in Europe, and warring nations professed common allegiances, they were certainly not impelled by a common logic. Austria made an almost immediate decision to respond to Franz Ferdinand's assassination by invading Serbia, not because its leaders cared a fig for the persons of the slain Archduke and his embarrassing wife, but because the murders represented the best justification they would ever have for settling accounts with a mortally troublesome neighbour.

The rulers of the Hapsburg Empire convinced themselves that military action was the only way out of their difficulties, not merely with Serbia, but with their own restless peoples. Finance minister Ritter von Bilinski said later: 'We decided on war quite early.' Vienna's military attaché in Belgrade reported that the killings had been planned and organised by the head of Serbian intelligence. Austria's rulers agreed that they thus represented a declaration of war, though Vienna had no more evidence to link them to the Serbs' monarchy or elected government than do modern historians. The war minister, Alexander von Krobatin, and Gen. Oskar Potiorek, commander-in-chief in Bosnia-Herzegovina, alike urged military action. Berchtold, often scorned by his peers as a ditherer, displayed an untimely resolution. On 30 June he spoke privately of the need for a 'final and fundamental reckoning' with Serbia.

Berchtold was surrounded by a group of young diplomats – Janós, Count Forgách; Alexander, Baron von Musulin; Alexander, Count Hoyos – who were convinced that an assertive and expansionist foreign policy was the best cure for the Empire's domestic ills. Forgách was a prime mover in the commitment to crush Serbia. Hoyos became responsible for ensuring Germany's support; he emphasised the recklessness prevailing in Vienna when he said: 'it is immaterial to us whether world war comes out of all this'. Musulin drafted the critical communications: an 'impetuous chatterbox', he later took pride in calling himself 'the man who caused the war'.

The Emperor Franz Joseph wrote personally to Kaiser Wilhelm saying: 'You too will be convinced after the latest terrible events in Bosnia that a [peaceful] reconciliation of the conflict between ourselves and Serbia is unthinkable.' On 4 July Berchtold dispatched Hoyos to Berlin, where the diplomat thereafter held a series of meetings with Wilhelm and his advisers, at which he was promised Germany's unconditional support for any course of action Austria chose to adopt – what later became notorious as 'the blank cheque', central plank of the case for German responsibility for the First World War. On the evening of 5 July, the Austrian envoy reported the Kaiser saying that 'if we really saw the necessity for military action against Serbia, he would think it regrettable if we did not take advantage of the present moment, which is favourable from our point of view'.

The Germans urged the Austrians to force the pace, denying the Serbians time to marshal diplomatic or military support; they wanted Vienna to confront St Petersburg with a swift *fait accompli* – Hapsburg troops occupying the Serb capital. When Hoyos went home, Arthur Zimmerman, the German under-secretary of state, estimated a 90 per cent probability of hostilities between Austria and Serbia. During the weeks that followed before Vienna's ultimatum was finally delivered, the Germans fumed at Austrian dilatoriness. Bethmann, the chancellor, showed himself vulnerable to moments of panic. Kurt Riezler, his confidential secretary and principal counsellor, wrote in his diary on 6 July, expressing dismay about a scenario somewhat troubling his master: 'an action against Serbia can lead to a world war. From a war, regardless of the outcome, the chancellor expects a revolution of everything that exists … Generally delusion all round, a thick fog over the people. The same in all of Europe. The future belongs to Russia, which … thrusts itself on us as a heavier and heavier nightmare.'

Riezler sought to reassure Bethmann by suggesting that it might be possible to achieve a triumph over Serbia by diplomacy alone, then added encouragingly: 'if war should come and the veil [of amity which masks the fundamental enmity between peoples] should fall, then the entire *Volk* will follow, driven by a sense of emergency and danger. Victory is liberation.' Amid such Wagnerian reflections and fantasies did Germany's political leaders enter the July crisis. At that stage, Bethmann and the Kaiser were doing almost all the talking for their country. Though Moltke assured Wilhelm that the army was ready to fight at any time, some historians claim that he was not directly consulted before the critical assurances were given to Austria.

After Hoyos returned to Vienna, Germany's leaders behaved with a nonchalance that conspiracists believe to have been theatrical. Bethmann spent most of the rest of the month on his estate at Hohenfinow on the Oder, though he paid several discreet visits to Berlin during which he consulted with the military. Moltke departed for a cure at Karlsbad – his second of the year – from which he returned only on 25 July, just in time for the showdown between Vienna and Belgrade. The Kaiser sailed on 6 July for his annual summer yachting trip in the North Sea, which continued until the 27th. Senior officers including Prussian war minister Erich von Falkenhayn went on leave; newspapers were urged to avoid wilful provocation of the French.

While some scholars regard all this as evidence of orchestrated deception, it is more plausible that the Germans at this stage sincerely believed that the Austro-Serbian war they had mandated could be localised, though they were fatalistic about the huge risk that this might not be so. Rear-Admiral Albert Hopman, a shrewd and informed observer, wrote in his diary on 6 July: 'In my opinion the situation is quite favourable for us, so favourable that a big and resolute statesman would exploit it to the uttermost.' Throughout the weeks that followed, Hopman persisted in his opinion, widely shared in Berlin, that Germany could gain important diplomatic capital from the Balkan crisis, at small cost. He wrote on 16 July: 'personally, I do not believe in war entanglement', and again on the 21st: 'Europe will not brawl because of Serbia.'

In Vienna, on the 7th Berchtold told the Austrian Council of Ministers that Germany was providing unqualified backing for drastic measures, 'even though our operations against Serbia should bring about the great war'. That day Baron Wladimir Giesl, the Austrian envoy to Belgrade, returned to his post after consultations in Vienna with clear instructions from the foreign minister: 'However the Serbs react to the ultimatum [then being drafted], you must break off relations and it must come to war.' Only Hungary's minister-president, Count István Tisza, deplored the threat of 'the dreadful calamity of a European war', and counselled caution. He told Count Julius Andrássy that blame for the actions of the unprincipled little group which killed the Archduke should not be pinned on an entire nation, and maintained this view until mid-July.

By contrast the Austrian army's chief of staff, Conrad, urged aggressive action. After the conflict ended Count Hoyos wrote: 'No one today can imagine just how much the belief in German power, in the invincibility of the German army, determined our thinking and how certain we all were that Germany ~~would easily win the war against France~~ [deleted in original] would provide us with the greatest guarantee of our safety should a European war result from our action against Serbia.'

Many Austrian soldiers were not merely untroubled by the possibility of provoking war with the Russian bear, but regarded such a showdown as an indispensable contribution to the elimination of the pan-Slav threat. Wolfgang Heller, a General Staff officer, noted in his diary on 24 July that he felt confident Serbia would reject Vienna's ultimatum, and was only worried that the Russians might not rise to the bait: 'real success cannot be achieved unless we can implement *Kriegsfall R* [the plan to fight Russia]. Only if Serbia and Montenegro cease to exist as independent states can a solution of the [Slav] question be achieved. It would be useless to go to war with Serbia without being resolved to erase it from the map; a so-called punitive campaign – "*eine Strafexpedition*" – would be worthless, a waste of every bullet; the southern Slav question must be solved radically, so that all southern Slavs are united under the Hapsburg flag.' Such views were widely held among Austria's nobles, generals, politicians and diplomats.

An Austro-Serb war was thus ordained. But was a regional Balkan conflict doomed to become a general European catastrophe? Did Serbia deserve to be saved from the fate Austria and Germany decreed for it? The irresponsibility of Serbian behaviour is almost indisputable, but it seems extravagant, on the evidence, to brand the country a rogue state, deserving of destruction. It is much less surprising that the Hapsburg Empire, in the febrile mood generated by its weakness and vulnerability, chose to start a war to punish Apis and his compatriots, than that its neighbour, great and rising Germany, should have risked a general conflagration for so marginal a purpose.

There seem several explanations. First, Germany's rulers, like many men of their generation, accepted the role of war as a natural means of fulfilling national ambitions and exercising power: Prussia had exploited this cost-effectively three times in the later nineteenth century. Georg Müller, head of Wilhelm's naval cabinet, told his master in 1911, 'war is not the worst of all evils', and this belief pervaded Berlin's thinking. The Kaiser and his key advisers underestimated the magnitude of the dominance their country was achieving through its economic and industrial prowess, without fighting anybody. They were profoundly mistaken to suppose that European hegemony could be secured only by the deployment of armies on battlefields.

But paranoia was a prominent feature of the German psyche at this period – a belief that the country's strategic position, far from progressively strengthening, was being weakened by the rise of socialism at home and the Entente's military capabilities abroad. Many German bankers and industrialists were morbidly convinced that the Western democracies were bent upon strangling German trade. Berlin's ambassador in Vienna made initial attempts to cool the Austrian government's bellicosity, but the Kaiser scribbled on his reports: 'Who has authorised him to do that? It is extremely stupid!' The Germans knew it was overwhelmingly likely that the Tsar would throw his protective mantle over Serbia – Nicholas had earlier committed himself to doing so. But Moltke and Bethmann Hollweg viewed Russia, to the point of obsession, as an existential threat; and if they had to fight Nicholas's army, they preferred to do so sooner rather than later. On 20 May 1914, sharing a railway compartment between Potsdam and Berlin, the chief of staff told foreign minister Jagow that within a few years Russia would be winning the arms race. If the price of anticipating such superiority was also to be a clash with France, Russia's ally – which Moltke assumed – the General Staff had planned meticulously for such a prospect, and professed to be confident of victory.

Bethmann was a natural government official rather than a leader. Lloyd George later recalled conversations with him during a 1908 visit to Germany to study its health-insurance law: 'an attractive but not an arresting personality ... an intelligent, industrious and eminently sensible bureaucrat, but he did not leave on my mind an impression of having met a man of power who might one day shake destiny'. Bethmann was also a vacillator, especially about the rival merits of peace and war. In 1912 he returned from a visit to Russia alarmed by the evidence of its rising might; and during the following year was heard to advocate a pre-emptive conflict. In April 1913 he lectured the Reichstag on the looming 'inevitable struggle' between Slavs and Teutons, and warned Vienna that Russia was bound to join any conflict between Austria and Serbia. In his better moments, however, the chancellor recognised the perils posed by a clash of arms. On 4 June 1914 he told the Bavarian ambassador that conservatives who imagined that a conflict would enable them to reassert their own domestic power, crushing the hated socialists, were mistaken: 'a world war with its incalculable ramifications will strengthen social democracy, which sermonises the virtues of peace'. War, he added, could easily cost some rulers their thrones.

Bethmann's judgement was not improved by personal isolation. His wife died in May 1914 after a long illness, and he was left to while away his leisure hours reading Plato in Greek. He had become almost politically friendless, especially in the Reichstag. Moltke had no time for Bethmann, whose career now rested solely in the hands of the Kaiser, his patron. The chancellor initially identified in the July crisis an opportunity to restore his personal authority and reputation by achieving a diplomatic coup for the Central Powers. He was a prime mover in encouraging the Kaiser to support Austria, and was highly selective about what cable traffic he showed his master, to preserve his steadiness of purpose. He believed that Germany should pursue its chosen course without fears of any response St Petersburg might see fit to make.

In tangled harness Bethmann, the Kaiser and Moltke made the critical decisions. Germany actively encouraged the Austrians to attack Serbia, and Berlin's three principal actors made no attempt to manage events in such a way as to avert a wider calamity. Therein lies the case for their culpability for what followed. It seems mistaken to argue that they entered the July crisis bent upon precipitating a general European conflict; but a pervasive German fatalism about such an outcome contributed largely to bringing it about. The Social Democrat leader August Bebel, a hero to millions of workers, delivered an impassioned warning following the 1911 Agadir crisis. 'Every nation will continue to arm for war until a day comes at which one or the other says: "Better a terrible end than a terror without end." [A nation may also say]: "If we delay any longer, we shall be the weaker instead of the stronger." Then the catastrophe will happen. Then in Europe the great mobilisation plans will be unleashed, by which sixteen to eighteen million men, the finest of many nations, armed with the best instruments of murder, will take the field against each other. The *Götterdämmerung* of the bourgeois world is approaching.'

Thomas Mann wrote that German intellectuals sang the praises of war 'as if in competition with each other, with deep passion, as if they and the people, whose voice they are, saw nothing better, nothing more beautiful than to fight many enemies'. Some conservatives were impressed by a 1912 bestseller written by Gen. Friedrich von Bernhardi, *Germany and the Next War*, which proclaimed a German 'duty to make war ... War is a biological necessity of the first importance ... Without war, inferior or decaying races would easily choke the growth of healthy, budding elements, and a universal decadence would follow ... Might gives the right to conquer or occupy.' Bernhardi was dismissed by Moltke, who called him 'a perfect dreamer', but the book was widely noticed in Britain, where Sir Arthur Conan Doyle and H.G. Wells were among those expressing repugnance. British opinion may have been coloured by the fact that their own nation had already done all the conquering and occupying it needed.

Fatalism about the desirability or inevitability of conflict was even more evident in the Hapsburg Empire. In March 1914 the influential military publication *Danzer's Armee-Zeitung* declared that the international situation had seldom looked graver. Incessant Balkan wars, to which had been added Italy's 1911 invasion and colonisation of Libya, were plainly mere overtures 'to the great conflagration which is inevitably awaiting us. We see that the arms race is no longer a means of sustaining a balance of power, as it has been for decades, but instead a frenzied and undisguised preparation for a conflict that may begin today or tomorrow.' *Danzer's* noted that Russia was still several years short of completing the strategic railway network indispensable to swift mobilisation, and thus an earlier war would be 'inconvenient for our enemies'. This led the writer to argue that it was in the strongest interests of Austria and its allies to strike before losing the initiative: 'Today, the balance is quite favourable, but heaven knows if this will remain so tomorrow! Sooner or later, hecatombs of blood must be sacrificed, so let us seize the moment. We have the strength – only the decision is wanting!'

On 14 July Count Berchtold presided over an important meeting at which the Empire's next steps were decided. Conrad raised the issue of timing: given the economic difficulties threatened by mobilising reservists in the midst of the harvest season, he wanted war delayed until 12 August. The foreign minister rejected such a postponement. 'The diplomatic situation will not hold so long,' he told the army chief, meaning that Entente pressure on Vienna to maintain the peace might become irresistible. The German ambassador was informed that Berchtold's staff was working on the wording of an ultimatum to Belgrade which was designed to be rejected.

Western Europe paid scant heed to the latest round of Balkan bickering. A note on *The Times*'s court and social page for 3 July declared: 'The Domestic Servant Problem is one of the most serious problems of the present day. With the idea of helping to its solution, *The Times* some months ago instituted a scheme whereby Lady Experts assist Ladies to obtain able and reliable Servants ...' On the 16th, the newspaper addressed the European situation in a second leader, urging that Serbia should volunteer to conduct an inquiry into Franz Ferdinand's assassination. It concluded dismissively that neither force nor the threat of force could play any useful part in Austria-Hungary's diplomacy towards Serbia: 'Any attempt to meet it in that fashion would constitute a fresh peril to European peace and that, we are confident, the EMPEROR and his most sagacious advisers clearly perceive.' Two days later *The Times*'s foreign page was led by a report on Mexico; the only European news was headed 'the Serbian scare'. On 17 July, Lloyd George told an audience of London businessmen that 'although you never get a perfectly blue sky in foreign affairs', some clouds seemed to be clearing. He asserted his confidence that the European problems would soon be solved. From the outset, Britain's politicians and press – anyway preoccupied with the Ulster crisis – found it hard to conceive that Austrian grievances against Serbia merited a resort to arms.

France, chronically politically unstable after experiencing seven changes of government between 1911 and 1914, was engaged with its own lurid domestic affairs, prominent among them the trial of Joseph Caillaux's wife Henriette for shooting dead *Le Figaro*'s editor Gaston Calmette. President Raymond Poincaré and René Viviani, his temporary prime minister, departed from Dunkirk early on the morning of 16 July aboard the battle-ship *France*, to pay a state visit to Russia. Both professed to welcome the trip as a holiday: Poincaré wrote later of 'sailing under the illusion of peace'. The ship's wireless facilities were primitive, and throughout their time at sea they found themselves almost incommunicado: 'a heavy mist falls on the billow, as if to hide Europe's shores'.

On the 20th the French party arrived at the landing stage of the Peterhof Palace, to be received by the imperial family and several of Nicholas II's ministers. Maurice Paléologue, the French ambassador, reported hearing the Tsar say as he waited to greet his French guests: 'I can't believe the [Kaiser] wants war ... If you knew him as I do ... how much theatricality [there is] in his posing! It is all the more important for us to be able to count on England in an emergency. Unless Germany has gone out of her mind altogether she will never attack Russia, France and England combined.' After the initial courtesies, Poincaré invited the views of Sergei Sazonov about the Sarajevo murders. According to the president's memoirs, the foreign minister was dismissive, and messages from the French embassy in Vienna, warning that the Austrians seemed likely to take drastic action, were not forwarded to St Petersburg for days. At the banquet which followed, Paléologue, who grew ever more euphoric and emotional as the visit proceeded, wrote: 'I shall long remember the dazzling display of jewels on the women's shoulders ... a fantastic shower of diamonds, pearls, rubies, sapphires, emeralds, topaz, beryls.' Here was a last flourish of the serene complacency of old Europe's ruling class.

René Viviani was an Englishman's idea of a stage Frenchman: fluent, erratic, emotional, impulsive and subject to fits of extreme rudeness. On the Russian trip, it was plain that his mind was fixed more on domestic issues than on foreign affairs: he was fearful that evidence embarrassing to himself would emerge from the Caillaux courtroom circus, and anxious about his mistress, an actress at the Comédie Française. When messages arrived from Paris, Poincaré became increasingly impatient to see anything that bore upon the European crisis, but Viviani seemed to care only for the Paris gossip. He said the Serbian issue would obviously be resolved, so there was no purpose in hastening home.

Poincaré, passionately committed to the Entente, led the discussions with the Russians, writing in his diary in theatrical self-justification: 'I have taken upon myself Viviani's responsibilities. I fear that he is hesitant and pusillanimous.' Paléologue noted: 'It was Poincaré who had the initiative. Before long he was doing all the talking; the Tsar simply nodded acquiescence, but his whole appearance showed his sincere approval. It radiated confidence and sympathy.' The ambassador was an unreliable witness, but right about the congenial mood of the talks.

There is a massive difficulty about assessing this Franco-Russian summit, as we should now call it, because no minutes were kept, and few relevant state papers survive. Memoirs written by some of the principals are evasive and perhaps actively deceitful about what took place. Poincaré and Sazonov alike claimed that they discussed generalities, because they knew nothing of the looming Austrian ultimatum to Serbia. This may well be untrue, because Russian codebreakers had cracked Vienna's diplomatic traffic. The Tsarist General Staff had a good grasp of Hapsburg plans and manoeuvres: Col. Alfred Redl, the homosexual Austrian intelligence chief who killed himself in 1913, was only the most notable of a network of agents in St Petersburg's pay. The Russians were much less well informed about Germany, though they had few doubts about its war plan for a grand envelopment in the West, after buying from a spy for 10,000 roubles the report of the German army's 1905 war games.

It is likely that the French and Russian delegations had intensive discussions about the Balkan crisis, and agreed a tough line. Poincaré believed that the Germans were bluffers: 'whenever we have taken a conciliatory approach to Germany she abused it; on the other hand, on each occasion when we have shown firmness, she has yielded'. Firmness was a perceived virtue which powerfully influenced the behaviour of all the Powers in July 1914. Some historians believe that in St Petersburg Poincaré stiffened the resolve for war of Sazonov – 'a sad wobbler', in the view of the British Foreign Office's Robert Vansittart. During a state banquet at the French embassy, the foreign minister spoke to the president in terms that echoed Conrad on the other side: he said that, if the crisis worsened, Russia would face great difficulties in conducting a mobilisation during the harvest. The fact that the Frenchman acknowledged in his memoirs a conversation about such a contingency suggests that he and Sazonov already viewed the Balkan situation more gravely than either afterwards admitted.

But it is easy to accept that France and Russia agreed on coordinating a tough response to the Austrian ultimatum to Serbia, even including a precautionary Russian mobilisation such as had taken place in the last Balkan crisis, without convicting them of precipitating a European war. The Tsar certainly had no enthusiasm for such a clash, and his generals knew that their military position vis-à-vis Germany would be much stronger in 1916. Russia's ambassadors to Paris, Vienna and Berlin, together with Gen. Yuri Danilov, the army's quartermaster-general and strongest personality, were absent from their posts until the Austrian ultimatum was delivered on 24 July, a further indication that St Petersburg did not anticipate hostilities. All that is known for sure of these meetings is that the Tsar proposed for himself a visit to France in 1915. On a scenic trip up the Neva, the Franco-Russian party passed shipyards where new battleships were under construction, but the workmen were on strike. Nicholas suggested that this represented an attempt by German agitators to blight the state visit, though Poincaré shrugged: 'pure speculation'.

On the 21st the president's party received all the ambassadors accredited to St Petersburg in their superb gold-embroidered uniforms and knee-breeches, and exchanged banalities with most. The German envoy said that he looked forward to visiting France with his French family later in the summer. Britain's Sir George Buchanan – 'cold, ponderous and extremely courteous', in the president's words, displayed alarm about the European situation and suggested that Vienna and St Petersburg should open a direct dialogue. Poincaré responded that such a course would be most dangerous, and wrote in his diary: 'This conversation leaves me pessimistic.' Count Friedrich Szapáry, the Hapsburg ambassador, disturbed the French president much more: 'He gives the impression that Austria-Hungary wishes to extend to all of Serbia responsibility for the crime committed [in Sarajevo] and possibly desires to humiliate her little neighbour. If I say nothing, that will make him suppose a violent initiative has the approval of France. I reply that Serbia has friends in Russia who would be astonished at this information, and such surprise would be shared elsewhere.'

Paléologue recorded Szapáry saying coldly to Poincaré: '*Monsieur le Président*, we cannot suffer a foreign government to allow plots against our polity to be hatched on its territory!' The president allegedly urged the need for caution on the part of all the European powers, adding: 'With a little goodwill this Serbian business is easy to settle. But it can just as easily become critical. Serbia has some very warm friends in the Russian people. And Russia has an ally, France. There are plenty of complications to be feared!' Szapáry bowed and left without saying a further word. Poincaré said to Viviani and Paléologue, according to the latter: 'I'm not satisfied with this conversation. The ambassador had obviously been instructed to say nothing ... Austria has a *coup de théâtre* in store for us. Sazonov must be firm and we must back him up ...' This account is disingenuous, but probably catches the tone of what was said.

A telegram arrived from Paris, reporting that Germany was offering Austria-Hungary its support. Viviani and Poincaré claimed to have agreed that this sounded like a bluff to increase pressure on the Serbs, but the French leaders were now becoming alarmed by the meagreness and tardiness of incoming information. The Germans shortly thereafter began jamming some French diplomatic wireless traffic. The mere fact that Berlin adopted such a measure places its role in the July crisis in an unsympathetic light, alongside its consistent mendacity in exchanges with the other Powers. If Germany seriously desired a peaceful outcome, this could scarcely be promoted by isolating France's leaders from unfolding developments, nor by lying about its own state of knowledge.

On the 23rd, Poincaré gave a dinner under an awning on the quarter-deck of the *France*, marred by a heavy rainstorm which doused the empress and her daughters. The president was irked that his naval officer showed little imagination or *chic* in its management of the evening. The dinner, he complained, needed a woman's touch. But the French delegation left St Petersburg a few hours later confident that the visit had been a success, and confirmed in France's commitment to Russia. Indeed, it is possible that Viviani's visible unease was fuelled by fears about how far his president went in promising support, though again there is no evidence about this. Poincaré speculated later that efforts made by Germany to deny him information during those critical days were prompted by fears that Russia and France might otherwise have concocted a credible peace initiative. This is implausible; but it is a matter of fact that the Austrians delayed presenting their ultimatum to Serbia until they were sure the French presidential party was at sea, sailing ever further from Russian shores. Only next day did Poincaré and Viviani begin to receive in successive fragments the text of the Austrian document as delivered.

Between 14 and 25 July, astonishingly, the two men received no dispatches from France's Belgrade mission, because the minister was ill. Meanwhile Paléologue in St Petersburg was persistently pressing on Sazonov the case for 'firmness'. In those days ambassadors were important people, as intermediaries and even sometimes as principals. Paléologue was an erratic personality, unafraid of war because he believed that the balance of military advantage now lay with Russia and France. But it remains hard to see why the St Petersburg summit should be condemned as a malign and conspiratorial affair, as some seek to do even in the absence of evidence to that effect.

It is true that Russia was competing fiercely with Germany for control of the Dardanelles and access to the Black Sea, but the latter issue influenced 1914 events only because it had intensified animosity and suspicion between the two nations. The Tsarist Empire had stronger motives than any nation in Europe to delay a showdown. At St Petersburg in July the two Entente Powers debated not a military initiative of their own, but an appropriate reaction to an Austrian one, which was evidently likely to be backed by the Germans. It was never plausible that Russia would acquiesce in Serbia's suppression, nor that Paris would leave St Petersburg unsupported. Both the Austrians and the Germans knew this, but declined to be deterred, because they believed they could win a war.

The final Austrian decision to invade Serbia, heedless of Belgrade's response to Vienna's demands, was reached at a secret meeting in Berchtold's house on 19 July. Count Tisza, the sole earlier dissenter, was now reconciled to the foreign minister's course; Hungarian public opinion had become as feverishly anti-Serb as was Austrian. Baron Musulin, who drafted Austria's ultimatum to Serbia, said proudly later that he 'sculpted and polished it like a precious stone', to 'astound the world with the eloquence of its accusation'. The day before its delivery, a draft was sent to Berlin, which the German government made no attempt to amend or soften, and afterwards mendaciously claimed that it had not seen before publication.

The document presented to Belgrade at 6 p.m. on 23 July denounced Serbia for promoting terror and murder in the Hapsburg Empire. The charges made in the ultimatum about the participation of the Black Hand in the Sarajevo plot were largely valid. But Clauses 5 and 6, demanding that the Austrians should be empowered themselves to investigate and arbitrate on Serbian soil, represented a surrender of sovereignty no nation could concede – nor was Serbia expected by Vienna to do so. Berchtold's missile was thus launched, and in flight.

2 THE RUSSIANS REACT

Nikola Pašić, the Serb prime minister, was away from Belgrade election-eering on 23 July – he made a habit of removing himself from the capital at moments of crisis, perhaps not accidentally. In his absence, the Austrian ultimatum was received by Serbia's finance minister, Dr Laza Paču. A frenzy of activity followed. Apis, one of those most responsible for the crisis, went to the house of his brother-in-law, Živan Živanović, and warned him gravely: 'The situation is very serious. Austria has delivered the ultimatum, the news has been passed on to Russia and the mobilisation orders are out.' Živanović, like many others, hastily escorted his family to the temporary safety of the countryside.

The Russian ambassador, the egregious Nikolai Hartwig, had died suddenly of a heart attack on 10 July; his deputy, Vasily Strandman, found himself in charge of the mission, which was modestly staffed. Strandman conscripted his wife and Lyudmila Nikolaevna, Hartwig's daughter, to help encipher the mounting pile of telegrams that had now to be dispatched to Sazonov in St Petersburg, creating a curious snapshot of diplomatic domesticity. Late that night, they were engaged on this task when a servant entered to report that Alexander, the twenty-six-year-old Prince Regent, was waiting below to discuss the ultimatum. The Russian told the young man, who was visibly emotional: 'The terms are very severe and offer little hope of a peaceful outcome.' Strandman said that unless they could be accepted in their entirety, Serbia must expect to have to fight. The Prince agreed, then asked simply, 'What will Russia do?' Strandman answered: 'I cannot say anything, because St Petersburg has not yet seen the ultimatum, and I have no instructions.' 'Yes, but what is your personal opinion?' Strandman said he thought it likely that Russia would offer Serbia some protection. Alexander then asked, 'What should we do next?' The Russian urged him to telegraph the Tsar.

The Prince, who had been educated in Russia, fell silent for a few moments, then said, 'Yes, my father the King will send a telegram.' Strandman urged: 'You yourself must tell [the Tsar] what has happened, give him your assessment of the situation and ask for help. You should sign, rather than the King.' Alexander demanded sharply, 'Why?' Strandman said: 'Because the Tsar knows and loves you, whereas he barely knows King Peter.' They argued the toss about signatories for several minutes. Strandman suggested copying the message to Italy's King Victor Emmanuel, who was married to Alexander's aunt. He also agreed to cable St Petersburg immediately, asking for 120,000 rifles and other military equipment desperately needed by the Serbs – the Russians had failed to deliver earlier promised arms consignments.

Western Europe and its leaders were slow to address the Austrian ultimatum with the urgency it demanded. France's president and prime minister were at sea. Raymond Recouly of *Le Figaro* described how, in Paris, he gained his own first intimations of the gravity of the crisis not from ministers or diplomats, but from financial journalists. Before the Austrians acted, between 12 and 15 July there was frenzied activity on the Vienna and Budapest bourses, probably driven by inside information. 'Everybody's selling everything for any price they can get,' *Le Figaro*'s financial editor told Recouly. Stock exchanges discounted the delusion in some chancelleries that Austria-Hungary intended to act temperately: they expected war.

Across the Hapsburg Empire and in Serbia, millions held their breath. A Graz schoolteacher wrote on the 23rd: 'nobody could think or speak about anything else'. In Serbia it was a season of lush blooming: gardens were full of roses, carnations, wallflowers, jasmine, lilac; pervasive scents of lime and acacia. Peasants drifted into Belgrade and other cities from surrounding villages, many accompanied by their families, to sell in the streets boiled eggs, plum brandy, cheese, bread. In the evenings the young gathered to sing songs, watched and heard by silent, grizzled old men. In the Serbian capital, Dr Slavka Mihajlović wrote on hearing of the ultimatum at her hospital: 'We are astounded. We look at each other aghast, but must go back to work ... We expected Serbia's relations with Austria to get tense, but we did not expect an ultimatum ... The whole town is in shock. Streets and cafés are filling up with anxious people ... It is less than a year since our little Serbia emerged from two bloody wars, with Turkey and Bulgaria. Some of the wounded still lie in hospitals – are we to see more bloodshed and more tragedy?'

The July crisis entered its critical phase on the 24th, when the terms of the Austrian ultimatum became known in the chancelleries of Europe. Sazonov said immediately: '*C'est la guérre européene.*' He told the Tsar that the Austrians would never have dared to act in such a fashion without German guarantors. Nicholas's response was cautious, but he convened a Council of Ministers to meet later that day. Sazonov then received Sir George Buchanan, who urged allowing time for diplomacy. Paléologue inevitably maintained his insistence upon toughness. What took place in St Petersburg during the ensuing four days ensured that the looming conflict would not be confined to the Balkans.

All the operational plans in 1914 were complex, that of the Russians most of all, because of the huge distances involved. Each mobilised soldier of the Tsar must travel an average of seven hundred miles to reach his regiment, against a German's average of two hundred. The strategic rail network required twelve days' warning of a call to arms, and troop concentrations would anyway be much slower than Germany's. An hour after receiving news of the ultimatum, Sazonov ordered the army to prepare to move onto a war footing. Later that day of the 24th, Peter Bark the finance minister instructed Foreign Ministry officials to arrange repatriation of a hundred million roubles of state funds lodged in Berlin.

Austria's commitment to war, and Germany's 'blank cheque' in support, predated every response by the Entente. During an earlier Balkan crisis in the winter of 1912–13, Russia adopted the same military precautions that it activated on 24 July 1914 – without provoking hostilities. Unless St Petersburg proposed to acquiesce in the Austrian invasion of Serbia, immediate warning orders to the Russian army represented not eagerness to precipitate a European catastrophe, but prudence. There was, however, a critical new factor. In 1912–13 Germany had declined to support a tough Austrian line in the Balkans: key elements of its own military preparedness were still lacking – the Rhine bridge at Remagen, the bridge at Karwendel across which Austrian heavy artillery could move northwards, the Kiel canal, a new Army Bill. Now those links were complete: Moltke's machine was at near-perfect pitch. St Petersburg and the rest of Europe knew that if Russia moved, Germany was almost bound to respond. Sazonov claimed that mobilisation was not a declaration of war; that the Tsar's army could remain for weeks at readiness, but passive – as it had done in the earlier crisis. But German policy was different and unequivocal: if the Kaiser's army mustered, it marched.

The Russian Council of Ministers' meeting on 24 July lasted two hours. Sazonov stressed Berlin's war preparations – which he probably exaggerated – and the unhappy past, in which Russian concessions to Austrian or German assertiveness had been treated as admissions of weakness. He argued that it was time to take a stand; that it would be an intolerable betrayal to allow Serbia to succumb. The two service ministers, Vladimir Sukhomlinov and Igor Grigorovich, said that, while the national rearmament programme was incomplete, the army and navy were ready to fight. Their contributions were important: had they spoken more cautiously – or perhaps, realistically – Russia might have drawn back.

Implausibly to foreign eyes, it was the agriculture minister whose remarks appear to have exercised the strongest influence. Alexander Krivoshein was a skilful court politicker with an extensive network of connections. He said that 'public opinion would not understand why, at a critical moment involving Russia's vital interests, the Imperial Government was reluctant to act boldly'. While recognising the dangers, he thought conciliation mistaken. The Tsar held a long private conversation with his uncle Grand Duke Nicholas, who commanded St Petersburg military district. It is unknown what was said, but it is likely that the Grand Duke expressed confidence both in France's support and in the power of its army: he had been much impressed by a 1912 visit, during which he viewed Joffre's soldiers. Moreover, he and his brother Peter were married to sisters, daughters of the King of Montenegro, whose impassioned influence was exercised to urge the Russians to fight the Austrians to the last gasp.

The Tsar remained deeply unhappy about the prospect of a conflict which, he well knew, could destroy his dynasty. He remarked thoughtfully on 24 July: 'Once [war] had broken out it would be difficult to stop.' But he nonetheless consented to the measures preparatory to mobilisation. In an effort to play the part of the ruler of a great power, a status to which Russia's claims were precarious, Nicholas acted not ignobly or wickedly, but rashly. He emulated Franz Joseph in setting a course for regime destruction – his own.

That evening, Sazonov told the Serbian ambassador that Russia would protect his country's independence. He offered Belgrade no 'blank cheque', instead urging acceptance of most of the terms of the Austrian ultimatum. But his commitment was decisive in persuading the Serbian government to reject a portion of Vienna's demands: without the Russians, absolute surrender was its only option. Sazonov felt confident that his country could count on France, while having no great expectation of support from Britain; he remarked gloomily that every British newspaper save *The Times* was backing Austria in the crisis. Many people in Britain, some of them holding office, were wholly unsympathetic to Russian intervention. They sympathised with the Austrians in viewing Serbia as a pestilential Balkan nuisance.

That day, while Europe held its breath, awaiting Serbia's response to Vienna's ultimatum, a violent thunderstorm struck central Europe. Outside the parliament building in Budapest a statue of Gyula Andrássy, one of the architects of the Dual Monarchy, was allegedly seen to totter. Troubled citizens told each other that their ancestors deemed such occurrences portents. But, as Finance Ministry official Lajos Thalloczy demanded in his diary: 'for whom?' That afternoon, expectant crowds gathered in the streets of Berlin, but by nightfall no further news was forthcoming.

Next day, Saturday the 25th, German teacher Gertrud Schädla described in her diary how her family lunged for their morning paper, desperate for the latest tidings. She wrote: 'Despite the danger that we shall be dragged into a war, people applaud Austria's muscular stance. The murder of the ducal couple demands harsh punishment.' As a gesture to the gravity of the international situation, the local sharpshooters' fair was cancelled, though booths and roundabouts had already been erected. Meanwhile Belgrade was thronged with worried people chattering in the streets, at their garden gates and in such cafés as The Russian Tsar. Each new edition of the papers was seized upon as eagerly as in Gertrud Schädla's house.

There were rumours – accurate enough – of Austrian troops gathering on the border, but still no panic: Serbs, with their boundless capacity for self-delusion, clung to a belief that somehow fate would pass them by.

On the evening of the 25th, Germany's Social Democrats staged protests against war. Bethmann rejected conservative demands for a blanket ban on assemblies, but decreed that they must be confined to halls, staying off the streets. Over 100,000 people attended rallies around the country, at which SPD leaders proclaimed that Austria was picking a fight Germany should not join.

All politicians find it hard to address with conviction more than one emergency at a time. This goes far to explain why the British government was slow to engage with events in Europe. Until the last week of July, the minds of senior ministers were fixed upon the Ulster crisis, to the near-exclusion of all else. Prime minister Herbert Asquith mentioned the assassinations just once, almost immediately after the event, in his intimate letters to Venetia Stanley, then not again until 24 July. In the intervening period, a Hungarian woman acquaintance called on David Lloyd George and harangued him about the rash insouciance with which the British were treating the reverberations of Sarajevo; she argued that unless Austrian anger could be assuaged, a war was inevitable. The chancellor was unimpressed, for which he later expressed regret. A *Times* leader on 3 July headed 'Efforts for Peace' related to Ulster, not Europe. It seemed entirely plausible that the United Kingdom was about to be plunged into a civil war, in which Protestant Ulstermen would be pitted against the Liberal government. Not only the Conservative Party, but also much of the British aristocracy and many of the army's officers, passionately supported the rebels.

In an age when every European nation measured power by breadth of empire, imperialists saw Britain's greatness imperilled if its other island was permitted to secede. The Ulster crisis fell upon a society already stricken by industrial strife: there was a protracted lock-out in the building trades, together with conflicts in the mines, on railways and in the engineering industry. In a July speech Lloyd George warned that the industrial and Irish confrontations were alike 'the gravest with which any government has had to deal for centuries'. He did not exaggerate. A historic constitutional clash beckoned, as King George V recognised when he summoned a conference of the warring parties at Buckingham Palace to seek a path to reconciliation.

Yet another *Times* leader, headed 'The King and the Crisis', on 20 July, referred to Ulster. Catholic passions were rising in step with those of Protestants: on Tuesday the 21st the *Manchester Guardian* reported that men of the Dublin Fusiliers, returning from camp training, were heard shouting: 'We will have Home Rule at any cost!' 'A nation once again!' A letter-writer to *The Economist* asked what would happen to Lord Roberts' rash public assertion – made in support of the army's Orange sympathis-ers – that soldiers must be allowed to exercise their consciences, if Irish nationalists wearing British khaki claimed such a right. There were extraordinary scenes as the foremost Home Rulers, Redmond and Dillon, walked towards Buckingham Palace to attend the King's conference: Irish Guardsmen in uniform cheered them on their way.

On 22 July Ulster still dominated the columns of *The Times*, but the paper admitted that the growing tension between Austria-Hungary and Serbia had become 'too serious to be ignored', though 'we have no wish to exaggerate the dangers ... a cool perception of their greatness may enable the Powers to conjure them before it is too late'. *The Times* found it so evident that war would threaten the very existence of Austria-Hungary that it cherished every hope the Emperor would act 'reasonably'. On the afternoon of the 24th, Asquith was obliged to tell the House of Commons that the King's Irish conference had broken down without a resolution. The cabinet plunged into vexed debate about the prospective boundaries of the six Ulster counties now scheduled for exclusion from immediate implementation of Home Rule – this was a concession extracted by the Protestant rebels at gunpoint. But then the foreign secre-tary, Sir Edward Grey, reported to his colleagues upon the draconian terms of the Austrian ultimatum to Serbia. Winston Churchill has described in immortal phrases how 'the parishes of Fermanagh and Tyrone faded back into the mists and squalls of Ireland, and a strange light began immediately, and by perceptible gradations, to fall and grow upon the map of Europe'.

Yet that night, few British people retired to their beds anticipating any consequences for themselves from the Balkan drama. It is only because European war caused the Irish crisis to be swept aside, the government to postpone implementation of Home Rule for the duration and then forever – because it was supplanted in 1921 by Irish partition and independence – that the savage hatreds, the magnitude of the threat to Britain's political fabric, are often today underrated. The Ulster imbroglio also significantly influenced Berlin's attitude: German leaders saw the British impaled upon their domestic troubles, and found it hard to imagine that a nation thus preoccupied and divided could menace their own purposes.

On the 25th, for the first time *The Times* acknowledged the gravity of the situation, saying – though still only in a second leader – that unless Austria-Hungary moderated its attitude towards Serbia, 'we stand upon the edge of war, and of a war fraught with dangers that are incalculable to all the Great Powers ... Austria-Hungary leaves a small and excitable Balkan kingdom to decide at a few hours' notice whether there is, or is not, to be a third Balkan war, and a Balkan war this time in which one of the Great Powers will be involved as a principal from the first.' It was widely remarked that, if Austria had been seriously interested in averting conflict, its ultimatum would have allowed a pause of more than forty-eight hours for the Serbian response, to give time for diplomacy to work.

But the British public still took more notice of such domestic trivia as 'the motor-horn nuisance' much discussed in *The Times*'s correspondence column. On 24 July Asquith mentioned the Balkans to Venetia Stanley in tones that still displayed Olympian detachment, though also sluggishly rising concern: 'Russia is trying to drag us in ... The curious thing is that on many, if not most, of the points Austria has a good and Serbia a very bad case, but the Austrians are quite the stupidest people in Europe ... and there is a brutality about their mode of procedure which will make most people think that it is a case of a big Power wantonly bullying a little one. Anyhow it is the most dangerous situation of the last 40 years, and may have incidentally the good effect of throwing into the background the lurid pictures of "civil war" in Ulster.' Asquith told the Archbishop of Canterbury that the Serbs deserved 'a thorough thrashing'. On the afternoon of the 25th he presided at a diplomatic garden party at 10 Downing Street, where a string orchestra played while the German ambassador rubbed shoulders with the Serbian minister, and the Lloyd Georges mingled with assorted peers.

That same Saturday night the attorney-general, Sir John Simon, addressed a gathering of Manchester Liberals at Altrincham. He told them: 'We have been so filled with our own political developments that some of us may not have noticed how serious a situation is threatening on the continent of Europe ... Let us resolve that the part which this country plays ... shall from beginning to end be the part of a mediator simply desirous of promoting better and more peaceful relations.' It is understandable that many Europeans, both allies and enemies, recoiled from such self-righteousness.

In the press announcement of house parties for the forthcoming Cowes yachting week, it was stated that 'Prince Henry of Prussia was to have been among the guests, but is unable to leave Germany at present owing to the crisis, though he may do so later should the situation improve.' Walter Cunliffe, governor of the Bank of England, asserted confidently to his guests at Inverewe in the Scottish Highlands that a great war was impossible, because 'the Germans haven't got the credits'. The financier Sir Ernest Cassell gave the same assurance to Mrs George Keppel's glittering summer house party across the Channel at Clingendaal House, near The Hague: a general European conflict could not be funded. However, a young guest declared that she must go home anyway – Violet Asquith wanted to be with her father in Downing Street. Some of the young men took a cue from her. Lord Lascelles, a Grenadier Guardsman, said to his friend Lord Castlerosse, 'We had better get back.' They motored to the coast, and caught a boat to England among other uneasy folk with the same idea.

Just before the 6 p.m. expiry of Austria's deadline on the 25th, Serbia's response was delivered by the prime minister personally to Austria's Baron Giesl. Pašić, conscious of the solemnity of the moment, wore an expression of mournful gravity. He said to Giesl in imperfect German: 'Part of your demands we have accepted, for the rest we place our hopes on your loyalty and chivalry as an Austrian general. With you we have always been very satisfied.' The Serbs accepted all Vienna's harsh terms save its requirement for Austrians to be granted authority on their soil. When this response became known in western Europe, there were some brief delusions that war was averted. 'People are relieved and at the same time disappointed to hear that Serbia is giving in,' wrote André Gide. But Vienna made no pretence of desiring a peaceful outcome: whatever the Serbian response, Baron Giesl had been instructed to remove himself to the border at Zemun by the 6.30 train.

News that the ultimatum had not been accepted in totality prompted an explosion of frivolous glee in Vienna, where crowds surged through the streets until the small hours. It has recently been suggested that Serbia's Nikola Pašić was also secretly enthused about a war that would commit Russia in support of Serbia's pan-Slav ambitions; while this is remotely possible, it is again wholly unproven and unprovable. But the Serbs knew their response would not satisfy Vienna, and their own mobilisation orders had been dispatched four hours earlier, at 2 p.m. That night government official Jovan Žujović, now in uniform, boarded a train carrying the General Staff eastward to the army's concentration area, while his brother, a doctor, reported to a divisional field hospital. After two recent conflicts and a mobilisation, the Serbs were more familiar with the routines than any other nation in Europe. But their army had not yet re-equipped after the Second Balkan War, and the government knew how ill-stocked were its arsenals – a further reason for doubting that Pašić welcomed hostilities.

Next morning Berchtold informed his Emperor – mendaciously – that the Serbs had fired on Austria's Danube steamers. Old Franz Joseph promptly signed the Empire's mobilisation order, saying enigmatically, '*Also doch!*' – 'So, after all!' Since the crisis began, his ministers had seriously debated only two matters: diplomatic measures to ensure German support, and the mechanics of Serbia's dismemberment after its conquest. Belgrade, the country's sole city of any stature, was to be annexed to the Hapsburg Empire, together with some additional territory. Other portions would be offered to Romania, Bulgaria, Greece and Montenegro, to reconcile them to the new dispensation. Serbia would thus cease to trouble the world; the pan-Slav movement would be deprived of its prime mover. Both Austria and Germany repeatedly lied about these intentions, assuring the Russians and the world that the Hapsburg government had no plans for imposing territorial changes.

Count István Burián wrote that 'across the whole of Europe our steps are rumbling like a storm which truly will decide our destiny'. Theodor Wolff, editor of the *Berliner Tageblatt*, asserted that the increasingly frenzied response to the appearance of each special edition on the streets of the capital reflected not merely a hunger for news, but each man's unwillingness to be alone, his yearning to share his own fears with others: 'Suddenly the crowds move. A couple of delivery vans appear, stormed by throngs of people. Some hold a white paper, others stare over their shoulders ... People stand in their autos and carriages, hanging out over the street, staring, waiting for certainty ... Never before has there been so much reading in the streets ... Everyone does it, the flower-sellers in front of Café Kranzler as eagerly as the elegant lady inside the café itself.'

An extra edition at 9.30 p.m. on the 25th reported that the Serbs had rejected Vienna's ultimatum. Few people cheered; most simply went home. But crowds gathered in front of the Austrian and Italian embassies screaming patriotic slogans: 'Down with Serbia!' Nationalists sang outside the chancellor's office. Café orchestras played '*Deutschland über alles*'. In

Wolff's words, 'the music rose sublimely to the heavens', followed by Austria's anthem '*Gott erhalte Franz den Kaiser*'. Kurt Riezler wrote: 'in the evening and on Sunday people were singing. The chancellor is much moved, deeply stirred and strengthened, especially since news [of such displays of popular emotion] is coming in from across the Empire. Among the people [there is] an enormous, if confused, urge for action, a yearning for a great movement ... to rise up for a great cause, to show one's powers.'

Joffre, France's chief of staff and commander-in-chief, found civilian politicians nervous, as well they might be, facing a huge crisis with the president and premier still abroad. The general told Messimy, the war minister, that he was quite prepared to handle a mobilisation in their absence: '*Monsieur le Ministre*, if we have to make war we shall do so.' Messimy responded emotionally: '*Bravo!*' On 25 July, without reference to Joffre, the minister telegraphed an order for all senior officers on leave to return to their units, which caused the general testily to remind him that there was a proper sequence for such measures, which Messimy had pre-empted. That night, French intelligence learned that German officers in Switzerland had been recalled from leave; guards were being placed on key bridges across the Kaiser's empire. It was nonetheless decided not to recall vacationing French soldiers, many of whom were still needed at home for the harvest.

In London Sir Edward Grey still harboured a huge though scarcely ignoble delusion: that Germany would exercise its influence upon Vienna to prevent a Balkan quarrel from escalating into a general European conflict. But that night of the 25th, the head of the Foreign Office's East and West Department, Sir Eyre Crowe, warned of the gravity of the situation. He wrote that everything now hinged upon the vital question of 'whether Germany is or is not determined to have this war now', and urged that the most likely way of preventing disaster was for Britain to make plain that it would not remain neutral in a conflict that engaged France and Russia. But at that moment there was no possibility that the cabinet or the House of Commons would have endorsed any such commitment, even had Grey asked for it – as he did not.

Europe now had a war: only its scale remained to be determined. Everything turned upon Russia. Jules Cambon, the French ambassador in Berlin, told his Belgian counterpart: 'Today the fate of France and the conservation of the peace of Europe depend upon a foreign will, that of the Tsar. What will he decide? And upon what advice? If he decides for war

France, the victim of her alliance, will follow the destiny of her ally on the battlefields.' It was taken for granted that Serbia would not have dared to reject even a part of Austria's ultimatum without being confident of Russia's support. At 1 a.m. on 26 July St Petersburg placed Russian Poland under martial law. Later that day, critical pre-mobilisation orders were issued. The army required a fortnight to be ready to fight, a month to be fully deployed, and thus every hour counted. Sazonov wanted only partial mobilisation; Russia had taken this same step in 1912 without precipitating a war. It seemed prudent to avoid directly provoking the Germans, and thus to hold back from activating the troops of Warsaw district, closest to their frontier. But when Danilov the quartermaster-general returned from the Caucasus that day, he explained to the foreign minister that a limited mobilisation would critically impede the full process.

On the 26th also, the minister of internal affairs published an order prohibiting publication or public mention of information about the armed forces, under the terms of Russia's treason laws. Notice was given that lighthouses and navigation lights were being doused in all Russian waters save the inland Caspian and Azov seas. The naval base at Sebastopol was closed to shipping, and Russian vessels at sea were instructed to halt radio transmissions. A series of domestic restrictions was introduced, starting with a 10 p.m. closure order for all St Petersburg restaurants. Next day all Germans and Austrians on Russian soil were ordered to settle their affairs and leave the country forthwith. From the 27th also, shipping in the Black Sea was warned that any craft steaming inshore during the hours of darkness was liable to be fired upon.

Soldiers began to move. Outside Moscow, the Sumskoi Hussars were recalled from exercises to barracks, where horses were reshod, campaign uniforms issued, harness and equipment checked. Men locked their personal possessions into chests which were labelled with the names and addresses of their next of kin. The officers' mess silver was sent to the State Bank for safekeeping, and cherished regimental banners were presented to a museum. The Serbian military attaché to Berlin noted that he travelled across Germany on 26–27 July without observing any warlike activity, but on crossing into Russian territory 'we noticed mobilisation steps being taken on a grand scale'. When Sir George Buchanan questioned Sazonov about Russia's scurrying soldiery, the foreign minister responded soothingly that they were merely responding to the ongoing industrial turbulence. The ambassador, however, was in no doubt that the army was preparing for war. That day, the 26th, Grey put to Prince Lichnowsky, the

German ambassador in London, Britain's proposed solution to the crisis: a four-power conference. Berlin promptly dismissed this, believing that such a gathering would be bound to condemn Austria. Here again was evidence of the German indifference to securing a diplomatic outcome.

In the last days of July, the weight of traffic flying between governments swamped the relatively primitive international communications system, so that vital cables became subject to chronic delay. Only a fraction of government messages were transmitted by diplomatic wireless: most relied upon the commercial telegraph network. Details of Russia's mobilisation were slow to reach the French government, for instance, because every message from its St Petersburg embassy had to be carried more than two miles to the public telegraph office. The British Foreign Office cipher clerks, only four in number, were overwhelmed: they worked in pairs, one reading out the groups, the other transcribing them onto a Post Office form – everything was done in longhand. Since five-number groups cost more to send, they made efforts to achieve terseness in the interests of economy. Once completed, a message was sealed in an envelope and taken by a messenger half a mile to London's central post office in The Strand for transmission.

German civilians were becoming increasingly conscious that they might have to fight. The prospect roused dismay among socialists, enthusiasm among conservatives. Wilhelm Kaisen was a twenty-seven-year-old Bremen plasterer, and a dedicated Social Democrat. On 26 July he wrote to his girlfriend Helene expressing revulsion at the prospect before Europe: 'War – those letters embrace such a dreadful ocean of blood and horror that they make us shudder to contemplate them.' Kaisen was full of hopes that the Socialist International would intervene to prevent conflict. If it failed to do so, he foresaw mutiny among soldiers, especially 'once murderous aircraft unleash perdition from the sky'. Across Europe in the last weekend of July, fears of the breaking storm prompted tens of thousands of hasty weddings. In the small town of Linden near Hanover, the register office married forty-six couples before finally closing at 11 o'clock on Sunday night. In Hanover itself, two hundred couples tied the knot.

Admiral Tirpitz had told a diplomat earlier in 1914, with doubtful accuracy, that the British had their newspapers under much better control than did Germany. 'In spite of your "liberty of the press", at a hint from your government your whole national press becomes unanimous on questions outside your domestic politics.' By contrast, German newspapers, said the admiral contemptuously, were 'ocean tramps', each representing the view of its own little party. There were 3,000 titles, fifty of them in

Berlin. Now, the *Berlin Post* urged that Austria should be left alone to pursue whatever course she chose. The *Rheinisch-Westfälische Zeitung* said on 24 July: 'we are not required to support Hapsburg wars of aggression'. *Vorwärts*, a Social Democratic publication, declared contemptuously on 27 July that 'only immature adolescents could be attracted to a warrior adventure that must turn Europe into a slaughterhouse stinking of blood and decay'.

Contrarily, in Freiburg the town's semi-official bulletin, *Freiburger Tagblatt*, asserted that Austria's looming war with Serbia 'holds sway completely over our city. Our whole life [has] played out as if we ourselves had to draw the sword – among families, in shops and public places, on the streets, in tram cars. These are genuine lofty sentiments, rooted in real German patriotism.' *Freiburger Zeitung* wrote of 'a wave of the highest patriotic enthusiasm [which] cascaded like a spring flood through the entire city'. Even the most pacifistic socialist papers said that if war came to Germany the working class would fight, rallying to the defence of the Fatherland. A German defeat would be 'unthinkable, horrible ... we do not desire that our women and children should be victims of the Cossack's bestialities'.

A liberal journalist wrote on 26 July in *Weser-Zeitung*: 'We cannot allow Austria to go under, for then we should ourselves be threatened with becoming subject to the greater Russian colossus, with its barbarism. We must fight now in order to secure for ourselves freedom and peace. The storm from east and west will be terrible but the skill, courage, and sacrifices of our army will prevail. Every German will feel the glorious duty of showing himself worthy of our forefathers [who fought] at Leipzig and Sedan.' But even the most strident editorialists hoped that France and Britain would remain neutral, leaving Germany to direct its undivided military attentions to Russia. The Berlin government, in one of its spasms of moderation, urged the Austrians initially to mobilise only sufficient forces to address Serbia.

But on 26 July, Jules Cambon warned German foreign minister Jagow that the British would not this time remain neutral, as they had in 1870. Jagow shrugged: 'you have your information and we have ours, which is completely different. We are confident of British neutrality.' Cambon was among those who always thereafter believed this a critical misapprehension – that if the Germans had known Britain would fight, they would not have risked war. His view seems mistaken, however. The key German decision-makers, Moltke foremost among them, had long before weighed the possibility and indeed likelihood of British intervention – and discounted it as irrelevant. The outcome of a brief continental struggle would be determined by the clash of vast armies, to which a British troop contribution would perforce be tiny, and the Royal Navy irrelevant.

At this stage, too, most of Britain's governing class remained indifferent to the fate of Serbia and strongly hostile to intervention. The British ambassador in Paris, Sir Francis Bertie, wrote on 27 July: 'It seems incredible that the Russian Government should plunge Europe into war in order to make themselves the protectors of the Serbians.' Many influential people questioned the wisdom of shattering European peace to save squalid little Serbia.

Meanwhile Berchtold, in Vienna, decided that it had become urgent to initiate military action: he wrote apprehensively that it was 'not impossible that the Triple Entente might yet try to achieve a peaceful solution of the conflict unless a clear situation is created by a declaration of war'. From Berlin, without Bethmann's knowledge, Moltke sent a message to Vienna urging general mobilisation and rejection of mediation; but this was decrypted and read by the Austrians only after they had already made their commitment to march. At 11 a.m. on Tuesday, 28 July, sitting at a little writing table in his study at Bad Ischl, the Emperor Franz Joseph signed a declaration of war, the document which would prove the death warrant of his own empire.

Early that afternoon, via telegraph, a copy of this missive reached the Serbian Foreign Ministry's temporary quarters in Niš. Officials at first suspected a hoax. One of them, Milan Stojadinović, later wrote: 'its form was so very unusual, in those days when the very etiquette of such things was still deemed important'. The language was undiplomatically crude and terse, but the Serbs eventually decided the telegram must be genuine. One of them bore it down the street to the Europa coffee house, where the prime minister was lunching with Strandman, Russia's acting envoy.

The Serb leader read the brief words with every eye in the place upon him. Then he crossed himself, passed the fatal document to his Russian companion, rose and addressed the company: 'Austria has declared war on us. Our cause is a just one. God will help us.' Another Foreign Ministry official hurried in, to report that a similarly worded communication had just reached the army high command in Kragujevac. Shortly afterwards, a message from St Petersburg reached Strandman, which he was ordered to deliver personally to Pašić. Signed by the Tsar, it declared that while Russia desired peace, it would not remain indifferent to the fate of Serbia. After reading this, Pašić once again crossed himself and said reverently and theatrically, 'Lord, great merciful Russian Tsar.'

In Paris, the sensation of 28 July was not, however, Austria's declaration of war, but instead that day's acquittal of Madame Caillaux for her admitted killing of Gaston Calmette. Amid worldwide amazement, a jury decided that *Le Figaro*'s coverage of her husband and of their relationship in the days when she was merely his mistress made it not unreasonable for her to have shot its editor. And all the while, France's leaders remained almost incommunicado on their Baltic cruise. The trip had become a nightmare: Poincaré and Viviani were obliged to continue with exchanges of courtesies in Stockholm and an apparently interminable sea passage while war clouds swept towards western Europe. Many of the wireless messages that reached them on the 26th proved indecipherable. President and prime minister conducted tense conversations, turning over the crisis. Poincaré wrote: 'M. Viviani and I come back always to the same question: what does Austria want? What does Germany want?'

Even if the contribution of the French president to the crisis was more proactive than he later admitted, he cannot have relished meandering across the Baltic while Europe's flames kindled and flared. In Paris, Joffre and France's soldiers were becoming acutely frustrated by the political paralysis. The general wrote crossly: 'The main preoccupation [of ministers] … was to make no move which could be construed as anything except a response to German initiatives. This timid attitude was largely the result of the absence of the heads of the government.' He was appalled on the 28th, when a 21 July dispatch reached Messimy from Cambon in Berlin, which had been 'incomprehensibly' delayed for a week, claiming that Germany had begun pre-mobilisation measures. The ambassador overstated the case, but the French now believed Moltke's forces to be a week ahead of themselves in preparedness, and still Messimy would not act in Viviani's absence.

The war minister's caution was prudent; but Joffre's fuming anger emphasises the urgency with which soldiers were now shouldering a path to the centre of the stage in France, Russia, Germany. As war loomed, every commander-in-chief was terrified of the consequences if the enemy was ready to fight first. Thus, each began to press his respective political leaders. The Russian chiefs of staff lamented to the president of the Duma the Tsar's indecision. Europe's armaments race and military contingency plans were not responsible for war, because they were symptoms rather than causes. But by the last days of July 1914 generals were pushing governments towards the abyss: they knew they would take the blame if their nation lost on the battlefield the deadly game of grandmother's footsteps that was now being played.

On the 27th, Poincaré and Viviani learned that the French press had become savagely critical of their absence from Paris. The two men decided to hasten home after refuelling at Copenhagen, and duly arrived at Dunkirk early on the morning of 29 July. The Germans had been insistently jamming communications between Paris, St Petersburg and Berlin, but it is hard to suggest that such mischief altered outcomes. The Russians were determined to react to Austria's assault on Serbia. The French government was committed to support them, strongly influenced by knowledge that if war came, the Germans would strike at France first. The powerful Eiffel Tower radio station enabled the Russian military attaché to maintain contact with St Petersburg through the crisis, overcoming German interference. The Baltic yachting trip of Poincaré and Viviani probably had little or no influence upon the course of history. The president favoured a policy of 'firmness' towards Germany; he is likely to have led his country to support Russia in the July crisis whether or not he had met Sazonov at St Petersburg.

Many French people recognised a growing likelihood that they would have to fight. On Sunday the 26th there were scenes of intense excitement on the streets of Paris: appearances by the usual weekend military bands were cheered; a Hapsburg flag was burnt by protesters outside the Austrian embassy. Most citizens faced the prospect of war without enthusiasm but with an overwhelming sense of resignation, placing blame squarely upon Germany. As printer Louis Derenne left his works in Orléans he heard a crowd shouting 'Mort aux Boches!', heedless of the fact that thus far the Austrians had been prime movers in the crisis. 'We are getting ready to enter a long tunnel full of blood and darkness,' wrote André Gide. The government gave no clear public signals of its intentions until Poincaré and Viviani reached the capital on the 29th, but it was generally assumed that if Russia fought, so too would France.

Joffre, on his own initiative, had told the Russians on the 27th that they could expect his country's full support. Both the chief of staff and Messimy, the war minister, urged Russia to hasten its mobilisation and deploy as rapidly as possible against Germany. They knew that its war plan required an immediate attack in the West. It was vital to French security that the Russians should realise as swiftly as possible a 'threat in being', to oblige Moltke to divide his forces. In Paris, a rush to hoard gold caused panic on the Bourse. In France, as across Europe, a collapse of credit was creating a huge financial crisis which was alleviated only by the intervention of governments. People milled on the boulevards and thronged cafés and restaurants, less in search of refreshment than of news and companionship.

In Berlin on Tuesday evening, the 28th, some thousands of people from working-class areas marched into the city centre singing socialist songs and crying out 'Down with the war!' and 'Long live social democracy!' They were prevented from entering the main thoroughfares by mounted police with drawn swords, though at about 10 p.m. a thousand broke through to the Unter den Linden. On the pavements, bystanders showed their disapproval by singing the rousing patriotic songs 'Wacht am Rhein' and 'Heil dir im Siegerkranz'. Half an hour later the police charged and cleared the street, to loud applause from patrons nursing their mugs of hot chocolate on the balconies of Café Bauer and Café Kranzler.

Twenty-eight people were arrested for chanting anti-war slogans, and thus causing 'public disturbance'. The right-wing press had a field day next morning, denouncing the demonstrators as 'a mob', and anti-war protesters as traitors. Some historians suggest that more Germans demonstrated against war than in its favour, which may well be true. But the conduct of the Kaiser, Moltke and Bethmann was wholly uninfluenced by exhibitions of dissent which they judged – correctly – would cease when the nation found itself committed. Far fewer Germans protested against war than had taken to the streets four years earlier, to demand Prussian voting reform.

The first significant strategic move by Britain came on Sunday, 26 July, when the Royal Navy's Home Fleet was due to disperse after a trial mobilisation. The staff of Northcliffe's *Daily Mail* believed that they played some role in the First Lord of the Admiralty's initiative that day. Amid looming crisis, they telegraphed him at his holiday rendezvous in Norfolk: 'Winston Churchill Pear Tree Cottage Overstrand: WAR DECLARED AUSTRIA SERBIA GERMAN FLEET CONCENTRATING MAY WE ASK IS IT TRUE BRITISH FLEET DEMOBILISING: *DAILY MAIL*'. This missive was delivered to Churchill on the nearby beach. He never responded, but spoke by telephone within the hour to the First Sea Lord, Prince Louis of Battenberg, and took the afternoon train back to London. Late that night, an order was issued to cancel the dispersal of the fleet, which two days later was dispatched to its war station at Scapa Flow in the Orkney Islands. Paul Cambon said later that Churchill rendered a great service to France by his impassioned support for intervention and his

order not to demobilise the fleet 'which we [the French] have never sufficiently recognised'.

Yet there was still among the British at large no sense of imminent peril.
Asquith wrote to Venetia Stanley on the 28th: 'We had a cabinet yesterday
... mainly to talk about war & peace. I am afraid that Grey's experiment
of a Conference *à quatre* won't come off, as the Germans refuse to take a
hand. The only real hope is that Austria & Russia may come to a deal
among themselves. But at this moment things don't look well, & Winston's
spirits are probably rising.' Churchill adopted a shamelessly cynical view,
mirroring that which was driving policy in Berlin: 'if war was inevitable
this was by far the most favourable opportunity and the only one that
would bring France, Russia and ourselves together'. He wrote that day to
his wife Clementine: 'My darling One & beautiful – Everything tends
towards catastrophe, & collapse. I am interested, geared-up & happy.'
Asquith ended his 28 July letter to Venetia Stanley on a bathetic note: 'It is
a slack evening of Supply at the House, so I am getting Violet to beat up
one or two people to dine at home & play Bridge.' The prime minister
showed no greater agitation the following evening, the 29th: 'I have just
finished an Army Council ... Rather interesting because it enables one to
realise what are the first steps in an actual war.'

Some people seized upon looming conflict as a profit-making opportunity. The Cotton Powder Company, whose impressive engraved copper-
plate letterhead announced its Kent works as 'manufacturers of Cordite,
Guncotton, Blasting Explosives, Distress Signals, Detonators etc', wrote on
29 July to the Serbian war minister. Its board offered to provide 10,000
rifle grenades, 'part of a contract for 80,000 which we are executing for
another foreign government ... This present order followed a previously
executed order for 25,000 which have been used up in actual hostilities
with the most satisfactory results ... 10,000 are packed ready for dispatch
and could be shipped within twenty-four hours. If desired the same
Grenade may be thrown by hand for close-quarter fighting.' There is no
record of whether such an order was placed by Belgrade, but the Cotton
Powder Company could not be accused of lacking zeal on behalf of British
enterprise.

On the evening of 28 July, Russian military intelligence reported that
three-quarters of the Austrian army was being mobilised, twelve out of
sixteen corps – many more troops than Vienna needed to tackle Serbia.
Though the Tsar had yet to sign the order, that night Russia's chief of staff
wired the senior officers of all military districts, warning that '30 July will

be proclaimed the first day of our general mobilisation.' The Tsar yielded to Sazonov's urgings, and agreed that general mobilisation should start next day. From 24 July the Russians had made military preparations ahead of any other nations save Austria and Serbia, yet every Russian decision was made against the background of the former's commitment to crush the Serbs by force. Hopes for peace crumbled in St Petersburg on the 29th, when word came that the Austrians had begun to bombard Belgrade.

Russia's politicians and diplomats united in a belief that they must fight. That day the head of mission in Sofia, A.A. Savinsky, an accustomed moderate, said that if the country gave way, 'our prestige in the Slav world and in the Balkans would perish never to return'. Aleksandr Giers in Constantinople said that if Russia bowed, Turkey and the Balkans would unfailingly swing into the Central Powers' camp. Another diplomat, Nikolai de Basily, replied with dignity to a friend – the Austrian military attaché – who warned of domestic catastrophe if the Tsar went to war: 'You commit a serious error of calculation in supposing the fear of revolution will prevent Russia from fulfilling its national duty.'

Bethmann Hollweg now warned St Petersburg that unless Russia halted its preparations, Germany would mobilise. This message reinforced Sazonov's conviction that a clash was unavoidable – but caused the Tsar to waver again. He had received a personal message from the Kaiser; in response, he insisted that Russia should draw back a step – albeit a fruitless step – and revert to partial mobilisation. But Sazonov remained insistent. At 5 o'clock on the following afternoon of 30 July, while still lamenting 'sending thousands and thousands of men to their deaths', Nicholas signed a general mobilisation order, to take effect next morning.

That evening, many Russian army units were alerted by telephone to expect a courier carrying secret instructions. The Sumskoi Hussars were ordered to readiness to entrain in thirty-six hours for Poland's frontier with East Prussia, while the grenadier regiment that shared their barracks outside Moscow headed for the Austrian border. Soldiers were issued with tinned emergency rations. Cornet Sokolov pointed out that these were dated 1904, but this did nothing to stem soldiers' curiosity. To the embarrassment of the Hussars' officers, within an hour the barracks was littered with empty tins. 'They were just like children!' wrote Vladimir Littauer in exasperation. He contrasted their behaviour with that of German stragglers whom they later captured, some of them starving. So disciplined were the Kaiser's soldiers that, in the absence of orders, not a man had touched his emergency rations.

After a last civilian passenger train crossed the border from East Prussia into Russia on 30 July, a Russian passenger who had hitherto remained silent burst into voluble expressions of frustration that he had not had a bomb to drop on the German rail bridge at Dirschau; he expressed glee that its guards were still wearing parade rather than field dress, showing that those 'pigs of Germans' were not quite ready. Russia's leaders understood that they were undertaking an adventure beyond their own national strength. It is most unlikely that they would have dared to move against the Central Powers in 1914 had they not been assured of the support of France. Diplomatically and even militarily, they might have done better to have delayed mobilisation until the Austrian army had started its invasion of Serbia. But the policy-makers in St Petersburg, especially Sazonov, were spurred by fears that delay would enable Germany literally to steal a march on them. Russia's prevarications about the exact pattern of its mobilisation were almost certainly irrelevant to the European outcome. Once St Petersburg made the decision to take military action of any kind against Austria, Germany was sure to respond.

The Russians made little attempt to conceal their extended preparations: the Tsar told the Kaiser without embarrassment on the night of 29 July, in one of their personal 'Nicky–Willy' communications: 'the military measures which have now come into force were decided five days ago for reasons of defence on account of Austria's preparations'. Those who today attribute to Russia principal responsibility for war are obliged to rely on the same argument as did the Kaiser in July 1914: that the Tsar should have preserved wider European peace by allowing Austria to conduct a limited war to crush Serbia. Such a case can be made; but it seems essential to acknowledge its terms, rather than attempt to construct a spurious indictment that the Russians were guilty of duplicity. The most important dates in the July crisis were the 23rd, when Austria made explicit its commitment to destroy Serbia, and the 24th, when Russia began to take active measures to respond. Unless or until evidence is forthcoming that the Serbian government was complicit in the plot to kill Franz Ferdinand, or that Russia had prior knowledge of the outrage, the Tsar's commitment to resist the attempt to extinguish Serbia seems justified. The best reason for Nicholas to have held back was not doubt about the legitimacy of Russia's action, but caution about the menace posed by belligerence to his own polity.

3 THE GERMANS MARCH

The only untenable view of the July crisis is that war was the consequence of a series of accidents. On the contrary: the leaders of all the great powers believed themselves to be acting rationally, in pursuit of coherent and attainable objectives. A large enigma nonetheless persists about the exercise of authority in Germany: who was in charge? During the previous decade, the dysfunctionality of the nation's governance had progressively worsened, even as its economic might increased. A new generation of elected politicians, many of them socialists, jostled for access to power outside palaces still dominated by the spurred topboots of a highly militarised autocracy. The Kaiser had become the symbol of his country's assertive nationalism rather than an executive ruler, but he continued to make erratic interventions. Around him rival personalities, institutions and political groupings vied for mastery. The army and navy were at loggerheads. The General Staff scarcely spoke to the War Ministry. The Empire's component states intermittently asserted themselves against Berlin.

A German author predicted in 1910 that during the period of political and military tension preceding any conflict, 'the press and its key instruments, telegraph and telephone, will exercise immense influence, which may be for either good or ill'. Moltke agreed. However great the power of the army, the chief of staff recognised that to induce millions of conscripted civilians to engage in a twentieth-century conflict, the cause must command popular support. 'Moltke told me,' recorded a Prussian officer in 1908, '... that the time of cabinet wars was over and that a war the German people did not want or did not understand, and would therefore not greet with sympathy, would be a very dangerous affair. If ... the people thought that the war had been conjured up in a frivolous fashion and was only intended to help the governing classes out of an embarrassment, then it would have to start with us having to fire on our own subjects.' This goes far to explain why Germany had refused to go to war alongside Austria in earlier Balkan crises. It shows why, in July 1914, Moltke attached such importance to ensuring that Germany was seen, above all by its own people, as a threatened victim and not as an aggressor. The European crisis was overlaid on domestic turbulence. Labour unrest, manifested in frequent strikes, alarmed the Berlin government as much as similar troubles elsewhere prompted British, French and Russian fears about social stability.

It is difficult to assess the Kaiser's conduct, because he changed his mind so often. Scribbled annotations on state documents emphasise his irredeemable intemperance: 'Fool yourself Mr Sazonov!'; 'Damnation!'; 'No!'; 'It's not for him to decide'; 'a tremendous piece of British insolence!'. The exclamation mark was his favoured instrument of policy-making. Wilhelm's reversions to caution always came too late to undo the damage inflicted by his more usual imprudence. He allegedly told Bethmann on 5 July: 'we should use all means to work against the growth of the Austro-Serbian controversy into an international conflict'. Yet next day he gave Vienna the 'blank cheque'.

On 27 July his initial reaction, on returning from his Norwegian yachting trip to read the Serbs' humble response to Vienna's ultimatum, was that he saw 'no more reason for a war'. But Bethmann that same day told the German ambassador to Austria: 'We must appear as the ones being forced into the war.' Gen. Erich von Falkenhayn, the Prussian war minister, met the Kaiser and Moltke on the 27th and recorded afterwards: 'It has now been decided to fight the matter through, regardless of the cost.' Three days later, on the 30th, the Bavarian Gen. Krafft von Dellmensingen wrote in his diary: 'The Kaiser absolutely wants peace and the Kaiserin is working towards it with all her might. He even wants to influence Austria and stop her continuing further. That would be the greatest disaster! We would lose all credit as allies.'

By that time, however, the general's court gossip was two days out of date. The Kaiser said on 28 July, 'the ball that is rolling can no longer be stopped', and seemed to mean it. One might liken his erratic behaviour to that of an amateur actor struggling to fill a monarch's part in a Shakespearean history piece. Wilhelm strove to keep up with the rest of the cast, to play the warrior emperor, while being chronically uncertain what this required: he was forever snatching at the wrong cue or delivering misplaced lines.

But if German policy had vacillated earlier in July, now the march to war had attained its own momentum. In Berlin on the 29th, Falkenhayn sought to force the pace: he declared that the time for prevarication was over; Germany could no longer wait for Russia to move, but must mobilise. Bethmann and Moltke remained anxious, for domestic reasons, to be seen to follow rather than lead Russia, but they knew the hour was nigh. An ultimatum to neutral Belgium was prepared, demanding a right of passage through the country for the German army. Bethmann then made a diplomatic blunder. At a moment when British sentiment was wavering, he dispatched an offer to Sir Edward Grey: would Britain undertake to remain neutral, in return for assurances about German respect for Belgian and French territorial integrity? This essay in blackmail, which made plain that the Germans were preparing to attack in the West, provoked outrage in London. 'There is something crude and almost childlike about German diplomacy,' wrote Asquith disdainfully. Grey responded curtly that in no circumstances could Britain entertain so shameful a proposal.

This news from London precipitated a brief crisis of nerves on the part of Wilhelm and Bethmann during the night of 29 July. It had become apparent that they were leading their country into the greatest military clash in history, with the British unlikely to remain neutral. The Kaiser suddenly proposed that the Austrians should agree merely to occupy Belgrade until their terms were met. At 2.55 a.m. on the 30th, Bethmann telegraphed Vienna urging acceptance of diplomatic mediation. His message reached Berchtold, however, only after Austrian mobilisation had begun, and on the same day as the telegram from Moltke, urging the Empire to reject mediation and deploy its army against Russia rather than Serbia. Thus, before the chief of staff knew of full Russian mobilisation, he emphasised his personal commitment to a wider war, and his readiness to exercise his influence in the diplomatic sphere in a fashion well beyond the usual compass of an army chief of staff. Berchtold asked Conrad after reading the two contradictory messages: 'Who rules in Berlin – Moltke or Bethmann?' The Austrians figuratively and perhaps literally shrugged, then continued their mobilisation and bombardment of Belgrade.

The answer to Berchtold's question was anyway now Moltke. Bethmann made no further attempt to dispute the chief of staff's insistence that the march to war must take its course. Moreover, the chancellor would soon become an advocate of far-reaching war aims, explicitly directed towards securing German mastery of Europe. Though both the Kaiser and Bethmann havered during July, they could never bring themselves to adopt the only measure that would probably have averted disaster: withdrawal of German support for an Austrian invasion of Serbia. By the last days of the month, Moltke and Falkenhayn were asserting military imperatives – and the soldiers' primacy in the decision-making process, now that war was inevitable – in a fashion that brooked no dissent. Wilhelm, like his chancellor, lacked strength to allow himself to be seen to draw back when the generals were insisting that his duty lay in acceptance of trial by combat. Falkenhayn had once argued that duelling must be maintained as a means of resolving personal disputes between officers, citing its importance 'for the honour of the army'. Now, in the same spirit, he sternly silenced the Kaiser's belated expressions of doubt: 'I reminded him that he was no longer in control of these matters.'

Moltke became the critical personality in Germany's endgame. The army was the country's most powerful institution, and he directed its motions. Part of the historic indictment against the chief of staff is that, even if the charge that from the outset he pressed for war is disputable, he endorsed such a course while harbouring huge doubts about its implications, and about Germany's prospects of success. If it was sufficiently wretched for a man as foolish as Conrad to have willed Armageddon, it seems even more base for one as intelligent as Moltke to have been complicit in this outcome. The most plausible explanation, supported by his subsequent conduct amidst the stress of war, is that like his royal master, the chief of staff was fundamentally a weak man seeking to masquerade as a strong one. In Vienna and Berlin alike – and in St Petersburg and Paris also, though to a lesser degree – there was now a fatal hunger for a showdown, a decision, in place of repeated inconclusive crises over a decade.

Many of Germany's soldiers, as well as its conservative politicians, believed that war offered a prospect of reversing the social democratic tide which they deemed a threat to national greatness as well as to their own authority. The generals also saw that within two or three years, enhanced Russian capabilities would remove Germany's last hopes of fulfilling Schlieffen's mystic vision – smashing France before turning east. Deterrence was bound to fail, with or without a British commitment to fight, because the Germans believed that in 1914 they had a better chance of defeating any Entente combination than they would ever enjoy again. Berlin merely sought to ensure that the Tsar bore the odium for initiating mobilisation, and for the Kaiser's mighty military response.

The Belgians suddenly recognised the peril facing their own country. Baron de Gaiffier d'Hestroy, political director of Belgium's Foreign Ministry, holidaying with his family in the Engadine, was hastily ordered home, and departed for Brussels on 29 July. He found that many trains had already been commandeered by the Germans or Austro-Hungarians for troop movements; only a chance meeting secured him a place homewards in the private carriage of a Belgian industrialist, reaching Brussels on the morning of the 30th.

Sir Francis Bertie wrote that day, quite mistakenly but in a fashion reflecting the mood in Paris: 'Things are hanging in the balance of peace and war. We are regarded as the deciding factor. The Italians suggested that they and we should both stand aside. A poor bargain for the French. I have written to Grey that the feeling here is that peace between the Powers depends on England and that if she declare herself *solidaire* with France and Russia there will be no war, for Germany will not face the danger to her of her supplies by sea being cut off by the British.' That afternoon of 30 July, it was learned that French pedestrians attempting to cross the frontier into Germany were being turned back, while some motor cars and even railway locomotives with the same intentions were detained; telephone links were severed.

All over France, people gathered to discuss the news. Work stopped in the little factories of Beaurepaire, in Isère; solemn crowds filled the streets, discussing the crisis with gravity rather than excitement. In the words of one local man, 'It was like a funeral. Our small town appeared to be in mourning.' In Germany on 30 July, a thousand customers of Freiburg's Municipal Savings Bank emptied their accounts, forcing it to restrict withdrawals, and there were matching queues outside most of the banks of Europe. Many shop-owners refused to accept payment in paper currency, while others shut their doors. In Le Havre, waiters warned restaurant customers before they ordered dinner that only gold rather than banknotes would be acceptable in payment.

There were still a few spasms of optimism: on the evening of the 30th, in the courtyard of the Palais Bourbon journalists thronged around M. Malvy of the Foreign Office, who told them of new exchanges between St Petersburg, Berlin and Vienna. 'As soon as the diplomats start talking,' he said, 'we may hope for an accommodation.' But late that night, as Raymond Recouly was writing his column at *Le Figaro*, a colleague burst into his office and cried: 'Henri de Rothschild is downstairs. He has been dining with a senior official of the Foreign Ministry, who told him that war was a matter of days away, perhaps even of hours.' Shortly afterwards a woman friend appeared, and asked the journalist whether she should cancel an intended motoring holiday in Belgium the following week. Without question, replied Recouly: 'If you are really determined to go driving, head instead for Biarritz or Marseille.'

By the evening of the 30th, Moltke was no longer willing to wait for the Russians to announce mobilisation. He told Bethmann that Germany must act. The two agreed that whatever the Tsar did, Germany would proclaim its own mobilisation at noon next day, the 31st. A few minutes before this deadline came, to the vast relief of the Germans, St Petersburg announced its own move. Berlin could thus go to war, having achieved its critical diplomatic purpose of seeing the Russians become first after Austria to draw the sword. Following an official 'declaration of a war threat' – *'Zustand der drohenden Kriegsgefahr'*, a legal definition – on the 31st, the army forthwith began to patrol Germany's borders. Some unauthorised crossings took place by troops of both sides, notably in Alsace. German pioneers blew up a railway bridge near Illfurt, following false reports that the French were at hand. Only on 3 August, however, did Berlin formally authorise its soldiers to invade French soil.

After the Kaiser signed Germany's mobilisation order at 5 p.m. on 1 August in the Sternensaal of his Berlin palace, with his usual instinct for the wrong gesture he ordered champagne to be served to his suite. The Bavarian Gen. von Wenninger visited the Prussian War Ministry soon after news of Russian mobilisation came through: 'Everywhere beaming faces, people shaking hands in the corridors, congratulating one another on having cleared the ditch.' Russia had acted in accordance with the ardent and freely avowed hopes of Wenninger, Moltke, Falkenhayn and their comrades; as Germany adopted pre-mobilisation measures on 31 July, they merely expressed fears that France might decline to follow suit, fail to enter the trap. Wilhelm despised the French as 'a feminine race, not manly like the Anglo-Saxons or Teutons', and this undoubtedly influenced his lack of apprehension about going to war with them.

There was one more internal crisis in Berlin that day: Moltke had already left the palace after the mobilisation decree ceremony when a telegram was brought to the Kaiser from Lichnowsky in London. This professed to bear an undertaking from Grey that Britain would remain neutral, and guarantee French neutrality, if Germany refrained from attacking France. Wilhelm exulted. Moltke was recalled, to be told that it was now only necessary to fight in the East. A legendary exchange followed: the chief of staff, appalled, said that the mobilisation plans could not be changed; such an upheaval would dispatch to the battlefield not an army, but a rabble. He was outraged that Wilhelm should seek to meddle when diplomacy was at an end; the issue was now that of conducting a war – the responsibility of himself.

It swiftly became plain that Lichnowsky's dispatch reflected a foolish misunderstanding of the British position. The French were mobilising, and Germany had its two-front war. But the conversation with Wilhelm had a devastating impact on Moltke. He returned to the General Staff building incandescent, his face mottled deep red. He told his adjutant: 'I want to wage a war against the French and the Russians, but not against such a Kaiser.' His wife later testified that she believed him to have suffered a slight stroke. Moltke's health was already fragile, his nerve unsteady. Now, on the brink of the collision of armies that he had done much to bring about, he showed the first signs of a moral and physical vulnerability which within six weeks would destroy him.

German mobilisation was accompanied by a declaration of war on Russia six days before the Austrians followed suit. A fourteen-year-old Bavarian schoolboy, Heinrich Himmler, wrote in his diary for 1 August: 'Played in the garden in the morning. Afternoon as well. 7.30 Germany declares war on Russia.' France was informed that its neutrality could be accepted only on condition that it surrendered its border fortresses to Germany 'as a gesture of sincerity'. Bethmann was furious that the military now marginalised him: it was a General Staff officer, Major Hans von Haeften, who drafted a declaration to the German people for the Kaiser to deliver. The chancellor and the general had always disliked and resented each other. Hereafter, their animosity became manifest. On the afternoon of 1 August crowds cheered the Kaiser as he motored from Potsdam down Berlin's Unter den Linden in the full-dress uniform of a cuirassier of the Guard. Wilhelm enthused: 'a wonderful confidence prevails ... unanimity and determination'. Journalist Theodor Wolff, a spectator, said of the crowd's enthusiasm for the Kaiser's appearance, 'It was a warm, sunny day. In the hot air there was already the sweaty breath of fever and the smell of blood.' A right-wing newspaper asserted that after Wilhelm had passed there was 'a holy mood among the crowd, worthy of the moment'. Strangers shook hands with each other.

Russia's mobilisation solved a critical political problem for Moltke. Germany's Social Democrats might well have continued to oppose war had their own country been seen as the first to move. As it was, though the government had already made its own secret commitment to march, Berlin could assert that Germany was merely responding to a Russian initiative – preparing to defend the Reich against Slavonic aggression. Admiral Müller wrote on 1 August: 'The mood is brilliant. The government has succeeded very well in making us appear as the attacked.' Moltke, after his fall, wrote to a fellow field-marshal: 'it is dreadful to be condemned to inactivity in this war which I prepared and initiated'. Nor was he alone among prominent Germans in avowing without embarrassment responsibility for the horrors that were now ordained. Foreign secretary Gottlieb

Jagow later told a woman friend that he was haunted by contemplation that Germany had 'wanted the war' which went so wrong. In 1916, shipping magnate Albert Ballin declined to meet Jagow because 'he wanted nothing further to do with a man who bore the responsibility for this whole dreadful disaster and for the deaths of so many hundreds of thousands of men'.

Wilhelm von Stumm, Jagow's close associate, told Theodor Wolff in February 1915: 'we were reconciled to the fact that we would have war with Russia ... If the war had not come now, we would have had it in two years' time under worse conditions ... No one could have foreseen that militarily not everything would work out as one had believed.' Prince von Bülow, a former chancellor, blamed Bethmann Hollweg for giving Austria the 5 July 'blank cheque'; he did not suggest that Germany sought war, but said the chancellor should have insisted upon prior consultation about the terms of Vienna's ultimatum to Belgrade, and condemned Berlin's rejection of Britain's proposal for a diplomatic conference.

During the last two days before and after mobilisation came, the German public mood became much less exuberant. On 31 July a *Frankfurter Zeitung* journalist recorded: 'Over everything hangs a great gravity, a frightening peace and tranquillity ... In their quiet rooms wives and young women sit, nursing their sombre thoughts about the immediate future ... a great fear of terrible things, of what may be to come.' Social democrat Wilhelm Heberlein said that in Hamburg news of mobilisation was grimly received: 'most people were depressed, as if waiting to be beheaded the following day'. The *Hamburger Echo* said that on the evening of 1 August 'the noisy mood which was ignited by a couple of unthinking fools in the first few days of this week is gone ... one seldom hears a joyous laugh on the street'.

That day Gertrud Schädla repeatedly visited Verden's town centre to garner the latest news, until finally at 6 p.m. she saw the mobilisation order posted. She described her community's mixed feelings: 'We were half happy because our government has behaved with nobility and firmness, half minded to cry because of our fears for the future.' She added later: 'Now all our fears have been realised, things that appeared both all too possible and yet impossible ... Our enemies in the east, the west and the north tormented us pitilessly. Now they will see that we fight back! ... We did not want war – if we did, we could have had it ten times during the past forty-three years of peace!' On Sunday, 2 August, Berlin police warned against extravagant displays of enthusiasm, such as crowds surging up to the Kaiser's car. For the first time, soldiers guarding public buildings appeared garbed in field grey. From the very onset of the struggle, Germany became the first power to characterise it not as a merely European affair, but as global war – *Weltkrieg*.

As Germany began to mobilise, in Paris Sir Francis Bertie called on the French prime minister, whom he found 'in a highly nervous state … Evidently the Germans want to hurry matters before the Russians can be ready.' France now lagged two days behind Germany's military preparations: Joffre told the government that every further twenty-four-hour delay represented a prospective loss of up to twelve miles of French territory when Moltke's offensive began. Some socialists remained implacably opposed to war, but their gestures towards peace were brushed aside. The sub-prefect of Isère was among many officials who banned public protests, prohibiting a socialist anti-war demonstration in Vienne on 31 July. Local unions planned another such rally in Grenoble for 2 August, but withdrew when it became plain it would receive little grassroots support, and would anyway be disallowed.

Jean Jaurès, France's great socialist leader, complained to his companion in a taxi taking them to a Paris restaurant on the evening of 31 July that the driver's manic haste would be the death of them. 'No,' said the other wryly, 'like all Parisian drivers he is a good socialist and union man.' It was not reckless speed that killed Jaurès that night, however, but instead a deranged fanatic who shot him in the back as he ate. This assassination prompted across Europe a wave of shock and horror far more emotional than that following the murder of Franz Ferdinand. Jaurès was recognised across frontiers as a political giant. *Le Temps* lamented that he was extinguished 'just at the moment when … his oratory was about to become a weapon of national defence'.

Raymond Recouly wrote of that night of Friday the 31st: 'As I came out of the paper with a friend, towards one in the morning, at the corner of the Rue Drouot we heard in the distance the sonorous clatter of a troop of cavalry. The cafés were just closing, but there were plenty of people about. The hooves resounded ever more loudly on the cobbles. A voice cried: "Here come the *cuirassiers*!" Something like an electric shock surged through the crowd. On every floor, windows opened. People stood up on benches, on the tables of cafés. A big taxi-driver hoisted himself up on the roof of his vehicle, at the risk of breaking it. Led by a band of children and young people, the horsemen appeared. In campaign kit, their helmets covered, gigantic in their long cloaks, they filled the roadway. A formidable clamour rose from every lip: "*Vive la France! Vive l'armée!*" The taxi-driver atop his vehicle looked frenzied. He cried more loudly than all the others, throwing his cap in the air and windmilling his arms.'

Later that night, a *Le Temps* office boy in front of the central post office in the Boulevard des Italiens saw the mobilisation order being posted. Just before 4 a.m. on 1 August, he ran into the newspaper manager's office crying, '*C'est affiché!*' The staff hurried outside to see for themselves. A crowd gathered before one of the post office windows to read the small blue sheet – Russia's was lilac in colour. 'Mobilisation is not war,' prime minister Viviani had insisted when he signed the order. But as Raymond Recouly said, 'no one believed him. If it was not war, it was in any event something equally terrible.' The French army was instructed not to approach within six miles of the German or Belgian frontiers, to ensure that the odium for territorial aggression rested squarely in Berlin.

Sir Francis Bertie wrote, as French troops began to muster: 'The populace is very calm. Here today it is "*vive l'Angleterre*", tomorrow it may be "*perfide Albion*". I was to have dined at Edmond de Rothschild's Boulogne-sur-Seine villa; the rendezvous was in Paris instead, for all his horses and automobiles have been appropriated. His electric brougham cannot go outside the *enceinte* [city perimeter] – no automobile can do so without a special permit. Our 4 footmen have left to join their regiments at once and the under-butler left 10 days ago; 3 other men have joined the colours. I have asked to be allowed to keep the French chauffeur.' There were violent demonstrations against German-owned businesses such as the Maggi food-processing company, which achieved a special virulence because small French milk-producers considered the giant a commercial menace. German and Austrian shops were looted while the police stood passively by. Viviani told the Chamber of Deputies: 'Germany has nothing to reproach us with. What is being attacked are the independence, dignity and security which the Triple Entente has secured for the benefit of Europe.' His words received thunderous applause.

The American novelist Edith Wharton, who was living in France, had spent July visiting Spain and the Balearics. She returned to Paris on 1 August, and found herself obliged to abandon plans to move on to England for the balance of the summer: 'everything seemed strange, ominous and unreal, like the yellow glare which precedes a storm. There were moments when I felt as if I had died, and woken up in an unknown world. And so I had.'

4 THE BRITISH DECIDE

Now, all Europe waited to learn what Asquith's government would do. In Vienna, Alexander Freud wrote disbelievingly to his brother Sigmund about the notion of Britain entering the war alongside Russia, arguing that 'a civilised people will not take the side of barbarians'. Many Germans, too, found it hard to comprehend the threat of British belligerence in a struggle they deemed none of Albion's business. Richard Stumpf, a sailor with the High Seas Fleet, expressed disgust that only weeks after a squadron of the Royal Navy had been received with every friendly honour at Kiel Regatta, its country should be considering entering hostilities: 'one feels bitter to think that [British behaviour] is really driven by jealousy, that wretched commercial envy is to blame'. The Germans delayed until 3 August their declaration of war on France, in hopes of preserving British neutrality. The Kaiser continued to think this plausible, because he was absurdly overimpressed by a conversation some time earlier between his brother and King George V. Prince Heinrich came home from a visit to London reporting the monarch's assurance that his country would stay out of any European conflict. Wilhelm thought Britain would be wise to do so in any event, since, as he cleverly observed, 'dreadnoughts have no wheels'.

A visitor to France wrote: 'no one who was not in Paris at the time can ever realize the intense anxiety of the French during those days of waiting for England to speak'. The Asquith government's intentions remained profoundly uncertain. A *Times* editorial on 29 July praised the country's unselfishness: 'It is our settled interest and traditional policy to uphold the balance of power in Europe'; to the Entente with France 'we shall remain faithful in the future, come what may'. The French, however, were merely exasperated by such pious expressions of good intentions. All they wanted to know was whether the British Army would fight beside them. And at that moment, the answer was that it would not.

Grey, Churchill, Haldane and Asquith wanted Britain to stand four-square with the other Entente partners: as early as 29 July, the foreign secretary privately threatened resignation if the government failed to do so. The First Lord of the Admiralty buffeted and cajoled his friend the Chancellor of the Exchequer to overcome Lloyd George's stubborn reluctance to see Britain committed to a continental conflict. Churchill suggested, absurdly, that participation need not cost much: 'Together we can carry a wide social policy ... The naval war will be cheap.' But as

Russia mobilised, most British people resisted the notion that their country should emulate its example. The *Daily News* asserted firmly on 29 July: 'the most effective work for peace that we can do is to make it clear that not a British life shall be sacrificed for the sake of Russian hegemony of the Slav world'. The Labour Party considered urging the unions to call a general strike if Asquith sought to join the struggle. 'All Europe Arming', ran the *Daily Mail*'s headline on 30 July, as if describing remote events, followed two days later by 'Europe Drifting to Disaster'. At a dinner on 31 July, Russian ambassador Count Benckendorff told the writer Maurice Baring that both he and the French envoy were bleakly convinced that England would not fight.

The leftist *Daily Chronicle* on 31 July applauded the absence of popular jingoism: 'Very welcome, and in comparison with what we experienced some while ago very remarkable, is the complete absence of anti-German sentiment. The last few years have done a great deal to reopen English eyes to our community of interest with the great people whose civilisation is in many ways the most akin in Europe to our own; and the bare idea of a ruinous conflict between us seems more unqualifiedly distasteful now than it has, perhaps, for a generation.' That day the *Manchester Guardian* became the first British newspaper to suggest that the country might be obliged to fight if France was attacked. However, the newspaper discounted any possibility of a German invasion of Belgium, because such action would breach Europe's 1839 treaty guaranteeing Belgian neutrality, to which Berlin as well as London was a signatory.

A soldier of the Royal Welch Fusiliers was awakened in his quarters in the Dorset town of Dorchester at 6 a.m. on that sunny Friday the 31st by the regimental band playing that jauntiest of ditties 'I Do Like to be Beside the Seaside'. Yet many British people now recognised that conflict was lapping very close to their shores. Norman Macleod, an Admiralty private secretary, 'felt rather apprehensive (1) because [I am] entirely ag[ain]st the idea of war (2) for fear of financial and economic crisis – people were buying in large stocks of food supplies. Bank rate up to 10% … I thought this trouble would restrain jingo feeling.' A delegation from the City called on the Chancellor of the Exchequer to argue that 'the only means of saving the world was for their own country to stay out of the conflict so that it might remain the great market, the economic arbiter of the world'. On 1 August the *Daily News* carried an article by its editor A.G. Gardiner, headed 'Why We Must Not Fight'. The writer demanded: 'Where in the wide world do our interests clash with Germany? Nowhere. With Russia we have potential conflicts over the whole of South-Eastern Europe and Southern Asia.' After the cabinet's meetings that Saturday, Paul Cambon told Grey – in French, through an interpreter, for he resolutely confined himself to his own language in official exchanges – that he flatly refused to communicate to Paris its resolution, 'or rather, lack of it'.

Many British people believed that responsibility for the unfolding nightmare rested in Belgrade and St Petersburg. *The Economist* warned that 'the provocation begun by Serbia has been continued by Russia. If a great war begins, Russian mobilization will be the proximate cause. And we fear that the poisonous articles of *The Times* have encouraged the Tsar to hope for British support.' A Viennese letter-writer to *The Economist*, Josef Redlich, demanded: 'Public opinion throughout the Austrian dominions, without distinction of party, has throbbed with the one question, How long Austria is to tolerate such a conception of neighbourliness as dominates Serbia?' Nine distinguished Cambridge academics wrote to *The Times*: 'We regard Germany as a nation leading the way in Arts and Sciences, and we have all learnt and are learning from German scholars. War upon her in the interests of Serbia and Russia will be a sin against civilisation. If by reason of honourable obligations we be unhappily involved in war, patriotism might still our mouths, but at this juncture we consider ourselves justified in protesting against being drawn into the struggle with a nation so near akin to our own.'

That night of 1 August, Grey dined with his private secretary at Brooks's Club in St James's Street; after leaving the table, for a while they played billiards together. Meanwhile the prime minister retired to bed nursing a grievance: the crisis had obliged him to cancel a country weekend in the company of Venetia Stanley, twenty-six-year-old object of his amorous, if unconsummated, obsession: 'I can honestly say that I have never had a more bitter disappointment,' Asquith wrote to her. He had some difficulty achieving unconsciousness, he said, 'but really I didn't sleep badly in that betwixt & between of sleeping & waking, thank God the vision of you kept floating about me and brought me rest and peace'. The British prime minister's prolific and compulsively indiscreet letters to Stanley do little to enhance his reputation, but provide a priceless insight into his thinking.

The most prominent left-wing newspapers – the *Daily Chronicle*, *Daily News* and *Manchester Guardian* – remained vehemently opposed to British intervention, but the government's attitude was contrarily hardening. On Sunday, 2 August, Asquith breakfasted with the German ambassador, and warned the emotional Lichnowsky of dire consequences should his nation's army fulfil its threat to march into neutral Belgium. Crowds gathered in Downing Street and Whitehall, and for the first time many anxious faces were seen. Conservative leader Bonar Law wrote to the prime minister, promising his party's support for a British declaration of war – a missive designed to hasten such an outcome.

The cabinet met, and learned from Grey that the French fleet had mobilised. France, he told them, now counted upon Britain to secure the Channel and the North Sea, having concentrated its own strength in the Mediterranean in conformity with a secret pact made at the 1912 Anglo-French naval talks. Some ministers were astonished, indeed confounded, to learn for the first time of this momentous commitment. But the cabinet – with varying degrees of reluctance – agreed to honour its terms, and to deploy warships to protect the northern French coast. The Germans promptly promised to stay out of the Channel if Britain remained neutral, but when Paul Cambon heard of the Royal Navy's commitment, his spirits soared: 'this was the decision I had been waiting for … A great country cannot half-make war. From the moment it decided to do so at sea, it was inescapably fated to do so also on land.'

The cabinet still rejected such a proposition, however. That evening of 2 August Sir John French, Chief of the Imperial General Staff until his March resignation over the 'Curragh Mutiny', made a bizarre telephone call: he sought guidance about the government's military intentions not from ministers, but from Sir George Riddell, owner of the *News of the World*. The little field-marshal asked Riddell: if war came, would an expeditionary force be sent to France, and who would command it? Riddell referred his questions to the government. Lloyd George sent back word that French should present himself at Downing Street at 10 o'clock next morning. When he did so, he was told there was still no question of Britain sending an army to the continent.

Now Belgium became the focus of British attention. At 3 p.m. on 2 August, the Belgian vice-consul in Cologne arrived at the Brussels Foreign Ministry to report that since 6 o'clock that morning he had been watching trains leaving the Rhine city's stations every three or four minutes, crammed with troops: they were heading not towards France, but instead for Aix-la-Chapelle and the Belgian border. When word followed that German troops had entered Luxembourg and were expected imminently to invade Belgium, the foreign minister M. Jean Davignon said emotionally to his colleague Baron Gaiffier: 'Let us go to mass and offer prayers for our poor country: never has it stood in such need of them!'

King Albert had visited Berlin in November 1913, and received a dark warning from the Kaiser and Moltke: 'small countries, such as Belgium, would be well-advised to rally to the side of the strong if they wished to retain their independence'. On 2 August the Belgian monarch was confronted with the meaning of this threat: Germany summarily demanded for its armies a right of passage through his country. The French were uncertain how the Brussels government would respond: they considered large parts of Belgium to be Germanophile. It was Albert's personal decision, as commander-in-chief of the armed forces as well as monarch, to reject Berlin's demand – with the overwhelming support of his people.

'The response [to Berlin's ultimatum] was very easy to draft,' said Baron Gaiffier. 'We only had to translate in plain language onto paper the feelings that moved each one of us. We were sure that we correctly interpreted the views of the whole country.' Yet that Sunday evening, though the Belgian government knew the worst, an innocence still pervaded the mood in Brussels, especially among its humbler citizens. At the end of a radiant summer's day, a host of walkers who had been promenading in the surrounding countryside strolled back into the city, many of them singing and clutching armfuls of flowers.

Britain was among the guarantors of Belgian neutrality under the 1839 European treaty, made soon after the country separated from Holland. Late on 2 August, the Germans warned the British government of their intention to march through King Albert's country, with or without his consent. At 7 o'clock next morning, Belgium's rejection of the ultimatum was conveyed to Berlin. When the news was published, Brussels burst forth with tricolour flags. Most Germans regarded this show of defiance with contemptuous pity. 'Oh, the poor fools,' the counsellor at the German legation kept repeating, as he gazed out on streets ablaze with national tokens. 'Oh, the poor fools. Why don't they get out of the way of the steamroller? We don't want to hurt them, but if they stand in our way they will be ground into the dirt. Oh, the poor fools!'

It has sometimes been suggested that King Albert's people would have fared better had the monarch bowed to the inevitable, and granted the German army free passage. But why should he, or the ruler of any sovereign nation, have done so? Throughout modern history, the protection of small states from aggression has often been considered by larger democracies to create a moral imperative. In 1914 *force majeure* constituted a more formidable influence upon events than international law. But the view adopted by most of the British people, as well as by their government, was that Germany's invasion of Belgium constituted an affront to morality as well as to the European order. Ironically, once the Germans were committed to violate Belgian neutrality – as secretly they had been for a decade – they would have done better to go the whole hog and attack without an ultimatum. The time-lag between threat and assault enabled King Albert to rally his people and foreign opinion, and also to prepare to resist. The Belgians organised a formidably effective programme of railway-tunnel demolitions, which limited enemy train movements through their country for months to come.

Apologists for Germany's behaviour argue now – as did the Berlin government then – that if the Kaiser's army had not violated Belgian neutrality, the allies would swiftly have done so. The only plausible evidence for this claim is that the British debated a possible blockade of Antwerp as a conduit to Germany, a contingency overtaken by events. They repeatedly warned the French against infringing Belgian territory, and Joffre acquiesced. Germany had hitherto been the clear winner, at the expense of Russia, in the game of managing events so as to avoid seeming the immediate aggressor. Moltke forfeited this status, however, the moment his armies crossed the Belgian frontier. Bismarck had warned his countrymen against such action, precisely because he anticipated its impact on foreign opinion. The assault on Belgium came as a heaven-sent deliverance to those members of Asquith's government already convinced that Britain must enter the European war. Without Belgium, the country would have joined the conflict divided, if at all. Moltke made a critical miscalculation: he was so convinced Britain would fight that he did not think the issue of Belgian neutrality would influence such an outcome one way or the other. He was quite wrong. The perceived martyrdom of King Albert and his people rallied to the cause of war millions of British people who had hitherto opposed it.

There were considerable ironies about Britain's rush to embrace 'gallant little Belgium'. During the Boer War, Albert's country had adopted a passionately anti-British posture. Belgium's deplorable record of inhumanity as the colonial power in the Congo was surpassed only by that of Germany in South-West Africa. British and French soldiers regarded the Belgian army with contempt, its officers as posturing dandies. Moreover, throughout the previous month the Belgian Catholic press had strongly supported Austria-Hungary's right to take military action against Serbia. One paper, *l'Express* of Liège, denounced the Franco-Russian Entente as 'the nightmare of all those who hold in their hearts a future of liberty, democracy and civilisation ... [it is] an alliance against nature'.

No matter. In London a few ministers still clung to a belief that the mere passage of the German army should not constitute a *casus belli*. But most of the British people here at last identified moral certainty amid a sea of Balkan and European confusions. A telegram was brought to Grey, at dinner with Haldane on Sunday evening, 2 August, warning that German action against Belgium was imminent. The two men drove immediately to Downing Street, where they detached Asquith from some private guests. They told him the news and asked for authority to mobilise the army. Haldane volunteered to become temporary war minister, as Asquith would obviously be too busy to continue to fill that role. The prime minister assented to both proposals.

On the morning of Monday, 3 August, a British bank holiday, *The Times* declared: 'Europe is to be the scene of the most terrible war that she has witnessed since the fall of the Roman Empire ... The blame must fall mainly upon Germany. She could have stayed the plague had she chosen to speak in Vienna as she speaks when she is in earnest. She has not chosen to do so.' Whitehall, bathed in brilliant sunshine, became impassable to traffic, so dense were the expectant crowds. At 11 a.m. the cabinet was told of King Albert's decision that Belgium would resist, yet still ministers agonised. Two, Sir John Simon and Lord Beauchamp, said they would resign rather than be complicit in a British commitment to war. But Lloyd George, a pivotal figure, at last overcame his own doubts, and accepted the case for fighting. A disappointed fellow Liberal complained that the chancellor 'lacked the courage of his convictions'. It is probably the case that Lloyd George was more strongly influenced by political fears of splitting the government and the Liberal Party – to the partisan advantage of the Conservatives – than by any fervour for the Entente's cause. Asquith made a telephone call to Dover to halt the imminent departure for Egypt of Lord Kitchener, Britain's most eminent soldier. The prime minister asked the field marshal to return to London. He was likely to be needed.

That morning George Lambert, the Admiralty's Civil Lord, ignorant of the latest momentous developments, said to the Financial Secretary: 'I wish the Cabinet would stop shilly-shallying and decide one thing or another.' The other official who, in the words of an eyewitness 'looked very pale and anxious, quite unlike Saturday', responded: 'I think they have decided.' But the British people remained deeply divided. Even amid the news from Belgium, civil servant Norman Macleod wrote on 3 August:

'Felt very unhappy about turn of events – danger of secret diplomatic engagements forcing people blindly into war – had it not been for financial reasons [I] would have resigned [my] post.' Sir George Riddell, proprietor of the *News of the World*, told Lloyd George of his 'feeling of intense exasperation … at the prospect of the government embarking on war'. Guy Fleetwood-Wilson protested in *The Times*'s correspondence column: 'I write as a "man in the street". Doubtless I am an abnormally dense one, because I cannot for the life of me see why this country should be dragged into this war.' Serbia, he asserted, 'is not worth the life of one single British Grenadier'.

But all over Britain military establishments were receiving the mobilisation order. Capt. Maurice Festing of the Royal Marines was exasperated to get the call while playing in a cricket match at the corps depot outside Deal: he had scored 66 not out and just fulfilled a cherished ambition by driving a ball through the window of the sergeants' mess. The colonel of the Royal Welch Fusiliers was attending a dinner party when an orderly bearing a message was announced. The guests were almost certain of its contents, but etiquette prevailed: the messenger was kept waiting until dinner was finished and the ladies had retired, before being permitted to deliver the regiment's mobilisation telegram.

Britain was the only major power to debate in parliament its entry into the war. At 3 o'clock that afternoon of 3 August, Grey, visibly strained and exhausted, rose in the Commons to make the government's first formal statement about the crisis. He was no great orator, and such grace time as he might have used to prepare a speech was stolen by Prince Lichnowsky, who called at his office to make a futile final plea for Britain not to regard the passage of German troops through just one small corner of Belgium as a *casus belli*. It was the two men's last meeting.

The floor of the House was packed, as were the Diplomatic and Strangers' Galleries. Asquith was expressionless as Grey invited the House to consider the crisis from the viewpoint of 'British interests, British honour and British obligation'. The foreign secretary told Members of the secret naval arrangement with France, and how the government had concluded that it could not leave the Germans free at will to bombard the French north coast, on Britain's doorstep. Tories cheered while Liberals sat silent, many unpersuaded. Then Grey, having spoken unimpressively about British interests and trade routes, was suddenly roused to a passion he had never before displayed, in describing the violation of Belgian neutrality. 'Could this country stand by and watch the direst crime that ever stained the face of history, and thus become participators in the sin?'

He reverted to a familiar but fundamental theme of British govern-ments for centuries – the European balance of power. Britain, he said, must take a stand 'against the unmeasured aggrandisement of any power whatsoever'. After seventy-five minutes, he concluded with a dramatic peroration and appeal: 'I do not believe for a moment that, at the end of this war, even if we stand aside, we should be able to undo what had happened ... to prevent the whole of the West of Europe opposite us from falling under the domination of a single power ... and we should, I believe, sacrifice our respect and good name and reputation before the world and should not escape the most serious and grave consequences.'

This last statement has become, for the past century, the focus of every argument about whether Britain should, or should not, have entered the First World War. The Commons, that afternoon, received his words with overwhelming acclaim. It was because Grey, through his twenty-nine years as an MP, had become known as a man of compulsive taciturnity, that his eloquence on this occasion achieved its remarkable effect. Simon and Beauchamp, having heard him, withdrew their resignations. The mood of the Liberal Party, instinctively pacifistic, underwent a dramatic shift towards war – though Parliament was never invited to vote on the final step.

'What happens now?' Churchill demanded as he and Grey left the House together. An ultimatum would be sent to Berlin, said the foreign secretary, demanding German withdrawal from Belgium within twenty-four hours. Sir Francis Bertie wrote: 'Grey's speech ... was splendid and has given much more satisfaction [in Paris] than I expected. Germany was deter-mined to have war and tried all she knew to lure us into abstention from the struggle.' Jules Cambon said after the conflict: 'We were extraordinarily fortunate that Britain's Liberal Party was then in government. Had it been in opposition, it would perhaps have delayed British intervention.' In this he was probably correct; it is by no means certain that if a Conservative government had been eager to fight, the Liberals would have fallen into step. Their contrarian instinct might have proved too strong, as it did for two minor cabinet members – Lord Morley and John Burns – who quit.

That night, even after all the dramas of the day, uncertainty persisted about what practical military measures Britain would adopt. The foreign secretary displayed awesome naïveté, and severely injured his reputation before posterity, when he told the Commons that, since Britain was a naval power, by entering the war 'we shall suffer but little more than we shall suffer if we stand aside'. Because such vestigial delusions persisted in government, no minister would authorise immediate dispatch of an army to the continent. This prevarication exasperated soldiers who knew that hours mattered in giving orders for a British Expeditionary Force to muster and sail before the German juggernaut swept into Belgium and France.

Coudourier de Chassigne, London correspondent of *Le Figaro*, rang Tom Clarke, news editor of the *Daily Mail*, in pursuit of tidings. 'Are you going to go to the help of France?' he demanded urgently. 'I know the whole British nation is with us, but this rotten "wait and see" government of yours, when will they move? Soon it will be too late. It is terrible … Cannot Lord Northcliffe and the *Daily Mail* do something?' An old Frenchman peered at a poster outside the local newspaper office in Nice and declared disgustedly: '*L'Angleterre se dégage! C'est ignoble.*' Early on that evening of 3 August, the German ambassador in Paris called upon René Viviani and read aloud to him a declaration of war, the moral force of which was blunted by its deceits. The document claimed that French aircraft had bombed Nuremberg and Karlsruhe, and overflown Belgium in breach of its neutrality. Viviani denied the charges, then the two men silently bowed and parted. Gen. Joffre took a formal farewell of Poincaré before leaving for his headquarters, from which, through the months that followed, he would exercise a power more absolute than that of any other national commander.

Just after 8 o'clock on the morning of 4 August, the first German troops crossed the Belgian border at Gemmenich, thirty miles from Liège. Belgian gendarmes made the futile but significant gesture of firing on them before taking to their heels. At noon, King Albert formally appealed for aid to Britain, as a guarantor of Belgian neutrality. Then, dressed in field uniform and mounted on a charger, he rode at the head of a little procession of carriages, one of which held his wife and children, to the parliament building in Brussels. Once dismounted and in the chamber, he created an inimitable moment of theatre by demanding of members: 'Gentlemen, are you unalterably decided to maintain intact the sacred gifts of our fore-fathers?' As one man they rose, shouting, '*Oui! Oui! Oui!*'

In Berlin the Kaiser summoned the Reichstag deputies to his palace. He received them in helmet and full regimentals, flanked by Bethmann in the uniform of the Dragoon Guards. He said nothing of Belgium, but instead declared the war to have been provoked by Serbia with the support of Russia: 'We draw the sword with a clear conscience and clean hands.' His speech prompted wild applause. By contrast, when Bethmann later addressed the Reichstag, he displayed a frankness that Tirpitz afterwards branded as madness: 'Our invasion of Belgium is contrary to international law, but this wrong – I speak openly – that we are committing – we will make right as soon as our military objective has been attained.' Social democrats applauded as enthusiastically as did conservatives.

Asquith and Grey found themselves cheered by crowds in Whitehall as they hastened to and from the Commons on 4 August. The prime minister wrote to Venetia Stanley: 'Winston, who has got on all his war-paint, is longing for a sea-fight in the early hours of tomorrow morning ... The whole thing fills me with sadness.' That afternoon, King George V's proclamation of mobilisation was read to the Commons, following which Asquith rehearsed to the House the British ultimatum to Germany, which required an answer by midnight – 11 p.m. London time. The final part of the document was finally dispatched only at 7 p.m., after Grey learned that the Kaiser's forces had entered Belgian territory. When Bethmann received it from the British ambassador, he claimed that 'my blood boiled at this hypocritical harping on Belgium which was not the thing that had driven England into war'. The chancellor delivered a harangue to Sir Edward Goschen, pinning upon Britain blame for war and all that followed, and concluding: 'all for just a word – "neutrality" – just for a scrap of paper'. The phrase passed into history. A host of Germans professed to regard British intervention as a betrayal.

In London as darkness fell, the cabinet met once more, to be told that Germany already considered itself at war with Britain. After further debate, they sat together in the Downing Street council room, waiting upon the clock chimes. As soon as Big Ben struck the first note of eleven, the government knew the worst. Twenty minutes later, the War Telegram was dispatched in plain language to the British Army. Norman Macleod perceived during the preceding twenty-hours 'an extraordinary change in public feeling – up till Monday at any rate strong anti-war party – "Neutrality League" forward – but German refusal to respect neutrality of Belgium absolutely destroyed it'. He noted 'another remarkable change. On Fri & Sat there had been panic in City & rush for food supplies. [By Monday] there was a feeling of complete confidence in the Govt – I have never seen anything like it, certainly not at the time of the Boer War.'

In the Royal Marine mess at Chatham on the night of 4 August a waiter handed a telegram to the corps commandant, who read it aloud: 'Commence hostilities against Germany at once.' This was received with

applause by the assembled officers, many of whom would be dead within
a year. Britain's dominions and colonies, led by India, Canada, Australia,
New Zealand and South Africa, were not consulted in any way about the
decision to fight: their governors-general merely issued proclamations on
their own authority, declaring them to be in a state of war with Germany,
alongside the Mother Country. Only a few old Boers' voices were raised in
demurral. One of them, Jacobus Deventer, summoned his commando
then telegraphed his former general, Louis Botha, now South Africa's
prime minister: 'All my burghers armed, mounted and ready. Whom do
we fight – the British or the Germans?' He eventually accepted an order to
join a force mustering to invade German South-West Africa, though some
others mounted a short-lived anti-British rebellion.

Even many intelligent and informed Europeans failed to grasp the gravity of the course of action to which they had committed themselves. This
is emphasised by the remarks of British leaders who expressed gratitude
that war had reprieved the country from a bloody showdown in Ireland.
In Grey's Commons speech of 3 August he made an almost frivolous aside:
'One thing I would say: the one bright spot in the very dreadful situation
is Ireland.' Sir William Birdwood, secretary to the government of India,
wrote: 'What a real piece of luck this war has been as regards Ireland – just
averted a Civil War and when it is over we may all be tired of fighting.'

Ramsay MacDonald, who resigned the Labour Party leadership when
his followers – like their German counterparts – decided to vote in favour
of war credits, won some cheers when he told the Commons that Britain
should have remained neutral, though when he went on to assert that 'in
the deepest parts of our hearts we believe that [would have been] right,
and that alone was consistent with the honour of this country and the
traditions of the party now in office', he was received with a derisive laughter that sensitive witnesses thought unseemly. Mr Ponsonby, MP for
Stirling Burghs, said that 'we were on the eve of a great war and he hated
to see people embarking on it with a light heart', which prompted some
assenting voices. Another MP, Mr Wedgwood, said that this was not going
to be 'one of the dear old wars of the 18th century … but a matter of
sustaining the civilisation which it had taken centuries to bring about'.
Perhaps the wisest comment, though at the time it received scant applause,
also came from Ramsay MacDonald: 'no war is at first unpopular'.

In the last days of the crisis, many of the principals – the greatest men
of their nations, the most powerful people in the world – experienced
moments when they shrank in size. They glimpsed the horror of the

consequences of the courses they were pursuing, and looked back over their shoulders in yearning. This was true of the Kaiser, Bethmann and Tsar Nicholas; but not, apparently, of any of the Austrians, or Moltke, or Sazonov. The French were astonishingly fatalistic about the need to support Russia, if only because they were convinced – almost certainly correctly – that the German army would anyway fall upon themselves as a partner in the Entente. The British, save a few wild men such as Churchill, were least eager for war, but identified in the violation of Belgium a justi-fication for joining the struggle. Because Britain was a Great Power, they believed that when great issues were at stake, it must be seen to play a great part.

In the last days of peace Vernon Kell, director of the British security service MI5, stayed at his office in Watergate House around the clock, organising arrests of known German agents. Although his infant organisation boasted a staff of only seventeen, he had forged effective links with county chief constables: between 3 and 16 August, twenty-two arrests were made. Some spies escaped in the fashion of Walter Rimann, a language teacher in Hull who caught the Zeebrugge ferry. It is thought that a few others remained undetected, but if so they made little contribution to Germany's war effort.

Most of those caught had been identified through the interception of their correspondence with Germany's intelligence service, the *Nachrichten-Abteilung*, under Home Office warrant – a system fostered by Winston Churchill. The Kaiser raged about the incompetence of his spy chiefs. Gustav Steinhauer, ringmaster of the British network, recorded Wilhelm demanding: 'Am I surrounded by dolts? Who is responsible?' German military intelligence had focused its efforts exclusively on France, leaving the navy to handle Britain. Steinhauer, who often travelled there in the pre-war period, had recruited agents chiefly by writing unsolicited letters to German expatriates; his most active 'postman' was Karl Ernst, a Pentonville barber, who approached seaman customers for information. German wartime intelligence in Britain never recovered from the 1914 round-up: as late as 21 August, Berlin was unaware that a British Expeditionary Force had been convoyed to France.

Meanwhile, Bernard Shaw wired his German translator: 'YOU AND I AT WAR CAN ABSURDITY GO NO FURTHER. MY FRIENDLIEST WISHES GO WITH YOU UNDER ALL CIRCUMSTANCES.' Lord Northcliffe said to his erstwhile Vienna correspondent Wickham Steed, 'Well it's come!' Steed answered, 'Yes, thank God!' Memories of Queen

Victoria caused many Russians to refer to England as '*Anglichanka*' – the Englishwoman. A peasant said in August 1914 that 'he was glad that the *Anglichanka* was with Russia, because first she was clever and would help; secondly, if things went badly with Russia, she was good and would help; thirdly, if it came to making peace, she was determined and would not give way'.

Fran Šuklje was a well-known Slovenian sage, sixty-five in 1914. On 4 August this unwilling subject of the Hapsburgs was sitting under the trees in the famous Stembur garden in Kandija when he read the news of Britain's declaration of war. He told the little crowd of disciples around him: 'Now you will give thanks to God if this war is over in three years.' His words quickly spread among his fellow citizens, 'whose unanimous judgement was that I had gone mad. They assume an outcome in three weeks, three months at the most.' In Berlin, Frederick Wiles of the *Daily Mail* described scenes at the British embassy that day: 'the realisation of what was now upon them turned the Germans into infuriated barbarians … Stones, keys, sticks, knives, umbrellas – any and everything which could be thrown were hurtling through the smashed windows.'

At an English country tennis party, the writer Jerome K. Jerome expressed 'relief and thankfulness … I was so afraid Grey would climb down at the last moment … It was Asquith I was doubtful of. I didn't think the old man had the grit … Thank God, we shan't read "Made in Germany" for some little time to come.' On the night of 4 August, as mindless crowds roared and sang outside Buckingham Palace, Maurice Baring watched a drunken man in evening dress harangue passers-by from the roof of a taxi in Trafalgar Square.

Even after war was declared, impassioned dissenters remained. On 5 August C.P. Scott argued in the *Manchester Guardian*: 'By some hidden contract England has been technically committed behind her back to the ruinous madness of a share in the violent gamble of a war between two militarist leagues … It will be a war in which we risk everything of which we are proud, and in which we stand to gain nothing … Some day we will regret it.' Many British people in the twenty-first century believe that Scott was right, chiefly in the light of the horror of the experience that followed, but also because they are unpersuaded that it was necessary to resist in arms the Kaiser's Germany at such cost.

Would any of the Entente Powers have acted differently had they known of the profound complicity of the Serbian army, though not the government, in the murder of Franz Ferdinand? Almost certainly not, because this was not why the Austrians and Germans acted, or their opponents reacted. The Russians simply considered the extinction of a small Slav state as an excessive and indeed intolerable punishment for the crime of Princip, and for that matter Apis. Unless France had swiftly declared its neutrality and surrendered its frontier fortresses as Germany demanded, its alliance with Russia would have caused Moltke to attack in the West. The British were entirely unmoved by Serbia's impending fate, and acted only in response to the German violation of Belgian neutrality and the threat to France. The various participants in what would soon become the Great War had very different motives for belligerence, and objectives with little in common. Three conflicts – that in the Balkans over East European issues, the continental struggle to determine whether German dominance should prevail, and the German challenge to British global naval mastery – accomplished a metamorphosis into a single over-arching one. Other issues, mostly involving land grabs, would become overlaid when other nations – notably Japan, Turkey and Italy – joined the struggle.

Many people in Britain have argued through the past century that the price of participation in the war was so appalling that no purpose could conceivably justify it; more than a few blame Sir Edward Grey for willing Britain's involvement. But, granted Germany's determination to dominate Europe and the likely consequences of such hegemony for Britain, would the foreign secretary have acted responsibly if he had taken no steps designed to avert such an outcome?

Lloyd George in his memoirs advanced a further popular argument against the conflict, laying blame upon the soldiers he hated: 'Had it not been for the professional zeal and haste with which the military staffs set in motion the plans which had already been agreed between them, the negotiations between the governments, which at that time had hardly begun, might well have continued, and war could, and probably would, have been averted.' This was nonsense. What happened was not 'war by accident', but war by ill-conceived Austrian design, with German support.

Today, as in 1914, any judgement about the necessity for British entry must be influenced by an assessment of the character of Kaiser Wilhelm II's empire. It seems frivolous to suggest, as do a few modern sensationalists, that a German victory would merely have created, half a century earlier, an entity resembling the European Union. Even if the Kaiser's regime cannot be equated with that of the Nazis, its policies could scarcely be characterised as enlightened. Dominance was its purpose, achieved by peaceful means if possible, but by war if necessary. The Germans' paranoia caused them to interpret as a hostile act any attempt to check or question their international assertiveness. Moreover, throughout the July crisis they, like the Austrians, consistently lied about their intentions and actions. By contrast, whatever the shortcomings of British conduct, the Asquith government told the truth as it saw this, to both its allies and its prospective foes.

The *Kaiserreich*'s record abroad was inhumane even by contemporary standards. Isabel Hull has written of 'a juggernaut of military extremism', unchecked by any effective civilian authority. Berlin mandated in advance and applauded after the event the 1904–07 genocide of the Herero and Namaqua peoples of German South-West Africa, an enormity far beyond the scope of any British colonial misdeed. German behaviour during the 1914 invasion of Belgium and France, including large-scale massacres of civilians endorsed at the highest level, cannot be compared with what took place in the Second World War, because there was no genocidal intent, but it conveyed a profoundly disturbing image of the character of the regime that aspired to rule Europe.

It seems mistaken to suppose that neutrality in 1914 would have yielded a happy outcome for the British Empire. The authoritarian and acquisitive instincts of Germany's leadership would scarcely have been moderated by triumph on the battlefield. The Kaiser's regime did not enter the war with a grand plan for world domination, but its leaders were in no doubt that they required huge booty as a reward for the victory they anticipated. Bethmann Hollweg drafted a personal list of demands on 9 September 1914, when Berlin saw victory within its grasp. 'The aim of the war,' he wrote, 'is to provide us with [security] guarantees, from east to west, for the foreseeable future, through the enfeeblement of our adversaries.'

France was to cede to Germany the Briey iron deposits; Belfort; a coastal strip from Dunkirk to Boulogne; the western slope of the Vosges mountains. Her strategic fortresses were to be demolished. Just as after 1870, cash reparations would be exacted sufficient to ensure that 'France is incapable of spending considerable sums on armaments for the next eighteen to twenty years'. Elsewhere, Luxembourg would be annexed outright; Belgium and Holland transformed into vassal states; Russia's borders drastically shrunken; a vast colonial empire created in central Africa; a German economic union extending from Scandinavia to Turkey.

Georges-Henri Soutou has convincingly argued that Bethmann was never as serious about his territorial demands – he strove to dissuade the Kaiser from insisting upon annexation of Belgium – as about the intention to impose a customs union on the continent. But whatever means Berlin proposed to employ, the purpose was not in doubt; in Soutou's words, 'it is well understood that customs union must thereby make possible Germany's control of Europe'. While other German leaders advanced different shopping lists, all took it for granted that the war could not end without their nation receiving what they deemed 'appropriate' territorial and financial rewards. Having vanquished its only important continental rivals, it is implausible that Germany would thereafter have been content to make a generous accommodation with a neutral Great Britain, or to acquiesce in its global naval mastery.

The Asquith government is often accused of opacity in European affairs, both strategic – between 1906 and 1914 – and tactical – during the July crisis. While Britain made itself a party to the Triple Entente, uncertainty persisted in all the capitals of Europe, London included, about whether it would join a European war. Yet the British had little power to control events. Though the Germans preferred not to fight them, they were seen in Berlin as marginal in a clash of continental forces. Only if Britain had adopted the domestically unacceptable course of creating a large standing army might it have been capable of playing an effective deterrent role in 1914. The most grievous British error was to suppose the nation could maintain its cherished balance of power on the continent without a credible mass of soldiers to support its diplomacy. But failure to create a conscript army can scarcely be characterised as warmongering.

The argument that Britain should have declared in advance of the 1914 crisis its determination to participate in any Russo-French clash with Germany ignores the nature of democracies, and the requirements of prudent statesmanship. No government could have commanded the support of Parliament for an open-ended commitment to join a European conflict without heed to the circumstances in which this evolved, and there is no reason why it should have done so. If in July 1914 Asquith had offered France and Russia unconditional support, he would have been guilty of the very recklessness – the issue of a 'blank cheque' – for which Germany has been justly condemned in its conduct towards Austria-Hungary, and to a lesser degree France also in its commitment to Russia.

Britain cherished the status quo, and was committed to peace, because it still appeared to be global top dog. The Asquith government harboured a sensible unease about Russia and the follies of which its government was capable; it had no desire to promote French bellicosity. Thus its only rational course in the decade preceding the war, and indeed in July 1914, was to offer its allies goodwill and provisional support, the scope and nature of which must depend on events and exact circumstances. The failure of this policy is self-evident: Britain's tentative approach to European commitments, and especially to the Entente, sufficed to involve it in history's greatest conflict, but not to prevent such a disaster. It nonetheless seems hard to conceive of any alternative pre-war British diplomatic path which would have commanded domestic political support, and persuaded Germany that the risk of war was unacceptable.

Those who claim that a general conflict was avoidable even after Austria declared war on Serbia, and who hold Russia responsible for what followed, imply that Austria and its German guarantor should have been allowed to have their way at gunpoint in the Balkans, in Belgium and indeed across Europe. Only the German ultimatum to Belgium enabled the war party in the British cabinet to obtain a mandate. It is sometimes said that this was a mere pretext – a figleaf – since Grey, Churchill and several of their colleagues were bent upon belligerence even before the issue of Belgium emerged. But it remains doubtful that they could have carried their point but for the violation of Belgian neutrality. It does not seem ignoble or foolish that much of the Commons and the British people seized upon this as a just *casus belli*, whereas they recoiled from going to war to support Serbia, or for that matter merely to fulfil Britain's illdefined commitment to the Triple Entente. Even if Germany is acquitted of pursuing a design for general European war in 1914, it still seems deserving of most blame, because it had power to prevent this and did not exercise it.

On 3 August the Kaiser told his orderlies to lay out field-grey uniform, topboots, brown gloves, and a helmet without plumes for his address to the Reichstag on the morrow. Then he decided that a more magnificent show was appropriate. He chose to appear in full dress, accompanied by every available senior officer in Berlin, adorned with their medals and sashes. In all his splendour as Germany's Supreme Warlord, with much emotion he told the assembled members next day: 'From the bottom of my heart I thank you for your expressions of love and fidelity. In the struggle now ahead of us, I see no more parties in my *Volk*' – '*Ich kenne keine Parteien mehr, ich kenne nur Deutsche*' – 'among us there are only Germans'. Wilhelm was now to experience a few joyous weeks of the military glory he had always dreamed of. Thereafter, however, the shades would close in upon him – and upon Europe.

'Dreadnoughts have no wheels!': German and Austrian officers savour the Supreme Warlord's wit.

STATESMEN

Opposite top: Poincaré and the Tsar during the July 1914 French state visit to St Petersburg.
Opposite below: Asquith and Lloyd George at The Wharf, the prime minister's Berkshire country home. *Below, clockwise from bottom left:* Pasic, Berchtold, Sazonov, Grey, Churchill, Bethmann Hollweg.

Every army, including that of the Tsar, solicited divine assistance before marching.

WARLORDS
Below, clockwise from left: Moltke, Ludendorff, Hindenburg, Kitchener, Lanrezac.
Opposite, clockwise from left: Conrad, Joffre, French, Haig, Falkenhayn, Franchet d'Espèrey.

Russians in Galicia.

3

'The Superb Spectacle of the World Bursting Into Flames'

1 MIGRATIONS

Across continental Europe, for the last time in history proclamations of war were accompanied musically as well as figuratively by a clarion call. In cities such as Freiburg a trumpeter and a police officer toured the city's main squares in a chugging automobile, halting at each one to rehearse the tidings. Most of the newly warring nations accomplished the transition from peace with doom-laden efficiency. Lt. Col. Gerhard Tappen, Moltke's chief of operations, admitted to a 'peculiar feeling' as he unlocked the office safe and withdrew Germany's 'Deployment Plan 1914/15', but mobilisation represented the greatest professional triumph of the chief of staff's career. Before war came, Berlin feared that socialist-inspired rail strikes might cause disruptions, but none occurred. There were few absentees among the four million men summoned to the colours.

Governments' contingency plans extended well beyond the mechanics of mobilisation. Maurice Hankey, secretary of Britain's Committee for Imperial Defence, had since 1910 produced annually updated editions of 'The War Book'. This was a red quarto volume, sub-headed in gold lettering 'Co-Ordination of departmental action on the OCCURRENCE OF STRAINED RELATIONS and on the OUTBREAK OF WAR'. The latest edition, circulated throughout Whitehall on 30 June 1914, contained 318 grey-blue pages, detailing the responsibilities of every department of state, first in the 'Precautionary stage': 'The Secretary of State [for foreign affairs], foreseeing the danger of this country being involved in war in the near future, decides to warn the Cabinet to this effect.' The War Book, with gentlemanly circumlocution, stressed the importance of discretion: 'The Under-Secretary of State specially instructs any member of his staff who may be concerned that the greatest reticence must be observed in regard to the existence of strained relations and all matters relating to precautionary measures.'

Thereafter, the Book catalogued all manner of necessary practical steps, such as the submission to Parliament of a Bill for the control of aliens, introduction of censorship, seizure of enemy merchant vessels, severance of enemy submarine telegraph cables, embodiment of the Channel Islands militia, and notice to neutral powers of an impending blockade of enemy ports. In addressing the management of telegraph traffic, an appendix stated: 'In order that the greatest number of telegrams requiring Priority over all others should be indicated, it has been assumed … that the war would be one in which the United Kingdom would find herself immediately opposed by the three countries forming the Triple Alliance.' The War Office was warned: 'Certain defensive measures against treacherous or surprise attacks become necessary.' The Admiralty chief censor's telegraphic address was to be 'Scoured, London'. The Home Office was instructed to alert chief constables 'to pay special attention to the movements of suspicious foreigners'. During the first days of August, all this came to pass.

Serbs were dismayed that their country had been obliged to mobilise before the harvest was gathered, instead of waiting for autumn, as at the start of the two previous Balkan wars, when the barns were full. Not only the departure of men caused dismay, but also the spectacle of precious carts and oxen being driven away to the army. Nonetheless, Tadija Pejović remarked that everybody around him was singing, 'because it is a Serb custom to sing when soldiers go to war'. Young and old alike had little notion how long their adventure might last. Uncomprehending children demanded to know why their homes were being broken up.

Generosity towards the enemy would soon be banished from every belligerent's public life, but in August vestiges survived. Britain's National Free Church Council adopted a resolution: 'The crime and horror of a universal war has fallen upon European civilization. It is useless to seek nicely to apportion blame.' H.W. Nevinson, Berlin correspondent of the *Daily News*, wrote of the young Germans whom he had watched march away: 'finely-built and well-trained fellows they are, of a stock so much like our own at its best'. He applauded the well-tilled countryside, the neat and well-behaved children, and all that Germany had done to advance the world's progress. In the same spirit, some British academics strove to sustain respect for the country that had now become their mortal enemy. 'Only ignorance can afford to mock at German culture,' wrote a Cambridge theologian.

A thirty-one-year-old schoolteacher living near Graz, who kept a diary in which she signed herself simply as 'Itha J', was an impassioned Austrian nationalist. She recoiled in disgust when her friend Martha described the bitterness of some men summoned to the colours. 'I am sorry,' Itha interrupted stiffly, 'but it is incomprehensible that any man should complain. I call it cowardice – it could be nothing else.' This was an age when classicism was an almost universal expression of literacy. Young Edouard Beer, one of four Belgian brothers who joined his country's armed forces, quoted Caesar with some complacency: '*Omnium Gallorum fortissimi sunt Belgae*' – 'The Belgians are bravest of all Gauls'.

Writer Sergei Kondurashkin was holidaying with his family in southern Russia, where he glimpsed a microcosm of his nation's vast mobilisation: 'The omnipotent state apparatus of names and numbers was able to search out people even in the remote gorges of Caucasian mountains, beneath the Amanaus glaciers. Couriers came galloping with telegrams for doctors, professors and engineers – everyone to the war! Private rail travel stopped, the post became irregular, and for a time private telegrams were rejected. It seemed that the pattern of ordinary life around us, formed over centuries, was coming to a halt, soundlessly breaking up, as war established its own norms.'

Russia's mobilised strength was on paper – full potential was never achieved – the largest of any belligerent, but most of those called to the colours had little notion of the cause. One man, Ivan Kuchernigo, described a scene in his village, where a policeman suddenly appeared, knocking on door after door to summon peasants to a meeting. They assembled amid general bewilderment and vain mutual questioning. Suddenly, the village elder called for silence: 'Here's what's afoot boys! An enemy has turned up! He has attacked our Mother Russia – *Matushku Rossiiu* – and our Father-Tsar needs our help, our enemy for now is Germany.' A buzz ran through the crowd: 'It's the Germans! The Germans.' The elder shouted for quiet again: 'OK boys, in order not to lose time messing with lists, whoever feels healthy and able to serve the Fatherland should show up in the office of the District Military Commander in Aleshka, and I advise you to bring with you two pairs of underwear, and they'll give you anything else there, just do it quick.' The crowd dispersed to their houses, forgetting work in the fields. Kuchernigo wrote: 'My God, how many tears were spilled when we had to go.' His five-year-old daughter sat in his arms, pressing against him and saying, 'Daddy, why are you going? Why are you leaving us? Who's going to earn money and get bread for us?' She embraced and kissed her father, whose own tears were soon flowing. 'I couldn't answer her questions, and just answered, "I'll be home soon, baby."'

In France mobilisation continued for fifteen days, with draftees reporting by age groups, the youngest first, the oldest last: arrivals at barracks were processed with astonishing speed. From the moment a man was received, inside twenty minutes he was stripped of his civilian clothes, bathed, uniformed and dispatched to his unit. With the reinforcement of its colonial mercenary regiments, most of them North African, France mustered 3.8 million trained soldiers, approximately equal to the forces of Germany. Seventeen-year-old peasant Ephraim Grenadou was attending a wake following the funeral of a young friend when mounted gendarmes trotted into his little town of Saint-Loup in Eure-et-Loir to post a stark white proclamation: *MOBILISATION GENERALE*. 'The schoolmaster shouted to us to sound the tocsin. Everyone crowded around the *Mairie*, having abandoned the fields in the midst of harvesting.' Men quizzed each other: 'When are you leaving?' 'The second day.' 'Me, the third.' 'Me, the 25th.' 'Oh, you will never go – we shall be back by then.' Next day Achilles, Saint-Loup's town crier, toured the community, proclaiming tidings preceded by trumpet calls: 'Everybody who has good boots should take them. You will be paid 15 francs.'

Two police automobiles brought the order to the church square of Valtilieu in Isère at 4.30 on the afternoon of 1 August. Immediately the local bell-ringer summoned the population; the village teacher described the effect: 'it seemed that suddenly the old feudal tocsin had returned to haunt us. Nobody spoke for a long while. Some were out of breath, others dumb with shock. Many still carried pitchforks in their hands. "What can it mean? What's going to happen to us?" asked the women. Wives, children, husbands – all were overcome by anguish and emotion. The wives clung to the arms of their husbands. The children, seeing their mothers weeping, started to cry too.' Most of the men resorted to the café, to discuss the practical issue of how the harvest was to be got in. The general mood was resolute.

Sergeant Paul Gourdant expressed dismay at leaving behind a bedridden wife and four children; he was distressed that the burden of caring for them would fall on his elderly parents. But religion provided a staff: 'God gave me strength to put aside all my fears and anxieties and to think only of the defence of my country.' Henri Perrin, who owned a little ironmongery in Vienne, hastened around the town settling debts, before painstakingly instructing his young wife about the shop's management in his absence. Then the family fell on their knees and prayed together. The Perrins explained to their two small children that 'Papa must go away for a while on business for the country.' At thousands of railway stations, clusters of stoical, anxious or openly emotional relatives surrounded each man as he boarded the train. One shouted gaily, 'All aboard for Berlin! And what fun we'll have there!' André Gide, a spectator, noted: 'People smiled, but did not applaud.' Some peasants treated the occasion as a holiday – these young men who had never experienced such an indulgence. A few fled to hide in the woods, but stern womenfolk drove most to report sheepishly to barracks.

Europe's vast migration created a corresponding social upheaval. 'So many men have left,' reported a French regional newspaper, *La Croix d'Isère*, 'that an atmosphere of sadness and doom pervades the small towns and villages of the Dauphiné.' The rector of Grenoble Academy wrote: 'all along the valley … the once familiar shouts and cries of farmers going to market, of animated "farm talk" in cafés and market squares, has given way to an anxious silence maintained by women, children and old men'. Machinery lay idle and bread ran short, with skilled workers gone and petrol stocks appropriated by the army. In Malleval, a public-spirited motorist siphoned the tank of his automobile, to provide just enough fuel to run a threshing machine for two days to finish the harvest.

Britain, alone among the belligerents, had no system of universal military service, and thus a relatively small professional army of 247,432 men, of which half was dispersed across the Empire. Unlike the continental powers, which mustered millions of trained conscripts, the British summoned into uniform only a further 145,347 reservists – ex-soldiers contractually liable to recall – and 268,777 men of the part-time Territorial Force. Although the process went relatively smoothly, some men wrenched from civilian life responded with reluctance and even truculence. Captain the Hon. Lionel Tennyson of the Rifle Brigade, grandson of the poet and an England cricketer who had spent the previous winter playing Test matches in South Africa, sentenced fifteen reservists who displayed symptoms of what would later be called 'bolshiness' to twenty-one days' 'CB' – Confinement to Barracks. This, he said, 'quietened them down a bit'.

Austria's army mustered with Ruritanian incompetence for the war its rulers had willed. Its principal strength lay in exotic parade uniforms and splendid bands. Some of the artillery still had 1899-vintage bronze barrels. The Hapsburgs' ruling class might enthuse about crushing Serbia, but most of them had traditionally escaped military service, leaving this to humbler folk. Relatively elderly men found themselves dispatched to the front, while fit younger ones were left behind to guard bridges and stations. Early casualty lists showed that among the dead were fathers of families aged forty-two and more. The call-up of doctors caused severe problems, especially in rural Alpine areas where communications were poor and horses, carts and carriages had been commandeered by the army. Conrad deliberately earmarked for his assault on Serbia formations recruited from Slav minorities. A brisk experience of crushing their racial brethren, Vienna deluded itself, would strengthen such Hapsburg subjects' loyalty to the Empire.

There was some confusion about which nations would take up arms for which side. An astonished Japanese was hugged in a Berlin street, because it was briefly rumoured that his country would back the Central Powers. The same was said of Italy, so that when homegoing Italian migrant workers met Hapsburg troops on their way to the front, the Austrians shouted enthusiastically '*Hoch Italien!*', and the workers replied with equal warmth '*Eviva Austria!*' But Italy's army was in a parlous state. Through most of the pre-war crisis, the country lacked a chief of staff because the incumbent had died on 1 July, and Count Luigi Cadorna was appointed to succeed him only on the 27th. Cadorna promised Italian support to the Germans – then found his pledge disowned by the foreign minister. Italy was interested in fighting only to secure territorial gains – parts of Serbia and Italian-speaking Hapsburg lands foremost among them. A constitutional tangle ensued. King Victor Emmanuel was willing to sign a mobilisation order at Cadorna's behest, to fight alongside Germany and Austria, but on 2 August the cabinet voted for neutrality. Italy was thus temporarily spared from the looming bloodbath, though many Austrians and Germans expressed disgust at an alleged betrayal.

Europe meanwhile teemed with civilian travellers struggling to return to their home countries. Geoffrey Clarke, an ex-Rifle Brigade officer living outside Paris, recorded a conversation with a railwayman he met on his local station platform. The Frenchman, off to join his regiment, asked where the Englishman was going, and was told he was heading home to rejoin the army. '*Ah!*' came the warm response, '*alors, nous serons ensemble.*' He extended a hand, saying as it was shaken, '*Au revoir, à bientôt.*' Half a million Russian migrant workers had to abandon their summer jobs in Germany. Thousands of German hotel and restaurant staff in Britain trooped aboard ferries bound for neutral Holland. Hundreds of English-language teachers in Berlin, lacking cash, found themselves stranded.

Eighty thousand American tourists hurried home, some of them in the steamship *Viking*, which they clubbed together to purchase. Railway stations were crowded with desperate people of many nationalities. London shoe-shop manager George Galpin had a German neighbour in Wimbledon who left for home just before war broke out. Galpin accompanied the man to Victoria station, where his new enemy joked, 'Don't worry too much – I'll see that you and your family are well treated when we come over to England!'

Peter Kollwitz, younger son of East Prussian painter Käthe, was born into a family dedicated to high art and leftist ideals. The war found him, aged seventeen, holidaying in Norway with three friends. Determined to enlist, they travelled homewards on a train from Bergen to Oslo with English and French tourists who embarrassed them by their friendliness. They eventually reached Berlin, 'talking excitedly about their new identity as fighters, lit up by sensuality and the thrill of imagined battle'. After some family argument, Peter's father signed the papers consenting to his under-age enlistment, then he and his elder brother Hans departed for barracks, leaving their parents 'weeping, weeping, weeping'. Peter left for the front, and a grave, bearing in his knapsack his mother's parting present, Goethe's *Faust*.

Some diplomats displayed rash insouciance by continuing to parade their protected status in the spirit of nineteenth-century gentlemen's wars. In Paris the Bavarian minister was seen dining at the Ritz on the evening of 2 August, while the Austrian ambassador Count Szécsen was insensitive enough to continue taking meals at the fashionable Cercle de l'Union club, much to the chagrin of its members, who eventually closed their doors to him. In Berlin, with reciprocal grumpiness French ambassador Jules Cambon was ordered by the Germans not to send his staff to dine at the Hotel Bristol, because it would be hard to ensure their safety. Cambon lost his temper: 'Where the devil do you want them to eat? As far as I know, the clientele of the Bristol is made up of well-brought-up people.' The ambassador telephoned the hotel and asked that food for his staff should be dispatched to the embassy. The manager replied that he would do this only if authorised by the Foreign Ministry. The messy process of burning secret papers occupied Cambon through the evening of 3 August and all next morning, until he and his staff took a train to neutral Denmark en route homewards.

There were flurries of excitement at sea, such as the escape of the battle-cruiser *Goeben* and her light-cruiser consort *Breslau* eastwards across the

Mediterranean, amid epic fumbling by the Royal Navy which enraged Winston Churchill. The German paper the *Lokal-Anzeiger* reported triumphantly the *Goeben*'s 2 August departure from Messina: 'the funnel smoke thickens; across the stillness echoes the noise of anchor chains being hauled up. A crowd, thousands strong, surges towards the harbour; then resounds clearly from *Goeben* the notes of "*Heil dir im Siegerkranz*". Officers and crew line the sides, heads bowed. Three rousing cheers for the Supreme Warlord ring across to the shore, where the crowd remains silent, impressed with the cheerful calm and confidence with which German sailors go forth to fight. Later, there are [false] reports of the wreckage of a British ship being sighted. One thing is certain: they are through!'

And so they were, to the chagrin of the Admiralty in London, after the Royal Navy bungled their pursuit. The two ships were granted passage through the Dardanelles. Once in the Bosphorus, the ruling Young Turks persuaded Berlin to present them, crews and all, to the Turkish navy – a spectacular *coup de théâtre*. *Goeben*'s successful defiance of British naval might significantly influenced Turkish opinion towards joining the Central Powers, though more important was the bitterness engendered by decades of British slights towards the Ottoman Empire, among them confiscation of Crete and Cyprus. Moreover, the Turks loathed and feared the Russians.

Among the gravest manifestations of war was the collapse of credit, which created a huge and immediate crisis for the City of London, the world's financial capital. For days there was real danger of a meltdown of the monetary system. This was averted only by the Chancellor's decision on 13 August that the Treasury must bear the strain: the Bank of England bought more than £350 million worth of outstanding bills of exchange. The sums were staggering, but this intervention saved the financial system.

2 PASSIONS

Some people responded with serenity to the new circumstance of European conflict. In Schneidemühl, Prussia, twelve-year-old Elfriede Kuhr asked her grandmother if Germany would win. 'We have never lost a war in my lifetime,' answered the old woman proudly, 'so we won't lose this one, either.' Her granddaughter was bemused that this supposedly earth-shattering event made little immediate impact on daily life: 'We eat white rolls and good meat and go for a walk as if nothing had happened.' It is a myth that most of the belligerents expected a short war. Ignorant people, and even some informed ones, cherished such a delusion partly because economists, with their accustomed paucity of judgement, assured them that Europe would swiftly run out of money. But many thoughtful soldiers of every nation recognised that a general European conflict could be protracted.

In Paris, *Faust* was still playing at the Opéra, and the press found space to report the death of a child run over by a milk float; a futurist conference continued its debate about the merits of excavating a tunnel under the Channel. But on 2 August the French capital declared a state of siege for the duration: the municipality surrendered to the military all public order responsibilities, with draconian powers of entry, and restriction on assemblies and entertainments. Three days later a law was passed 'repressing indiscretions of the press in wartime', forbidding publication of all military information save that authorised by the government or high command. Journalists were barred from entering combat zones. In the months that followed, Joffre, as army commander-in-chief, wielded the powers almost of a national dictator, provoking the envy of his German counterpart Moltke, shackled to the Kaiser. The doors of many Paris businesses bore signs declaring, with a mixture of regret and pride: '*Maison fermé à cause du départ du patron et des employés sous le drapeau français*.' Cafés and bars now closed at 8 p.m., restaurants at 9.30 p.m. Cavalrymen bivouacked on the boulevards, tethering their horses to chestnut trees. By ten, the most vibrant city in Europe was almost silent.

Germany's parliament agreed on 5 August to fund a war loan of 5,000 million marks, supported by the Social Democrats, even though most of their members opposed the conflict. War had become an accomplished fact, and thus patriotism trumped former convictions, as it did also in Britain and France. Socialists, sensitive to conservative taunts that they were mere *vaterlandslose Gesellen* – 'stateless folk', felt compelled to rally beneath the flag. Moreover, fear and detestation of Russia were as passionate on the left as on the right. Most Germans sincerely believed that their country was encircled by enemies. The *Münchner Neueste Nachrichten* reflected bitterly on 7 August about the renewal of all-too-familiar foreign hostility, a 'hatred against Germanness, this time coming from the east'. The semi-official *Kölnische Zeitung* declared: 'Now that England has shown its hand, everyone can see what is at stake: the most powerful conspiracy in the history of the world.'

The newspaper *Neue Preußische Zeitung* was the first to employ the word *Burgfrieden* to describe Germany's new political truce. It derived from a medieval custom, forbidding private strife within the walls of an embattled castle. Now, *Burgfrieden* became once more a common currency. In the same spirit in France, on 4 August prime minister René Viviani coined a phrase that passed into the French language – *l'union sacrée*: '*Dans la guerre qui s'engage, la France [...] sera héroïquement défendue par tous ses fils, dont rien ne brisera devant l'ennemi l'union sacrée*' – 'In the coming war, France will be heroically defended by all its sons, whose sacred union in the face of the enemy will be indissoluble.' There was much press bellicosity. The clerical *Croix d'Isère* declared the struggle '*la guerre purificatrice*', visited upon France as a punishment for its sins under the Third Republic. 'That was the idea everywhere,' wrote another contemporary, 'that war would clear the air, make things pleasanter all around afterwards.' The socialist paper *Le Droit du peuple* adopted a phrase: 'the war for peace'.

In Britain also, reconciliation became a prevailing theme. On 11 August the government welcomed the excuse to remit all suffragettes' jail sentences. Among the famous Pankhurst family, Sylvia continued to plead for peace, but her sister Christabel and their mother Emmeline denounced 'the German peril'. The executive of Britain's Trades Union Congress declared that it identified the war with 'the preservation and maintenance of free and unfettered democratic government'. More than a few people believed, as do some modern historians, that hostilities with Germany averted a violent collision between British workers, employers and the government.

John Redmond, leader of the Irish Home Rulers, made a supremely enlightened conciliatory gesture when he declared in the House of Commons: 'there are in Ireland two large bodies of Volunteers. One of them sprang into existence in the South. I say to the Government that they may tomorrow withdraw every one of their troops from Ireland. I say that the coasts of Ireland will be defended from foreign invasion by her sons, and for this purpose armed Nationalist Catholics in the South will be only too glad to join arms with the armed Protestant Ulstermen in the North.' Redmond sat down to deafening applause, but he proved to have thus forfeited his status as the standard-bearer of Irish nationalism, and destroyed his political career.

Daily Mail executive Tom Clarke wrote in his diary on 5 August: 'The mock warfare of Ulster is already forgotten. People speak of it in whispers of shame. The history of the past few days is a nightmare ... Now we have taken the plunge one feels better already ... [The British people] know we are in for a hard thing. They are confident, but not cocky. Everybody is thinking to-day of the North Sea. The decisive battle might be fought there even this night.' *The Times* editorialised, in a fashion richer in schoolboy romanticism than intellectual rigour: '[The people of Britain] feel and know that they are summoned to draw [the sword] in the old cause – that once again, in the words which King William inscribed upon his standard, they will "maintain the liberties of Europe". It is the cause for which Wellington fought in the Peninsula and Nelson at Trafalgar – the cause of the weak against the strong, of the small peoples against their overwhelming neighbours, of law against brute force.'

War prompted many acts of private generosity. Some were useful, others not, and most were vulnerable to abuse. A French grandee who donated his cherished motor car to the nation's service was infuriated to glimpse it in the Rue de Rivoli a few days later, occupied by the minister of war's mistress. Alois Fürst zu Löwenstein-Wertheim-Rosenberg was a rich German aristocrat with little interest in military affairs, who had previously avoided service. But now, like many of his kind, he offered a splendid automobile to the Bavarian army along with his own services as its driver, in order to have 'a small share in the national sacrifice'. He also turned his castle at Kleinheubach into a hospital, deemed suitable for ten officers and twenty other ranks, and paid all its expenses. He was given the rank of lieutenant, and after a fortnight's delay while his overworked tailor made uniforms, set off towards the front.

Rich people not called upon to expose themselves to shot and shell instead offered money to the common weal. King George V's name led a list of donors to Britain's 'National Relief Fund' with a gift of £5,000, the Queen adding 1,000 guineas. Sir Ernest Cassel and Lord Northcliffe each gave £5,000, Lord Derby £2,000 and lesser folk smaller amounts, but nobody could immediately decide what worthy purpose the cash should be applied to. A Serbian Relief Fund was established, which raised £100,000 by September. The Duke of Sutherland initiated a scheme whereby the aristocracy opened its vast country houses for use as hospitals, but many of the 250 residences offered proved unsuitable because of the inadequacy of their drains. The Duke then went further and announced that he could also deliver a convalescent hospital in London with a full staff ready to receive patients. A sceptical Admiralty official went to investigate, and was astonished to discover that there was indeed a ducal medical support facility in Victoria Street: it had been established on behalf of the Ulster Volunteers, in anticipation of an Irish civil war.

Millions of Germans began to contribute to *Liebesgaben* – gifts of food, drink, tobacco and clothing for soldiers – but sometimes enthusiasm for aiding the afflicted was deemed to go too far. The *Norddeutsche Allgemeine Zeitung* warned wealthy women against inviting the children of the poor into their homes, because acquaintance with a living standard so much superior to their own was likely to make humble folk dissatisfied. Some commercial enterprises embraced new opportunities. Courtaulds textile manufacturers advertised waterproof black crêpe 'for fashionable mourning'. Burberry began to market 'active service kit': 'Every officer will want his Burberry waterproof.' The tailors Thresher & Glenny did fine business making uniforms, and Ross enjoyed a booming sale of binoculars. A manufacturer of two-seater fast cars recommended them as suitable 'for officers and others'. In Paris knitwear shops began to offer such unsummery clothing as thick underwear and stockings, appropriate for campaigning. There were complaints that London gunmakers Webley & Scott now charged £10 for a revolver which they had sold in July for only five guineas.

Such 'profiteering' provoked public anger. Food hoarding caused some German shopkeepers to close their doors, and almost all to raise prices. In Munich the cost of potatoes doubled, flour rose by 45 per cent, salt trebled. In Hamburg a group of angry women stormed the stall of one alleged profiteer, belabouring its owner with his own sausages. The *Deutsche Volkszeitung* reported an altercation about potatoes between customers and a woman vegetable-seller demanding twelve pfennigs a kilo instead of the usual six or seven. She declared defiantly: 'Well, if you don't like the price I will sell my potatoes to the Russians!' A minor riot followed, until police rescued her from furious citizens.

Meanwhile, magazines filled their pages with photographs and sketches of soldiers and military equipment. Newspapers carried war news, chiefly spurious, to the exclusion of almost all else. In mathematics classes, children were taught to add and subtract soldiers and ships. Innumerable war poems were written, almost uniformly dreadful: 'Use me, England, in thine hour of need,' wrote Elizabeth, daughter of poet laureate Robert Bridges. 'Give then, England, If my life thou need, Gift yet fairer, Death, thy cause to feed.' In London Madame Tussaud's waxwork museum transferred the Kaiser from its Royal Gallery to the Chamber of Horrors. The famous British sense of humour suffered immediate war damage: Bernard Shaw found himself in trouble after penning an article urging both sides to shoot their officers and go home. Libraries and bookshops removed his works from their shelves, while the literary panjandrum J.C. Squire called for him to be tarred and feathered. Shaw remained impenitent, jeering that if the allies were serious about smashing Germany, the rational method would be to kill all its women.

On 2 August, a company of the Sherwood Foresters marched into the Armstrong shipyard on the Tyne and deployed around an almost completed dreadnought. She was destined to become the pride of Turkey's fleet, and five hundred of the Sultan's sailors were waiting expectantly aboard an old passenger ship downriver, ready to take her over. Winston Churchill decreed otherwise; the Royal Navy's need took precedence, and within weeks the *Reshadieh*, renamed the *Erin*, joined the Grand Fleet at Scapa Flow; a second battleship, the *Sultan Osman I*, became the *Agincourt*. Though Britain offered the Turks £1,000 a day for the ships' use, together with their return or full value at the conclusion of hostilities, Turkish opinion was outraged by the loss of the two vessels, which had been partly funded by public subscription. Inflamed sentiment contributed mightily to Constantinople's decision, a few days later, to welcome the *Goeben* and *Breslau*. Turkish neutrality was obviously precarious.

Europe struggled to adjust to new allegiances and animosities. In Vienna Franz Joseph sought to display the solidarity of the monarchs' trade union by rejecting a proposal from his War Ministry that the 27th Infantry should drop its title as 'the King of the Belgians' Own'; the Austrian 12th Hussars likewise continued to be known as 'King Edward VII's Own'. But Britain's royal family hastily stripped its German relations of British honours: the Kaiser dispatched to Buckingham Palace his uniforms as an admiral of the fleet and field-marshal. There was a rush to rechristen popular venues with patriotic names. Le Jardin du Roi de Württemberg in Nice changed its name to Alsace-Lorraine Square. Berlin's Grand Café became the Café Unity, displaying a constantly updated war map on its wall and having the latest dispatches from the front read aloud to patrons. Many German restaurants deleted French and English words and phrases from their menus, which confused diners who could not understand what they were ordering when the fare was described in their own language. Meanwhile in France, Pilsner beer was relabelled Bière de la Meuse.

Spy fever overtook Europe. In Münster, a notably Catholic city, civilians seized several nuns as alleged Russian spies; police arrested the civic head gardener four times because he affected a suit of apparently English cut. British newspapers reported from Brussels: 'five German spies disguised as priests have been arrested here'. Russian agents were alleged to have bombed German bridges and poisoned water supplies, obliging Munich police to tour the streets reassuring the public that it could safely drink from taps. In Belgrade several men were arrested for allegedly making torch signals from the Moskva Hotel to Austrian gunners at Zemun.

Paris's Hôtel Astoria was closed amid charges that its German manager had installed on the roof apparatus for intercepting French wireless messages; the British ambassador heard a rumour that the man was summarily shot, which he disbelieved, but wrote resignedly that he expected 'there will be a good many *tueries*'. A letter was published in *The Times* alerting readers to the peril posed to national security by prominent British residents of Teutonic origin: 'During the last quarter of a century, numbers of highly-placed aliens, some naturalized, some not, who are known to be in close communication with German and financial circles, have bought their way into British society.' The writer urged telephone taps and a close watch on such 'highly-placed sympathizers', and ended with a dark warning: 'I do not wish to be an alarmist, but I know what I am writing about.' This nasty missive was signed only 'S'.

In Berlin the famous Danish-born actress Asta Nielsen was walking down the Unter den Linden when she suddenly and incomprehensibly found herself denounced: 'my hat was thrown down so that my black hair appeared. "A Russian," I heard someone yell behind me, and a hand grabbed my hair. I yelled, full of fear and pain. In front of me a man turned around and recognised me. He yelled my name to the excited people behind me; they let me go and began to curse each other. One of them started flailing his arms as if he was crazy, and hit one of the others in the face. Blood flowed. "You cannot stay here," my saviour said. "The people have completely lost their senses. They no longer know what they are doing."'

Everywhere there was an insatiable hunger for information. Newspapers were torn from vendors whenever a new edition arrived, and café patrons addressed themselves to complete strangers. Rumour ran wild. In St Petersburg, it was said that Emperor Franz Joseph was dead. Austrian soldiers in Mostar heard that revolution had broken out in France, where the president of the republic had been assassinated. Wiseacres on the terraces of Nice predicted that hunger would force Germany to quit the war within weeks. A local resident wrote on 5 August: 'There is no authentic war news – either by land or by sea: all that appears in the papers is invention.' In Germany that week the *Hannoverscher Courier* delivered a vituperative denunciation: 'Animals! ... Yesterday a French surgeon and two disguised French officers attempted to poison fountains with cholera bacilli. They were court-martialled and shot.' It was also alleged that mobs of Belgians were murdering German civilians: Moltke's soldiers claimed to have captured a Belgian with his pockets full of German fingers, severed for their rings.

Russians drifted towards local railway stations, where news was likely to come first: papers from Moscow took days to reach remote areas, and contained little of substance when they did so. Country-dwellers wandered out onto highways and quizzed travellers for scraps of intelligence: 'one was delighted to encounter a simple Cossack', wrote Sergei Kondurashkin in the Caucasus, 'and listen greedily to his naïve words, waiting patiently while the millstones of his memory ground slowly into motion'. When two days' newspapers belatedly arrived, the Kondurashkin family and friends crowded onto the verandah of their holiday *dacha* twenty strong, aged from eight to sixty, and including children, students, clerks, professors, doctors. One of their number was voted the clearest speaker, and nominated to read the paper aloud to the rest, a Chekhovian moment. He then rehearsed the bleak budget of tidings – declarations of war; German incursions into Poland and Russian moves into East Prussia; the arrival in Warsaw of the first PoWs.

There was intense, almost uniformly ill-founded speculation about what the conflict would be like. German pundits offered especially optimistic predictions: a writer in the *Braunschweigische Anzeigen* declared that modern weapons and tactics would diminish fatalities: 'To be sure, some clashes may be notably severe, but it is certain that overall losses will decrease. The vast hordes of men now being mobilised do not face experiences as violent as many people imagine. Battle will be no slaughter' – '*Die Schlacht wird kein Schlachten*'. There was intense British concern about a supposed German invasion threat, which prompted many civilians to enlist in local rifle clubs. People gaped in wonder at the sight of anti-aircraft guns being mounted on Admiralty Arch and London's bridges; the navy urged the War Office to deploy some planes in Hyde Park.

Such fears were mirrored across the North Sea. Anna Treplin, living in the German port of Cuxhaven, was alarmed by the prospect of British warships shelling the harbour, and with it the seaside home she and her three children occupied. Just as pre-war British readers had been excited by Erskine Childers' thriller about the German menace, *The Riddle of the Sands*, so many Germans had read the mirror-image shocker entitled *1906*. This 1905 work by the pseudonymous author 'Seestern' – a journalist named Ferdinand

Grauthoff – anticipated an Anglo-French naval assault on Cuxhaven, and a gunnery duel between allied warships and coastal fortresses. Frau Treplin decamped to Hamburg with her nerves and her offspring.

The legend that Europe welcomed the conflict is today heavily qualified, if not discredited. Rural communities of all nationalities were stunned and profoundly dismayed; most of those who cheered in the streets were the urban young, without responsibilities. Thoughtful people were appalled. Michel Corday, a French senior civil servant, wrote: 'Every thought and event caused by the outbreak of war came as a bitter and mortal blow struck against the great conviction that was in my heart: the concept of permanent progress, of movement towards ever greater happiness. I had never believed that something like this could happen.'

But some romantics and nationalists enthused, like the Austrian woman Itha J, who wrote lyrically about 'the grandeur of the times ... the superb spectacle of the world bursting into flames'. Even as she sobbed at the station on 2 August, bidding farewell to her husband, a lieutenant, she rhapsodised about 'this wonderful young [generation], who depart to face battle and death with laughter and cheering. Nobody shivers, nobody sobs – isn't such an army ordained to gain victory?' Germany experienced the most conspicuous surge of euphoria, influenced by the remembered glories of victory over France in 1870. Its Red Cross had to urge people to give soldiers less chocolate, because it was making them sick. On 2 August a journalist on the *Tägliche Rundschau* wrote: 'what Germany has experienced in recent days has been a miraculous self-renewal, in which everything petty and alien has been shed; it has represented a supremely powerful recognition of our true self'.

At the Reichstag session of 4 August, Bethmann Hollweg asserted that the date would live for eternity as one of Germany's greatest. Falkenhayn told the chancellor: 'Even if we go under as a result of this, it was beautiful,' and many of his compatriots agreed. On 14 August Bethmann's secretary Riezler exulted: 'war, war, the *Volk* has arisen – it is as if there were nothing there before and now suddenly it is powerful and moving ... on the surface the greatest confusion and yet the most meaningful order; by now millions have already crossed the Rhine'. A young girl, Gertrud Bäumer, wrote with a mawkish sentimentality typical of the moment in Germany that war increased the store of love in the world, 'for it taught one to love one's neighbour more than oneself'.

In Britain, by contrast, while Norman Macleod at the Admiralty acknowledged a 'feeling of confidence in Navy & Army & determination to set about the great business as well as possible', he added, 'there is certainly no martial ardour. Of course men are enlisting and volunteering fast enough and everybody has become a military and naval expert, but there is an absence of that joy in fighting – glory of battle – which was so marked at beginning of the Boer War and shortly before it – Kiplingism quite forgotten – the horrors of war are not for a moment lost sight of.' *The Economist* asserted the grave significance of unfolding events, and their implications for civilisation: 'Since last week millions of men have been drawn from the field and the factory to slay one another by order of the warlords of Europe. It is perhaps the greatest tragedy of human history … In the opinion of many shrewd judges, a social upheaval, a tremendous revolution, is the certain consequence. It may perhaps be the last time that the working classes of the Continent will allow themselves to be marched to destruction at the dictates of diplomacy and by the order of their warlords.' The magazine expressed doubts about how Britain's disaffected working class and alienated Irish subjects would respond to the advent of war. 'It has been freely stated,' declared one of its correspondents, 'that in the North of England there is still a good deal of apathy.'

So there was. Tens of thousands of volunteers quickly offered themselves to the army, but many more potential recruits decided to stay at home. A Mr Doyle of the Manor House, Birtley, in Co. Durham, wrote to the *Yorkshire Post*: 'The important work of instructing the public as to the meaning of the war should begin in real earnest. A few days ago, in passing through one of the larger villages, I stopped to see a dozen or so young men who had joined the colours being drilled in a field. Six times as many were lying up against the fence passively looking on. I enquired of one of them, a well set-up, athletic young fellow, why he was a spectator and not a participant. He looked at me squarely and said: "Because it isn't worthwhile; we could be of no use for six months, and by that time there will be no enemy. Germany will be off the map." Another young man said: "It's no business of ours this foreign war. Austria and Serbia should be let fight it out. Germany didn't want to come in until compelled by Russia, and we should have kept out of it. Anyhow, we're all right; the fleet will keep us safe."'

But others were inspired to don khaki. The writer A.P. Herbert, an instinctive iconoclast, nonetheless wrote long afterwards, denouncing the satirical musical *Oh, What a Lovely War!*, which suggested that he and his generation were 'duped into the Forces by damsels singing patriotic songs, or bullied in by peremptory posters'. He declared his own lasting conviction that Britain had gone to war for a just cause, and remained impenitent about his own commitment to fight for it. Most British intellectual opinion agreed. Thomas Hardy believed that 'England was innocent for once ... the war began because the Germans wanted to fight.' Sir Walter Raleigh, Oxford's professor of history, confided to a friend: 'I've often known this must come when I've heard the Germans talk about their destiny and their plans for achieving it. I'm glad I've lived to see it, and sick that I'm not in it.' Many men idealised the prospect of military service, as did C.E. Montague in his autobiographical novel *Rough Justice*: 'Always to have just some one plain and not hard thing to do; to be free to give yourself up ... to whole days of rude health, to let yourself go, with a will, in the swing of marching, the patterned dances of drills ... with the blithe or grave calls blown on bugles to lead you through the busy, easy days.' Montague was described by a friend as 'the only man whose hair turned black in a single night through courage'. At the age of forty-seven, though initially opposed to the war, he dyed his white hair black in order to join the Grenadier Guards.

Few families in Britain embraced the coming of war with as much jingo enthusiasm as Robert Emmet's. He was a rich East Coast American, forty-three years old, since 1900 living and fox-hunting in Warwickshire. His bank-holiday house party at Moreton Paddox was largely composed of cavalry and reserve officers, 'who worked themselves into a frenzy of anxiety' lest the government flinch from a declaration of war 'which appeared the natural and even inevitable reply to Germany's wanton invasion of Belgium'. The telephone was in constant service, to quiz porters at the men's London clubs about the latest news. On the following Tuesday Emmet, who had served as a lieutenant with the New York National Guard in the Spanish-American War, took his entire family to London. Installed in their usual quarters at Claridge's Hotel, he addressed his wife and three teenage sons. He saw only two alternatives, he said: to disappear quietly back to the safety of neutral America, or stay and fight. He made plain his personal view, then invited a vote among the assembled company. His three sons unhesitatingly opted to stay, 'Their mother, in her turn, courageously voting "aye" as well, the decision being made unanimous by my final vote. A great load was lifted off my mind.'

Returning to Warwickshire that week of the war's outbreak, Major Emmet hoisted the Stars and Stripes on his lawn. He intended this as a gesture of solidarity with Britain, but the neighbourhood unfortunately misconstrued it. Emmet's brother-in-law telephoned to say that unless he lowered the flag, it was not impossible that the house would be burned down. People supposed that he was attempting to proclaim his own neutrality and safeguard his property in the event of a German invasion. Emmet was outraged, and persisted in defiance for three days before prudently lowering Old Glory. Soon afterwards he handed over the Paddox to become a hospital, which it remained for the rest of the war, while he himself trained cavalry recruits and his sons enlisted.

Throughout Europe, families adjusted their domestic economies to the prospect of a new austerity. The haste with which staff were shed caused much hardship. Many German women servants found themselves without a place, and were soon crowding around city soup kitchens. Violet Asquith complained to Venetia Stanley about the crass conduct of Lord Elcho, in whose house she and her father spent a weekend. The peer 'issued an abrupt ultimatum to all his employees servants etc. – to join the Army or leave his service – & has then gone off to London leaving poor Lady Elcho' – Arthur Balfour's long-service lover – 'to cope with the situation – which he created without consulting her in any sort of way. It is too cruel as the people here have hardly heard of the war.'

Shortage of raw materials forced many factories to reduce or halt production, so that in Germany unemployment rose from 2.7 per cent in July to 22.7 per cent in August. Salesmen working on commission saw their incomes vanish. A pastor in Berlin's Moabit tenement quarter observed that enthusiasm for the struggle was a luxury only intellectuals could indulge. The *Rheinische Zeitung* noted: 'a tense mood prevails during the late hours in our working-class districts. There is no noise, no songs. One hears sobbing and sees men looking grave … no strident patriotic slogans, no hurrahs, instead work and sacrifice.' A journalist visiting the London East End's Hoxton, 'a stronghold of penury at all times', found its people 'threatened by a very disaster of distress under the shock of war'. There was special hardship in Lancashire, where one-fifth of cotton looms stopped, and a further one-seventh were reduced to short-time working. Over 100,000 cotton workers were idle, with half Burnley suddenly unemployed, and one-third of Preston.

Jewish historian Gustav Mayer on 12 August found his father bewailing the collapse of business at his drapery shop in Berlin's Zehlendorf. In Freiburg some 10,000 men, much of the city's workforce, went to the army, so that one firm lost 154 out of its 231 workers; Ditler's furniture manufactory lost forty-five men, a third of its employees, and a local publisher was deprived of over a hundred, most of them printers. The building trade collapsed almost overnight. Textile and leather-goods manufacturers found themselves suffering acutely from raw-material shortages.

It is hard to overstate the social and economic impact of the mass mobilisation of horses, which created difficulties not merely for agriculture, but for every form of transport. Though the world would soon become motorised, in 1914 horses and oxen were the customary means of moving goods and people anywhere that a train could not go. In the German countryside near Halle, a pastor asserted that farmers were more upset by the requisitioning of their animals and wagons than by the conscription of their workers. In England, too, horses were ruthlessly commandeered, though on a generous scale of compensation – £40 for a troop horse and £60 for an officer's charger, which enabled some owners to recycle indifferent hunters. Lt. Guy Harcourt-Vernon of the Grenadier Guards wrote home exhibiting a blend of optimism, bewilderment and opportunism: 'This war ought to end as soon as the Russians march on Berlin say 4 to 6 months, but I hope they won't bicker over the spoils like the Balkan war. I wonder if they will send us after all. Are they commandeering horses? If so, let "Child" go, but stand out for £60 if they will give it. It is probably more than I shall get any other way.' At the Tower of London, long rows of purchased horses stood tethered in the moat.

In the harvest fields of the vast Yorkshire estate of Sledmere, on 5 August wagoners were handed mobilisation papers. After serving in South Africa Sir Mark Sykes MP, the local grandee, had become convinced that a future war would expose a shortage of army transport. He thus persuaded the War Office to acquiesce in a scheme whereby his own neighbours' agricultural workers should be enlisted as volunteer drivers. These men received no military training, but were subject to call-up. Sykes mustered drivers at his own expense, grading them as 'Wagoner', 'Foreman' and 'Roadmaster', with appropriate brass lapel badges. In 1913 the War Office took over responsibility for paying the men annual bounties of between one and four sovereigns. Wagoners called the former 'the silly quid', because it seemed so easily earned – by driving a timed run around a figure-of-eight obstacle course at Sledmere. By 8 p.m. on 5 August, more than eight hundred such men had assembled at the Army Service Corps' Bradford depot, where they drew uniforms and received a little hasty training. Within weeks, most were driving in France.

* * *

The war had not been precipitated by popular nationalistic fervour, but by the decisions of tiny groups of individuals in seven governments. In most countries before hostilities began, only small numbers of people attended demonstrations in favour of belligerence, and there is no evidence that these influenced policy. Instead, it was the fact of conflict which precipitated displays of patriotism and rallied societies to their respective causes. Many people who had strongly opposed fighting decided that the debating season was now over: national solidarity had become a duty. A Protestant clergyman in the Black Forest noted that Catholics who had hitherto ignored his existence now greeted him with 'Hello, pastor.' Twelve-year-old Elfriede Kuhr, living with her grandparents in Schneidemühl, wrote on 3 August: 'We have to learn new songs about the glory of war. The enthusiasm in our town is growing by the hour. People wander through the streets in groups shouting "Down With Serbia! Long live Germany!" Everyone wears black, white and red pompoms in their buttonholes or black, white and red bows.'

Field-Marshal Lord Roberts, the British public's beloved 'Bobs', wrote in *The Times* on 6 August: '"my country right or wrong and right or wrong my country" is the sentiment most treasured in the breast of anyone worthy of the name of man'. Even Ramsay MacDonald, the pacifist former Labour leader, urged that 'those who can enlist ought to enlist and those who are working in munition factories should do so wholeheartedly'. Ritual political reconciliations took place in communities all over France. On 4 August in Paris a message from President Poincaré was read to a packed Chamber of Deputies, calling for an end to the factional and class struggles that had riven the Third Republic. This was received with rapturous applause, followed by handshaking between political enemies. The phrase '*la patrie en danger*' was heard on many lips, a manifestation of the *union sacrée*. In France as in Germany, such solidarity was interpreted as a triumph for the political right, reflecting the eclipse of the socialists who had opposed belligerence.

In the first days of August, the Labour Party sponsored 'Stop the War' rallies in several British cities and towns. The Fabian Beatrice Webb attended one of these in Trafalgar Square, which was addressed by Keir Hardie and George Lansbury. She found herself untouched by either its manner or its message, writing afterwards: 'It was an undignified and futile exhibition, this singing of *The Red Flag* and passing of well-worn radical resolutions in favour of universal peace.' She noted with approval that even many extreme pacifists 'are agreeing that we had to stand by

Belgium'. Webb nonetheless recoiled from 'the disgusting misuse of religion' to stimulate patriotism. She may have been thinking of the Bishop of London, who declared: 'This is the greatest fight ever made for the Christian religion ... a choice between the nailed hand and the mailed fist.'

At St Petersburg's Nikolaevsky, Baltiysky and Varshavsky stations, thousands of men lit candles at the trackside icons as they departed to join their regiments. The Catholic Archbishop of Freiburg spoke to his flock of the war as a *Heimsuchung* – an affliction sent by God to test believers. A chaplain proclaimed stentoriously: 'Rage over Germany, you great holy war of freedom. Tear down all that is rotten and sick, heal the wounds on the body of our German people and let a breed grow, a new breed, full of reverence for God, faithfulness to duty and brotherly love.' In the Hapsburg Empire the Bishop of Sekau exulted in a belief that the war would introduce a new (spiritual) order: 'This is the end of culture without God, without Christ, [and of] high politics without religion.'

The most spectacular displays of apparently spontaneous support for the war took place in Russia. On 4 August the German embassy in St Petersburg was sacked by a mob, a hapless caretaker murdered. To the British correspondent Arthur Ransome, a Russian paraphrased the old Roman pronouncement of Carthage's doom: '*Germania delenda est.*' Two days later in the capital, a quarter of a million people gathered to sing patriotic songs. Even in provincial cities, far from the metropolitan elite, crowds thronged the streets, some carrying portraits of Nicholas II decorated with flags. 'Long live the Tsar and the People!' they cried.

Yet despite such displays of fervour in some cities, not many Russians deluded themselves that the struggle would do them any good: few wars ever had. Scepticism – indeed, cynicism – intensified lower down the social scale. The historian Allan Wildman has written that Russia's peasants thought it 'a fruitless venture of the upper classes for which they would have to pay'. Menshikov, *Novoe Vremya*'s chief columnist, wrote: 'There isn't nowadays among the masses that faith, that capacity to catch fire, that there was in the days of Suvorov and Napoleon.' In Riga, alongside celebratory banners appeared others proclaiming 'Down with the war'.

In some places there were riots to protest against conscription, or at least to vent rage about the incompetence with which it was being implemented. An official telegraphed from Tomsk: 'Reservists are producing disorder almost everywhere ... in Novosibirsk a mob of reservists sacked stores and began to sack the bazaar, the disorders were stopped with the assistance of [troops] ... The mobs threw stones at them.' When somebody fired a shot which wounded a soldier, troops opened fire on the crowd, killing two civilians and seriously wounding two more. Meanwhile reservists pillaged liquor stores in several villages; some demonstrated furiously for food, and against the requisitioning of their horses, indispensable to agricultural activity.

In Paris, artist Paul Maze reported to the Invalides to volunteer for the army, only to discover that no more men were being immediately accepted. A hoary old sergeant dismissed the crestfallen youth with the words, 'Why worry? You'll get all you want before the end.' Maze, who was bilingual, joined the disembarking British Expeditionary Force at Le Havre as an interpreter, and eventually became a decorated officer. Many young men in all countries, especially artists and writers, were less enthusiastic than curious about the prospect of seeing a battlefield. Viennese-born Ludwig Wittgenstein, who was twenty-five, at first saw it as offering an escape from his own tortured philosophical confusions and uncertainties, intensified by study at Cambridge under Bertrand Russell. He volunteered for military service, and recorded in his coded diary delight at the civilised reception he received. 'Will I be able to work now??' he asked himself on 9 August. 'I am curious about my future life! The military authorities in Vienna were extraordinarily civil. Officials who had to deal with thousands of men every day answered my questions politely and at length. Such things cheer me up enormously; they remind me of the way things are done in England.' Within days, however, Wittgenstein's spirits sagged. Dispatched to serve as a searchlight operator aboard the picket boat *Goplana* on the Vistula, he found the company of ordinary sailors not merely unwelcome, but repellent: 'The crew are miserable pigs! They display no enthusiasm, unbelievable brutishness, stupidity and wickedness! So it is untrue that a shared great cause (the war) ennobles humanity.'

German Paul Hub, a twenty-four-year-old from Stetten, a village near Stuttgart, volunteered after getting engaged to his twenty-one-year-old girlfriend Maria. He departed for the front on 4 August, writing to his parents: 'Please keep my washing a little longer, until I ask you for it. Unpack my clothes in the meantime … Maria's letters are in the engagement case, together with my watchchains and other keepsakes that remind me of the happy times I've had with her. Please look after them. I hope I'll be coming back.' Like many others, Hub was to be disappointed.

The conflict created some remarkable new allegiances. In the last days of July 1914, British novelist and civil servant Erskine Childers committed high treason. He sailed his yacht *Asgard* into the Irish harbour of Howth, delivering to militant nationalists a cargo of rifles smuggled from Germany. Yet a month later, the forty-four-year-old Childers was recruited by the First Lord of the Admiralty, Winston Churchill – who was ignorant of the *Asgard*'s adventures – to become a naval reserve officer and advise on Germany's North Sea coast. Childers had cruised for years in the Friesian Islands before he wrote his 1903 thriller *The Riddle of the Sands*, the plot of which centred on a German invasion conspiracy against Britain. Now, the author drafted a memorandum for the Admiralty proposing seizure of Borkum and Juist islands as springboards for an amphibious assault on Germany: 'The plan of invasion up the Ems valley ... seems to present the best opportunity of ending the war by a decisive stroke,' he wrote. He concluded: 'The writer ventures to hope that he may have the honour of being employed, if the service permits, whether in aeroplane work or in any other capacity, if any of the operations sketched in this memorandum are undertaken.'

On 20 August Childers was taken aboard the seaplane carrier HMS *Engadine*, accepted as an intelligence officer, where his Irish comrades might have been surprised to discover him two days later saluting Admiral Sir John Jellicoe and shaking hands with Winston Churchill on their visit to the ship. He wrote: 'The atmosphere on board is one of cheerful optimism. It would be ridiculous, though more accurate perhaps, to call it pessimism – so sanguine and jovial is the anticipation of a certain doom in our gimcrack pleasure boat with its popguns and delicate, butterfly planes. But indeed no human being can forecast our destiny because the whole enterprise is new in war: an incalculable experiment.' Childers was one of a limited number of men of all nationalities enthralled by the notion of playing a part in the twentieth century's first great conflict, which engaged its most exhilarating new machines, magic carpets to the skies.

3 DEPARTURES

With the exception of Churchill and Haldane, the members of the British cabinet lacked the smallest understanding of military affairs, and knew it. Indeed, in that era politicians of all nationalities expected to leave strategy and military science exclusively in the hands of their soldiers, an abrogation they would lament before they were much older. Asquith would like to have reappointed Haldane, architect of radical and brilliant army reforms in the previous decade, as secretary of state for war. He felt unable to do so, however, because the Lord Chancellor was the victim of a vicious press campaign led by *The Times*, which damned him as a 'pro-German'. The appointment was given instead to 'K of K' – Field-Marshal Earl Kitchener of Khartoum, Britain's foremost soldier. This was hugely popular with the public, and the new minister possessed unusual qualifications: partly brought up in Switzerland, he spoke fluent French. In 1870 he had briefly served in a French field-ambulance unit, an adventure cut short when he contracted pneumonia after making a balloon ascent to view the Army of the Loire.

But the grim, austere, taciturn Kitchener also had notable limitations. He was not merely unpolitical, he deplored politicians. Lloyd George wrote of his 'loud staccato voice' in cabinet meetings, and of 'that remote look in his eyes, directed at no one in particular, which was a sure indication of his unease amid surroundings with which he was not familiar. He was sitting in council with men belonging to the profession with which he had wrestled all his life, and for which, in his heart, he had the usual mixture of military contempt and apprehension.'

Kitchener was a loner who did not change his ways at the War Office. He had always thought poorly of France's forces, telling Lloyd George in 1911 that, in the event of war, the Germans would 'walk through them like partridges'. He was nonetheless an able soldier, whose great contribution in 1914 was to insist that Britain must plan for a long war. He found himself struggling to transform a force of imperial skirmishers into a host fit for continental war. The regulars, reserves, Territorials and a ragtag of militias provided Britain with 733,514 more or less trained men scattered around the world. Everyone recognised that much bigger numbers would be needed, but unfortunately Kitchener bungled the expansion programme. The obvious course would have been to build on the existing Territorial Force framework, but the new secretary for war despised the 'Terriers' and was also conscious that they were not automatically liable for overseas service. He decided to create a 'New Army', whose officers and men would alike be novices. The chaos which followed, and the tribulations which hundreds of thousands of eager young recruits suffered between August 1914 and their immolation in France the following year, make a sorry story.

One among many August volunteers was Robert Cude, a twenty-one-year-old factory worker from South London. He first tried to join the navy, and was sent to Devonport for a trade test, which he failed because of 'my inability to stomach orders'. With three mates from his factory, he promptly joined the East Kent Regiment. They arrived at its Canterbury depot to find no food and no quarters, and were obliged to doss down on the barrack square. They were then moved to a camp at Purfleet, where each tent bulged with twenty-two occupants. 'What a cosmopolitan crew we are!' wrote Cude. 'All manner of wearing apparel ... Parades every few minutes. Am sick of this playing at soldiers. Dinner comes up. Menu: "Warm water with pieces of a substance which was termed meat floating on top".' When Cude and his comrades were given three days' leave while the authorities worked out how to handle them, one man in five never came back.

Many volunteers were rejected. The writer Jerome K. Jerome, author of the immortal Edwardian romp *Three Men in a Boat*, became an ambulance driver with the French after being denied a King's uniform – unsurprisingly, since he was fifty-five. An advertisement for potential officers placed by one regiment asserted without embarrassment that 'preference will be given to public school men of good appearance and address', but even some such applicants were refused. *The Times* published a letter from joint signatories who called themselves 'Eight Unattached'. The writers expressed disgust at having been rejected for commissions as too old at thirty-plus, though 'absolutely fit and game for active service'. They proposed instead to join the ranks, but wished to do so with others of similar social background: 'all public school men of similar age and qualifications are invited to attend an informal meeting at the address below – 59a Brook Street W – to discuss the formation of a "Legion of Marksmen".' Here was the spirit that bred 'pals' battalions, which later suffered appallingly in France.

Some patriots decided that if insufficient young men were volunteering for military service, women could 'do their bit' by shaming them into doing so. Bernard Hamley was playing golf with a friend on Wimbledon Common, and just congratulating himself on a fine tee shot, when two girls came out of the nearby clubhouse. One said sharply, 'That was a good shot, wasn't it? I hope you will be making as good a shot against the Germans,' before presenting both players with white feathers. The men then identified themselves as officers in the 1st London Rifle Brigade, granted a few hours' leave of absence. 'The young females were somewhat crestfallen and made some inadequate excuses.'

Stephen Lang told a woman who gave him a feather in Camden High Street that he was only seventeen, and anyway worked on the railways – a 'reserved occupation'. The young woman said crossly, 'Heard that one before,' and pushed the feather up his nose. A recruiting sergeant to whom Lang gave the same explanation said, 'Nineteen? That's a good age.'

'But I'm only seventeen – born in 1898.'

'1896 – that's fine. The war's the only thing this bastard's fit for' – and enrolled him.

Some women were eager to put themselves in harm's way, but found it hard to identify a role. Gladys Winterbottom was an exception. Her husband Archie was a subaltern with the 5th Dragoons. Impatient with the notion that there could be no place on a battlefield for wives and mothers, she packed her children off to the country and offered herself and the Winterbottom motor car to the Cavalry Division at Aldershot. Maj. Gen. Edmund Allenby, its commander, familiarly known to his staff as 'the Bull', found time to sign a testimonial for her on 14 August: 'This is to certify that I have been driven in motor cars by Mrs A. Winterbottom. I know her to be a thoroughly efficient driver, and I confidently recommend her for employment.' When the army nonetheless proved unwilling to employ her in the theatre of war, she became an ambulance driver with a British volunteer unit that joined the Belgians, and within weeks was serving under fire.

The allies, as they began to deploy, were fortified by knowledge that they enjoyed a comfortable paper superiority over their enemies. The combined Russian, French, British and Belgian populations of 279 million people were pitted against the Central Powers' 120 millions; their armies mobilised 199 infantry divisions against 137, fifty cavalry formations against twenty-two. More than half this military strength was Russian, and it was thus that people fantasised enthusiastically about the appearance of some portion of the Tsarist host on west European battlefields.

Dispositions had been settled long before. The Germans dispatched seven armies westwards, to implement Moltke's variant of the Schlieffen concept, a vast envelopment of the French army designed to achieve its swift destruction. The Austrians sent almost half their soldiers to invade Serbia, the rest to confront the Russians in Galicia, where Russian Poland bordered the Hapsburg Empire. The Serbs prepared to defend their western frontiers against the Austrians. The Russians committed two armies to invade East Prussia, and four more to fight the Austrians. France began to implement Plan XVII; until 6 August, French troops were forbidden to enter Belgium or French aircraft to overfly it, to ensure that the Germans bore indisputable responsibility for breaching the country's neutrality.

Only Britain dithered about how to commence military operations, just as it had hesitated about whether to fight at all. The cabinet appointed a War Council, which met for the first time at Downing Street, under Asquith's chairmanship, at 4 p.m. on 5 August. Its immediate dilemma was

Rival Concentrations on the Western Front, August 1914

N

0   20   40
Miles

Antwerp

Schelde

Demer   Diest

Louvain   Hasselt   FIRST ARMY (von Kluck)

BRUSSELS   2   3   St   Trond

Wavre   6   5   Gette   Liège   SECOND ARMY (von Bülow)

B E L G I U M   Gembloux   Namur   Malmédy   SECOND ARMY

Mons   17 August   Perwez   4   Meuse   8 August

Charleroi   25 Aug.   8 Inf.Bde.   Dinant   THIRD ARMY (von Hausen)

Valenciennes   Sambre   Givet   Sordet

Maubeuge   I CORPS   Sordet's Cavalry Corps

B.E.F.   Meuse   Mézières   Neufchâteau   FOURTH ARMY (Grand Duke of Württemberg)   THIRD ARMY

Concentration   FIFTH ARMY (Lanrezac)   LUX.   Trier

Area   Longwy   LUXEMBOURG

La Fère   16 Aug.   FOURTH ARMY

Aisne   FOURTH ARMY (Langle de Carry)   FIFTH ARMY (Imperial Crown Prince of Prussia)   FOURTH ARMY

Laon   THIRD ARMY (Ruffey)   Thionville   FIFTH ARMY Moselle Position

Reims   Verdun   Metz   G E R M A N Y

Épernay   Châlons-sur-Marne   St Mihiel   SIXTH ARMY   SIXTH ARMY (Crown Prince of Bavaria)

F R A N C E   Commercy   Château-Salins   Saarburg   Strasbourg

Vitry-le-François   Marne   Tour   NANCY   Bruche   SEVENTH ARMY (von Heeringen)

Lunéville   19 Aug   Col   SEVENTH ARMY

SECOND ARMY   FIRST ARMY (Dubail)   de Saales   Rhine

(de Castelnau)   III   COLMAR   Neu-Breisach

Charmes   19 Aug   10 Aug

Épinal   7 Aug.   Thann   MULHOUSE

Langres   8 Aug   Altkirch

"THE PENTAGON"   Belfort   BASLE

Dijon   Besançon   S W I T Z E R L A N D

British Expeditionary Force (beginning concentration 14 August)
French armies (concentration areas on 14 August)
Belgian army (positions on 17 August)
German armies (concentration areas on 14 August)
German armies (positions on 17 August)
Military fortresses or fortified towns
Defended areas

THE CAMPAIGN IN ALSACE

7 August French from Belfort take Altkirch and Thann

8 August French capture Mulhouse

10 August Germans from Colmar and Neu-Breisach retake Mulhouse

19 August French reoccupy Mulhouse; other forces move towards Colmar

28 August French retire, leaving a small force to occupy Thann to decide whether to dispatch the nation's little army across the Channel. Though Grey and such soldiers as Henry Wilson always intended this to happen, and had promised the French that it would, some important people remained strongly hostile. They believed that the country could, and should, fight an exclusively naval campaign. Much of Britain's pre-war planning for a continental struggle had focused on waging economic war upon Germany through blockade, but these schemes atrophied, partly because of Foreign Office unwillingness to upset neutrals – and a desire to sustain British trade. Fear of precipitating a disastrous global financial collapse, such as already loomed, was another critical incentive for caution. Moreover, amid a crisis in which the fate of Europe seemed likely to be settled in weeks, there was little interest in a blockade which must take many months to achieve an impact. There were serious proponents of a scheme to exploit the Royal Navy's command of the sea by putting ashore a landing force on Germany's Baltic coast, thus opening a second front.

Lord Northcliffe, the most powerful newspaper magnate in Europe, owner of *The Times* and the *Daily Mail*, was at first vehemently opposed to any continental commitment. 'What is this I hear about a British Expeditionary Force for France?' he cried to his senior executives. 'It is nonsense. Not a single soldier shall leave this country. We have a superb Fleet, which shall give all the assistance in its power, but I will not support the sending out of this country of a single British soldier. What about invasion? What about our own country? Not a single soldier will go with my consent. Say so in the paper tomorrow.' Yet this was a rare moment when the press lord's assembled editors persuaded him to change his mind: Northcliffe's newspapers endorsed dispatch of a BEF.

At the War Council meeting of 5 August, some outlandish suggestions were made. Field-Marshal Sir John French profoundly mistrusted Britain's allies. He hankered after conducting a private British war, as far removed as possible from any activities in which the French army might choose to engage. At Downing Street, he proposed taking up positions around Antwerp. Lt. Gen. Sir Douglas Haig, who would command a corps, wrote following the meeting: 'I trembled at the reckless way Sir J. French spoke about "the advantages" of the BEF operating from Antwerp against the powerful and still intact German army!' Haig, who would eventually become the most famous – or notorious – British general of the war, voiced prudent fears about the risk of defeat in detail 'if we separated from the French at the outset of the campaign', and expressed agreement with Kitchener that the war would not be short.

Fifty-three in 1914, Haig was an intelligent and relatively well-educated man who had entered Sandhurst late after spending three years at Oxford. No aristocrat – he was the scion of a Scottish whisky-distilling family – he had gained a reputation as an able administrator and an effective field commander. Haig's posthumous reputation suffered grievously from publication of his wartime diaries, which exposed an apparent callousness about the horrendous losses on the Western Front, and a distasteful bent for palace intrigue: he exploited ruthlessly for his own purposes his wife Doris's position as a maid of honour to the Queen. He was a man of his time, class and condition who will never command the affection of posterity, but against the drear backcloth of the 1914–18 Western Front, where no general of any nationality much enhanced his reputation, Haig was an abler soldier than caricature allows.

At the 5 August War Council meeting, however, he suggested that Britain should hold back from sending any troops to the continent for several months, until a stronger army could be appropriately organised, trained and equipped. Such an idea appalled Henry Wilson, who rightly pointed out that the fate of France would be settled within weeks, if not days: Britain's ally needed immediately whatever men the country could send. The government's decision to dispatch an expeditionary force was overwhelmingly attributable to Wilson. Seldom in history has a single relatively junior general exercised such a profound influence.

Next day, the War Council authorised the movement to France of a BEF consisting of one cavalry and four infantry divisions. Two infantry formations – the balance of the army available for immediate deployment – were temporarily held back for home defence, which included suppression of potential civil disorder among the disaffected working class. In consequence, the BEF's strength would initially be dwarfed by that of France, and even of Belgium. Nonetheless, this represented the government's most important strategic decision of the war. Given the instinctive insularity of most British politicians as well as citizens, the inevitability of the country joining the continental land struggle should never be assumed.

Command of the BEF was given, as expected, to French, a sixty-one-year-old cavalryman of Irish lineage thought to have distinguished himself in the Boer War. He had been messily involved in the 'Curragh Mutiny' a few months earlier, during which he resigned as Chief of the Imperial General Staff. Though reinstated, he himself feared his career at an end. The Liberal government and many society wives found Sir John sympathetic, but his qualifications for high command were meagre. A man of strong prejudices but limited intellect, he had never commanded large forces. He spoke scarcely a word of French, though on the continent he would have to work closely with Britain's key ally. Haig wrote on 11 August: 'I know that French is quite unfit for this great Command at a time of crisis in our Nation's History,' and most of his peers agreed. Wilson would probably have been named as French's chief of staff – he was the only British senior soldier who enjoyed the confidence of Joffre – but he had been deeply compromised by support for the Orange cause in the Ulster crisis. He was thus obliged to content himself with the curious title of sub-chief of staff, under Sir Archibald Murray.

Lloyd George later looked back on the discussions and confusions of those days: 'it was my first experience of the fallibility of the Military Leaders – the stubborn miscalculation, muddle and lack of co-ordination, which resulted in mowing down the flower of the finest armies ever put in the field by France and England'. These were the words of a politician whom the war made extravagantly bitter against soldiers; the Chancellor's abuse of Kitchener, especially, was overdone. The best that can be said of French was that his subsequent conduct as a commander-in-chief in the field was little more egregious than that of his counterparts of the other European armies, on both sides.

Kitchener's instructions to Sir John, issued on 10 August, included a critical passage, which throughout the weeks that followed the C-in-C interpreted as a mandate for pusillanimity: 'It must be recognised from the outset that the numerical strength of the British force – and its contingent reinforcements – is strictly limited, and with this consideration kept strictly in view it will be obvious that the greatest care must be exercised towards a minimum of losses and wastage ... The high courage and discipline of your troops should, and certainly will, have fair and full opportunity of display during the campaign, but officers may well be reminded that in this – their first – experience of European warfare, a greater measure of caution must be employed than under former conditions of hostilities against an untrained adversary.' In other words, Kitchener knew that the coming collision would bear no resemblance to the massacres he himself had conducted in the Sudan sixteen years earlier, pitting artillery and Gatling guns against Dervish spearmen.

Late in 1912, after the second Morocco crisis, a Railways Executive Committee had been established, to plan their management in the event of war. This now swung into action with impressive efficiency, transporting the BEF to its embarkation ports. But even as French's men were being conveyed across the Channel, shielded by the Royal Navy's protecting guns, wrangling persisted at the War Office about what they should do when they arrived. Kitchener expected the Germans to advance across the Meuse, and thus favoured a British concentration at Amiens, well back from the Belgian frontier. Henry Wilson expressed impatience about the secretary for war's attitude, writing after a meeting on the afternoon of 12 August: 'he still thinks the Germans are coming north of the Meuse in great force, and will swamp us before we concentrate'.

Kitchener's judgement was correct – indeed, his strategic assessment showed far more powerful insight than that of France's general staff – but Wilson was justified in asserting that the foremost objective of British forces must be to frustrate a lightning German triumph – a blitzkrieg, though the word had not then been invented. That sultry day at the War Office, Kitchener gave way to Wilson's view, and agreed that the BEF should advance towards the frontier fortress city of Maubeuge, on the left of the French army.

All was now movement, haste. The *Illustrated London News* carried a photograph of horses being collected and branded at the London stables of the big newsagents' chain WH Smith. Volunteer drill halls and depots were customarily located in city centres, and thus one mobilised battery of Territorial horse artillery drove through the heart of London's financial district on its way to war. In Paris a fashionable priest, Abbé Mugnier, sat at a café outside the Gare du Nord hearing the confessions of gilded young men leaving for the front: 'Quick, *Monsieur l'Abbé*, my train's nearly due out!' A visitor at the mansion of Comte Greffulhe at 8, Rue d'Astorg passed in the courtyard a cluster of young men whom he vaguely recognised – then identified as the Count's footmen, leaving to join their regiments. Within the echoing, deserted rooms where so many glittering parties had been held, he found the house's master being served a cold lunch brought in from a restaurant by his butler, a last gesture before this man, too, doffed the Count's livery to join the garrison of Belfort.

Along thousands of miles of Europe's railway tracks, trainloads of soldiers rolled at sedate speed towards their appointed battlefields, proclaiming a somewhat affected dislike for the enemy. Frenchmen chalked the sides of their carriages with such slogans as '*Mort aux Boches!*'; British soldiers favoured 'Hang the Kaiser!' German troop trains were decorated with freshly cut green boughs. A Freiburger among the crowd watching his city's infantry regiment march out on 6 August was impressed by the men's spotless uniforms and looks of determination. 'Suddenly a cheer: the machine-gun company came ... Then the field kitchens ... Then the ration- and pack-wagons; all the horses in new livery, all the wagons, all the equipment in top condition. It was a wonderful sight.' In Schneidemühl Elfriede Kuhr saw the town's regiment march to the station sturdily singing '*Die Wacht am Rhein*' amid applauding crowds. 'Shoulder to shoulder they streamed onto the platform like a grey tidal wave. All the soldiers had long garlands of flowers around their necks or pinned on their breasts. Asters, stocks and roses stuck out of the rifle barrels as if they were intended to shoot flowers at the enemy. The soldiers' faces were serious. I had expected them to be laughing and exultant.' The German moral code of the day demanded that young women serving at station charity canteens should be chaperoned by older matrons. A local mayor warned censoriously: 'Behind the army that bears arms follows the army of love.'

Little Elfriede cried out to a tall soldier leaning out of a window as the train rolled away from the crowd on the platform, '*Leb wohl!*' – 'Farewell!' The man called back good-naturedly, '*Auf wiedersehen, Mädel.*' In 312 hours 11,000 trains carried 119,754 officers, 2.1 million men and 600,000 horses across Germany to concentration areas on the frontiers of France, Belgium and Luxembourg. The infantry, cavalry and artillery of Moltke's seven western armies crossed the Rhine bridges in 560 trains a day, each of fifty-four wagons.

Deep in Russia, Sergei Kondurashkin watched other long trains laden with troops lurch away northwards, carriage buffers bumping against each other: 'Women bade them farewell with howling and wailing. Weak with grief, they would collapse on each other's breasts, [crying out]: "Oh, wasn't he my good one? Wasn't he my loved one?"' As the horses and men of the Sumskoi Hussars jingled and clattered through Moscow, a passer-by blessed the soldiers and presented an icon to the officer commanding the machine-gun platoon.

Lt. Vladimir Littauer's parents lived in St Petersburg, and he had no time to visit Moscow's central telephone office, the only place from which he might have placed a call to tell them of his departure. In any event, he wrote later, they would have expressed little emotion. Their attitude was that their son had chosen a military career, and part of his contract was to fight: 'They would simply have wished me luck and said "God protect you."' At the station, many horses resisted boarding the dark-red wooden freight cars. But somehow they were loaded and the regiment set off. As successive trains coasted south-west through Rzhev station, Russia's soldiers bound for the front glimpsed the figure of a white-haired old sergeant who stiffly saluted their occupants, tears pouring down his cheeks.

There were other lachrymose moments. Prince Lichnowsky cried cease-lessly on leaving the German embassy in London, while the King of Württemberg sobbed as he watched his regiments departing for the front. Winston Churchill cried when he bade farewell to Henry Wilson, en route for France, causing the staff officer to write: 'I never liked him so much.' Though some of the British soldiers who set forth were veterans of colo-nial wars, others knew astonishingly little of their trade. Among the Irish Guards' officers was Lt. Lord Castlerosse, who had scarcely done a day's military training in his life: his commanding officer was merely a family friend who agreed to take the young man to war as a personal favour; the Guards made their own rules of enlistment. A British expatriate returning home from Calais passed in the Channel one of the steamers carrying the BEF southwards. He heard a stentorian voice bellow from among hundreds of men arrayed along its rails, 'We'll die hearty!' The Englishman reflected, with the condescension of his age and kind, 'What splendid phrases this war is bringing forth from the throats of simple men!'

At 5 a.m. on 3 August, Charles Stein and his comrades of the Belgian Grenadiers were awakened by bugle calls. Two hours later they paraded, and were issued with field dressings. Their colonel addressed the regiment, telling them that it seemed inevitable Belgium must fight to defend itself. As one man, they cried '*Vive le Roi! Vive la Belgique! Vive le colonel!*' They marched out past crowds of onlookers, some of whom cheered, but others – especially women – cried.

Nevertheless, battle still seemed an unfrightening and indeed exciting idea. Jože Cvelbar was a promising young artist, now setting off to serve as an Austrian infantryman. He wrote in confusion to a friend: 'Only God knows if I shall come back; but if I do, it will be as a man. I understand how men grow up in such circumstances … This year, so many things have overwhelmed me. I have awoken from my dreams. I had been planning to travel to Venice.' Lt. Charles de Gaulle wrote: 'Goodbye, my rooms, my books, my familiar objects. How much more intense life does seem, and how the smallest trifles stand out in relief, when perhaps everything may be coming to an end.' But he professed himself undaunted, as befitted a professional soldier, anticipating the 'unknown adventure' which he 'glori-fied in advance … without horror'. Capt. Plieux de Diusse was one of those who cherished high and joyful illusions: 'The front – magic words evoking such glory and heroism which combines every finest and noblest human quality. The banishment of self in the interests of defending the nation ... It is with barely concealed excitement that I set off.'

On Sunday, 16 August a jovial, ebullient party, clad in field grey but glittering with orders and decorations, gathered at the Potsdam station to board eleven trains bearing the Kaiser, Moltke and their staffs to a new advanced headquarters at Coblenz. The chief of staff had said a few days earlier, 'If there is any justice left in the world, then we must win this war,' and this was still Moltke's mood. To the disgust of subordinates, in deference to his frail health his wife Eliza and her maid had been given the Kaiser's leave to accompany them, providing domestic solace for the man who had done more than any other to bring war about. As the carriages slid out of the station on their overnight journey, the uniformed passengers were impressed by the meticulous arrangements – every compartment named, seats for meals allocated as soon as the train set forth. A few, however, were troubled by the extravagant comfort, delicious food and wine. One wrote wonderingly, 'Are we real warriors, or sybarites?'

A ten-year-old boy named Yves Congar, who lived just inside the Franco-German border at Sedan, had written exuberantly on 29 July: 'I can only think about war. I would like to be a soldier and fight.' Instead, however, a few days later the first brutal manifestations of the reality of conflict descended upon his community: the vanguard of the German host crossed the frontier into France. Those who occupied Sedan pitilessly appropriated cars, horses, wine, food – even domestic telephones. Yves Congar's father was among those seized as a hostage for the community's obedience.

Gingerly toes dipped in the war's inaugural trickles of blood. The first dead soldier seen by Florence Farmborough, an Englishwoman serving as a volunteer nurse in Russia, was a little officer's groom named Vasily who expired in hospital after being kicked in the head by his master's horse as he left for the front. She crept into the mortuary to look at a body 'so small and thin and wizened that he looked more like a child than a grown man. His set face was grey-white, never had I seen that strange colour on a face before, and his cheeks had sunken into hollows.' Sugarlumps had been placed on the man's eyelids, to keep them closed. Henceforward, across the battlefields of Europe, the dead would be denied such refinements. The overture was ended. The fantasies of the first days of war were now overtaken by terrible realities.

4

Disaster on the Drina

The Western Front would become the cockpit of the war, but it was in the east that the killing began, when Conrad Hötzendorf's Austro-Hungarian army launched its campaign of vengeance against Serbia. In the early hours of 29 July Belgrade's citizens were awakened by gunfire from the direction of the riverside frontier fortress of Zemun. A few hours later Austrian shallow-draft naval monitors steamed down the Sava and the Danube and began shelling the Serb capital, hitting some buildings near the cathedral. The streets quickly emptied. There was a thunderous explosion as Serbian soldiers detonated charges which wrecked the river bridge linking their country with the Hapsburg Empire. To the engineers' satisfaction, the rubble fell on an Austrian gunboat, most of whose crew drowned.

Crowds of would-be fugitives besieged three trains at Belgrade station, raising steam to depart eastwards. When at last they puffed forth, colourfully attired families and their portable possessions crowded even the carriage roofs. Panic broke out when the first train was bracketed by shells from Austrian warships on the river: 'The sound of gunfire and explosions of shells mingled with terrible crying and screaming from terrified children and women,' wrote Sveta Milutinović. 'Luckily no one was hit, because the chief engineer dashed through the killing zone at full speed and then turned towards Topčider ... [Meanwhile in Belgrade,] after the first barrage, many women started dressing up their male children in shawls and skirts, believing that enemy soldiers would not mistreat girls.'

Serb Foreign Office official Živan Živanović wrote: 'The war that Austria-Hungary declared on Serbia in July 1914 came as suddenly and unexpectedly as any earthquake, fire or great inundation. Did not Serbia, after the Balkan wars, need peace more than ever?' Such assertions were disingenuous: Živanović was brother-in-law to 'Apis' – Dragutin Dimitrijević, sponsor of Franz Ferdinand's assassins. Even if the Serbian people did not deserve the cataclysm which descended upon their country following Austria-Hungary's declaration of war, those privy to the Black Hand's machinations could scarcely profess injured innocence. But that, of course, is what they did.

Serbia's leaders knew they could not aspire to absolute military victory over Austria. If, however, their army could merely stay in the ring until their mighty allies triumphed on battlefields elsewhere, war would be worth something – indeed, everything. A pan-Slav state, Yugoslavia, could rise from the ashes of the Hapsburg Empire. In schools, children were taught the geography of former Serb lands – Macedonia, Dalmatia, Bosnia, Herzegovina, Croatia, Banat and Bachka – as part of their own. The view across the Danube, wrote a sympathetic English visitor, 'is dear to every Serbian, who looks longingly across at his old empire, and the homes of his compatriots dotted among the tender browns and blues and yellows of the plains'. For such things they were happy to fight: an ancient national poem proclaimed 'I am a Serbian, born to be a soldier.'

Meanwhile on the other side, the Austrian ruling caste embarked upon its chosen war oblivious of the gulf between its army's peacock self-image and the sclerotic reality. Alexander von-Brosch Aarenau was a prominent general who had served for years as an aide to Franz Ferdinand. He wrote exultantly on 29 July: 'More than America, Austria is a country with boundless potential. It has suddenly passed from humiliation and exhaustion, indolence, frivolity and cowardice, into a mood of such iron calm, dynamism and gravity that one becomes very proud of one's fatherland and its leaders! How impressive was the ultimatum [to Serbia]; how smoothly … mobilisation followed; and now, to render impossible any gratuitous interference despite the growling of the Russian bear, comes the declaration of war – surprising even to a soldier! Each stroke has followed the last in such a fashion that Bismarck and Moltke [the Elder] together would not have been able to conclude matters in a manner more worthy, energetic, and … skilful. Serbia has been caught totally off guard … and now stumbles along with the Great Powers which are completely stunned, and already realise that any intervention would be useless.' Arenau's remarks emphasise the complacency with which Austria's commanders, Conrad foremost among them, viewed the continental catastrophe. Their mood infected ordinary citizens. Sigmund Freud wrote: 'Perhaps for the first time in 30 years I feel an Austrian, and would like to try again with this Empire, for which there is so little hope. The mood is excellent everywhere. A valiant initiative has had a liberating effect.'

Austria had plunged Europe into a great war to punish – indeed, destroy – Serbia. But the Central Powers now faced much larger and more dangerous opponents. Close cooperation was essential, to deal with the allies on the battlefield. On 30 July Lt. Col. Karl von Kageneck, the German military attaché in Vienna, pleaded with Moltke's deputy 'to play with absolutely open cards in order not to repeat the [negative] experience of all coalition wars'. In absolute contradiction of this, however, nothing was done to make collaboration effective. Reason should have persuaded Conrad to dispatch only a small force to frustrate any initiative by the Serbs, while the overwhelming bulk of the Austrian army met the threat from the Russians, northwards in Polish Galicia. The Serbs should have been addressed only if and when the Russians were beaten.

The Kaiser wrote to Vienna on 31 July: 'in this hard struggle it is of the highest importance that Austria should direct her principal strength against Russia and not divide it by launching a simultaneous offensive against Serbia. This is all the more important as a large part of my army will be tied down by France. In this gigantic struggle which we are embarking upon shoulder to shoulder, Serbia plays a quite subordinate role, which demands only the most absolutely necessary defensive measures.' This was common sense, but Conrad ignored it. Passion and muddled thinking, in this as in much else, persuaded the Austrian chief of staff to divide his forces. He committed nineteen divisions to fight Serbia's eleven, and sent another thirty to meet fifty Russian formations in Galicia. The Germans and Austrians shared blame for failure to coordinate a strategy; each nation merely did as seemed best to its own commanders. Conrad tasked two armies in Bosnia, initially separated by seventy miles, to invade Serbia and its junior ally Montenegro from the west. A third army in Hungary was made available for three August weeks only – as if for a limited theatre run – before it was redeployed to Galicia. This force was to strike south across the Sava river west of Belgrade.

Operations against Serbia were commanded by Gen. Oskar Potiorek, governor of Bosnia. The man who had bungled Franz Ferdinand's security arrangements in Sarajevo was invited a month later to direct a crucial military operation. Potiorek was a bachelor who had devoted his life monastically to his profession, while remaining ignorant of every aspect of it that was either modern or important; he had never seen a day's action. The Austrian army was poorly trained and equipped, and its Slav soldiers were disaffected. Commanders neglected such tiresome details as artillery ballistics; Potiorek was personally responsible for frustrating the purchase of modern mountain guns, which would have been invaluable in Serbian terrain. Infantry–artillery coordination was non-existent. At a 1906 strategy conference, Potiorek cut short staff speculation about supply problems: 'waging war means going hungry! If I start an operation today with 200,000 men, I know I can attain my objectives with just 100,000 of them.'

Any delusion that Conrad and his subordinates were chivalrous cavaliers, adorned with the graces of a Vienna ballroom, vanished in the face of their brutish conduct of the war. Even before invading Serbia, they opened a second front against their own minorities suspected of disloyalty: on 26 July military rule was imposed on Bosnia and Herzegovina. Hundreds of Serbs were arrested, including three members of the Austrian parliament. In Slovenia martial law was introduced, proclaimed by local officials borne from district to district in horse-drawn carriages. At each crossroads a little procession halted, a drummer beat a roll to summon attention, then a dignitary clad in black coat and top hat read the proclamation.

Passers-by scarcely heeded the ceremony because, in the words of Slovenian Valentin Oblak, 'they did not realise the full implications' of the decree, which were draconian indeed. Opposition newspapers were shut down; fifty executions were carried out in Dubrovnik and more elsewhere. In Austria some Czechs were badly beaten up – one such victim died in Linz – for allegedly shouting 'Up with Serbia!' A consequence of such actions was to provoke some thousands of the Empire's two million Serb subjects to cross the border and enlist in Belgrade's army.

The people of Serbia, meanwhile, were not merely fiercely nationalistic; they also knew the business of soldiering. In the recent Balkan wars, they had gained experience such as the Hapsburg armies lacked. They were unafraid of sacrifice: foreign visitors often remarked upon the popularity of *Coriolanus*, bloodiest of Shakespeare's plays, with Serbian theatre audiences. They saw conflict with Austria as offering a unique opportunity to advance the pan-Slav cause. Out of a population of less than four million, they mobilised an astonishing half a million men, of whom four-fifths were now deployed on the western frontier, while their Montenegrin allies, 45,000 strong, took up positions further south.

They would be fighting in their own mountains, with aid from local partisans – *komitadji*, as they were known. *The Times*'s military correspondent wrote that the Serbian army was 'not to be despised', and would give the Austrians 'much trouble', which proved prescient. There was a classless comradeship among Serb soldiers, who acknowledged few

distinctions of rank: a private might salute an officer, then shake hands
with him if they knew each other back at home, in a fashion implausible
in any other warring army. 'We are all peasants in Serbia – that is our
pride,' a Serbian colonel told an American correspondent. They were short
of weapons, however – a third of the men mobilised in 1914 lacked rifles,
and local ammunition production was sluggish. At the end of July, so
desperate was the country's need that police conducted a house-to-house
search for rifles. Uniforms were threadbare leftovers from the Balkan wars;
many conscripts could only be provided with tunics and hats – *šajkače* –
and some did not even get those. The chief of staff told the War Ministry
that new recruits should be instructed to bring from home their own
clothing and boots, because 'there would be no uniforms, at least initially'.
But the Serbs liked fighting, and were good at it. At first, they approached
the war as a romantic adventure: every regiment advanced towards the
front led by two or three gypsies, playing bagpipes or their national style
of fiddle, singing love songs, paeans to victory, epic chants.

Živan Živanović, brother-in-law of Apis, described the febrile optimism: 'The people of Živkovci were saying: "We have beaten the Turks, we
have seen off the Bulgarians, now it's the [Austrians'] turn; if God wills we
shall show them who are the better men."' Geologist Tadija Pejović
marvelled at the spirit of soldiers whom he saw marching towards the
front from the army's rear base at Kragujevac, armed only with spades and
mattocks. They joked exuberantly: 'These are to bury all the dead
Germans!' – '*Schwaben*', Serbs' generic term alike for the subjects of Franz
Joseph and Wilhelm II. And while the Austrians fielded only 10cm guns
and lacked heavy artillery, the Serbs had modern 15cm howitzers, and
soon showed that they knew how to use them.

Their chief of staff, Marshal Radomir Putnik, was a competent soldier,
though sixty-seven years old; few Serbs were troubled by his close association with the Black Hand. The July crisis caught the tough veteran taking
the waters at a Hungarian spa, having left his country's war plans locked
in a Belgrade safe to which only he had a key. Subordinates had to use
guncotton to gain access to the documents; the Austrians, in the last courteous gesture of the war, allowed the general to return home across their
territory. After a brief brush with pneumonia, by 5 August Putnik was at
his post, directing operations.

The Serb government knew that Belgrade, on the country's Danube
frontier with Hungary, was immediately vulnerable, and evacuated east to
Niš its archives and personnel, together with such key envoys as Russia's

Vasily Strandman. Amid the chaos of mobilisation, the trains crawled, taking twice the normal time to complete the journey. Once ensconced in their new quarters, Serbian ministers besieged the Russian mission with demands for arms and equipment – their first request was for 200,000 uniforms and four wireless transmitters.

A fundamental insouciance nonetheless persisted, described by Finance Ministry civil servant Milan Stojadinović. 'We were still oblivious of what we and our country were getting into … We were convinced: Serbia is going to win. I could not understand then and I cannot understand now: whence this optimism? Whence this insane belief in victory? There were four million of us against forty-five [million]. And yet this faith in assured victory made us embrace the war contented, merry, happy, singing songs. Throughout my own ministry, for the two days and nights needed to prepare for the move [to Niš], one song was constantly repeated with glowing eyes and full hearts, sung by one group in their room, as another rested next door:

> 'Bulgaria, traitor,
> Came to fight at Bregalnica [a battle in the Second Balkan War].
> Go, go Austria!
> To await the same fate!'

But when the Austrians began to shell the Serbian capital from their Danube gunboats and batteries on the Hungarian shore opposite, Belgrade's citizens suffered terribly. Policemen hurried from street to street through rubble and broken glass, dust and bleeding people, thunderous detonations; they warned citizens to take refuge or fly. Many seized what possessions they could carry, then trudged towards the precarious safety of the countryside, or paid small fortunes for a cart or carriage to drive them there. When Živan Živanović first glimpsed Belgrade under bombardment, 'I felt how much the Old Town deserved the name it was given by the Turks: "the home of wars". From every side shells were exploding upon the city.'

Slavka Mihajlović, a doctor who had served in her country's earlier conflicts, marvelled at the fashion in which those who lingered in the capital adjusted to the new reality: 'As soon as the gunfire paused for a time, coffee houses reopened and people hastened back to them. Over a glass of wine and *rakija* they gathered the latest news before hurrying home, anticipating a new outbreak of shelling. Enemy fire ranged constantly over

Serbia, 1914

1 Serbia's Strategic Isolation

0 100 200
Miles

Berlin
POLAND
GERMANY
RUSSIA
Vienna
AUSTRIA-HUNGARY
ROMANIA
Belgrade
SERBIA
BULGARIA
ITALY
MONTENEGRO
GREECE
Constantinople
TURKEY

2 Austria's August "Strafexpedition"

12-24 August

AUSTRIAN SECOND ARMY

Sr. Mitrovica
Pancevo
Sava
Shabatz
Belgrade
Danube
AUSTRIAN FIFTH ARMY
XIII CORPS VIII CORPS
Jadar
Mt Cer
MAIN SERBIAN FORCE
Kolubara
Srebrnica
Drina
Valjevo (Putnik's H.Q.)
AUSTRIAN SIXTH ARMY
SERBIAN UZHITSE (UŽICE) GROUP
Uzhitse

Serbian units guarding Belgrade

0 10 20
Miles

3 Austrian November Advance

- ⇢⇢⇢ Austrian advances 6-30 Nov.
- ⇢⇢⇢ Austrian front line 30 Nov.
- ▬▬▬ Serbian front line 30 Nov.

0   20
Miles

Sr. Mitrovica
Sava
Velino Selo
Drina
Sava
Zemin
Pancevo
Belgrade
Danube
Sabac
Loznitsa
Jadar
Lesnica
Valjevo
Kolubara
Rama
Mt Cer
Railway to Turkey
Srebrnica
Uzhitse
W. Morava
Kragujevac
Putnik's H.Q.
Niš

4 Serbian December Counter-Attacks

⬅ Serbian advances 3-15 December

0   20
Miles

15 December, Austrians expelled from Serbia

1-14 December, Serbian capital occupied by Austrians

Sava
Sr. Mitrovica
Sabac
Velino Selo
Sava
Zemin
Pancevo
Belgrade
Danube
Jadar
Loznitsa
Lesnica
Kolubara
Rama
Mt Cer
Valjevo
Drina
Srebrnica
SERBIAN FRONT LINE 2 December
Kragujevac
Uzhitse
W. Morava
Niš

different parts of the city, seeking to spread terror as widely as possible ... There were lots of problems with food. At every lull in the firing one saw women, children and old people hurrying hither and thither with baskets, trying to fulfil their needs as quickly as possible.'

Jovan Žujović of the Foreign Ministry spent 6 August helping staff at Belgrade's Geological Institute pack up its precious collection of meteorites. But having done so, they could find no means to remove the crates before the Austrians recommenced shelling. Next day Žujović laboured among a crowd of citizens trying to save the French Association's library, set ablaze by shells. It nonetheless burned to the ground, followed that night by much of the city university. It became obvious, wrote the diarist bitterly, that the Austrians were targeting cultural institutions. He removed the meteorite collection to his own home for safekeeping.

Meanwhile, further south and west, shrouded in dust clouds, two Austrian armies tramped across Bosnia towards the Serb and Montenegrin frontiers at the Drina river. Infantrymen, bent under sixty-pound packs, sweated prodigiously in the summer heat. They had been issued with extra rations of canned meat, which most now discarded rather than carry – to their later regret, because the army's field kitchens and supply carts lagged far behind its soldiers. 'On Monday we marched through Jablanica to Rama,' wrote Matija Malešič of Graf von Lacy's regiment. 'The heat was terrible. Thirsty, thirsty, thirsty, our kit heavy as lead, unbearable heat and yet we must keep going, keep going. It is so hard that a man instinctively asks himself why he was brought into this world. Was it just to suffer?'

Austrian drivers battered the army's few precious motor vehicles at reckless speed along rough, unmetalled Balkan tracks. Volunteer chauffeur Alex Pallavicini wrote despairingly on 6 August: 'If we go on like this our cars will soon be wrecked. People seem to think an automobile is indestructible.' Crowds of men, interminable columns of carts and gun batteries, clogged every Bosnian approach route to the front, making it difficult to get rations to the vanguards. 'It is hard to believe this logjam will ever break,' wrote Pallavicini after a day spent amidst the traffic chaos. 'It took me over nine hours to cover 40 km.' Some soldiers told Cpl. Egon Kisch that they had found the body of a comrade whose head and arms had been cut off by the Serbs, the skin flayed from his legs. Kisch wrote with sensible caution: 'If this story is true – which I doubt – then the Serbs mutilated this poor guy not out of delight in bestiality, but to frighten us before we meet them in action.'

As they approached the Drina river, men were bemused by what Kisch described as 'big, buzzing flies' filling the air. Then these innocents grasped that they were hearing their first passing bullets. On 10 August, Potiorek's troops began operations to cross the river at three points between fifty and a hundred miles west and south of Belgrade. At Batar, one formation advanced across a newly built pontoon bridge linking Bosnia and Serbia, led by a band playing martial airs. A Serb shell fell in its midst, killing some musicians, blasting others into the water. Their music stopped.

The bulk of the Austro-Hungarian troops gathered in darkness on the west bank, preparing to cross at dawn, covered by a bombardment. Suddenly their own shells started falling short, exploding in the water or among waiting infantrymen. Cpl. Kisch saw one round detonate atop a tree beneath which a divisional commander and his staff were gathered in their finery. '*Herrgott!*' expostulated the shaken general. 'That could have done for us. We'd better get back.' At daybreak, however, the Serb defenders retreated from the far bank, conceding the passage of the Drina to the invaders.

Potiorek seemed untroubled by these embarrassments, which bordered on farce. He wrote in his diary with some complacency on 12 August: 'Today my war has begun.' Only on the 15th were the Austrians firmly established on the eastern shore, and moving sluggishly forward. Alex Pallavicini wrote: 'The whole horizon is filled with pillars of smoke which mark our troops' advance. New fires keep appearing: the ubiquitous straw stacks seem to be put there for that purpose. Heavy firing from enemy artillery. The spectacle resembled a splendid field exercise.' By contrast, Cpl. Kisch's narrative is a tale of woe: incessant marching interrupted only by snatched dozes in open fields; clothing and kit soaked by river crossings. 'Though the enemy was in front of us, we faced other and more terrible foes: the packs on our backs; exhaustion; rough scrub that tore clothes and skin to shreds; stinging nettles; hunger; frost at night after the heat of the afternoons – thus, we advanced to Lešnica. Occasionally we passed a *kutja* [wooden house] or a pillaged village. Chickens provided the only sign of life.'

The invasion of Serbia provoked widespread resistance by armed civilians. The French had employed such tactics in their 1870–71 war with Prussia, and they would be widely used in World War II. But in 1914 Serbia was the only front where they became commonplace – to the fury of the Austrians. Alex Pallavicini reported being shot at by guerrillas who exploited the cover of huge cornfields, several miles behind the front. As one Austrian unit was advancing through a wood, a *komitadji* suddenly appeared and fired point-blank at Lt. Hugo Schulz, who fell dead. The Serb, in his turn, was riddled with bullets, but the Austrians gazing down on his corpse noted that his eyes were still open, his features set in a grin, 'apparently contented that he had exchanged his own life for that of an enemy officer'. Most partisans adopted a subtler approach, waiting until enemy troops had passed before firing into their backs, prompting chaos and wild outbreaks of shooting.

'[Our men] scattered like startled chickens,' wrote Egon Kisch, 'firing right and left, ahead and behind without an enemy in sight or any order given. Thus they wounded our own people in large numbers ... Only a few men fired, but they did a lot of mischief. Beside me a corporal constantly blew his whistle in an effort to stop the shooting. Suddenly I heard a body fall, turned and saw him lying on the ground, blood gushing from his forehead. A moment later, he became still. It took ten minutes before whistles and shouted orders caused the firing to stop, so that we could resume the advance. There were awful sights in our path: an occasional dead Serb, and many more wounded comrades from our own regiment. This was our first skirmish.'

The Austrians were determined that their war should be waged according to their rules. They deemed guerrilla activity an affront, and moreover feared that any Serb success would rouse sympathetic Slav minorities within the Empire. Inside Hapsburg Bosnia, they adopted a policy of pre-emptive repression: groups of Franz Joseph's Serb subjects were herded aboard trains as hostages, threatened with summary execution in the event of any *komitadji* sabotage attack. Meanwhile, in Serbia, a corps commander told his officers to ensure that their men were aware of 'our moral and numerical superiority to the point of fanaticism'. The chief of Austrian intelligence, Col. Oskar von Hranilović, had warned that the army was likely to meet guerrillas. It was agreed that resistance would be met by ruthless application of *Kriegsnotwehrrecht*, the martial law of self-defence.

Thus thousands of Serb civilians, most of them innocent, were summarily shot or hanged. On 16 August, for instance, five '*Tschuzen*' – Slovene or Croatian peasants – were dragged in front of the colonel of the 11th Infantry, denounced as alleged partisans. The regimental adjutant demanded: 'Who saw them fire?' Some voices answered promptly: 'The captain and ten men.' The hapless peasants were led before an embankment, ordered to kneel, and shot. Alex Pallavicini's account of other such incidents is rich in circumstantial detail, but it seems rash to accept at face value his allegations against the Serb victims. He described how, on 17 August, his column was fired upon from a cornfield behind the front. Austrian patrols sent to investigate returned with sixty-three prisoners; they claimed that some women and children among them were caught carrying rifles, and that they had found a priest in possession of grenades.

'An hour later,' Pallavicini wrote, 'only a mass grave was visible. In order not to upset [our] soldiers by [the sound of] shooting, these people were bayoneted to death. The priest's beard had supposedly been ripped off – our men were that angry after the atrocities committed [against them]. In the afternoon I motored to Losnitza, where fourteen [Serbs] swung from a gallows. Oberstleutnant Kokotović had given orders to hang them. From rooftops our troops were still being fired upon. The hatred for us is boundless, and everyone is our enemy. The population is so deceitful that I must always anticipate being shot down by a child or an old woman, though to our faces they appear servile … We are not fighting against an army of 300,000 but against a whole nation. This seems a war driven by religious fervour. The priests are the worst agitators and monasteries the main centres of agitation.'

A striking feature of the many executions of civilians carried out on the Eastern Front, especially by the Austro-Hungarians in Serbia, is that they were photographed, and the images published. This was because, far from being a source of embarrassment to Vienna, the punitive killing of alleged *francs-tireurs* or spies was an important aspect of its policy; Conrad wanted as many people as possible to know about them. Hangmen presented bodies for the camera like sportsmen displaying animal trophies. An Austrian officer in Serbia recorded on 24 August:

I met a column of thirty [alleged *francs-tireurs*] assembled for execution. They were accompanied by a crowd of people including Prince Odescalchi and Lieutenant Weiss who could not refrain from boxing the ears of the poor wretches, bound as they were. We tried to restrain them but it was absolutely impossible. The execution place was at the edge of the woods behind the monastery. The [condemned Serbs] had to dig their own graves. Then they were sat down in front of the pit and bayoneted five at a time, three infantrymen stabbed each. A gruesome spectacle. Odescalchi behaved like a wild animal and would have liked to take part. It was terrible to see earth being heaped on the victims while some still lived – and indeed tried to climb out of the grave – and to see some of those rising from the grave. Our men behaved like savages. I could not stand the sight, and left them to it.

Gen. Kasimir Lütgendorf, a divisional commander in Serbia, caused 120 inhabitants of the town of Šabac to be shot on 17 August, allegedly following street fighting. In reality, the Serb army had evacuated Šabac without offering resistance, leaving behind only women, children and old people. It remains a mystery why Lütgendorf ordered these executions, though he was equally merciless to his own men. That same evening of 17 August, the general received a report on three men – Private Josef Ebert and medical orderlies Franz Buzek and Josef Douhlik – who had drunk themselves into a stupor on looted schnapps, then fired their rifles wildly.

Lütgendorf without further ado ordered the miscreants' execution, as an example to others. Disdaining to waste bullets, he decreed that they should be publicly bayoneted. The following night, as the wretched men loudly protested their innocence, they were led before Šabac's church in front of a large crowd, and absolved by a priest. There was a delay, because the designated bayonet squad declined to do its part, and had to be replaced. Black farce ensued, when the corps commander Gen. Karl Tersztyanzky arrived and ran forward, waving his cap and shouting 'Stop, stop!' to the executioners. He was too late: the three soldiers were dead. In 1920, Lütgendorf was tried and convicted for their killing by an Austrian court. He was never, however, indicted for the murder of Šabac's civilians. It is estimated that around 3,500 civilians were summarily killed by the Austrians during the first two weeks of their August campaign. Conrad was impenitent, claiming that 'the population, among them women, had taken part in the fighting and committed atrocities against Austrian troops … Anyone who knows the cultural level and mentality of the Balkan peoples will not be surprised about this.' Hungarians, traditional enemies of the Serbs, are alleged to have been responsible for some of the worst crimes against civilians.

Meanwhile in the forward areas, Austrian soldiers were gnawed by a growing conviction that the enemy knew his business much better than did their own commanders. Serbian gunners had surveyed terrain and registered targets in advance. Their tactics were ingenious and skilful: in the face of one attack on 18 August, the Serbs made a brisk withdrawal, then turned to deliver a hail of fire from a prepared fieldwork. The Austrian pursuit collapsed as soldiers threw themselves behind whatever cover they could find. Their foes began tossing grenades, which alarmed the Hapsburg troops, who had never seen such weapons. One Serb called out in German, 'Officers, step forward!' A captain named Wagner reflexively obeyed – and was shot down. Austrian commanders remained stubbornly unwilling to learn caution. When a headquarters was warned of Serbian field fortifications and concrete bunkers barring the way up a hillside ahead, staff dismissed the warning, because 'such a way of fighting seemed to them implausible'. Their troops paid the price in casualties.

Austrian soldiers were bewildered by a torrent of confused orders and counter-orders. As Serb volleys and salvoes scoured advancing columns, newcomers to battle strove to find figures of speech to describe its hellish sounds. Austrian doctor Johann Bachmann likened rifle fire to raindrops pattering on a roof during a storm, and artillery to the flat noise made by banging a stick hard on an extended umbrella, followed by a reverberation 'resembling a strongly-struck bass string. As a music-lover, I tried to judge the weight and decided that it approximated to the "a" of a bass note.' The Austrian commissariat almost collapsed. Driven to desperation by hunger, soldiers scavenged for food in the packs of dead and wounded comrades.

The invaders attacked Serbians entrenched on high ground at a position designated as Hill 404. After a fierce artillery and small-arms duel the defenders retreated, but the Austrians suffered heavy losses, especially among officers who rode forward on their chargers, sabres flashing in the sunlight, 'as if they wanted to offer the *komitadji* the most distinctive possible target', in the words of a wondering soldier. As that little battle died away, the invaders moved on to enter the village of Slatina. Here, for the first time, they met some civilians, who displayed astonishment on discovering that most of the enemy troops ravaging their countryside were Czechs, and thus their own 'Slav brethren'.

Cpl. Kisch dropped a prized cake of soap into the village pond, where it vanished forever. 'I looked wistfully after it,' he wrote, 'a last fragment of civilisation.' He was irked by a growing belief that everyone in Europe save himself was making money out of the war. On a captured position, he studied a miscellany of ammunition used by the Serbs. Many bullets, he observed crossly, were of Austrian and German manufacture: Hirtenberger Patronen-, Zündhütchen- und Metallwarenfabrik vorm. Keller & Co., Manfred Weiß Budapest; he picked up Turkish cartridges made by Deutsche Metallpatronenfabrik of Karlsruhe; Russian ammunition overprinted *Niemiezkaja fabrike oruschia I munizii, Berlin.* 'Other boxes come from Paris or from Liège, or prudently bear no imprint.'

The decisive phase of this first Serbian campaign began on 15 August, when the Austrians set out to assault formations defending Mount Cer, some twenty miles east of the Drina. It was a plateau, twelve miles long by four wide, rising amid mountains as high as 3,000 feet, looking down upon expansive cornfields. Heavily burdened Austrian infantry found the ascent hard going, and their artillery could not accompany them. *Komitadji* guerrillas sniped from surrounding woodland. On the evening of the 15th, in a torrential rainstorm, the invaders reached high ground. At 1 a.m., Serb troops closed in on the Austrian bivouacs, announcing themselves to unsuspecting sentries as Croatian Hapsburgs. Then, in darkness, they poured murderous rifle fire into the slumbering and wholly disorganised enemy. Serb soldiers cried out '*Kuku Mayka!*' – 'Holy Mother, help me!' – but their enemies needed divine assistance more.

Most of the Austrians' officers were killed while attempting to rally their men, including Joseph Fiedler, who became the first of thirty-five Hapsburg colonels to perish in those days. The divisional commander seized a rifle and fought at close quarters alongside his staff. A confused mêlée continued for hours, until at dawn both sides subsided into temporary exhaustion. Thereafter, the Serbs brought up reinforcements and artillery. Watched by their monarch King Peter from a nearby peak, they pounded the demoralised Austrians until at last they fell back.

The Serbs paid dearly for success, losing forty-seven officers and almost 3,000 men; in one regiment all four battalion commanders and all but three of sixteen company commanders were wounded or killed. Cavalry harassing Austrian rearguards suddenly found themselves facing machine-guns, which in a minute or two of firing annihilated two squadrons rash enough to charge them; here was a first earnest of the terrible vulnerability of horse soldiers to modern weapons, which would find conclusive proof in France. But Austrian losses were far heavier. Throughout the battle and in its aftermath, guerrillas harassed them at every turn. Mount Cer entered Serb folklore as a historic triumph. On 20 August, the survivors of the battle stumbled back into Bosnia from where they had started, having suffered 28,000 casualties and presented the Entente with its first victory of the war. The logical Austrian response would have been to sack Potiorek, who had presided over the fiasco. But court influence in Vienna sufficed to save the general's command, and indeed that of Conrad. Blame was instead laid upon the wretched Czech troops who spearheaded the operation; they were said to have let down their Emperor. An official investigation into the disaster at Mount Cer concluded that the ethnic German troops had been the only ones present who did their duty.

The Serbs were not strong enough to exploit success by immediately pursuing the retreating enemy westwards. But on the 20th, at Conrad's insistence the Hapsburg army facing Serbia on the Hungarian border began to leave for Galicia, seriously weakening Potiorek's forces. Some Austrian troops briefly continued their advance into Serbia, but in a state of demoralisation and privation. Infantryman Matija Malešič wrote on 21 August: 'amid horrendous heat, our road leads us from Konjice up into the hills. We are not allowed to drink water as we wish, although we are marching right beside [a river]. Everything resembles manoeuvres, and yet is so different.' He added three days later: 'Only now have I realised that this is going to be for real; how horrible will be the struggle against a tough, skilled and brave nation which is fighting for its existence – literally, for its "to be or not to be". It is a beautiful starry night, I am lying on bare soil; I have just prayed and looked up in the sky thinking how much I miss Carniola [his home region of Slovenia], my mother and the idyllic life I failed properly to appreciate. I will probably never be granted the opportunity to enjoy it again.'

Soon, the remaining Austrian columns in Serbia bowed to the inevitable and fell back. Men's throats were so parched that when a thunderstorm erupted, they held out their mess tins to catch the falling rain. Every unit left in its wake a litter of packs, hats, sabres, rifles. Austrian reserve officer Lt. Roland Wüster used his revolver for the first time, to try to kill a horse that had foundered. After he had fired three times at the beast, however, it struggled to its feet and walked slowly away from him. An exasperated superior ordered the bemused young officer to finish the job with a pick-axe. Wounded men were abandoned at field hospitals, for lack of transport to evacuate them. Egon Kisch wrote despairingly: 'The army is beaten and indeed routed, now engaged in full-scale headlong retreat.' He himself purchased a seat on a cart for two cigarettes: 'A rampaging horde fled back towards the border in mindless terror. Drivers whipped up their horses ... officers and soldiers alike weaved paths between columns of carts or tramped along the ditch beside the roadside.'

Alex Pallavicini described panic in the Austrian ranks when a distant dust cloud, and reports that a baggage train was under attack, suggested that the Serbs were at their heels. Generals and staff officers sprang into their cars and drove across the Drina, ignoring the screams of wounded men, desperate not to be abandoned. 'The road is strewn with people and horses, dead and wounded. Everybody made a rush for the bridges. The whole migration continued to Brčko [on the Austrian shore]. Many horses drowned in the Drina.' Serb artillery hastened their flight with salvoes of shrapnel shells, for the fugitives were readily visible. Many Austrian horses, badly wounded, died lingering deaths because none of the fleeing men would spare a moment or a bullet to end their misery. Another soldier wrote: 'The army is beaten and in headless, wild and chaotic flight ... An unruly mob bolted in mad fear towards the frontier ... Men were trampling over one another in their haste.'

Austrian teacher Itha J, a bellicose nationalist, wrote in her diary on 17 August: 'We feel heartache, thinking of our soldiers out there in the fields. They perform their duties amid filth and mud, lying in swamps and trenches! We haven't had a war for fifty years, and our men are not used to stresses like this.' How right she was. By the evening of 24 August, no Austrian remained on Serbian soil save 4,500 prisoners in Serb hands. The Serbs had lost 16,000 dead and wounded, the Austrians more than twice as many, a toll that would have seemed very terrible save in the context of the slaughter which soon overtook all Europe. The Hapsburg Empire, served by incompetent officers and unwilling soldiers, had inflicted humiliation upon itself. A tiny Balkan country proved able to maul the invading Austrians to such effect that only a rabble fell back across the Drina.

Back at home, even as Franz Joseph's army suffered disaster, the Austrian people were celebrating fantasy newspaper reports of its alleged triumphs. Itha J wrote in her diary on 22 August: 'Wonderful! Wonderful! Our hearts overflow with exultation, we have won a glorious and valiant victory after a hard struggle against the gang of Serb fanatics, beating thirty Serb battalions ... It is said that we have lost many, many of our brave men. But victory is ours ... We stayed in the cafés far into the night, waiting upon every detail.' Next day, however, her mood changed abruptly. Much sobered, she found herself asking why, after beating 'thirty Serb battalions', the Austrian victors had 'moved back to their old positions'. She reflected uneasily: 'it is said that "an orderly retreat was unimpeded by the enemy". But why retreat if they have won? All kinds of rumour are rife in the town. Officers say we have far too few troops in Serbia ... One said that 8,000 men of our beloved Viennese *Deutschmeister* [Regiment] have been so badly beaten by the Serbs that there are only four hundred survivors. Isn't that appalling? And who is to blame?'

Men of the broken Austrian units now bivouacking behind the west bank of the Drina cursed their commanders: 'our generals are inept old donkeys ... The people who started this thing are responsible for hundreds of thousands of tragedies.' At Lanja, in Bosnia, one regiment held a mail parade. As name after name was called in vain, voices from the ranks shouted, 'He's dead!' The first casualty lists were published. In a single week, Cpl. Kisch's unit had lost sixty-nine officers, twenty-three of them killed, and a thousand men. This represented 71 per cent officer casualties, 25 per cent of other ranks. One battalion's doctor wrote wretchedly home, saying that eight officers and two hundred men of his unit had been lost, '[our men] suffer terribly from hunger, and ... fighting in Serbia is rendered very difficult by the fact that the entire population is engaged in the struggle'. Further south, even the tiny Montenegrin army proved able to evict its share of invaders.

By late August, all over the Hapsburg Empire it was known that Franz Joseph's army had suffered terrible losses in Serbia; there were reports, which proved accurate, that the Sava river was full of floating Austrian corpses. Itha J wrote: 'The heart stops, one wants to scream – and to erase this awful image from one's imagination.' The government produced a new version of events, announcing that the punitive expedition into Serbia was unimportant to the nation's war effort, which fooled no one. 'The impression made by this bulletin was appalling,' wrote Slovenian priest Dr Eugen Lampe. 'Everyone lapsed from triumphalism into melancholy. If we cannot cope with the Serbs, what will happen in Russia?' What indeed? Austrian soldiers recoiled in disgust when newspapers rehearsing such statements reached their positions. They were told that with Russia's entry into the war, the Serb front had become 'a mere sideshow'; that movement into Serbia had been intended only as a raid. Following its success, units had 'withdrawn to prepare for another incursion'. Egon Kisch and his comrades were infuriated by such 'wholly dishonest and deceitful' claims.

Austrian officers responded to defeat by imposing harsh, indeed savage, measures to improve discipline before the next battle. As a penalty for eating their emergency rations, some soldiers were bound to trees all day under the sun. Kisch found this dismayingly reminiscent of the treatment American 'Red Indians' administered to captured white men. Bored soldiers were marched out of their camps to exercise, allegedly to sustain morale, while their commanders planned a renewal of the campaign. Kisch wrote with heavy sarcasm that six to eight hours' drill each day 'is indeed the best way to make everybody feel jolly'.

On 28 August, the Serbs staged a modest incursion of their own into Hapsburg territory: troops crossed the Sava river west of Belgrade, and occupied the Hungarian town of Zemun. The commander of the Austrians' Danube flotilla reported that local people 'welcomed Serbian troops with great enthusiasm, throwing flowers and waving flags'. Next day the Sava railway bridge between Belgrade and the enemy bank, which had been wrecked by the Serbs at the onset of hostilities, was sufficiently repaired to enable foot traffic. Jovan Žujović was one of those who crossed northwards, to view his battered city from the former Austrian gun positions, and to take some photographs. Many of the inhabitants of Hungarian Zemun, meanwhile, seized the opportunity to cross to Belgrade. Of Serb race and sympathies, they had no desire to be within reach of retribution when the Austrians returned. Meanwhile, further south, early in September, some forty Serb and Montenegrin battalions crossed into Bosnia, where desultory fighting took place during the weeks that followed.

The Serbian government, having gained a respite, struggled to procure aid of all kinds from its allies, which posed severe practical difficulties for a landlocked country with poor communications. On 7 September, Britain's foreign secretary wrote with the elaborate formality of the times: 'Sir E. Grey presents his compliments to the Serbian Minister and … has the honour to inform him that a telegram has been received from His Majesty's *Chargé d'Affaires* at Cairo reporting that instructions have been given to allow the exportation of 3,000 sacks of rice to Serbia.' But the hapless Serbs were in need of far more than a few days' supply of rice. Their war, far from being won, had scarcely started.

Early in September, the Austrians launched a second invasion. Reinforcements arrived to fill the depleted ranks of Potiorek's regiments. Every unit was provided with a Slovak guide. One battalion's officers, unable to speak the language of their own appointed man, sought to explain to him by dumb show that he was now subject to military justice, and would face execution if he deserted. The wretched peasant misinterpreted this as a warning that he was to be hanged out of hand, and collapsed into a sobbing heap, shrieking his innocence.

As Egon Kisch marched back towards the Drina with his comrades, he tried to persuade himself that being shot at would be less disagreeable the second time. 'Water doesn't feel so cold once you are in it,' he wrote in his diary. 'It is surely the same with gunfire. But before you dive in, you shiver and your teeth chatter.' Yet the Austrians' renewed invasion of Serbia began as disastrously as the first. On 8 September near Velino Selo, men began to board assault boats to cross the Drina, under heavy small-arms fire. Of

Kisch's platoon of twenty men, only ten were aboard when the boat pushed off, the others having prudently melted away. Their paddle seemed interminable as Serbian bullets whipped the water. When they reached the east bank, the boat was beset by men already wounded, desperate for a passage back to safety. Thousands of Austrians of three regiments milled around the bridgehead in confusion, unable to advance in the face of fire from the Serbians' concrete emplacements.

Night fell. All through the hours of darkness the bedraggled Austrians huddled by the water. Early on the morning of 9 September, a withdrawal was ordered. Only twelve boats, each holding forty men, remained undamaged to carry back the survivors, and thus the evacuation continued for hours. Most men discarded their arms and equipment. As Austrians impatient for passage yelled in rage and despair at the boatmen, Serb infantry ran forward to the river bank and emptied their rifles into the fugitives. Some boats sank under artillery fire, while many men drowned because they could not swim, or were crippled by wounds. Fugitives mobbed the overloaded craft, and were repulsed with increasing ruthlessness by their crews. Egon Kisch escaped by crossing in the water, clinging unnoticed to the transom of a boat being paddled to the Bosnian shore.

For a week after the disaster, Austrian corpses drifted in the Sava and Drina rivers. Elsewhere, some units advanced into Serbia with less initial difficulty, but for no greater military advantage. NCO Matija Malešič wrote despairingly on 16 September: 'How hungry I am and full of thoughts about home and what life will be like when I return ... There are lots of things I could write about but I must take care not to fill up too much paper, since God knows how long this struggle will continue, and paper is scarce. I must focus on the most important thing – and God knows who may get this diary if I fall. It is better if one keeps a lot to oneself. What will happen to me? ... I am all sickness; I have no sensation in my feet due to frostbite, only where the skin has been broken; the hearing in my right ear has gone. I doubt that I am still the same human being that once I was.'

Even as this new disaster was unfolding, other Austrian forces renewed their assault across the Sava. In darkness on 14 September, troops forded the river just north of its junction with the Drina. Once established on the eastern bank, they repulsed a Serb counter-attack. But during the days that followed, they found it impossible to make further progress, and lay hemmed into a narrow perimeter. There were scores of cases of self-inflicted wounds. Potiorek contemptuously ordered his soldiers to try harder, 'without timidity about casualties', but they proved unable to advance beyond the Paranica peninsula. After weeks of inconclusive fighting, once more the Austrians retired across the Drina into Bosnia.

Neither side was strong enough to force a decisive outcome. Further south, the Serbs and Montenegrins were forced to relinquish their footholds in Bosnia. After their withdrawal, in accordance with the spirit in which war was being waged in this region of liquid loyalties, the Austrians hanged or shot out of hand local people who had been rash enough to show sympathy for their temporary occupiers. Gen. Potiorek complained: 'Our Serbs fight on Serbia's side not only in Herzegovina but also at Visegrad, where the population worked covertly against our troops when they were withdrawing.' A Bosnian priest named Vid Parežanin, hanged by the Austrians for allegedly signalling information to the enemy, shouted as the noose was put around his neck, 'Long live Serbia. Long live the Serbian army. Long live great Russia!'

Austrian Dr Jochan Bachmann recorded several occasions on which 'Serbian-sympathising Bosnian trash' allegedly spied for the Serbian army. He mentioned an old peasant couple suspected of such behaviour: the husband was hanged, the wife shot, their home looted and burned. But even Bachmann was appalled by the fate of a Serbian prisoner wounded in the head. Having tended him overnight and laid him in a barn near the Visegrad road, the doctor looked for the man at daybreak, to change his dressings before the regiment marched out. He learned that the prisoner had been hanged, having earned the displeasure of the regiment's colonel by shouting denunciations of Austria through the night. 'Such an order was beyond my understanding, and reflected gross insensitivity,' wrote Bachmann. 'The poor wretch had contracted meningitis from his wound, and his ravings were the result of feverish delirium.'

The same fate was meted out to substantial numbers of Serb residents of the Hapsburg Empire who crossed the border to enlist in the Serbian army, wherever they fell into Austrian hands. This did not deter 452 of 70,000 Austro-Hungarian prisoners now held by Belgrade from joining the Serbian ranks. Vienna imposed a further spate of repressive measures in its Bosnian colony, designed to strengthen the inhabitants' loyalties. The use of Cyrillic script in schools was banned. Austro-Hungarian troops were given draconian orders about the treatment of terrorist suspects. They were warned about Serb *komitadji* guerrillas, and instructed to fire at the slightest provocation, even at women and children, 'because they too can throw bombs and grenades'. The struggle lapsed into a protracted

two-front war: almost a million Serbs and Austrians fought in the north
on the Sava river, and in the mountains east of the Drina.

It was a minor grotesquerie of the time, that even as they did so, in neighbouring Bosnia the trial of the men whose actions had started it all
dragged wretchedly on. An Austro-Hungarian officer posted to Sarajevo
watched the twice-daily procession of the accused conspirators in the
assassination of Franz Ferdinand between the barracks in which they were
confined and the courthouse where proceedings were held: 'first came a
strong guard, then the felons, flanked by more guards, with a further detail
bringing up the rear. All the criminals were bound by chains and chained
to each other, so that escape was impossible. Princip was always at their
centre. He looked pretty unimpressive, with his dark hair, pale features,
and small, slight figure … The transfer was usually accompanied by
booing and Tyrolean invective from watching soldiers, which Princip met
with a cynical grin.'

Only slowly did the leaders of Serbia and Austria come to understand
that they were locked in an embrace which was imposing disaster upon
both. War reduced the former country to a wasteland and cost the lives of
three-quarters of a million people – one in six Serbs, by far the highest
proportion of the population of any belligerent nation to perish in the
conflict. In this respect only, the Austrians achieved their purpose: Serbia
suffered a dreadful punishment for the role of some of its people in the
killing of the Archduke. Meanwhile, however, Conrad's army endured
humiliations such as no later success could erase. Here, the world heard
the bell toll for the looming collapse of the Hapsburg Empire. But Balkan
chimes were swiftly drowned out by vast, deafening concussions across
other battlefields of both western and eastern Europe.

5

Death with Flags and Trumpets

1 THE EXECUTION OF PLAN XVII

Throughout the first fortnight of August, under brilliant skies the armies of France, Germany, Belgium and Britain marched from their detrainment points towards collisions with the enemy amid golden cornfields and wondering peasant spectators. Millions of men traversed many miles each day, some on foot, others on horses or carts, a few in primitive motor vehicles. 'The dust clung to our hair, eyebrows and beards,' wrote Paul Lintier on the 14th, 'and by the time a column of Paris motor buses had gone by us, we were as white as the road itself,' for relatively few of France's highways were metalled. Each German corps, accompanied by 2,400 wagons and 14,000 horses, filled twelve miles of road.

While the German and British armies had adopted uniforms of grey-green and khaki respectively, the French and Belgians retained the brilliant hues of the nineteenth century. Fantastically, the soldiers of France advanced towards the enemy's fire beneath regimental colours, to the music of drums and trumpets. More than a few French headstones of 1914 bear the succinct inscription after a man's name, '*clarion*' – 'trumpeter'. Many units deployed full bands, and some officers affected white gloves. All the belligerents were led into action by commanders armed with swords and mounted on chargers.

From September onwards, the armies burrowed deep into the earth, but the dominant characteristic of the August battles in France and Belgium was that the motions of infantry, cavalry and artillery were alike readily visible. Masses of men advanced against devastatingly powerful modern armaments in the same fashion as warriors since ancient times. The consequences were unsurprising, save to some generals. On 22 August 1914 the French army suffered casualties on a scale never thereafter in the war surpassed by any nation in a single day. Its commander-in-chief, Gen.

Joseph Joffre, orchestrated a series of battles which, to a spectator, resembled those of the nineteenth century in all respects save the dearth of military genius. The conviction of French senior soldiers that spirit alone – '*cran*' – could overcome firepower was responsible for rendering more than a quarter of a million of their young countrymen casualties inside three weeks. The Germans lost almost one-third as many – their own dying time came later.

One day in 1909, a tourist wandered through the streets of the great fortress of Liège, the gateway to Belgium astride the Meuse. A joyless figure, his jowly features set in a perpetual frown, he gazed keenly not upon architectural gems, but instead towards the ring of modern forts protecting the city's approaches. This was Col. Erich Ludendorff, forty-four years old, an obsessive warrior deemed one of the most brilliant stars of the German army. He was inspecting its designated future battlefield, knowing that seizure of Liège and a subsequent sweep through neutral Belgium were crucial elements in Germany's plan for the destruction of the French army. This had been conceived in the first years of the century by chief of staff Count Alfred von Schlieffen, who envisaged thrusting across Dutch territory. Moltke adopted instead a line of march through Liège, because it was decided that Holland should be quarantined as a neutral conduit to the outside world – a 'windpipe' for Germany – in which role it indeed proved serviceable.

No precisely ordered 'Schlieffen plan' ever existed, and it seems more appropriate to speak of an indisputable 'Schlieffen concept', which identified two fundamentals: the need quickly to smash France before turning on Russia, and the intent to do so through a vast outflanking movement, making the right wing the focus of German strength and hopes. In 1913, Ludendorff was removed from the post of chief of operations on the General Staff, allegedly because of his dogged, wearisome insistence that more manpower would be indispensable if Germany's fabulous war vision was to be fulfilled. But a year later he found himself back before Liège, playing a prominent personal role amid the thunder and rattle of gunfire.

Falkenhayn said at the beginning of August: 'It is critical that we use the prevailing euphoria before it goes up in smoke.' This Moltke sought to do, unleashing against Liège the first big assault of the western war. The city was defended by a garrison of 40,000 reinforced by a field division – far more men than the attackers had anticipated meeting. The local German corps commander, Gen. Otto von Emmich, issued a proclamation to

Belgians: 'we want a clear road to attack those who wish to attack us. I give my assurance that the Belgian population will not have to suffer the horrors of war.'

But instead of 'a clear road', on 5 August the first waves of his Westphalian and Hanoverian soldiers met ferocious artillery and small-arms fire. These green troops, who had never heard a shot fired in anger, were thrown back with heavy loss. A Belgian officer wrote: 'As line after line of German infantry advanced, we simply mowed them down ... They made no attempt at deploying but came on ... almost shoulder to shoulder, until, as we shot them down, the fallen were heaped one on top of the other, in an awful barricade of dead and wounded men that threatened to mask our guns and cause us trouble.' The German army started its war in a fashion the rest of Europe would emulate in the weeks that followed, and at Liège Moltke harvested a first crop of grieving widows and mothers.

The Belgian government was rash enough to issue a triumphalist communiqué: 'We are completely victorious. All the German attacks have been repulsed.' But Emmich had hardly started: in the days that followed, his men pressed successive attacks supported by fierce bombardments. Casualties mounted: one brigade lost over half its men, including the commander and a regimental colonel; in another attack at Vise, thirty officers and 1,150 men became casualties. On 6 August an unwelcome novelty was introduced, when a Zeppelin airship staged the first-ever bombing raid on a European city, killing nine Liègeois.

Before war came, Henry Wilson had vainly begged the Belgians to strengthen Liège and Namur. Now they discovered the vulnerability of their fortresses to sustained assault. Gen. Gérard Leman, Liège's garrison commander, abandoned efforts to hold a continuous perimeter. He dispatched almost half his men to join the Belgian field army, thereafter relying upon interlocking fire from the bastions to check a German break-through. The forts at Liège, like those defending France's eastern frontier, were constructed of concrete strengthened by vast earth banks. Ditches covered by machine-guns – though insufficient of them – held enemy infantry at bay. Each fort's defences were dominated by guns mounted on tracks in casemates and steel cupolas which, though weighing over a hundred tons apiece, could be hand-cranked and trained.

Five German corps, 150,000 men, pressed in upon the city. A growing number of attackers exploited darkness to infiltrate between the forts. They were ordered to advance with unloaded weapons, to prevent careless soldiers shooting each other, but muddle persisted, redeemed only by

some purposeful leadership. In a notably theatrical gesture, on the morning of 7 August Ludendorff hastened forward, rallied some despondent
units wilting under Belgian fire, and personally led them into Liège's abandoned citadel. For this action he won – pretty easily – Germany's highest
decoration, the Pour le Mérite. The nation was informed that the city was
taken: '*Lüttich ist gefallen.*' A week earlier, few of the Kaiser's subjects were
as enthusiastic about war as had been the Prussians in 1870, but now the
capture of Liège launched a wave of popular enthusiasm which persisted
into September. The Germans, like most peoples, recoiled from carnage
but loved victories, especially when these came quickly. Towns and cities
exulted, with singing and dancing in the streets. Next day schoolchildren
were assembled to share the rejoicing, then granted a holiday.

Celebration was premature. Despite the citadel's fall, the Belgians held
out stubbornly in most of the surrounding forts. On 8 August, Gen. Karl
von Einem took over responsibility for the siege. He abandoned frontal
attacks and deployed 60,000 troops in an encircling 'ring of steel' pending
the arrival of heavy artillery. The Belgians kept firing: the first casualties
suffered by Dr Lorenz Treplin's regiment were three men who rashly left
their posts in the captured fort of Barchon to bathe in the Meuse, where
an exploding shell severely cut and bruised them. Otherwise, wrote the
surgeon on 11 August, his life was boring – 'stupor and tranquillity'; he
asked his wife to send him a book to pass the time. She told their children
Papa was in a place where he was obliged to speak in French. Four-year-
old Ingeborg wailed, 'But then I shan't be able to understand him when he
comes home!'

Civilians in the path of the armies wearied of war very swiftly. 'You
cannot think how miserable life is here,' Ghent doctor's wife Madame
Jeanne van Bleyenberghe wrote to a friend. 'Many people are ruined.
Pierre had thought to send me to England ... but I don't want to be so far
away and not be able to come back when I want and besides it is too late.'
Worse, much worse, now befell her country. The assault on Liège provoked
the first manifestations of a month-long German frenzy about supposed
francs-tireurs opposing their advance. This prompted the Kaiser's army to
behave with extraordinary savagery. On the night of 4 August, troops in
the village of Bernau panicked amid unexplained shooting which cost the
lives of eleven Germans. Next day, ten villagers were murdered in retaliation, including a family of five hiding in a cellar. The following night, a
Belgian shell landed in the hamlet of Saint-Hadelin, wounding some
Germans posted there. A local teacher was accused of betraying their

position by signalling to the fort of Fléron, and was promptly shot along with several of his family. The first mass executions also took place that day. A hysterical officer, Maj. Gen. von Kraewel, explained the repulse of his troops' attacks by claiming that 'the entire population in Liège and the suburbs participated in the fighting'. Between the 4th and 7th, Kraewel's brigade shot 117 civilians, whom he claimed had engaged in 'mass resistance'.

Likewise another brigade, embittered after suffering a repulse, vented frustration about its losses on the village of Soumagne, where 118 inhabitants were shot or bayoneted and a hundred houses destroyed. German soldiers told survivors: 'It is your brothers who are firing on us from the fort of Fléron.' On the 6th, two hundred civilians from the communities of Romsée and Olne were used as a human shield by Germans advancing on the forts of Embourg and Chaudfontaine. Other hostages were held captive and unfed on the Meuse bridges for several days, to deter Belgian artillery from destroying them. On 8 August infantrymen herded into a nearby meadow seventy-two inhabitants of Melen, including eight women and four girls under thirteen, and executed them. When the local burgomaster arrived in hopes of identifying and burying the dead, he too was shot; most of the village was burned. Sixty-four people likewise perished in Olne and Saint-Hadelin, and another forty in Riessonart. By 8 August, some 850 civilians had been killed around Liège and 1,300 buildings punitively burned by the Germans, to appease their hysteria or assert their dominance. A local tax inspector at Francorchamps, whose father had been murdered, protested to a German officer that no local citizen had raised a hand against his forces. The soldier shrugged and responded in French: 'It doesn't matter. At Liège you kill our men. We also have the right to kill you.'

The Belgians' emplacements were proof against field artillery; only the heaviest metal cast by Krupp and Skoda could penetrate their casemates. Graf Harry Kessler, a forty-six-year-old reservist *Rittmeister* commanding an ammunition train outside Liège, was surprised one morning to meet Austrian artillerymen. They told him they had arrived 'hotfoot from Trieste', bringing four batteries of Skoda 305mm howitzers. These vast weapons opened fire on 12 August, soon accompanied by four 420mm Krupp monsters, each with a crew of two hundred men, which were fired electrically from a distance of three hundred yards, and delivered armour-piercing projectiles. The defence of Liège was terminated by violent eruptions of earth and concrete, rendings of steel and human flesh: in one place, a single shell killed three hundred defenders. Gen. Leman was carried unconscious, choked by fumes, from the ruins of Fort de Loncin. Thirty-odd shells sufficed for each bastion: those on the right bank of the Meuse fell on the 13th, while the river's left bank was cleared three days later.

The capture of Liège had cost the attackers 5,300 casualties. The eleven-day siege did not impose a matching delay on the German advance, because the mass of the Kaiser's armies had anyway needed time to concentrate before they swept onwards. Some formations were already hastening down a twelve-mile-wide corridor to the French frontier, through which two vast armies must somehow squeeze. But the struggle for Liège did cause disruption: the invaders' right flanking armies were denied the quick passage they needed to achieve their long, long crossing of Belgium and northern France before Joffre's forces could redeploy to meet them.

Some pre-war German military pundits had argued that a swift, devastating, absolute war was preferable to a sustained and limited conflict. One such author wrote in 1913: 'Ruthless destruction of the enemy's forces and weapons is the most humane objective, strange as that sounds. The more generously and widely the term "humanity" is defined, the less effectual war-making becomes ... [and thus] the longer a war will last, and the more heavily its consequences will weigh upon the entire existence of the belligerents. Only uninhibited commitment of every element of strength can achieve the swift and decisive overthrow of the enemy.' This was what Moltke was attempting in August 1914.

In the first weeks of the European war, the armies of France also made their own dramatic attempt to force an outcome, before German operations had attained full momentum. Along hundreds of miles of the interface between the belligerents from Belgium to the Swiss border, Joffre's formations began to move forward in fulfilment of Plan XVII. The exotic horsemen of Gen. Jean-François Sordet's cavalry corps, clad in Napoleonic finery, made a dash towards Liège ahead of the French Fifth Army, to be greeted with wild enthusiasm by Belgian civilians everywhere along their road. But on 8 August, ten miles from the city, Sordet's dragoons and lancers met German forces. They fell back, having merely exhausted their unhappy mounts; gleaming French helmets, breastplates and horsehair plumes were not matched by effective weapons. British cavalry carried infantry rifles and were trained for dismounted action, but Sordet's men had only swords and 1890-model carbines – little more use than pistols.

A light-cavalry sergeant later described the frustrations his regiment suffered when it attempted to charge enemy horsemen in Belgium, only to meet the deadly fire of German infantry, which emptied many saddles: 'That's what happened over and over again – perhaps twenty or thirty times.' At each encounter, their numbers shrank. Horse management was a critical military skill, but that of the French army was lamentable. Sordet's cavalry rode thirty-five miles a day through the first weeks of the campaign, and some regiments covered far greater distances: the 9th Cuirassiers recorded in their war diary that they moved a hundred miles in just forty-eight hours. Soon their horses – exhausted by carrying a weight of 250 pounds apiece, poorly fed, stinking from untended saddle sores – were foundering in scores. Unlike British cavalrymen, who were trained to lead their animals as much as possible, to husband their strength for action, the French – and Germans – rode many hapless beasts to death.

As the armies brushed and skirmished in these early encounters, many men flaunted their innocence. Pte. Charles Stein of the Belgian Grenadiers saw German shells bursting, and delighted in their perceived beauty – until he saw his own compatriots fleeing in consequence. On the night of the 11th, a frightened sentry in Stein's unit shot a cow which grazed too close to his post. A company of German reservists likewise glimpsed shadowy movements in early-morning mist, and opened a heavy fire which killed several cattle and a returning patrol before order was restored. When a dud shell landed near French Capt. Plieux de Diusse, he bent curiously to pick it up until a veteran shouted that he would burn himself – de Diusse had no inkling that projectiles were hot.

Even as Moltke's columns tramped across Belgium, further south the first serious clashes unfolded between his formations and those of Joffre. On 3 August the French advanced into the 'lost provinces' annexed by Prussia after its victory in 1871. It is doubtful how many Frenchmen in 1914 nursed real emotion about Alsace-Lorraine. One young blood questioned some years earlier shrugged that their loss was 'a historical event … I don't think that this question interests the youth of today or the country, nor does it interest me.' In 1908 the newspaper *La Patrie* asserted, 'for most Frenchmen the dismemberment is an event as distant as the Seven Years War'.

But those who minded did so passionately. Gen. Louis-Napoléon Conneau, for instance, who commanded a cavalry corps in 1914, observed a pre-war ritual of bivouacking with his regiment of dragoons for one night each year beside a frontier post marking the gateway to Alsace. More than a few such men, now at the head of France's armies, shed tears as they set forth to liberate people whom they regarded as oppressed fellow countrymen – though 380,000 Alsace-Lorrainers eventually fought as conscripts in the German army. The province of Alsace, German-speaking but French-ruled for most of its modern history, extends about a hundred miles from north to south, but is less than forty miles deep. Its western landscape is dominated by the Vosges mountains – *Vogesen* to Germans, just as Alsace was *Elsass* and Lorraine *Lothringen*. The frontier between France and Alsace ran along a steep, densely forested ridge rising in places to 3,000 feet.

In the north, the Germans had constructed the vast fortress of Mutzig, with a network of underground bunkers, to protect the approach to Strasbourg. In the south, towards the textile town of Mulhouse, between the Vosges and the Alps lay the old floodplain of the Rhine. This constituted a corridor barely twenty miles wide, which alone offered ready access to an army. Most of the province was rustic peasant country, known for cheese, wine and lace-making. It had little strategic significance, because it was a cul-de-sac: beyond lay southern Germany's hills and forests, major obstacles. Moreover, the Alsatian front was much more readily reinforced and supplied from Germany than from France. But Moltke correctly anticipated that, in the event of war, the French army would find irresistible the lure of recovering the eastern provinces.

The Germans who deployed to defend Alsace gazed in wonder at the first French soldiers they glimpsed before them, clad in the same long blue overcoats, red trousers and képis their fathers of the Prussian army had known and vanquished back in 1870. One of the Kaiser's men wrote home: 'They really look like something out of a picture-book.' Joffre and his officers could not complain that they were unwarned about the folly of adherence to brilliant plumage. In the spring of 1914 Col. Serret, military attaché in Berlin, submitted a long report about his hosts' latest manoeuvres. He identified the importance of their howitzers and heavy artillery, which senior officers in Paris discounted. He emphasised the benefits of German grey-green uniforms in reducing visibility, and urged that French soldiers should not merely abandon their traditional garb, but also forswear shining sword hilts, cooking utensils, even buttons. He quoted the Kaiser: '[For centuries] we have believed that military dress should be aesthetically pleasing ... fighting at close quarters, in order to kill it was important to be able to recognise each other. Now that we deploy some kilometres apart, we should not show ourselves.' Wilhelm, said Serret, regretted the passing of brilliantly attired soldiers, but declared that war had now become 'a melancholy and dirty affair'.

The colonel was infuriated by a contrarian article which appeared in *Le Temps* of 30 April. This claimed that other nations regretted adopting drab uniforms, and that France was fortunate to have rejected such folly. Serret wrote again to the War Ministry, deploring the fact that old-fashioned uniforms made its men the most conspicuous in the world: 'This difference in visibility, where the most insignificant [French] soldier must attract immediate attention, would have a more serious [adverse] effect on morale than being asked to fight with an inferior rifle.' He added that the gleaming French army 'would hold the record for visibility in the face of its adversaries'. In July a new regulation belatedly introduced sensible new greyish-blue service dress – the '*bleu horizon*' – but this had not yet been issued when the killing began.

Though Gen. Yvon Dubail's 260,000 men in Alsace constituted the biggest of France's five armies – reorganised as seven during the weeks ahead – commanders in the south were instructed by Joffre that their task was merely to engage and contain the largest possible enemy forces, while their comrades further north struck the decisive blows. The Germans at first offered no serious resistance: on the road to Mulhouse, Dubail's men suffered only a hundred casualties. At 3 p.m. on 8 August, the French people were invited to rejoice that the tricolour flew once more over the city, which the enemy had evacuated. The liberators' arrival was greeted with repeated renderings of the *Marseillaise* and dancing in the streets. Gen. Louis Bonneau, the local French commander, who was himself a son of the province, staged a two-hour victory parade, and issued a bombastic proclamation: 'Children of Alsace, after forty-four years of painful waiting, French soldiers once more tread the soil of your noble land. They are the first labourers in a great work of revenge.'

Celebrations were short-lived. Twenty-four hours later, the Germans committed massive reinforcements and counter-attacked. In oppressive heat, there was confused fighting in woods and vineyards, in which not all the Kaiser's soldiers proved themselves heroes. When Maj. Otto Teschner ordered a frontal attack, only his officers and a few men obeyed – others clung to the shelter of a gravel pit. Teschner was obliged to threaten to shoot waverers, to stem a panic-stricken rush to the rear. Another officer, sent to discover what was happening at the front, met streams of men fleeing: 'They told me that they had been beaten and wanted to [retreat] across the Rhine.' But then the tide turned. The Germans prevailed, the French abandoned Mulhouse. Bonneau, much shaken, ordered a general retreat back across the frontier to Belfort.

Joffre was infuriated by both the military reverse and the moral humiliation. He castigated Bonneau for halting his advance to celebrate in Mulhouse, when he should have pushed on to destroy the Rhine bridges. The commander-in-chief had intended that a display of *panache* in Alsace should lift the spirits of the entire army. Here now, instead, was Bonneau asserting that he was pressed, and demanding reinforcements. The general and his principal subordinate were sacked, being held responsible for conducting the retreat 'in an indescribable disorder, a chaos of horse, guns and stragglers'. Joffre nonetheless concealed news of the repulse from the French public: here was an early manifestation of the high-handed manner in which France's C-in-C would exercise his command.

The Kaiser's allies, however, were swiftly informed of this triumph. 'In the evening news spread of a splendid German victory over the French at [Mulhouse],' wrote Austrian schoolteacher Itha J. 'These Germans! Are they really the rising new force? Is the old glory of France destined to fall, its star to wane and fade?' But many German soldiers in Alsace were as shocked and traumatised as their French enemies by this first brief experience of battle. On 10 August, an artillery officer said to Sgt. Wilhelm Kaisen: 'For so long, one looked forward to war, but now that we see its harsh reality one turns away with a shudder.' Kaisen wrote to his girlfriend Helene: 'His words burned into my consciousness, for I know others think the same. Just as he spoke, someone rushed in, reporting that France was asking for peace. You cannot imagine how enthusiastically that story was received. Oh, these madmen. They don't know what it's all about – that a struggle for existence has begun which will be fought to the last pfennig. This war will be Europe's last.'

Further north, thirty-seven-year-old warrant officer Ernst Klopper – a peacetime artist from Pforzheim – succumbed to melancholy as he contemplated the battlefield. His dead comrades were laid out in rows for burial, while the French village which they had died to capture was almost burnt out. Klopper was distressed by the clamorous appeals for food, water, rescue from horses, pigs and cattle trapped in their stalls and pens. 'I do not like to record these wicked atrocities,' he wrote in his diary. 'I never saw anything sadder than a battlefield with so many victims dead and wounded. Despite our victory, I feel deeply depressed. It looks as though the ancient Huns had been here: everything is smashed to pieces.

Kitchens, trunks, cellars ransacked for food and drink. Even the manure heaps are burning.'

Millions of men in their first actions shared the confusion of Jacques Rivière, twenty-eight-year-old French intellectual and friend of André Gide. As he and his comrades watched houses collapse and burn under fire, they somehow fancied themselves attending a military tournament, a fantasy war, a firework display staged in a vast arena. Observing cavalry manoeuvring across the front, Rivière wondered how they would distinguish between French and German horsemen at a distance, and swiftly discovered this was impossible. His unit opened a brisk fire on their own dragoons, fortunately without effect. Hearing shellfire, like all novice warriors they were uncertain whether it was outgoing or incoming. Ever more fanciful figures of speech occurred to Rivière: three Uhlans jogging with upraised lances across a meadow on the distant horizon 'look like vessels tossing on the distant billow'.

But some young men displayed, briefly at least, a burning enthusiasm. Lucien Laby, a twenty-two-year-old military medical student who had been mobilised as a stretcher-bearer, felt so frustrated by his non-combatant role that on 10 August he asserted that he stripped off his red cross armband to go freelancing with a few comrades in search of Germans to kill. He wrote in his diary that his passions were roused by reports of enemy atrocities, including stories of ambulances being fired on. 'We tell no one because these little amateur expeditions would be repressed.' Claiming to have achieved his purpose, he returned to his appointed role. 'For a long time I have been longing to do this and now I shall do my duty as a medic with a much lighter heart.'

The first clashes in Alsace were crude affairs. The rival armies repeatedly committed men to attack in huddled masses, direct from the line of march, without attempting to deploy in open order. Commanders shrugged that such tactics were inescapable when so many unexpected encounter battles took place. Men advancing shoulder to shoulder were more likely than a scattered rabble to preserve momentum. But the consequences were devastating whenever French or German attackers met the machine-guns and artillery of their opponents.

Professional soldiers had had plenty of time to contemplate this prospect: almost a decade earlier in Manchuria, automatic weapons did immense execution, watched by many European military observers. Following that experience, the Germans adopted Maxim guns for their own army – 12,500 were in service by 1914, designated the MG08, with many more in production. There is a popular myth that Moltke's regiments deployed proportionately more automatic weapons than the BEF, but this was not so. The British Vickers, sighted up to 2,900 yards, was likewise a modification of the Maxim, which became the begetter of most heavy machine-guns for the next half-century, though in the first weeks of the war British newspapers used the French word for automatic weapons – '*mitrailleuses*'.

The Russians also used a Maxim variant, chambered for a slightly lighter bullet than the British and Germans used. All such guns were water-cooled and weighed around forty pounds, plus boxed ammunition belts which added fifteen pounds apiece. They were normally served by a crew of three, and were accurate to 1,100 yards. Their bullets scoured a 'beaten zone' of some square yards around the aiming point, which increased killing power. The French favoured their own clip-fed, air-cooled Hotchkiss, a good gun despite a tendency to jam, but initially had fewer automatic weapons than did the Germans and British. In Joffre's armies the machine-gun later came to be known, with heavy irony, as the '*arme noble*', and every commander complained that he did not have enough of them. In August, however, no dashing officer wished to be associated with such ungentlemanly technology. What was remarkable in 1914 was that relatively few machine-guns generated prodigious carnage.

Joseph Césaire Joffre, commander-in-chief and for a season near-dictator of France, directed its military destinies from GQG, his *Grand-Quartier-Générale*, located at a school in the Place Royer-Collard in the little Marneside town of Vitry-le-François. He commuted to work each morning at 5 o'clock from the nearby house of a certain M. Chapron, a retired engineer officer – Joffre himself was an engineer – with whom he was billeted. Each day at 11 a.m. he returned to Chapron's for lunch, a ritual which enhanced his reputation for unshakeable calm. Only during the month of August 1914 did he abandon the additional custom of a postprandial snooze. Dinner took place at 6.30; as in British officers' messes, military 'shop' was barred from the headquarters staff's conversation. Thereafter, a brief evening conference was held – *le petit rapport* – and at 9 p.m. the commander-in-chief retired to bed.

Most British generals took pride in their personal appearance, but Joffre's often verged on the slovenly. His corpulence was the object of some mockery: it was claimed that the regulation requiring every French officer to be capable of riding a horse with conviction had to be waived in his favour. He was sixty-two in 1914, and native talent had propelled his rise from humble origins as one of eleven children of a cooper. Most of his career had been spent in France's colonies, but when the post of chief of staff of the army fell vacant in 1911 Joseph Gallieni, the obvious candidate, asserted vehemently that Joffre, and not he, must be the man. The general was famously a listener rather than a talker. He unsettled and indeed alarmed subordinate army commanders by sitting for hours in their head-quarters, through conferences and crises, often without interjecting a word.

A technician devoid of intellectual pretensions, he abhorred detail, and interested himself only in big decisions. He was supported at GQG by a group of men who, while not fools, thought and acted within a tightly-laced corset of convention; displays of imagination were unwelcome. Gen. Ferdinand Foch, probably France's ablest and most inspirational soldier of his generation, is said to have warned a General Staff officer back in 1911 that Moltke would attempt a grand envelopment: 'Tell General Joffre … Never forget this: the Germans will put thirty-five army corps into the field against us, with their right wing on the Channel coast.' GQG, however, declined to acknowledge the critical importance of the north. Joffre committed the cardinal error of focusing his energies almost exclusively upon his own offensive along the German border. In the first three weeks of hostilities, he showed scant interest in his enemies' intentions.

If the commander-in-chief had been prudent, he would at least have delayed his own grand initiative until he knew that the Russians had started operations in the East. Soon after hostilities began, intelligence warned that the Germans looked unexpectedly strong in Belgium. But on 11 August, Joffre ordered his armies to start their main attacks – the advance into Alsace had been a mere *bon-bouche*. Two days later one-third of his total strength, many of the men peasants with the straw scarcely yet brushed from their hair, marched towards the Germans in Alsace-Lorraine. Cpl. Bernard Delabeye's brigade was told with careless insouciance that its mission was to 'lay siege to Strasbourg'. But the soldier viewed his briga-dier and such braggadocio with scorn: 'with his black coat and red trou-sers he seems a survivor of Solferino [in 1859]'. Delabeye thought no better of his colonel, who ordered them forward: 'He is old and does not know about the deadly fire of an invisible enemy, which begins even before the attack. Under the deluge of shells and machine-gun fire the men run in every direction. The myth of the swift bayonet assault evaporates. The first to die fall without having glimpsed the enemy. When first [we] do see

Germans, they are greyish shapes fifty metres distant, only identifiable by the spike on their helmets. Then follows a retreat which almost becomes a rout.'

Col. Serret, France's pre-war attaché in Berlin, had always worried that his country's officers included an excess of dilettantes, rather than serious professionals schooled in modern tactics. He wrote in one of his reports: 'France makes me think of a factory in which there are too many engineers and inventors but not enough foremen such as Germany has in abundance. Does modern warfare with its heavy armies demand a genius or hard labour?' The French army had institutionalised the promotion of officers known to be elderly, incompetent or both, solely because of their seniority or connections. In 1914 this policy exacted a heavy toll: from top to bottom of society, within a fortnight of mobilisation tens of thousands of households were plunged into grief. A countess living in Nice had a sister-in-law who professed to be a spiritualist medium. Some months before the war, this woman predicted that the countess's son would die of a gunshot wound at the age of twenty. In Alsace, the medium's prediction was fulfilled.

On the other side in Lorraine, the German Sixth Army was commanded by forty-five-year-old Crown Prince Rupprecht of Bavaria, who also controlled Seventh Army on his left, in southern Alsace. In those days, and for the last time, German armies sustained their regional integrity: Rupprecht's formations were overwhelmingly composed of Bavarians. Moltke had instructed him to sustain a strategic defensive – simply to tie down the largest possible French forces, while the grand envelopment took place in the north. Now, therefore, the two German armies waited upon the motions of Joffre.

The French took Mulhouse once more on 19 August, inflicting considerable slaughter on their enemies. They themselves also suffered heavy losses, however, and this time received a cautious reception from the inhabitants. Those who rejoiced at their earlier arrival had suffered brutal retribution when the Germans returned, and now Alsatians feared a repetition. Gen. Paul-Marie Pau contented himself with taking the city, and declined to push on to the east. Further north, on 14 August the Second Army of Gen. Edouard de Castelnau entered western Lorraine – open countryside interspersed with coal- and salt-mining districts – in the accustomed French manner, led by mounted officers, colour-bearers and bands. The Germans did not seriously dispute their passage, because they had prepared an elaborate reception some twenty miles eastwards. Alsace-Lorraine was well supplied with strategic railways, stations with

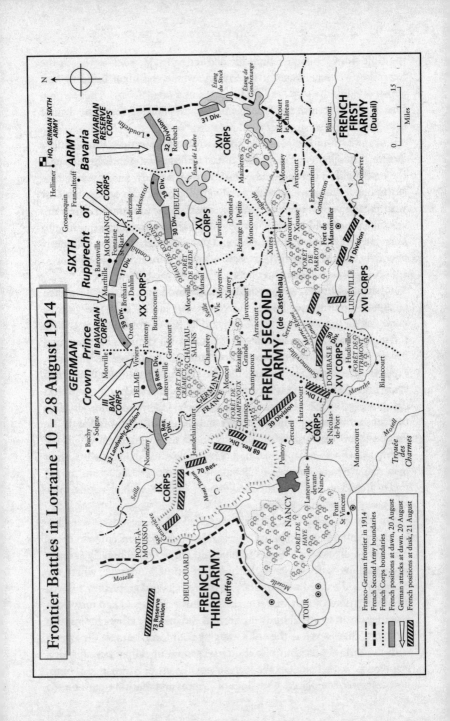

Frontier Battles in Lorraine 10 – 28 August 1914

multiple sidings purpose-built for detraining troops such as that at the Lorraine frontier village of Chambrey, where the main building was constructed in the style, and on the scale, of a small *Schloss*. The German intention was to lure the French into a sack, allowing them to advance until they could be struck from three sides.

On the 17th in London, *The Times* wrote optimistically about Joffre's armies, through the fog of ignorance and misinformation which shrouded the battlefield: 'They are ready, and more than ready, and it will not be surprising if they now move forward in the spirit which corresponds best with French military genius.' And so they did. For four days, Castelnau's advance proceeded slowly. German rearguards overreacted, pausing to burn every village they abandoned, and putting up a resistance sufficiently energetic to impede their prospects of luring forward the French, who suffered a thousand casualties before 9 a.m. on the 15th.

Castelnau himself had opposed the offensive into Lorraine: he argued with notable prudence that his forces should merely hold their strong positions on the hills around Nancy, and let the enemy do the attacking. Joffre, however, was insistent that the offensive should go ahead, and progress in the first few days convinced him of its success. Further south, First Army overran Sarrebourg. On the evening of the 19th, Castelnau again urged caution on his local corps commander, Ferdinand Foch. Next day, however, Foch and his neighbours launched their formations in close columns across rolling country broken only by expanses of woodland. The French threw forward 320 battalions and a thousand guns, which the Germans, who as it happened had chosen the same day to deliver their own massive blow, met with 328 battalions and over 1,600 guns. In the midst of Alsace-Lorraine, the rival attacks collided with shocking force and heavy losses on both sides.

On the left, where the French deployed on an east–west axis, the Germans simply stood their ground and let Foch's soldiers come to them. The splendidly arrayed masses of blue and red marched bravely across a wide, shallow valley towards the hilltop town of Morhange, where the occupiers had created a big military base. From its eminence, they enjoyed an uninterrupted south-westerly view for miles. They had had forty-four years' leisure in which to study the ground and measure ranges for just this moment. They used it to the full, arranging their forces to meet the French with the formal precision of a military tattoo – or rather, perhaps, of a Napoleonic battlefield. On the plateau north-west of Morhange 150mm howitzers were emplaced, with lines of 77mms and machine-guns on the tiered lower slopes of the same heights. French aviators warned their commanders of the strength – indeed, near-impregnability – of the German position, but they were ignored. The attackers pressed forward in two vast columns, between the Forêt de Cremecy and the Forêt de Bride. Here was a battle which is today known only to specialist students of the war, yet was awesome in its scale and character.

Consider the spectacle confronting the Germans on the commanding heights that morning: under Foch's orders some 43,000 French soldiers advanced across the open fields below Morhange in full view of the enemy, to meet a hail of fire which ravaged their ranks. Two divisions were wrecked; a French officer described 'a sublime chaos, infantrymen, gunners with their clumsy wagons, combat supplies, regimental stores, brilliant motor cars of our brilliant staffs all meeting, criss-crossing, not knowing what to do or where to go'. Behind the killing ground lay the hamlet of Fontaine Saint-Barbe. This became a casualty-clearing station for the French, though the medical facilities were overwhelmed. By afternoon, around Fontaine's pump and communal washing place lay hundreds of groaning and bleeding men, many in extremis. Meanwhile, even worse things were happening on Foch's right, where the entire neighbouring corps broke and fled, exposing his flank.

The Germans began to press the reeling French from three sides. They launched Bavarian infantry to complete what the guns had begun. Foch's corps admitted 5,000 casualties in the day's fighting below Morhange, of whom 1,500 lie buried in a single cemetery: the real total may have been twice as many. Many of the dead bore Alsatian names, while 158 by some accident of fate were of Russian descent or citizenship – men whose names were crudely misrepresented on their gravestones as those of Picofay Borrisof, Nicolai Bororghin, Fryaje Dimitry. Among the dead also lay a *sous-lieutenant* of light infantry, Charles de Curières de Castelnau. Before the war, as Joffre's chief of staff, Charles's father the general shared in the creation of Plan XVII. He had nonetheless opposed the Lorraine offensive, only to be overruled by Joffre, who bore overwhelming responsibility for the horrors that befell French arms in the blood-logged fields before Morhange. Local inhabitants also paid heavily. In the valley lay the village of Dahlin. After the battle the victorious Bavarians razed its houses, executed its priest and deported the inhabitants, for allegedly displaying sympathy for the French. The victorious Prince Rupprecht wandered with his aides through the nearby forest of Dieuze, marvelling at the chaos of abandoned weapons, clothing and equipment.

On the night of the 20th, Castelnau, who was furious with his subordinates, ordered a full retreat, fifteen miles back inside France to the Meurthe river and the heights known as the Grand Couronné of Nancy, which protected that city. A few days later, on the 24th, a reporter for *Le Matin* gave its readers an account which offered one of the few glimpses accorded to the French people of the disasters befalling their armies: 'Companies, battalions passed in indescribable disorder. Mixed in with the soldiers are women carrying children on their arms ... girls in their Sunday best, old people carrying or dragging a bizarre mixture of objects. Entire regiments were falling back in disorder. One had the impression that discipline had completely collapsed.'

The commanding general had adopted a custom of reading aloud to his staff each morning the names of officers who had fallen the previous day. On 21 August there was a momentary break in his voice as he pronounced the words 'Charles Castelnau' – the first of his three sons to die in the war. Then his voice recovered, and he continued the recital to the end. On the Lorraine front, however, matters were not as bad as they looked: Castelnau was able to regroup his army remarkably quickly and effectively. The Germans had suffered sufficiently severely that they did not immediately press Foch's men as they withdrew, but they were also able to drive back Castelnau's northern and southern neighbours, and every French soldier found the experience painful. Before quitting Sarrebourg, Gen. Comte Louis de Maud'huy stood at attention with his staff amid heavy German shellfire while massed bands played the *Marche Lorraine*.

Foch kept his job, indeed was soon promoted to an army command, because Joffre admired his energy and '*cran*', even if he could scarcely applaud his achievement, at Morhange. It remains bewildering that the French commander-in-chief permitted, far less incited, the Lorraine offensive, because he never supposed that decisive results could be achieved there. Even before Morhange he was already shifting forces north, removing one corps from Castelnau and diverting another destined for his sector. Joffre had always told his commanders that their job was to tie down the maximum German forces, rather than to win the war, which would be contrived further north. If this was so, it is extraordinary that he accepted huge losses in pursuit of secondary objectives.

But in August 1914 every commander was prodigal with manpower and careless about casualties – only much later were the belligerents obliged to recognise that flesh and blood were finite resources. The Kaiser declared with his usual extravagance that the Lorraine fighting on 20

August had produced 'the greatest victory in the history of warfare'. At the heart of the frustration of German purposes in August 1914 lay a failure, by Wilhelm and his generals alike, to understand the magnitude of operations that would be necessary to secure a decision rather than a mere local success in a struggle between twentieth-century industrialised nations. When battlefields were populated by millions, killing mere tens of thousands of the enemy did not suffice.

Yet in those days, the French disaster at Morhange was matched elsewhere. The banquet of slaughter in Alsace-Lorraine represented only one part of Joffre's disastrous achievement. Even as it unfolded, elsewhere along the front other French armies were suffering still bloodier fates in piecemeal encounters with the Germans. The most northerly, Gen. Charles Lanrezac's Fifth, a quarter of a million men strong, advanced into Belgium, up the Meuse past Sedan and Mezières as far as Dinant, before meeting the Germans. On the night of 14 August, after a long march Lt. Charles de Gaulle's regiment collapsed into exhausted sleep slumped against houses on Dinant's streets. Early the following morning, German shells began to fall on the town. The defenders, after experiencing a few moments of confusion, galvanised themselves. Amid a crackle of German small-arms fire, the French soldiers ran forward across a railway line, heading for a bridge over the Meuse now threatened by the enemy.

De Gaulle himself had covered only twenty yards when 'something struck my knee like a whiplash, making me trip. I dropped, and Sergeant Debout fell on top of me, killed outright. Then there was an appalling hail of bullets all round. I could hear the muffled sound of them hitting the dead and wounded scattered over the ground. I extricated myself from my neighbours, corpses or little better.' The young lieutenant astonished himself by surviving a long crawl to the Meuse bridge, where he helped to rally what was left of the regiment. At nightfall, he clambered aboard a cart carrying casualties to the rear. He was operated on for a bullet wound in the right fibula which had paralysed the sciatic nerve, but curiously caused him no pain. His regiment, along with the entire Fifth Army, began to retreat.

Joffre and most of his senior officers expected the decisive battles to be fought by Lanrezac's southerly neighbours in the centre of the line, on the Ardennes front. GQG had been handicapped in making France's war plans by uncertainty about what part, if any, the British might play. Even now, as the little BEF tramped towards the Franco-Belgian border, the French high command displayed scant interest in what might, or might not, be happening up there. Joffre received a stream of reports from French airmen and from intelligence officers that large forces of Germans were crossing the front northwards, towards his left flank. The Belgians also described enemy masses traversing their country in long, grey-green columns. This merely led Joffre to the conclusion that since Moltke's forces – whose overall numbers he much underestimated – were so strong on both flanks, they must be weak in the centre. Instead of focusing on the northern threat, the commander-in-chief addressed his large person to France's own, supposedly decisive, thrust into Luxembourg and southern Belgium through the Ardennes. On 21 August he gave the order – among the most fateful in French history – for nine corps of Third and Fourth Armies to attack between Charleroi and Verdun, while the Fifth did likewise on the Sambre.

The BEF's Sir Henry Wilson wrote home that day: 'It is at once a glorious and melancholy thought, that by this day week the greatest action that the world has ever heard of will have been fought.' GQG told Third and Fourth Armies' commanders to expect no serious opposition; in truth, however, they were advancing against ten German corps, commanded by the Kaiser's son, Crown Prince Wilhelm. 'Little Willy' and his chief of staff were bent upon glory. Reconnaissance clearly revealed French intentions. Heedless of Moltke's injunctions to adopt a defensive posture, the Germans had no intention of playing a passive role while others won the critical victories in accordance with Schlieffen. Thus, they unleashed a series of murderous – and, on the French side, disastrously ill-coordinated – encounter battles across a sixty-mile front.

On the morning of the 22nd, several French columns advanced into the Ardennes amid thick mist. At Ethe, a subordinate general expressed concern to his divisional commander about continuing to push forward blindly. A young officer who heard their conversation said later: 'I can still hear Trentinian, very haughty, looking down from his horse and saying, "you are being extremely cautious, general!" So we went on.' They collided with advancing German forces which, despite being taken by surprise, rallied impressively, and after fierce fighting inflicted a bloody repulse on Trentinian's division. Likewise just north of Virton, cavalry trotting ahead approached Belle Vue farm, atop a steep hill, and met heavy German fire. A wire fence prevented the horsemen from attempting a flank movement. A day of chaos and blood ensued. The streets of Virton became jammed with French infantry, cavalry and guns – the latter impotent in the fog.

The Germans sought to advance, ordered by their officers to identify themselves to each other by singing. Their opponents likewise struck up the Marseillaise, the last tune many of the choristers ever sang. As one French infantry unit took up position, its men seemed gloomy. An officer named Captain Kerquence ordered them to run through their drill movements under fire, which the regimental history claimed unconvincingly 'brought back snap and spirit into the battalion'.

Suddenly, the fog cleared. The French infantry, cavalry and artillery batteries found themselves exposed in full view of German gunners on the hilltop. When the legendary 'soixante-quinze', a superb quick-firing 75mm gun, was first employed in combat, some officers opposed the introduction of a shield screening its crew, saying that 'Frenchmen must look the enemy in the face'. Fortunately for the gunners, such bravado was overcome. But shields were of little service when, as at Virton, crews found themselves under high-angle howitzer fire. Cavalry of the 12th Hussars were likewise shot down wholesale.

The French infantry renewed their advance uphill in short rushes. Their Field Service Regulations assumed that in twenty seconds an assault line could move fifty yards before an enemy could reload. A survivor of Virton observed bitterly: 'the people who wrote those regulations had simply forgotten the existence of such things as machine-guns. We could distinctly hear two of those "coffee-grinders" at work; every time our men got up to advance, the line got thinner. Finally our captain gave the order: "Fix bayonets and charge!" It was mid-day by now, and … devilish hot. Our men, in full kit, started running heavily up that grassy slope, drums beating, bugles sounding the charge. We didn't even reach those Wurtembergers. We were all shot down before we got to them. I was hit and lay there until I was picked up later.'

The subsequent course of the battle around Virton proved less one-sided than its commencement. French infantry at last overran the thin German line, but their corps commander failed to exploit local success. Both sides ended the day much chastened by their losses, but it was the French who fell back. 'The battle was lost. I knew neither why nor how,' wrote gunner Paul Lintier, whose battery limbered up and retreated soon after noon. '… I now noticed shells bursting over some woods a long way off to the south-west. It looked as though our flank must have been completely turned … The drivers urged on their horses, while the rest of us jumped down off the limbers to lighten the load and ran along in extended order on either flank of the column. Halfway up the steep hillside a broken-down infantry wagon was straddled right across the way. A wretched white horse was straining in the shafts while the driver shouted and pushed at one of the wheels. One of our corporals hailed the infantry-man: "Get on, you there!" … He turned a pitiful face to us and I could see the tears in his eyes. "Get on? Tell me how!"' Lintier and his comrades helped to push the wagon back on the road. 'It was nearly two o'clock. The air was hot and oppressive.'

The Germans lost 283 killed and 1,187 wounded in the action at Virton, but French casualties were heavier. On two occasions during the Ardennes fighting on 22 August, entire French formations broke and ran; the dead lay stacked like folding chairs, overlapping each other where they fell. As always, the mounted men were slaughtered: two brigade commanders were killed, along with every officer of one regiment; another lost a third of its strength. That evening, Third Army's commanders at first harboured delusions about renewing the attack next day; their men were ordered to entrench, employing their only tools to hand – mess tins. But it was soon recognised that regiments almost bereft of leaders were unfit to fight again. A survivor, stunned by his experiences, stood muttering again and again, 'Mown down! Ah … Mown down!' The inhabitants of Virton after-wards suffered severely at the hands of the Germans, who accused them of signalling to French artillery. The Kaiser gave both his son and Prince Rupprecht the Iron Cross First and Second Class.

Further north on that same dreadful 22nd, elements of the French Fourth Army advanced up a forest road which took a column through the village of Bellefontaine. One regiment was led by Colonel Charles Mangin, author of a deplorable 1910 book entitled *La Force noir*. This sought to justify France's plans to exploit colonial mercenaries to make good its shortfall of white manpower against the Germans. Mangin wrote: 'In future battles these primitives, for whom life counts so little and whose young blood flows so ardently, as if eager to be shed, will certainly attain the old "French fury" and will reinvigorate it if necessary.' Now that war had come, Moroccans, Senegalese, Algerians and suchlike were indeed hurled foremost into its flames. By 1918, France's black soldiers had suffered a death rate three times higher than that of their white comrades, because they were so often selected for suicidal tasks.

On 22 August Mangin's troops advanced until, as they approached the village of Tertigny, the Germans opened fire from neighbouring wood-land. Bitter fighting followed; Mangin led a bayonet charge, while street fighting developed in Bellefontaine, which came under heavy shellfire.

That evening, French survivors retired to the edge of the forest, having lost eight company commanders and more than a third of the regiment. Another French formation which suffered dreadfully that day was the 3rd Colonial Infantry Division, which, despite its title, was composed of white troops, and considered a crack formation. Its units advanced in column through the village of Rossignol, and thence up a narrow road where its vanguard entered the Foret d'Anlier. The French had failed to reconnoitre: horse, foot and guns merely marched into the woodland led by the Chasseurs d'Afrique, nicknamed 'les marsouins' – 'porpoises' – because of an old naval connection. They encountered German columns marching in the opposite direction. Both sides' officers were equally astonished, but the Germans quickly deployed and dug in, to meet a succession of suicidal French frontal attacks.

The colonial infantry's commander rejected subordinates' repeated urgings to withdraw, and instead fed ever more men forward, into the killing ground. German reinforcements worked steadily around their flanks until the division was surrounded, its only line of retreat across the river Semoy cut when German artillery severed its bridge. Horses, men, carts and guns milled in chaos in and around Rossignol under shellfire, until the fortunate contrived to surrender. The 3rd DIC lost 228 officers and 10,272 other ranks, including 3,800 men taken prisoner; two generals were killed, one wounded and captured. Indeed, almost all the French commanders perished: among the divisional artillery, only a single officer survived. After the war, a memorial was erected by the father of one of the dead, Lt. Paul Feunette. The grieving parent never forgave himself, because he had responded to his son's pre-war sowing of wild oats by insisting that he should join the Chasseurs d'Afrique 'to sort him out'. After the French retreated, the Germans conducted another orgy of violence against civilians, murdering 122 people in Rossignol on 26 August.

Other French Fourth Army advances upon Longwy and Neufchâteau met similar disastrous fates to those further south. The fighting on this one day, the 22nd, cost the French army 27,000 men killed, in addition to wounded and prisoners in proportion. This was a much larger loss than the British suffered on 1 July 1916, first day of the battle of Somme, which is often wrongly cited as the First World War's high blood mark. Extraordinarily incompetent French local and higher leadership missed several opportunities to turn the tables on the Germans, even just possibly denying Joffre a chance of a strategic victory in the Ardennes. More than a few senior officers lost offspring: Foch's only son and son-in-law both perished. The casualties of August 1914 dealt a blow from which the French army never fully recovered – it is remarkable that it recovered at all. The Germans also suffered heavily on 22 August, but their leadership and tactical skills, above all speed of response to surprise encounters, proved far superior to those of the French. Fourth Army commander Langle de Cary, who had himself bungled deplorably, observed laconically to Joffre: 'On the whole, results hardly satisfactory.' The C-in-C urged a renewal of the assault, but Langle ignored him and withdrew.

Further south, French fortunes briefly improved. Edouard Cœurdevey wrote on 23 August: 'Exhausting week. We have followed the rapid advance of our troops and here we are in Alsace. Received fresh supplies on the field of battle. Trenches, burned houses, sacked station, shelled-out church, houses with bullet-holes, crosses in the corner of a wood, a convoy of prisoners. So many sad things, especially the prisoners: this troop of haggard-looking, filthy, exhausted men with their heads hung down, without any arms or equipment, dressed any old how.' But after this brief spasm of optimism, French tribulations were renewed. When Castelnau fell back from Lorraine, his neighbours in Alsace had no choice but to do likewise, or face being outflanked. '5 a.m. movement order – retire to the rear,' Cœurdevey recorded on 24 August. 'No other explanation. It seems that we are in the light. The Alsatians who had welcomed us without enthusiasm see us leave without regret. Alsace has been denationalised during these past forty-five years. France seemed to have forgotten it and accepted the mutilation, Germany maltreated it so it lacks a fatherland. Poor things! The example of Belgium must make them understand that there are not three solutions, but two: either France or Germany.'

Paul Deschanel, president of France's Chamber of Deputies, later told Sir Francis Bertie that the entire incursion into Alsace-Lorraine had been 'theatrical and a great error'. André Gide scribbled in his diary: 'The Mulhouse business; any other nation would have avoided that ... Mistakes made in France are due to love of the dramatic remark or gesture.' There was never a realistic prospect that the southern assaults could achieve useful success; they were undertaken – as the Germans had coldly antici-pated – merely to restore the glory of France, an objective better post-poned unless or until her armies had prevailed elsewhere.

Moltke's armies had also been shaken by the severity of the fighting among the woods and vineyards of Alsace. In the Vosges French *chasseurs-alpins*, specialist mountain troops, inflicted severe casualties. The German recapture of Mulhouse was a shambles, undertaken without reconnaissance.

One officer, a Maj. Leist, deplored his difficulties in stemming panic when cut off from effective higher command: 'There can be no talk of a connection with the regiment. Not a single regimental order was passed down during the entire battle.' Sgt. Otto Breinlinger wrote that after the Mulhouse fighting, his company was reduced from 250 men to sixteen.

It was nonetheless unequivocally Joffre's forces which suffered most disastrously from the mid-August battles. Jacques Rivière's regiment fought its first action – or rather, joined the roll of victims – with Third Army north of Nancy. He and his comrades of a reserve unit were awaiting an order to move when suddenly their captain cried, 'Get down! Get down!' with an urgency he had never displayed on exercises. Rivière heard a 'silky, tearing sound' as the first of scores of incoming shells tore through the air overhead. There was a moment of panic as violent noises among the trees of a nearby wood suggested that the enemy was approaching. Then they saw that it was their officer's horse, which had broken loose and bolted. Shells began falling in fours among the Frenchmen, raising plumes of smoke in neat diamond pattern.

At daybreak on 24 August, the advancing Germans took Rivière prisoner. He marvelled at the fact that when the enemy overran the trenches from which he and his comrades had been shooting for hours, their conquerors displayed no ill-will: 'It was finished, and that was that.' German methods, he thought, were coolly clinical. They kept firing only until their enemy was overcome, then, when they had gained the desired result, they concluded the business with no more emotion than an accountant aligned pens and paper on his desk. 'From that comes their success in war,' reflected Rivière. 'Military operations as practised today seem made for them ... They do what is necessary, taking the job to its conclusion (in a fashion impossible for a Frenchman) ... They plunder and set fire to places in just the same (methodical) way.' André Gide wrote likewise: 'With us, the army remained an instrument; with [the Germans] it is an organ; so that, without much exaggeration, it could be said that, for that organ, war was the necessary function.'

President Poincaré's military liaison officer, Col. Marie-Jean Pénelon, was prone to display absurd optimism. But now, when the politician asked, 'Is it defeat?' Pénelon answered succinctly: '*Oui, M. le Président.*' Beyond lives, the loss of terrain deprived France of much of its capacity for producing coal, iron and steel. Poincaré wrote bleakly on 24 August: 'Where now are the illusions on which we have been feeding for the last fortnight? From now on, salvation can lie only in the strength of our resistance.'

Many French soldiers recognised that the Kaiser's host had shown itself a more formidable fighting machine than their own. Jacques Rivière, in captivity, gazed with respect on German troops detraining at a railhead, then marching off towards the battlefield in 'an unending and well-ordered procession'. This was, he thought, 'an army made for war, and not an army making war because such a fate fell upon it', such as that of France.

Yet Rivière and many of his compatriots conferred excessive respect on the enemy. There was no doubt of the energy, efficiency and motivation of Moltke's NCOs and soldiers, but few officers revealed evidence of tactical genius. When German infantry attacked, their huddled formations suffered as grievously as did the French. The shells of '*soixante-quinzes*', together with machine-gun and rifle fire, fell with deadly effect upon enemy advances. On both sides, the futility of many officers' displays of courage evoked astonishment and even revulsion among those they led. A German spectator wrote of a scene on 18 August when the Kaiser's Grenadiers first marched into battle: 'Even before the fight had started, his Royal Highness Prince Joachim Albrecht [of Prussia] and the head of the machine-gun company rode ahead on reconnaissance, bafflingly exposing themselves to the enemy's fire without dismounting.' The entire regimental staff stood among the forward troops throughout the subsequent battle. On the 22nd, another German regimental history recorded: 'The crude assaults by the 131st Infantry have cut deeply into its ranks.' Karl Gruber, a Freiburg architect now serving as a company commander, found his men pestering him insistently, demanding, 'Lieutenant, will we be in Paris soon?' 'Lieutenant, won't the murdering soon stop?' In August the Duke of Württemberg's Fourth Army admitted 20,000 casualties, the Crown Prince's Fifth almost as many.

Moreover, the Germans' machinery of command began to expose grievous flaws, and their senior officers failings of judgement and character. Joffre presided over catastrophe in the 'Battles of the Frontiers', but at least there was no doubt of his authority over his armies, and close supervision of their operations. Moltke, by contrast, left his subordinates in the field to execute his design almost without intervention or coordination. He sought to make a virtue of delegation, saying that his own most important responsibility was not to micro-manage his generals, but instead to control the Kaiser.

The coming of war had thrust upon Wilhelm the nominal role of Supreme Warlord: the chief of staff was fearful that his master might seek to translate this into a reality; that if he got near the front, he would attempt to meddle with the conduct of operations. Thus Moltke exerted himself to quarantine the Kaiser from battlefield influence. On 16 August imperial headquarters were established in Coblenz, where Wilhelm took up residence in the castle and Moltke's staff occupied the Hotel Union. His signals chief, incomprehensibly and with serious consequences for command communications, was installed elsewhere, in Bad Ems. Lt. Col. Gerhard Tappen, chief of operations and a key figure, loathed by subordinates for his overbearing manner and unwavering rudeness, urged Moltke to get closer to the action. The chief of staff argued unconvincingly that the intervening countryside was still insecure. In truth, he appeared to see his own function as that of the chairman of a corporate board, rather than as its chief operating officer. The consequence was that Germany's seven field army commanders in the West were left to conduct the largest military operation in history in the manner each thought best.

Napoleon wrote that the presence of the general is everything, that he is not merely the head but the very all of an army: 'it was not the Roman army which conquered Gaul, but Caesar; it was not the Carthaginian army which caused the republican army to tremble at the gates of Rome, but Hannibal; it was not the Macedonian army which reached the Indus, but Alexander'. By 1914, personality had become less important, and mass more so, than a century earlier. But Bonaparte's thesis was not invalidated. Though the French, in the first three weeks of the war, had made the most disastrous command blunders, the Germans would thereafter emulate them.

For a brief season, however, the Kaiser's soldiers saw themselves as conquerors, relishing their opportunities to snatch fruits of victory, large and small. On 22 August Pte. Vogel of the Silesian 105th Regiment and two other men of his unit broke into a French grocery store and looted it. Vogel was laden with booty when he met his battalion's adjutant. 'What good things have you got in that box?' demanded the officer. 'Biscuits, *Herr Leutnant*.' 'May I have some?' 'Certainly, sir.' Vogel described how next day six French soldiers advanced into the German lines under a white flag to give themselves up. Most of their comrades, wrote the German, had retired into a nearby forest, leaving behind hundreds of dead who 'stank like the plague'. But this evidently became Vogel's own fate soon afterwards, for his diary fell into British hands, its pages soaked in blood.

All the while that the soldiers were struggling around the frontiers, in homes across Europe tens of millions of civilians awaited tidings from the battlefield. Helene Schweida wrote to her boyfriend Wilhelm Kaisen from

Bremen on 18 August: 'We civilians know nothing. After the fevered excitement in the first days of mobilisation, now a quiet has descended. Bremen will soon be a city of women.' In the first weeks of war, every society experienced successive waves of jubilation and dejection amid news from the front which was scanty and often wildly mistaken. In August, most of the rash rejoicing took place in Germany. On the afternoon of the 21st, news of victories in Lorraine unleashed a round of celebrations in German towns and cities. In Freiburg, for instance, many a house decked itself out with German and Badenese flags, church bells rang, the imperial colours were raised over the cathedral, there was wild cheering in the streets for the Kaiser and the army. Excited crowds gathered around the Victory Monument in the city's central square.

In France, to an extraordinary degree the population, along with the government and its British allies, were kept in ignorance about what was taking place, the slaughters and retreats. But there were sufficient hints to dismay informed people. An elderly dowager in Nice, disgusted by hearing reports that the local Provençal regiments were performing poorly in Lorraine, asserted contemptuously that the local male population expected to live on its womankind. British ambassador Sir Francis Bertie wrote on the 16th: 'I think that the French system of announcing only French successes and captures of men and guns is foolish, for they have no doubt lost many men and some guns and when the truth comes out there will be a great outcry here.' He added a fortnight later: 'There is much more description and truth in *The Times* than in any of the French newspapers,' though this was no high compliment.

Among the first intrusions of war upon the home front was the arrival of wounded men in provincial towns. Grenoble, for instance, received its first trainload on 22 August, and by September the town was caring for 2,000 casualties. Most had been dispatched straight from the front, to be distributed among towns and villages as local authorities saw fit. The high command issued orders that for morale reasons, the civilian population was to have the minimum possible contact with the wounded. But each arriving train was met by crowds of spectators who asked anxious questions, to which shrugs were the most common response. A *chasseur-alpin* said: 'We soldiers were usually as much in the dark about the military situation as the civilians. Our platoon, our company, our unit, that was all we knew or generally cared about.'

After the first weeks, however, many people were chilled by the swiftness of the ebb of civilian curiosity about the casualties, and sympathy for their plight. In Narbonne, barrel-maker Louis Barthas noted bitterly that when the town's hospitals overflowed, mayoral appeals for citizens to take wounded men into their homes fell mostly upon deaf ears. The wounded languished for hours on stretchers laid down around the station, no one knowing where to send them. For months the medical facilities of all the belligerents, and especially of the French, were overwhelmed by hundreds of thousands of lacerated and maimed men. Many died whom even the crude treatments of the time might have saved, had these been available. But often they were not.

French morale did not collapse following the slaughters of those first dreadful weeks; most of the men of Joffre's armies remained amazingly staunch. But a new sobriety tempered the spirit of millions. A French officer wrote dryly to an English friend: 'Self-evidently, what is happening is not taking place in a theatre; the situation and timing of the acts are not regulated by whistle-blast; and members of the audience impatient for their suppers may find that the action continues a little longer than they would wish ... We will fight the enemy to our last man, and to the expenditure of our last *écu*, and rest assured that long before these are reached, Germany will be on its back.' But as the failed French offensives melted away, Moltke's great assault gathered momentum. The clashes of mid-August served only as an overture for those of the weeks that followed, that would decide the war.

2 'GERMAN BEASTLINESS'

A significant and conspicuously ugly aspect of the first weeks of Germany's campaign in the west was the misconduct of its army towards civilians, approved at the highest level. The policy of institutionalised ruthlessness which the invaders initiated at Liège was thereafter extended across every area they occupied. Conditioned by their 1870–71 experiences of meeting civilian guerrillas in France, in 1914 they showed themselves obsessed with the alleged threat posed by *francs-tireurs*, in breach of the laws of war. One soldier recorded in his diary near Andenne on 19 August: 'Our cavalry patrols, we hear, are being shot at in the villages again and again. Several poor fellows have already lost their lives. Disgraceful! An honest bullet in honest battle – yes, then one has shed one's blood for the Fatherland. But to be shot from ambush, from the window of a house, the gun-barrel hidden behind flowerpots, no, that is not a nice soldierly death.'

An officer's letter published in the newspaper *Deutsche Tageszeitung* on 19 August said: 'We have to shoot practically every town and village to smithereens ... because civilians, above all women, shoot at the troops as they march past. Yesterday civilians shot at the infantry from the church tower in X, and wiped out half a company of brave soldiers. The civilians were fetched down and executed and the village was left in flames. A woman chopped off the head of an injured Uhlan. She was caught and had to carry the head to Y, where she was killed. My magnificent men are full of courage. They are ardent for vengeance. They protect their officers, and whenever they catch *francs-tireurs*, they string them up from the roadside trees.' This account seems wildly fanciful, but paranoia about guerrillas was ubiquitous. A German assured some French prisoners they were safe – 'all soldiers are comrades' – then brandished his bayonet menacingly as he added, 'But as for *francs-tireurs* ...'

Reports of the enemy's conduct in Belgium – 'German beastliness' – soon made headlines in every allied newspaper. A wounded Irish soldier in Dover hospital told Asquith, the prime minister, that he had seen with his own eyes Germans driving a screen of women and children in front of their troops. Such incidents occurred, though sometimes witnesses may merely have seen refugees fleeing spontaneously ahead of attackers. Some accounts, however, were grossly exaggerated: there were tales of babies impaled on Hunnish bayonets, of mothers' hands cut off by Prussian grenadiers. British naval cadet Geoffrey Harper wrote in his diary on 24 August after hearing of atrocities in Belgium: 'It is utter rot saying that the Germans are "a cultured race" or a civilised race. If the greater part of their army is capable of doing what it is doing, the rest of the race must be the same. From now onwards I shall of course regard every German – man, woman and child, from the Kaiser downwards – not as a poor and uneducated savage, but as a wilful savage.'

There was a fierce argument in Britain's newspapers about whether its own civilian population should resist if the country was invaded. H.G. Wells and Sir Arthur Conan Doyle urged that it should, but a correspondent to *The Times* strongly disagreed, citing the futility of Belgian civilian resistance, which did no harm to the Germans, but prompted severe reprisals: 'Let no one doubt what would be the consequences. We should be treated to the ghastly and maddening spectacle of blazing villages, brutal executions, and all the nameless horrors that the retaliation of an exasperated soldiery usually involves.'

Before long, it became known that some reports of German behaviour in Belgium had been exaggerated, or entirely manufactured, for propaganda purposes. A violent reaction followed. An American in Paris one day entered the offices of the Foyer Franco-Belge, a group to which André Gide was giving help, and scornfully offered a large donation if its staff could introduce him to a single child who had been mutilated by the German invaders. This incident followed publication of a newspaper article by Jean Richepin, claiming that the hands of 4,000 children in occupied territories had been cut off by the enemy.

Many British soldiers – at least in the early stages of the war, before gas and protracted slaughter hardened attitudes – respected the Germans as 'honourable adversaries'. They were disgusted by newspaper atrocity stories, at odds with their own experience. Maj. Bertie Trevor wrote home in September, applauding a sporting enemy: 'We fought the Guard Corps … a good lot … The German atrocities (so-called) to the wounded are much exaggerated.' The *New Statesman* declared its scepticism about tales of the enemy's alleged enormities against civilians: 'It seems to be universally the case that, if one's enemy does not commit atrocities, one has to invent them for him in order to hate him as he requires to be hated.' Bernard Shaw contemptuously compared the cry of newspapers for German atrocity stories to 'the clamour of an agonisingly wounded combatant for morphia'.

As late as 1928, Labour MP Arthur Ponsonby published a book entitled *Falsehood in Wartime*, claiming that 1914 'atrocities' were wilful inventions by allied governments, designed to stimulate hatred for the enemy. His work was acclaimed by liberal opinion and became unsurprisingly popular in Germany, where it was later republished by the Nazis. Around Europe to this day, many people believe that allegations of German war crimes had scant basis in reality. The issue became entwined with the postwar British liberal conviction that all the belligerents shared moral and political responsibility for the catastrophe that had taken place, and that all were equally guilty of crimes against humanity.

Such a view is at odds with the contemporary evidence. Modern research shows that, while some press reports of atrocities were fabrications, the German army in Belgium and France indeed behaved with systemic inhumanity. British and French soldiers occasionally executed innocent French and Belgian civilians as spies, but nothing is recorded or even alleged against the Western allies remotely on the scale of German massacres. Obsessed with an alleged threat from *francs-tireurs*, the Kaiser's army murdered civilians and hostages in large numbers. The most

authoritative recent chroniclers of German war crimes, John Horne and
Alan Kramer, write: 'We can state categorically that there was neither
collective civilian resistance nor military action by *franc-tireur* units [as
there had been during the 1870–71 Franco-Prussian War]. There were a
few isolated cases of individual civilians firing on Germans, but none of
these incidents provoked mass executions such as those of Dinant,
Louvain, or Liège in Belgium and others in France.'

From early August onwards, rumours of *francs-tireurs'* activity, and
details of their alleged atrocities, spread feverishly among German formations. These fed soldiers' willingness both to believe the worst whenever
they heard gunfire behind the front, and to exact summary retribution. A
policy of extreme severity was sanctioned at the highest level. The Kaiser
wrote on 9 August: 'The population of Belgium ... behaved in a diabolical,
not to say, bestial manner, not one iota better than the Cossacks. They
tormented the wounded, beat them to death, killed doctors and medical
orderlies, fired secretly ... on men harmlessly standing in the street ... The
King of the Belgians has to be notified at once that since his people have
placed themselves outside all observance of European customs ... they
will be treated accordingly.'

A sample of incidents which provoked appalling German responses
included one in Belgian Luxembourg on the night of 12 August: a woman
in Arlon accidentally severed a field telephone wire by opening her shutters on it. She was denounced as a saboteur; the local commander ordered
the razing of the village and payment of an indemnity. A police officer
taken hostage was executed the following night, after German cavalry
claimed to have been fired on. At Jarny in Luxembourg on 10 August, an
Italian who shot his own dog in compliance with a German edict about
controlling pet animals prompted allegations of *franc-tireur* activity,
which caused fifteen Italians to be shot. Tactical battlefield setbacks often
prompted murderous displays of spite towards civilians. On 11 August,
after German dragoons were forced to withdraw under fire, they claimed
to have been attacked by villagers in Bazailles. Twenty-five of its inhabitants were thereupon shot, forty-five houses burned. In Vise on the 16th,
drunken Königsberg Pioneers claimed to have been attacked. Twenty-five
inhabitants were shot, 631 deported to Germany; the town was pillaged
and six hundred houses burned.

Some German units punished enemy troops for resisting them: two
Belgian regiments held up an advance on Aarschot on 19 August, which
provoked the affronted invaders to kill twenty prisoners and throw their

bodies into the river Demer. Later that day, a brigade commander named Col. Stenger was shot and killed, probably by 'friendly fire'. A certain Capt. Karge ordered seventy-six male hostages to be shot immediately, in batches of three, as a reprisal. The burning and looting of Aarschot continued through that night. On 28 August a further thousand of the town's inhabitants were herded into Louvain, where some were shot on arrival. Four hundred were later deported to Germany, including monks of the Sacred Heart order from the local monastery. In all, 156 inhabitants of Aarschot perished.

Even some German officers seem to have had misgivings about the ruthlessness of such actions. After 262 civilians of both sexes and all ages were murdered in Andenne-Seilles, a newly appointed town commander, Capt. Becker, ordered that 'a festival of reconciliation' should be held on 28 August, which local people regarded as evidence of German discomfort. But incidents involving the exploitation of civilians as human shields remained relatively commonplace, including one during the taking of Namur, where two priests were among those killed fulfilling this role. In Namur also, which was occupied on the evening of 23 August, four hundred hostages were assembled in a riding school, to be addressed by a German officer in halting French: 'Our soldiers have been fired on. We are going to act as we did at Andenne. Andenne [is] finished ... The inhabitants tried to poison our soldiers, fired on our soldiers ... You too are going to be shot because you've fired on our soldiers right near here, in the Grand Place. You Belgians have also cut off our soldiers' noses, ears, eyes and fingers.' Instead, and most unusually, that evening the hostages were abruptly freed.

The incendiary catastrophe visited on the old city of Louvain was provoked by an unexplained outbreak of firing at 8 o'clock on the evening of 25 August. Soldiers ran into houses, dragged men out for beating, and in some cases shot them. That night at 11.30 soldiers broke into the university library and set it on fire, then prevented Belgian firemen from fighting the blaze, which consumed 300,000 volumes. Shooting and arson continued through the 26th, until 2,000 buildings had been destroyed. Some 10,000 inhabitants of Louvain were driven from the town, of whom 1,500 were deported to Germany.

The occupiers convinced themselves that Belgian clergy were foremost in inciting resistance. A young Jesuit, Father Dupierreux, was among four hundred Louvain priests and academics herded into a field outside Brussels, then searched for weapons. A diary was found on Dupierreux in which he had written a passage which his captors read aloud: 'Decidedly,

I do not like the Germans. I learned that centuries ago it was the barbarians who burned unfortified towns, pillaged houses and assassinated innocent townsfolk. The Germans have done exactly the same thing ... This people can be proud of its *Kultur*.' The priest was executed on the spot.

'The inhabitants of Seilles attacked our pioneers building a bridge across the Meuse, killing twenty of them,' Harry Graf Kessler wrote in his diary on 22 August. 'As a punishment approx. 200 citizens were court-martialled and shot. No house still has a roof or windows; bare burned walls stand street by street, and more terrible – household effects, family pictures, broken mirrors, overturned tables and chairs ... A family sits on the pavement before one house that is still burning: they watch until the last rafters collapse crying and crying ... Every [German] convoy we met between Seilles and Bierwart carried pillage ... our soldiers get used to drinking and looting. In Liège whole platoons get drunk daily on wine and schnapps from burnt-out houses. It will be hard to stop this sort of thing.'

At Leffe, outside Dinant, on 23 August German troops convinced them-selves that they faced widespread civilian resistance. Cpl. Franz Stiebing described what followed: 'We pushed on past house by house, under fire from almost every building, and we arrested the male inhabitants, who almost all carried weapons. They were summarily executed in the street. Only children under 15, old people and women were spared ... I did not see if anyone from my battalion was killed or injured in this street fighting. But I saw the corpses of at least 180 *francs-tireurs*.' Forty-three men were taken from the church and executed, among a total of 312 Leffe inhabit-ants killed.

It is unnecessary to persist in detailing such episodes. Kramer and Horne record 129 'major' documented atrocities during the first weeks of the war – 101 in Belgium and twenty-eight in France – in which a total of 5,146 civilians were killed in cold blood. There were also 383 'minor' inci-dents, involving fewer than ten deaths, which accounted for a further 1,100 people. A grand total of around 6,427 civilians are known to have been deliberately killed by the Germans during their 1914 operations. Some 65 per cent of the 'major' incidents were prompted by allegations that civilian *francs-tireurs* had fired on soldiers. The killings were carried out by men of every German army. Atrocities declined steeply only when the front stabilised in October.

It is interesting to contrast these statistics with the Eastern Front. A German official report declared that 101 civilians perished during the Russian invasion of East Prussia. It recorded only two 'major incidents':

one at Santoopen on 28 August, where nineteen Germans were executed, another at Christiankehmen on 11 September, where fourteen civilians died. The German report concluded: 'Russian atrocities have … turned out to be grossly exaggerated … It is reported that Russian troops have behaved correctly everywhere towards the inhabitants. If individual towns and villages were burned down, this occurred almost without exception during artillery duels.' Erich Ludendorff sought to contrast the supposedly 'shocking' behaviour of Belgian people towards the Kaiser's army with the fact that 'many of the Russian troops behaved in exemplary fashion in East Prussia'.

The atrocity issue has been addressed at some length here, because it plays an important part in the evolution of allied public sentiment about the war, together with associated myths and legends. From the first weeks, some sceptics within the allied camp denounced tales of German 'frightfulness' as mere propaganda. Six American correspondents in Germany, headed by Irving S. Cobb of the *Saturday Evening Post*, sent a joint wire to the Associated Press on 7 September dismissing published accounts of horrors: 'In spirit we unite in rendering the reports of German atrocities groundless, as far as we are able to … After spending two weeks with and accompanying the troops upward of 100 miles we are unable to report a single instance unprovoked.'

This naïve proclamation sat oddly with such German newspaper reports as those of the *Kölnische Zeitung* four days earlier; far from denying stories of savage reprisals, it sought instead to justify them: 'Our brave fellows were not prepared for the resistance of the inhabitants of the towns and villages which they were obliged to occupy. How could they expect to be shot at from windows and cellars? At first they were petrified with horror at such crimes, and only when their officers ordered it did they adopt punitive measures, burn houses, execute civilians.' Modern researchers have assembled evidence which seems hard to question. A mood of hysteria overtook the Kaiser's army in Belgium and France during August 1914, matched by a determination swiftly and ruthlessly to assert its supremacy. There was also, among some soldiers, a desire to wreak revenge on any victims to hand for battlefield setbacks and casualties. Unauthorised misdeeds are committed by every army in every war, but in this case the German hierarchy formally endorsed the legitimacy of its soldiers' conduct.

Many well-intentioned allied people, both soldiers and civilians, after discovering that some outrageous contemporary charges against the

German army were false, thereupon concluded that all 'atrocity stories' should be disbelieved. Such a view grew among the British, especially, because of their respect for pre-war German culture. They were naïve. Their enemies indeed committed actions in Belgium and France in 1914 unworthy of a civilised society. In defence of German conduct, it is sometimes asserted that other European nations and their armies also behaved barbarously at times. The Russians were guilty of widespread atrocities against Polish Jews in 1914–15. The Belgians' conduct in their Congo colony was consistently appalling. The record of British imperial security forces in India and Africa was tarnished by excesses towards civilians, as was that of the French in their overseas possessions. The British also sometimes acted deplorably during the 1920–21 independence struggle in Ireland.

But the German policy – and policy it was – of seizing large numbers of hostages and murdering them wholesale in response to resistance, largely or wholly imagined, was unmatched in scale in Western Europe during that era. The excesses of the Kaiser's nation cannot reasonably be compared with those of the Nazi regime that followed a generation later. But they make it more difficult to accept the indulgent view of some historians that a German victory in the conflict of 1914–18 would have represented the triumph of a nation and a cause morally indistinguishable from those of the allies.

3 LANREZAC ENCOUNTERS SCHLIEFFEN

All the while that the French armies had been hurling themselves upon the Germans along almost the entire length of France's eastern frontier, the hosts of Moltke's right wing tramped, tramped, tramped towards the centre of the stage, which they would dominate in the days ahead. In Belgium and northern France, rather than in Luxembourg, Alsace or Lorraine, the fate of Europe would be decided. Almost 600,000 German soldiers of two armies passed Brussels, then swept on southward towards the frontier of the two nations. In their path stood the French Fifth Army, soon to be joined by the British Expeditionary Force, together mustering just half the enemy's strength.

Joffre still cherished hopes that Belgian forces might strike at the German right flank when, as he wrongly expected, Moltke turned south of the Meuse. After the loss of Liège, the Belgians would most sensibly have retired to the frontier fortress of Namur, within reach of the main

French army. But King Albert cared less for prudence than for clinging to national soil. He determined instead to fall back on his northern fortress of Antwerp, there to hold out until the allies marched to his relief – he himself reached the city on 20 August. Joffre's GQG dismissed the Belgians' insistent and accurate warnings, that the principal might of the German army was now surging through their country, headed for France.

On the afternoon of 21 August, however, the commander of the French Fifth Army, Gen. Charles Lanrezac, suddenly recognised the strength of the enemy bearing down upon him. His formations lay beneath the descending mace of the German right wing, the critical stroke in Moltke's implementation of the Schlieffen concept. Lanrezac's force comprised four corps, and was three times as large as the little British Expeditionary Force coming up on his left, but it was nonetheless heavily outnumbered by the Germans. At that stage, GQG was still expecting Fifth Army to join with its neighbours further south in renewing Joffre's grand offensive. Instead, its commander defied orders, abandoned his attacking role and began to pull back south of the Sambre, with the Germans crowding on his heels.

Lanrezac, sixty-two years old, has had a poor press from historians, and it is easy to understand why. Though a clever man, one of his nation's leading military intellectuals, he was also a boorish and ineffectual one, prey to a despondency beyond pessimism. He disdained the British, who returned his contempt with interest. He referred to the BEF as 'L'armée W[ilson]', because its sub-chief of staff was the only senior officer capable of speaking French, and thus deserving of notice. But Lanrezac's grasp of developments in mid-August 1914 was much superior to that of Joffre. He was among the first French generals to realise that the Germans were advancing through Belgium in huge strength, and vainly urged the commander-in-chief to abandon his thrust in the Ardennes, 'that death-trap'. The repeated retreats which Lanrezac ordered on his own initiative seemed to Joffre as well as to the British pusillanimous. But they preserved Fifth Army for important service under a better commander. More immediately, Lanrezac's handling of his forces denied the Germans the decisive clash in the north they were impatient to bring about.

The commander-in-chief did not at first press his subordinate to attack. Thus Fifth Army was largely supine until, on 21 August, Karl von Bülow's formations fell upon it near Charleroi. This heavily-built-up industrial region was poor country in which to fight a defensive battle, because it was difficult for artillery or infantry to gain a clear sight of the foe. That day, the Germans seized bridges across the Sambre, and held them against

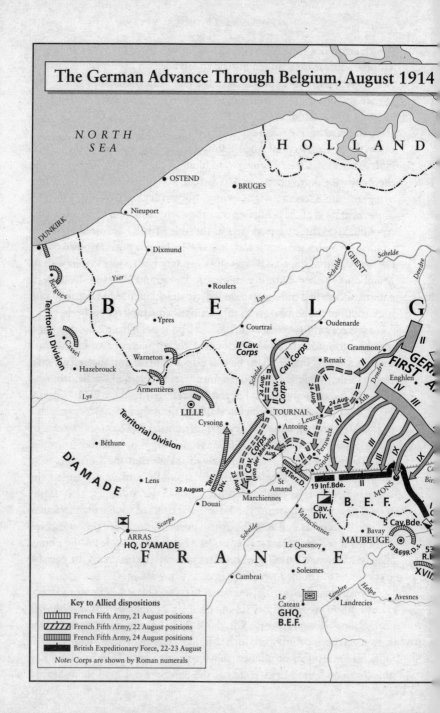

The German Advance Through Belgium, August 1914

NORTH SEA

HOLLAND

OSTEND

BRUGES

Nieuport

DUNKIRK

Dixmund

Bergues

Yser

Roulers

Territorial Division

B   E

Ypres

Courtrai

L

Oudenarde

Schelde

GHENT

Schelde

Dendre

G

Lys

II Cav. Corps

Grammont

II

Cassei

Warneton

Hazebrouck

Armentières

Lys

LILLE

Cysoing

Béthune

Territorial Division

D'AMADE

Lens

Douai

Marchiennes

St Amand

ARRAS
HQ, D'AMADE

Scarpe

FRANCE

Cambrai

Solesmes

Schelde

Renaix

II Cav.
Corps

24 Aug.

II Cav.
Corps

Schelde

TOURNAI

Antoing

Leuze

II Cav. Corps
(von der Marwitz)

Peruwelz

Condé

Valenciennes

84 Terr.D.

19 Inf. Bde.

Cav.
Div.

B.E.F.

Bavay

MAUBEUGE

Le Quesnoy

Sambre

Le Cateau
GHQ,
B.E.F.

Helpe

Landrecies

Ath

24 Aug.

Enghlen

FIRST A.

GER

II

II

IV

III

IX

24 Aug.

IV

III

IX

IV

III

Cô

Bir

MONS

5 Cav. Bde.

53

53&69 R.D.

R.D

XVII

Avesnes

Aug.

23 August

II Cav. Corps

23 Aug.

Terr.
Div.

Terr.
Div.

Key to Allied dispositions

French Fifth Army, 21 August positions
French Fifth Army, 22 August positions
French Fifth Army, 24 August positions
British Expeditionary Force, 22-23 August

Note: Corps are shown by Roman numerals

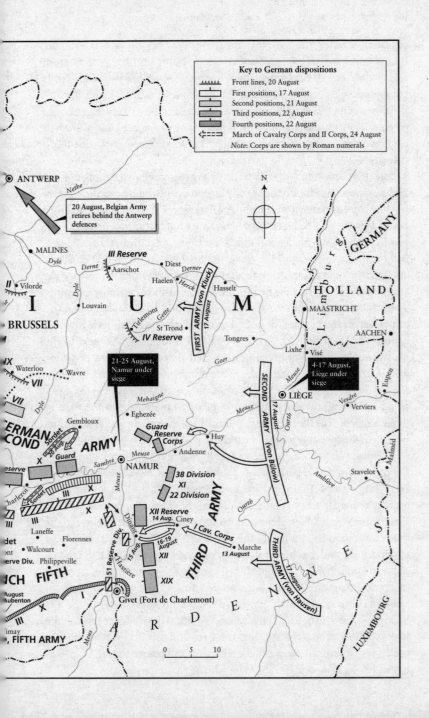

Key to German dispositions

ᴧᴧᴧᴧᴧ	Front lines, 20 August
▭	First positions, 17 August
▬	Second positions, 21 August
▬	Third positions, 22 August
▬	Fourth positions, 22 August
◁┅═┅▷	March of Cavalry Corps and II Corps, 24 August

Note: Corps are shown by Roman numerals

⊙ ANTWERP

Nethe

20 August, Belgian Army retires behind the Antwerp defences

• MALINES

Dyle   Derne • Aarschot   • Diest   Derner   HOLLAND

II • Vilorde   Haelen • Herck   • Hasselt   GERMANY

Dyle   • Louvain   Tirlemont   Gette   MAASTRICHT

BRUSSELS   St Trond   FIRST ARMY (von Kluck) 17 August   AACHEN

IV Reserve   • Tongres   Lixhe • Visé

IX   Waterloo   Wavre   Geer   Eupen

VII   21-25 August, Namur under siege   SECOND ARMY (von Bülow) 17 August   LIÈGE   4-17 August, Liège under siege   Vesdre

VII   Dyle   Mehaigne   Meuse   ⊙ LIÈGE   • Verviers

ERMAN   Gembloux   • Eghezée   Meuse   Ourthe   Malméd

COND   Sordet 20 Aug   Guard Reserve Corps   • Huy   Vesdre

Reserve   X   Guard   Meuse   • Andenne   Stavelot •   Ambleve

Charleroi   III   X   Sambre   ⊙ NAMUR   38 Division XI   Ourthe

III   • Laneffe   • Florennes   XII Reserve 14 Aug. Ciney   I Cav. Corps   THIRD ARMY (von Hausen) 17 August   S

det   • Walcourt   Dinant   16-19 August   • Marche 13 August

erve Div.   • Philippeville   51 Reserve Div.   15 Aug   XII

NCH FIFTH   August   Hastière   XIX   THIRD ARMY

ubenton   X   I   Givet (Fort de Charlemont)   D   E   N   LUXEMBOURG

III

imay   Meus   FIFTH ARMY   ⌐ 0   5   10 ⌐   R   D   E   N repeated counter-attacks. Next morning, France's bloodsoaked 22nd, Bülow and his staff motored to a vantage point on high ground from which they could view operations. Lanrezac gave his two local corps commanders on the opposite side of the valley no orders, and thus on their own initiative they did what was expected of every French general in August. They attacked, committing their men to a succession of massed charges to recapture the river bridges. These were repulsed with 6,000 casualties.

The destruction of two colonial infantry regiments, 1st Tirailleurs and 2nd Zouaves, passed into the bloody legend of the time. There was other-worldly close-quarter strife around the Tirailleurs' colours, which changed hands repeatedly. The regiment's report later noted, ungrammatically but vividly: 'the colour-bearer was killed five times'. Lt. Edward Louis Spears, British liaison officer with Lanrezac, wrote of the regiment that attacked: 'As if at manoeuvres, in dense formation, bugles blowing, drums beating and flags flying, it had dashed to the assault with the utmost gallantry. These brave men, in the face of machine-guns and artillery whose gunners can never have dreamed of such targets ... were driven back in some confusion.' Most of Fifth Army, we should remember, was new to the ghastly experiences that French forces further south had been enduring for a fortnight. Spears met some of Lanrezac's men preparing to renew their assaults: 'they were like eager children, as gay as if this were the dawn of a holiday and they were presently going to march down the road to make a day of it at the local fair'. Within a few hours, their radiant spirits were extinguished in a storm of machine-gun fire and high explosives.

Lt. Spears – in those days he spelled his name 'Spiers' – became one of the most remarkable participants in the drama of 1914. He was twenty-eight, and an upbringing in France had conferred on him a talent rare among contemporary British soldiers – he spoke accentless French. Despite his youth and junior rank, from the first days of the campaign he made himself indispensable to the senior officers of the two allies, whose eminence intimidated him not at all. Four years later the French ambas-sador in London described Spears as '[a] most dangerous person ... a very able and intriguing Jew who insinuates himself everywhere'. Many of Spears's compatriots shared such disdainful sentiments. Later in the war Winston Churchill befriended him, and sceptical comrades sneered at the two as fellow mountebanks. But the British liaison officer became an eyewitness to crucial inter-allied exchanges, and later published a narra-tive of his experiences, *Liaison 1914*, which is a masterpiece.

On Fifth Army's front on 22 August, having crushed French attacks, the Germans launched their own advance. By late afternoon Lanrezac's centre was collapsing, and his army had fallen back in disorder some six miles. Just three German divisions had inflicted a major defeat on nine French formations. The general was at first minded to counter-attack next day. However, when confronted with bad news from every sector, at 9.30 p.m. on 23 August he ordered a general retreat, hoping to turn and meet the Germans again on better terms, in new positions further south. He was not a moment too soon: though Bülow's army had also suffered severe losses in the Sambre battles, its divisions were now deploying in strength south of the river. The French commander's egregious error was that, having acted sensibly in defiance of orders, he left both Joffre and his nearby British allies supposing that he intended imminently to resume the offensive – which he did not.

Between 20 and 23 August, 40,000 French soldiers died. By 29 August, total French casualties since the war began reached 260,000, including 75,000 dead. The Third and Fourth Armies in the Ardennes had suffered worst – of the Third's 80,000 infantrymen, 13,000 had fallen. By the evening of 23 August, the 'Battles of the Frontiers' were over. They would remain the entire war's bloodiest daily clashes of arms. And even as Lanrezac's men were falling back, a few miles westwards the British Expeditionary Force met the Germans for the first time, at the dreary little Belgian industrial town of Mons.

6

The British Fight

On 3 August *The Times*'s military correspondent, that intelligent cad Col. Charles à Court Repington, declared that the Franco-German frontier would become the focus of the war's first big military operations. He added fiercely: 'If our troops fail at the rendezvous, history will assign our cowardice as the cause' – meaning the sluggishness of Asquith's government in agreeing to deploy British troops on the continent. On the 10th, Repington warned: 'We must be prepared for a desperate enterprise on the part of the entire German navy, and for the attempted cooperation of the German army in an attack on us.' Two days later he wrote sombrely: 'We should not be under any illusion that the approaching *Massenschlacht* will be anything less than the most frightfully destructive collision of modern history,' adding on 15 August: 'It is at least possible that the war may last a long time.'

That day the British Expeditionary Force's commander-in-chief, Sir John French, arrived at Paris's Gare du Nord, to be greeted by a large crowd undeterred by drizzling rain. Following the field-marshal's subsequent meeting with France's leaders at the Elysée Palace, Sir Francis Bertie described René Viviani as 'harassed, nervous and anxious'. Meanwhile 'the minister for war was more anxious to display his knowledge of English than to impart valuable information'. Amid huge uncertainties and apprehensions, it is scarcely surprising that the nerves of the principal players, none of them young men, were stretched to the limit. Bertie was probably unaware that Joffre was telling his government – never mind the people of France – almost nothing about events on the battlefield.

It is an enduring British conceit that the First World War began in earnest only on 23 August, when the 'Old Contemptibles' of the BEF drubbed the Kaiser's hosts at Mons, thus saving England by their exertions and Europe by their example. In truth, of course, the French army had been engaged in murderous strife for almost three weeks before the first of the King-Emperor's soldiers fired a shot in anger; Serbia, Poland and East Prussia were already steeped in blood.

In northern France during the first exchanges of the war the British contribution, though significant, was entirely subordinate to that of the vastly larger allied forces. Against 1,077 German infantry battalions, at the start of the campaign the French deployed 1,108, the Belgians 120 and the BEF ... fifty-two. It is unlikely that the Kaiser ever spoke of Britain's 'contemptible little army', as popular myth asserts, but its absurdly inadequate size justified such an appellation. French's initial force comprised sixteen regiments of cavalry, the aforesaid fifty-two battalions of infantry, sixteen brigades of field guns, five batteries of horse artillery, four heavy batteries, eight field companies of Royal Engineers, together with service corps and suchlike supporting contingents. Later in the war – from 1916, as France became increasingly exhausted – Britain assumed a major role on the Western Front. In August 1914, however, the BEF conducted only a long retirement interrupted by two holding actions. German miscalculation and bungling, together with French mass and courage, did much more than British pluck to deny the Kaiser his victory parade down the Champs-Elysées. But this does not diminish the fascination with which posterity views the BEF's first actions.

The Anglo-Saxon allies were warmly welcomed to the continent. After a march on 13 August Lt. Guy Harcourt-Vernon wrote: 'Last mile ½ battalion fell out to be seized by inhabitants & dosed with water and cider. Discipline appalling.' Unit adjutants visited brigade paymasters to exchange officers' English gold sovereigns for local francs. A café in the Place Gambetta of Amiens adopted a custom which had spread through all Europe's warring camps: at 9 p.m., closing time, uniformed and civilian patrons alike rose and stood at attention while the band played in succession each allied national anthem. But the old women who supervised the local public baths treated their foréign visitors – by no means mistakenly – as lambs destined for slaughter. They mopped their eyes as they distributed free tea, saying, '*Pauvres petits anglais, ils vont bientôt être tués.*'

The right wing of Moltke's armies had farthest to march to do its part in the vast envelopment of Joffre's forces. After smashing a path through Liège, two corps were detached to pursue the Belgian army, retiring northwestwards towards the fortress of Antwerp in hopes of eventual French succour; to occupy Brussels; and to secure lines of communication. These diversions significantly weakened the main 'Schlieffen' thrust south. Belgian forces were incapable of major offensive action, and could most sensibly have been masked until the French were beaten, then mopped up at leisure.

The third week of August found the adjoining armies of Alexander von Kluck and Karl von Bülow, more than half a million men, plodding doggedly southwards through Belgium towards the French frontier. Some eyewitnesses who watched their progress were stricken with awe at what seemed an irresistible phenomenon. Richard Harding Davis, an American novelist and journalist, described their triumphal entry into Brussels at 3.20 p.m. on 20 August: 'No longer was it regiments of men marching, but something uncanny, inhuman, a force of nature like a landslide, a tidal wave or lava sweeping down a mountain. It was not of this earth, but mysterious, ghostlike.' Harding Davis marvelled at the sense of power projected by thousands of men singing 'Fatherland, my Fatherland' 'like blows from a giant piledriver'.

As for their commanders, Kluck was sixty-eight years old, of non-noble background, a tough, leathery professional who had risen on merit. Bülow was also sixty-eight, a Prussian aristocrat to whom Kluck was subordinate, though in the field the latter not infrequently ignored the fact. Moltke considered Bülow the ablest of his generals, and had thus entrusted him with the most critical responsibilities, but both he and Kluck were old men, well past fitness to assume leading roles in the greatest military operations in history, as would soon become apparent. Within Bülow's two armies both men and beasts were already feeling their feet. In just one German cavalry division, seventy horses died of exhaustion in the first fortnight of the campaign, and most of the others could scarcely raise a trot. No system was adopted for regularly resting marching men, the better to husband their strength and minister to blistered feet.

Towards them tramped the columns of the British Expeditionary Force, advancing through gently undulating countryside, basking in welcomes as warm as those its soldiers had everywhere met since disembarking at the Channel ports. 'These French people are certainly enthusiastic beyond British comprehension,' wrote Lord Bernard Gordon-Lennox of the Grenadiers, 'and it would do old England a world of good to see the unbounded patriotism and *bonne camaraderie* displayed on all sides.' Some men remarked on the profusion of mistletoe in the branches of roadside trees, though relatively few would live to kiss any woman beneath

Christmas boughs. Recalled reservists made up at least half of the strength of every BEF unit: fresh from soft civilian life and wearing unbroken boots, they struggled to keep up.

Guy Harcourt-Vernon scribbled on the 22nd: 'All day men have been gorging themselves on pears & apples. Farmer says better us than Prussians. Hear, hear!' The BEF's C-in-C had agreed to halt his force at the Mons–Condé canal just inside Belgium, where it could protect Lanrezac's left, while French cavalry filled the intervening gap. But then Fifth Army received a bloody nose at Charleroi, and yielded ground. The British and French thus became perilously misaligned, with the BEF still advancing blithely, even as Lanrezac's men were falling back.

When the khaki columns reached Mons, some thirty-five miles south of Brussels, soldiers whose faces were already reddened by the summer sun stripped off their tunics and began to dig in, to no great effect, amid the clutter of a suburban and industrial region. Buildings limited fields of fire. Towards nightfall insects began to swarm out of the waterways, causing thousands of men to curse freely as they slapped bites. In the distance to the south-east, some heard the crump of guns on Fifth Army's front. Sir John French learned of the repulses that had been inflicted on his allies, but did not comprehend their scale – the facts that the French army had lost a quarter of its mobilised strength, while Lanrezac's left was nine miles behind the British.

The little field-marshal remained buoyant about allied prospects. He knew there were Germans in the offing, but displayed a bizarre insouciance about placing his troops in their path. The BEF's highly competent chief of intelligence, Col. George MacDonogh, gave warnings based on air reconnaissance and messages from Lanrezac's staff, that three German corps were bearing down upon him. Sir John dismissed this threat, proposing to continue an advance towards Soignies. When he personally interviewed an RFC pilot who had gazed down on Kluck's masses, the C-in-C revealed obvious disbelief, and changed the subject to quiz the troubled young man paternalistically about his aeroplane.

The first British shots of the war were fired early on the morning of the 22nd. Cavalry from C Squadron of the 4th Royal Irish Dragoon Guards were deployed at the top of a gentle slope about three miles north of the Mons–Condé canal. They saw approaching from a dip ahead of them a German lancer patrol, including an officer smoking a cigar. Capt. Charles Hornby led two troops cantering down the road, sparks flying from the cobbles, in pursuit of the enemy, who took flight. There was a mêlée a mile on, in which the British took five prisoners from the startled Germans, hampered by their lances. Cpl. Ted Thomas used his rifle: after years on the ranges, where one waited several seconds for a paper target to be marked, he was amazed by the promptness with which a German horseman dropped from his saddle – the first enemy to fall to a British bullet. Hornby returned exultant, reporting that his own victim had died like a gentleman, at the point of a sword. He gave his weapon to the regimental armourer to be sharpened, expressing idiot regret at the necessity to have the blood wiped off. His brigadier had promised a DSO to the first officer to kill a German with the new pattern cavalry sword, and Hornby duly received this decoration.

That evening of 22 August, a message arrived from Lanrezac suggesting to Sir John French that the entire BEF should wheel to the right, and attack the flank of Bülow's advance. Open flanks are where armies lose battles, and even wars, if an enemy can contrive to strike at them. But such a British manoeuvre would have been madness in the circumstances: Kluck's six corps, close at hand beyond Bülow's formations, could have engulfed them, facing the wrong way. The C-in-C refused, almost his last wise decision of the campaign, and retired to bed with no sense of impending doom or even of bad trouble.

The two divisions of Gen. Sir Horace Smith-Dorrien's II Corps spent the night of the 22nd bivouacked along the Mons–Condé canal, with the cavalry covering their left, commanded by Allenby. Haig's I Corps deployed in a quarter-circle on the right, reaching back towards Lanrezac's Fifth Army. The BEF's positions were anything but ideal for meeting an attack: the sixteen-mile canal was neither wide nor deep enough to constitute a major obstacle, averaging barely twenty yards of breadth. On some stretches of the overall twenty-six-mile British front the ground on the north bank sloped down to the water amid either woodland or clusters of buildings, both offering cover to an approaching enemy.

Smith-Dorrien's corps was given a much longer front than Haig's. The British were too few to man a continuous line – some battalions were responsible for 2,000 yards – and thus they concentrated around the bridges, leaving wide gaps that an attacker could exploit, especially with the aid of the barges moored at intervals along the towpath. North-east of Mons the canal bent back into a half-loop, creating a dangerous salient for the companies of Royal Fusiliers and Middlesex holding that sector. As the light began to fade on the 22nd, Lt. Col. Charles Hull of the Middlesex, whose rigid notions of discipline inspired both respect and fear, rode around the battalion's positions with his adjutant, Tom Wollocombe. Hull exploded into anger when he heard a company commander urge his men to blaze away at a German aeroplane: the colonel said they would soon need every round of ammunition they carried. As darkness fell, the British heard a distant, unexplained rattle of musketry, which helped to preserve the watchfulness of pickets.

Partly because they expected soon to advance again, but chiefly because they had not yet been galvanised by the ruthless imperatives of war, the defenders failed to use their hours of grace before the Germans' arrival to prepare the canal's eighteen bridges for demolition. They merely erected some half-hearted barricades, and covered the approaches with machine-guns. Engineers laid a few precautionary charges; a sapper at one bridge set off on a bicycle to find some detonators, with which he was unprovided. Just before dawn on 23 August, Sir John French conferred briefly with his two corps commanders at Smith-Dorrien's headquarters in the Château de Sars. He seemed in ebullient form, asserting against all evidence that only one or at most two German corps were at hand. He told his generals to be prepared alternatively to advance, hold their line or pull back. Then he rattled away in his motor car to visit an infantry brigade at Valenciennes, playing no further part in the battle which now developed. Here was extraordinary behaviour by a commander-in-chief responsible for Britain's only field army, starting its first continental campaign for a century, with the enemy known to be at hand. French seemed to lack any sense of the gravity of the moment. His subordinates, down to platoon level, were given no clear briefings whatsoever, save that they should expect to defend their positions for a day or so.

In the small hours, an order reached units in the line: 'you will stand to arms at 4.30 a.m. today. Transport to be loaded up and horses saddled. Acknowledge.' At 6 a.m., a further instruction arrived, to dispatch battalion baggage carts to the rear. Men were later grateful for this – their kits could never have been got away under fire, once battle was joined. During the tense hour or two while they lay on their weapons awaiting the enemy, the Middlesex received a superbly inconsequential message from division, complaining that one of their officers had ridden away from a Belgian blacksmith's forge at Taisnières without paying for his horse's reshoeing. Most men used the pause to improve their positions under the friendly eyes of local people, clad in their Sunday best. Neither soldiers nor civilians displayed much sense of peril, which only devastation and death would provide. Officers pored over maps which were unhelpful, because lacking detail. The first brushes with German patrols took place in a light drizzle, but soon afterwards the sun broke through. Cavalry pickets cantered back into the lines. Enemy artillery began to drop shells on Smith-Dorrien's units, rudely interrupting some men at breakfast.

These were soldiers of an army which, for half a century past, had known only colonial campaigns, most often against natives armed with spears, though the Boers had shown them what modern small arms could do. The average age of the BEF was twenty-five, and many younger soldiers had never shot to kill. But there were also present old sweats who had fought Dervishes and Pathans: when a Guards sergeant-major set about forming his battalion's baggage carts into a defensive circle outside a Belgian village, he dubbed it – echo of Kitchener's Sudan – a 'zareba'.

The BEF was small but its soldiers, thanks largely to Richard Haldane, were the best-equipped Britain had ever sent to war. They had the superb .303 short magazine Lee-Enfield rifle, the cavalry had the Vickers machine-gun, whilst the infantry used the older Maxim variant. Some men wore leather personal accoutrements, while others had already been issued with the canvas webbing and ammunition pouches which were becoming standard. Both were well-designed, as was the British pack. Men valued their puttees, despite the pernickety bother of winding the long cotton wrappings around their legs. Puttees were warm, and provided ankle support on rough ground and long marches, or in muddy trenches. The BEF's most serious deficiencies were of numbers, heavy artillery and motor transport. In the autumn of 1914, French countryfolk grew accustomed to the sight of requisitioned lorries still bearing the names of their London store owners – Harrods, Maples, Whiteleys – and motor bicycles ridden by eager young civilians who had volunteered their services as dispatch riders. Vans belonging to the caterers J. Lyons soon bore wounded men from London stations to hospitals.

This was an army many of whose officers appeared physically indistinguishable from each other, their features adorned with uniform tightly-clipped moustaches. They took it for granted that – with the exceptions of the Army Service Corps, Pioneers and suchlike – they were gentlemen who regarded horses rather than motors as their natural means of personal transport; members of the same club, many of whom knew each other. When Tom Bridges found himself unhorsed in the path of the enemy, he was rescued by a passing staff officer in a Rolls-Royce, who proved to have been at school with him. After peacetime years in which promotion

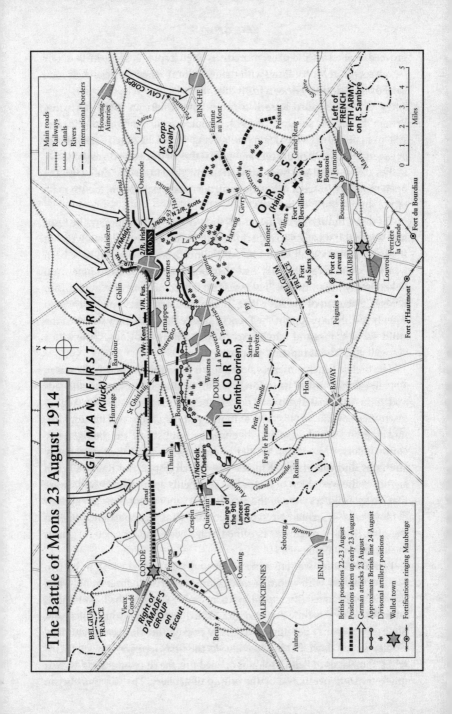

The Battle of Mons 23 August 1914

Legend
- Main roads
- Railways
- Canals
- Rivers
- International borders

GERMAN FIRST ARMY (Kluck)

IX Corps Cavalry

I CAV. CORPS

I CORPS (Haig)

II CORPS (Smith-Dorrien)

Left of FRENCH FIFTH ARMY on R. Sambre

Right of D'AMADE'S GROUP on R. Escaut

Charge of the 9th Lancers (24th)

BELGIUM / FRANCE

Places: Houdeng-Aimeries, Binche, Estinne au Mont, Peissant, Grand Reng, Fort de Boussois, Jeumont, Maubert, La Haine, Osterode, MONS, Harmignies, Rouveroy, Givry, Bonnet, Villers, Fort Bersillies, Boussois, MAUBEUGE, Louvroil, Ferrière la Grande, Fort du Bourdiau, Fort d'Hautmont, Maisières, Ghlin, Cuesmes, Nouvelles, Fort des Sarts, Fort de Leveau, Feignies, Jemappes, Quaregnon, Wasmes, La Bouverie, Frameries, Sars-la-Bruyère, BAVAY, Baudour, Hautrage, St Ghislain, Boussu, DOUR, Petit Honnelle, Hon, Jenlain, Thulin, Fayt le Franc, Grand Honnelle, Roisin, Sebourg, Crespin, Quievrain, Quiévrain, Audregnies, CONDÉ, Vieux Condé, Fresnes, Onnaing, VALENCIENNES, Bruay, Aulnoy

Units: 4/Midx., 2/R. Irish, 4/R. Fus., 8/R., 2/R. Scots, 1/R. Fus., 1/N. Fus., 1/W. Kent, 1/Norfolk, 1/Cheshire

Scale: 0 1 2 3 4 5 Miles

N

Map key (bottom):
- British positions 22–23 August
- Positions taken up early 23 August
- German attacks 23 August
- Approximate British line 24 August
- Divisional artillery positions
- Walled town
- Fortifications ringing Maubeuge

proceeded at a tortoise pace, more than a few captains aged thirty-six or -seven served at Mons, along with many majors in their forties. Their men were overwhelmingly drawn from the industrial underclass or rural peasantry. Charles Edward Russell, a prominent American socialist visiting Britain during the summer of 1914, deplored manifestations of the class system in uniform. Watching recruits being drilled, he noted the disparity between the heights of officers and men – the former were on average five inches taller – and the poor appearance of the latter: 'the dull eyes, the open mouths that seem ready to drool, the vacant expression, the stigmata of the slum – terrible spectacle'.

Yet some, though by no means all, such victims of privation made resolute soldiers. It was rash to expect them to think much for themselves, but the same limitation afflicted most of their officers. Few would have been wearing khaki serge that day had they been capable of scraping a meal ticket by any other means. 'There was no hatred of Germany,' wrote Tom Bridges, a veteran of the Boer War. 'In the true mercenary spirit we would equally readily have fought the French.' Beside the canal, they smashed the windows of homes and warehouses to create firing positions, some with a vestigial guilt about injuring property.

The first of Kluck's infantry began to push downhill towards the water, shielded along most of its unlovely length by drab houses, mine pitheads and industrial installations. Though the German army was a mighty instrument of war, at this critical moment it displayed weaknesses, foremost among which was intelligence. In August, all the belligerents' commanders vied with each other in misjudgements of their opponents' strengths and intentions. Kluck's was the largest of the Kaiser's seven armies in the west. Men of its leading regiments approached Mons aware that British soldiers were in the vicinity, but ignorant of their strength or deployments – German aircraft played no useful reconnaissance role on the 23rd. Kluck himself was esteemed by his peers, but revealed no genius in this, his first battle of 1914.

Pte. Sid Godley was enjoying coffee and rolls brought to him by two Belgian children, with whom he made clumsy efforts at conversation, when their little party was interrupted by an incoming German shell. He recalled later: 'I said to this little boy and girl, "You'd better sling your 'ooks now, otherwise you may get hurt." Well, they packed their basket up and left.' Godley settled down behind his rifle. As the first Germans showed themselves, thousands of British soldiers opened fire, the rippling crackle of their musketry soon overborne by the crump of artillery. The Germans began crowding around the dangerous salient north-east of Mons, at Nimy, where the bridges were defended by the Royal Fusiliers, who had the 4th Middlesex to their right behind Obourg: legend has it that the Fusiliers were warned of the enemy's approach by the stationmaster's daughter. Col. Hull, commanding the Middlesex, was a small-arms enthusiast who had taken pains to ensure that his men could shoot straight, and that day they did him proud. Successive German rushes were checked by murderous rifle-fire. Huddled grey-green corpses, surmounted by Pickelhaube helmets, soon littered the north bank. But Kluck's men, in their turn, took up firing positions and were soon inflicting casualties on the ill-concealed British.

One of Hull's men, Pte. Jack, said later: 'When the firing began, I was frightened by the noise. I'd never heard anything like it. Most of the shells were bursting well behind us, but there was also a strange whistling sound as the bullets came over. There were four of us in a rifle-pit and our officer walked over to us and I remember thinking, "Get down, you silly bugger." Later on I heard the poor man was killed. Then the man next to me was hit. I was firing away and suddenly he gave a sort of grunt and lay still. I'd never seen a dead man before.' Guy Harcourt-Vernon wrote: 'Funny to notice how everyone ducks at the sound of a bullet. You know it is past you, but down goes your head every time.' Soon, too many bullets and shells were passing for any man to have time to duck. Most concentrated upon ramming clip after five-round clip into their hot weapons, though too much has been made of the rifleman's notional fifteen-rounds-a-minute capability. Any unit which sustained such a rate of fire would speedily have exhausted its ammunition.

Most of the Germans surging forward were as new to war as the British. Some experienced brief euphoria, such as was later described by Walter Bloem, a captain in the Brandenburg Grenadiers. As he advanced, 'a shout of triumph, a wild, unearthly singing surged within me, uplifting and inspiring me, filling all my senses. I had overcome fear; I had conquered my mortal bodily self.' At first, Kluck's men advanced in masses, direct from their line of march, and suffered in consequence. A British NCO wrote: 'They were in solid, square blocks, standing out sharply against the skyline, and you couldn't help hitting them … They crept nearer and nearer, and then our officers gave the word … They seemed to stagger like a drunk man hit suddenly between the eyes, after which they made a run for us, shouting some outlandish cry that we couldn't make out.'

In the same spirit a Gordon Highlander recounted: 'Poor devils of infantry! They advanced in companies of quite 150 men in files five deep, and our rifle has a flat trajectory up to 600 yards. Guess the result. We could steady our rifles on the trench and take deliberate aim. The first company were simply blasted away to Heaven by a volley at 700 yards, and in their insane formation every bullet was almost sure to find two billets. The other companies kept advancing very slowly, using their dead comrades as cover, but they had absolutely no chance.' The war would become overwhelmingly a contest between rival machine-guns and artillery pieces, but for a brief season in the late summer of 1914, the rifle displayed its powers against bodies of men exposing themselves in plain view.

However, the British grossly overestimated the casualties their riflemen inflicted. Many of the Germans who dropped to the ground were merely taking cover. Kluck's units broke up into smaller groups that manoeuvred more subtly, supported by howitzers which caused steadily mounting casualties. Far from behaving like the mindless squareheads of British caricature, many Germans used fire and manoeuvre effectively. Smith-Dorrien's companies deployed in advanced positions beyond the canal fell back to the south bank. 'God! How their artillery do fire!' exclaimed a Gordon: the shelling was a new and unwelcome experience for almost every member of the BEF. 'The men were digging little holes for themselves to sit in,' wrote Tom Wollocombe, 'and most of them were getting a bit jumpy, not being used to such living.' By the standards of the French battles a few days earlier, never mind those of Ypres two months later, British losses were slight. But for troops with no experience of the firepower of a modern European army, that August day on the canal bank seemed terrible enough. There was little German activity on the right, where Haig's corps was deployed, but on Smith-Dorrien's front information from prisoners and the badges of enemy dead revealed the presence of elements of two corps, pressing especially hard on the north-eastern salient.

But it should be stressed that, while Kluck led a much bigger army than French, the numbers of troops actively engaged on each side at Mons on 23 August were roughly equal. Praise has been lavished upon British heroism, less upon equally notable German courage. While significant numbers of Kluck's men were shot down at the approaches to the water, scores worked forward to seek footholds on the south bank, some of which were secured within ninety minutes of the battle's beginning. Memorable among the Germans was Oskar Niemeyer, a Hamburger. East of the rail crossing at Nimy defended by Royal Fusiliers stood a pedestrian bridge, which could be swung across the canal by pedal power. The British had parked this along their own bank. Niemeyer dived into the water, swam across, and under fire pedalled the span almost to the north bank before being shot down, a feat that would have won him a Victoria Cross had he been wearing khaki that morning. The dead man's comrades were able to toss a rope to secure the bridge and pull it to their side; then they began to dash across.

Such actions at a dozen points during the course of the morning exposed some British units to enfilading fire, and indeed threatened them with isolation. Shortly before 1 p.m., the Middlesex received a foolishly tardy message from division: 'you will decide when bridges and boats within your zones should be destroyed'. Tom Wollocombe wrote: 'it was too late. The enemy were across or crossing.' The defenders at Mons were much too thinly spread to generate the intensity of violence necessary to halt Kluck's host. British artillery batteries, close behind the infantry, suffered almost as severely from German fire as did riflemen. 'Our faithful gunners stuck to their pieces magnificently,' said Wollocombe. One of them, Sgt. William Edgington, wrote in his diary with notable understatement: 'A very trying day – Germans seemed to be all around us.' The Middlesex were among units which received no direct artillery support, because their nearest gunners could not see targets, and were obliged merely to hurl shells in the general direction of the enemy.

Though the British mauled Kluck's leading regiments, as the day wore on their own casualties rose; meanwhile, the trickle of Germans crossing the canal swelled into strong streams. Early in the afternoon, Douglas Haig crawled to the crest of a low hill three miles north of Le Bonnet and overlooking the battlefield, accompanied by a staff officer, and viewed in grim silence 'masses of grey-clad figures advancing' upon his neighbours of II Corps. So accurate was enemy artillery fire in some sectors that Smith-Dorrien's soldiers, like those of every other nation that August, became morbidly convinced that spies must be spotting for the enemy's batteries. Eventually, unit by unit II Corps began to fall back, its men scrambling in small groups towards the rear, platoons taking turns to cover each other's withdrawal, some soldiers supporting wounded mates. The difficulty was to make retreat a disciplined manoeuvre, not a headlong flight. When Col. Hull saw one of his platoons retiring under the orders of a sergeant – its two company officers had been hit – he told his adjutant to identify the NCO. After a glance through his field glasses, Tom Wollocombe gave the name, causing Hull to say furiously, 'if Sgt. — had not had any order to retire, he would have him shot'. In the event, the suspect proved to be on the battalion's 'Missing' list that night, so escaped the threatened firing squad.

Pte. Sid Godley took over a Royal Fusiliers machine-gun at Nimy after its crew was killed, to such effect that both he and Lt. Maurice Dease were awarded Victoria Crosses – the latter posthumously – for their defence of the rail bridge. Godley, though wounded in several places, allegedly kept firing to cover the retirement of the battalion, until that evening his position was overrun by the Germans, and he became a prisoner. Sceptics have cast doubt on the reality of this action, pointing out that no German account mentions having encountered such resistance: they suggest that the feats of Dease and Godley were chiefly attested by the latter, while the high command was eager to identify plausible heroes. But there is no dispute about the courage of Capt. Theodore Wright of the Royal Engineers, who at 3 p.m. began a brave but hopelessly belated journey along the canal, to attempt demolition of five bridges along a three-mile front. Wright's party was under fire most of the way, and his driver was understandably alarmed by the experience of threading a path across a battlefield in a car containing eight crates of guncotton.

Shot at from three sides, the engineer was eventually successful in destroying the crossing at Jemappes. While he was working on another at Mariette, he sent off his vehicle to take a wounded man to the rear. He was then grazed on the head by a shell fragment, and found himself without electricity to detonate his charges. He hastily ran a cable to the mains of a nearby house. Still getting no live current, he tried again and again to achieve a contact, while men of the Northumberland Fusiliers provided covering fire. Then exhaustion caused Wright to slip into the canal. An NCO, Sgt. Smith, fished his officer out, but by now it was 5 p.m., and the Germans were shooting at them from a range of thirty yards. The engineers abandoned their efforts and retired. For this gallant day's work, and others before he was later killed, Wright received a VC. It was all in vain: only one bridge on the British front was ever blown – the necessary orders had been given far too late.

By nightfall, the Germans held Mons. There is no reliable record of their losses, but Walter Bloem's battalion commander of the Brandenburgers lapsed into emotional lamentations: 'You are the only company commander left … [it is] a mere wreck, my proud, beautiful battalion!' Their regiment had lost killed one battalion commander and his adjutant, three company and six platoon commanders; a further sixteen officers were wounded; other ranks had suffered in proportion.

Bloem reflected miserably: 'Our first battle is a heavy, an unheard-of heavy defeat, and against the English, the English we laughed at.'

Though this remark is often quoted in celebration of the BEF's achievement, it was a wild exaggeration, reflecting the writer's sensitivity to losses, common to all novice warriors. Bloem's battalion suffered much heavier casualties than any other German unit that day. The British had been unable to frustrate Kluck's advance, merely delaying it by a day before relinquishing their positions to the enemy. Another German regimental narrative recorded triumphantly that at nightfall 'the spirit of victory was overwhelming, and was enjoyed to the full'. I Corps and Allenby's cavalry had scarcely been engaged. The good fortune of Mons was that enemy bungling allowed the BEF to withdraw almost intact, having lost an estimated 1,600 men, many of them taken prisoner. A former travelling salesman from Hamburg who spoke fluent English marshalled some of the latter good-humouredly: 'Gentlemen, please, four by four!' Almost half of the losses fell on just two battalions – 4th Middlesex with over four hundred, and 2nd Royal Irish with more than three hundred; several units were obliged to abandon their precious machine-guns. German total casualties were roughly similar, but with a much higher proportion of killed and wounded, rather than prisoners.

The British regarded their allies with contempt. Yet it was critical to the brief stand at Mons and the subsequent escape of II Corps that a scratch force of French territorials led by Gen. Albert d'Amade covered Smith-Dorrien's left flank. Even as the little British action was being fought, Lanrezac's Fifth Army suffered far more heavily, at Charleroi. Further south still, in the Ardennes on the 23rd and 24th the Fourth French and Fourth German armies lost 18,000 dead between them. In woods near Bertrix, an entire French corps panicked and fled, abandoning its artillery. Elsewhere the Germans began to bombard the fortress of Namur, garrisoned by 35,000 French and Belgian troops, and took it two days later at a cost of only nine hundred casualties. Their Third Army, commanded by Gen. Max von Hausen, prepared to cross the Meuse at Dinant using pontoons and barges. Hausen had fought with the Austrian army against the Prussians in 1866. Now sixty-seven and Saxony's war minister, he saw an opportunity for his forces to envelop Lanrezac. Franchet d'Espèrey, ablest of Fifth Army's corps commanders, on his own initiative launched a counter-attack, which pushed back the Germans. Late that night, Hausen's men nonetheless secured the town – and conducted a brutal massacre among its population. But Franchet d'Espèrey had won time for Fifth Army's withdrawal, and Hausen lost over 4,000 men.

By comparison with all these engagements, British doings at Mons receded in significance – though not in the minds of Sir John French and his senior officers. At 3 o'clock on the afternoon of the 23rd, the C-in-C returned from his trip to Valenciennes, still prey to delusions that the allies might soon renew their advance. By nightfall, however, he was forced to recognise reality, to accept Col. MacDonogh's assessment that his army faced an overwhelmingly powerful enemy. Kluck's men were crowding in upon II Corps' right – now south and west of Mons – and threatened to isolate it from I Corps; finally and most disturbing, Sir John knew Lanrezac had begun to withdraw Fifth Army from the Sambre valley, heedless of Joffre's wishes to the contrary. The BEF had started the day nine miles ahead of the French. Now, that gap was about to widen dangerously, inviting the Germans to fill it. Sir John acknowledged that his own command must pull back fast, to avert almost inevitable destruction.

The BEF bivouacked for the night some three miles south of Mons, its men expecting to fight on their new line next morning. That evening Tom Wollocombe 'even had time to think that a battle was a wonderfully exciting thing when it was in progress … our men, instead of being downcast, were much impressed with the superiority of their rifle fire and extended order manoeuvring, over the enemy's fire and movements "*en masse*"'. But at 1 a.m. on the 24th, GHQ issued new orders for a retreat, unassisted by guidance about how this was to be carried out, which was left to the corps commanders. Here was renewed evidence of incompetence at British headquarters, especially by Murray and Wilson, who simply did not know their jobs as staff officers. The only man who did was quartermaster-general Sir William 'Wully' Robertson, who through the weeks that followed improvised a supply system for the BEF with energy and skill.

In the space of a few hours, Sir John French had lapsed from jaunty confidence into gloom, even panic. Now, he talked at one moment of leading his force to take refuge in the old fortress of Maubeuge; at another, of withdrawing north-westwards to Amiens, severing all contact with his allies. A few days' experience of campaigning caused the British C-in-C to leap to the hyperbolic conclusion that French soldiers were not people with whom he could do business, not 'proper chaps' with whom he wished to continue fighting a war. Such an attitude would merely have invited ridicule, did it not threaten grave consequences for the allied cause.

Meanwhile in Paris that morning of the 24th, Joffre told Messimy, the war minister, that for the time being the French army had no choice save to abandon the offensive, which had failed. The nation's strategy was discredited. The French army had almost spent itself in futile attacks; it could aspire only to a protracted defence. 'Our object,' the commander-in-chief told the politician, 'must be to last out as long as possible, trying to wear out the enemy, and to resume the offensive when the time comes.' In the face of the news from the north, Joffre's vast illusions about German deployments and intentions were at last falling away. He understood Moltke's purpose.

Hitherto, the C-in-C had paid only casual attention to the left wing. Hereafter, it became the focus of all his fears – and then of his hopes. Next day, the 25th, he issued to his commanders, copied to Sir John French, his later famous *Instruction Général No. 2*, declaring an intention to start transferring large forces northwards, to create a new army on the left of the BEF. He was anxious to confront the peril on his flank with forces which he could rely upon to accept his orders – as the British would not. But Joffre's immensely complex redeployment could not be completed before 2 September, an eternity away, in the circumstances of the moment. Much must necessarily happen, for good or ill, before that day came, some of it to the BEF.

It is hard for an army exchanging fire with an advancing adversary to break off contact and retreat in good order. At first light on the 24th, the Germans began once more to press II Corps. Many units that day experienced skirmishes, though with slight loss, before falling back to bivouacs a few miles further southwards. A notorious incident took place when the 9th Lancers and Dragoon Guards charged German guns at Audregnies across a mile of open ground, an extraordinary piece of folly even by the standards of British cavalry. They were led by Lt. Col. David Campbell, a famous horseman who had once won a Grand National steeplechase riding his own horse, The Soarer. Tom Bridges was one of many men at Audregnies astride heavyweight hunters which a few months earlier had been jumping fences in the Shires, before being purchased by the army. An unexpected sunken road caused many fallers; German guns unhorsed more men, who sought cover behind corn stooks, from which they returned fire. Bridges' mount Umslopoogas was killed.

Eventually the British withdrew, having suffered eighty human casualties – fewer than they deserved – and rather more equine ones. Fourteen-year-old German schoolboy Heinrich Himmler wrote exultantly in his diary: 'Our troops advance to the west of the Meuse towards Maubeuge. An English cavalry brigade is there and is beaten, really beaten! Hurray!' That day Maj. 'Ma' Jeffreys of the Grenadiers – in Haig's corps – described 'a long and trying march … in great heat and over very bad and dusty roads. The men very tired and rather puzzled as to what we are at.' Jeffreys was disgusted by a large number of Coldstream stragglers whom he encountered on the road, and insisted that his own men should be denied opportunities to lag behind: the only concession to the most exhausted was to place their packs and rifles on the battalion's baggage carts.

Bernard Gordon-Lennox deplored the supposed secrecy which kept officers in ignorance of GHQ's plans and intentions: 'most disheartening. No one knows what one is driving at, where anyone is, what we have got against us, or anything at all, and what is told us generally turns out to be entirely wrong.' In truth, of course, this mystification derived not from GHQ's sense of discretion, but rather from its incompetence and indecision. Failure to brief subordinates about the purpose and context of their activities proved a chronic British command weakness throughout the campaign.

The same pattern was repeated on 25 August. Beside the ruins of the old Roman forum in Bavay, southward paths divided. A single road could not possibly carry the entire BEF and a mob of civilian fugitives. It was decided to dispatch I Corps by the route which ran east of the great forest of Mormal, while II Corps took an almost parallel line on its west side. All day, a traffic jam persisted in Bavay, as French's jumbled formations struggled through. 'I have never been so tired,' wrote Capt. Guy Blewitt of the Oxf & Bucks, 'as in the last 46 hours I had no sleep, covered 40 miles besides having the anxiety of a rearguard. At nearing Bavay it was evident that things were serious, the road being packed – cavalry with their horses, cavalrymen who had lost their horses, ambulance wagons, refugees, bicycles, perambulators, guns, infantry in fours, infantrymen who had lost their units and infantrymen whose units didn't know where they were required and were sleeping by the side of the road. The cobbles of Bavay made one's feet sorer and we were very glad to be turned into a stubble field to bivouac; here fires were soon burning and we got some food to eat and straw to sleep on.'

Traffic control throughout the retreat was poor, and in those innocent first days the British lacked the ruthlessness necessary to clear their road of fleeing civilians and vehicles. Guy Blewitt saw a very old Belgian, obviously at his last gasp, being wheeled past on a cart. The Englishman winced at the irony when the old man summoned just enough strength to cry in a high, fluty voice, '*Vive l'Angleterre!*' By contrast, some units which had been cheered when they advanced now found themselves booed as they retired: local people divined the price they would pay for allied defeat when the Germans arrived. Lt. Rose of the Wiltshires described the night of 25 August: 'The whole way back there were two lines of vehicles, guns, ambulances etc, going the same way along one not very broad road, the infantry in no sort of formation … It was dark except for the fitful flashes of lightning and glow of burning houses in the various villages which had been set alight by shellfire … The rain came down in torrents. The men were very tired; they had had no rations for two days, but they were not demoralised in the least.'

On that same day of the 25th, 2nd Grenadiers marched almost fifteen miles, oppressed by the heat, troubled by blistered feet and impeded by refugees pushing barrows and handcarts. A British officer gazed with pity upon an old woman torn between her urge to seek safety, and a deep peasant instinct against abandoning her farm. 'But who will feed the pigs if I go?' she cried. Sixty miles northwards, in Ghent, Belgian housewife Jeanne van Bleyenberghe wrote to a friend: 'It makes you cry to see all those poor people with numerous children, who left behind their cow, their pig and all that they earned by hard work … We have only had three weeks of war and already it seems years to me.'

The Grenadiers finally halted just south of the Sambre in the town of Landrecies, where Haig had established a new corps headquarters. Guardsmen had gratefully thrown off their kit and made themselves comfortable in billets, when around 5 p.m. an alarm was given. The inhabitants retired to their cellars as panicky troopers of the Irish Horse ran down the main street shouting, 'The Germans are on us!' It transpired that an enemy cavalry patrol had appeared at the outskirts of the town, then hastily retired. Men of the Coldstream were deployed to guard the Sambre bridge approach, taking up position around a farm on rising ground five hundred yards north of the river. Their first intimation of activity came when they heard the sound of voices which they later claimed were lustily singing the *Marseillaise*.

Instead of French soldiers, however, a German officer advanced to the barricade of furniture erected by the Guards. In a notable stroke of initiative, matched by equally striking British negligence – Haig wrote crossly in his diary, 'their guard does not seem to have been very alert' – the German was able to seize an unattended Maxim gun, and retire clutching it. Thereafter, there was a general mêlée as darkness descended, during which a Guardsman named George Wyatt won a VC by running out under heavy fire to extinguish a blaze in stacked cornsacks which threatened the British position. His regiment, however, scarcely distinguished itself at Landrecies.

The British were aggrieved by the perfidy of their enemies supposedly singing French songs to mask their approach, but the Germans were expecting to find billets, and not enemies, in Landrecies. Their column was led by a field-kitchen wagon; if indeed they were singing France's national anthem it is likely they chose the tune because it sounded well, rather than as a *ruse de guerre*. Neither side displayed much tactical skill. A senior officer thought the Guards were 'very sleepy and the measures taken were rather half-hearted'. But a few enemy shells fell in the town and Grenadiers sallied forth to support the Coldstream. An officer wrote: 'they seem pushing devils, these Germans', but then added, 'the moment the Dutchmen' – a corruption of *Deutscher Mann* – 'tried to advance a deadly rapid fire was poured into them. They charged pluckily three or four times, but each time they were mown down.'

The scrimmage at Landrecies – for it was no more – cost each side around 120 casualties. The British stood to until dawn, dozing and shivering in the darkness: the harsh night chill was among the unwelcome surprises of the campaign. They then withdrew from the town, relieved that the enemy allowed them to decamp unscathed. Most of the Grenadiers lost their kits, because the battalion baggage carts had been incorporated in street barricades. 'Ma' Jeffreys wrote: 'I like most others kept falling asleep as I marched along … We still know nothing about the general course of the war.'

The most important consequence of the brush at Landrecies was that it caused Haig, the corps commander, temporarily to succumb to panic. The British regarded the German assault on them as far more serious than it was, initially claiming that the enemy had lost eight hundred dead. Haig was feeling desperately unwell, weakened by an outbreak of 'the runs' and a heroic dose of bicarbonate of soda. During the night's exchange of fire and confusion in the streets he persuaded himself – and Sir John French – that his force was threatened with disaster. Corps commander and headquarters fled away southwards. Through at least the next five days, Haig manifested a defeatism which few of his subordinates afterwards forgot. He focused his energies upon saving his own corps, almost heedless of the fate of Smith-Dorrien's. Col. James Edmonds, a divisional chief of staff who later became British official historian of the war, wrote brutally of this episode in a 1930 private letter to an old comrade: 'D.H. had ... been thoroughly shaken by the business at Landrecies, had drawn his revolver and spoken of "selling our lives dearly". Undoubtedly he also thought Smith-D[orrien] was in a bad way. In any case, he played a selfish game, marched off leaving Smith-D in the lurch, although the firing at Le Cateau and march of the Germans across the front of his rearguard was reported [to Haig].'

When Sir John French should have been worrying about Smith-Dorrien's formations, which were gravely exposed as the Germans continued to press relentlessly upon them, instead he chafed about a non-existent threat to Haig's formations. These continued on their weary way southwards, scarcely troubled by the enemy, while their comrades fought the bloodiest action of the retreat.

2 LE CATEAU: 'WHERE THE FUN COMES IN, I DON'T KNOW'

Brilliant late-August sunshine, warming and lighting the French countryside, mocked the condition of the warring armies, milling in a fog of misapprehensions and uncertainties. On the 25th the British II Corps suffered many frustrations: dense masses of refugee traffic enforced halts on its retreating columns; units fell behind amid local difficulties – the Royal Irish Rifles were delayed by a long train of artillery crossing the battalion's line of march. That evening their colonel, Wilkinson Bird, reported to his brigadier that the men were too exhausted both to march and to fight through the night, if they had to continue serving as rearguard. At 10 p.m. the battalion entered Le Cateau, twenty-five miles south of Mons. Bird went to the post office and telephoned Corps HQ, who told him to keep marching to the village of Bertry, three miles west.

He emerged into the brightly-lit town square, thronged with wagons, stragglers, soldiers eating and drinking in restaurants. One of his officers asked, 'Are you going to halt, sir?' Bird answered tersely, 'No – damned sight too dangerous.' He knew that once his men fell out, it would take hours to herd them onto the move again. The battalion trudged up the hill out of the town into rustic darkness – and became lost. At 2 a.m. they blundered into Reumont, a mile short of Bertry, where they found 3rd Division's headquarters. Bird asked for a meal for his men. A staff officer said, 'You won't get it, because we are retreating again at four, and yesterday it took five hours to get under way.' The riflemen collapsed into sleep in a nearby cluster of farm buildings. Some officers procured a meal at a little café in nearby Maurois.

The previous evening, II Corps had issued Operation Order No. 6, which began: 'The Army will continue its retirement tomorrow.' In the small hours of the 26th, however, Smith-Dorrien felt compelled to reconsider. Many of his units were in the same exhausted and hungry condition as the Irish Rifles, and some were still tramping through the darkness towards Le Cateau. He reckoned that if the corps tried to move on southwards that day, its cohesion must collapse; lagging units would be overrun by Germans hard on their heels.

Generals' personalities sometimes lack colour, but this could not be said of Sir Horace Smith-Dorrien. Twelfth in a family of sixteen children, as a young transport officer in Zululand he was one of the few survivors of the 1879 disaster at Isandlwana, following which he was nominated for a VC for his efforts to save other fugitives. Thereafter he gained extensive experience of colonial wars, and fought at Omdurman – he became a lifelong friend of Kitchener. He emerged from the Boer War with an enhanced reputation, and thereafter held a succession of commands. A committed army reformer, he especially promoted musketry and was an evangelist for machine-guns. In July 1914, Smith-Dorrien was sent to address several thousand public-school cadets at their summer camp, where he astonished an almost uniformly jingoistic audience by asserting that 'war should be avoided at almost any cost; war would solve nothing; the whole of Europe and more besides would be reduced to ruin; the loss of life would be so large that whole populations would be decimated'. At the time most of his cadet listeners recoiled from such heresy, but those fortunate enough to survive until 1918 came to look back with respect on Smith-Dorrien's frankness and independence of thought.

He took command of II Corps unexpectedly, after the sudden expiry from a heart attack of Lt. Gen. Sir James Grierson. A self-indulgent lifestyle and excessive girth had ill prepared Grierson for the stresses of active service, but his death was a loss because, as a former military attaché in Berlin, he knew the German army intimately. Kitchener imposed Smith-Dorrien as a replacement against the bitter opposition of French, who detested him. Though generally calm and robust, the new corps commander was prone to outbursts of extreme temper which caused subordinates to quail, and had indeed provoked his chief of staff to try to resign his post after Mons.

This, then, was the man in charge at Le Cateau on 26 August. Early in the small hours, Smith-Dorrien consulted such senior officers as he could convene. Allenby, commanding the cavalry, reported that both his men and his horses were 'pretty well played out'. He said that unless II Corps began to withdraw before dawn, the enemy was so close that a battle would be unavoidable. Hubert Hamilton, commanding 3rd Division, said his men could not possibly move before 9 a.m. The 5th Division was even more scattered, and 4th Division – which had detrained from the Channel ports only on the night of the 24th, and still lacked most of its support units – was entangled in a rearguard action. Smith-Dorrien asked Allenby if he would accept his orders. Yes, said the cavalryman. 'Very well, gentlemen, we will fight,' said the corps commander in a manner that would read well to history, 'and I will ask General Snow [commanding 4 Div] to act under me as well.'

All the officers present heaved a sigh of relief. After the chaos and confusion of purpose which had attended them for three days past, here was a clear decision, which they welcomed. So too, at first, did Sir John French, when informed in a message delivered to GHQ by automobile that half his army was to conduct a second battle of the campaign without benefit of the commander-in-chief's guiding hand or assistance. French later very publicly recanted, castigating Smith-Dorrien in his memoirs. Given II Corps' predicament, however, it is hard to see how its commander could have acted otherwise. He proposed to try to inflict 'a stopping blow' on the Germans, to gain a breathing space in which to resume his retirement. He expected I Corps to support him, and was given no hint by French that Haig was continuing to withdraw, leaving II Corps' right flank in the air.

At 7 a.m. Smith-Dorrien was summoned to take a call on the railway telephone network, which proved to be from Henry Wilson. The sub-chief of staff said the C-in-C had now decided that II Corps should resume its retreat. Too late, said Smith-Dorrien; his troops were already in action, and could not disengage before dark. Wilson afterwards claimed to have said, 'Good luck to you; yours is the first cheerful voice I have heard for three days.' But Sir Henry also appears to have expressed extreme gloom about II Corps' prospects. Later that day James Edmonds met Smith-Dorrien, who complained how little he knew about what was going on, and about having been obliged to make so big a decision. Edmonds replied reassuringly, 'You needn't bother your head about that, sir. You have done the right thing.' The general said that GHQ appeared to differ: 'that fellow

Wilson told me on the telephone this morning that if I stood to fight there would be another Sedan' – referring to the disaster that befell the French there in 1870.

When Sir John French's chief of staff received Smith-Dorrien's message that he planned to halt and make a stand at Le Cateau, Sir Archibald Murray was convinced that it was all up with the BEF. In a manner that might be deemed tiresomely theatrical had it not been authentic, he collapsed in a dead faint. A colleague implausibly named 'Fido' Childs said, 'Don't call a doctor: I have a pint of champagne.' James Edmonds wrote sardonically: 'And that they poured into Murray about 5 a.m.! ... "Curly" Birch, who was riding about the field in a towering rage looking for the cavalry brigades which Allenby had lost, told me that the instructions of GHQ were "to save the cavalry and horse artillery". It was a time of near-madness at French's headquarters, which enjoyed no accession of sanity as the day unfolded.

Now and for days ahead, the C-in-C and his staff were prey to defeatism and indeed panic. Joffre witnessed this for himself when he arrived at Saint-Quentin later in the morning, to confer about his new campaign plan with the British and Lanrezac of Fifth Army, even as Smith-Dorrien's men were fighting for their lives a few miles northwards. The generals met in a gloomy, over-furnished bourgeois mansion off the main street, where Sir John French had established himself. Lanrezac was in a vile temper, and had earlier that morning abused both Joffre and French to his own staff in a fashion that dismayed and even disgusted them. He professed agreement when Joffre said that it was essential for Fifth Army to keep counter-attacking, to sustain pressure on the Germans, and promised that as soon as his retreating army had got clear of the woods around Avesnes, where artillery could not deploy effectively, he would resume the offensive in open country.

Joffre was not to know that, in reality, Lanrezac had no intention of doing anything of the sort. On the 26th, while the British fought at Le Cateau, Fifth Army continued its drifting retreat; the only French forces which saw significant action that day were Sordet's cavalry and the scratch group of territorial divisions on Smith-Dorrien's left. Tom Wollocombe of the Middlesex was one of the few British officers to acknowledge hand-somely the contribution of their allies: 'the French troops ... under General D'Amade took a lot of pressure off us'. Meanwhile at Saint-Quentin, Joffre was shocked by the wild words of the British C-in-C, who railed at the fashion in which the BEF had been exposed to disaster since the moment it reached the front, for lack of French support. Their conference took place in a shuttered and thus darkened room where, according to Spears, 'everyone spoke in an undertone as if there were a corpse in the next room'. Protracted interpretation was necessary, since few of the British present spoke French, and neither Joffre nor his subordinates were fluent in English.

France's commander-in-chief began to explain his counter-offensive plan – General Instruction No. 2. He was dismayed to learn that the BEF's C-in-C knew nothing about this: Sir Archibald Murray, in a state of physical and mental collapse, had failed to show his chief the critical document. Joffre summarised his intention to create a new 'mass of manoeuvre' with the French Fourth and Fifth Armies on the right of the BEF, then bring up fresh forces on its left. He urged upon his British allies the need to stand their ground and launch a counter-attack, for which he promised French support.

Sir John was unmoved by any of this: he merely insisted that he intended to continue his own withdrawal. Spears wrote: 'The sense of doom was as evident in that room as when a jury is about to return a verdict of guilty on a capital charge.' When the meeting ended, Sir John French drove away southward, taking his headquarters with him, almost heedless of Smith-Dorrien's battle further north. Spears again: 'It was perhaps the worst day of all at GHQ. Nerves were bad, morale was low, and there was much confusion. The staff wanted heartening, and Sir John's departure had the contrary effect.'

Joffre wrote in his memoirs: 'I carried away with me a serious impression as to the fragility of our extreme left, and I anxiously asked myself if it could hold out long enough to enable me to effect the new grouping of our forces.' The allies' principal commander was confronted by the vast, looming German menace; by doubts about the nerve and competence of Lanrezac in the most gravely threatened sector; and finally by a British C-in-C alienated from his allies and visibly unmanned by the crisis. One British corps was retreating on a different axis from that which GHQ had decreed, while the other had started a critical battle on its own initiative. The Saint-Quentin conference ended in indecision, its only outcome British acquiescence in Lanrezac's further retirement. Joffre departed without having made any attempt to impose his personality, to force Sir John French's hand. Both the allied commanders-in-chief seemed bereft of that most vital of all battlefield qualities: grip.

In fairness to the BEF's commander, Joffre's assurances of Lanrezac's cooperation proved worthless. But this scarcely justified Sir John's growing determination, in effect, to wash his hands of the campaign. To say that French's headquarters was not a happy place, his staff not a united team, would be an understatement. Beyond the fact that the commander-in-chief did not enjoy the confidence of his subordinates, his chief of staff was detested by Henry Wilson, who was bitterly resentful that he did not have Murray's job; all the more so when the latter kept his position even after suffering a nervous collapse.

Years later, Murray wrote to an old comrade: 'to me it was a period of sorrow and humiliation ... As you know, the senior members of [GHQ] entirely ignored me as far as possible, continually thwarted me, even altered my instructions ... I have never before, or since, had a disloyal staff to work with ... Why did I stay with this War Office clique when I knew that I was not wanted? It was my mistake ... I wanted to see Sir John through. I had been so many years with him, and knew better than anyone how his health, temper and temperament rendered him unfit, in my opinion, for the crisis we had to face.' He concluded that if Wilson had been less disloyal, 'I should not have had to struggle with Sir John unaided'. The only sentiment shared by French, Murray and Wilson was lack of confidence in each other, an alarming state of affairs at the summit of an army in the field. Indeed, personal relationships between almost all the most senior British officers in France ranged between frigid and poisonous. They would not improve during the year ahead, and intrigue became endemic. Henry Wilson, for instance, once told French that Kitchener was as much the enemy of the BEF as Moltke or Falkenhayn. The only band of brothers to which Britain's generals might be likened was that of Cain and Abel.

Once early-morning mist cleared on the 26th, a succession of RFC pilots landed back at their fields from scouting missions to report enemy forces clogging every approach road for miles in front of II Corps: '[the airmen's] maps were black with lines showing columns of German troops', in the words of a staff officer. A single infantry regiment of three battalions, 233 horses and seventy wagons occupied two miles of road; six of these were closing fast upon Le Cateau, celebrated as the home of Matisse. 'A sun-baked drowsy little place it seemed,' in the words of a British officer, 'on the eve of being flung into history to the accompaniment of the roar of great guns ... unconscious of its fate, the little town looked as if nothing could ever rouse it.' The action Smith-Dorrien fought on 26 August, 568th anniversary of Crécy, proved much bloodier than Mons – indeed, as costly in British lives as was D-Day in June 1944, a world war later. It was utterly unlike almost everything that happened to its survivors in the ensuing four years. This was the last significant battle the British Army would ever fight in which a man standing on the rising ground a mile or so north-west of Le Cateau might have beheld most of the day's critical points within his own range of vision.

The little town nestled in a valley, where it was invisible to the 60,000 troops who took up positions across ten miles of green and golden fields in the open, rolling countryside above. The corn had been cut, and stood in ordered stooks on the stubble, interspersed with expanses of sugar beet and clover, together with occasional haystacks, reaching as far as the eye could see. One soldier thought the place resembled a familiar exercise ground – 'Salisbury Plain without the trees'. Smith-Dorrien deployed his exhausted corps on unfavourable terrain, without benefit of much reconnaissance. Some units, especially those on the right nearest to Le Cateau, found themselves defending positions which were soon overlooked by the advancing Germans, who could bring up men in dead ground. Critics later argued that the British would have fared better holding a higher ridgeline half a mile further south. Smith-Dorrien would have shrugged: 'Needs must.'

Some local townspeople came out to help the British entrench. Nearest to Le Cateau, the Yorkshires settled into shallow rifle-pits dug by Royal Engineers, with the Suffolks on their right. The Norfolks struggled to cut down a lone tree on their position, which offered a conspicuous aiming point for enemy gunners. Signals detachments cantered across the appointed battlefield, laying telephone cable from whirling drums mounted on wagons. But this was in desperately short supply, because so much had been used and lost at Mons. The most important means of communication throughout the August 1914 campaign were the superbly efficient French civilian and railway telephone networks. An official historian later wrote: 'At the outset of the campaign we had an intercommunication system where, through favourable circumstances, the forward circuits were more numerous than was again achieved until much later in the war.' At times in August, however, units were reduced to sending messages by lamp or semaphore flag. The most reliable method of communication remained that of thousands of years past: dispatching messengers afoot or on horseback. On the field of Le Cateau, gallopers were a familiar sight, dashing from unit to unit, delivering orders at mortal hazard.

The battle unfolded piecemeal, broadly from right to left of the British line. German artillery began firing at 6 a.m., and soon afterwards Kluck's men entered the town of Le Cateau, which was undefended, and pushed British pickets back up the hill at its eastern edge. One of the attackers, Lt. Kuhlorn, recalled later: 'I gave my platoon the orders "On your feet! Forward! Go!" and we advanced in short rushes. When I looked around during a pause, I found I had about eight men and some NCOs with me. The remainder had stayed where they were.' But, a few yards at a time, he and his regiment pushed forward. By 9 a.m., Kluck's guns were bringing down heavy fire on the Suffolks and Yorkshires and their supporting batteries, all in plain view, plunging them into an ordeal which continued for many hours thereafter. The Suffolks' colonel was among the first to fall; before long one British artillery battery had lost all its officers, and was firing only a single gun. By mid-morning Smith-Dorrien's right was outflanked, so that for the rest of the day the Germans were shooting at the Suffolks and Yorkshires from three sides, and had machine-guns sited to enfilade the British positions.

Some of II Corps' units further north were still marching to their appointed places in the line after the battle started. At 7 a.m. a panting cyclist orderly pedalled up to the farmhouse where Col. Bird of the Irish Rifles had snatched an hour or two's sleep, with orders to march at once to Bertry. Bird was at first mystified about where to find his men. He roused Capt. Dillon, the adjutant, fast asleep in an armchair. 'I'm awfully sorry, sir,' said Dillon. 'I remember sitting down, then nothing more until you woke me.' An hour later, with his companies trudging dozily behind him, Bird rode into Bertry, where outside Corps HQ he met Smith-Dorrien. 'Will your men fight?' demanded the general. Yes, said Bird. The lean, intense corps commander ran his eyes down the column. 'Your men look very well … [They] just want a damned good fight and no more of this retreating.' The Irish Rifles were dispatched two miles north-west to Caudry station, in the centre of the British line.

A staff officer later reported that once the die was cast, Smith-Dorrien wanted no interference from his C-in-C. '[He] was most anxious that Sir John should not come – he spoke for quite a long time on this point, after which a few casual remarks about his left and right flanks both being in the air, but that he was confident of giving the Germans a good fight even if he was running the risk of being surrounded.' Around 10 a.m., masses of German infantry began advancing across the stubble fields west of Le Cateau. Kluck believed that he was deploying his IV Corps against six BEF divisions, which were retreating south-westwards. In consequence of this misapprehension, his formations stumbled upon the British in a succession of uncoordinated encounters that denied the Germans the chance to throw their full weight behind the punches.

Kluck's soldiers were quite as tired as their opponents, having marched thirty miles the previous day. Contrary to British claims of overwhelming numbers of attackers thrown against II Corps, only six regiments, together with three or four Jäger battalions of skirmishers and several thousand dismounted cavalry, came into action against Smith-Dorrien on 26 August. This was a formidable force, backed by excellent artillery. But Le Cateau cannot credibly be portrayed as the David-and-Goliath clash of British myth: the respective forces were about equal.

Just as at Mons, wherever enemy masses appeared within rifle range, they were mauled. 'It is impossible to miss German infantry,' wrote forty-three-year-old Maj. Bertie Trevor, a company commander in the Yorkshires. 'They come on in heaps.' But the defenders in their turn suffered from artillery fire, which caused especially severe losses in British batteries, deployed as conspicuously as were their forebears on the ridge of Mont Saint-Jean, at Waterloo in 1815. Indeed, the first Duke of Wellington would have seen much at Le Cateau that was familiar to him: enemy troops advancing in close-packed columns; drivers lashing lathered artillery teams forward to unlimber; gallopers bearing orders hastening hither and thither.

A German officer wrote wonderingly: 'I did not think it possible that flesh and blood could survive so great an onslaught ... Our men attacked with the utmost determination, but again and again they were driven back by those incomparable soldiers. Regardless of loss, the English artillery came forward to protect their infantrymen and in full view of our own guns kept up a devastating fire.' Another German participant, Lt. Schacht of a machine-gun company, observed more sceptically: 'We could see a [British] battery which, according to our doctrine, was located far too far forward, in amongst the line of infantrymen, to which we had already approached very closely. Right! Sights at 1,400 metres! Rapid fire. Slightly short. Higher! Soon we could observe the effect. There could not be greater activity around an upturned antheap. Everywhere men and horses were milling around, falling down, and in among all this brouhaha was constant tack-tack-tack.'

When Smith-Dorrien ordered forward men of his slender reserve to reinforce the threatened right, few were able to cover the distance, across ground swept by German fire. Bertie Trevor of the Yorkshires later described the battle as 'too terrible for words ... We fired 350 rounds a man in my company, and did a good deal of execution. But we were in an absolute trap – it is a marvel that anyone there is alive & untouched. Until one has been for hours pelted at with lyddite & shrapnel, machine-guns and rifles, one cannot understand war. Where the fun comes in, I don't know.' A circling German aircraft, dropping spasmodic coloured smoke-bombs to mark targets for the artillery, contributed a contemporary touch to a nineteenth-century battle. On Smith-Dorrien's right, by 10 a.m. one artillery battery had lost all its officers, and retained only a single gun in action. This was a day when the county battalions of the British Army – Yorkshires, Suffolks, Cornwalls, Argyll & Sutherland Highlanders and East Surreys – conducted themselves with a stubborn steadiness and profes-sionalism in which their senior officers – with the notable exception of the corps commander – showed themselves deficient.

On the British left, the day began with a small disaster. The 1st King's Own had marched all night. Dawn found them on the Ligny road, waiting in column of companies for a promised breakfast. Capt. R.G. Beaumont spotted some horsemen on the horizon who looked neither British nor French, but he was sharply put down by his colonel for talking nonsense when he suggested they might be German. The enemy, snapped the CO, was at least three hours away. The welcome rattle of carts caused voices to call, 'Here come the cookers!' Men piled arms and took out their mess tins, even as the distant horsemen brought up wheeled vehicles of their own, and offloaded them in plain sight. These were German cavalry, and they were permitted unmolested to deploy machine-guns. As almost a thou-sand British soldiers crowded around their breakfast, the Maxims opened fire.

The first bursts killed the King's colonel, and prompted a panic-stricken flight by three companies, who abandoned their piled rifles. Almost all those who tried to run were cut down: only men who embraced the earth escaped the slaughter. The unit's second-in-command eventually rallied enough survivors to retrieve their weapons and bring in most of the wounded. But in the space of a couple of minutes the King's had suffered four hundred casualties – a murderous demonstration of the price of exposure. Among the witnesses of this embarrassment was a platoon commander of the neighbouring Warwicks, Lt. Bernard Montgomery, later the field-marshal, who thought poorly of most aspects of British command and control that day. The King's thereafter held their ground for a time, assisted by the fact that they faced only German cavalry and skirmishers. But as horsemen of Gen. Georg von Marwitz's corps worked around behind the battalion's left flank, its survivors withdrew.

When Germans exposed themselves in their turn, they suffered as heavily as Smith-Dorrien's men: a battery unlimbered and opened fire in front of the Hampshires, whose rifles immediately obliged the gunners to retire. Both sides' field artillery laboured under the handicap that crews needed to be able to see their targets – so-called direct fire. Forward observation officers linked by telephone to gun positions were not then available. It was a terrible business, recalling the British disaster at Colenso in the Boer War, to invite gunners and horse teams to deploy within sight and range of German rifle as well as artillery fire; yet this happened all day at Le Cateau, and again and again through that first campaign. British guns fired over open sights, as the term went, at ranges of 1,200 yards – no more than Wellington's artillery knew. The Germans were better equipped to deliver indirect fire from concealed positions through their heavier howitzers, but both sides were constrained by the limited ammunition supplies they carried. The barrages seemed brutal to those who endured them, especially without benefit of trenches, but were mere miniatures of those that followed in subsequent battles.

It is characteristic of even the fiercest actions, that not all the participants are engaged all the time. At Le Cateau, though some units were severely punished, others had an astonishingly quiet morning in sectors initially untroubled by the Germans. Tom Wollocombe of the Middlesex recorded that around 11.30 he 'got quite a good lunch' at the battalion mess in the rear. Once back in the forward positions, for some time 'we sat there talking and joking, and began to get quite bored'. Even when German shellfire began to fall around them, Wollocombe was chiefly fascinated by the spectacle of four black cows, grazing unconcernedly. One eventually received a direct hit and was killed, but the other three chewed the cud until the end of the battle. A German participant was similarly bemused by seeing a flock of sheep, bleating furiously, cross the front amid the cannonade.

Lt. Roebbling, an infantryman, found that although he peered intently towards the British positions through his telescope, he could not identify an enemy to fire at: 'At the same time things were whistling past or crashing into the ground. Then all of a sudden the man two to my right called out "*Adieu* Subenbach, I've had it!" Corporal Subenbach said: "Don't say

that, Busse! Keep your chin up!" A little later comes a groan: "Oh, I've
only got it in the shoulder and ear!"' Roebbling asked for the wounded
man's rifle and some ammunition, but still could not see anything to
shoot at. Shrapnel began to burst around them, and a bullet hit the sling
of his weapon, tearing open the lieutenant's hand. One of his men applied
a field dressing.

The young officer sensed British fire slackening as German shelling
took its toll. But when Lt. Fricke leapt to his feet waving a sword and
ordered his men forward, he was promptly shot down. Roebbling then
watched his company commander, son of an officer of the Franco-Prussian
War, meet the same fate: 'The sword which his father had dropped when
he lay mortally wounded at the head of the same 7th Company before
Beaumont in 1870 fell to the ground for ever.' At Caudry, Lt. von Davier
raised a laugh to steady his men under fire by wailing satirically: 'I have
lost my monocle. Anybody who finds it should give it to me later!' His
enemies would have applauded.

The Germans began to press the British centre only around noon, and
suffered considerably when they did so. Col. Hull of the Middlesex made
his men wait until the enemy closed to five hundred yards. Their rippling
fire then took effect, but dismounted German cavalry meanwhile infil-
trated Caudry. The Royal Irish Rifles, holding part of the little town, were
urged to make a counter-attack. To the relief of Col. Bird, that order was
overruled by a senior officer who said: 'what we want to do is stop and
exhaust the Germans'. Soon after 1 p.m., shellfire began to fall in the vicinity. Bird saw British soldiers running towards the rear. All the transport
horses of the Middlesex were killed, and houses were soon blazing. 'There
were a lot of men making their way back in a disgraceful manner, even
NCOs,' wrote signals officer Alexander Johnston, who was in the town. 'It
makes one sad and anxious for the future to see Englishmen behave like
this, as the fire was not really heavy nor the losses great. Of course these
were only the bad men or men whose officers had been hit and were therefore out of control, and one always found plenty of splendid fellows holding on gamely.'

Col. Bird was attempting to check fugitives from Caudry when he
suddenly met his brigadier slumped in the saddle of a charger, being led
rearwards by two staff officers. 'Hullo, sir,' said the colonel. 'I hope you are
not hurt.' The brigadier mumbled in response, 'No, I am just going back
for a while,' and left the battlefield. The senior officer's retirement was
excused by the fact that he had been concussed by a shell, but later in the

war humble rankers would be shot for doing the same thing. The Germans were temporarily evicted from the southern half of Caudry by a counter-attack delivered by a scratch group of British troops led by the divisional commander's aide-de-camp.

Meanwhile on the right, II Corps' predicament was worsening. Smith-Dorrien had counted on Haig for support, and instead I Corps' formations were still retreating, scarcely pursued, while GHQ made no attempt to turn them back. Thus the German assault on the exposed flank at Le Cateau was unimpeded. Infantry and gun batteries faced a storm of artillery and machine-gun fire from an enemy who could now observe almost every yard of the British positions. Pte. Fred Petch of the Suffolks was firing at some Germans attempting to creep up a little gully on his right when one machine-gun bullet ricocheted off the stock of his rifle, and a second went through his left hip and out through his right leg, 'which left me pretty well paralysed'. When there was a brief lull in German movements and firing, George Reynolds of the Yorkshires said, 'it was as if the referee had blown his whistle. We lay there and wondered what the second half would be like.'

More of the same, was the answer. Soon after noon, it became plain that the British must pull back – some men were already trickling towards the rear. Several units withdrew intact, but others remained as German infantry worked around behind them, up the hill from Le Cateau. 'About 2.30 the situation was as bad as it could be,' wrote Bertie Trevor of the Yorkshires. 'The ridge on our right ... was shelled to pieces, and we were getting it from the Maxims half-right at about 900 yards, as well as volumes of shell – H[igh] E[xplosive] and shrapnel. Half the men were hit and the ammunition was running out ... One battalion had held up its hands and I remember the German Guards coming up and taking them prisoners, and executing a parade march round them.'

The most urgent problem became that of extricating the British artillery. Some batteries were firing from positions alongside the infantry; these needed to bring forward horse teams, limber up and retire, within range of every German within a mile. The men holding Smith-Dorrien's right witnessed a series of displays of extraordinary, absurdly old-fashioned gallantry as again and again gunners galloped forward to bring away their pieces amid a rain of shell and small-arms fire. Infantrymen sprang to their feet cheering at the spectacle of one battery's horses charging down a forward slope in plain view of the Germans. On the other side, Lt. Schacht and his fellow machine-gunners watched in

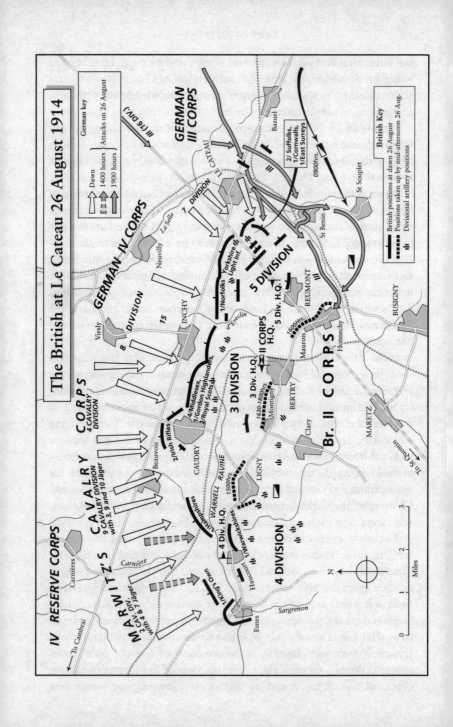

The British at Le Cateau 26 August 1914

German key

⇧ Dawn
⇧ Attacks on 26 August

⇧ Dawn
⇧ 1400 hours
⇧ 1900 hours

British Key

▬ British positions at dawn 26 August
┅ Positions taken up by mid-afternoon 26 Aug.
⊪ Divisional artillery positions

GERMAN III CORPS

GERMAN IV CORPS

III (16 DIV)

Bazuel

2/ Suffolks,
1/ Cornwalls,
1/ East Surreys

0900hrs.

St Souplet

LE CATEAU

7 DIVISION

La Selle

Neuvilly

St Benin

Yorkshire H.
Light Inf.

5 DIVISION

1/ Norfolks

Viesly

8 DIVISION

15

INCHY

d'Ercin

5 Div. H.Q.

REUMONT

BUSIGNY

GERMAN IV CORPS

II CORPS H.Q.

1600Hrs.

Maurois

Honnechy

Br. II CORPS

4/ Middlesex,
1/ Gordon Highlanders,
2/ Royal Scots

3 DIVISION

3 Div. H.Q.

Montigny

1630–1800hrs

BERTRY

Clary

MARETZ

To St Quentin

CAVALRY CORPS
4 CAVALRY DIVISION

Beauvois

2/ Irish Rifles

CAUDRY

WARNELL RAVINE

LIGNY

1500hrs

MARWITZ'S CAVALRY CORPS
9 CAVALRY DIVISION
with 3, 9 and 10 Jäger

Carnières

1/ Hampshires

4 Div. H.Q.

1/ Warwickshires

Haucourt

4 DIVISION

MARWITZ'S
2 CAV. DIV.
with 4 & 7 Jäger

Carnière

1/ King's own

Esnes

Sargrenon

IV RESERVE CORPS

To Cambrai

Carnières

N

Miles
0   1   2   3

ght among the flashes appeared a dark mass. It was the
s approaching at a mad gallop. We could not help but
hey mad?" No, with extraordinary bravery they were
to pull out their batteries at the last minute ... In a hectic
velve machine-guns poured bullets at the sacrificial victims.
readful tangle it was up there ... one [horse] remained standing
this wild hail of fire; started to graze; whinnied for water and
its head tiredly.'

gain and again bullets struck and shells exploded among horses and
ers, who collapsed in thrashing, bloody heaps. Two guns were extracted
from the carnage and taken to the rear, but the neighbouring batteries had
to be abandoned, breech-blocks removed. VCs were awarded to an officer
and two drivers who dashed within two hundred yards of approaching
German infantry, and somehow carried away one of two howitzers – the
second team that made the attempt was shot to pieces. The Suffolks, Argy
& Sutherlands and Yorkshire Light Infantry covered the retirement of 5
Division at mid-afternoon, before those three units were progressi
demolished where they stood. At 3 p.m., Maj. Trevor of the Yorkshir
back the survivors of his own company. Two men beside him we
down as they crossed a cornfield, 'however, we retired at a walk
Aldershot fashion, and 3 times we turned and tried to answe
Then it became a case of each man running to some trenches
under a murderous fire ... We retired through the guns, the g
dead all around.'

Smith-Dorrien stood by the roadside watching his tro
units in unsurprising disorder, but most soldiers in re
heart. 'It was a wonderful sight,' he wrote later, 'men smc
apparently quite unconcerned, and walking steadily do
formation of any sort, and men of all units mixed up t
at the time to a crowd coming away from a race meeti
fanciful view: Smith-Dorrien's corps had been
nineteenth-century battle while exposed to the
century weapons, and no sane participant had
Moreover, it was mistaken to pretend that all his
Officers drew their revolvers to arrest the flight
In Caudry at mid-afternoon, Col. Wilkinson
had taken over command of his brigade – wa
attack. When he gave the order to a major c
battalion, that officer looked Bird in the

sir, that the men will not again attack. T[...]
they defend?' 'Yes – I think so.'

Bird, desperate for information[...]
was galloping by: 'Hi! Hi! Tell [...]
Division smashed to pieces on [...]
on our left. Goodbye.' This was an e[...]
British were under heavy pressure, but [...]
people who should have known better. Ale[...]
dismayed when his brigadier ordered a withdrawa[...]
that we ought to have stuck onto the town somehow. [...]
try showed no inclination to assault.' But shellfire had [...]
defenders' spirits. Wilkinson Bird told the major of the neig[...]
battalion that his men must act as rearguard. The officer responded[...]
do my best, sir, but I must warn you that, after what they have bee[...]
through, the men may not withstand a strong attack.' Though some British
gunners displayed great gallantry that afternoon, a battery commander
whom Bird requested to support his brigade refused, saying that he could
not expose his men to German small arms. Bird gave the officer a direct
order, but soon learned from an orderly that the battery withdrew the
moment Germans began to fire on it from Ligny. This was prudent, but
inglorious.

A mounted orderly at last gave Bird's brigade the signal to pull back.
Hundreds of soldiers rose from where they had lain in the stubble and
[be]gan running southward towards a bridge beneath a railway line that lay
[be]hind the British front. One spectator thought the scene resembled 'the
[sta]rt of a big cross-country champion foot race'. Bird and the units' adju-
[tan]ts mounted, to ensure that their men could see them: 'We sat and
[wat]ched the panic. First came drivers wildly lashing their teams, which
[ras]hed past with guns and carriages covered with infantrymen clinging to
[the]m. Then, after an interval, a mob of men now walking because out of
[breat]h ... Towards the end of the crowd came the officers walking singly
[in] pairs.'

[...]ll, iron-willed CO of the Middlesex, was seen to be the last man of
[his div]ision to retreat. Some artillery teams headed smartly for the rear
[withou]t making any attempt to salvage their guns, which prompted young
[men] of the Irish Rifles to volunteer to fetch in the abandoned pieces.
[It was] obviously impossible, however, in the absence of horses and
[...] the Rifles that day lost five officers and sixty men killed or missing
[or ta]ken prisoner – and a further twenty-nine wounded. Wilkinson

Bird survived unscathed, but lost a leg in another action three weeks later. Lt. Siegener, a German infantryman, described how his men began to advance as they saw the British withdraw: 'Our losses had been, and continued to be, great, but we wanted to get on. 200 metres to our front was a trench that was still occupied. But already white flags were being displayed over there. The men had their hands up and they surrendered. An officer came up and handed over his sword, but there was still fire coming down on us from further up. I pointed this out and threatened to shoot him immediately. The Briton waved towards the rear and the shooting stopped.'

On the right, the Yorkshires conducted a sacrificial stand. By 4.30, they were cut off; a German bugler sounded the British ceasefire, seeking to avert further slaughter. The remains of the battalion fought on; one of its officers, forty-two-year-old Maj. Cal Yate, led nineteen survivors in a final bayonet charge, in which he fell badly wounded. It is always disputable whether such actions are heroic or merely foolishly futile; in this case, Yate was given a VC, awarded posthumously since he died as a prisoner in Germany, allegedly attempting to escape. Some Yorkshires were bayoneted when they were finally overrun, but most were spared by the Germans, who also treated the wounded humanely. When the few men who escaped to II Corps' main body reformed, it was found that seventeen officers including the Yorkshires' colonel were lost, together with most of their NCOs and men. Bertie Trevor assumed command of what was left.

In the British centre, the Gordon Highlanders failed to receive the signal to withdraw, which was given around 5 p.m. by a galloper who thought 250 yards close enough to ride towards the embattled unit. Only one subaltern saw him wave; being heavily engaged at the time, he said nothing. Three platoons slipped away on their own initiative, and eventually regained the British lines. The rest continued firing from the Audencourt ridge until nightfall, along with some stragglers from the Royal Scots and Royal Irish. There was then a strange row between the Gordons' CO and another officer – confusingly named Brevet Colonel W.E. Gordon, a South African war VC. Gordon claimed the right to supersede the commanding officer, and took command of the party, which set off southwards in darkness. In the village of Bertry, some officers entered a bar which they found occupied by Germans, whom they later implausibly claimed to have engaged with their revolvers and killed. Almost all the 750-strong party eventually surrendered. Details of their forlorn odyssey, which obviously included bitter recriminations between senior officers, have been lost with time. A wounded Scottish officer described how a young German lieutenant offered him chocolate and demanded, 'Why have you English come against us? It is no use. We shall be in Paris in three days.' The Gordons' travails at Le Cateau led to bitter post-war controversy, and even a libel action involving one officer concerned. Unkind critics referred to the batallion mockingly as 'the Kaiser's Own'.

Gen. Sordet's French cavalry, which had come into action further west, along with their 75mm guns, played an invaluable role in covering the British withdrawal, which continued through the hours of darkness. Gen. Henri de Ferron's territorial division also attacked German formations deploying towards Le Cateau. Without this support, Kluck's men could have turned Smith-Dorrien's left flank during the afternoon, with disastrous consequences. Enemy shells continued to fall upon some of II Corps' positions for hours after they were abandoned. 'The British had withdrawn so skilfully that we had not noticed anything,' wrote cavalryman Capt. Freiherr von der Horst. Smith-Dorrien had concluded a stubborn defensive stand by performing the most difficult of all battlefield manoeuvres – disengagement from close contact with the enemy.

German gunner captain Fritz Schneider observed that 26 August was a glorious day in his regiment's history, 'but the British also fought bravely. That must be recognised. Despite heavy and bloody losses, they held their positions … When, later that evening, we found ourselves on the road in Beauvois a group of forty to fifty prisoners were being led past. They were all tall, well-built men whose bearing and clothing made an outstanding impression. What a contrast to the short, pale and anxious Frenchmen in their grubby uniforms, whom we had captured two days previously in Tournai!' The most popular booty from the battlefield proved to be scores of discarded British greatcoats, whose quality the victors appreciated.

German failure to encircle and shatter Smith-Dorrien's command reflected poorly on Kluck's competence, as well as showing the strength of the resistance his regiments faced. On 26 August II Corps held a position in which its most likely fate was destruction. Smith-Dorrien kept his nerve, and instead extricated his force in tolerable order. As at Mons, however, this was certainly no British triumph. His men had merely checked their pursuers for a few hours and escaped catastrophe, chiefly because their enemies were slow to concentrate superior strength against them. II Corps had abandoned thirty-eight guns, and officially recorded the loss of 7,812 men at Le Cateau, a serious toll for a small army, though many stragglers reappeared in the days that followed. Around 5,000 seems a realistic British casualty total for the battle, of which perhaps seven hundred were killed, 2,500 taken prisoner and the rest wounded.

As II Corps continued its withdrawal, staff officers stood by roadsides directing men towards their own units, identification not assisted by the fact that so many had given their cap badges to French or Belgian civilians. Tom Wollocombe of the Middlesex described the spectacle, and his own mingled emotions, as they retreated: 'the road … was absolutely ghastly – dead and wounded horses and men strewn all the way, and limbers, guns, ambulances, wagons, carts and all kinds of things running away and bumping into one another without drivers. I marched on that evening feeling fit as a fiddle, although I was nearly done when I went into action. An enemy is a wonderful stimulant.'

Smith-Dorrien's men had won a twelve-hour start on their enemies, who made no attempt at close pursuit. Analysis of regimental casualty figures suggests that Kluck's losses at Le Cateau were about half those of Smith-Dorrien: few Germans became prisoners, as did the British left behind on the battlefield. Kluck's returns show battle casualties of just over 7,000 for the ten-day period embracing both Mons and Le Cateau. The German First Army during the entire month of August admitted only 2,863 men killed or missing, with a further 7,869 wounded. Such losses had only marginal significance when Kluck's entire command numbered 217,384. He was at least equally troubled by a sick list of 8,000, mostly men too footsore to march. British official historians argued in the 1920s that the Germans wilfully understated their losses, but there seems no reason to believe this. The BEF fought staunchly in both its significant August battles, but its fire injured the enemy much less grievously than optimists supposed then and romantics have imagined since.

German soldiers emerged from the two encounters with respect for British determination and musketry, but commanders saw nothing to make them flinch. Moltke expressed satisfaction at the outcome of Le Cateau: Kluck's formations continued to advance, while the BEF kept on retreating. The British constructed a heroic legend by focusing upon individual acts of courage, and glossing over the stark 'big picture'. It was probably the case that Smith-Dorrien had no choice save to fight a battle. But he found himself in an unholy mess in the beet and stubble fields that day, from which he was fortunate to escape, with under-acknowledged French assistance.

That night of the 26th, Haig sent a telegram to GHQ which Edmonds, the official historian, later suggested was prompted by a bad conscience:

'No news of II Corps except sound of guns from the direction of Le Cateau and Beaumont. Can I Corps be of any assistance?' No, of course it could not. The day was done, and also one of the less creditable passages in Haig's military career. Edmonds – whose spleen or even malice should be acknowledged – said that I Corps' commander always refused to discuss Le Cateau except to express his opinion that Smith-Dorrien was wrong to have fought there. The historian commented with relish: 'I fancy Haig was none too proud of August 1914.' The resolve and professionalism of Britain's soldiers narrowly sufficed to compensate for the follies and inadequacies of their senior officers. The most significant contribution of the two actions at Mons and Le Cateau was to check the momentum of Kluck's advance: every day the Germans failed to traverse more miles across France represented a gain for Joffre's redeployment. Time was critical, and Moltke was running short of it.

7

The Retreat

It is a peculiarly British trait to find glory in retreats – to Corunna in 1809, from Kabul in 1842, to Dunkirk in 1940 – and from Mons in 1914. In Belgium and France that August, the BEF suffered the consequences of the Asquith government's policy, reprising that of many British administrations throughout history, of pursuing gesture strategy. Ministers committed an absurdly small army to the continent, where it became entangled in a clash between major European land powers. Only as a consequence of luck, French mass and German fumbling did the BEF escape a disaster which its inadequate size and the incompetence of its commander-in-chief made likely. It should never be forgotten that the French army's general withdrawal from eastern France was much more important strategically, being on a far larger scale, than that of the British alongside it from Mons. The experiences of Joffre's soldiers further east mirrored those of the BEF.

For eleven days following Le Cateau, in oppressive heat interrupted by sporadic thunderstorms, long columns of men, horses and wagons trudged southward, sometimes dozing as they marched or rode. Gunner Sgt. William Edgington wrote on the 26th: 'marched to St. Quentin in heavy rain & all feeling very much the want of sleep. No rations … all ranks are very much depressed owing not only to the fact of us continually retiring, but at the total absence of any information; we appear to be simply driven blindly back.' Some stragglers, no longer able to bear the pain of their feet, the misery of motion, slipped away from the road into nearby woods or fields and fell into blissful sleep, awakening to face captivity or death at German hands. A few such men were hidden by Belgian or French people after becoming separated from the army; some were betrayed, and in a few cases shot, many months later. There were occasional little actions as rearguard units fell behind and found themselves cut off.

The experience of Le Cateau pushed some British officers and men further than they could endure. Late on the night of 27 August Tom Bridges led his squadron of dragoons clattering along the *pavé* into the central square of Saint-Quentin, where he was dismayed to find two or three hundred exhausted soldiers lying prostrate, impervious to imprecations or kicks. Bridges was even more shocked to discover that two battalions – the Warwicks and the Dublin Fusiliers – had piled arms at the railway station, after their commanding officers handed to Saint-Quentin's mayor a written undertaking of surrender, to save the town from bombardment. Bridges retrieved this damning document from the Frenchman. But when he sent a messenger to tell the two colonels that his cavalrymen would cover their battalions' escape, the troops refused to move unless a train was produced to carry them. Bridges thereupon declared that if they failed to set off within thirty minutes, he would leave no British soldier alive in the town. Under this threat, the men sullenly scrambled to their feet and began to move. The major then turned his mind to the stragglers in the town square. He contemplated their somnolent forms and thought, 'If only I had a band!' His eye fell on a toyshop, and he saw means to create one. Equipping himself and his trumpeter with a drum and a tin whistle, the two marched round and round the square, manically playing 'The British Grenadiers' and 'Tipperary'.

Soldiers began to laugh, then to cheer. Bridges harangued them, shouting that he would take them back to their regiments. One by one they roused themselves and fell in. Darkness had fallen. Bridges and his trumpeter, reinforced by a brace of mouth organs, led his motley column out of Saint-Quentin. Some of them indeed rejoined II Corps' line of march, but four days later 291 men of the Warwicks were still missing, listed as 'stragglers'. Both defaulting colonels, John Elkington of the Warwicks and Arthur Mainwaring of the Dublin Fusiliers, were cashiered for their attempted surrender: on 14 September, Army Orders recorded their convictions for 'behaving in a scandalous manner unbecoming to the character of an officer and a gentleman'. Elkington, though forty-nine years old, responded in a manner worthy of fiction by joining the French Foreign Legion, with which he was badly wounded and won the Legion of Honour, Croix de Guerre and Médaille Militaire. King George V later reinstated him in the British Army and gave him a DSO in recognition of his extraordinary efforts to secure rehabilitation. One of the Warwicks' young officers was Bernard Montgomery, who in his later memoirs made it plain that he did not think much of Elkington, and recognised a shambles when he saw one, at Le Cateau.

Another battalion's CO, by contrast, spoke of the aftermath of the battle with partisan regimental pride: 'I ran into what appeared to be a disorganised mass of soldiers of all sorts of units, mixed up together. They were leisurely retiring, but in no sort of formation. There was no panic, only disorganisation. [Then] I sighted the Wiltshires, marching along the road all in good order, ready for action wherever required.' They reached Saint-Quentin, twenty miles south-east of their battlefield, early on the 27th. By dawn the following day, II Corps was at the Somme, thirty-five miles from Le Cateau, having shown that most of its men could march as hard as they could fight.

If Sir John French's contribution to the conduct of the British campaign since Mons had been erratic and inglorious, it was his good fortune that the enemy did worse. Kluck, commanding far larger forces, manoeuvred them ineptly, missing repeated opportunities to trap the vulnerable British. On the 27th the German general compounded earlier mistakes by maintaining his army's southerly line of march, while the British veered south-eastwards on a line towards Paris, untroubled by the enemy. That day, the French divisions on their left received most of Kluck's attentions.

One consequence of the C-in-C's moral collapse – for it is hard to define his conduct as anything less – is that it caused his liaison officer with GQG, Col. Charles Huguet, to report to Joffre in the most despondent and defeatist terms. The Frenchman declared on the 26th: 'battle lost by the British Army, which seems to have lost all cohesion'. In the days that followed, gloom took hold in the rear areas of the BEF. Huguet sent a further message on the 27th in which he asserted: 'conditions are such that for the moment the British Army no longer exists. It will not be in a condition to take the field again until it has been thoroughly rested and reconstituted.' The colonel is often castigated by British writers for his pessimism, but this is unjust. What Huguet said merely reflected the hysterical view prevailing at GHQ in general, and in the mind of its commander-in-chief in particular.

The muddle of stragglers, and the conspicuous distress of some senior officers, bred a virus of panic which eventually spread to London. Huguet suggested that Sir John French might insist upon withdrawing the BEF to Le Havre. The C-in-C was indeed attracted to a fantastic notion that his army might retire from the campaign for a few weeks, to reorganise and refit, while his senior staff officers did nothing to restore confidence. Henry Wilson sent a message to 4th Division's commander: 'Throw overboard all ammunition and impediments not absolutely required, and load up your lame ducks on all transport, horse and mechanical, and hustle along.' The same order was given to II Corps. Smith-Dorrien immediately countermanded it, only to be rebuked by Sir John French for having done so.

The despondency at the top was almost entirely unjustified. Haig's I Corps had scarcely been engaged. Most of II Corps' units were suffering from nothing worse than exhaustion; the fighting spirit of most of its units was not critically impaired. Men were bewildered that they continued to flee before the enemy. Since they could not see the great grey masses of Kluck's and Bülow's armies, they were cockily confident that, on the Germans' showing thus far, they could lick them. Their commander-in-chief, however, saw only one choice: opposed by overwhelmingly superior numbers, and alongside allies in whom he had lost all confidence, the BEF must continue its flight, if possible as far as the sea. Only the robust good sense of quartermaster-general Sir William Robertson, who organised dumps of ammunition and rations along the army's line of retreat, enabled the troops to remain fed and capable of fighting.

The BEF marched two hundred miles between Mons and the Marne, averaging four hours' sleep a night. Three exhausted Irish Guardsmen, literally sleepwalking, shuffled southwards clinging to the belt of their adjutant, Lord Desmond Fitzgerald. On 28 August Guy Harcourt-Vernon wrote: 'Marches are much slower now, but we cover the ground somehow.' At halts, they cut wire from farm fences to make defensive entanglements, and dug potatoes from the fields with a sense of guilty delight at being licensed to steal. Bizarrely, on 29 August the Grenadiers spent two hours holding a routine pay parade.

And spasmodically they scuffled with Germans. The Connaught Rangers had made a notable contribution to the culture of the war by singing 'It's a Long Way to Tipperary' as they first disembarked in France. George Curnock, *Daily Mail* star reporter, heard the song and mentioned it in a dispatch. The paper's news editor wrote in his diary: 'The chief [Lord Northcliffe] has given us orders to boom it, to print the music so that everybody shall know it. He says, thanks to Curnock's genius, we shall soon have everybody singing it.' And so they did. But on 26 August the Connaught Rangers had a much less happy experience. They were acting as rearguard when they failed to receive an order to retire; six officers and 280 men were lost, including their colonel, almost all taken prisoner.

On 27 August, 2nd Royal Munster Fusiliers suffered even more severely. The unit was commanded by an officer of French descent named Paul

Charrier, who three weeks earlier had enthused about the prospect of fighting the Germans, his people's hereditary foes. North of Etreux, the Munsters fell victim to yet another of the campaign's communications breakdowns: missing an order to pull back, they were cut off. The Irish soldiers attempted to escape down roadside ditches while a Maxim gun kept the enemy at bay. They were finally cornered in an orchard, where they fought until evening, when the Germans used a herd of cattle to mask their final assault. Four wounded Munsters officers and 240 men were taken prisoner, while ten officers and 118 other ranks were killed – including Charrier, a figure of notable eccentricity who fought wearing a sola topee; he was twice wounded leading counter-attacks before succumbing. Another of the dead was a certain Lt. Awdry, said to have fallen with his sword in his hand, whose brother later achieved an incongruous celebrity as author of the children's tales of *Thomas the Tank Engine*.

Elsewhere, driver Horace Goatham's best mate in his 18-pounder battery put a hand over his horse's back to mount, and promptly received a bullet through it. Goatham somehow pushed the man onto another horse and whipped up the gun team. After a time, however, his mate slumped in the saddle from loss of blood, then slid to the ground. The gunners were fortunate enough to meet a field ambulance wagon which picked up the wounded man, who reached safety, as others did not. Goatham's worst subsequent experience came when his battery reached a river where the bridge had been blown. Only a precarious Royal Engineers' pontoon offered a route southwards, with German shrapnel bursting around it. 'We had to wait till the shells burst, then gallop like hell over, one gun at a time. We lost one team, blown all over the shop. My off horse got hit, but we got clear. If ever men deserved to be decorated, every manjack of those REs did, for as fast as one got bowled over and fell in the water another would run along the bridge and jump in the [pontoon] boat to replace him.'

A sergeant of the Oxf & Bucks shouted repeatedly during those days, 'Stick it lads! We are making history!' If such histrionics read well to posterity, however, they merely exasperated the weary men whom he addressed. Cpl. Bernard Denore of the Berkshires was better pleased when his pal Ginger Gilmore found a mouth organ and staggered along at the head of the company playing tunes 'despite the fact that his feet were bound in blood-soaked rags ... Mostly he played "The Irish Emigrant". Which is a good marching tune ... An officer asked me if I wanted a turn on his horse, but I looked at the fellow on it and said, "No thanks."' Others

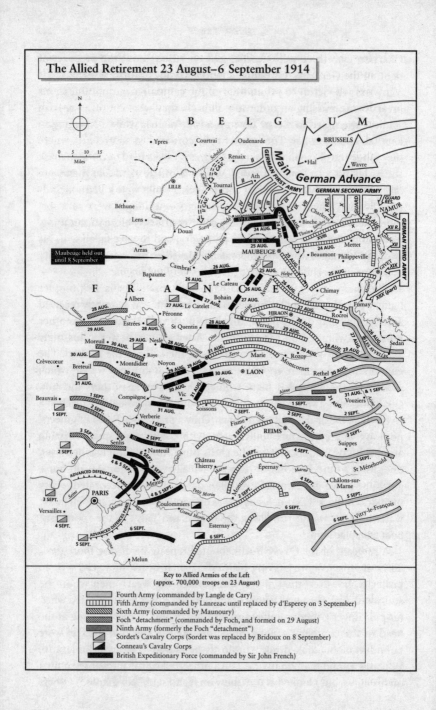

The Allied Retirement 23 August–6 September 1914

N

0 5 10 15
Miles

B E L G I U M

Ypres • Courtrai • Oudenarde

Renaix • BRUSSELS

Hal • Wavre

Schelde

CAV.

Tournai

Ath

Main German Advance

GERMAN FIRST ARMY

GERMAN SECOND ARMY

GUARD RES.

NAMUR

Charleroi

IX RES.

GUARD

IX

Béthune

Lens

Douai

Canal

Escaut (Schelde)

LILLE

Scarpe

Condé

Valenciennes

23 AUG.

24 AUG.

25 AUG.

Binche

Thuin

Sambre

XVIII

X

VII RES.

XII R.

GERMAN THIRD ARMY

Arras

Scarpe

Cambrai

MAUBEUGE

24 AUG.

25 AUG.

Mettet

XII

Dinant

Beaumont • Philippeville

CIVET

XIX

Maubeuge held out until 8 September

F R A N C E

26 AUG.

Bapaume

26 AUG.

25 AUG.

Le Cateau

Bohain

Chimay

Fumay

25 AUG.

Helpe

Sambre

XIIX (part)

Amiens

Albert

27 AUG. Le Catelet

27 AUG.

Guise

Oise

HIRSON

27 AUG.

Rocroi

Sedan

28 AUG.

Estrées

Péronne

28 AUG. St Quentin

28 AUG.

Vervins

28 AUG.

29 AUG.

LES AYVELLES

27 AUG.

28 AUG.

29 AUG.

Moreuil

30 AUG.

29 AUG. Nesle

28 AUG.

Crozat

31 AUG.

Serre

Marie

Montcornet

30 AUG.

28 AUG.

29 AUG.

Crèvecœur

Breteuil

Montdidier

Roye

Noyon

29 AUG.

30 AUG.

LAON

Rethel

30 AUG.

31 AUG.

30 AUG.

Aisne

Beauvais

Compiègne

Oise

30 AUG.

Vic

31 AUG.

Aisne

Aisne

31 AUG. & 1 SEPT.

Vouziers

1 SEPT.

1 SEPT.

Aisne

Soissons

2 SEPT.

Vesle

1 SEPT.

31 AUG.

2 SEPT.

Verberie

Néry

1 SEPT.

Fismes

3 SEPT.

REIMS

2 SEPT.

Aisne

3 SEPT.

Suippes

3 SEPT.

Senlis

2 SEPT.

Nanteuil

6 SEPT.

3 SEPT.

Château Thierry

Marne

4 SEPT.

Épernay

4 SEPT.

St Ménehould

4 & 5 SEPT.

Meaux

4 & 5 SEPT.

Montmirail

2 SEPT.

Châlons-sur-Marne

ADVANCED DEFENCES OF PARIS

3 SEPT.

PARIS

Marne

Lagny

Coulommiers

Marne

Petit Morin

5 SEPT.

Seine

Versailles

4 SEPT.

ADVANCED DEFENCES PARIS

Grand Morin

Esternay

6 SEPT.

Vitry-le-François

5 SEPT.

6 SEPT.

6 SEPT.

Melun

Seine

Key to Allied Armies of the Left
(appox. 700,000 troops on 23 August)

	Fourth Army (commanded by Langle de Cary)
	Fifth Army (commanded by Lanrezac until replaced by d'Esperey on 3 September)
	Sixth Army (commanded by Maunoury)
	Foch "detachment" (commanded by Foch, and formed on 29 August)
	Ninth Army (formerly the Foch "detachment")
	Sordet's Cavalry Corps (Sordet was replaced by Bridoux on 8 September)
	Conneau's Cavalry Corps
	British Expeditionary Force (commanded by Sir John French)

were less unselfish. When the medical officer of the Royal Welch dismounted to attend a wounded man, he asked a passing Cameronian to hold his reins. The man promptly scrambled into the saddle and cantered away, leaving the hapless doctor to continue his own progress on foot.

Horses soon began to go lame in large numbers, many because they needed shoeing, and there were no smithies at hand. Limping and dead animals littered the line of march, along with discarded carts and equipment. Driver Charles Harrison and his mates subsisted chiefly on raw vegetables picked from roadside fields. Several later found themselves in trouble for losing their caps, which slipped off as their heads slumped in sleep, even as they rode. And all the while the retreating army competed for road space with dense columns of refugees, incongruously clad in their Sunday best, because that was what they always wore for leaving their own villages – as some now did at the commencement of a four-year exile.

The manner in which the campaign flooded across France, swamping a large tract of a great country not yet adjusted to war, produced some bizarre encounters. When the Royal Flying Corps headquarters staff found themselves in need of automobile tyres and headlights, on 29 August an officer simply drove to the Daimler showroom in Paris and purchased as many as his vehicle could carry, paying in gold sovereigns from a bulging portmanteau entrusted to him for such purposes. '*Les anglais sont épatants*,' marvelled the French salesman, shaking his head in admiration for these 'wonderful' people. The jumble of ancient and modern was illustrated by the experience of exhausted RFC pilots, who one night during the retreat slept fully dressed on a straw stack in a barn, while their machines in a neighbouring field were guarded by a squadron of the Northern Irish Horse.

A staff officer dispatched on a liaison mission from I Corps met Smith-Dorrien and his staff on the 29th, and recorded in his diary that he found the mood at II Corps utterly different from that of GHQ, and anything but cast down: 'quite calm, approachable and pleasant; not too busy to say a cheery word or two, and quite unfluttered'. But some officers felt that the morale of the entire BEF was sagging. Col. George Morris of the Irish Guards – who would be killed two days later – was 'very gloomy', telling a fellow officer 'it was the old story of allies failing to get on together and that everything was going wrong … we should be re-embarking for England in a fortnight'. Guy Harcourt-Vernon wrote home on 29 August: 'the marches have been awful & unless we get a day of rest soon we shan't have a man in the ranks'. But then he added, after a few hours' priceless repose: 'We shall be able to carry on for a long time yet. It is wonderful what a different view of life you take after a sleep & meal.' Yet still they continued to retreat southwards day after day, as did the French armies on their right.

On 25 August Lt. Col. Gerhard Tappen, Chief of the *Operationsabteilung* of the General Staff, declared with satisfaction: 'In six weeks we shall have the whole job done.' Whatever the significance of Mons, Le Cateau and comparable French actions in allied minds, the only reality that seemed to matter to most Germans was that they continued to advance, and to repulse every French counter-attack. By the 27th the high command had tacitly, if not explicitly, abandoned its plan to encircle Paris from the west, deciding that it was now necessary only to hound the beaten foe to destruction. The German army's successes spawned a huge misjudgement. After inflicting vast casualties on the French, Moltke and his subordinates failed to recognise that, in history's greatest clash of arms, even such carnage did not suffice to destroy an enemy's powers of resistance. A fatal complacency overtook the Kaiser's commanders in the last days of August and the first of September: they persuaded themselves that a coherent strategy was no longer necessary to complete their triumph.

Yet in some places, notably the Lorraine front, the advancing Germans were now suffering almost as severely as the retreating French. On 25 August Joffre's forces launched a counter-attack in the Trouée des Charmes between Tour and Epinal, a difficult country of steep hills and rivers. In what became known as the Battle of the Mortagne, some 225,000 French soldiers clashed with 300,000 of Prince Rupprecht's men. Fighting petered out in a draw on 28 August, but the Bavarians had bled freely for small advantage – one historian estimates that they suffered 66,000 casualties in Alsace-Lorraine. The Germans' advance slowed, especially that of Hausen's Third Army: at least until early September, Moltke's commanders acknowledged a need to keep step with neighbours, which sometimes required holding back their own men. On the evening of the 29th came a decisive moment: Bülow invited Kluck, his subordinate, to change his axis of advance, to wheel inward – further east – to strike a killing blow at Lanrezac's Fifth Army. This initiative was duly adopted without authorisation from the chief of staff, yet it represented a critical departure from even OHL's modified version of the Schlieffen concept. Next day Moltke acquiesced. He too seemed to suppose that it was now merely necessarily

SERBIA

Above: Serbian troops advance.
Left: Serbian C-in-C Putnik.
Below left: Potiorek, Austrian
field commander. *Below right:*
Corporal Egon Kisch (*left*) and
comrade.

Austrian troops in Serbia conduct punitive mass executions of civilians, a ritual often photographed and publicised to discourage *francs-tireurs*.

Above: An Austrian siege piece of the type used to destroy the Liège forts.
Left: Kluck, commanding the German First Army.

Left: Bülow, commanding Second Army.

Some of Joffre's men, before the deluge.

Belgians doing their modest best.

75s – the legendary French *soixante-quinzes* – in action.

to herd the shattered French armies south-eastwards, towards the Swiss frontier.

The formidably powerful Eiffel Tower radio station intercepted the German signals about this movement; within hours, a copy of the critical order was on Joffre's desk. Whatever the commander-in-chief's earlier blunders, he immediately understood the significance of the German decision to cross the French front before Paris, and discerned a great opportunity beckoning for the allies. With stunning hubris, Bülow had ordered Kluck to execute a parade march in the face of an undefeated foe. Falkenhayn warned Moltke on 30 August that the French army had not collapsed – instead, it was conducting an orderly withdrawal. If Joffre was indeed beaten, the Prussian war minister demanded, where was the great haul of captured guns and equipment, the vast mass of prisoners that should be falling into the victors' hands?

Moltke professed to dismiss Falkenhayn's strictures, but in truth they added to the discomfiture of a commander already prey to feverish secret anxieties of his own. He had earlier felt sufficiently convinced of imminent triumph in the West to propose the dispatch of six corps to East Prussia, and eventually to send two. But on that same 30 August, to Admiral Müller he spoke much as Falkenhayn had done to himself, expressing unease about the absence of the flotsam associated with shattered armies: 'Contrary to the Kaiser's fantasies, we have pushed the French back, but they are not yet beaten. That has still to happen. Where are our prisoners?' On 1 September, the chief of staff's spirits briefly revived. He became excited by a prospect of achieving a new envelopment between Verdun and Reims. But, as so often in those days, the Germans advanced too slowly and Joffre's forces withdrew too fast to make this possible. Moltke's anguish intensified. Were the victories that so thrilled his royal master mere occupations of Belgian and French real estate? To subordinates, he avowed unease. But since he had abdicated operational direction of the armies, his apprehension exercised no influence upon the conduct of Kluck and Bülow in the critical days that followed.

It is mistaken, however, thus to burden the two army commanders with responsibility for the looming collapse of Germany's fantasy of victory in 1914. Rather, they became prisoners of the fundamental unsoundness of their nation's war plan. It is unlikely that any grand design could have produced a swift, conclusive outcome unless the allied armies suffered total moral collapse – which they did not. But Moltke had progressively abandoned even his own diluted version of Schlieffen, weakening the right, and on 24 August agreeing that Crown Prince Rupprecht's Bavarians should pursue Castelnau's retreating army towards Nancy. As German complacency grew, Schlieffen's sophisticated if flawed vision was supplanted by the crude pursuit of objectives of opportunity. The Kaiser's commanders saw themselves sustaining a headlong advance, while the French and British fled before them. Bülow, Kluck and their counterparts further south were more disturbed by the effects of exhaustion on men and horses than by their battle casualties. They supposed that the hard fighting was already behind them.

Back in Berlin, Bethmann Hollweg's confidant Kurt Riezler wrote: 'One is already beginning to make plans for the victory booty … We looked at the map today. I always preach the erection of vassal states. Today the chancellor had me come to him, asked me about peace conditions and my ideas.' He added a few days later, in lyrical mood: 'We Germans have … awakened powers in ourselves the magnitude of which we would never have imagined. Above all, we have discovered a spiritual essence through which we can concentrate these powers.'

On the other side in the last days of August, while Joffre grasped a gleam of possibility of redeeming the ghastly defeats that had befallen French arms under his leadership, few of his subordinates shared his kindling hopes, and certainly not the senior officers of the BEF. They experienced only the reality of continuing flight from the enemy, ever further southwards. On the 27th, Joffre signalled Lanrezac at his headquarters at Marle. Fifth Army was continuing its withdrawal, across the river Oise: GQG told its commander that he must now wheel his left-hand corps to the west, and launch an attack on Kluck's left flank, to relieve pressure on the BEF. After the C-in-C's departure, Lanrezac exploded in fury, denouncing both Joffre and the British with a fury that shocked his staff. He saw no prospect of such an attack succeeding, and believed that he would merely thrust his army into the jaws of a German vice. Sir John French, meanwhile, showed no interest in anything Lanrezac might or might not do, and continued his retirement.

On the 28th, momentously, Joffre in his long black overcoat appeared in person at Fifth Army's headquarters. At first, his demeanour was cordial and flattering, identifying several officers for praise. But then followed an explosion of rage, and an explicit threat: if Fifth Army failed to attack next day, Lanrezac would be sacked. A liaison officer was dispatched to Haig and Smith-Dorrien, informing them of what was to happen, and seeking their cooperation. Near Lucy the Frenchman found the British I Corps commander receiving an excited report from an RFC pilot, who had just landed to confirm that Kluck's flank was exposed, his columns veering eastward. Haig passed word to Lanrezac that a great opportunity beckoned; he would be happy to support a major counter-attack, and his formations could move at 5 a.m. next day.

During the hours that followed, however, some British units brawled with the Germans, and suffered delays. Haig sent word first that his own move must be delayed until 5.30 a.m., then that he needed a further postponement until midday. Finally, he said he could do nothing without the assent of Sir John French. This was abruptly refused: the C-in-C declared that I Corps needed a rest day. Lanrezac was incandescent, Joffre despondent. Spears, who had to endure both voluble and mute reproaches from Fifth Army's staff, wrote: 'the French considered that the British were running away at the critical moment, while the British were persuaded that they had been treated so badly that they could place no further reliance on their Allies'. Fifth Army's attack proceeded anyway.

Guise nestles in the deep valley of the Oise, where open fields are interspersed with dense woodlands on the hillsides both north and south of the river. There are views for miles, landmarked with farms bearing such sardonic names as '*Désolation*' and '*Monchagrin*'. Here, next morning, Lanrezac ordered forward his formations – the left driving at Kluck, the right against Bülow. Initially, the latter of these thrusts met some success, driving back the Germans up to three miles. 'He manipulated his units with the skill of a master at the great game of war,' wrote Spears, 'but he played his hand without zest or faith.' The second part of this statement was manifestly true; but the claim seems unfounded that, for once in his life, on 29 August Lanrezac played the part of an inspirational commander.

On the left, Fifth Army's main attack was thrown back with heavy casualties. Before the assault, the Germans captured a corps chief of staff whose papers showed that the principal French objectives lay on Kluck's front. Bülow, next door, could thus be confident that he had nothing important to fear. When the French advanced towards Saint-Quentin, the Germans were ready: some ground the attackers won at heavy cost was soon lost again. Only further north, around Guise, did Fifth Army make significant progress, pushing forward on both sides of the town to exploit a gap between Kluck's and Bülow's armies. German local command broke down, and German artillery caused substantial casualties by firing on one of its own Guards units.

The vanguard French brigade driving towards Le Hérie was led by the corps commander, Louis Franchet d'Espèrey, who would later prove one of the outstanding French generals of the war. He was fortunate that he survived to do so, because on 29 August he rode his horse towards the German line south of Guise, amid his regiments with colours flying and bands playing. Bülow became sufficiently concerned by the vigour of the attack to solicit support from his neighbor Hausen, who responded that he had his hands full on his own front. Bülow also urged Kluck to pivot still more sharply southward, further foreshortening the great German sweep.

Lanrezac sent a new appeal to the British for support, met by a renewed refusal from their C-in-C, conveyed by Henry Wilson. The latter thought Fifth Army's attack madness because it could lead nowhere, against over-whelmingly superior forces. That night, Wilson drove to Reims to meet Joffre, and begged him to order a withdrawal before Kluck and Bülow closed in upon Lanrezac, perhaps precipitating disaster. Joffre indeed instructed Fifth Army to resume its retreat, though it is unlikely that his decision was influenced by Wilson. Bülow reported to Moltke that he had gained a victory – but added that his men were too tired to march next day. Thus Lanrezac, and the corpses of several thousand men, secured another breathing space. Franchet d'Espèrey was the only general to emerge with credit from the actions at Guise.

Confusion among both armies about their respective positions prompted droll incidents in those days, among soldiers who became victims of misinformation. A smart young German cavalry officer was driven into the village of La Fère in a dusty motor car, which halted outside the post office. Oblivious of French soldiers standing around, whom presumably he supposed to be prisoners, he marched inside, bought and wrote some postcards. On reappearing, he was abruptly seized by the military bystanders, along with his driver, who proved to be a former Berlin taxi-driver. The officer sulked terribly about his ignominious capture and refused to speak, but the driver expressed himself forcefully in condemnation of the war. A French officer gleefully showed Louis Spears the German's postcards, retrieved from the post office, which described the British as running 'like sheep'.

Next day, 30 August, the Kaiser and Moltke belatedly shifted their head-quarters forward from Coblenz to Luxembourg, where the latter set up shop in a schoolhouse. Radio messages to and from the fronts required passage through several relay stations, with delays sometimes amounting to an amazing twenty hours. The army commanders were not much troubled by this problem, because it liberated them from unwelcome interference by the chief of staff. But the consequence was that Moltke's lack of grip upon the campaign became institutionalised. Each of his subordinates acted as seemed to him best.

That same day, Sir John French dispatched one of his most notorious communications, writing to Joffre from a new headquarters in the palace at Compiègne: 'I feel it very necessary to impress on you that the British Army cannot under any circumstances take its place in the front line for at least ten days. I require men and guns to make good casualties ... You will understand that I cannot meet your wishes to fill the gap between the Fifth and Sixth Armies.' Sir John declared his intention to retire beyond the Seine. This was a devastating telegram. It is extraordinary that an officer capable of sending it should ever have been entrusted with command of an army in the field, and even more remarkable that he retained such a role for more than a year thereafter. Sir John French's conduct between Mons and the Marne exposed him as a poltroon – not the first nor the last such figure to achieve military eminence, but nonetheless a heavy handicap for the allied cause. Sir James Edmonds characterised French as 'a vain, ignorant and vindictive old man with an unsavoury society backing'. If this was cruel, it is hard to suggest that it was unjust. Several of French's key subordinates had also been found wanting, notable among them Murray, Wilson and in some measure Haig, though the last would rehabilitate himself two months later at Ypres.

The best that can be said of the limitations of Britain's generals is that most of their counterparts of all the rival armies exposed large shortcomings in August 1914. Their conduct was perhaps no worse than that of many peer groups in civilian society, facing wholly unfamiliar challenges and circumstances of unprecedented magnitude, but in war the penalties for bewilderment are paid with lives. Moltke, a sick man from the outset, was now visibly ailing; he declined to impose personal control on the decisive phase of the campaign he had willed, probably because he had no idea how to do so. He and his subordinates proved unable to exploit the institutional superiority of the German army to forge a decisive victory. In part, this is attributable to the fact that they sought to fulfil ambitions beyond the powers of their armies in the pre-motorised age. The technologies of mobility and communication lagged critically behind the enhancement of firepower. But it remains remarkable that Moltke left Kluck and Bülow such immense latitude, and unsurprising that they blundered.

On the French side, Joffre had launched Plan XVII with dreadful consequences for his country and its army. Many of his subordinates had been found wanting in the Battles of the Frontiers. Lanrezac was a soldier of some gifts, who nonetheless proved to lack the moral strength for high command. The merits of Joffre's insistence on fighting at Guise on 29 August remain as keenly debated as those of Smith-Dorrien's stand at Le Cateau. It was plain that Lanrezac could only deliver a 'stopping blow', at heavy cost in casualties. The balance of evidence suggests that the battle represented an acceptable gamble, for it inflicted a further check and significant losses on the Germans.

But in the days that followed, the allied retreat continued, as did the growth of demoralisation among the troops. Joffre still clung to hopes for a major counter-offensive on his left; throughout those last days of August French men, guns and horses packed scores of trains moving up from the south. But to those marching and always marching, the only meaningful realities were those of the heat, the road, and their torn, bruised, blistered feet. Elsewhere in their weary bodies, almost four hundred years earlier Montaigne wrote: 'I have seen many soldiers inconvenienced by the irregularity of their bowels.' By late August, men of every army found constipation or diarrhoea compounding their sufferings as they stumbled across France in shared confusion. Marc Bloch, French conscript and later a historian murdered by the Nazis, wrote in a mood mirroring that of his nation: 'I stand bad news better than uncertainty ... Oh, what bitter days of retreat, of weariness, boredom and anxiety!'

On the morning of 1 September, for the first time since Le Cateau excepting skirmishes, the Germans caught up with elements of the BEF. Kluck was not looking for the British, in whose affairs he had lost interest; he was pushing south-eastwards towards Lanrezac. But in consequence his leading elements crossed the British sector as they headed towards Château-Thierry and bridges across the Marne. The first encounter with French's units came thirty-five miles north of Paris, at Néry. A British cavalry brigade which occupied the village during the night took the best billets, and quartered many of their mounts in a big farmyard beside the church. L Battery of the Royal Horse Artillery, last to arrive, was forced to make such shift as it could for the night in an orchard immediately south of the village, just short of a big sugar factory. Néry stood beside a deep, narrow valley thick with brushwood on the east side. Beyond, some six hundred yards from the village lay more high ground. 1 September dawned in thick mist. L Battery was assembled ready to march. Then a delay was ordered; limber poles were let down, and some teams were led away to water at the sugar factory.

A succession of shocks followed. First, a Hussars' picket dashed into the village to report German horse at hand. The mist suddenly lifted, and at 5.40 a.m. a dozen enemy field pieces from Marwitz's cavalry division began to fire on the British at point-blank range, less than a thousand yards, from the hill across the narrow valley. The Bays' mounts bolted in panic down the village street. Many of the British cavalry were invisible to the Germans among the houses, but L Battery's orchard was in plain sight – a perfect, unmissable target. Salvo after salvo landed with devastating effect. Horses reared, broke free and stampeded, men scuttled for cover, seized equipment, strove to harness teams.

Most of L Battery was limbered up, drivers and gunners preparing to mount and move. German fire fell upon them with stunning effect, bringing down whole teams in a chaos of mingled animal and human flesh. Capt. Edward Bradbury, the second-in-command, shouted, 'Come on – who's for the guns?' and led a handful of men in a dash through the shellfire to respond. They contrived to get three pieces into action, but two were quickly silenced. The last gun kept firing under the barrage until only Bradbury, Sgt. Nelson and Battery-Sgt.-Maj. Dorrell remained alive to work it, surrounded by dead and dying horses and gunners.

Bradbury, a keen steeplechase rider just turned thirty-three, had a leg blown off as he shifted ammunition, but continued giving fire orders until he collapsed from loss of blood. As he was carried dying to the rear, he passed the commanding officer of the Bays and called out, 'Halloa, colonel, they have been giving us a warm time, haven't they?' Bradbury's other two gunners kept their piece in action as long as they had rounds. L Battery's destruction was a miniature disaster involving the loss of five officers and forty-nine men. It is reasonable to doubt whether its single gun achieved much in the desperate circumstances of that morning; but it is characteristic of military iconography that the actions of Bradbury and his two comrades were rewarded with VCs and passed into legend, celebrated by a superbly heroic painting, while the retribution the British immediately afterwards inflicted on the Germans is almost forgotten.

The Hussars' machine-guns were deployed in Néry to fire across the valley, inflicting terrible casualties on the enemy gunners and horses. Lt. Algy Lunn then brought the Bays' Vickers into action also. Soon barrels were white hot, steam was hissing from condensers. Lunn and his men frantically refilled ammunition belts to sustain the fire. Infantry of the Middlesex and Royal Fusiliers, billeted in a neighbouring village, doubled to the scene, and began skirmishing forward on the northern side of Néry, while two squadrons of the 5th Dragoon Guards circled southward and opened dismounted fire on the Germans from the other flank. I Battery of the Royal Horse Artillery joined in at 8 a.m., to important effect, around the time the last of L Battery's pieces fell silent.

Marwitz's cavalry fell back in disarray, abandoning eight of their twelve guns and seventy-eight prisoners. A German doctor who was among them protested vigorously about the confiscation of his binoculars and his grey horse, which he insisted were private property – he waved a French-language edition of the Geneva Convention to support his argument. The victorious cavalry took both anyway. The British disputed fiercely among themselves about who deserved credit for giving the Germans a belated comeuppance. What was for sure is that it was a costly day for both sides, and especially for their horses: between three and four hundred perished around Néry. 'It is one of the worst things in the war,' wrote Harry Dillon of the Oxf & Bucks, 'dead horses everywhere and the stink is fearful. The corpses of men get moved or disposed of somehow, but there is no time to deal with the horses.'

There was debate about who, if anybody, deserved VCs. Sgt.-Maj. Dorrell was widely thought to have been decorated partly because he was a 'good chap': he had enlisted underage at sixteen, served in the Boer War and risen the hard way to warrant officer's rank. It is no slur upon the courage of some of those who received Britain's highest decoration in the first weeks of the war to observe that a few months later, amid relentless carnage, the bar for the award was raised: for the rest of the war men had to achieve and suffer more to receive it. A British memorial at the scene of L Battery's destruction asserts with shameless nationalistic immodesty: 'The Battle of the Marne was won at Néry.' This claim reflects the fact that the German cavalry were roughly handled on 1 September. In truth, however, what took place was no more than a minor incident in the vast epic of the retreat of two million men.

Further east, between 10.45 a.m. and 2 p.m. on the same day, there was another such encounter. A rearguard of Haig's corps, retiring along one of the few tracks through the huge forest of Villers-Cotterêts, became entangled in confused fighting which proved the Guards brigade's costliest action of the month. The forest runs along the spine of a ridge. Its dense summer foliage made it impossible for formed bodies of men to move

except on rides, and hard to spot targets to shoot. The British were acutely
sensitive to the threat of being outflanked and cut off by Germans infil-
trating between the trees. The Grenadiers' No. 4 company lost heavily
delivering a counter-attack with the bayonet. Maj. 'Ma' Jeffreys met the
brigade-major leading a horse on which sat slumped his brigadier, 'badly
wounded and obviously in great pain'. The staff officer shouted to Jeffreys
that the enemy was being held, but the battalion would soon have to withdraw. Then a hard-hit Coldstream, Stephen Burton, staggered towards
Jeffreys. He said, 'For God's sake get me out of this or I shall be captured
– I can't get much further.' With difficulty, the Grenadier hoisted Burton
onto a pack horse, and detailed a transport man to lead him towards the
rear.

One Guardsman was bending down to offer his mate a piece of sausage
when a bullet struck his boot, ricocheted into his mouth and out of the
top of his head. The Grenadiers had two platoons cut off and destroyed,
fighting almost to the last man. In all, they lost four officers and 160 other
ranks; the huge, adolescent figure of nineteen-year-old Lt. George Cecil
was last seen leading a bayonet charge, sword in hand. Soon afterwards
Jeffreys found himself in temporary command of his battalion, and supervised its withdrawal by bounds. 'The Germans did not press us at all,' he
wrote. 'They had evidently not only lost heavily but got very mixed up in
the thick forest, and we could hear them shouting orders and blowing little
horns, apparently to rally their men.'

Lord Castlerosse of the Irish Guards was among the casualties left
behind. He was shepherding some stragglers under machine-gun fire
when he put up his hand to brush off a wasp. A bullet struck his arm,
inflicting shocking damage and causing him to collapse unconscious. He
awoke to find a column of German troops marching past. The commanding officer of one battalion, noticing the British officer, stopped to remark
conversationally, 'Do you know that the Duke of Connaught is the colonel
of this regiment? Why do you make war on your cousins?' Some hours
later Castlerosse, in agony and untended, found himself the object of
unwelcome attention from a German soldier prodding him with a bayonet. An officer in the uniform of the Death's Head Hussars stopped,
rebuked the prisoner's tormentor, and summoned a medical orderly to
tend his wound. He then wrote his own name – von Cramm, father of a
later three-time Wimbledon tennis finalist – in Castlerosse's field note-
book, saying, 'If ever a German should fall into your hands be kind to him
as I have been to you.'

The Guards suffered three hundred casualties at Villers-Cotterêts, and another brigade covering their withdrawal lost 160. On the credit side, by evening on 1 September the gap between the two British corps, which had caused such dismay and apprehension since they split at Bavay on 25 August, was at last closed. But small parties of German cavalry continued to infiltrate here and there, causing moments of confusion. Maj. Gen. Charles Monro, commanding 2nd Division, glimpsed distant horsemen and shouted to Jeffreys, 'They've got their cavalry round! Quick! Get these men to change front and open fire!' The Grenadier, mercifully calmer than his superior, saw that the horses were white and said, 'But it's the Scots Greys, sir,' to which the 'tired and overwrought' Monro responded, 'Thank God! Thank God!' The Royal Welch had a similar experience, opening fire on the 19th Hussars under orders from an over-excited general.

Sir John French was in a worse muddle. That day his headquarters abandoned with unseemly haste the château at Dammartin in which it had been housed. Maj. Christopher Baker-Carr wrote: 'The departure was a panic-stricken flight. Rumours of thousands of Uhlans in the woods nearby arrived every moment. Typewriters and office equipment were flung into waiting lorries, drawn up in serried ranks in front of the château. It was a pitch-black night, lit up by a hundred dazzling headlights. With much difficulty I collected my quota of passengers and got clear of the seething mass of vehicles.' Nearby, 'Wully' Robertson was just sitting down to eat roast mutton when the alarm came; his dinner was hastily wrapped in newspaper and tossed on the floor of a lorry, to be eaten cold next day. Nobody remembered to tell the adjutant-general, Sir Nevil Macready, dining with his staff in their quarters, that the C-in-C had decamped; on learning the news, he scrambled crossly after the fugitives. Baker-Carr, however, returned to Dammartin later that night, to collect some washing he could ill afford to lose. Finding the little town quiet, he enjoyed a good night's sleep there.

Bob Barnard was one of many British soldiers by now utterly exhausted, as well as bewildered that they continued to retreat while seeing so few Germans. He wrote: 'We didn't know where we were going no more than fly, but I remember the day was September 1st when we saw the first sign-post which said "Paris". I was quite pleased at that, as I had never been to Paris.' Barnard was not going there now, however: the path of the British retreat lay southwards. Many of those who followed it would perish without ever glimpsing the French capital's delights.

* * *

Just at the moment when Moltke's unease about his armies' strategic predicament was about to precipitate the decisive moral crisis of his career, the Kaiser's subjects were rejoicing at the prospect of imminent triumph. On 1 September *Vossische Zeitung* editorialised: 'The mind is scarcely able to grasp the news being given to the German people about their victories in both east and west. It represents a divine judgement, as it were, branding our antagonists as the criminal originators of this fearful war.' Half a century earlier, industrialist and banker Gustav Mavissen wrote wonderingly amid the euphoria after Prussia's 1866 victory over Austria: 'I am no devotee of Mars ... but the trophies of war exercise a magic charm on the child of peace. One's eyes are involuntarily riveted on, and one's spirit goes along with, the unending rows of men who acclaim the god of the moment – success.' So it was again in Germany during the first days of September 1914.

Its foes did not dissent from such triumphalism: in the British ranks there was profound pessimism, if not quite despair. Many of the BEF's officers felt ready to wash their hands of their allies – figuratively, and almost literally, to take to the boats. James Harper, a staff captain, wrote bitterly: 'the damned French Army never appears at all. There has been a bad strategy somewhere ... The men are losing their confidence, I'm afraid.' News that the French government was evacuating Paris swept through the BEF, causing gunner NCO William Edgington to write, 'which all seems to point to disaster, and all that we get from the allies is that mythical French cavalry corps'.

Guy Harcourt-Vernon wrote: 'personally, I don't believe the French have properly mobilised, & that we are being used to keep back the whole German army to give them time. Whatever happens the British Army has done its duty ... for the last week we have been fighting alone.' He added a week later: 'I can't feel really cheerful about this war, I simply can't believe in these Frenchmen. Time after time, we have been told that there are French Corps on either side of us & we are going to take up a position, but every day it is the same & back we go ... Can you wonder that we are feeling worn & weary & disheartened?' No British senior officer made the smallest attempt to persuade his subordinates that the French were doing their own part manfully – or, if he had no accurate intelligence to that effect, at least to pretend to it. The institutional chauvinism of the British Army had a deplorable effect in rendering unattainable, at a critical time, the mutual respect indispensable to every successful alliance.

The retreat from Mons cost the BEF 15,000 men killed, wounded and captured, together with forty-two guns lost, most of these losses being in

II Corps. They were only a tiny fraction of French casualties, but profoundly shocking to their commanders. It seemed to them, as well as to the Kaiser's generals, entirely plausible that German victory was at hand. It was fortunate for the allied cause that the spirit of France, far from being extinguished, was soon to achieve a historic redemption.

Tannenberg: 'Alas, How Many Thousands Lie There Bleeding!'

The peoples of Europe were awed by the scale of the forces unleashed across the continent. 'Russian society had not experienced such emotions since the 1812 war,' wrote Sergei Kondurashkin. 'A great battle was to be fought on the threshold of one's own home. Men who had been reservists for as long as seventeen years were called up – six million men … A sea of people against another sea of people … One's imagination was unable to grasp the scale of the coming events.' But once even the Russian hosts were dispersed across fronts of many hundreds of miles – three times the length of those contested in the west – suddenly they became much less impressive than when passing in review across parade grounds. A dominant theme of the campaigns of 1914 was the mismatch between the towering ambitions of Europe's warlords, and the inadequate means with which they set about fulfilling them.

On the Eastern Front, reason should have told the Stavka – the Tsar's high command – that Germany was the critical enemy: if Russia could achieve quick victories against the Kaiser's relatively small army in East Prussia, the impact on the whole war would be dramatic, conceivably decisive. That is what the French government wanted, and implored the Russians to attempt. Contradictorily, however, Gen. Alexei Speyer, most respected of Russia's strategic planners, urged smashing the Austrians before making any attempt to take on the Germans. The Stavka, which established itself in a pine forest beside a railway junction at Baranovichi in Belorussia, deliberated, wavered, then committed the mirror error of Conrad Hötzendorf's. The Russians divided their armies, and attempted to attack both foes simultaneously. Two-thirds of their immediately available forces – 1.2 million men – were sent to fight the Austro-Hungarians in southern Poland, while half that number attacked the Germans in East Prussia.

Moltke had taken a large risk by deploying only a blocking force to hold the Russians in play, and now his gamble was to be put to the test. The

Kaiser's eastern subjects were acutely conscious of the proximity of a hated and feared enemy to their homes. Berlin's *Neue Preußische Zeitung* was known as 'the Cross newspaper' – *Kreuzzeitung* – because its masthead bore an iron cross. On 6 August 1914 it spoke of the 'cross of Prussia's Teutonic Knights' rising again to fight the barbarians from the east. During the first weeks of war, memories of the knights were often invoked. Fears ran deep that 'Russian hordes' might sweep forth towards Berlin, wrecking and pillaging.

In the late summer of 1914, from every corner of Nicholas II's empire the armed might of Mother Russia converged upon its Polish colony, focus of operations against both Germany and Austria. The Tsar wanted to take personal command of his armies in the field, but was persuaded instead to appoint a figurehead commander-in-chief, his uncle Grand Duke Nicholas – often known as 'Nicholas the tall' to distinguish him from the Emperor, 'Nicholas the short'. The Grand Duke's personal train crawled slowly along the Vitebsk line towards the theatre of war. Three-course lunches and dinners were served, with plenty of claret and Madeira. The French military attaché, Gen. Marquis de Laguiche, expostulated in frustration, 'Think of me – with thirty-eight years' service, having dreamt so much of this moment, and now stuck here when the hour has come.'

Amid desultory time-passing conversation, the Grand Duke told British military attaché Maj. Gen. Alfred Knox of his impatience to get to England for some shooting once the war was disposed of – he was a passionate hunter. He spoke of his distaste for the Germans, and said that once they had been beaten the *Kaiserreich* must be broken up. As royal soldiers go, Nicholas commanded some respect, but he had always been a trainer of troops rather than a field commander. He lacked both the delegated authority and the force of personality effectively to coordinate the operations of Russia's generals in Poland. When at last they reached Baranovichi on the morning of Sunday the 16th, flippancy was still to the fore. A Foreign Ministry official said to Knox, 'you soldiers ought to be very pleased that we have arranged such a nice war for you'. He received a cautious response: 'We must wait and see whether it will be such a nice war after all.'

Train after train bore to Warsaw and beyond horse, foot and guns of one of the most exotic military hosts the world has ever seen. Many infantry officers were of peasant stock, while most generals and cavalry leaders were aristocrats. Not all Russian commanders were incompetents, although in the early months of the war they displayed no more military genius than most of their French and Austrian counterparts. Especially in the early months, cavalry played a much larger role on the Eastern Front than in the west. Foreign observers never failed to be impressed by the exotic regiments of the Tsar – Don, Turkistan and Ural Cossacks, the latter 'big, red-bearded, wild-looking men'. Officers carried their maps in their high hats; many enemies were killed with the lance. And there were astounding numbers of Russian horse: to conduct one raid, Gen. Novikov's corps deployed 140 squadrons. As for the men, correspondent Alexei Ksyunin wrote: 'The yellow and purple robes of the Turkmens appeared blindingly brilliant against the background of village houses. They wore enormous sheepskin hats, above dark features and wild hair which made them seem picturesque and majestic. Galloping on their horses they caused no less panic than armoured vehicles. I offered cigarettes and tried to talk to them. It was useless, for they didn't speak any Russian. They could say only "Thank you, sir," and nothing more.'

An American correspondent described a squadron of Kubanski Cossacks: 'a hundred half-savage giants, dressed in the ancient panoply of that curious Slavic people whose main business is war, and who serve the Tsar in battle from their fifteenth to their sixtieth years; high fur hats, long caftans laced in at the waist and coloured dull pink or blue or green with slanting cartridge pockets on each breast, curved yataghans inlaid with gold and silver, daggers hilted with uncut gems, and boots with sharp toes turned up … They were like overgrown children.' First Army's cavalry were commanded by the old Khan of Nakhichevan, who was found weeping in his tent one morning because he was too crippled by haemorrhoids to mount his horse.

Some of the Tsar's officers were conscientious professionals, but others behaved towards their men like country landlords among serfs. Foreigners were shocked by commanders who, when their regiments halted for the night, set off in search of women, leaving horses and men to shift for themselves. Cossacks were sometimes seen thrashing their whips to halt fleeing infantry. Provisioning arrangements were casual: the army was expected to subsist chiefly off the land, though every column carried supplies of *sukhari*, a dried black bread which substituted for biscuit, packed loose in sacks.

Poland was the Russian Empire's critical salient: there the Tsar's armies could grapple their foes, but were also threatened by counter-strokes. Russian soldiers newly arrived in the region were impressed by the living conditions of rural Poles, whose houses were adorned with such unfamiliar refinements as soft furniture and lace curtains. German settlers lived among

A View of the Eastern Front, 1914–18

N

0   100   200
Miles

Gulf of Finland

Revel • • Narva   **ST PETERSBURG**
(Petrograd)

BALTIC SEA

Gulf of Riga

• Pskov

Libau •   Riga •   • Moscow

Memel •   Dvinsk •

Königsberg •   Kovno •   *Dvina*

Danzig •   **EAST
PRUSSIA**   Vilna •   Smolensk •

G E R M A N Y   *Masuria*   Grodno •   Minsk •

Tannenberg •   *Narew*   *Niemen*

• Prasnysz

Vistula   Warsaw •   Brest-
Litovsk •   Pinsk •   *Pripet*

P O L A N D   Ivangorod •   **R U S S I A**

Łódz •

Breslau •   Radom •   Lublin •   Cholm •   *Pripet
Marshes*   *Desna*

Oder   Oderburg •   Kovel •

Cracow •   Krasnik •   Lutsk •

Tarnow •   Jaroslav •   Rovno •   Kiev •

G A L I C I A   Przemysl •   Dubno •   *Dnieper*

San   Lemberg •   Brody •

Carpathian Mountains   Tarnopol •   *Vorskla*

A U S T R I A   Stanislau •

• Bratislava   Miskolc •   Czernowitz •   *Dniester*

Danube   • Budapest   Debrecen •   *BUKOVINA*   *Bug*   Nikolaiev •

H U N G A R Y   Cluj •   Kishinev •   *Pruth*

Szeged •   *TRANSYLVANIA*   *MOLDAVIA*   Odessa •

• Timișoara   Sibiu •   *BESS-
ARABIA*

R O M A N I A   *BLACK SEA*

BELGRADE •   *WALLACHIA*   *DOBRUDJA*

SERBIA   BUCHAREST •

Danube

B U L G A R I A

**MONTE-
NEGRO**

the peasants, and in that polyglot region it was hard to guess what language might prove comprehensible to local people. When a Russian officer demanded first in Polish, then in Russian, whether a farming family had any produce to sell, he was met by blank stares. He fared better in German, but the old farmer, already embittered by experience, responded, 'What produce?' He shifted in his chair, looking scared. The officer said, 'How come you didn't store anything in the summer?' 'We sold everything.'

The Eastern theatre of war must be understood as a colonial region, in which Russians, Austrians and Germans alike ruled minorities – Poles, Bosnians, Czechs, Serbs, Jews – whose loyalty to their respective empires was anything but assured. This reinforced paranoia about spies and saboteurs, even stronger here than on the Western Front, as the armies of three empires began to skirmish across their respective frontiers. Jews were considered the natural prey of any passing Russian patriot. The Belobeevsky infantry regiment's train halted for two hours at the Polish station of Tłusz. Many men slipped away into the town, seizing goods for which they declined to pay Jewish shopkeepers. In response the traders put up their shutters, prompting the soldiers to break down doors and commence uninhibited looting, while their officers stood by and watched. The episode would have gone unremarked had not a passing general expressed outrage. The next day in Lublin, twenty Jewish stores were systematically pillaged by troops. Josh Sanborn has written: 'soldiers knew that their word would be honoured over that of a Jew, and even the murder of robbed Jews went largely unpunished'.

A Russian gendarme telegraphed to his superior, reporting that in Vyshov 'in the guise of buying horses, two Germans arrived who stayed the night in the barn of the Jew Gurman and then went to Ostrolenka'. On 18 August in Tarchin, an outbreak of fires as Russian troops marched through the town was immediately blamed upon Jews 'with the goal of letting the enemy know where our troops were moving'. Fourteen such hapless men were arrested. Unusually, they were later freed when the local police chief concluded that the fires had started accidentally, but their pillaged goods were not returned or compensated. Through the months that followed, a series of pogroms against Jewish communities was conducted chiefly, though not exclusively, by Cossacks. A considerable number of Jews took flight to Warsaw, from whence they were forcibly deported eastwards.

Lt. Andrei Lobanov-Rostovsky was a twenty-two-year-old sapper, bookish, widely travelled, the son of an aristocratic diplomat. He described how in a small Polish town his unit of newly mobilised soldiers murdered eight Jews following an outbreak of spy fever. That afternoon, as the men prepared for mass they saw a partial eclipse of the sun; this caused the superstitious soldiers to become troubled about their deeds of the morning. But their consciences were quieted soon enough: Russian troops in Poland seized anything they could snatch on their line of march, heedless of the fact that the victims were supposedly their own compatriots. For the overwhelming majority of the Tsar's subjects, foreigners began in the next village to their own. Though Gen. Paul Rennenkampf issued stern edicts against looting on Russian territory, and on 10 August announced that four men had been shot for robbing civilians, his subordinates made little or no attempt to enforce his orders. Pillage had a severe impact on local trade, harming both civilians and soldiers. Commissary officers, struggling to feed their men, found it hard to secure local produce, even where the army was willing to pay.

On the other side, in the first days of the war the Germans acted as savagely as in Belgium, destroying the Polish border towns of Kalitz and Częstochowa, taking hostages and murdering civilians. After occupying Kalitz on 2 August, the invaders became obsessed by reports of civilian snipers, and began firing at will on the inhabitants. Suspected 'ringleaders of *francs-tireurs*' were taken hostage along with civil and religious dignitaries: 750 people were soon in custody. There was widespread rape, pillage and arson. The Germans admitted to executing eleven civilians, but locals said the real total was much higher. When the invaders withdrew, from mere spite they unleashed an artillery bombardment on the town, obliging tens of thousands of Poles to flee.

The Russian Sumskoi Hussars, who detrained at Suvalki on 3 August, rode towards the East Prussian border through a contraflow of dusty, desperate refugees, trekking away from the front on foot, or driving carts laden with their scanty possessions. Mutual fears provoked civilian migrations alike in Poland, East Prussia and Galicia. A woman refugee at a Red Cross depot in Schneidemühl kept crying out, 'Where can we go? Where can we go?' She looked down at twelve-year-old Elfriede Kuhr and said, 'A girl like you can have no idea what it's like, can you?' Elfriede wrote: 'Tears ran down her chubby red cheeks.' A few days later the child wrote with pathetic naïveté: 'Gretel and I now play a game in the yard in which her old doll is a refugee child that has no more nappies. She has painted its behind red, to show that it is sore.'

In 1914, East Prussia had not experienced war for a century – a long respite, in the turbulent history of the region. Across its vast, open, underpopulated flatlands, at first each side's lancers roamed at will, like naval privateers of bygone ages, engaging like-minded foes or attacking villages according to the whim of their commanders. Often the only means by which a patrol could discern the whereabouts of the enemy was by scanning the horizon for pillars of smoke, beacons of domestic tragedy. Cavalry officer Nikolai Gumilev grew accustomed to coming upon houses whose owners had just fled, sometimes leaving behind coffee on the stove, knitting on the table, open books. As he availed himself of such creature comforts, 'I remembered the children's story about the little girl who entered the house of the bear family, and I was constantly expecting to hear the angry demand: "Who ate my porridge? Who slept in my bed?"'

In the East Prussian border village of Popowen, south of Lyck, in the first days of August fearful peasants saw flames creeping rapidly closer, as neighbouring communities were torched. One day they glimpsed a lone Russian horseman looking down on them from a nearby hillside, rifle poised. He was soon followed by a troop of his comrades who departed after cutting the telegraph wire. Nobody could decide what to do for the best. Schoolteacher Johann Sczuka fled with his family and a cartload of possessions, only to return a few days later when all still seemed normal, save for thirsty and unmilked cows lowing on abandoned farms.

Back home, the Sczukas' two young daughters were dispatched to scour the area for stray chickens and any other source of food. On their wanderings, the children chanced upon a man cycling from another village. As he spoke to them, they suddenly saw distant figures descending in their direction from the hills. The cyclist urged the girls to make themselves scarce. He himself rashly lingered, only to be shot down a few moments later, to the horror of the young spectators. The newcomers were Russians. The children dashed for home, heedless of nettles that stung their legs and rough ground on which ten-year-old Elisabeth lost her shoes. Exhausted, they took refuge in the family house and awaited the next act.

Through the days that followed, between 10 and 15 August, patrols of both armies drifted through the area. Local people warned a German cavalry troop that there were Russians in a nearby wood, but the men advanced anyway – and were fired upon. Dashing cavaliers learnt harsh lessons. Capt. Lazarev, a squadron commander of the Sumskoi Hussars, found his men reluctant to advance in the face of German fire. Seeking to inspire them by example, he galloped headlong towards the enemy – and was promptly shot out of his saddle. Another Russian officer expressed amazement at how quickly one adjusted to the horrors of war, especially the corpses. They rotted fast in the summer heat, skin darkening, mouths gaping and teeth gleaming so that they were readily visible at a distance. 'But it is only the first impression that is ghastly,' he said. 'After that, one becomes almost indifferent.'

The Sumskoi Hussars dismounted to approach a German position, then were crestfallen to find themselves almost horseless: their mounts, terrified by artillery fire, broke free from their pickets and bolted. Many men were obliged to plod ignominiously towards the rear on foot, though one who still had his horse carried a wounded cornet slung across the saddle. A mile back the soldiers were relieved to meet their commanding officer, who had recaptured most of the animals. A day or two later, when Lt. Vladimir Littauer's squadron found itself suddenly facing rifle fire, one of his troopers pointed towards a farm and shouted, 'There they are – look!' They spotted two figures disappearing behind some buildings. Littauer led twenty dismounted men up a convenient ditch, which he later realised marked the Russian frontier with East Prussia. On reaching the farm they found no one. 'We didn't know any better than to set it on fire,' he wrote. 'This was something our troops were always afterwards doing in similar circumstances.'

The farm they destroyed was on Russian soil, but the young hussar noted 'something crazy was happening on the German side: houses, haystacks and sheds were ablaze everywhere' – more wretched consequences of *franc-tireur* fever. Russian units were swept by rumours of a Cossack who asked an East Prussian woman for milk, and was shot dead; of a cavalry division commander who leant from his saddle to ask another woman if she had seen any German troops, only to be greeted by a revolver shot. Civilians on both sides of the border suffered in consequence of such fantasies.

Just eleven German infantry divisions and one of cavalry – 15 per cent of the Kaiser's host – were deployed for the defence of East Prussia. The inhabitants of this rustic outpost of the Wilhelmine Empire, a flat, melancholy land of cattle, lakes, forests and pasture, had cause for resentment towards their rulers, who had knowingly exposed them to devastation by the rival hosts in order to fulfil their grand strategic vision in France. The role of the relatively small Eighth Army in the east commanded by Gen. Maximilian Prittwitz und Gaffron was not to destroy the Tsar's forces, an impossible task, but merely to hold a line as best it could; to purchase time until the western legions had crushed the French and could shuttle east for

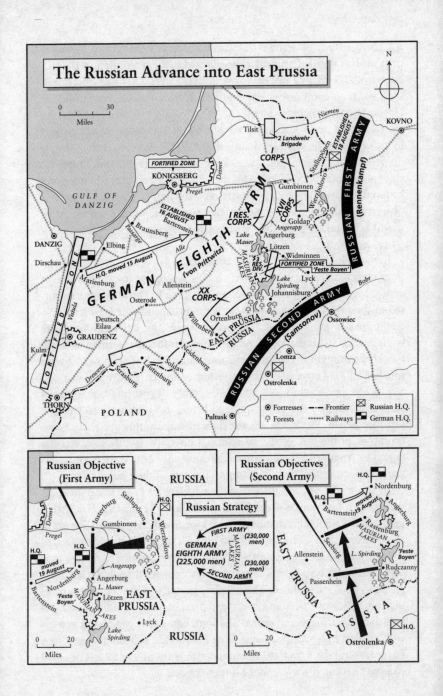

The Russian Advance into East Prussia

0 — 30
Miles

N

KOVNO

Niemen

Tilsit

2 Landwehr Brigade

ESTABLISHED 18 AUGUST

RUSSIAN FIRST ARMY (Rennenkampf)

Stallupönen

CORPS

Wierzbolovo

FORTIFIED ZONE

KÖNIGSBERG

Pregel

Deime

XVII CORPS

Gumbinnen

GULF OF DANZIG

Braunsberg

ESTABLISHED 16 AUGUST

Bartenstein

I RES. CORPS

Angerapp

Goldap

Passarge

EIGHTH ARMY (von Prittwitz)

Angerburg

DANZIG

Elbing

Alle

Lake Mauer

Lötzen

Dirschau

H.Q. moved 15 August

MASURIAN LAKES

3 RES. DIV.

Widminnen

Marienburg

Allenstein

Lyck

FORTIFIED ZONE 'Feste Boyen'

Bobr

GERMAN

XX CORPS

Lake Spirding

Johannisburg

RUSSIAN SECOND ARMY (Samsonov)

Osterode

FORTIFIED ZONE

Deutsch Eilau

Willenberg

Ortenburg

EAST PRUSSIA

Ossowiec

GRAUDENZ

RUSSIA

Kulm

Neidenburg

Lomza

Drewenz

Soldau

Strasburg

Laurenburg

Ostrolenka

THORN

POLAND

Pultusk

Vistula

⊙ Fortresses ---- Frontier ⊠ Russian H.Q.
♧ Forests ++++ Railways ▧ German H.Q.

Russian Objective (First Army)

RUSSIA

Insterburg

Stallupönen

H.Q.

Deime

Pregel

Gumbinnen

Wierzbolovo

H.Q.

H.Q. moved 19 August

Nordenburg

Angerapp

Bartenstein

'Feste Boyen'

Angerburg

L. Mauer

EAST PRUSSIA

Lötzen

MASURIAN LAKES

Lyck

RUSSIA

Lake Spirding

0 — 20
Miles

Russian Strategy

FIRST ARMY (230,000 men)

GERMAN EIGHTH ARMY (225,000 men)

MASURIAN LAKES

SECOND ARMY (230,000 men)

Russian Objectives (Second Army)

H.Q.

Nordenburg

moved 19 August

Angerburg

H.Q.

Bartenstein

Rastenburg

MASURIAN LAKES

Seeburg

'Feste Boyen'

Allenstein

L. Spirding

EAST PRUSSIA

Rudczanny

Passenheim

RUSSIA

H.Q.

Ostrolenka

0 — 20
Miles

a decisive settling of accounts. Prittwitz's officers were very conscious of their orphan status. The formations allotted to them represented the left-overs from Germany's vast deployment in the west. They had a makeshift staff, and their commander was confused by mixed messages from Berlin. Having been instructed before the war that his role was merely to keep the enemy in play, on 14 August Moltke urged him to manoeuvre aggressively in the event that he faced a full-scale thrust: 'If the Russians come – simply no defence but attack, attack, attack.' Lt. Col. Max Hoffmann, Prittwitz's chief of operations, confided to his diary that he found the responsibilities he faced 'gigantic, and more of a strain on the nerves than I expected'. He observed cynically that if the campaign went well, his general would be hailed as a great captain, while 'if things do not go well, they will blame us' – the army staff.

Even as Moltke's western legions approached Brussels, Prittwitz's formations met cavalry patrols which were harbingers of two invading armies of almost four times the Germans' numerical strength. The Russians committed to their northern offensive 480 battalions against the Germans' 130; 5,800 Russian guns against 774. Sukhomlinov, the war minister, wrote complacently in his diary on 9 August: 'it seems that the German wolf will quickly be brought to bay: all are against him'. The French, however, were much dismayed by the Russian division of forces. Before the war, the Stavka had professed to accept the importance of ensuring that its forces were concentrated and fully equipped before any advance into German territory began. But in the middle days of August, this prudent resolve crumbled in the face of the overriding imperative swiftly to divert the enemy's strength and attention from the campaign in the West: the Russians started operations while still lacking 20 per cent of their infantry.

In the midst of East Prussia lay a necklace of large water features surrounded by swamps – the Masurian Lakes. The Russian First Army under Gen. Paul Rennenkampf advanced westwards from a startline north of the lakes, while a few days behind him Aleksandr Samsonov's Second Army launched itself on a southern axis. The two commanders were thus separated by time, space and some mutual animosity, though the latter has probably been exaggerated. The invaders posted a grandiloquent proclamation: 'To you Prussians, we the representatives of Russia present ourselves as harbingers of united Slavdom.' Samsonov conducted himself with reckless braggadocio, dispatching his wireless transmitter back into Poland, then riding forward to reconnoitre without any means of rapid communication. Most telephone lines were cut.

Within hours, almost every Russian horseman screening the left flank of Rennenkampf's army was riding with a cheese dangling from his saddle, after looting a cheese factory in the town of Mirunsken. 'A cavalryman is used to many odours,' wrote one, 'but never before or after did we smell as we did then.' For days, they feasted upon a diet of pillaged sausage, ham, pork, geese, chickens, such as few of the Tsar's soldiers had ever known. If a Russian mount was shot or went lame, the rider exchanged it for a German one: farm horses grazed in the fields, and there were plenty of loose cavalry animals. When the Sumskoi Hussars passed a stud farm, they appropriated all the horses they could catch, muttering teasing words that became commonplace throughout the army, about 'presents from the grateful local population'. Vladimir Littauer acquired a handsome four-year-old thoroughbred chestnut, but found it vile-tempered.

From the outset, cavalrymen were forced to recognise their vulnerability. Two Hussar squadrons advancing on a village were driven back by rifle fire from a handful of Germans. They retreated, having suffered significant casualties. Littauer struggled to lift a bleeding NCO into a saddle while bullets whipped up dust around them. He suddenly reflected, in a fashion typical of a Russian gentleman among peasants, 'Why am I helping this man? I hardly know him. Why should I be helping him?' Then another officer cried out, 'Watch out for the civilians!' As if in proof of his words, a shot rang out from a nearby wood, wounding a cornet. As usual, this was attributed to *francs-tireurs*.

The German inhabitants of East Prussia endured Russian looting with grim resignation, but recoiled in fury when they saw local members of the Polish minority joining the pillage of abandoned homes. Schoolteacher Johann Sczuka solemnly noted the names of all whom he recognised – especially his own pupils – with a view to future retribution. He rebuked a woman he met near his village, laden with booty, but she brushed him off and marched defiantly onwards, clutching her spoils. Some Russian officers showed themselves surprisingly humane and sensitive. Martos, one of Samsonov's corps commanders, expressed embarrassment about being billeted in a house still adorned with the possessions and photographs of its German owners, now fugitives. One day when he encountered some children roaming unattended on the battlefield, he removed them to the rear in his own car.

The long columns plodding forward into German territory filled observers with wonder at their exotic character and mingling of modern and primitive equipment. Many of the infantry lacked high boots. Supply arrangements were chaotic and inadequate, hampered by poor roads and few railways in their rear. The Russian army rejected howitzers as a 'cowards' weapon', because they could be fired by men beyond sight of their enemies; for artillery support, they relied exclusively upon field guns. Communications were hampered by a shortage of radios, and commanders were obliged to signal in plain language, because each corps used a different cipher. The invaders owned a total of just twenty-five telephones and eighty miles of wire. The cavalry were trained to act chiefly as mounted infantry, filling gaps between corps, and made little attempt to fulfil the vital reconnaissance role. Most of Russia's few available aircraft had been sent to Galicia, and those in East Prussia were temporarily grounded for lack of fuel.

In 1910 German writer Heino von Basedow described his impressions of the Tsar's army in terms which reflected widespread foreign opinion: 'The Russian soldier is impulsive as a child. He is easily excited by rabble-rousers (towards revolt) but equally readily restored to submission.' Basedow was amazed by the careless culture of the Tsar's soldiers, symbolised by the rakish angle at which each man wore his cap. An NCO calling 'ras-dwa' at the front of a marching column in hopes of maintaining its step and precision could not prevent a man in the rear rank from casually munching an apple. Soldiers supposedly marching at attention would nonetheless raise an unfailing hand to cross themselves when they passed a church or roadside icon. Meanwhile a grenadier might seat himself on a roadside marker and hawk his platoon's bread to all comers. Such a way of soldiering did not inspire German respect. Alfred Knox noted the same casualness on the battlefield, where he was astonished to see Russian artillerymen sleeping huddled against their gunshields, minutes before they were due to open fire.

Rennenkampf and Samsonov groped forward, sharing with the Germans uncertainty about each other's whereabouts. The Russians occupied the town of Lyck, only to be almost immediately obliged to evacuate it. This news failed to reach a Tsarist officer who drove smartly up to the Königlicher Hof hotel and stepped out of his automobile to find himself a prisoner of war; it profited him nothing that his compatriots recaptured Lyck a few hours later. There were daily clashes between patrols of the rival armies, riding hither and thither between towns and villages, sometimes firing on their own side in the general confusion.

Many German and Russian soldiers were exhausted by epic marches before they even began to fight. Some of Samsonov's men trudged 204 miles from Białystok in fifteen days. One of Prittwitz's corps spent twelve days footslogging from Darkehmen – 186 miles – and then immediately engaged the enemy on the morning of 20 August. Its commander, Gen. August von Mackensen, ordered an assault on Rennenkampf's army near the village and rail junction of Gumbinnen, some twenty miles inside East Prussia. The Germans drove in the Russian flanks with impressive ease. In the centre, however, they suffered a bloody repulse which made their other gains worthless. Advancing across open ground in extended lines – *Schützenlinien* – they met the fire of two entrenched divisions. Mackensen's men had been marching twenty hours without sleep; their waterbottles were empty. Their tactics were no more subtle than those of the French army in Alsace-Lorraine, and were similarly rewarded.

One Russian regiment's 3,000 rifles and eight machine-guns fired 800,000 rounds that day. Its supporting artillery did formidable execution: Russian gunnery showed an excellence it would reprise on future battlefields. Thousands of Germans were mown down – one man in four – while many of the survivors fled in panic, and kept running for hours. A Grenadier lieutenant sought to encourage his men by shouting defiantly that the Russians were hopeless marksmen, until he fell dead with a bullet in his breast. Thousands of wounded lay untended. Mackensen's cavalry became separated from the infantry, and rejoined only days later, worn out. At nightfall, the Gumbinnen battlefield was strewn with the casualties of both sides. When at last some of these were brought into field hospitals, a Russian officer noticed a German private soldier, prostrate on a stretcher, smoking a cigar. Though this stogie was no costly product of Cuba, the Hussar nonetheless marvelled at the wealth of an enemy society which permitted a humble rifleman access to such a luxury as no Russian ranker could dream of.

The Prussian formations had been savagely mauled. They were rallied by their officers only with difficulty during the ensuing night. Next day, the German high command experienced a rapid series of mood changes. Some senior officers believed there was a chance to roll up Rennenkampf's army by renewing the action, exploiting the previous day's successes on the flanks. But Prittwitz, badly shaken by his losses, flinched from taking such a risk. Moltke had told him that his prime responsibility was to keep the army intact. Thus, the commander-in-chief made a drastic decision: to disengage and undertake a strategic retreat, more than a hundred miles west towards the Vistula.

This order enraged Max Hoffmann and many of his comrades, who considered the withdrawal wholly unnecessary. It also precipitated chaos in the rear areas of the army. On 22 August the military authorities ordered that all cattle and corn must be shipped west across the Vistula, beyond reach of the Russians. Then refugees began hastening the same way. Westbound movements of livestock, produce and people collided head-long with reinforcements and supplies heading east. For some days, panic prevailed among civilians behind the German front. Almost a million East Prussians left their homes in the face of the Russian threat – around a quarter of the entire population – most with only such possessions as they could carry on their backs.

The flood of refugees surging into the border town of Schneidemühl persuaded many of its own inhabitants to flee westwards. Carts laden with household possessions, creaking towards the station, became a familiar sight in the streets. The newcomers brought shocking tales of destruction, alleged rape and murder, causing the Kuhr family's nervous housekeeper Marie to threaten to decamp. The townspeople debated what to do with a refugee boy who had lost his parents. A mother wept, because she had mislaid her children on the road from the east. A farmer's wife asserted bleakly that 'not a stone was left standing' in the community from which she had fled: 'everything was burning … we could take away only our clothes and a little bit of money'. Elsewhere along the East Prussian fron-tier, at Elbing station local authorities posted a despairing sign: 'This town is completely full of refugees. Please keep moving.' Germany's pre-war planning to meet a Russian invasion included measures to dam the Nogat river. Inundations along its course would block the path to central Prussia, at the cost of flooding large tracts of farmland and many villages. Prittwitz's staff repeatedly changed their minds about whether to initiate this drastic step. In the end, no flooding took place, because it was bound to provoke a huge new refugee migration.

On the Russian side, success at Gumbinnen prompted a wave of euphoria which swept back to St Petersburg and thereafter across the Tsar's empire. The Russians deluded themselves that the Germans were in full retreat towards the coastal fortress of Königsberg. Rennenkampf made one of the decisive mistakes of the campaign. Complacent in the wake of his little victory, he was also short of supplies, especially ammunition. He decided to give his men a rest and refill his limbers before advancing further. He made no attempt to pursue the retreating enemy. If, instead, he had immediately exploited southwards, momentous consequences might have ensued for Germany. As it was, Rennenkampf simply sat down upon the battlefield.

Meanwhile Samsonov, informed of Gumbinnen, saw an opportunity to cut off Prittwitz's beaten forces and achieve a historic triumph. His army hastened forward to garner the spoils of Rennenkampf's success, an initiative which represented a calamitous misreading of the Germans' condition and intentions. In the days after Gumbinnen, Prittwitz's brilliant chief of operations persuaded his general to reverse the earlier decision to make for the Vistula. Max Hoffmann argued that great opportunities still beckoned. Reconnaissance showed that Rennenkampf was going nowhere fast. The colonel urged that if a weak screen was left behind to watch the Russian First Army, Prittwitz could exploit the Germans' excellent rail network to shift two corps southwards to meet Samsonov, and with luck deal him a crippling blow. As Second Army pushed forward, it looked amazingly vulnerable, especially on the flanks.

The Germans had often wargamed just such a scenario for defeating a Russian invasion force, but it is remarkable that Prittwitz agreed to the bold new plan, given his shaken state. One of the critical manoeuvres of the war thus began. And even as troops boarded trains taking them southwards, the high command intervened. In Coblenz, a disbelieving Moltke had learned of Gumbinnen, and of Prittwitz's planned retreat to the Vistula. He exploded into furious and indeed tearful rage, then telephoned each of the corps commanders in East Prussia to invite their opinions. In turn they asserted that Prittwitz's order was mistaken and unnecessary. On the afternoon of 22 August, Eighth Army's headquarters at Marienburg on the western border of East Prussia received a terse message: Prittwitz was dismissed. Old Gen. Paul von Hindenburg had been summoned out of retirement to relieve him; he would be accompanied into the field by a new army chief of staff, the bleak, moody Erich Ludendorff, fresh from his heroics at Liège.

Hindenburg, a stolid sixty-six-year-old, had served as an infantry officer in Prussia's wars against Austria in 1866, and against France four years later. He retired from the army in 1911, and thereafter devoted himself to his pipe, daily readings of newspapers, and a little Italian tourism. When Germany mobilised, to his disappointment he was not at first recalled to the colours. The corpulent Hindenburg growled crossly, 'I sit like an old woman in front of the stove.' But on the afternoon of 22 August a telegram reached his flat in Hanover: was he available for immediate service? He responded instantly and tersely: 'Am ready.' At 4 a.m. next day a special train, already carrying his chief of staff, stopped briefly to collect him from a darkened platform at Hanover station; it then hastened onwards to East Prussia.

Hindenburg's appointment represented window-dressing. He was not even the first choice for the job – merely an officer of appropriate seniority to command Eighth Army, whose home happened to be situated on the line that his chief of staff must travel to reach East Prussia. The latter was the man Berlin expected to transform the campaign, selected before Moltke gave a thought to identifying a figurehead commander-in-chief. Ludendorff was a commoner, forty-nine years old, who had risen by sheer ability through the ranks of an army dominated by aristocrats. A dour professional warrior to every last extremity of his being, he considered war the natural business of mankind. He had served on the General Staff under Schlieffen, who remained his idol. For a decade he had enthusiastically endorsed the core principle of German planning – that East Prussia should be lightly held while France was disposed of.

A man of chilly rationality though highly nervous temperament, in 1904 he indulged the sole romantic gesture of his life by falling in love with a married mother of four children, Frau Margarethe Pernet. They met in the street in a rainstorm, when he gallantly offered her the shelter of his umbrella. She divorced her husband, married Ludendorff, and the two achieved a notably successful partnership. Now, Moltke wrote to him: 'You have before you a new and difficult task … I know no other man in whom I have such absolute trust. You may yet be able to save the situation in the east. You must not be angry with me for calling you away from a post in which you are, perhaps, on the threshold of a decisive action which, please God, will be conclusive … The Kaiser, too, has confidence in you.' This last assertion was untrue. Ludendorff collected his Pour le Mérite for Liège from Wilhelm an hour before his train departed for the East. But the Kaiser was furious that Moltke had not consulted him about either appointment to Eighth Army, and considered the new chief of staff a vulgar and ambitious adventurer.

The two generals, who would establish one of the most famous military double acts in history, reached Marienburg on 23 August. They received a gloomy, icily formal reception from Prittwitz's dejected staff. Max Hoffmann certainly harboured doubts about the newcomers: both were unknown quantities, and Ludendorff bore the air of a man who knew that he had everything to prove. Hoffmann's plan to concentrate against Samsonov had already been set in motion, and thereafter events evolved with stunning speed. Moltke made a momentous decision, to shift six corps to strengthen Eighth Army. Ludendorff said he had neither wish nor need for the proposed reinforcements, which would weaken the Western

Front at a critical moment. He was told they were coming anyway, and he should plan to use them. In the end, Moltke sent just two corps, which arrived after the momentous clash with Samsonov had taken place. But German critics ever thereafter cited this redeployment as evidence of the chief of staff's tottering judgement, cracking nerve.

At Marienburg, less than twenty-four hours after Hindenburg assumed command, two enemy plain-language radio signals were intercepted. These revealed that the forces of Rennenkampf and Samsonov had drifted so far apart that they could not support each other. The morse of First Army's obliging commander also informed the Germans of the lines of march of each of Samsonov's corps. In the new wireless age, all the belligerents had much to learn about security of the ether – on the Western Front, the French intercepted important enemy signals *en clair*, and broke several German ciphers – but the consequences of this Russian lapse were especially significant. Hindenburg and Ludendorff were surveying the operational area, driving towards a hill south of Montowo, when the messages reached Max Hoffmann at army headquarters. He immediately set off by car in pursuit of his chiefs, clutching the texts. His driver raced alongside the generals' open motor; the colonel leaned across and thrust the flimsies into Ludendorff's hand. After he had read them, both cars halted. The Germans conferred about the significance of the news.

Hoffmannn was now Ludendorff's deputy. He was the brilliant, bullet-headed Prussian staff officer of caricature, a Russian specialist who had for years studied the Tsarist army, not least as a German observer of the Russo-Japanese war. He knew that effective coordination between Rennenkampf and Samsonov was implausible. The Russians' indiscretion offered their enemies a chance to smash them in detail. Hoffmann could claim credit for having inspired the German concentration in the south, but it was Ludendorff who now presided over its implementation. The Germans' 1891, 1898 and 1899 manoeuvres had addressed just such a scenario in East Prussia, and proposed precisely the response Eighth Army now adopted. Ludendorff concentrated his formations slightly further south and east than his subordinate had intended. As for the slow, stolid Hindenburg's role, years later Hoffmann conducted a party of army cadets around the field of Tannenberg. 'Here,' he told them scornfully, 'is where Hindenburg slept before the battle; here is where he slept after the battle; and here is where he slept during it.'

The approaching encounter would represent a collision between the most professional army in Europe and the most careless. The Russians' neglect of reconnaissance, logistics, medical facilities, concentration of force and common prudence could not be adequately redeemed by mass, good artillery and peasant courage. Aleksandr Samsonov was fifty-four, a jovially uxorious figure who had been on leave in the Caucasus with his wife when summoned to take up war duties. In East Prussia, he often expressed concern that he heard no news from home – any more than his men did. He chaffed the soldiers: 'Where do you come from?' 'Are you married?' 'Well, your wife won't know you when you get back. Look at the beard you have grown!' 'Have you any children? When I went to war in 1904 I left a daughter one and a half years old, and when I came back she ran away from me.'

Samsonov's chief of staff, Postovsky, was unflatteringly nicknamed by comrades 'the mad mullah'. He characterised the advance of Second Army as an 'adventure', an unfortunate word for an offensive on which his nation's fortunes in large measure turned. Samsonov was dependent for communication with Rennenkampf and with his own rear headquarters upon couriers travelling by car to a distant wireless transmitter, and some-times even as far as Warsaw. In the last week of August, the general fooled himself that the Germans were fleeing, and that his task was merely to exploit Rennenkampf's victory. The army intelligence staff was so weak that they could not even read captured documents, for lack of a German-speaker to translate them. In Samsonov's haste to cross the supposed enemy line of retreat, he left behind one corps on his right among the Masurian Lakes, another on his left. Three corps proceeded northwards, dispersed across a front of almost sixty miles, with no effective cavalry screen to warn of enemy movements.

Hindenburg's formations were meanwhile tramping south, hampered by heat exhaustion and long columns of refugees, fleeing before the Russians. Soldiers displayed impenitent ruthlessness in driving civilians off the roads, overturning carts to make way for artillery; cavalry columns and baggage wagons trampled cherished household possessions into the dust. The fact that many of the German troops were themselves local resi-dents prompted some painful incidents during the campaign. A certain L/Cpl. Schwald found his artillery battery called upon to destroy Eydtkuhnen, his home town, when it was occupied by the Russians, and Col. Emil Hell had to shell his own house in Gross-Grieben.

Hindenburg's Eighth Army was poised to strike one of the great mili-tary blows of history, at a moment when Russia's western allies were both utterly ignorant of and amazingly complacent about events. On 24 August,

The Battle of Tannenberg 24–29 August 1914

1 The Pre-Battle Situation

- German infantry
- German cavalry
- Russian infantry
- Russian cavalry

BALTIC SEA

RUSSIA
EAST PRUSSIA

Memel
Tilsit

Labiau

Königsberg
Pregel
Deime
Wehlau
Allenburg
Insterburg
Inster
Gumbinnen

RENNENKAMPF

I Corps (by rail)
I Res. Corps
XVII Corps

Zinten
Pr. Eilau
H.Q. GERMAN
EIGHTH ARMY

Braunsberg

Nordenburg
Goldap
Angerapp

Danzig

Mülhausen
moved 22 August
Alle
Bartenstein
Korschen
Gerdauen
Omet
Angerburg

Elbing
Nogat
Heilsberg
Bischof-stein
Rastenburg
Lake Mauer
'Feste Boyen'

Dirschau
Passarge
Wormditt
MASURIAN LAKES

moved 23 August
Marienburg
Seeburg
Bischofsburg
Lake Spirding

moved 24 August
Saalfeld
Locken
Allenstein
23–25 Aug.
Sensburg
22–25 Aug.

Vistula
Riesenburg
moved 24 Aug.
HINDENBURG
Osterode
Ortenburg
Rudczanny
Johannisburg

I Corps 23–24 Aug.
Löbau
LUDENDORFF
25 Aug.
25 Aug.
Jedwabno
21–23 Aug.
21 Aug.

Graudenz
Deutsch Eilau
Neumark
Gilgenburg
Usdau
Neidenburg
EAST PRUSSIA
RUSSIA

Strasburg
Lautenburg
25 Aug.
Soldau
21–23 Aug.
Yarnov
H.Q. RUSSIAN
SECOND ARMY
Łomza

22 Aug.
Mlawa
Ostrolenka

Thorn
Drewenze
SAMSONOV
Narew

N

0 10 20 30 40 50
Miles

the military correspondent of *The Times* told the British people: 'In the East all continues to go well.' An editorial asserted: 'before very long there will be hosts of Russians within German territory, as the Germans will discover to their cost'. Yet that same day brought the first encounter of what became known as the Battle of Tannenberg, though the critical actions were fought some miles distant from the village. At first, a single Russian and German corps clashed head to head. Ludendorff, visiting the local headquarters, told its commander histrionically that his formations must 'hold to the last man' to buy time for Hindenburg's left wing to come up. Thus all day Russians and Germans ravaged each other, as Samsonov's men advanced again and again across open ground, striving for a breakthrough.

By evening, to men as yet unaccustomed to heavy loss, the bloodshed seemed very terrible: one Russian regiment had lost nine company commanders out of sixteen; a company of 190 men finished the day seventy strong, all its officers dead. Yet when evening came, the Germans fell back. Samsonov was exultant: once again, it seemed to him, the enemy was retreating before Russian might. Next morning, imbued with the highest hopes, he ordered his army to resume its advance, oblivious that the Germans had shifted their ground the previous night only to align neighbouring corps. When Samsonov's soldiers advanced on the 25th, they met overwhelming firepower from three sides, smashing into their columns. By nightfall, the Germans knew that they were achieving important results, but also recognised that these were not yet conclusive. Hindenburg slumbered heavily, while Ludendorff's nerves did not allow him to sleep at all.

On 26 August, Samsonov's right wing renewed its advance, to meet pounding artillery and raking small-arms fire from two German corps. Yet that night, dinner at Hindenburg's staff mess was eaten in dead silence. An alarming report had come in: Rennenkampf's army was said to be marching, moving to support Samsonov in a fashion that could transform the battle by falling on the German flank or rear. For some time Ludendorff furiously rolled his bread around the table. Then he suddenly demanded a private conference with Hindenburg. That night the old general played a useful role, calming his subordinate's tormented spirit. At last word came that the report about Rennenkampf was false; First Army's formations had not moved. Samsonov's battered forces were on their own.

The 27th brought another spasm of alarm to Eighth Army headquarters. Officials at the post office of Allenstein, deep in the German rear,

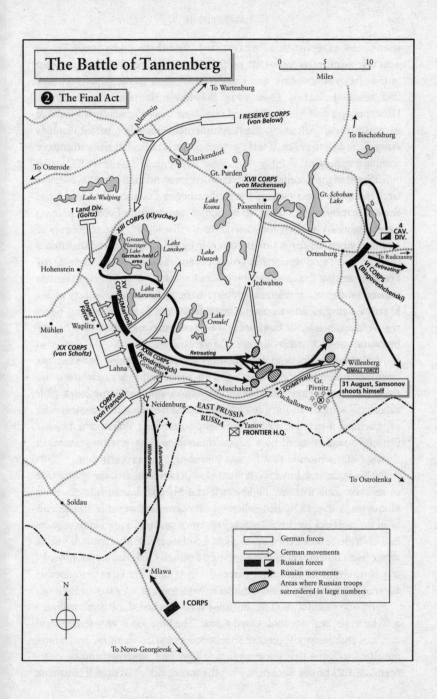

The Battle of Tannenberg

2 The Final Act

0 5 10
Miles

To Wartenburg

To Bischofsburg

To Osterode

Allenstein

I RESERVE CORPS
(von Below)

Klankendorf

Gt. Purden

XVII CORPS
(von Mackensen)

Gt. Schoban
Lake

Lake Wulping

1 Land Div.
(Goltz)

XIII CORPS (Klyuchev)

Lake
Kosna

Passenheim

4
CAV.
DIV.

To Rudczanny

Grosser
Plautziger
Lake German-held
area

Lake Lansker

Lake
Dluszek

Ortenburg

Retreating

VI CORPS
(Blagoveshchenski)

Hohenstein

XV
CORPS (Martos)

Lake Maransen

Jedwabno

Mühlen

Unger's
Force

Waplitz

XX CORPS
(von Scholtz)

Lahna

Lake Omulef

Retreating

XXIII CORPS
(Kondratovich)
Grünfliess

Muschaken

Willenberg
SMALL FORCE

SCHMETTAU

Gr.
Pivnitz

31 August, Samsonov
shoots himself

I CORPS
(von François)

Neidenburg

EAST PRUSSIA
RUSSIA

Puchallowen

Yanov
FRONTIER H.Q.

To Ostrolenka

Withdrawing

Advancing

Soldau

To Rudczanny

Mlawa

N

I CORPS

To Novo-Georgievsk

	German forces
	German movements
	Russian forces
	Russian movements
	Areas where Russian troops surrendered in large numbers

telephoned to report that Russians had entered their city. Some Tsarist soldiers, awesomely ignorant of the world beyond their villages and impressed by Allenstein's size, gazed around them in the belief that they had reached Berlin. They were granted little time for gawping. Hindenburg's staff hastily diverted reinforcements whose trains were due to pass through Allenstein, then resumed the pounding of Samsonov's army. That day, the 27th, it was the turn of the Russian left flank to endure terrible punishment.

Tannenberg has sometimes been called an 'accidental miracle', because Gen. Hermann von François, ordered earlier by Ludendorff to attack the Russian left, was late taking up his appointed position because his men were exhausted by their long march to the battlefield. The consequence was that when his corps finally struck, it found itself behind Samsonov's rear, poised to complete his envelopment. The Germans considered François among the foremost heroes of the battle. One of his regiments massed its entire complement of automatic weapons in a battery of six Maxims, firing in unison on the bewildered and broken Russians. Soon the Germans saw white flags being waved on poles and rifles – the first of thousands of such symbols across the vast battlefield.

At Usdau, the Prussian 41st Infantry stormed enemy positions across open ground, and after bitter hand-to-hand fighting, drove back the opposing forces. They found that they had vanquished Samsonov's 85th Infantry – whose honorary colonel was the Kaiser. That day, the Russians experienced a new kind of harassment when their Polish rear base at Ostrołęka was bombed by a Zeppelin airship. Slow, ghastly realisation dawned on Samsonov that he was presiding over a catastrophe. Eighth Army headquarters, however, remained reluctant to believe the magnitude of its own good fortune: Ludendorff and his staff lapsed into renewed gloom on Friday, 28 August, when reports came in that some attacks had been thrown back by fierce Russian resistance, and that a few German units had even given themselves up. Only at 4 o'clock in the afternoon did news arrive that François's corps was bursting through the Russian rear, provoking consternation and mass surrenders. At last, the German generals allowed themselves to exult, confident that a huge victory was unfolding.

Samsonov's chief of staff, Postovsky, dispatched the British military attaché to the rear. He told Alfred Knox: 'The position is very serious and it is not right that a foreigner should see the state we're in.' Samsonov admitted to Knox that his army was falling back in chaos, adding enigmatically that he did not know what the future held, 'but even if the worst

happened, it would not affect the ultimate result of the war'. Soon afterwards, the Germans threw a final heavy punch at the Russian centre. The
remnants of Second Army began to fall back in chaos towards the Polish
frontier. Over half Samsonov's 230,000 men were dead, wounded or
captured; his three attacking corps were shattered. Corpses lay scattered
for miles among the region's profusion of wild lupins.

Tens of thousands of bewildered Russians around Ortensburg and
Neidenburg found themselves trapped against lakes, wandering lost in
forests, or seeking places to ford rivers. The beaten army fell apart, each
fragment desperately seeking its own path to escape the relentless
Germans. Hindenburg sought, and received, the Kaiser's consent to name
his victorious battlefield Tannenberg. Though the village was some
distance removed, its name possessed a powerful resonance. There, in
1410, the knights of the Teutonic Order had suffered a historic defeat at
the hands of the Poles and Lithuanians. Now, that outcome was reversed.

Max Hoffmann professed surprise at receiving an Iron Cross for his
own role: 'I had never imagined that one could earn this most beautiful
military decoration sitting on the telephone.' But then he preened himself:
'I saw that there must be somebody who keeps a cool head and overcomes
difficulties and crises with boundless ruthlessness and commitment to
victory.' On 31 August, Hoffmann toured the battlefield with Gen. Count
Dohna. When they reached a railhead where thousands of Russian PoWs
awaited transport to cages, Dohna asked Hoffmann, 'Well, how many prisoners will it be?' Hoffmann guessed 30–40,000; Dohna thought 20,000 at
most. Hoffmann invited Dohna to wager him a mark for every prisoner
over or under 20,000 the Germans counted. Dohna declined, but
Hoffmann would have won a fortune – the final total of PoWs was 92,000,
along with 350 Russian guns.

To gain this critical victory, the Germans had suffered only 12,000 casualties out of the 150,000 men Hindenburg committed to battle. The Kaiser,
with his accustomed felicity of judgement, suggested that the Russians
captured at Tannenberg should be herded into the Courland peninsula on
the Baltic and 'starved to death'. The grandfatherly figure of Hindenburg
achieved lasting heroic status in Germany. He was made a field marshal,
and huge wooden images of him were erected in many towns, plated with
metal nails bought by citizens to raise funds for the Red Cross. 'Our
Hindenburg' achieved a stature and authority which soon alarmed the
Kaiser and gnawed at Ludendorff, who knew his commander-in-chief for
the heavy old bull he was.

'Our hearts are full of gratitude,' wrote schoolteacher Gertrud Schädla in Verden, on hearing news of Tannenberg, 'and above all hope that the war will not last too long into the winter. But alas, how many thousands lie there bleeding!' Samsonov himself escaped from the carnage, having lost everything including his maps. When darkness fell, he and his aides could read their compass only by striking matches; when these were gone, they stumbled wearily on a course set by guesswork. The general was asthmatic, and soon had to lean on the shoulders of his aides to keep going. On 31 August, when Alfred Knox enquired about the whereabouts of the beaten commander, a Russian mutely drew his hand across his throat. Samsonov had finally paused to address his little cluster of staff officers: 'The Emperor trusted me. How can I face him after such a disaster?' He then shot himself, leaving his men to escape into Poland as best they could.

Many other Russian senior officers perished. One corps commander – the same Martos who had displayed such solicitude for local children – was wounded by a shell which hit his car. He was accompanied by Aleksandra Aleksandrovna, the wife of an officer of the Muromski Regiment, who spoke German and was acting as an interpreter. She was last seen fleeing into woodland. Russian survivors of Tannenberg asserted bitterly that their commanders acted as if they had at their disposal such millions of men 'that it does not matter how many are thrown to their deaths'. Alfred Knox wrote: 'It looks as if the Russians were too simple and good-natured to wage modern war.' This was a kindly way of acknowledging the unfitness of Samsonov and his professional kin to enter the ring against Ludendorff and the German army. The Russian presented his troops to the enemy like successive courses of a banquet, to be devoured in detail. The Tsar's forces almost invariably cracked in the face of flank attacks, while in the centre the Germans were able to fight a succession of defensive actions on the most favourable terms, before advancing to pursue their stricken foe.

As in every battle, many factors had contributed to German victory: Hoffmann's prescience, Ludendorff's skill, Russian incompetence – and a dusting of luck. Hindenburg became overnight the idol of the German people, while almost every officer in the Kaiser's uniform saluted the perceived genius of Ludendorff. Above all, the Germans knew that they had demonstrated the fundamental superiority of their soldiers to those of Russia. Their condescension, if not contempt, towards the Russian army persisted, with baleful consequences, into the Second World War.

* * *

It was now the turn of Rennenkampf to suffer the same fate as Samsonov. During the first week of September, the schoolchildren of Schneidemühl, near Germany's eastern frontier, watched fascinated as crowded troop trains passed through the town every half-hour, bound for the east: these were the two corps dispatched by Moltke from the Western Front to reinforce Hindenburg. On the morning of the 9th, the Germans attacked First Army amid the Masurian Lakes, which gave their name to the battle. First, the Russians' left flank was turned; then their right and centre collapsed. Hindenburg's triumph became complete. Within days, the Russians were withdrawing from East Prussia, pillaging the border villages with the cruel spite of defeat. Passing through Johannisberg, Tartars wanted to carry off a statue of Bismarck. Their general demurred, roaring that such an action 'would cause an international incident'. The Tartars took the statue anyway, no doubt arguing that the war was already sufficient of an international incident.

The Sczuka family watched the ebbing of the tide of Russian might which had swept over their community. Rennenkampf's army, now heavily reduced, trudged past Popowen's little houses for days. The villagers saw wounded men; others who had lost weapons and equipment; brokendown horses and carts which were thrust aside into roadside ditches when they lost a wheel or their hapless animals collapsed. Little Elisabeth Sczuka felt a surge of pity for an exhausted donkey, whipped along by its Russian master. Some of her neighbours suffered terribly from the rancour of the defeated. An elderly couple named Olschewski were driven from their cottage by a Russian officer wielding a knout, who then applied a match to the straw of their bed; flames devoured the building. But the Sczukas nonetheless rejoiced in victory. Loyal Germans all, they sat in the candlelit safety of their home, singing the Prussian anthem '*Heil dir im Siegerkranz*' around the family piano, while Rennenkampf's stragglers passed outside all night.

The Russian First Army escaped total destruction only by the speed of its flight – twenty-five miles a day, which left its pursuers far behind. German cavalry proved no more effective than anybody else's in fulfilling their traditional function of pursuing a beaten foe; the rifle fire of Russian rearguards prevented them from closing in. Rennenkampf's formations were battered and beaten, but most survived to fight another day. The Germans had accomplished their immediate purpose, smashing the invasion of East Prussia. In the months that followed, the enemy maintained a threatening presence across the border, and indeed would again cross in force. But it no longer seemed plausible that a 'Russian steamroller' would thrust into Germany by that route.

The Western allies were slow to grasp the severity of the disasters the Tsar's armies had suffered at Tannenberg and the Masurian Lakes. Amidst the torrents of competing and mutually contradictory propaganda unleashed by all the belligerents, in London and Paris German reports of Hindenburg's triumphs were disbelieved. The Russians strove to conceal from their allies the scale of their humiliation, and were in considerable degree successful. Good news from Galicia, further south, was allowed to mask sombre tidings from East Prussia. So vast were Russia's human resources that the destruction of Samsonov's army and the mauling of Rennenkampf's seemed to represent no irreversible catastrophe for the Tsar's military power – merely the collapse of his immediate and most dramatic hopes.

It is sometimes suggested that Russia's August offensive played a decisive role in deciding the outcome of the war, by persuading Moltke to transfer two corps from the west at a critical moment, shifting the balance of German forces in the east against those in the west from 1:10 to 1:8. This seems most unlikely. More plausibly, Germany's resources were simply insufficient to fulfil its towering ambitions in France, while conducting simultaneous operations of any kind in the East. Germany's Tannenberg triumph was also a disaster for its leaders and for those of its people who craved peace and hoped for an early negotiated end of the struggle. National euphoria prompted a surge of faith in the prospect that an absolute victory was attainable, above all in the mind of Erich Ludendorff.

The most conspicuous victim of those first eastern battles was Russian military self-confidence, which never recovered from its 1914 humiliations in East Prussia. Many officers recognised that they reflected the Tsarist army's institutional inadequacy, together with a dearth of competent commanders, which would dog its battlefield performance to the end of its struggle in 1917. The Russian soldier displayed formidable willingness for suffering, and sometimes astonishing courage. These qualities made possible successes against the Austrians, but not against the Kaiser's army.

Earlier Russian exultation was replaced by weeks of extreme alarm, indeed panic. Anticipating a German thrust into Poland, the bridges of Warsaw were prepared for demolition, while government officials and families packed their bags in readiness for flight. But the Germans were temporarily content. They had frustrated Russia's grand ambitions. Almost the entire attention of the Kaiser and his generals focused upon the Western Front, where the fate of their huge strategic gamble was now being decided.

9

The Hour of Joffre

1 PARIS AT BAY

August witnessed a remarkably comprehensive transformation of France's capital into a war city – if not besieged, at least in imminent peril of such a fate. All public buildings including museums were closed. Motor buses were requisitioned by the government, while taxis for a time vanished from the streets. The Metro ran on, with women serving as ticket-collectors, but became so stiflingly overcrowded that many people preferred to walk. The most conspicuous street sounds were the klaxons of ambulances transporting wounded men from stations to hospitals. Many shops shut because their staff had gone to the army, as did all theatres save a few 'moving-picture houses'. More than 50,000 people, almost all of them women, attended a service at Notre Dame to offer prayers for France.

Some commodities became scarce. There was plenty of milk – cattle grazed in the Bois de Boulogne – but butter was in short supply for lack of hands to churn it, and bakers stopped making croissants and all forms of 'fancy bread'. There was little horsemeat to be had, because so many animals had been taken by the army that farmers deemed it more profitable to keep their remaining stock on the hoof, as prospective mounts, than to send them for slaughter. The Parc de Belleville was closed to the public so that it could accommodate sheep and cattle; its lake was drained and stocked with rabbits, a further precautionary measure in case the capital had to endure a siege.

Among many incongruities, one morning passers-by were startled to see a flock of sheep being driven along the Rue de Rivoli towards the eastern railway. The army took over the Hôtel George Cinq. The Grand Palais provided quarters for 2,000 marines in place of its usual works of art. Versailles became an armed camp. The night sky over the capital was pierced by scores of searchlight beams, probing for enemy aircraft. A daily crowd of onlookers surrounded the American hospital at Neuilly, watching wounded men being brought in. Army volunteers of many nationalities presented themselves for medical inspection at the Cour des Invalides. It was considered a reflection of respective societies' health that doctors rejected half the Russian applicants, one-third of Poles, 11 per cent of Italians, 4 per cent of the English, and no Americans. The British ambassador expressed irritation that Lord Kitchener allowed the King's subjects to opt for French service. The five hundred men who had already come forward, wrote Sir Francis Bertie crossly, should properly have joined their own country's army.

The most acute famine was that of news: the only tidings of the war came in three terse, anodyne bulletins posted at intervals through the day by the War Ministry. First news of the murderous fighting in Alsace reached Parisians through a five-day-old copy of an Italian newspaper, whose correspondent had filed a story from Basle. Many domestic titles closed down, and those that survived offered poor fare, because the price of paper soared, and thousands of printers as well as journalists had been mobilised. André Gide was so avid for information that he took nine newspapers a day. Marcel Proust admitted to seven: he found most bereft of enlightenment, but admired the military commentaries of Henri Bidou in the *Journal des débats* – 'clear and remarkable, the only decent things I've read about the war'. His confidence was somewhat shaken, however, when Bidou accepted a second and simultaneous role as the paper's dramatic critic: 'I wonder he doesn't get mixed up!'

In consequence of the shroud of secrecy with which Joffre and the government overlaid military operations, the nation was traumatised when, on 28 August, the government issued an abrupt communiqué announcing that 'our lines extend from the Somme to the Vosges'. It was a devastating shock, to be thus casually informed that the enemy had advanced deep into the heart of France. 'From what mad optimism we descended!' lamented Gide. 'The newspapers had done their job so well that everyone began to imagine that our army had only to show itself to put the entire German army to rout.' Now, instead, people became resigned to a siege of the capital, a prospect rendered more plausible when, on the 29th, a Taube monoplane dropped five small bombs on the city.

On 30 August the nation learned that the government was decamping to Bordeaux, taking with it the gold reserves of the Bank of France, and that the Germans held Compiègne. At the British embassy Sir Francis Bertie burned his confidential papers. He wrote bleakly, 'The Germans seem sure to succeed in occupying Paris,' and soon afterwards himself scuttled away to Bordeaux, along with most of the diplomatic corps. The rail journey took fourteen hours instead of the usual seven; Bertie complained that his staff was crowded into three compartments while the Russians had commandeered eight, to accommodate not merely their diplomatic families but also servants with children.

Civil servant Michel Corday, who had left Paris with his department, wrote disdainfully of his ministerial masters: 'it is sad to see these men now ... riding around in their cars ... climbing into their special trains, see how gladly and openly they bask in their power'. There was much mockery of refugee ministers who did themselves well at the famous restaurant Au Chapon Fin; wits rechristened it *Au Capon Fin*, substituting 'coward' for 'capon'. One evening over aperitifs, Corday and some politicians discussed, curiously tastelessly, a linguistic oddity that had suddenly assumed relevance: why was it that there was a word for a woman who had lost her husband – widow – but none for a mother who had lost her child? An absurd contest developed between rival military censors established in Paris and Bordeaux: each in turn exasperated journalists by approving for publication material which the other had blue-pencilled. The rules governing news were thought less stringent in Bordeaux, but France, like all the belligerent nations, banned enumeration of total losses.

Seeing the government quit the capital, a million humbler refugees did likewise. Among these was Proust, who set forth for his beloved Cabourg on the Normandy coast. The five-hour trip stretched to twenty-two, and on arrival he found the town's little hospital crowded with wounded soldiers. Each day thereafter, he took them small gifts – playing cards, games, chocolates. A cluster of fugitive duchesses assisted in the establishment of soup kitchens for Belgian refugees, but the novelist noted that the local *cocottes* proved rather more competent in fulfilling this role.

One of war minister Adolphe Messimy's last acts before leaving for Bordeaux was to appoint Gen. Joseph Gallieni military governor of Paris. A lean, gaunt, bespectacled sixty-five-year-old with long experience of colonial warfare, Gallieni had waived his claims upon France's supreme command back in 1911, deferring to Joffre. He was, in the words of Lloyd George, who met him in those days, 'evidently a very ill man; he looked sallow, shrunken and haunted. Death seemed to be chasing the particles of life out of his veins.' Gallieni had retired from the army that April, but when recalled to the colours in this supreme emergency he summoned up reserves of energy, resolution and insight – not to mention wit – which served France well. He, like Lanrezac, had earlier visited GQG at Vitry-le-François, and on 14 August vainly advised Joffre against an offensive in the Ardennes.

Now, Gallieni seemed a man for the hour. While Frenchmen are supposed by Anglo-Saxons to be chronically susceptible to displays of emotion, even the old general was surprised to be warmly kissed by Messimy when he accepted the military governorship on the 26th. He threw himself immediately into organising a defensive perimeter around the capital, though he had few illusions that, if the Germans broke through the French field army, Paris could again withstand such a siege as it had experienced in 1870. Gallieni fumed at the prevarications of bureaucrats, who seemed incapable of adjusting from the tempo of peace to that of extreme national peril: house demolitions essential to create fields of fire had not been carried out, for fear of distressing local communities.

On 27 August the government fell, and a reshuffle took place. Thereafter René Viviani remained prime minister, albeit a widely discredited one, but two socialists joined the government for the first time. Assembly deputies were disgusted by Messimy's evident inability to exercise any control over Joffre – to Poincaré's fury, the C-in-C even refused to allow the president to visit the front. Messimy was thus forced out of the War Ministry. His replacement by Alexandre Millerand did nothing to ease the difficulties of Gallieni. The governor inherited a 100,000-strong Paris garrison, but these men were the scrapings of the army, not a coherent fighting force. To hold the capital in the face of a German assault, the governor concluded, he would need three regular corps – reserve formations were useless – and there was no prospect Joffre would give them to him.

An Englishman in the first days of September lamented the emptiness of the most brilliant city in Europe. The terraces of fashionable cafés were almost deserted. One famous *boulevardier* sat alone and mournful, 'deserted by his court'. A caustic Paris editor claimed that the road from the city to Fontainebleau was strewn with automobiles ditched because their owners, accustomed to entrusting the driving of them to chauffeurs, had themselves taken the wheel in order to flee, only to founder. The Invalides was besieged by frightened people desperate to secure military permits to quit the city, and long queues snaked around station ticket offices. Parisians watched disconsolately as trees were felled to create obstacles and loopholed wooden barriers were erected across streets. One afternoon a crowd in the Bois de Boulogne gawked at an eagle wheeling high in the sky, and debated its significance. Was this a bronze symbol of

Napoleon, or the family bird of the Hohenzollerns? Instead of either it proved to be a vulture, escaped from a zoo.

2 SIR JOHN DESPAIRS

Later in the autumn of 1914 Lloyd George, Britain's Chancellor of the Exchequer, held a conversation with Castelnau, commanding Second Army. As they discussed the difficulties confronting the allies, the Welshman made some reference to France's greatest soldier. 'Ah, Napoleon, Napoleon!' mused the general. 'If he were here now, he would have thought of the "something else".' But then, asked if France could expel the Germans, Castelnau shrugged simply: '*Il le faut!*' His assertion that the invaders' removal was not an option, but a compelling necessity, was an important statement of France's strategic predicament from the end of August 1914 until the armistice more than four years later. It signified the fact that Germany occupied large areas of French and Belgian territory. Thereafter, the allies felt obliged to sustain offensive operations, to dispossess the Kaiser's armies of their gains.

But how? Admirers of Gallieni afterwards argued that he deserved credit for the great reversal of fortune which the French army contrived in September 1914, not least because confidence in Joffre fell so low. In the early weeks of the war the C-in-C had presided over a succession of blood-baths, which cost the lives of more than 100,000 young men in attempts to fulfil Plan XVII. The commander-in-chief had utterly misread German deployments and intentions, and led his country's armies to disaster. Had Joffre fallen dead on 1 September, history would remember him only as a bungler and butcher. He would later commit further misjudgements and preside over more costly failures which prompted his dismissal in December 1916.

Nonetheless, during a few short weeks in late August and September 1914, while the general did not establish a claim to be considered one of history's outstanding soldiers, he contrived for himself a moment of greatness. His first notable achievement was that, after the disasters of the Frontiers battles, he suffered no personal collapse of nerve. His generation of European generals had been conditioned to anticipate heavy losses in any great clash; far from being traumatised by the casualty lists, most senior officers regarded a stoical response as a critical measure of their virility. But this did not prevent several commanders on both sides from succumbing to despair in the autumn of 1914.

Joffre did not. Belatedly this slow, heavy, strong man grasped the enemy's intention. He preserved his self-discipline when others, French, British and German alike, conspicuously lost theirs; he displayed an Olympian calm and an iron will which proved decisive in averting the triumph of the Kaiser's armies. Joffre's transition, from the role of abattoir superintendent in the Battles of the Frontiers to that of allied saviour, began on 25 August, the day on which he initiated a major transfer of forces northwards from Alsace-Lorraine. Relying upon formidable pre-war French fortifications to contain larger numbers of Germans, he re-deployed twenty infantry and three cavalry divisions to the centre and left of the allied line. The movement required immensely complex train scheduling, and would not be completed until 1 September. Meanwhile the retreat of the allied left continued, but in the centre of the front French armies launched some important and effective counter-attacks – for instance, on 25 August against German forces driving for Nancy. Castelnau, who commanded in that sector, showed conspicuous skill in directing the defence against Prince Rupprecht's advance from Morhange.

For all Joffre's bulk, in those days he displayed remarkable energy. He hated the telephone as a medium of command communication. In contrast to Moltke, who never quit his headquarters until 11 September, the Frenchman drove hundreds of miles, on dusty roads clogged with troops and refugees, to meet his generals. His car was chauffeured at breakneck speeds by a former racing driver, Georges Bouillot, who had earned the appointment by winning the 1912 and 1913 French Grand Prix; the commander-in-chief's hurtling convoy became a familiar sight in the rear areas of the armies.

The British continued to fall back roughly in step with the three French armies withdrawing on their right, which fought much fiercer and more costly rearguard actions than Mons or Le Cateau. Lanrezac still believed that the British II Corps had been effectively destroyed in the battle on the 26th, which reinforced his staff's disdain for their Anglo-Saxon allies. Joffre was obliged to acquiesce in the continuing retreat, because the new Sixth Army which he had begun to build on the extreme left flank could not be ready to fight for a week. It was plain that the original plan outlined in his 25 August *Instruction Générale No. 2* was impracticable, because the positions he had identified for his counter-attack were already falling to the Germans. But was the concept still valid, of a great thrust in the north? The British C-in-C and his officers were uninterested, preoccupied only with salvaging their little force from what they deemed a French disaster.

By 28 August, the allies had fallen back south of the Somme. Three days later they began to cross the Aisne, and passed through the champagne country, abandoning Reims.

New mishaps further poisoned relations between the allies. On the afternoon of the 30th, Lanrezac's staff sent a message to GHQ, asking that the British should blow an important bridge across the Oise at Bailly. Only after the lapse of several hours was a party of sappers belatedly dispatched with explosives. Seven men led by a captain dismounted from their lorry two miles short of the bridge. As they approached it on foot in darkness carrying charges, they met German infantry who had pre-empted them, whose fire killed the British officer and drove off the engineers. Next day, the 31st, Fifth Army's retreat continued under a blazing sun. The French badly needed help from Allenby's cavalry to protect their left. Louis Spears adopted the imaginative expedient of telephoning a succession of post-mistresses at likely places where British troops might be found. At last one responded positively; she fetched a gendarme who proved most helpful, and he in turn brought to the telephone an English Hussar with whom the liaison officer had once served. This officer promised to pass on the message, and to try himself to get some cavalry deployed in the gap between the two armies; not much happened, however.

GHQ, meanwhile, was almost incommunicado as it repeatedly shifted position southwards, having lapsed into a mute sulk. Sir John and his staff, as Spears saw it, now 'showed little interest in events not directly affecting the British Army'. The 31st was chiefly important as the day on which the British C-in-C overreached himself. He dispatched to London a telegram in which he vented at length his disgust towards the French and the campaign he was obliged to share with them. 'I do not see why I should again be called upon to run the risk of absolute disaster in order a second time to save them,' he wrote. 'I do not think you understand the shattered condition of the Second Army Corps, and how it paralyses my powers of offence.'

This display of petulance, by the soldier leading Britain's only army in the field, stunned the War Cabinet. Sir John's telegram reached London at a critical moment. For almost the first month of the conflict, the vast events unfolding on the continent, and their own little force's part in them, had been shrouded in mystery and misinformation. Early news-paper reports were sparse, but unfailingly cheerful. *The Times* of 17 August bore the optimistic headline 'Germans Driven from Dinant'. In a familiar tradition, many officers writing home from the BEF made light of their ordeal. Harry Dillon, a thirty-year-old-year-old captain in the Oxf &

Bucks, enthused on 29 August: 'I am very fit and everything is going top-hole. We have done a great march – it has been fearful work, 25 hours with hardly a stop once and it has been going on so far almost continuously for days. One's feet throb so one can hardly stick it at times. We have bumped into the absolute flower of the German army and have laid them low absolutely in thousands ... The swine are doing all sorts of low-down things. In one case they drove civilian women and children in front of them ... On another occasion they dressed in French uniforms and came up shouting ... We have had the best of them everywhere.'

Beyond this sort of nonsense, designed to lift the spirits of families at home, even the prime minister remained blithely ignorant of the scale of the battles fought by the French, dwarfing British experiences. Asquith twice read through the telegram reporting the action at Mons before observing resignedly to Kitchener, 'I suppose you're doing everything that's possible.' He referred repeatedly to alleged French unwillingness to fight, citing the British Army's view that its allies were in a state of 'funk'. In cabinet on 24 August there was some brief discussion of a possible evacuation of the BEF via Dunkirk, though thereafter nerves somewhat steadied. Maurice Bonham Carter, a member of the Downing Street staff, wrote to Violet Asquith on 28 August with characteristic nationalistic complacency: 'Our people have done wonders & have really I think saved the situation for the French.' Asquith himself expressed similar sentiments on 29 August: 'The Belgians ... are really gallant fellows – and so far compare very favourably with the French – and are now collecting their forces.' Britain's leader seemed to lack any sense of the sheer scale of events, military and otherwise. The same day, he wrote casually to Venetia Stanley about the possibility that the Russians might dispatch three or four army corps to France via Archangel: 'don't you think this is rather a good idea?' Two days later, he followed up with some scribbled lines which he prefaced SECRET: 'the Russians can't come – it wd take them about 6 weeks to get to Archangel!'

Asquith was a man of high intelligence and sensibility, yet he wrote of vital strategic issues as if he were discussing the tiresome inability of some guests to attend a garden party. Through August, with his nation at war, he resumed his accustomed practice of weekending in the country. Driving back from one such idyll in Kent, he encountered a broken-down fellow motorist, and companionably towed his vehicle into the nearest town. On the same journey, he gave a lift to two small children returning from holiday in Margate to the shop in Lewisham where they lived, one of them sitting on the prime minister's knee.

There is no reason to attribute cynical motives to these trifling good deeds. Neither yielded any crowd-pleasing photo-opportunity; they simply reflected paternalistic good nature. But it is hard to imagine Winston Churchill, as national leader a conflict later, behaving in such a fashion amid the burning urgencies of a similar crisis. Almost everything Asquith said and did in 1914 reflected the conduct of a measured man responding in measured terms to the unfolding of a measureless European catastrophe. He had neither skills nor inclination to exercise control of military operations, which he left to Kitchener and the War Office. It is not to his discredit that he was no warrior. But he was no more appropriate a national leader in such a vast emergency than was Neville Chamberlain in 1940.

The British people, meanwhile, knew even less about events on the continent. *The Times* asserted confidently on 18 August: 'The one thing clear is that the German Army has not yet assumed the offensive in the wholesale and impetuous fashion we were led to expect by the military professors.' Three days later, it became plain that this was the opposite of the truth, and the *Chronicle* told its readers: 'The tremendous battle which in all likelihood will decide the fate of Europe and remodel its map has evidently begun.' Thereafter, for ten long days the public was denied significant tidings, which fed a widespread apathy, especially among the socially and politically disaffected 'lower orders'.

The headmaster of Eton, Edward Lyttelton, wrote a letter to *The Times*, published on the 24th, expressing dismay at what he saw as the moral debility of such people: 'the notion among many of our working men seems to be that if Germany wins they will be no worse off than they are now. If this idea is not combated, we may yet be done for.' Following a rural weekend party, parliamentary lawyer Hugh Godley wrote to Violet Asquith, also on 24 August: 'It is extraordinary to think how little the people in the country districts seem to know or think about all that is going on … They are really much more interested in their own affairs.' That same day, the combination of supposed Russian success in East Prussia and Serbian victories over the Austrians prompted a spasm of wild press optimism. There were predictions that the Tsar's forces would soon take Königsberg, then drive on towards Danzig. The charlatan Horatio Bottomley scaled heights of maudlin sentimentality, proclaiming in *John Bull*: 'Let every Briton look with calm confidence and firm resolve to the Golden Eventide when the sounds of battles shall be silenced and, with the women and children, we will foregather to talk of the victory of our dear, lost comrades and the newborn world, in which the Prince of Peace shall be King.'

But then reports of French misfortunes began to seep through Whitehall and Westminster. Admiralty civil servant Norman Macleod wrote irritably in his diary on 24 August: 'If [the] French cannot defend their own country, it seems hopeless to help them.' Next day *The Times*'s military correspondent predicted – correctly, though two days after the event had taken place – that the British army at Mons would be obliged to conform to the French retreat further south. On that same 25 August, Norman Macleod had a bleak conversation with the Fourth Sea Lord, Capt. Cecil Lambert, 'who took a most gloomy view of the situation – French Army in his opinion wd not make a good stand: "I'm afraid they'll let the Germans through. Well, we must make up our minds to go through with it, we're in the same position as 120 years ago."' But Macleod noted that by the same afternoon, Lambert had cheered up: 'our men had done wonderfully well and come off with little loss on the whole – situation more hopeful'.

The *Daily Mail*'s news editor wrote in his diary on 26 August: 'Published first British casualties. Over 2,000. How enormous they seem, and the war is only beginning. Everybody talks about them in horrified whispers.' In those early weeks, until numbers overwhelmed space, *The Times* published brief biographies of fallen officers, for instance: 'Lt. Claude Henry was born in 1881 and joined the Royal Worcestershire Regiment in 1903 … From 1909 until last July he was employed with the West African Frontier Force … Captain Dugald Stewart Gilkison was born in 1880 and joined the Scottish Rifles in 1899. He served under Sir Redvers Buller in the Ladysmith Relief Army.' Such profiles were accompanied by photographs, some painfully incongruous, like that of Lt. A.F.H. Round of the Essex Regiment in his football kit. In the same vein, after the cruiser *Amphion* fell victim to a mine in the North Sea, *The Times* published a full list of the hundreds of her crew saved, a nicety of a sort that would soon have to be abandoned.

An advertisement in the paper reflected the awesome ingenuousness about the struggle on the continent which persisted at home: 'India's magnificent loyalty in the Empire's hour of need has stirred the admiration of the world. Indian princes and Indian peasants, Indian troops and Indian treasure – all are being placed at Britain's service with touching devotion. You can do India a small service in return – and gain by it. Use Pure Indian Tea at home, insist on getting Pure Indian Tea in public tearooms and restaurants.'

The French and British policy of denying press access to the armies had many malign consequences. The public suffered anguish in the absence of any word about the fate of their soldiers. Since correspondents had no sources of news save meagre official bulletins, they set about exploring the front on their own account. Most were repulsed: there was a story, possibly not apocryphal, of a group of reporters detained en route to the battlefield, and brought before Horace Smith-Dorrien. One proclaimed himself the representative of *The Times*, which caused the general to respond tartly that he hoped his employer, Lord Northcliffe, would reward him handsomely for his enterprise and zeal, but for his own part he was dispatching the press group under guard to Tours, to cool their heels until the war was disposed of.

In the absence of front-line dispatches from correspondents, pundits were thrown back on speculation and tittle-tattle from the front. Editors began to publish letters dispatched by soldiers to their loved ones at home, then forwarded to newspapers by wives and mothers enthralled by their men's exploits. It soon emerged that many such reminiscences were embroideries or outright falsehoods. The Rifle Brigade was enraged to discover that a soldier on its ration strength named Curtis had written a letter, which received prominent press exposure, detailing his own heroics in the retreat. In reality, the man was a straggler who drifted to the rear without seeing action.

Meanwhile the *Illustrated London News* of 29 August described British troops at Mons as 'victorious'. Their retreat, Charles Lowe asserted comfortingly, resembled that of Wellington's army from Quatre Bras in 1815: 'it was only a question of *un peu reculer pour mieux sauter*, and Waterloo was the result … They gave the French a lesson then, and now – almost in the same place – they are setting them an example.' In the face of such breathtaking condescension, it is scarcely surprising that Joffre and his subordinates succumbed to exasperation.

Then, on 29 August, newspaper readers received a stunning shock: wholly unheralded news that the campaign on the continent was going very badly indeed. *The Times* published a report from a correspondent, datelined Amiens, 28 August: 'the situation in the north appears to be very grave'. Amid the chaos of retreat, reporters had at last been able to talk to some soldiers, who painted a bleak picture. Worse followed: *The Times*'s reporter Arthur Moore was bicycling along a road when he met stragglers from the BEF. Having heard their tales, he withdrew to write a further detailed report on the plight of the British Army, which caused a sensation when it was published in a special edition on 31 August. It depicted the BEF as having suffered absolute defeat: 'It is important that the nation should now realize certain things,' Moore wrote. 'Bitter truths, but we can face them. We have to cut our losses, to take stock of the situation, to set our teeth ... I saw fear on no man's face. It was a retreating and a broken army, but it was not an army of hunted men ... Our losses are very great. I have seen the broken bits of many regiments ... To sum up, the first great German effort has succeeded. We have to face the fact that the British Expeditionary Force, which bore the great weight of the blow, has suffered terrible losses and requires immediate and immense reinforcement.' He concluded that the German army had also suffered heavily: 'It is possible that its limits have been reached.'

The Times editorialised flatulently: 'The British Army has surpassed all the glories of its long history, and has won fresh and imperishable renown ... Though forced to retire by the overwhelming strength and persistence of the foe, it preserves an unbroken if battered line.' It is hard to exaggerate the impact of the paper's report on public opinion. Its publication enraged the rest of the British press, which had obeyed government injunctions to sustain morale with a diet of platitudes. Asquith denounced the story, and dismissed Moore's conclusion that the army was broken. But the storm about the *Times* dispatch was still raging when the commander-in-chief's secret telegram arrived, offering much the same view of the BEF's condition as that of the 'sensationalist' press correspondent. Both were wrong, and exaggerated grossly. But French's defeatism threatened dire consequences: he informed the prime minister that he proposed to retire beyond the Seine and establish a new logistical base at the port of La Rochelle. The C-in-C no doubt thought of himself as Sir John Moore in Spain a century earlier, saving his gallant little force by retreat to Corunna.

The wildest rumours were circulating in London, reflecting cruelly and unjustly upon the French army. Norman Macleod recorded in his diary reports of a wholesale collapse; of the British C-in-C supposedly threatening to withdraw the BEF to England; of a French cavalry division allegedly refusing to support hard-pressed British troops, 'saying they were tired'; of the BEF fighting continuously for eleven days until 'flesh and blood could stand no more'. The Fourth Sea Lord told Macleod wearily that it looked as if Britain would once more have to save the French in spite of themselves, as Wellington had once saved the Spanish. Next day, this dignitary confided: 'the French have been told that they must fight or go to the devil'.

Such, then, was the fevered climate at Westminster and in Whitehall amidst which the cabinet received Sir John French's telegram. It was an incomparably grave matter, that the C-in-C of Britain's army in the field should advise washing his hands of the campaign, which was what his proposal amounted to. The notion of the BEF unilaterally disowning France's army threatened devastating consequences for the allied cause. The cabinet made a critical and by no means inevitable decision: Anglo-French solidarity must transcend all other considerations. The field-marshal must be overruled. He would be given a direct order to keep the BEF alongside the armies of Joffre in the line. The secretary for war, K of K, was dispatched forthwith to Paris to ensure that Sir John did as he was told. The C-in-C must abandon his shamelessly base attempt to desert France.

3 SEEDS OF HOPE

On 1 September in the French capital, even as L Battery and the Guards brigade were fighting their little battles at Néry and Villers-Cotteret, a momentous meeting took place at the British embassy, Pauline Borghese's former palace in the Rue Saint-Honoré. Kitchener, hotfoot from London, chose this rendezvous with Sir John French, summoned from Compiègne. The C-in-C later professed disgust, first at having to leave his headquarters to meet Kitchener at all, and second that his fellow field-marshal, now a mere civilian war minister, attended in uniform. French denounced the visit as an unwonted political interference with his own 'executive command and authority', and summarily rejected Kitchener's proposal to see for himself the BEF in the field. In truth, the C-in-C must have felt sorely inadequate in the company of a much cleverer soldier than himself, who wore the French commemorative medal for the campaign of 1870–71, belatedly presented to Kitchener the previous year. Following a tense and indeed acrimonious meeting, an uneasy compromise about operational plans was agreed: Sir John should continue the BEF's withdrawal, but was ordered to act in close conformity with Joffre's plans, while taking care to secure his flanks.

In the four days that followed, French's determination to exploit to the limit the escape clause about flanks drove Joffre and his comrades towards despair. The British C-in-C interpreted these orders as empowering him to reject repeated pleas to participate in an allied counter-offensive. French's overriding purpose was to keep his men marching until the Seine

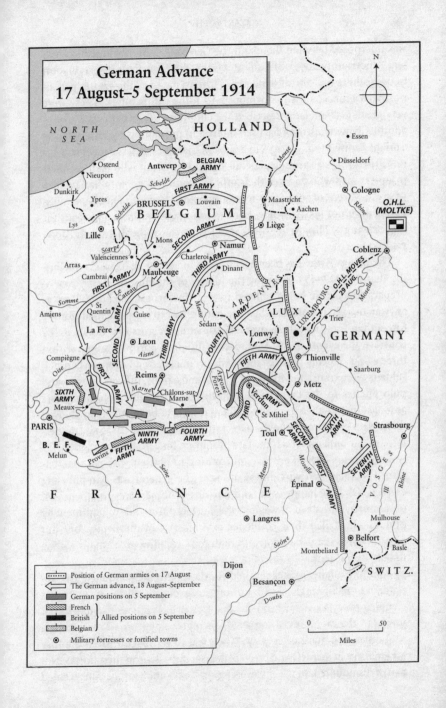

German Advance
17 August–5 September 1914

NORTH SEA

HOLLAND

• Essen

• Düsseldorf

Ostend
Nieuport

Antwerp

BELGIAN ARMY

Maastricht

⊙ Cologne

Rhine

Dunkirk

Schelde

FIRST ARMY

BRUSSELS • Louvain

BELGIUM

Aachen

O.H.L. (MOLTKE)

Ypres

Lille ⊙

Schelde

Mons

SECOND ARMY

Liège

Lys

Scarpe

Valenciennes

Charleroi

• Namur

THIRD ARMY

Meuse

Coblenz ⊙

Arras

Cambrai

Maubeuge

Dinant

ARDENNES

LUX

O.H.L. MOVES 29 AUG.

• Trier

GERMANY

Somme

Le Cateau

FIRST ARMY

St Quentin

Guise

Meuse

Sedan

LUXEMBOURG

Lonwy

Moselle

Amiens

La Fère

SECOND ARMY

• Laon

Aisne

FOURTH ARMY

FIFTH ARMY

Thionville

• Saarburg

Compiègne

THIRD ARMY

Reims

Argonne Forest

• Metz

Oise

FIRST ARMY

Marne

Châlons-sur-Marne

THIRD ARMY

Verdun

St Mihiel

SECOND ARMY

SIXTH ARMY

Meaux

SIXTH ARMY

NINTH ARMY

FOURTH ARMY

Toul

SIXTH ARMY

Strasbourg

PARIS

B. E. F.

Melun

Provins

FIFTH ARMY

Seine

FIRST ARMY

Moselle

SEVENTH ARMY

VOSGES

Rhine

F R A N C E

Meuse

Épinal

Langres

Saône

Mulhouse

⊙ Belfort

Basle

Montbeliard

SWITZ.

⊙ Dijon

Besançon

Doubs

N

Position of German armies on 17 August
The German advance, 18 August–September
German positions on 5 September
French ⎫
British ⎬ Allied positions on 5 September
Belgian ⎭
⊙ Military fortresses or fortified towns

0   50
Miles

was interposed between them and the Germans. John Terraine has written: 'Uncertainty about British intentions, their apparent determination to do nothing but retreat while the Germans over-ran the greater part of northern France, added enormously to Joffre's difficulties.' These were very great. Gallieni later described the condition of the nation's armies – admittedly with a strong partisan interest in promoting a vision of chaos until he himself took a grip – in a fashion that nonetheless carries conviction. He wrote of meeting generals behind the front who had lost their troops; troops who had lost their officers; commanders who had no idea where they were, or where they were supposed to be going. On 2 September, Paris's governor spoke by telephone to Joffre, who expressed his fears for the left wing of Fifth Army 'because of the inertia of the British who don't want to march'.

The British Army has been accustomed in almost all its wars – including that of 1939–45 – to enjoy the luxury of months, or even years, of preparation before being obliged to fight in earnest. Such a delay was anyway usually inevitable when the nation had to muster expeditionary forces then transport them overseas, sometimes across vast distances. By contrast, the events of 1914 imposed a uniquely abrupt trauma: within three weeks of being plunged into a wholly unexpected European conflict, soldiers were translated from parade grounds, pubs, officers' messes and polo pitches to the carnage of a battlefield. For some – commanders amongst them – the change proved too drastic to be borne. They showed themselves unable to make the necessary psychological leap to rise to their roles in a drama on which the fate of Europe hinged. On the night of 31 August, Spears heard Lanrezac murmuring to himself with an unaccustomed softness and wistfulness of tone. The general was paraphrasing Horace: 'Oh how happy is he who remains at home, caressing the breast of his mistress, instead of waging war!' Such capitulations to sentiment by officers who failed their countries in August 1914 merit pity, but not sympathy. No man should accept high responsibility unless he is willing to bear its burdens.

For those on urgent business in those days, movement around Paris was rendered maddeningly slow by throngs of troops, vehicles and refugees clogging every byway behind the front. A British officer found himself forced to abandon his car and walk one night, along a road blocked by a motionless regiment of cavalry: 'The great towering cuirassiers, clumsy and massive in helmets and breastplates, sat impassive on their horses. Not a man dismounted. In the still evening air the booming of the guns seemed very near. A gust of wind animated the horsetail plumes that hung down each man's back, then the long steel-clad column was still again.' An officer of Fifth Army's staff, Commandant Lamotte, was obliged to drive repeatedly into Paris to urge the military-map printers to greater exertions. They were confronted by an insatiable demand for sheets covering France, while tens of thousands of paper representations of western Germany, carefully stockpiled in expectation of Joffre's grand advance, mouldered in a vault through the balance of the conflict.

The last days of August and the first of September witnessed some allied heroism, but also scenes reflecting ignobility and squalor. Disgust was often expressed about German pillage in France, which was real enough; less was said about the excesses of retreating French and British soldiers, some of whom looted ruthlessly – especially alcohol. Edouard Cœurdevey recoiled from the spectacle of destruction created in Le Mesnil-Amelot in the Oise not by the enemy, but by French colonial troops: 'The owners of the big farms live in unimaginably luxurious houses: crystal vases, pianos, billiard tables, sumptuous beds, all of which have been overrun by a savage soldiery. They have ripped open everything closed, thrown the contents onto the floor, pillaged what they pleased, dirtied everything that was no use to them, broken family portraits, thrown linen and women's underwear on the floor, scattered provisions everywhere on beds, billiard tables and pianos. China lies smashed on the ground; some [soldiers] have [defecated] on the beds. The Germans wouldn't have done worse.'

The armies' medical facilities were overwhelmed by the scale of casualties. Around a third of British wounded who reached dressing stations subsequently died of gangrene. In the French army, medical aide Lucien Laby recorded that his own ambulance alone collected 406 casualties in the first month of the war, 650 in the second. Often, it was impossible to evacuate them during daylight, and by night they were hard to locate even with the aid of some of the French army's 'chiens sanitaires' – 150 dogs specially trained for the role. Laby became accustomed to making summary and ruthless judgements: he abandoned those with no prospect of survival, and in some cases claims to have ended their sufferings with his pistol. His only equipment was a supply of dressings; he staunched one man's haemorrhage by placing two hardtack biscuits on the wounds and applying a bandage as tightly as possible.

Inside dressing stations there were no lights, and often deep mud. Laby wrote: 'What horrors! How many wounded men! All of them beg us to look after them and to take them first. A cellar is full of them as well as the whole house – in every room and on all the beds.' Even evacuees fortunate enough to find space on overcrowded trains could expect little relief in the rear. Many received their first hospital treatment only after a lapse of four or five days. Tetanus was a massive killer. A chaplain at the American hospital in Neuilly described how he and colleagues asked each man where he was hit. 'Several silently point to their throat, their head, their side. Some lift their covers to show great black patches surrounded by splashes of red. There is a sickly odour … This morning I gave absolution to a Lyonnais: his brain laid open, half his body paralysed but still quite conscious and sensible and able to answer yes or no to questions asked him.'

More than a few able-bodied soldiers exploited the chaos of the retreat to slip away from their units, some to rejoin later, professing to have become lost, others content to lag behind and become prisoners. Sir John French and his staff were not the only senior officers to succumb to defeatism: Gen. Joseph de Maistre, chief of staff of First Army, later told Spears that during the August disasters he seriously contemplated shooting himself. The British officer described a scene on 1 September, as men of Fifth Army continued to fall back north-east of Paris: 'They looked like ghosts in Hades expiating by their fearful endless march the sins of the world. Heads down, red trousers and blue coats indistinguishable for dust, bumping into transport, into abandoned carts, into each other, they shuffled down the endless roads, their eyes filled with dust that dimmed the scalding landscape, so that they saw clearly only the foreground of discarded packs, prostrate men, and an occasional abandoned gun.'

Civilians struggled to avert the consequences of the tidal wave sweeping over their communities, some great and some small. The mayor of a hamlet named Défricheur interrupted a party of soldiers sweating as they dug a grave for a horse, to complain bitterly that it was too close to people's houses. Grumbling, the soldiers moved away to begin their labours anew in a field. Few units on either side found time to bury dead men, never mind dead animals. 'It is extraordinary how one gets used to this nomadic life,' wrote Edouard Cœurdevey, 'sleeping and eating here and there and not thinking of anything important because we know nothing. We see neither letters nor newspapers and cannot share in the drama which is unfolding … We march, stupid and mute – slaves of the god of war.'

Only a handful of the uniformed millions engaged on both sides of this movement of humanity, resembling a terrible animal migration, had any hint of the change of fortunes that was stirring. Joffre could boast some strategic gains from the events of August. Albeit at dreadful cost, the French onslaughts in Alsace-Lorraine had made it impossible for the Germans to shift troops to reinforce their right flank in Belgium. The Entente armies were growing stronger, as troops arrived from overseas colonies; Italy's declaration of neutrality allowed France to remove the defenders of its southern border to reinforce the Western Front. Thanks to Fifth Army, d'Amade's Territorials and the BEF, the Germans had lost the race to achieve decisive success in the north before Joffre redeployed to present first a shield and then a sword against their advance.

Throughout late August and early September, trains from the south crammed with men, vehicles, guns, horses were offloading north of Paris, joining the new Sixth Army of Gen. Joseph Manoury. German Alois Löwenstein, a mere lieutenant, wrote home that the French fought hard, and were well-led. 'Above all,' he said, 'they have the capacity to move huge masses of troops quickly & thus to attack our weakest points with superior numbers.' This remark reflected a sharper awareness than was displayed by Löwenstein's immeasurable superiors of the General Staff about the capabilities of the French railway system, now being exploited to critical effect.

Joffre placed Sixth Army under the authority of Gallieni, but vetoed the governor's request for an additional corps to join the garrison of the capital: the fate of Paris must hang upon a great battle to be fought out of sight of its splendours. Privately, Joffre railed against what he considered the precipitate British retreat, which made it impossible to fight where he had wished, around Amiens. He nonetheless displayed almost oriental courtesy towards Sir John French and his subordinates, to their faces. Though the BEF constituted only 3 per cent of allied strength, its support was indispensable to a counter-offensive. The British were marching – albeit towards the rear – between Fifth and Sixth Armies; that was where they must be persuaded to stay.

Increasing evidence showed that Kluck had made a critical error: instead of encircling Paris, as Schlieffen had envisaged, or even making straight for the capital, he was pivoting his forces eastward, shortening the German stroke. He thus began to march across the front of the embryo army of Manoury, of whose existence the Germans were ignorant. Kluck's action reflected the absolute conviction among Moltke's generals that the critical actions of the campaign had been fought. Germany already held over 100,000 French prisoners; it now apparently remained only to garner the fruits of its triumph. Victory fever swept the Hohenzollern Empire:

even in Berlin working-class areas, hitherto strongly hostile to the conflict, for the first time flags became visible at tenement windows. In the euphoria of the moment, novice German gunner Herbert Sulzbach set off for the front on 2 September frustrated that he was not already with his nation's victorious army at the gates of Paris: 'I was seized by a strange feeling, a mixture of happiness, exhilaration, pride, the emotion of saying goodbye, and consciousness of the greatness of the hour.'

During the past century, fierce controversy has swirled around the frustration of German hopes of absolute victory in 1914. It is sometimes suggested that Moltke's grand envelopment failed only because he lacked vision and boldness properly to implement Schlieffen. Much is also made of the swerve north of Paris at the end of August, on the initiative of Bülow, as a fatal betrayal of a brilliant conception. Both theses are unconvincing. It is unlikely that any strategy would have enabled the Germans to achieve a decision in 1914, when the Western allies mobilised forces broadly comparable with those of Moltke, unless those adversaries suffered an absolute collapse.

The chief of staff was bitterly criticised by his own compatriots, during and after the war, for weakening the German right in order to reinforce further south. It is true that Moltke showed an anxiety to ensure that every yard of German soil was defended, where history's great captains might have accepted a need to yield ground elsewhere, in order to ensure a sufficiency of strength at the decisive point; he certainly erred in supporting Prince Rupprecht's drive on Nancy. But this was a new world of warfare, pitting against each other forces of unprecedented vastness. The French army had become a much more impressive instrument than it was in 1870 or 1906, when Schlieffen retired. No responsible commander could have left exposed sectors in which Joffre's men were known to be formidably strong.

Transcending all else is the probability that Schlieffen's vision of a grand envelopment was incapable of fulfilment by an army dependent for mobility on the feet of its men and the hooves of its horses. The technologies of mobility and communication lagged far behind the twentieth-century revolution in the destructive power of weapons. In the pre-motorised age, defenders proved able to redeploy and reinforce more swiftly than attackers advanced, by the exploitation of rail links. It was a disastrous collective delusion, to suppose that a formula could be identified for achieving quick victory over three of the greatest powers in Europe. It is unlikely that even a Bonaparte could have contrived a different outcome in 1914. Like more than a few commanders and military sages in history, Count Alfred Schlieffen's fatal limitation was that he lacked the grasp of logistics fundamental to all modern military operations: the daily weight of supply necessary to support an army in the field had doubled even since 1870. Rather than a strategist of genius, Schlieffen proved to be a fantasist who brought doom upon his foolish disciples.

On 1 September, the French secured intelligence which confirmed Kluck's change of direction. A haversack caked with blood was brought from the front to one of Lanrezac's staff officers. It had been taken from the body of a German cavalry officer and contained food, clothing and papers, together with a map. This not only revealed the deployments of every corps in Kluck's army, but was also marked with pencil lines showing their intended bivouacs for that night – all of them north-east of Paris. Here was confirmation that the capital had been abandoned as Kluck's immediate objective. The right wing of the German army was passing across the allied front, exposing itself to counter-attack.

A stream of intercepted signals emphasised the exhaustion of the enemy's troops, together with mounting supply and transport difficulties. Moltke's armies, and the horsepower on which their logistics were critically dependent, found themselves in grave difficulties far beyond their railheads, with animals at best inadequately fed, at worst suffering the ill-digested consequences of a diet of green corn. It was becoming evident that German reserve formations, which Moltke had designated for a key role, were struggling to fulfil this. Men fresh from civilian life were as unfit as their allied counterparts, and lacked adequate artillery fire support. As for their ailing beasts, one decrypted message pleaded for three lorry-loads of horseshoes and as many nails as could be found for the Guards Cavalry Division at Noyon. Kluck's First Army alone had 84,000 horses, requiring almost two million pounds of fodder a day: thousands of animals were flagging or collapsing. There was an acute shortage of the wagons necessary for carrying hay.

Veterinary surgeons were also lacking: though even an infantry brigade had 480 horses, all the vets had been allocated to the cavalry and artillery. Many horses were tended by inexperienced and indeed starkly ignorant men, whose mistreatment hastened the animals' demise. Meanwhile technology was of limited value, because all the armies suffered from the unreliability of primitive motor vehicles. The diary of Lt. Edward Hacker, commanding a section of the Army Service Corps in the BEF, recorded a day during the retreat: 'One of our lorries (a Thorney) over-heated at the brake and caught fire. Another, (a Wolseley) got its oil feed choked ... We broke a petrol pipe on a Halley, which we had to braze up.' This sort of daily experience was common to the motorised sections of every army in France, including the Kaiser's. Serviceability rates were low, and fell fast amid the stresses of the campaign. During the German advance, every column had drastically breached the army's peacetime regulation that its motor vehicles should travel only sixty miles a day, so as to permit maintenance. By September, two-thirds of Moltke's 4,000 lorries had broken down.

Lanrezac's formations were now deployed just south of the Aisne, sixty miles north-east of Paris. Manoury's army, whose very existence remained unknown to the Germans, was massing forty miles north of the capital. And somewhat to the rear of both was the BEF. The cooperation of the British was essential, to launch the smashing blow against Kluck's open flank that Joffre wanted. If Sir John French and his men merely sat on their hands while Joffre's armies advanced, there would be a gaping, intolerable interval between them. 'But I cannot ask [the British] to do this, having so far obtained nothing from them,' the general wrote to the war minister on 1 September, adding gloomily, 'in any case I do not know whether they would consent to this'. His foremost problem in the days that followed, as he prepared his counterstroke, was to persuade the boundlessly foolish, childishly sullen British C-in-C to participate.

Fortunately for Joffre and the allied cause, Kitchener that day made it plain to Sir John that under no circumstances would the British government countenance a unilateral withdrawal, abandoning France. The secretary for war copied to the C-in-C his telegram to the War Cabinet, dispatched on Wednesday evening: 'French's troops are now engaged in the fighting line, where he will remain conforming to the movements of the French army, though at the same time acting with caution to avoid being in any way unsupported on his flanks.' Kitchener himself was later in no doubt that his conversation, and subsequent instructions, were decisive in compelling Sir John to abandon his intention to lead the BEF as rapidly as possible towards the coast.

After the battles of September had been fought, Gallieni sought credit for conceiving and executing the plan of attack which now unfolded. This was extravagant. Joffre was committed to launch a counter-offensive in the north before Gallieni was even appointed. Both men reached the same conclusion independently, and Joffre was in charge. But the governor's

energy and ingenuity were critical to massing Manoury's army, and thereafter urging it into the fray. His contribution was symbolised by the
manner in which he mobilised the capital's entire transport resources to
move forward troops – the legendary 'taxi-cabs of the Marne'. The cabs
were conscripted, sure enough, but they carried forward just 4,000 men, a
single brigade, to join the 150,000 soldiers of Sixth Army. Gallieni nonetheless deserves his place among the inspirational figures of the moment,
when many weaker vessels were cracking.

Foremost among these was, of course, Charles Lanrezac. On 3
September, with much reluctance because they were old comrades, Joffre
sacked him. Fifth Army's commander was *Limogé*, to use the contemporary French phrase for officers who were relieved of their posts, and
dispatched figuratively, if not geographically, to the rear area barracks of
Limoges. Lanrezac's bitterness was not assuaged by the fact that Joffre in
those days also purged many other generals who had been found wanting:
in all, three army chiefs, ten corps and thirty-eight divisional commanders
were replaced.

News of these wholesale changes quickly reached the BEF. Sir John
French was delighted, though no man more richly deserved to be *Limogé*
than himself. Humbler British officers were also heartened: on 4 September
Guy Harcourt-Vernon heard a rumour that the neighbouring French
armies had acquired new generals 'young and full of ardour'. He was told
that their predecessors had been shot for cowardice: 'I wonder if that was
true or not.' Some of it was. While Joffre did not shoot failed generals, he
authorised a ruthless programme of executions of ordinary soldiers found
guilty of desertion or cowardice, *pour encourager les autres*. 'Men who
abandon their units,' Joffre wrote in an order of 2 September, 'if there be
any such, are to be hunted down and immediately shot.' This achieved a
prompt and useful effect, causing men to recognise the likely consequences
if they fled the battlefield. In 1914, most of the French army displayed
courage and determination, especially so given its men's ghastly experiences in August. But its will to fight was stiffened by draconian sanctions
enforced by firing squads.

Lanrezac was replaced by his foremost corps commander, Louis
Franchet d'Espèrey, the tigerish officer who had distinguished himself in
the fighting at Dinant and Guise, and would eventually become one of the
most admired French generals of the war. Spears wrote that 'his head
reminded me of a howitzer shell'. The new army commander's first address
to his own staff on 4 September conveyed a galvanic shock: he warned that

those who failed in their duty would be shot; that Fifth Army must prepare to fight the battle of its life. In the mood of the time, comrades pitied those who suffered execution, but few questioned the necessity for extreme penalties. Jules Allard was a former gendarme, now conscripted as a military policeman, who accompanied a chaplain and a lawyer to carry news of a capital sentence to one condemned private. All three then attended the execution, Allard recording laconically: 'He refuses a blindfold. He himself gives the order to shoot; the doctor checks that he is indeed dead. He died as he should have lived.'

On 3 September, Gallieni took time out from his labours organising the capital's defences to visit the few members of the diplomatic corps who had not joined the flight to Bordeaux. He was cordially received by the American and Spanish ambassadors, the latter of whom made it plain that he would welcome a German victory. His Norwegian counterpart not only shared such sympathies, but suggested that he himself might play the role of armistice intermediary when the Germans arrived.

The commander-in-chief, meanwhile, passed hours brooding in silence at his headquarters, pondering his moment. Spears sketched the scene at Bar-sur-Aube, whither GQG had now transferred itself: 'Joffre spent the whole broiling afternoon sitting in the shade of a big weeping ash in the bare courtyard of the school in which the staff were working. Voices could be heard faintly and occasionally through the open windows of the classrooms; now and then the clanging of a telephone bell was perceptible. From time to time a much louder tone broke into the droning silence as some exasperated officer tried to make himself heard down a bad line. But in the courtyard no movement, nothing but waves of heat rising from the wide gravelled space where a big man was thinking.' Gallieni dispatched a message to Manoury, ordering Sixth Army to be ready to attack next day, the 5th. But was this possible? Would the British collaborate in such an operation?

The omens were not good. Haig wrote to his wife on 3 September: 'The French are most unreliable. One cannot believe a word they say.' Next day he told Sir John French that his own corps was exhausted: 'we could hold a position but they could not attack or move at the "double". Smith-Dorrien arrived and concurred in all I had said. Sir J.Fr. agreed that [the BEF] must retire at once behind the Seine in order to refit.' Here was the British commander-in-chief, four days after the meeting at which Kitchener had insisted that the BEF must stay in the line alongside the French, still chafing to separate himself from them.

On 4 September Franchet d'Espèrey left his headquarters – where, heavens knows, he had enough to occupy him – to drive to Bray for a first meeting with Sir John French. On arrival, to his fury he found no sign of the British. At last Henry Wilson appeared, making excuses for his chief's absence. Franchet d'Espèrey explained that his own army would attack next day. Would the British be marching on his left flank? Wilson said he could make no commitment on his chief's behalf. The Frenchman departed in a sulphurous humour, as well he might. Murray, the BEF's chief of staff, was already involved in tense discussions with Gallieni and Manoury about exactly when and where Sixth Army would attack, not assisted by having himself taken a violent dislike to the governor of Paris. On the 4th, they eventually evolved a plan which required a day's delay – until the 6th – to enable the British to withdraw a few miles further, clearing space for Sixth Army to deploy a little more eastward and attack south of the river Marne. Joffre and Franchet d'Espèrey had anticipated advancing on 5 September across a much wider front, from roughly where the armies stood, north of the Marne.

Fortuitously, in London on the 4th representatives of the British, French and Russian governments sought to emphasise their solidarity by signing an agreement, which became known as the Declaration of London, whereby each pledged not to conclude a separate peace with Germany. This had been prompted in considerable degree by Russian fears that France's dire predicament might prompt its government to throw in the towel. But the French had their own concerns, about the sorry British showing. That same evening on the battlefield, Col. Huguet reported to GQG that Sir John French had decided to continue the BEF's retreat on 5 and 6 September, professing a need to give further consideration to his ally's attack plan. Joffre, Franchet d'Espèrey, Manoury and Gallieni could have been forgiven for wishing the British C-in-C at the bottom of the sea; and must privately have said as much to each other.

At 8 o'clock that evening of the 4th, at Bar-sur-Aube Joffre was dining off his favourite dish, a *gigot à la Bretonne*, in an atmosphere of acute strain, depression and gloom which oppressed his staff. Suddenly, a staff officer burst in: 'his black uniform was grey with dust, so was his face and beard. It filled his eyes which were sore with it, and made him blink in the light. He took a step forward, saluted and said, "*Mon général*, General Franchet d'Espèrey has asked me to tell you that the English are prepared to assume the offensive."' Sir John French had grudgingly and belatedly agreed to conform to the instructions of his government. The commander-in-chief lifted both arms to heaven. 'Then we can march!' he exclaimed. Even if Spears' account above is exaggeratedly theatrical, its sense is valid. Somehow Murray and Wilson had persuaded the little field-marshal that the British must at least present an appearance of coopera-tion with the French offensive. Joffre decreed that the allies' Marne operations should commence on 6 September. At 9.15 p.m., Sir John French telegraphed formal assent for the BEF's participation.

That same day, Kluck had signalled to the German Supreme Command: 'As a consequence of difficult and incessant fighting,' he said, his army 'had reached the limits of its strength … Prompt reinforcements are urgently desired.' Here was Kluck's almost explicit admission that the triumphalism of his own words and actions during the past week had been misplaced. Walter Bloem described the state of his company: 'Unshaved, and scarcely washed at all for days … faces covered with stubbly beard, they looked like prehistoric savages. Their coats were covered with dust and spattered with blood from bandaging the wounded, blackened with powder-smoke, and torn threadbare by thorns and barbed wire.'

On the evening of 4 September, Moltke had finally and explicitly aban-doned the Schlieffen concept: he acknowledged a French threat to his right wing, if not yet its gravity. He decreed that the final big attacks of the war would be made in the centre and on the left of the German line, to achieve a closure around Verdun. He urged Kluck and Bülow to cooperate closely with each other, and ordered First Army to turn to face Paris, in case the allies launched a counter-attack from that direction. Kluck ignored the chief of staff's admittedly vague directive: he blundered on, in pursuit of Lanrezac. Hausen, commanding Third Army, on that evening of the 4th reported that he had given his army a rest day for the morrow, which meant that he could not cooperate with Bülow's planned attack. Moltke raised no objection, but once again German sluggishness cost an impor-tant opportunity: if Hausen had kept going, he might have pushed into a gap between the opposing forces of Ferdinand Foch – now commanding the newly-created Ninth Army – and Langle de Cary; but he did not. Thus did the invaders of France win themselves to death.

The war did not stop while the allies prepared to launch their offensive. The dying continued on almost every front, through almost every hour: the French were obliged to fight hard to resist a major German attack on the Couronné de Nancy, even as Sixth Army was massing in the north. Charles Péguy – celebrated poet, socialist and publisher – was shot in the head at Villeroy on 4 September at the age of forty-one, and his death became a symbol of France's sacrifice, just as the stolid image of 'Papa' Joffre was soon elevated as the embodiment of his nation's determination to prevail.

It was known to no one on either side, of course, that the Germans had now attained the extreme limit of their advance across France. Old Mme Lemaire, intimate of Proust and 'The Mistress' of one of Paris's great artistic salons, was at her château at Reveillon, Seine-et-Marne, on 5 September when the enemy's vanguard reached the area. She was walking in the garden with her daughter Suzette when a German cavalry officer jumped the boundary hedge and checked his horse at their feet. Clapping a monocle to his eye, the intruder cried: 'I wanted to see Madeleine Lemaire, and now I have!' Then he tugged his reins and galloped away. Here was a vivid manifestation of the freemasonry of Europe's cultured classes; that night a German unit occupied the house.

Even as troops poured out of Paris towards the front and Manoury's men took up their new positions, uncertainty persisted about the exact deployments of Fifth and Sixth Armies and the BEF. Early next afternoon, Joffre drove to the château of Vaux-le-Pénil, at Melun, where Sir John French was billeted. The story of what followed, brilliantly if histrionically recounted by Spears, has often been told but remains indispensable to any narrative of 1914. Entering the hall, Joffre exchanged greetings with the small group of French and British officers present, all the men still standing. 'At once,' wrote Spears, 'he began to speak in that low, toneless, albino voice of his, saying that he had felt it his duty to come to thank Sir John personally for having taken a decision on which the fate of Europe might well depend.' The British field-marshal bowed.

Then Joffre expounded his plan.

We hung on his every word. We saw as he evoked it the immense battle-field over which the corps, drawn by the magnet of his will, were moving like pieces of intricate machinery until they clicked into their appointed places. We saw trains in long processions labouring under the weight of their human freight, great piles of shells mounting up by the sides of the ready and silent guns … Joffre seemed to be pointing the Germans out to us – blundering blindly on, hastening to their fate, their huge, massive, dusty columns rushing towards the precipice over which they would soon be rolling. As a prophet he was heard with absolute faith. We were listening to the story of the victory of the Marne, and we absolutely believed … Then, turning full on Sir John, with an appeal so intense as to be irresistible, clasping both his own hands so as to hurt them, General Joffre said:

'*Monsieur le Maréchal, c'est la France qui vous supplie.*' His hands fell to his sides wearily. The effort he had made had exhausted him.

French witnesses attributed different words to Joffre: '*Il y a de l'honneur de l'Angleterre, Monsieur le Maréchal!*' This phrase, warning that Britain's honour was at stake, would have been less pleading, and thus seems more credible. What is beyond doubt is that Joffre appealed passionately to Sir John. The British C-in-C struggled to say something in response in the Frenchman's own language. Then, abandoning the attempt, he turned to a staff officer: 'Damn it, I can't explain. Tell him that all that men can do our fellows will do.' On that note, the two commanders-in-chief parted.

While this narrative of the encounter makes irresistible reading, and the outcome recorded by Spears represented an appropriately moving fulfilment, reality was harsher. British participation in the Marne offensive would be very slight, very slow, and embarrassingly half-hearted even according to the testimony of British participants. The best that could be said was that Sir John French's troops took their place in the line while the neighbouring formations of Manoury and Franchet d'Espèrey, together with the new Ninth Army of Foch, did the fighting. In those days, and especially between 1 and 5 September, the personality of Joffre sustained a calm resolution which alone made it possible to arrest and then partially to reverse the huge, cruel defeats of August. Whatever further failures and disappointments lay ahead, as the allies commenced what would become known as the Battle of the Marne, Joffre showed himself a great commander of armies. Late on 5 September, Gallieni telegraphed his forces with untrammelled exuberance: '*Demain, en avant!*'

10

The Nemesis of Moltke

1 THE MARNE

Before embarking upon their great western offensive, or indeed upon the war, the Germans should have pondered the fact that throughout history, swift outcomes of conflicts between approximate equals have been rarities. Even Marlborough's battlefield triumphs over the French, and those of Bonaparte over his many enemies, proved inconclusive. Wellington's victory at Waterloo and the elder Moltke's at Sedan were exceptions to the more general course of warfare. The armies of 1914 were equipped to inflict appalling human and material destruction upon their enemies, but the technology of movement lagged. Worse, the vast mobilised masses had outgrown the ability of their commanders quickly to communicate with them.

Wirelesses, less than a generation old, were few and heavy, available only to higher headquarters; they lacked range and reliability. The 'spark' sets of 1914 were also incapable of fine-tuning, so that signals were dispersed across all known long-wave frequencies, and were thus readily susceptible to interception. Valve technology, which made possible transmissions on a narrow band, was invented in the United States only in 1913, and was not widely used in Europe until two years later. Furthermore, many of the ciphers employed by the belligerents were broken by their enemies. In static positions, formations were accessible by telegraph or telephone, but once in motion they could receive messages only from couriers, some using motor cars, but many still horsed.

The more ambitious a general's objectives – and those of the German army in 1914 were supremely ambitious – the harder it became to control his men's movements. A delay was inevitable of hours, sometimes extending to days, between the issue of orders across thousands of square miles of operational activity and their implementation. Once a formation was committed to a given course of action, it was often as hard to change this as to steer a dreadnought from the bridge by dispatching hands below to manhandle its rudders. The reversal of German fortunes that took place in early September was principally influenced by the vast fallacy of Schlieffen, in lesser degree by Moltke's infirmity of leadership, but also by the technical difficulties of directing the motions of six German armies, fighting on foreign soil. French defeats and retreats had at least the compensating merit that they enabled Joffre to exploit the communications systems of his own country, much to his advantage.

It is characteristic of war, however, that commanders see all the difficulties on their own side. The British especially, in the mood of the moment, failed to grasp the fact that their opponents were in deepening trouble. Germany's war plan required millions of men, many of them newly recalled from soft civilian life, to march vast distances across western Europe carrying heavy loads in summer heat. By early September, the invaders of France found their columns losing cohesion, as weaker soldiers marched more slowly, and stragglers dropped out altogether. Time and energy were wasted by map-reading errors, misplaced orders and changes of objective. Units overtaking each other on the road lost coherence. Lack of sleep and denial of regular halts imposed an ever heavier toll. The historian of one German reserve regiment deplored command confusion which caused its lines of march to meander and diverge, adding to men's exhaustion.

The first two days of September passed without a single message from the German First or Second Armies reaching Moltke's headquarters, the *Oberste Heeresleitung* – OHL. On the evening of the 1st, Moltke signalled Kluck: 'What is your situation? Request immediate reply,' and received none. On the 4th, an angry message from Kluck to Moltke was delayed in transmission by sixteen hours. And all through this critical period, Joffre's forces were massing in the north. On 23 August, the day of Mons, the three armies of the German right wing comprised 24.5 divisions, facing 17.5 allied formations. By the time Joffre completed his redeployment on 6 September, he was able to commit forty-one divisions to his Marne offensive. To achieve this, he drastically weakened his front in the south; but strong pre-war French frontier fortifications compensated for inferiority of manpower. In Alsace-Lorraine the onus was now on the Germans to attack. A month of twentieth-century war had already demonstrated the advantages enjoyed by defenders, especially where they held prepared positions.

One of Moltke's more serious errors was to accede to Crown Prince Rupprecht of Bavaria's demand to exploit westwards his army's success at

Morhange. Moltke cursed the ruling dynasty, which burdened him not merely with the Kaiser, but also with two princelings and a grand duke as army commanders: 'Joffre is a lucky man,' he growled. 'In France a prince means nothing.' He claimed to feel unable to post liaison officers to report directly to OHL from the armies' headquarters, because their presence would be resented.

But for all Moltke's excuses, overwhelming blame for the chaos lay with himself. He vacillated constantly: at first he endorsed Rupprecht's thrust, but then two days later declared that he wished only to 'fix' the French on the Lorraine front. Rupprecht pushed forward anyway, bent upon storming the heavily fortified three-hundred-foot ridge known as the Grand Couronné de Nancy. Throughout early September, the Prince's offensive caused the French much concern. North of the city the Germans pressed forward to the long, low ridge protecting Verdun, creating what later became known as the Saint-Mihiel salient. But on the high ground of the Couronné itself Castelnau – 'the rock', as he became known – conducted a superbly dogged defence.

The main assault there began on the night of 3 September, and provoked savage fighting as swarms of field-grey figures strove to reach the high ground. Key positions were taken and retaken, so that the dead of the rival armies lay mingled among a chaos of abandoned weapons, loose ammunition and equipment. German officer casualties were especially heavy. The defence hung by a thread, and on the afternoon of the 5th Castelnau urged a strategic withdrawal. Joffre rejected his plea, insisting that Second Army must hold. Committed to his grand counter-offensive in the north, he continued to strip divisions from Castelnau, even while the outcome around Nancy was still undecided. On 7 September the Germans captured the key village of Sainte-Geneviève. Then the French retook it, in a struggle that continued into darkness.

On the same day, the 450-strong garrison of the fort of Troyon fought off a massive German onslaught. In these clashes the Baden corps suffered 10,000 casualties – German frontal assaults were as costly of lives as French ones. On 10 September Castelnau counter-attacked, pushing back the Germans several miles and capturing huge supply dumps in Lunéville. The line of the Meurthe was secured, Nancy saved. Rupprecht's men blew the river bridges, knowing they would not be needing them again in a hurry. One Bavarian regiment lost a thousand men as it fell back on 11 September. Rupprecht's chief of staff blamed failure at Nancy upon Moltke's repeated changes of heart. In truth, the latter should never have acquiesced in the attempt. While the French were obliged to fight desperately on several fronts simultaneously, so were the Germans, and the division of effort contributed to their looming strategic failure.

Joffre's armies holding the line in the centre and south made a critical commitment to France's northern offensive. The defiant phrase '*Ils ne passeront pas*' was applied to Verdun only in 1916, but it could as well have been coined in September 1914, when the Germans first hammered at the gates of the great fortress network. If the armies of Castelnau and his northerly neighbour had cracked, everything done on the Marne would have been in vain. Rupprecht's repulse on the Grand Couronné was as serious for Germany as had been the Morhange disaster for France. It has received less notice from posterity than it deserves, because in those same days much more celebrated events were taking place further north.

In early September, failures of intelligence once again exercised a critical influence on events – and they were German failures. Kluck's army was marching south, its right flank bypassing Paris which lay thirty miles to the west. His scouting aircraft reported great columns of enemy retreating south. The Germans did not look – or anyway, not hard enough – towards the west. Commanders ignored some pilots' reports of French concentrations in front of Paris and behind Kluck's flank. There Manoury's Sixth Army was massing, 150,000 strong. The general was a sixty-six-year-old gunner, recalled from retirement in 1914, and now leading seven reserve divisions. The German commanders, fixated with their belief that the French, and less importantly the British, were beaten enemies, remained heedless. They merely wrangled among themselves about how best to seal their triumph. Kluck pressed on in pursuit of the BEF and Fifth Army, and continued to fail to catch them.

Even while Joffre was still cajoling Sir John French to fight, Manoury began to push eastward, crowding Kluck's right flank along the river Ourcq, a tributary of the Marne. Many French officers were sceptical about their orders for the offensive. Seeing the exhaustion and demoralisation of the men, not to mention their own towering sense of defeat, they found it hard to believe that the army was capable of a big attack; a few formally protested to their commanders. Such appeals were dismissed. On 6 September Fifth and Sixth Armies began their advance.

The first hero of the Marne battles – for there were scores, along a hundred miles of front – was a German. Kluck had left a single weak corps of 22,800 reservists commanded by Gen. Hans von Gronau to screen his

The Battle of the Marne 6–10 September 1914

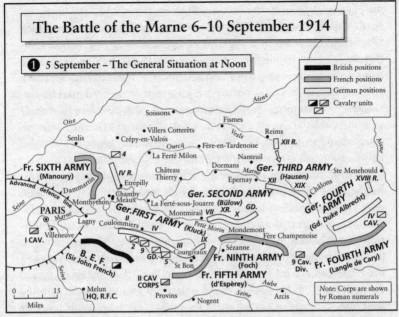

1 5 September – The General Situation at Noon

■	British positions
▬	French positions
□	German positions
◪ ◩	Cavalry units

Aisne

Oise

Soissons • • Fismes

Senlis • • Villers Cotterêts • Crépy-en-Valois Vesle Reims

Ourcq • Fère-en-Tardenoise XII R.

4 • La Ferté Milon Dormans Nanteuil Ger. THIRD ARMY

Fr. SIXTH ARMY (Manoury) IV R. Château Thierry Marne (Hausen) Ste Menehould XVIII R.

Advanced defence line Dammartin Etrepilly Epernay XII Châlons XIX Ger. FOURTH ARMY

Seine Monthython Chamby Meaux Ger. SECOND ARMY (Bülow) GD. (Gd. Duke Albrecht)

PARIS Marne La Ferté-sous-Jouarre XR. X IV CAV.

Lagny Coulommiers Ger. FIRST ARMY (Kluck) Montmirail VII

I CAV. Villeneuve II IV Petit Morin Mondement Fère Champenoise

B.E.F. (Sir John French) 2 III IX Sézanne Fr. FOURTH ARMY

GD. 5 Courgivaux Fr. NINTH ARMY 9 Cav. (Langle de Cary)

Seine St Bon (Foch) Div.

0   15 Melun Fr. FIFTH ARMY

Miles HQ, R.F.C. (d'Espèrey) Aube Arcis

Provins • Nogent • Seine

Note: Corps are shown by Roman numerals

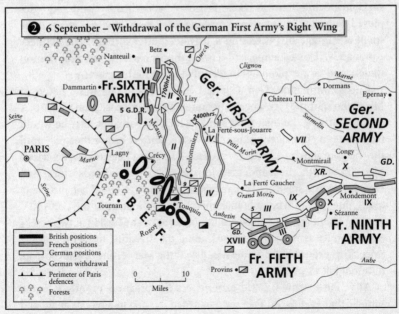

2 6 September – Withdrawal of the German First Army's Right Wing

Nanteuil • Betz • 4 Ourcq

VII Clignon Marne

Dammartin Fr.SIXTH ARMY 1700hrs. Lizy Château Thierry Dormans Epernay •

5 G.D.R. 2400hrs. Ger. SECOND ARMY

Seine Meaux La Ferté-sous-Jouarre Surmelin

PARIS Marne II IV VII Congy

Lagny Crécy Coulommiers Petit Morin Montmirail • X GD.

III Ger. FIRST ARMY XR.

II 9 La Ferté Gaucher IX

B.E.F. IV Grand Morin X Mondement

Touquin 5 III X IX

Rozoy F. Aubetin III • Sézanne Fr. NINTH ARMY

Tournan GD. I

XVIII III Fr. NINTH ARMY

Provins • Fr. FIFTH ARMY Aube

■	British positions
▬	French positions
□	German positions
⇨	German withdrawal
⊥⊥⊥	Perimeter of Paris defences
♧ ♧	Forests

0   10
Miles

rear, facing Paris in positions centred upon the heights of Monthyon, north-west of Meaux. When Manoury's vanguards met the Germans, their advance was blunted by a superbly energetic display of generalship by Gronau, though much outnumbered. German artillery checked Sixth Army's momentum; surprise was lost. Gronau then pulled back six miles, and just before midnight on the 6th informed army headquarters that Manoury was coming. His own corps suffered 4,200 casualties, but made a critical contribution to averting any risk of outright German collapse. Kluck made an immediate, drastic, momentous decision: to swing his entire command to face the new threat, then counter-attack.

Meanwhile Franchet d'Espèrey's Fifth Army was marching against Bülow, some of its officers still imbued with the reckless spirit of August. Gen. Philippe Pétain rode forward personally to address his regiments. He declared the retreat at an end: they were to attack. He broadcast these as glad tidings, and some of his listeners seemed willing to believe him. But on the morning of the 6th, when the men were ordered to advance upon their first objective, the village of Saint-Bon, they baulked. Pétain dismounted from his horse, walked quickly to join the infantry on the start line, then personally led them forward – and defied probability by surviving. Saint-Bon was taken; French guns dashed forward and redeployed. Soon the infantry were pushing on. Pétain's division enjoyed the small advantage of possessing a private spotter aircraft. His artillery commander, Col. Estienne, had secured this by barter for an ammunition wagon, and now exploited it to identify targets for his guns.

Corps commander Gen. Comte Louis de Maud'huy was a native of Metz who quit the city when it became a Prussian possession in 1870. A devout Catholic, he then took a vow, which he had kept, that he would never enter a place of entertainment – café, concert hall or theatre – until the tricolour flew once more over Alsace-Lorraine. Douglas Haig described Maud'huy with the condescension he displayed towards almost all Frenchmen as 'a small active man: about 58, sandy coloured hair, probably dye! Quite the old type of French man seen on the stage of the Louis XIV period.' Maud'huy had survived the bloodbath at Morhange two weeks earlier, and was now bent upon leading his divisions to victory at any price. This proved high: on the first day of the Marne, one brigade lost six hundred killed.

After Fifth Army's torrid experiences the previous month, it was a miracle that Franchet d'Espèrey persuaded its men to advance at all, and in just sufficient cases to display the energy which proved vital to success.

Afterwards Kluck wonderingly observed: 'That men who have had to retreat for fifteen days, having had to sleep on the ground, half dead from fatigue, could at the sound of the bugle pick up their rifles and attack, was something we Germans had never appreciated, this was a possibility that no one had ever considered in our military colleges'.

But 6 September became a day of renewed carnage, and of mortal fears for the Joffre offensive. One regiment, ordered to take the village of Vareddes, reprised the tactics of August by advancing behind its colours with drums beating. Twenty officers fell in the first half-hour; Col. Chaulet, their commander, was hit in the arm and shoulder, but removed the bloody rags of his tunic and bare-breasted led a bayonet charge across fifteen hundred yards of open ground. The village of Chambry changed hands three times before at nightfall Zouave attackers finally held it securely, the churchyard strewn with their richly-attired dead. A Moroccan brigade is alleged to have decapitated German corpses, and the record of France's colonial troops makes this as believable as similar stories about Britain's Gurkhas. Twenty-seven-year-old reserve officer Lt. Paul Tuffnau, scion of a Bordeaux wine family, watched the French advance across a beetroot field:

> Their march forward is magnificent but too fast, too close together … We advance with them, but my machine-gunners are way behind. Finally here comes Chamoutin, all upset: 'Poor Maire … A bullet in the heart' … Some men try to crawl to the rear, hiding in the beetroot. I go over and threaten them with my pistol. They claim they are wounded or helping a casualty. Bullets whistle by non-stop, from all directions. It is quite a job to get the men to stand up.

Tuffnau's machine-gunners refused his repeated imprecations to advance.

> The charge falters, stops. Mulleret, the colour-bearer, lies on his back on the other side of the road, his head on a sack. Behind a haystack, I see the colours, a few men and a colonel, shaking like a leaf, his tunic undone, his right arm in a sling, shirt covered in blood.
>
> I am bandaging Mulleret, who is wounded below the left shoulder. His eyes are closed, his face still has some colour. 'Is that you Tuffra?' He takes my hand, squeezes it tightly. 'You won't leave me? … Unfasten my belt, under the shirt … I have some gold in my belt. Leave that. But take my pistol.'

Soon afterwards the regiment launched another charge into a storm of musketry and shellfire. Once again Tuffnau found himself struggling to stop his men fleeing:

> 'Halt! Turn around! Forward!' I keep shouting, and these brave soldiers do turn around. I notice Dumesnil who is holding the flag. A sergeant close to me breaks into the *Marseillaise* and everyone joins in. But amid the incredible din Valmy's song is drowned out.

One by one they crawled to the rear. Tuffnau fell asleep in a trench as the sun set behind the French line. By nightfall of 6 September, on the French left wing Sixth Army had advanced between two and three miles. Far across the front, darkness was broken by the glare from burning villages, set ablaze during the day's fighting. Further east, Fifth Army was struggling to hold modest gains under German bombardment: each day of the Marne, Moltke's guns expended more ammunition than the Prussians had used in the entire 1870 war. Charles Mangin, one of Franchet d'Espèrey's divisional commanders, ran forward to the village of Courgivaux to check French soldiers fleeing under shellfire, and to persuade them to hold on. His men complained that they had not eaten for two days.

And even as the forces of Manoury and Franchet d'Espèrey gained some ground, elsewhere French affairs remained unpromising. Foch's newly formed Ninth Army held a ridge line sixty miles south-east of Paris behind a poplar-lined stream named Le Petit Morin, in the marshes of Saint-Gond. It was a desolate, uninviting region, offering attackers only a few causeway crossing places. Foot soldiers could wade through waist-deep, but the marshes were impassable for vehicles. Foch, a civil servant's son from Tarbes, sixty-three in 1914, was famously clever, authoritarian, decisive and monosyllabic – though he was also one of the few French officers who spoke fluent English. Fortunately for those who needed to understand his wishes, he acquired as chief of staff Col. Maxime Weygand, whom he soon nicknamed 'my encyclopedia'. Weygand brilliantly interpreted Foch's clipped phrases and orders, and the two formed a historic partnership. The Ninth Army's left wing was committed to a night attack through the marshes in the early hours of 6 September, led by a Moroccan brigade. Just before dawn, as they marched up the causeway towards Congy, the darkness was pierced by a blaze of German searchlights and a torrent of fire. The French advance was halted in its tracks.

The Germans, meanwhile, were attacking elsewhere on their own account, pushing up the hillside south of the marshes. At daybreak, a divisional headquarters in the Château de Mondement came under heavy artillery fire. While the local French commander, the magnificently monocled Gen. Humbert, watched the fighting's progress through his field glasses from a window, the château's owner, a certain M. Jacob, periodically raised the trapdoor of the cellar, where he and his family had taken refuge, to enquire about the state of the battle. Jacob, who had a weak heart, died a few days later from the strain of the unwelcome excitements he had suffered.

Further north, Foch's infantry floundered all day in the swamp: whenever they attempted to emerge on the eastern side, German machine-gunners harrowed them. At 4 p.m., the attacking regiment was ordered to withdraw, having lost a third of its numbers. Another unit in front of Villeneuve fled under fire. Its men were reassembled, given a ferocious dressing-down, and sent back to the battle. One difficulty common to all Joffre's soldiers was that *poilus* were still culturally resistant to using their spades – and paid the price. 'The French soldier knew nothing of the trench,' Weygand said later. 'No one had taught him how to dig in, at least not systematically. When it had to be done you had to assume his disgust.' Maurice Gamelin agreed: 'The idea of organising any kind of defence aroused an almost innate repugnance; digging into the earth was believed to be a dishonourable gesture for loyal fighters who in their heart of hearts wanted to offer themselves up to danger with their chests exposed. It was an instinctive thing, which seemed to have passed down into our age of machines and merciless economic warfare from the reckless chivalry of Agincourt or the elaborate graces of Fontenoy.' The Germans, by contrast, were never embarrassed to use entrenching tools whenever they halted. As they continued to press forward strongly on the road to Sézanne, at the western end of the Saint-Gond marshes, no one doubted that on Foch's front the battle was going their way.

But by far the most important event of 6 September was Kluck's response to Manoury's attacks. The German commander shifted men fast from his left, in front of the BEF, which was doing nothing to inconvenience him, to reinforce the threatened sector. On 5 September, Kluck's formations held a west–east front. By the close of the 6th, his army was redeploying on a north–south line, and he was counter-attacking Manoury fiercely. The fact that he felt able to do so reflected a shameful British failure of will, potentially disastrous for the allied cause. The people of

France hung in suspense, knowing that a great battle was being fought, but utterly ignorant of its progress. One man wounded in the early clashes described his reception on arriving in his home town of Grenoble aboard a hospital train: 'It was extraordinary. Flowers, chocolate, wine ... we were fêted like heroes, but we couldn't answer the questions: "How far are the Germans from Paris?" "Are we on the retreat?" And the Grenoblers, like all of France, demanded to know: "What are the British doing?"'

What indeed? The leaders of the French army fulminated at the tardiness of the BEF on 6 September. Kluck's reinforcements were marching pell-mell across their front, highly vulnerable to an energetic assault. But the British had started the day ten miles behind their allies, and thereafter advanced with painful sluggishness. Lt. Lionel Tennyson's only comment on his unit's leisurely march that day, while the French on both sides were fighting for their lives, was: 'we passed Jimmy Rothschild's beautiful house, and saw masses of pheasants running about everywhere, and longed to be able to stop and get some'.

That afternoon the Rothschilds' English gamekeeper surprised in a shed on the estate Pte. Thomas Highgate of the Royal West Kents, who had made a personal decision that the glories of the Marne offensive were not for him: he was clad in stolen civilian clothes, which damned him. Highgate was shot by firing squad on 8 September, a ceremony watched by two companies of his comrades, in accordance with a directive from Horace Smith-Dorrien. Straggling, trending towards desertion, was a serious problem: the corps commander wanted the execution to have the maximum possible deterrent effect. Orders to the provost-marshal specified that Highgate should be killed 'as publicly as possible', and so he was.

On 6 September, for some hours Sir Douglas Haig halted his own corps' advance in the face of vague reports of enemy forces ahead. He thus ended the day seven miles short of his objectives, having lost just seven men killed and forty-four wounded. In the wasteful way of war, British sappers who had demolished a big stone bridge at Frilport only a few days earlier, during the retreat, now found themselves obliged to build a new river crossing to enable the infantry to retrace their steps. The most exciting thing to befall pilots of the RFC billeted in a girls' school on 6 September was that they donned the pupils' nightgowns over their uniforms and staged an epic pillow-fight. Next day, Monday the 7th, while Manoury's army on their left sought to resume its offensive, in torrential rain the BEF marched just fourteen miles, and once again fought scarcely at all.

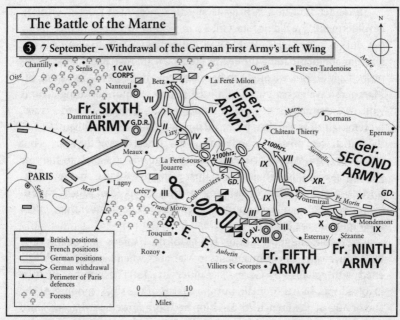

The Battle of the Marne

3 7 September – Withdrawal of the German First Army's Left Wing

Chantilly • Senlis • **1 CAV. CORPS** Betz • La Ferté Milon • Fère-en-Tardenoise

Oise

Nanteuil • VII

Fr. SIXTH ARMY Dammartin • G.D.R.

II Lizy 5

Meaux •

La Ferté-sous-Jouarre

PARIS

Seine

Lagny •

Crécy •

Grand Morin

III

II

Touquin •

Rozoy •

Ourcq

Ger. FIRST ARMY

IV

Marne • Dormans

Château Thierry • Epernay

2100hrs. VII Surmelin

Ger. SECOND ARMY

IX XR.

Montmirail X GD.

I

X Mondemont IX

Esternay • Sézanne

Fr. FIFTH ARMY

Fr. NINTH ARMY

Villiers St Georges •

Aubetin

	British positions
	French positions
	German positions
	German withdrawal
	Perimeter of Paris defences
	Forests

0   10
Miles

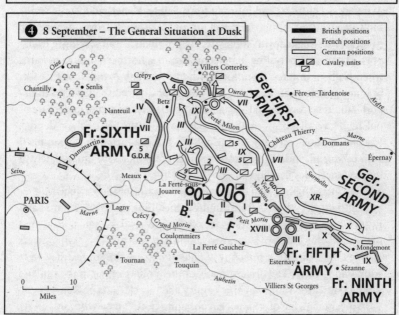

4 8 September – The General Situation at Dusk

	British positions
	French positions
	German positions
	Cavalry units

Oise • Creil

Chantilly • Senlis

Crépy • Villers Cotterêts

Betz

Nanteuil • IV

Fr. SIXTH ARMY Dammartin 5 G.D.R.

Meaux •

Seine

PARIS

Lagny •

Crécy

Grand Morin

III **B. E. F.**

Coulommiers

Tournan •

Touquin •

Aubetin

Ourcq

IX La Ferté Milon

Ger. FIRST ARMY

VII

III

5 IX

2 5

9 III

La Ferté-sous-Jouarre

Vieux Maisons

Petit Morin

La Ferté Gaucher

Villiers St Georges •

Fère-en-Tardenoise

Ardre

Château Thierry • Dormans

Marne • Épernay

Surmelin

Ger. SECOND ARMY

XR.

X

XVIII I X Mondemont

III IX

Esternay • Sézanne

Fr. FIFTH ARMY

Fr. NINTH ARMY

0   10
Miles

Alexander Johnston, a brigade signals officer in II Corps, wrote in bewilderment: 'We did not start till 5 p.m. I cannot understand this. Surely our duty is according to Field Service Regulations "not to spare man or horse or gun in pursuing the enemy etc" ... Heard that, had our 1st Corps pushed a bit more, we ought to have cornered those Germans last night.' Marwitz's cavalry rearguard mounted a succession of harassing actions which were entirely successful in reducing the British advance to a crawl. It seems fair to assert that, in accordance with the wishes of their C-in-C, the British were present in body during the critical days of the Marne, but absent in spirit. All the armies dispatched streams of signals to the rear protesting about the exhaustion of their respective soldiers, but it is striking to contrast the BEF's casual progress with the speed of Kluck's shift of front: his men marched almost forty miles on 7 September, more than forty miles on the 8th.

Meanwhile, the most famous legend of the battle is that of the Paris taxis which carried reinforcements to Manoury when his line was threatened with collapse by German counter-attacks. The number of men involved was, in truth, small, but the charm of the story endures. At the end of August, the French 7th Division had been moved north from Third Army in a nightmare rail journey from Sainte-Menehould: some trains took twenty-four hours to travel six miles around Troyes, where the network was clogged with supply trains, ambulance trains, refugee transport. The men were resting in billets at Pantin, a northern suburb of Paris, when Gallieni ordered them forthwith to join Sixth Army. Told that few military vehicles were available, the governor directed that civilian transport should be conscripted. A staff officer telephoned to the prefecture of police: 'Have all taxis – without exception – returned to their depots. Instruct the taxi companies by telephone to have their vehicles supplied with petrol, oil, and, where necessary, tyres, and then sent immediately to the Esplanade des Invalides.'

Soon after 10 p.m., one of the longest columns of motor vehicles ever by that date assembled – four hundred, including a few private cars and twenty-four-seat open buses – set off to find its passengers. That first night, and the following day, proved anti-climactic. The staff officers charged with directing the convoy failed to locate the troops they were supposed to carry. The drivers, many of them old men, sat in the sun and waited hour after hour, watching cavalry and bicycle units pass en route to the front, and giving occasional encouraging cries: '*Vive les dragons!*'; '*Vive les cyclistes!*'

Only on the evening of the 7th did the taxis rendezvous with the 104th Infantry Brigade in the village of La Barrière. The troops were disbelieving when they discovered that they were to be carried to battle in taxis – most had never ridden in such luxury in their lives. But when they had clambered aboard, crammed in weapons and kit, through deep darkness the column set off for Sixth Army. The soldiers slept, like all soldiers at every opportunity, unless awakened by the clash of injured metal and the muted curses that accompanied minor collisions.

Paul Lintier was among Manoury's men who witnessed the passage of the reinforcements through a village already crowded with men and horses. A vehicle 'ploughing its way through the throng, forced a confused wave of men and beasts against me, the weight of which flattened me against the wall. Another car followed in its wake, then others and still others, in endless, silent procession. The moon had risen, and its rays reflected on the shiny peaks of taxi-drivers' caps. Inside the cabs, one could make out the bent heads of sleeping soldiers. Someone asked, 'Wounded?' and a passing voice replied, 'No, Seventh Division. From Paris. Going into the line …' The passengers were finally decanted near Nanteuil. The 'taxi-cabs of the Marne' had carried 4,000 Frenchmen thirty miles, to play their part in a battle that embraced almost a million. The drivers, whose meters had been ticking throughout their odyssey, were paid a quarter of the amount shown, 130 francs, or around £5 sterling – at least a fortnight's wages.

At 11.40 a.m. on 7 September, Franchet d'Espèrey issued a general order: 'the enemy is in retreat along the whole front. The Fifth Army will make every effort to reach Petit Morin river [at Montmirail] tonight.' That day, to their initial disbelief, his men found themselves advancing unopposed. The Germans in front of them had gone, marching north-west to confront Manoury's offensive. Only Kluck's dead remained. That night, Charles Mangin billeted himself in the Château de Joiselle, which the previous night had been occupied by Duke Günther of Schleswig-Holstein, the Kaiser's brother-in-law. Louis Maud'huy hoped to find matching comforts in the château of Saint-Martin du Boschet, where lights were showing. But he arrived to discover the building crowded with German wounded, accompanied by a few medical orderlies who snapped to attention. 'Bad luck!' muttered the general, closing the door behind him as he left. 'Never mind. I suppose there's a barn somewhere?' He and his staff slept on straw that night.

Further east, on the front of Foch's Ninth Army, the fighting in the marshes of Saint-Gond continued as bitterly as ever. French 75s halted Bülow's attempts to advance, and on the morning of 7 September the German commander ordered a withdrawal behind the Petit Morin. To his left, however, Hausen decided that the French must be weak in his own sector – as indeed they were. The general's army was reduced to 82,000 men, and he himself was semi-delirious, suffering a sickness which was later identified as typhus. But Hausen demanded the launch of an energetic new assault, heedless of losses, which should start in the early-morning darkness of 8 September. Two German Guards divisions advanced in silence until with a rush they overran the sleeping men of two regiments, bayoneting many hapless French soldiers where they lay. Survivors fled.

The Germans pressed on, and soon fell upon reserve units, also slumbering with arms piled and no guards posted. They too died or ran – one infantry regiment, bivouacked two miles behind the front, lost fifteen officers and six hundred men. Foch and his corps commanders awoke at dawn to discover that their entire right wing was collapsing, thousands of men flying in panic. His staff telephoned their southerly neighbours to seek assistance, and was told Fourth Army could do nothing. Instead, Foch agreed with Franchet d'Espèrey, on his left, that they should together attempt an attack on the opposite wing, in the hope of forcing the Germans to abandon their push.

At lunchtime, however, the situation was still desperate: the Germans had advanced eight miles since dawn, and nothing seemed capable of stopping them. A lieutenant of the Zouaves described how his battalion counter-attacked behind a giant officer named d'Urbal: 'At the attack on Etrepilly he went forward with just a walking-stick, smoking his pipe. He absolutely refused to lie down. "A French officer isn't afraid of Germans," he said: and, a second later, he was shot through the head.' The counter-attack failed. On Foch's front, absolute disaster seemed imminent. And matters were no better in Sixth Army's sector. At a critical moment, some infantry units broke and ran in the face of Kluck's hammer blow. A colonel named Robert Nivelle, who became a brief and disastrous commander-in-chief later in the war, responded to the spectacle of the fleeing men by riding forward at the head of his own artillery battery, unlimbering their 75s and opening fire on the Germans at point-blank range. Some infantry rallied around his guns, which represented success, but unfortunately for the later interests of the French army Nivelle himself survived.

That day of the 8th, Gallieni drove personally to Manoury's headquarters at Saint-Soupplets, though the sick old general suffered agonies on the rough road. 'I have come to put your mind at rest,' he said magnificently. 'You are up against three German army corps, at least, and your advance has been checked. But don't worry ...' He meant that Sixth Army was doing its job of pinning Kluck's forces, while Franchet d'Espèrey and Foch made the critical thrusts, with token support from the BEF. That evening, Manoury promised to hang on somehow, until pressure elsewhere made Kluck's position untenable.

But on 8 September the outcome of the battle, perhaps also of the war, still hung in the balance. Both sides found themselves faced with a succession of revolving doors – they advanced in one sector, only to find themselves driven back in another. The French Sixth and Ninth Armies were in acute peril. Kluck was convinced that by next day, he would have accomplished Manoury's defeat. Foch's artillery was in constant action, some guns firing a thousand rounds a day. His soldiers wavered – some displayed a marked unwillingness to accept orders to go forward. In the course of the Marne battles, there were several episodes in which entire French regiments broke and fled.

Spears tells a story of how he once found himself with Maud'huy when they encountered a firing squad leading a soldier to execution for his part in such a collapse: 'Maud'huy gave a look, then held up his hand so that the party halted, and with his characteristic quick step went up to the doomed man. He asked what he had been condemned for. It was for abandoning his post.' Maud'huy then explained to the soldier the importance of discipline, the necessity of example; how some men could do their duty without sanctions but others, less strong, needed to recognise the cost of failure. The soldier nodded. Maud'huy held out his hand and said: "Yours also is a way of dying for France."' The general motioned the party to proceed. Spears asserts that this exchange reconciled the prisoner to his fate, which seems unlikely. What is certain is that the French army found such examples essential, to induce others to hold the line in 1914.

Through 8 September Franchet d'Espèrey continued to batter at Bülow's army, which was now under heavy pressure, its flanks exposed. The German commander began to pull in his right wing, widening the gap with his neighbour. Critically, and amazingly, communications between Bülow and Kluck, and between both generals and Moltke, had almost collapsed. Each German commander was fighting his own battle, in profound ignorance of what was happening elsewhere, and no guiding hand was imposing coordination. Moltke learned from wireless intercepts that the BEF was advancing into the void between Kluck and Bülow, but he was befogged about the general situation. He also allowed himself to become alarmed by the threat to his lines of communication posed by the Belgians, who had briefly sortied from Antwerp on 25–26 August; and from a possible British descent on the Belgian coast.

This was the moment when the fate of the Western Front hung by a thread: Castelnau was telling Joffre that he might have to abandon Nancy; Ninth Army's right wing had crumbled; Maurice Sarrail's Third Army was conducting a ferocious struggle to defend the Revigny Gap covering Verdun. Messages of elaborate courtesy but increasing urgency flew from Joffre to British GHQ, pleading with Sir John French to hasten the advance of the BEF. Yet at every approach to woodland, British commanders halted to reconnoitre. Their units crossed the Petit Morin almost unopposed, but by the evening of 8 September had still not reached the Marne. Maj. Tom Bridges wrote: 'Our pursuit could not be called vigorous, but then we were still a somewhat jaded army.' This was true enough; but what of the condition of the French, who had endured vastly worse things?

All hinged upon which army cracked. Around 1 p.m. on 8 September, the German Guards corps advancing against Foch's right wing halted, exhausted. Their early-morning bayonet charge had been a triumph, but there were no reserves to exploit it: the three divisions which had advanced eight miles had lost a fifth of their strength. The rest of the men were gnawingly hungry, not having received rations for at least one day, and in some cases two. Most collapsed into sleep where they stopped. The weather deteriorated, bringing drizzle and mist. Fighting in the Saint-Gond marshes became confused, with some of Foch's units attacking and some Germans falling back, while elsewhere French retreats continued. Several Ninth Army units ordered to advance refused to do so. All the combatants were in a condition of extreme exhaustion and demoralisation.

That evening, Foch presented an optimistic picture to GQG, which included direct deceits about the progress of some of his formations, and about the setbacks, withdrawals and even routs which others had experienced. The truth was that both his flanks had been squeezed, while his centre was holding only precariously. Legend has it that Foch now asserted: 'My right is driven in, my left is falling back. Excellent. I attack with my centre.' According to senior staff officers, these sentiments were put into the general's mouth afterwards by Lt. André Tardieu, his voluble interpreter, who was much given to such melodramatic pronouncements. The reality was that Ninth Army was rescued from a desperate plight less by its own efforts than by the pressure on the Germans to respond to their difficulties elsewhere.

It is a historic irony that just as Joffre and his army commanders from Lorraine to Paris were reduced to gnawing uncertainty about whether their line could hold or their offensives continue, Moltke in his turn studied the map in his Luxembourg schoolhouse and told his staff in ashen tones: 'We know nothing! It's terrible!' Though the BEF was moving very slowly, Germany's chief of staff was appalled by the spectacle of Sir John French's divisions advancing towards the yawning gap between Bülow and Kluck, who were fighting entirely separate battles, heedless of each other's purposes. Moltke radioed no orders to First or Second Army on 7 September – had he done so, they would probably have been ignored. Instead, all day he anguished. OHL had to endure a personal visit from Crown Prince Rupprecht, who complained bitterly about being obliged to surrender six ammunition columns to his neighbours, which he said would weaken Sixth Army's attack on Nancy. Moltke was feeble enough to give way to Rupprecht's demands. Then, amid the near-total breakdown of communication with his northern army commanders, the chief of staff determined to dispatch a liaison officer, Lt. Col. Richard Hentsch, to visit each headquarters in turn. This would provoke the most dramatic manifestation of delegated authority in military history.

Tappen, Moltke's principal staff officer, often employed such emissaries, and mandated to them far-reaching powers. Hentsch was forty-five, an NCO's son who had originally joined the Saxon rather than the Prussian army. He gained a reputation for brilliance and clear thinking, though gall-bladder troubles rendered him irascible, and he smoked heavily. No one knows precisely what orders Moltke gave Hentsch in their private conversation before his departure by motor, with a second car following in case of emergencies. But there is no doubt that the colonel was given verbal authority to use Moltke's name to impose redeployments, if these seemed necessary. It was an extraordinary way for a general to exercise command in the midst of the greatest campaign in history, but it was what Moltke did. Hentsch set forth from the girls' school in which the chief of staff's headquarters were located soon after 11 a.m. on the 8th, even as Frenchmen and Germans were slaughtering each other in dreadful numbers along two hundred miles of front. Moltke then endured many hours of suspense, as he waited to hear back from his emissary.

Hentsch made a personal decision to visit all the army headquarters, rather than merely those of Bülow and Kluck. To junior officers accompanying him, he voiced some concern that Moltke had not given him orders in writing. But he thought this would prove no difficulty, and it did not. He began his travels in the Argonne. At 4 p.m. he made a first telephone call to Luxembourg, to report that in the centre of the front he found both Fourth and Fifth Armies in satisfactory condition. He reached the same conclusion about Hausen's Third – not realising that its dashing advance of the morning had now run out of steam. Hausen still believed that he was on the brink of rolling up Foch's line, and at 8 p.m. Moltke received a radio message to this effect.

Then, in the small hours, came another missive from Hentsch, this time dispatched from the headquarters of Bülow's Second Army at the Château de Montmort. One of the most important radio messages of the war, it was taken to Moltke, who was still at his desk. He was writing to his wife, as he did almost daily, in tones verging upon hysteria: 'I cannot find words to describe the crushing burden of responsibility that has weighed on my shoulders during the last few days, and still weighs upon me today. The appalling difficulties of our present situation hang before my eyes like a dark curtain through which I can see nothing. The whole world is in league against us; it would seem that every country is bent on destroying Germany, once and for all.'

The thunderbolt from Hentsch that fell upon Moltke at 2 a.m. on 9 September was a report that old Bülow was acutely alarmed about his predicament. His right wing was cracking under pressure from Franchet d'Espèrey and Foch; the French heavily outnumbered Second Army, whose effective fighting strength had fallen from 260,000 men to 154,000. Bülow had heard nothing from Kluck, but reported an eighteen-mile gap between First and Second Armies. This breach was still widening, and the British were advancing towards it. At some point in discussion with Hentsch, either Bülow or one of his staff used the word 'Schlacke' – 'ashes' – to describe the threatened fate of Second Army. Bülow asked the colonel to use OHL's authority to get Kluck to close up on his flank. Hentsch, speaking in cool and measured terms, told the general this was impossible when Kluck's army was heavily engaged, and facing in the opposite direction. Even as they were speaking, a message arrived reporting that Maud'huy had broken through Einem's corps, and was threatening Montmirail.

Bülow was an old man in poor health, and Otto Lauenstein, his chief of staff, was also ailing – he died of heart disease in 1916. After five weeks of vast responsibility and stress, both had had enough. Hentsch, a mere lieutenant-colonel, hereupon told Second Army's commander that he had Moltke's personal mandate to authorise a withdrawal by First and Second Armies. He proposed that such a movement should commence forthwith, so that Kluck and Bülow's forces should reunite at Fismes on the Vesle river some thirty miles east, just short of Reims. Bülow appeared to assent with relief to this proposal, with its vast consequences for the battle and the war. Hentsch signalled Moltke: 'situation at 2.Army serious, but not desperate'. Then he went to bed.

At 5 o'clock next morning, the 9th, Hentsch held a further and final discussion with Bülow's staff, in the absence of the general himself, who had succumbed to a succession of crying fits during the night. Air reconnaissance showed the French advancing fast on Second Army's front. Against this background, the morning meeting confirmed the previous night's decision to retreat. Lt. Col. Hentsch had acted prudently; the course of action he adopted was almost certainly unavoidable. But the intervention of this very junior officer at a critical moment of the war would remain a focus of controversy for the ensuing century.

On leaving Bülow, the colonel set off to motor fifty miles to Kluck's headquarters at Mareuil through the chaotic and crowded rear areas of two embattled armies and a terrorised and fleeing civilian population. His messages had already reduced Moltke to demoralisation and indeed abject defeatism: he wrote in yet another letter to his wife: 'It goes badly. The battles east of Paris will not end in our favour … And we will certainly be made to pay for all that has been destroyed.' At 9.02 a.m., Bülow's troops received the order to begin a withdrawal.

Further south, however, Hausen was continuing his onslaught against Foch's right. At dawn, German troops had seized the Château de Mondement, putting to flight a Moroccan regiment; all morning the Germans kept up a bombardment of the precarious French line, together with infantry attacks which threatened to give them command of high ground from which they could dominate the region. It was profoundly fortunate for the allies that thirty miles westward, their luck dramatically improved. Heavy rain had fallen during the night. On the morning of the 9th, French infantry advancing on Montmirail met no opposition. They found Bülow's soldiers gone, leaving behind all the detritus of an army, together with an astounding number of empty wine bottles – broken glass carpeted the road. By a notable omission, reflecting their disarray and demoralisation, the Germans failed to destroy the Marne bridges. This was a turning point, a decisive moment of the First World War.

That day British cavalry, followed by men of Haig's I Corps, at last crossed the Marne, as did II Corps lower down. On 9 September gunner William Edgington wrote: 'everyone much more cheerful now that the retirement of the Germans is assured … In the afternoon we saw most of the German army in retreat, a marvellous sight, column after column of them in countless numbers.' Seeing the road littered with weapons and equipment, Edgington was fascinated and rather shocked that one of the abandoned German vehicles proved to be laden with women's underclothes. The fox-hunting cavalryman Col. David Campbell contrived to lead a charge at Moncel from which he emerged beaming, despite having received a German lance thrust. 'Best fifteen minutes of my life!' he exclaimed happily.

Though the BEF was now advancing into a void, Sir John French ordered another halt, to allow his forces – reinforcements had arrived from England, creating a third corps alongside those of Haig and Smith-Dorrien – to realign with each other. Major Jeffreys of the Grenadiers wrote caustically: 'It's a precious slow pursuit and the German rear-guards seem to delay us very successfully, judging from the constant checks.' A rumour reached Haig on the 9th that his French neighbours had suffered a 'heavy defeat', which intensified his caution.

Senior British officers lacked drive, will and competence, rather than courage. Indeed, like their French counterparts British commanders frequently displayed a foolish readiness to expose their persons. A staff captain watching divisional commander Aylmer Hunter-Weston standing on the street in La Ferté, heedless of bullets smacking into the wall behind him, wrote: 'his nerve is wonderful, in fact he is much too brave for a general'. Col. Le Marchant of the East Lancashires was likewise standing in full view, having just received orders for an attack on 9 September, when a German bullet felled him. A few days later Colonels Sir Evelyn Bradford of the Seaforths and Henry Biddulph of the Rifle Brigade stood on open ground peering at a map with Capt. Jimmy Brownlow. One of them had just muttered the words 'general advance' when two shells burst beside them. Bradford, a former Hampshire county cricketer, was killed instantly, and Brownlow hideously wounded in the head. Biddulph found his cap blown thirty yards by the blast, but was otherwise unscathed. He was less fortunate next day, when he had to be evacuated after being shot in the

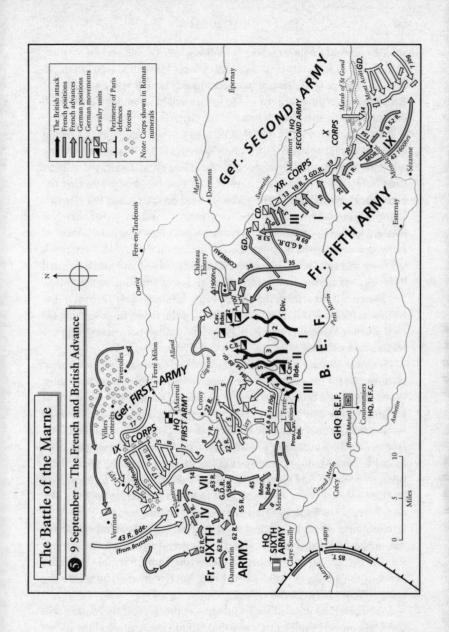

The Battle of the Marne

5 9 September – The French and British Advance

Legend

- The British attack
- French positions
- French advances
- German positions
- German movements
- Cavalry units
- Perimeter of Paris defences
- Forests

Note: Corps shown in Roman numerals

N →

Ger. SECOND ARMY

Ger. FIRST ARMY

Fr. FIFTH ARMY

Fr. SIXTH ARMY

B. E. F.

XR. CORPS

X CORPS

IX CORPS

VII

IV

Épernay

Dormans

Château Thierry

Fère-en-Tardenois

Surmelin

Marsh of St Gond

Mont Août

Esternay

Sézanne

Montmort

SECOND ARMY HQ

CONNEAU

Villers Cotterêts

Faverolles

Vernines

La Ferté Milon

Mareuil

Allard

Crouy

Lizy

L. Ferté sous-J.

Prov. Cav. Bde.

Dammartin

Meaux

Mor. Bde.

Nanteuil

Schafenburg

Crécy

Lagny

Coulommiers

GHQ B.E.F.
(from Melun)

HQ R.F.C.

HQ SIXTH ARMY
Claye Souilly

HQ FIRST ARMY

Aubetin

Grand Morin

Petit Morin

Clignon

Ourcq

Marne

Marne

0   5   10
Miles

(from Brussels)

43 R. Bde.

62 R.
62 R.

55 R.

G.D.R.
56 R.

53 R.

45

R.
R.

3.4.9 & 10 lbg.

22 R.
5

8 R.
22 R.
3

4
3 Cav. Bde.
5 C.B.
5
5
4
5
8 69

1 Cav. Bdes.

2
3
1 Div.
1
2
3

5
8
7
4
8
17
5
17
8
7
69 R.
4 G.D.R.
53 R.
2 GD.R.
19 R.
13

CO
GD

38
35
36

3.700 hrs
1900 hrs

20
19
20
51 R.
51 R.
MOR.

14
54
51
Monts 42 1600 hrs

7 J09
-18 & 52 R.

85 T.

ankle by a Royal Engineer who was cleaning his rifle. But these were mere battlefield incidents rather than consequences of sustained German resistance. Nobody at GHQ sought to inject urgency into British motions. The C-in-C's overarching concern was to ensure that his command did not fall victim to any further French betrayals or German surprises.

That same morning of the 9th, Col. Hentsch had one more important call to make. He reached Kluck's headquarters at 11.30 a.m. only after a nightmare journey on logjammed roads; at one point, Landwehr soldiers fired on his car. Everywhere nervous men told the staff group that the French had crossed the Marne and were hard on their heels. But Hentsch found Kluck and his staff confident – justly confident – that they had halted Manoury's advance in its tracks. Now, said the general's chief of staff, they were poised to inflict absolute defeat on the French. Manoury's left wing was collapsing, his troops were demoralised and much reduced by losses. Yet here suddenly was Moltke's emissary, announcing that Bülow was beaten and in retreat; that Kluck must fall back likewise, or find the BEF assaulting his rear. Hentsch emphasised the threat by describing his own journey through a chaos of stragglers, ambulance convoys, supply wagons and refugees.

First Army's officers replied that they refused to worry about any threat from the BEF. One said later: 'we knew from previous experience how slowly the British operated'. Hentsch disagreed. Though Joffre had not as yet grasped the extent of the thirty-mile gap between the two German armies, the German staff officer judged that it posed a mortal threat. He invoked Moltke's authority to insist that First Army must disengage from its battle with Manoury, and start falling back towards the river Aisne, between Soissons and Compiègne. Kluck's chief of staff, Hermann von Kuhl, assented. A corps was dispatched to screen the retreat from the BEF and Franchet d'Espèrey. Hentsch set off on his return journey to Luxembourg, which he reached at 12.40 p.m. on 10 September. Moltke had meanwhile issued his own order for a general retreat, on the grounds that the British were on the brink of effecting an irretrievable severance between the armies of Bülow and Kluck, merely by marching into the yawning space between them.

Historians have puzzled interminably over the fact that the momentous conversation between Hentsch and the staff of First Army, and the subsequent decision, took place in the absence of Kluck, who was a mere three hundred yards away, at his command post. No sense of panic or desperation seems to have afflicted the parties to the debate. They – though not

Moltke – were still convinced of their overwhelmingly advantageous strategic situation. The prospect of a grand envelopment in the north had obviously faded, but hopes persisted of a decisive breakthrough further south, at Verdun. On 9 September in Luxembourg the Kaiser initially expressed violent dissent when informed of Moltke's decision – or rather, perhaps, acquiescence in Hentsch's decision – that the German armies of the right wing must withdraw to the Aisne. 'No, no, no! It is out of the question!' said the 'All Highest'. But after a stormy meeting, Moltke departed to dictate a formal instruction for the retreat. He wrote resignedly to his wife: 'Whatever happens, I must take the consequences, and share my country's fate.'

Even as the German withdrawal began, on Foch's front bitter fighting continued on the high ground above the marshes, where the Germans had pushed towards the plateau and held the Château de Mondement against repeated counter-attacks – its approaches were heaped with French dead. But then on the morning of 10 September, one of Foch's divisions spearheaded an attack across the Saint-Gond marshes at La Fère-Champenoise, and encountered no resistance. The Germans had gone. Mondement was reoccupied after gunners manhandled forward two artillery pieces which blasted breaches in the park walls from a range of three hundred yards. When sufficient masonry crumbled to allow the attackers to swarm in, they were amazed to find only dead Germans; there too, the living ones had decamped.

It was the same on Manoury's Sixth Army front, to the north-west: Paul Lintier's battery near Nanteuil awoke on the sunlit morning of the 10th, and found that silence had descended: not a shot was to be heard. 'The enemy has cleared off in the night,' a passing infantry colonel told the gunners' commander. 'What's that?' expostulated the disbelieving major. 'Yes. We've got orders to move forward … The Germans are retreating all along the line.' The two officers grinned at each other. 'That means –' 'Yes, it's a victory.' Lintier wrote: 'The news, as it passed from mouth to mouth, shook us with joy. Victory, victory … when we were so far from expecting it!'

Many of Germany's soldiers were as bewildered and angered by their retreat from the Marne as had been their British counterparts retiring from Mons less than three weeks earlier. Tappen, linchpin of Moltke's staff, had declared that 'whoever now perseveres is the victor' – yet here was the German army breaking off its offensive. Cavalryman Gen. George Wichura was 'decimated', his men's morale 'terrible, everywhere confused looks'. One regiment of Third Army called the order to retire 'a thunder-bolt', its colonel writing, 'I saw many men cry, the tears rolling down their cheeks.' Gen. Oskar von Hutier of 1st Guards Division demanded, 'Have they all gone crazy?' Gen. Paul Flack wrote in disbelief: 'This could not be … Victory was ours.' Here was an early manifestation of a deep, passion-ate, almost hysterical sense of betrayal, a belief that dark forces had robbed the nation of a triumph that should justly have been Germany's, which would loom large in its descent into trauma and fantasy after 1918. 'They have totally lost control of their nerves at OHL,' Prince Rupprecht wrote contemptuously in his war diary. The Bavarian Karl Wenninger wrote of the mood at Moltke's headquarters on the 10th as 'quiet as a mortuary. One tiptoes around … best not to address [the staff] – not to ask.'

On 11 September, Moltke left his headquarters in Luxembourg with Tappen to pay personal visits to the field commanders. A significant encounter took place later that day, when he met Hausen at Third Army's headquarters. From there, he spoke by telephone to Bülow. All the news was bad, he said: Hausen himself was sick; his army had suffered 15,000 casualties in the first ten days of September, and the troops who remained were exhausted. The French were thrusting forward with a momentum which threatened Third Army with outflanking. On Hausen's left, Duke Albrecht was demanding assistance to cope with his own difficulties, which the Saxon felt obliged to provide.

Lionel Tennyson of the BEF wrote in his diary that 'rumours have reached us of the Russians coming to relieve us through England, tho it sounds hardly credible'. Amazingly, Moltke allowed himself to be impressed and alarmed by the same fantasy. He had always feared a British amphibious descent on Schleswig-Holstein. In Belgium, there were reports of British troops landing behind the front. In truth, four battalions which had been put ashore at Ostend almost immediately re-embarked, leaving behind only a trainload of dead horses, shot by their owners for lack of shipping to evacuate them. But Moltke did not yet know this. His appetite for risk, never large, was sated. He determined to dispatch ten divisions from the French front to Belgium; and to maintain his commitment to a general retreat in the west.

That day, Gen. Karl Einem was driving to Third Army to relieve the ailing Hausen. Passing through Reims, by chance he met Moltke, whom he found to be 'a totally broken … man'. The chief of staff rambled: 'My God, how could this possibly have happened?' Einem exploded: 'You yourself ought to know the answer to that best of all! How could you ever have remained at Luxembourg and allowed the reins of leadership totally to slip from your hands?' Moltke protested feebly that he could not have dragged the Kaiser halfway around France in the wake of the army. Einem said: 'if your great-uncle could take his King ... to Sedan, you and the Kaiser could at least have come close enough to the front to keep the reins in your hands'.

What followed was not a rout. The German armies fell back eastwards, leaving behind in scores of French towns and villages scenes of sack and squalor that much dismayed Joffre's advancing troops. But there was no great allied haul of prisoners and captured guns. The Germans quickly selected the positions at which they would halt and fight again – on high ground behind the Aisne, whither pioneers were dispatched to start digging. By the evening of 13 September, the crisis threatening the armies of Kluck and Bülow had passed: they were safely back across the river, occupying the ridge of the Chemin des Dames. Franchet d'Espèrey on the 14th rejected Joffre's urging to hasten forward, saying, 'it is not rear-guards that are in front of us, but an organised position'. The pursuit by the allies, and especially by the BEF, was painfully slow. French ammunition stocks were almost exhausted. The troops were too tired, and had suffered too much, to move with the speed that would have been necessary to seize any chance of transforming a French triumph into a German catastrophe.

But the high-water-mark of Moltke's assault in the west had passed. '*La bataille de la Marne s'achève une victoire incontestable*,' declared Joffre. Gen. Moriz Lyncker, chief of the Kaiser's military cabinet, agreed: 'in sum one must appreciate that [our] entire operation ... has been utterly unsuccess-ful ... Moltke is totally crushed by events; his nerves are not up to the situation.' A staff officer wrote: 'The nervousness of the general was displayed outwardly, particularly in that he walked ceaselessly up and down the room and exhaled with a whistling sound through his teeth ... There was a general view that General von Moltke was unequal to his great task on account of his physical condition, and that he let the heads of departments do as they pleased.' Lyncker told the Kaiser on the 14th that Moltke must go. The chief of staff became the foremost of thirty-three German generals dismissed, though his removal was not publicly acknowl-edged for several months. He received little sympathy from his peers, and deserves none from history. No man had done more to precipitate the calamity of European war; yet, having got his way, Moltke proved incapable of effectively conducting his nation's armies. He died in 1916, aged sixty-eight.

While the Kaiser was never allowed to influence battlefield operations, until late 1916 he retained one critical power, that of appointing and dismissing the army chief of staff. In September 1914 he chose his own man, Prussian war minister Erich von Falkenhayn, to assume control of Germany's war machine. Falkenhayn noted laconically on taking over command: 'Schlieffen's notes are at an end and therewith also Moltke's wits.' At this critical moment, it seemed to the leaders of Germany preferable to apportion to individuals responsibility for detailed failures, rather than to acknowledge that the nation's entire programme for waging war, so confidently set in motion less than two months earlier, had proved a catastrophe for their country and for the world. Hew Strachan has written: 'The army blamed Kluck for having disobeyed orders and created the gap [between his own army and Bülow's], Bülow for having been the first to decide to retreat, Hentsch for having ordered the First Army to conform, Hausen and Crown Prince Rupprecht for not having achieved the breakthroughs that would have retrieved the situation, and Moltke for having failed to prove himself a true *Feldherr*.'

An eternity past, on 24 August, the local school administration for Hanover province adopted a custom which had since been emulated all over Germany. Following a report of any major victory on land or at sea, teachers delivered a patriotic homily to their pupils, then gave them a celebratory holiday for the rest of the day. No one, however, had decided how to respond when instead a battle was lost. The German government's answer was to decline to admit the fact. It said nothing to its Austrian allies about the Marne; it also lied to its own people, though the deceit was not much believed. Even amid a torrent of newspaper propaganda, asserting that the battle left Germany in a favourable position, intelligent civilians understood that their nation had suffered a serious setback. Anna Treplin wrote to her husband at the front: 'This much is certain, that you have retreated an enormous distance.'

Gertrud Schädla described the 'agony' of awaiting news of her three brothers, all serving with the army in Belgium. She worried about the impact upon them of the experience of war: 'How will the sight of a battlefield cut into the hearts of those who survive?' At last, on 13 September, she received a letter from her youngest brother Gottfried, nicknamed 'Friedel'. He was writing, he said grimly, on notepaper taken from the pack of a dead Frenchman; he could scarcely understand how he had survived the 'hundreds of perils' he encountered every day: 'You can't imagine how horrible it is to face furious artillery fire, able only to lie motionless, calling upon God.'

The decision to withdraw to the Aisne remains intensely controversial. Some historians, not all of them German, believe that Moltke's collapse of nerve, Hentsch's almost casual nod to Bülow's and Kluck's retreat, denied the Kaiser a victory that was within his reach; that the Germans retained the balance of advantage on the Marne front, had their commanders displayed the resolution and united purpose to exploit this. It is certainly true that mystery, unlikely ever to be resolved, shrouds important details of German decision-making between 8 and 12 September. Some formations were performing much more effectively than their French opponents; both Foch and Manoury stood perilously close to defeat.

But there is overwhelming evidence that the French had fought the Germans to a standstill. Some of Kluck's men had marched four hundred miles between 17 August and 12 September, and been in continuous action for nine days. Kluck and Bülow had contrived for themselves untenable positions. Franchet d'Espèrey's Fifth Army, well-led and in formidable strength, was pressing upon them. Joffre, by notable generalship and iron will, had contrived a superiority of mass against the German right wing which his subordinates ably exploited. The French armies further south played their part nobly, by holding the line under savage pressure while those in the north secured the victory.

The final German folly of early September was a night bayonet assault on the 10th by almost 100,000 reservists of the Crown Prince's Fifth Army at Vaux-Marie, north of Sainte-Menehould. Moltke first approved the operation, then – becoming alarmed about casualties among the besiegers of Nancy – recanted. Wilhelm threatened the chief of staff with an appeal to his father the Kaiser, and Moltke grudgingly agreed. The consequence was a disaster. The attackers failed to achieve a breakthrough, and French artillery, the 'black butchers', punished the packed ranks of infantry mercilessly. At 7.45 a.m. the French counter-attacked, driving back the milling, panic-stricken Germans. Some units lost as many as 40 per cent of their officers. That night Gen. Maurice Sarrail tersely messaged Joffre: 'Situation satisfactory.' Much has been said above about bloody French blunders in the first weeks of war, but the Germans did not long lag behind in follies, this one notable among them. The limitations of Germany's royal army commanders were emphasised by the fact that Crown Prince Wilhelm buoyantly assured Moltke that his 10 September operation had been 'a great success'.

Contrary to the view of the German army's apologists, the Marne represented not merely a failure by Moltke – who had to acquiesce in reality – but a historic victory for the French army, which imposed due punishment upon German hubris. The French were able to exploit some advantages: as defenders of their native soil they had better communications and much shorter supply lines than the Germans, who were playing away. The French command system worked incomparably better than the German one. If Joffre had been sacked on 25 August – which the disastrous failure of his Plan XVII and consequent casualties merited – he would be remembered as one of history's military embarrassments. But thereafter he proved, like the hedgehog, that he knew one big thing. The Marne concentration represented a gamble by the commander-in-chief, which worked. It is hard to overstate the significance of Joffre's triumph of the will over Moltke in determining the fate of Europe. Moreover, the C-in-C's personal contribution was matched by that of the men of his armies, who revealed fortitude at a moment when they might have been forgiven for succumbing to despair.

Some historians argue that Bülow suffered a collapse of nerve less explicable, and more serious in its consequences, than that of Moltke. But this seems to ignore the simple fact that by 9 September Second Army's commander had been outfought by Franchet d'Espèrey. As for Kluck, if he considered Moltke's – or rather Hentsch's – intervention unmerited, why did he not contest it, as he had disputed many previous directives from OHL? It is more plausible that he, too, tacitly recognised that the German armies in the west had overreached themselves strategically, tactically and logistically. Not for a moment did Kluck and his peers suppose that the 9 September decisions implied that Germany was losing the war. But they acknowledged a need to draw back and regroup.

Thereafter the allies failed to seize their moment to transform the enemy's discomfiture into his destruction, because they lacked sufficient means and energy after the traumas of August. The BEF might have achieved important results by pressing hard upon the retreating Germans, but declined to do so. The British suffered only 1,701 casualties in the entire Marne battle – less than some French brigades. Had the matter been left in the C-in-C's hands, the BEF would not have participated at all. It was the decision of Asquith and Kitchener, not that of Sir John French, to join the counter-offensive. It is unlikely that more vigorous British action could have turned Joffre's victory into German catastrophe, but it could certainly have increased the enemy's losses, especially in prisoners, and made the retirement of Kluck and Bülow a less comfortable affair.

After weeks of gloom and terrible fears for the outcome of the war, success on the Marne inspired an outbreak of euphoria in the allied camp. Sir Edward Grey wrote to a government colleague on 14 September: 'The general news of the war is almost too good to be true.' Lt. Charles de Gaulle was among those who deluded himself that the Marne offensive would prove the decisive stroke of the war: 'The enemy will not be able to halt our pursuit ... and we shall have all the glory of having beaten the army that thought itself the finest in the world ... and this without the Russians having been absolutely necessary to us.' Other soldiers were more cautious, however. Edouard Cœurdevey welcomed the discovery that the Germans had abandoned a village in the path of his unit, but declined to join the extravagant rejoicing: 'This would be marvellous if France was to be quickly liberated ... but I am sceptical about the illusions of my comrades who already imagine themselves on the Rhine. I know the Germans' organisation, their immense reserves of energy, impressive scales of equipment. I believe it will be hard. My comrades mock my doubts but they don't know Germany – its pride and Prussian organisation.'

But it was plain to informed Germans that they had lost their bet on a swift outcome. At the Imperial Naval Office, Albert Hopman wrung his hands: 'The whole situation is very unfortunate,' he wrote, and resulted from the 'sins of earlier years'. He castigated the government as lacking strong personalities: 'Our system did not know how to bring strength and intellect into the front rank of politics and government ... It is sad, too sad, poor Germany.' A few days later, he described the war as an 'incredible folly' by those responsible for Germany's foreign policy. The only consolation he could identify was 'the spirit of the nation. This can only be sustained by extensive democratic concessions. Otherwise there undoubtedly will be revolution, and the [Hohenzollern] dynasty will fall. It is doubtful that our politicians have the sense [to act to pre-empt this].'

A surge of overpowering relief swept France. On 15 September Edouard Vaillant wrote in *l'Humanité*: 'it is the beginning of the annihilation of Prussian imperialism. It is, indeed, the beginning of the definitive victory of the allied armies.' The term 'the miracle of the Marne' was first coined in December by Maurice Barrès. He described the battle as the 'eternal French miracle, the miracle of Joan of Arc, the saint and patron of France'.

At that time, the Catholic Church in France was calling for a religious revival: a cleric followed Barrès by publishing leaflets entitled 'The Miracle of the Marne'. Soldiers' view of the September experience was, unsurprisingly, warier and less romantic. A colonel named Desfontaines wrote on the 25th: 'we have experienced the most painful period of war: physical exhaustion; lack of supplies; irreplaceable losses of officers'.

After 1918, the Marne became part of the German army's invention of the 'stab in the back'. Its official history asserted: 'The massive, historic battle on the Ourq and the Marne was stopped! The German right-wing armies created a retreat out of assured victory!' Ludendorff wrote in 1934: 'The army was not defeated on the Marne in 1914. It was the victor.' This was fantasy. The myth of German invincibility had been laid bare, and the French army had risen superbly from the ashes of defeat. Joffre's men experienced a spiritual renewal in the exultation of their advance, regaining from the occupiers many precious miles of the soil of France. Capt. Plieux de Diusse found himself billeted one night with an unfriendly old woman who had lately had the Germans staying in her house. As he climbed into bed, de Diusse momentarily wondered whether she had changed the sheets since their departure. Then he shrugged: 'What a question for a soldier in the middle of a campaign … I shall sleep well.'

2 'STALEMATE IN OUR FAVOUR'

The Germans withdrew in good order from the Marne, and chose with skill their ground on which to turn and stand. Moltke, in the last significant orders he issued before surrendering command, directed the armies south of Reims to abandon their assaults – notably around Verdun and Nancy – and dig in. Troops thus became available for new initiatives elsewhere, notably in the great void of western Belgium and northern France, still unharrowed by the armies. On 14 September, the chief of staff received the Kaiser's command to report himself sick, though since the news was concealed from the German people, for weeks he lingered wretchedly at OHL, which he quit only for a frustrating sortie to the Antwerp front.

Falkenhayn, who assumed Moltke's operational responsibilities, was younger at fifty-three than any other army commander, a chilly, unclubbable Guards officer who was socially acceptable to the Kaiser, as Ludendorff, for instance, was not. He was quick and shrewd – among those who from the outset predicted a long war – but sometimes

Left: Smith-Dorrien, who chose to fight at Le Cateau. ***Bottom left:*** Wilson – 'that poisonous tho' clever ruffian' – with Foch and Col. Huguet. ***Bottom right:*** Murray, the BEF's chief of staff, who wrote of Sir John French: 'I knew better than anyone how his health, temper and temperament rendered him unfit… for the crisis we had to face.'

WILLS'S CIGARETTES.

LT.-GEN. SIR A. J. MURRAY.

A spectacle familiar to countless French and British troops in the summer of 1914: Germans advance.

Top: Frenchmen display the offensive spirit so prized by Joffre. ***Above left:*** Austro-Hungarian cavalry struggle in Galicia. ***Above right:*** British soldiers deploy on their first battlefield; and (***opposite***) await the enemy.

THE EASTERN FRONT

Left: Samsonov. *Opposite:* Russians pay the price for their commanders' boldness and (*below*) are taken prisoner in tens of thousands after Tannenberg. *Opposite bottom:* Rennenkampf.

Fortunino Matania's painting of L Battery's action at Néry.

One of the few apparently authentic photographic images of the retreat: men of the Middlesex under fire.

indecisive. A driven man who required little sleep and would often commune with corps commanders in the small hours, he was also a lonely one, and intensely secretive. A much stabler personality than Moltke, in the course of the ensuing two years as Germany's principal warlord, Falkenhayn would display considerable gifts. He nonetheless faced the same intractable problems as his predecessor. Col. Gerhard Tappen, architect of Germany's invasion of France, remained operations officer, which made it unlikely that strategy would change. Falkenhayn at first refused to regard the setback on the Marne as decisive. His immediate task was to take a grip, exercise authority and impose coordination upon the army commanders as Moltke had so lamentably failed to do.

Almost immediately, tensions developed between himself and Tappen. The new chief of staff favoured a resurrection of the grand envelopment plan, shifting troops into Belgium to sweep around behind the allied flank, where it hung in the air with almost two hundred miles of empty space beyond. Tappen, by contrast, wanted to resume the attack in the centre, between Soissons and Reims. In the short term the operations officer's view prevailed, partly because only limited railway capacity was available to move troops across the front: most lines ran east–west rather than south–north, and the heavily sabotaged Belgian system was in chaos. The Germans staged a series of attacks which were ill-planned, costly and unsuccessful.

The allies, meanwhile, sought to convert success on the Marne into strategic triumph twenty-five miles further north, in a month-long series of clashes which became known as the Battle of the Aisne. The slow-flowing river lies in a valley, behind which a wooded hill rises steeply for three hundred feet. Northwards beyond the ridge crest is open farmland, climbing gently, along which runs a road, some twenty-one miles long, modestly famous in French history as Le Chemin des Dames, named for Louis XV's daughters Adélaïde and Victoire, who drove along it to visit the Countess of Narbonne at the Château de la Bove.

As the French advanced, some men scavenged 'vulgar trophies from the bodies of the Germans, covered in mud and blood ... they load sacks with German coats and helmets which they will not be able to keep', in the disdainful words of Edouard Cœurdevey. One September night, Cœurdevey's sergeant dragged in an enemy soldier who had lain for five days and nights in the open, immobilised by a broken thigh. 'We shudder with horror at the thought of the agony of these wounded men, unable to move to save themselves either from the heat of the sun or the cold of the

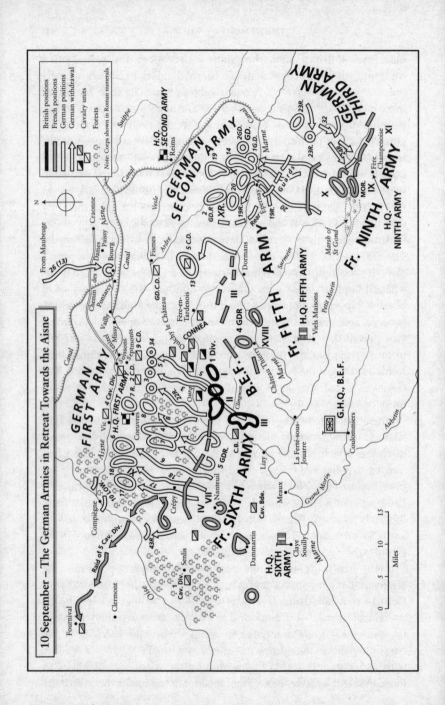

10 September – The German Armies in Retreat Towards the Aisne

night or shelter from the rain. This poor man gave his saviour his medals, his buttons and offered him money.'

Eastwards lay the hills around Reims and the woods of the Argonne, where Franchet d'Espèrey's Fifth Army was attacking. Its formations had advanced from the Marne as slowly as the British, but with better excuse after their travails of the preceding month. They retook Reims, then maintained attacks beyond it well into October, at high cost and making small progress. From 17 to 19 September, the Germans shelled the city, inflicting massive damage on its cathedral. This vandalism prompted outrage and a new surge of alarm in the French capital: Parisians became convinced that if their own city came within German artillery range the Louvre, Invalides, Notre Dame and every other treasure of their heritage would be condemned, and it is hard to suppose their fears groundless.

Between Manoury and Franchet d'Espèrey, through the second week of September the British continued their slow advance northwards, meeting heavy rain but little resistance. 'As I feared,' wrote Alexander Johnston on the 11th, 'we have let the Germans get clear away with very little loss ... Surely we should have harried the enemy as much as possible.' But most of the BEF succumbed to a surge of optimism. On 13 September Capt. Harry Dillon of the Oxf & Bucks wrote home: 'Everything is going well and I think the Germans are done. Yesterday after sleeping out in the rain we came up with them. We were under pretty sharp infantry fire for some time but no casualties, the regiment captured 116 prisoners including 5 officers ... I don't mind this show except for marching and being always wet and short of sleep etc.'

Yet even as the BEF closed up on the Aisne, a new German Seventh Army hastened forward to fill the gap between Kluck and Bülow. Some of these reinforcements force-marched to the river, taking up positions mere hours or even minutes before the British arrived. The German VII Reserve Corps covered forty miles, to reach the crest just in time to forestall Sir John French's vanguard. On 13 September a month of bloody fighting began, in which the allies strove for a breakthrough on the Chemin des Dames. Joffre's forces north and east of Reims bore a heavy share, but subsequent attention has focused chiefly upon operations in the British sector, because there it was thought – probably mistakenly – that spectacular opportunities existed for unhinging the German line, by crossing the river, cresting the ridge, then pushing on across the open country beyond. 'Looking back,' wrote Louis Spears, 'I am deeply thankful that none of those who gazed across the Aisne ... had the faintest glimmering of what was awaiting them. They were untroubled by visions of mud and soaking trenches … years of misery ahead.'

The first British crossing was the most successful. On the evening of 12 September, the 11th Infantry Brigade settled into billets at Septmonts, tired after a fifteen-mile march and soaked through by a long spell of rain. They had been resting for only two hours, however, when the men were roused, ordered to don their stiff, sodden webbing and equipment, and set forth again. Brigadier Aylmer Hunter-Weston learned that the Germans had bungled demolition of the Aisne bridge at Venizel, a few miles ahead. The span was fractured, but not severed: a reconnaissance party reported that it should be passable by careful men.

Hunter-Weston, with an urgency unusual among BEF commanders that autumn, insisted that his brigade should make the crossing immediately, exploiting darkness. Staff officer Lionel Tennyson wrote of the brigadier: 'As a man I do not like him much, nor does anybody. He is very fussy and has the reputation of rather losing his head, and being rather incompetent.' But that night before the Aisne, Hunter-Weston for once acted effectively. At 2 a.m., in single file with five-yard intervals between each man, the infantry started to shuffle over the rickety structure, guided only by a single hooded light on the eastern shore. The fractured ironwork quivered and shook as each man made his nervous passage, sixty feet above the flow. Within an hour, the reassembled battalions were squelching in water meadows below the ridge on the north bank. The troops had not eaten for twenty-four hours, and were cold and miserably wet – not a man of the BEF possessed clothing that was genuinely weatherproof. But with less than three hours of darkness remaining, Hunter-Weston once more imposed a driving will, insisting that the exhausted infantry press on to the high ground. His enterprise was rewarded: at dawn the men of the Somersets, Hampshires and Rifle Brigade surprised German pickets, who fled to their main line.

The newcomers dug in on the lip of the ridge. They were overlooked by strong German positions higher up the hill, but at least they were on the right side of the river. The British official history comments tartly: 'Had other divisions been equally enterprising – and their marches on the 12th been shorter – the fighting on the 13th might have had a different result.' In other words, the rest of the BEF approached the Aisne in the same leisurely fashion with which it had advanced from the Marne, failing to make serious attempts to cross the river until daylight on the 13th, when clashes took place at a dozen crossing points. The Germans had positioned a formidable array of heavy guns and mortars beyond the ridge line. From the heights, their observers could watch every movement, and pour down fire on the valley. A British gunner officer wrote ruefully: 'The advance proceeded with insufficient momentum, which permitted the Germans to prepare a strong defensive position ... from which we failed to dislodge them.'

At Bourg-et-Comin, a machine-gun ravaged the crossing of British cavalry: Lord Gerald Fitzgerald of the 4th Dragoon Guards, just thirty-three days married, took a bullet between the eyes. Infantry reached the north bank of the Aisne by traversing an aqueduct the Germans had failed to destroy, but a deluge of shells fell upon the village of Bourg as soon as the British occupied it. Engineers struggling to build a pontoon bridge suffered severely from artillery and snipers. One raft suffered a direct hit, blowing a dozen sappers into the water, most of them dead. Three bold men, stark naked, swam out from the shore to retrieve the raft as bullets whipped the water around them. One was shot, but the other two hoisted themselves aboard and steered the clumsy craft to the bank, saving the lives of five wounded engineers stranded upon it.

Below the village of Paissy, the West Surreys lost a hundred men crossing the river under fire. At Pontarcy, thousands of infantry reached the east bank across another half-demolished bridge, but German shelling continued relentlessly, as did heavy rain. At Vailly, scores of French's men were hit while running the gauntlet of enemy fire as they crossed a plank bridge. At Missy, engineers struggled in darkness through the early hours of 14 September to ferry horses over the river on rafts. 'We had an awful time ... as the banks were very steep and the current pretty strong,' wrote Lt. Jimmy Davenport of the Bedfords. A fellow officer, Maj. Singer, slipped and fell in the water as he was pushing off a raft, and found himself clinging precariously to the edge with his head within inches of a horse's hooves. Halfway across the animal started kicking out, and the hapless major was obliged to twist and wriggle frantically to avoid a killing blow. Several horses leapt overboard into the current, and were recovered only hours later.

By the morning of 14 September, thousands of British troops were established on the northern bank of the Aisne – but in a wretched predicament. Soaking wet, exhausted and mostly unfed for many hours, they clung to positions just above the woods that ran the length of the Chemin des Dames. At every point they were overlooked by Germans on the open farmland eastward, which rose gently uphill. Through the days that followed, the British struggled to breast the crest, while the Germans made repeated attempts to drive them back to the river. Both sides failed, with heavy loss. In the dismal weather, spirits sagged. They would have sunk further had either army known that, though much more dying would take place there, the front on the Chemin des Dames would remain almost unchanged through the next four years.

Pte. Charles Mackenzie of the Cameron Highlanders wrote after being wounded in both legs on 14 September: 'It is a terrible place out yonder – nothing but heaps of bodies and plenty of blood. We lost a lot of men … there are only 300 left out of 1400'. The Coldstream and Scots Guards also suffered heavily. The Connaught Rangers crossed the Aisne at Pont d'Arcy during the night of 13 September and found themselves in the village of Soupir, dominated by a splendid château which had belonged to Gaston Calmette, the editor of *Le Figaro* sensationally murdered by Madame Caillaux. They had no orders to go further that night, but their commander Maj. William Sarsfield, in a notable display of initiative, decided that since they must seize the high ground some time, the sooner the better. He led his men up a winding track through woods from the village that eventually emerged onto open ground at a big farm named 'La Cour de Soupir'. There, they established themselves and waited for dawn. At 9.45 a.m., in the usual torrential rain, the 2nd Grenadiers arrived, with no inkling that the Irish soldiers were ahead of them. Simultaneously the Germans launched a powerful infantry attack on the farm, obliging both regiments to make the best shift they could to hold them off amid a crackle of musketry, with no maps and scant idea of who was where. The subsequent messy, confused, costly little battle surged to and fro around the farms and surrounding woods.

Grenadier Guy Harcourt-Vernon wrote: 'We stop a lot of Connaught Rangers who are "retiring" rather in disorder & hear that their regt has been cut up in an ambush and their major has told them to retire. We take possession of them all & fall them in with us. We meet crowds of little detachments like ours … Can see that if anyone gets funky, everyone will be firing into everyone else. That's the worst of these wood fights, you can't see & there is no one directing. Hear firing on my right & halt to let the men get up to me; they have straggled appallingly. Suddenly see grey uniforms in front, poop off & almost immediately am hit.' Harcourt-Vernon was shot in the groin, briefly captured, then freed and dispatched to hospital an hour later, when the Germans were forced back.

It became a day of desperate local actions in a dozen places, of attack and counter-attack, a steady drain of losses to German riflemen who sniped from vantage points in tree branches. The Coldstream and then the Irish Guards arrived to give support. Men of four battalions fought sporadically through the day, bewildered about everything save the need to shoot at the enemy wherever he appeared. At one point, just as the Grenadiers started an attack some two hundred Germans lying in a root field north of the farm suddenly rose to their feet, put up their hands, and advanced waving a white flag. British soldiers were marshalling these dejected figures as prisoners when another enemy infantry unit began firing on the mingled men without discrimination. George Jeffreys of the Grenadiers wrote: 'I don't believe there was any intentional treachery on the part of the Germans. Their leading line had had enough and meant to surrender. Incidentally they had hardly any ammunition left. Their supports in rear, however, had no intention of surrendering and opened fire when they got a good target. I had no idea what good cover a root field could give to men lying down; they were as invisible in it as partridges.'

No general directed the Soupir battle – battalions and companies simply fought as best they could. Officer losses were crippling. In the Guards regiments which boasted so many aristocrats, blue blood flowed freely: as Lord Guernsey spoke to Lord Arthur Hay, both fell dead to bullets fired by a single skilful German rifleman. The Connaught Rangers suffered 250 casualties, the Grenadiers 120, the Coldstream 178. A young Grenadier private named Parsons collected twelve stragglers of another battalion lacking an officer or NCO, and commanded them all day with notable efficiency, a performance which won him promotion and a mention in dispatches. But Parsons, like so many others, would be dead within weeks.

That evening the Guards dug in, while shells fell on British billets behind the front, half a mile down the hill in Soupir village. Of that night Jeffreys wrote: 'I tried to sleep, but it was too cold, and a row of German wounded … continuously calling out "*Kamerad*" also kept me awake – I had never before realized the meaning of "My wounds stink and are corrupt." These undressed wounds did stink and were corrupt!' When a Connaught Ranger offered Jeffreys a mug of tea, the major was so disgusted by recollections of the Connaughts' alleged poor showing during the retreat that he was tempted to decline, but eventually succumbed to temptation.

The fighting at Cour de Soupir continued through the days that followed, as did the losses. The Germans launched big attacks and made small gains, from which they had to be dislodged. Each clash cost lives, and the British in their turn achieved no important advance. On the afternoon of 16 September, a German shell landed in a quarry on the lip of which a Grenadier company was deployed; all the British wounded lay inside. More than half the Grenadiers, fifty-nine men, were killed immediately, along with eleven men of other units and the only medical officer on the position – Dr Huggan, a celebrated Scottish international rugby player. Class distinction prevailed even in death. The Grenadiers' George Jeffreys read the burial service by torchlight over the British and German other ranks, who were committed to large pits dug by a crossroads. Meanwhile the bodies of the fallen British officers were dispatched down the hill, to be interred in Soupir churchyard.

Capt. Lionel Thurston of the Oxf & Bucks, which joined the Soupir battle, wrote to his family on 20 September: 'A week ago … we came up against the Germans in a prepared position and since then we have not budged an inch, it has been HELL … The place here is a regular cockpit; 150 oxen were roasted to death two days ago, and all the cows have been shot and yesterday, out of the remaining five pigs only two escaped.' Capt. Rosslyn Evelegh was killed by a shell when he rashly exposed himself to put a wounded pig out of its misery. Thurston concluded fastidiously: 'There are about 500 dead Germans lying about 800 yards from our trenches and I really think something should be done about it as they have been there for four days.'

Bernard Gordon-Lennox wrote: 'We were subject to a hell of a bombardment all day … We could from the trenches see a good deal of the German position and could see them digging like blazes too, but their guns are awful hard to find. Throughout the day shrapnel was bursting right over and on us. Ma [Jeffreys] and Doctor Howell, short and fat, came round. Howell says he is giving up "going for strolls".' Some British gunners made a bourgeois little calculation that the afternoon's bombardment of their sector had cost the Germans £35,000 in shells. The new CO of the Grenadiers, Wilfrid Abel-Smith, wrote to his wife: 'The men are splendid and I think their bravery in disregarding danger is largely due to British stupidity. I don't think they realize their danger, which is a great blessing, and makes them stand like rocks, when the highly-strung foreigners can't stick it. But the men are tired, I can see that.'

Though Soupir became especially notorious as a scene of British frustration and blood-letting, the BEF suffered similar experiences along the length of the Chemin des Dames, as did the French on their right. The sugar factory at Cerny became a place of special ill-repute. Casualties bore notably heavily on a handful of regiments. Between 15 and 17 September, the Loyal North Lancashires attacking Troyon lost nine officers killed and five wounded, together with five hundred other ranks. One company, which crossed the Aisne two hundred strong, found itself reduced to two officers and twenty-five men. On the 20th the West Yorkshires were outflanked in a disastrous little action which caused most of the battalion to surrender. The Germans suffered in like measure. Warrant Officer Ernst Nopper recorded on 23 September that his company had shrunk from two hundred men to seventy-four: 'Major Zeppelin wanted to shoot himself when he heard of these losses.'

The men who fought on the Aisne found the experience far worse than anything that had happened to them at Mons or Le Cateau, because the battle was so protracted. On the Chemin des Dames, they began to explore the new nature of warfare, in which operations were continuous and battles went on for weeks on end without respite or decision. Barrages sometimes persisted for hours, with shells landing around a given position at intervals of seconds. A German officer wounded in September said presciently, 'in this war the last word will be spoken by the artillery'. The occupants of the trenches appeared men of mud: baths were a distant memory; few even among the officers contrived to shave; much of the BEF had been wearing the same clothing since Mons.

The character of the struggle was changing, as men grasped a simple message: those who wished to survive must make themselves invisible. Soldiers newly arrived on the Aisne battlefield were struck by its apparent emptiness, at all times save when an attack was in progress. Only the crack and whizz of bullets, the crump of shells, showed that a war was being carried on. At night, they learned to curse the single jumpy soldier, on one side or the other, who fired a shot which provoked a storm of musketry and shelling along the front. Haig asserted on 14 September that 'it was impossible to rely on some of the regiments in the 3rd Division which had been so severely handled at Mons and Le Cateau'. On the 20th he described how the West Yorkshires 'ran away' and had to be forcibly restrained and herded forward again by dragoons.

Back in Britain on 22 September *The Times* wrote: '"Are the Germans giving way?" is the question on all lips.' No, they were not. When Julian Grenfell scowled at a German officer and some men whom they took prisoner, thinking of his own men killed by them, the German looked him in the face and saluted. Grenfell repented of his own anger: 'I have never seen a man look so proud and resolute and smart and confident, in his hour of bitterness. It made me feel terribly ashamed of myself.' Capt. John Macready of the Bedfords wrote:

> Had we but known it, this was the beginning of trench warfare … There was, of course, no wire, and trenches were far apart, the intervening ground being covered with fire. Patrolling went on nightly, through the Boche's lines and back again. We lost many men through sniping, so much so that in one of Allason's forward platoons, no movement whatsoever could be made in daylight. The morale of this post was definitely down … The weather became hot and the smell of dead bodies in the woods was dreadful, both Germans and our own had fallen in odd places and not been discovered. Carcasses of horses and cattle were even worse. Bit by bit we got them buried, but it takes some doing to bury a cow which has swollen to three times its normal size.

British casualties on the Aisne averaged 2,000 a day. One soldier wrote: 'Troops are beginning to get downhearted here, as the Germans have proven themselves to be a better army than we thought … Germans held this same position and beat the French in the 1870 war.' A German artillery NCO, Wilhelm Kaisen, wrote on 2 October: 'I have seen attacks which have caused men to shake their heads in disbelief because they were so mindlessly conducted. Even English officers see that an assault on a front of 6–800 metres against a well-prepared position is a waste of human life.' He asserted that infantrymen went into attacks carrying far too much equipment, making their movements painfully slow, and deplored the grim repetition of horrors: 'First, we shell a village for a day, until everything is destroyed. Then infantry advance with bayonets fixed, and a murderous struggle develops. I watched some Bavarians who discarded their tunics and fought in shirtsleeves, reversing their rifles and laying about them with the stocks. Then enemy artillery fire starts, and an impenetrable pall of smoke and flame descends. Anyone who escapes unscathed is blessed with luck.'

A few months later, when field censorship was established, Kaisen's letter would never have reached its destination, because he asserted that so disastrous were infantry losses that without replacements, neighbouring regiments would have ceased to exist. Within minutes of one lieutenant joining Kaisen's own battery, the young man received a chance shell splinter in the back which rendered him a corpse. Stocks of ammunition of pre-war manufacture were exhausted, making gunners of all the armies dependent on hasty wartime production, of much inferior reliability and accuracy. 'The Germans are brave to the point of utter foolishness,' Capt. Ernest Shepherd of the BEF wrote to a friend in Alabama – implausibly, although himself British he was a former member of the Alabama National Guard. 'Fancy a thousand men massed in regimental formation … coming on unfalteringly to trenches manned by the finest shooting soldiers in the world … This is a very ghastly business, and there has never been its like before.' In truth, of course, there had been its like before – the US Civil War, as Shepherd might have been expected to know. But the collective British consciousness took little heed of the precedent.

Only a few men on either side still affected braggadocio, like a German soldier who wrote home on 4 October: 'one does not take the Englishman seriously over here … You should have seen how those fellows could run … We popped them in cold blood amid gales of laughter. They went down like flies at ranges of up to 12–1300 metres.' So did Germans. On 21 September, Dr Lorenz Treplin told his wife that only a third of his regiment remained; six of its officers had been killed and a further thirty wounded: 'it is terrible how modern war goes on and on'. By now, few men in any army advanced towards the front with any of the illusions of August. German soldier Kresten Andresen, one of the doomed, wrote in his diary on 28 September: 'We are so benumbed that we march off to war without tears and without terror and yet we all know we are on our way into the jaws of Hell. But clad in a stiff uniform, a heart does not beat as it wants to. We aren't ourselves. We're hardly human any longer, at most we are well-drilled automatons who perform every action without any great reflection. O, Lord God, if only we could become human again.'

The Battle of the Aisne officially ended on 16 October, when the BEF relinquished its positions to French territorials. The month-long struggle became a focus of impassioned debate during the years that followed, and indeed after the war. Had Sir John French's army missed a great opportunity, by its sluggishness in pushing forward to the Aisne, crossing the river and exploiting beyond? Could a breakthrough have been achieved by concentrating force on a narrow front, rather than crossing the Aisne in a dozen places? From the outset of the Marne offensive, the British moved embarrassingly slowly, against weak opposition. They never pressed the retreating Germans, who were able to choose their ground on the Aisne, siting their guns at leisure to punish the allies as they crossed the river and strove to exploit beyond it.

More dash and drive might indeed have enabled the BEF to reach the eastern bank with less exertion and fewer losses. But, that said, it is most unlikely that an important strategic opportunity was lost. On the Marne, the German army had been forced into an untenable predicament, but not shattered. Reinforcements were rushed forward to the Chemin des Dames, even as the British scrambled upwards towards the ridge. British field artillery in the valley below, capable only of flat-trajectory fire, could offer negligible support to the hapless infantry above, while German howitzers enjoyed full play. Attempts to reach the high ground were never likely to succeed when men were required to advance fully exposed across open fields – and the Germans were equally handicapped when attacking the other way. The Aisne battle emphasised the lessons of everything that had happened since August: on favourable ground where other things were more or less equal, defenders were hugely advantaged over attackers.

Strange novelties manifested themselves. Cavalrymen clamoured to be issued with bayonets, because they almost invariably fought dismounted. Some artillery horses had been conscripted from farms, and bucked in terror when first they heard their guns go into action. Drivers struggled to control wildly rearing, kicking beasts through the weeks necessary to master their new role – if they lived that long. British soldiers stopped complaining that they were being mocked when enemy units' bands played the tune of the British national anthem, as one did on the Aisne front on 18 September. It was explained to them that the music of 'God Save the King' was also that of 'Heil dir im Siegerkranz', the Kaiser's anthem. Nobody could explain to the soldiers of any army, however, why it was that the heaviest fighting so often took place on Sundays.

On 16 September, Sir John French visited in hospital a group of wounded British officers who asked him what was happening. The commander-in-chief replied: 'at present, stalemate in our favour', which caused one of his hearers to write home in some bewilderment, 'whatever that means'. The C-in-C wrote to King George V, in a letter which gained widespread post-war attention: 'I think the battle of the Aisne is very typical of what battles in the future are most likely to resemble. Siege operations will enter largely into the tactical problems – the spade will be as great a necessity as the rifle, and the heaviest calibres and types of artillery will be brought up in support on either side.'

French's view, and his gloom, were shared on the other side of the hill. Schlieffen had always feared that a campaign of movement might give way to paralysis: 'all along the line the corps will try, as in siege warfare, to come to grips with the enemy from position to position, day and night, advancing, digging in, advancing again, digging in again, etc., using every means of modern science to dislodge the enemy behind his cover'. Now, Schlieffen's apprehension had become reality. 'This trench- and siege-warfare is horrible!' lamented Prince Rupprecht's chief of staff. Grenadier George Jeffreys wrote wearily, shortly before his battalion was relieved by French Territorials: 'One day very like another. There is nearly always shelling.' Freddie Guest, one of Sir John French's ADCs, described the incessant German attacks to a friend at home: 'It beats me how they can get their men to do it,' but added bleakly: 'I am afraid you will see another big casualty list soon.'

The BEF could take pride in the stubbornness with which it held its ground on the Aisne through a month of savage fighting, which gravely depleted many units. But, if the allies had not lost the battle, nor had they won it. Both sides now strove desperately to identify ground somewhere between Switzerland and the sea where manoeuvre might achieve a decision in the vast contest to which they were committed.

'Poor Devils, They Fought Their Ships Like Men'

The clash of armies in continental Europe dominated the First World War, at least until Germany launched its major U-boat campaign in 1917. Yet the British people nursed a persistent delusion that the Royal Navy would fight a great battle against the German High Seas Fleet, because this was what their heritage – and vast expenditure on dreadnoughts – had conditioned them to expect. They wanted a naval showdown, because they believed this would suit their interests, and nursed lasting resentment that they were not allowed to have it. A 'Trafalgar complex' dogged British thinking in 1914, in defiance of the simple logic that the Germans were unlikely to accept an engagement they could not expect to win, because so heavily outnumbered. In the first months of war every detail of the activities of the Royal Navy excited the British public more than anything their soldiers did, though the sailors' role was much less immediately significant.

The English Channel on the morning of 30 July presented a strange spectacle, following the eastward night passage of the Grand Fleet towards its war station at Scapa Flow. Tables, armchairs, even pianos bobbed in its wake: crews had hurled overboard from the columns of great warships every kind of inflammable furniture and fittings, in anticipation of an imminent collision with the enemy. A similar purge was conducted in the German High Seas Fleet. Admiral Franz von Hipper noted in his diary: 'The living spaces look bad. Everything that might burn has been torn out. Cosiness suffers severely from that.'

Junior officers on both sides, and even some senior ones, sustained for more than four years an eagerness to fight which was all the stronger because almost untested. Europe's soldiers quickly learned that war was a ghastly matter for mankind in general and themselves in particular. Sailors did not. Naval cadet Geoffrey Harper of HMS *Endymion* expressed adolescent delight at the expiry of Britain's ultimatum to Germany: 'Very good news.' Lt. Francis Pridham of *Weymouth* noted on 4 August: 'Very great excitement and enthusiasm on board.' Commander John McLeod wrote to his mother: 'If it comes off, it is for me personally what I joined the Navy for. I feel perfectly placid and free from care.'

Filson Young, a journalist who served on the wartime staff of Vice-Admiral Sir David Beatty, principal ornament of the battlecruiser squadron, wrote: 'One profound difference between the Navy and the Army was … [that] when war broke out the life of the Army was revolutionized; it was bodily transferred to a different country, its whole organization and environment were profoundly changed. But the Navy continued to move in its familiar element; its peace routine was so entirely designed for war conditions that the imminence of tremendous issues hardly affected its daily life; instead of having to be ready to fight at twelve hours' notice, it was ready at a moment's.' Britain's seamen, fortified by sublime professional confidence, sought an early opportunity to demonstrate in action their superiority over the enemy.

Yet this did not come. Through the weary months that followed, occupants of the wardrooms and messes of Admiral Sir John Jellicoe's squadrons and flotillas sheepishly replaced the fixtures and fittings they had precipitately ditched in the excitement of taking up war stations. As early as 17 August, Geoffrey Harper lamented: 'The German "High Seas Fleet" has stowed itself away in some port in a blue funk and our own ships can't find anything to blow up – except mines.' He categorised the enemy as 'skulking cowards'.

No British admiral since Lord Howard of Effingham in 1588 had held under his command Britain's entire battlefleet strength. Churchill famously wrote that Jellicoe could 'lose the war in an afternoon' if he blundered on a scale that permitted the Germans to gain dominance of the seas around Britain. Such a belief exercised a critical influence on his contemporaries, and on many historians afterwards. In truth, however, and not for the first or last time, the First Lord employed peerless language to overstate a case. It is unlikely that any stroke by the German surface fleet could have changed the face of the conflict; it lacked the means to impose a blockade on Britain, even if Jellicoe had suffered severe losses. The Royal Navy's grip upon the northern and southern exits from the North Sea precluded serious German interference with Atlantic trade, until U-boats became a major menace in 1917.

The navy, and especially Rear-Admiral Sir Edmund Slade, the economic warfare expert who served as director of naval intelligence from 1907 to

1909, had long feared a surface campaign against British commerce, which seemed a more realistic option for the Germans than a direct challenge to the Grand Fleet. The Admiralty sought to pre-empt such a threat by preparing a fleet of 'defensively-armed merchant carriers' – civilian ships modified to carry guns – of which forty were in service by 1914. Ironically, given the howls of outrage when *Lusitania* was sunk by a U-boat in 1915, both that Cunard liner and her sister ship *Mauretania* had received large government subsidies for their construction because they were earmarked for war service as armed merchant cruisers, though never employed in the role. Following the outbreak of war, the Admiralty expressed fears that some of the twenty-one German liners sheltering in neutral New York might be fitted with guns and sally forth into the Atlantic, wreaking havoc upon trade and vulnerable to destruction only by British battlecruisers. But Grand-Admiral Tirpitz was slow to explore the potential of an economic warfare campaign: British merchantmen were molested by only a handful of German surface raiders, which were soon hunted down and sunk.

The guardians of Britain's naval mastery, the crews of scores of warships anchored in serried ranks inside Scapa Flow, would have preferred to fulfil their duties against a more rewarding backdrop than the Orkney Islands, chosen as the only anchorage in the eastern British Isles large enough for the Grand Fleet that could be protected from hostile intrusion. Treeless Scapa appealed chiefly to bird-watchers, with its summer profusion of guillemots, terns, kittiwakes, skuas, razorbills. For sailors allowed ashore, there was a muddy football pitch, a dismal canteen and an officers' golf course on the island of Flotta, where each battleship maintained an assigned hole. Even some captains and admirals were to be found assuaging boredom by tending little vegetable gardens. Below decks, illicit gambling flourished.

But at least the Grand Fleet was free to plough the North Sea when it chose. Its enemies were not, and the men of the High Seas Fleet languished in their inglorious predicament. When crews returned to Wilhelmshaven to coal after brief sorties, they ventured ashore apprehensively: Germany expected them to fight, and they were not fighting. 'Boredom feeds depression,' wrote Seaman Richard Stumpf. 'Everywhere people express disgruntlement at our inactivity.' In the forward turret of Stumpf's ship *Helgoland*, a map of the Western Front was marked daily with the latest German advances. It became a focus of attention for a rotating crowd of gloomy sailors, who contrasted the army's triumphs with their own inertia. They complained that the ship's officers intensified kit inspections merely to alleviate the mind-numbing tedium of awakening each morning to an unchanging view of Schillig Roads.

The British economic blockade of Germany was in the early war years largely ineffectual, because of divisions of responsibility and uncertainty of purpose in Whitehall: the Foreign Office was preoccupied with avoiding a diplomatic showdown with neutrals, above all the United States. The Board of Trade strove to sustain British commerce. Not only did a steady flow of vital commodities reach Germany via Scandinavia and Rotterdam, but so too did large quantities of British exports, including Welsh coal and Cadbury's chocolate. Extraordinary as it may seem, the City of London continued to finance and insure many cargoes destined for Germany, and some of these were carried in British ships. The navy was denied authorisation to take the critical step towards implementing a blockade, laying minefields across the North Sea. There were chronic doubts and disputes about the legality of a tight blockade, which the United States – among others – saw as breaching both the 1856 Declaration of Paris and the 1909 Declaration of London. The Germans missed an important diplomatic trick by failing to mobilise neutral opinion against British blockading operations, while themselves incurring intense odium when they later launched unrestricted U-boat warfare. The British failure until 1917 to create a convincing blockade of Germany was an extraordinary manifestation of the government's failure to grip the imperatives of total war.

During August, Jellicoe's light forces busied themselves patrolling the North Sea, sinking enemy fishing vessels and warning British and neutral ships of the outbreak of war. In those days before radio receivers became universal, many vessels remained oblivious of Europe's turmoil until they entered a port. On 9 August, a German cruiser captured a Belgian schooner whose crew had no notion they had become enemies. An ignorantly friendly German trawler's crew cheered lustily as the British cruiser *Southampton* closed in to seize her. One of *Southampton*'s officers, Lt. Stephen King-Hall, observed wryly that his own wardroom's noticeboard still bore a five-week-old postcard from officers of the battleship *Schleswig-Holstein* who had visited them during Kiel regatta. 'We all hope to see you again,' the Kaiser's men had written.

Southampton was party to several minor skirmishes around Britain's coasts: one occurred early on Monday, 10 August, just north of Kinnaird Head, when jangling alarm bells summoned sailors from their hammocks to action stations. They stumbled sleepily onto the upper decks in the dawn, to find their sister ship *Birmingham* firing her guns at a target invisible to them in the haze. Suddenly the conning tower of a German submarine broke the surface of the sea, water cascading off its plates, midway between the two warships. *Birmingham* swung her helm and rammed. Moments later, only a black pool of oil marked the grave of U15, first of its tribe sunk by the Royal Navy. There were similar excitements across the North Sea: on 21 August off Borkum, lookouts on SMS *Rostock* sighted a British submarine and narrowly evaded two of its torpedoes. One of the cruiser's officers, Lt. Reinhold Knobloch, noted: 'This … was a salutary lesson for us. We saw that the enemy was indeed something real.'

Despite such brief scurries, a sense of anti-climax suffused British and German mess decks alike. Few sailors were rich in imagination, and most responded with shameless immaturity to the catastrophe of European war. Lt. Rudolph Firle, commanding a German torpedo-boat flotilla, wrote as early as 6 August: 'It becomes deeply boring. One imagined the war as if there was a "Hurrah" immediately after the declaration, followed by an attack and outcome … Enemy not here to be seen, so it's hard to maintain morale.' Reinhold Knobloch felt the same: 'Morale slides because we thought the war would be something different … Nothing is going on … A tremendous carelessness and boredom prevails on board. The men of the army are envied.'

Filson Young wrote: 'The naval mind was in the position of a swimmer who has trained and practised for a contest, brought himself to the pink of condition, and stands, stripped and ready, on the edge of the diving-board waiting for the word to go – and is expected to continue holding himself in that attitude of expectation for three or four years. Nothing more trying to the spirit could possibly be devised.' For years the British government had lavished a quarter of its entire tax revenue on the country's beloved navy. Politicians as well as the public now expected a return on their money. While the army was too small to exercise much immediate influence on the land war, surely the Royal Navy could strike out, humbling the Kaiser's pretensions in Britain's natural element?

Churchill was eager to land an army on the German coast. As First Lord of the Admiralty, since his appointment in 1911 he had treated the Royal Navy with proprietorial enthusiasm. He sought to indulge a personal whim by christening one of the Grand Fleet's new battleships *Oliver Cromwell*, a proposal not unreasonably vetoed by King George V. Now, Churchill's dearest wish was to see 'his' fleet fight. He behaved more like its commander-in-chief than a mere political overseer, and intervened constantly in operational matters, to the fury of the admirals. He was also accused of surrounding himself with indifferent officers whose only merit was a willingness to do his bidding. But voices of reason were successful in opposing the First Lord's amphibious fantasies, fortunately for those who would have had to sacrifice their lives to realise them.

If there was to be no landing on German shores, how then could the navy make its strength felt? The British were confronted with the difficulty of fighting a great land power. The High Seas Fleet commanded by Admiral Friedrich von Ingenohl had no intention of challenging the British in the North Sea, unless or until it could do so on favourable terms. Its big ships put to sea only on rare occasions, when there seemed a chance of catching a detachment of the Grand Fleet unsupported by its main strength.

Thus the first weeks of war passed at sea in bathos and disappointment; in place of a great action, there was only a series of incidents – colourful enough, to be sure, but bereft of grandeur. Every naval officer yearned to fight his war like a gentleman. Reinhold Knobloch felt embarrassed when his ship was employed to destroy some British trawlers, after their crews had been taken off: 'It does not make us feel good to sink unarmed steamers.' Captain Karl von Müller of the light cruiser *Emden*, raiding British commerce in the Pacific and Indian Oceans, was one of the few German naval officers who inspired the admiration of his foes. Lt. William Parry noted: 'She [the *Emden*] is undoubtedly doing jolly well, and moreover is behaving in a gentlemanly way.'

To romantics, Britain's First Lord foremost among them, it all seemed deeply disappointing. Here was the Grand Fleet, gowned and bejewelled like some noble heiress for a naval ball in the midst of the North Sea, and no guests would come. The sailors should have anticipated such a situation, but for years before the outbreak of war, both sides' admiralties were vague about what would follow mobilisation and implementation of defensive measures. 'The Navy are very bad at war,' wrote Churchill impatiently in 1912. 'Their one idea is to fight bull-headed.' This was not entirely fair, given the amount of energy senior sailors devoted to planning blockades, but it was true that fleet action was their chief preoccupation. Meawhile on the other side, intelligent German officers understood that the Kaiser's naval enthusiasm had sufficed to expend many millions of marks to create a substantial navy – but not one strong enough to meet Jellicoe's squadrons with a realistic prospect of victory.

At Coblenz on 18 August Falkenhayn demanded of Tirpitz why the High Seas Fleet had not struck out at the allies. The grand-admiral

answered: because such a course would be suicidal – comparable to marching a single army corps against St Petersburg. Falkenhayn said contemptuously, 'in that case the fleet is useless. It would be better to bring its sailors
ashore.' Tirpitz pressed his argument: the duty of the High Seas Fleet was
to protect Germany's interests afloat, and these would scarcely be advanced
by hurling it headlong against the superior might of the allies. The admiral
later confided to his staff that he feared the navy would become a scape-
goat for the nation's disappointments in the war, and he was not far wrong.
The incoherence of the pre-war vision of Germany's most famous sailor
was laid bare. Tirpitz, far from being the architect of his nation's naval
greatness, proved merely to have persuaded his master, the Kaiser, to waste
prodigious resources on an enormous armed yacht squadron.

Jellicoe, meanwhile, recognised that his most important duty was to
preserve Britain's superiority at sea, by eschewing recklessness and even
boldness. 'It was quite clear that the Commander-in-Chief's principal
concern was to protect his Fleet from danger,' wrote one of Beatty's officers
of the battlecruiser squadron. 'His strategy was not a little puzzling to that
part of the Fleet which was operating in the North Sea itself, and hoped
for nothing better than to come to immediate grips with the enemy.'
During Fleet exercises, when 'enemy' destroyers launched torpedo attacks
Jellicoe invariably turned away, causing a battlecruiser officer to assert
caustically, 'If he does that when the Germans attack he can't be defeated,
but he can't win.'

Yet though the Royal Navy fumbled some early skirmishes at sea, it
nonetheless played a significant role in denying victory to Germany in
1914. The BEF was transported to France without losing a man to enemy
action, an operation masterminded by Sir Edmund Slade. Despite minor
German interference with trade routes, and some sinkings of merchantmen, allied commerce continued almost unimpeded, a priceless advantage
over the Central Powers. The German and Austrian press denounced the
allied blockade as the warmaking of cowardice: 'They Want to Starve us
Out!' read one headline. Whatever its shortcomings in implementation,
the Royal Navy's interdiction of enemy shipping movements caused the
Central Powers substantial difficulties from an early stage of the war. That
autumn, all the warring armies found themselves short of baggage and
draught animals, vital to mobility, because hundreds of thousands of
horses and mules had foundered or been killed. The British and French
were able to purchase replacements in the United States, Argentina,
Australia, and ship them to Europe. The Germans, however, could not do

this. They were obliged to depend on conscripting ever more beasts from the continental territories under their control, where agriculture was already crippled by loss of draught animals. Transport shortages hampered the German army's operations. Lack of imported fertilisers impacted severely upon German food production. These were humdrum issues, viewed against popular expectations of a Nelsonian clash. But naval lieutenant Hermann Graf von Schweinitz was half-right when he wrote in his diary, shaking his head at Britain's mighty array of warships: 'They control the oceans on all sides ... That makes all our victories on land irrelevant.'

The longer allied planners contemplated their position, the more appealing it seemed to avoid any grand gamble, to focus instead on maintaining the status quo, in a fashion which coincided with German thinking. Admiral Hugo von Pohl, later naval C-in-C, declared: 'nothing could turn out better for the English, and nothing could so damage our [reputation], as that our fleet should be the loser in a serious engagement'. Hipper, commanding Germany's battlecruisers, wrote on 6 August: 'If we were to risk battle now ... we would not only gain no success but our High Seas Fleet would disappear in a trice – the best possible outcome for England.' For both sides deterrence and defence, preservation of assets in being, became the dominant theme of the next four years, at the expense of offensive action.

Yet elements of the Grand Fleet were always at sea, exercising or patrolling in all weathers. Sailings, often at night, were intensely romantic events for those stationed on upper decks, one of whom wrote: 'The dark shapes round you melted into the surrounding void, the loom of the land faded into the universal blackness, and there set in that blowing which was the wind of destiny, which would not cease until you touched the shores of death or of home again. Before you and on either hand was absolute blackness; behind you one shadow of grosser blackness, which was the ship astern; and from blackness into blackness, nose to tail, thirty thousand tons apiece, we were rushing at twenty miles an hour. And that was ... routine.'

Routine did not suffice, however, for the Royal Navy's eager spirits: senior officers began to think furiously about how they might carry the struggle to the enemy. Two Young Turks – submarine commodore Roger Keyes and Harwich destroyer commodore Reginald Tyrwhitt, conceived the idea of surprising the German light forces which by day and night swept Heligoland Bight, the High Seas Fleet's home waters. They proposed luring some of Ingenohl's destroyers within range of the guns and torpedoes of a superior force of British warships and submarines, at a low tide when German dreadnoughts could not get out of harbour across the Jade bar. The Admiralty initially rejected this notion out of hand. Keyes was an officer of modest intelligence but immense dash and energy. He had made his name as the hero of many adventures in China's 1900 Boxer Rising, for instance once conning a railway train through a throng of enemies, holding a revolver against the engineer's head. Now, figuratively speaking, he used an equally bold gambit – appealing over the heads of the admirals, direct to the First Lord. Churchill immediately embraced Keyes's plan, and ordered its execution.

Three surfaced British submarines were to provide bait to tempt the Germans to pursuit. Behind them, some fifty small warships would approach within a few miles of the Kaiser's principal naval base. If the raid went wrong and the High Seas Fleet's dreadnoughts became involved, a fiasco could follow: no unarmoured ship could survive the fire of one which mounted heavy guns. The only insurance designed into the original plan was that two British battlecruisers should lurk forty miles north-westwards. The operation was designed to resurrect sixteenth-century memories of Drake at Cadiz and 'singeing the King of Spain's beard'. But such was the Admiralty's hamfistedness that it was launched without Jellicoe being consulted or informed until 26 August, the day it began.

Keyes's submarines were first to sail, accompanied by their commodore in the destroyer *Lurcher*. Lt. Oswald Frewen of the destroyer *Lookout*, also earmarked to participate, noted that he disliked having two days' notice of a battle: 'I would have preferred it to come upon us suddenly. I am imaginative, & also constitutionally pessimistic, & I do not in the least require 2 days to think things over!' Next day Frewen's ship put to sea with Tyrwhitt's flotillas, thirty-two destroyers in all. The commodore flew his flag in the brand-new light cruiser *Arethusa*, which proved a mistake, because the vessel was unready to fight.

Jellicoe – cautious, sensible, instinctively controlling – now voiced alarm about the whole business. Committed to concentration of force, he proposed to take the Grand Fleet to sea, and cruise where he could intervene if opportunity beckoned or disaster threatened. The Admiralty dismissed this idea, but grudgingly authorised him to commit the rest of the battlecruiser squadron. Beatty thus sailed for Heligoland early on 27 August – the day after Le Cateau – with six light cruisers in support. Jellicoe then took his own decision to defy the Admiralty and lead his major units south, though only in a distant supporting role. This was an operation conceived on impulse and fumbled into execution, which none-theless became a significant marker buoy in the history of the war at sea: the first occasion on which the Royal Navy sallied in strength, with a pros-pect of battle. Column upon column of lean grey ships steamed forth across the North Sea from their several anchorages. Some captains were bent upon doing something great for England; others sought merely to avert a disaster.

The age of the dreadnought had created a new hierarchy of twentieth-century seamen: officers of the big ships, almost all deemed 'gentlemen' save the engineers, enjoyed considerable comforts and kept some state, in port at least. Three nights a week the ship's band played outside Beatty's cabin as he and his guests dined in mess undress uniform; on other evenings, the musicians performed outside the wardroom. Among humbler personnel, working conditions varied. Engine-room staffs laboured deep in the hulls, amid heat, noise and filth resembling that of a steelworks. 'The least informed could always tell when we were going to sea,' wrote an officer, 'by the songs that used to rise from the messdecks as soon as the orders to the engine-room department to raise steam had been given; the whole ship began to murmur with strange music, like a hive.' Not everyone approved of the choristers: a stoker petty officer requested *Lion*'s senior engineering officer: 'Please to make an order that the men at the furnaces were not to sing in action, as he found it impossible to make himself heard in D boiler room.'

In oil-fired ships working conditions were tolerable, save in very hot weather, but feeding coal to the furnaces of older vessels was a gruelling routine, and bunker replenishment was every crew's dirtiest and most detested duty. Stokers and trimmers below the waterline were among the least likely men to survive a sinking, and well they knew it. Through every moment at sea, they were vulnerable to an inrushing torrent if the ship struck a mine or was torpedoed. Elsewhere, seamen and heavy guns' crews of large vessels enjoyed the privileges of effective heating and ventilation, and most were protected from the elements. There was plenty to eat – far more than working-class civilians enjoyed in peace or war. Aboard a British battlecruiser, some 2,000 eggs were cooked each morning, a further 1,000 at night; a seaman would think nothing of eating six eggs for breakfast.

Those who served aboard light cruisers, destroyers and smaller vessels, however, endured in heavy weather conditions almost as harsh as those of Nelson's era. On watch or manning turretless guns in action, on decks and even bridges only a few feet above the sea, they were forever drenched, numbed and shivering, whipped by half-frozen spray, with no prospect when their watches ended of drying bodies or clothing in the dankness of the mess decks. Yet the men who manned small, fast surface ships and submarines prided themselves that they were members of an elite. U-boat officer Johannes Spies exulted in his lifestyle, despite its chronic stench and discomfort: 'In the clear seawater, when the sun is shining the silvery air bubbles sparkle all over the boat's hull and rise as in an aquarium. At times when the boat was lying still on the sea bottom we could observe fish swimming by the ports of our conning tower, attracted by the electric light shining through.' Destroyer crews likewise revelled in the thrill of rushing across the sea at speeds exceeding 30 mph. As one such 'ocean greyhound' left its anchorage, a fanciful listener likened the whisper of its racing hull through the water to the tearing of silk. There was human hardship aboard, but also romance.

The battlecruisers' commander, Vice-Admiral Sir David Beatty, who would play a significant role in Heligoland Bight, was already acclaimed as the most dashing sailor of his time, a star alike of the bridge and the chaise-longue. He was blessed with some ability, intense pugnacity and boundless self-esteem. His favourite journalist, Filson Young, described Beatty as 'young, distinguished-looking indeed, but more with the distinction of Pall Mall than of Plymouth Hoe'. Beatty first sprang to public notice commanding a Nile gunboat in Kitchener's 1898 Khartoum campaign, and achieved financial security by marrying Ethel, daughter of Chicago department-store tycoon Marshall Field. Critics considered the admiral a cad of the first water, citing his dalliances with junior officers' wives and penchant for shooting sitting gamebirds.

He was nonetheless a man after Winston Churchill's heart: before the war the First Lord had rescued Beatty's career from the breaker's yard when he was placed on half-pay following a contemptuous and almost unprecedented rejection of the post of second-in-command of the Atlantic Fleet. Churchill gave him instead the service's juiciest plum, the battle-cruiser squadron. In 1914 Beatty was forty-three, an age at which the average naval officer aspired to a mere captaincy. *Lion*, in which he flew his flag, became the most publicised ship of the 1914–18 war. Most of Beatty's officers adored him, but before the war was done his promotion of unworthy favourites and neglect of technical issues, especially communications, would expose dangerous shortcomings; Beatty possessed less of Nelson's genius – and luck – than he and the British public supposed.

In the early morning of 28 August, however, such revelations lay in the future, as British forces converged on Heligoland Bight. Most were blithely unaware of each other's presence, thanks to the operation's slapdash preparation as a 'come-as-you-are' party. Beatty signalled his squadron as it sailed: 'Know very little, shall hope to learn more as we go along.' The Royal Navy suffered not merely from a confused chain of command, but also from inadequate communications. Its wirelesses were less powerful than those of the Germans. An Admiralty telegram informing Keyes and Tyrwhitt that Beatty would be joining the operation failed to reach them before they sailed: the destroyer commodore discovered that the battle-cruisers were coming only when he met Commodore William Goodenough's light cruisers at sea. Exchanges in action relied chiefly on Nelson's technology – flag signals. Over short distances these were more reliable than wireless, but they became unreadable in poor weather, and their eighteenth-century efficacy was impaired in the twentieth by increased warship speeds and funnel smoke. Beatty's flag-lieutenant was an epic bungler, whose shortcomings adversely influenced British operations in the North Sea through the ensuing two years.

At first light, the three submarines acting as bait surfaced as planned and advanced close to the island of Heligoland, where they were duly spotted by the Germans. Action was brought on by one of Hipper's destroyers, which at 7 a.m. sighted Tyrwhitt's flotillas and warned the admiral. Low tide prevented German heavy units from putting to sea, as Keyes and Tyrwhitt had anticipated, but Hipper ordered eight light cruisers to sail as fast as they could raise steam, which took some ships three hours. A confused, desultory series of destroyer actions meanwhile began, as if several fox hunts were simultaneously pursuing quarry across the same country. The British ships exposed themselves within range of shore batteries, but were spared their attentions because visibility fell to 5,000 yards, mist blinding the gunners.

At 8 a.m., Tyrwhitt's skirmishing activities were interrupted by the appearance of the first two of Hipper's light cruisers, *Frauenlob* and *Stettin*. In accordance with doctrine, the British turned and fell back on their own cruisers, *Arethusa* and *Fearless*, which joined a fierce exchange of fire. Now, however, the British flagship revealed its unreadiness: all but one of its guns jammed and fell silent. The Germans hit the 3,500-ton *Arethusa* again and again, the accuracy of their fire displaying an embarrassing superiority over that of Goodenough's ships. Back in August 1913, the British naval attaché in Berlin, Capt. Hugh Watson, wrote in a valedictory dispatch: 'I see no reason to think the German naval officers ... are inferior to their British comrades ... From what I know ... I think that in the day of trial [they] will be proved more capable than the officers of navies with which we are politically more closely allied.' He meant the French and Russians, and he was right, as was revealed on 28 August. The German navy was a young service, devoid of any heritage comparable with that of its foe, but in Heligoland Bight its seamen showed courage and skill.

Arethusa was saved because her one remaining 6-inch gun achieved a lucky hit, exploding on *Frauenlob*'s bridge, which was reduced to a tangle of twisted steel. Thirty-seven of the crew were killed or wounded, including the captain. The German ship was obliged to turn and limp away, leaving *Arethusa* in desperate straits, having lost speed and begun to take in water. Almost immediately, Tyrwhitt's ships met a new group of their German counterparts, homebound from patrol; five destroyers escaped, but one was trapped and sunk in a hail of fire, her colours flying and guns blazing to the last.

The British had just started to rescue survivors when the cruiser *Stettin* raced back into action, after a brief withdrawal to bring its boilers to full power. Tyrwhitt's destroyers turned away as shells bracketed them, abandoning two of their boats full of German prisoners and ten British sailors. These orphans were pondering their fate on a temporarily empty sea when Keyes's submarine E-4 surfaced alongside, took aboard Tyrwhitt's sailors and three German officers 'as a sample', then submerged again. Everybody was determined to be seen to behave honourably: E-4's captain left the enemy with water, biscuits, a compass and course for Heligoland, fourteen miles away.

The time was still not much after 8 a.m., but an eventful day was unfolding in the Bight. During the next hour, there were some minutes of farce after Roger Keyes spotted four-funnel cruisers. Having no notion that any such British ships were at sea, he reported them by radio to the distant battlecruiser *Invincible* as enemies, and hastily fled in little *Lurcher*. When this confusion was sorted out, Keyes expressed alarm lest his submarines, still unaware that the big ships were in fact British, tried to sink them. One such attempt mercifully failed, as did *Southampton*'s effort to ram the offending British E-boat.

At 10.17, Tyrwhitt exploited a lull in the battle to heave to – taking a huge risk in seas where U-boats might naturally be expected. He called *Fearless* alongside his crippled *Arethusa*; for twenty minutes, the two ships lay dead in the water while their crews laboured frantically to clear jammed guns and restore power. By the time this was achieved, the British had been in Heligoland Bight some four hours, and it was obvious enemy reinforcements must be on the way. The tide remained too low for big ships to move, but three more of Hipper's light cruisers appeared just as *Arethusa* restarted her engines, and commenced firing on the British raiding force.

This development was scarcely unexpected, but caused Tyrwhitt to signal Beatty, still almost two hours' steaming away: 'Am attacked by large cruiser … Respectfully request that I may be supported. Am hard pressed.' The commodore gained a respite when the German light cruisers turned away in the face of a massed British destroyer torpedo attack. But Beatty recognised that a hornets' nest was stirring in Heligoland Bight. He did not know what enemy forces, and especially submarines, might face him there, but felt personally challenged by Tyrwhitt's signal. High on the bridge of *Lion*, he turned to Ernle Chatfield, his flag captain: 'What do you think we should do? I ought to go forward and support Tyrwhitt, but if I lose one of these valuable ships, the country will not forgive me.' Chatfield responded, with the easy enthusiasm of the man not in charge, 'surely we should go'. At 11.35 Beatty swung his mighty column – *Lion*, *Queen Mary*, *Princess Royal*, *Invincible* and *New Zealand* – at twenty-seven knots towards the Bight.

In sailors' eyes, each giant had its own defined character: *Queen Mary* and *New Zealand* were deemed crack ships; *Princess Royal* was the jolliest socially; *Lion* seemed a trifle gloomy, perhaps because of the weighty presence of the admiral and his staff. Now, all these embodiments of British naval prestige were steaming hard towards the Kaiser's front door. Beatty's decision to intervene was brave and probably inevitable, given that he had been sent with orders to provide support for Tyrwhitt, but nonetheless highly dangerous. In Nelson's time, it was an extraordinary occurrence for a line-of-battle ship to fall victim to any save a vessel of comparable size. In 1914, by contrast, while dreadnoughts remained impregnable to smaller ships' guns, they were highly vulnerable to mines and torpedoes, the latter enabling small warships to wield immense destructive power, in a fashion that seemed monstrously unfair to the schoolboy minds of some sailors.

Geoffrey Harper wrote: 'I always had a feeling against submarines and nothing would induce me to go in for them because I always thought they were not exactly the Navy, and now I have become quite certain … It is rotten and underhand and like stabbing a man in the back … I am not the only one who is against submarine warfare, I come across people everywhere whose general opinion is: It's not fair, I don't like it. Of course our submarines are as much to blame as the enemy's. Anyone, of any nationality, who serves in a submarine is not playing the game.' Such nonsenses aside, at midday on 28 August Beatty's squadron was taking a considerable chance by advancing towards the unknown perils of the Bight, for the honour of the Royal Navy more than for any more substantial prize.

Ahead of the battlecruisers, the action was drifting westwards: the 4,350-ton *Mainz* joined the fray, firing hard at British destroyers, of which eleven launched torpedoes at the light cruiser without effect. Tyrwhitt's ships felt the heat of *Mainz*'s superbly accurate fire: its first salvo hit *Laurel*, detonating shells in her ready racks, blowing away the after funnel and severely wounding the captain; *Liberty*'s mast disappeared overboard, her bridge was hit and her captain killed; *Laertes* received a full salvo which temporarily stopped her dead in the water. Disaster again threatened the British, until *Mainz* astonished them by turning away at full speed. German lookouts had spotted three of Commodore Goodenough's cruisers closing fast. Their ship, however, retired too late: within seconds, British 6-inch shells were hitting *Mainz* hard. Tyrwhitt's destroyers launched another flurry of torpedoes, at the cost of themselves taking a succession of gunfire hits from the doughty German. Almost all the torpedoes missed, but just one struck *Mainz*, inflicting grievous damage upon her propulsion system. Slowing in the water, she became an easy mark for the British cruisers, which now steamed past in succession, pounding her from end to end.

'Every salvo they fired brought a perfect tornado of hits,' said *Mainz*'s first lieutenant later. 'I counted every salvo by the flash: one, two, three, four, five, then the shells would reach us, scattering death and destruction. Every broadside that struck us shook the whole ship.' On *Southampton*, Stephen King-Hall wrote:

A most extraordinary feeling of exultation filled the mind. One longed for more yellow flashes; one wanted to hurt her, to torture her; and one said to oneself, 'Ha! There's another! Give her hell!', as if by speaking one could make the guns hit her. Though she was being hit, she was not being hit enough, as at the range of 10,000 yards in that mist it was nearly impossible to see the splashes of the shells and thus control the fire. Also she still had the legs of us. To our dismay, the mist came down, and for five minutes we drove on without sight of her.

Down below, in complete ignorance of what had been happening, the stokers forced the boilers until our turbines could take no more, and the safety valves lifting, the steam roared up the exhaust pipes at the side of the funnels with a deafening roar. Suddenly – everything happens suddenly in a naval action with ships moving at 30 miles an hour – we came on top of the *Mainz* only 7,000 yards away, and the range decreasing every moment. Something had happened to her whilst she was in the mist, for she was lying nearly stopped ... We closed down on her, hitting with every salvo. At irregular intervals one of her after guns fired a solitary shot, which passed miles overhead. In ten minutes she was silenced and lay a smoking, battered wreck, her foremost anchor flush with the water. Ant-like figures could be seen jumping into the water as we approached. The sun dispersed the mist, and we steamed slowly to within 300 yards of her, flying as we did so the signal 'DO YOU SURRENDER?', in international code. As we stopped, the mainmast slowly leant forward and, like a great tree, quite gradually lay down along the deck.

By 12.50 it was obvious *Mainz* was finished, and Roger Keyes ordered *Lurcher* alongside. He wrote: 'She had settled considerably by the bows, the after part was crowded with men, many terribly wounded; the battery was a ghastly shambles, amidships she was a smouldering furnace, two of her funnels had collapsed and the wreckage appeared to be red-hot; the heat scorched one's face as far off as the bridge of the *Lurcher*, everything was dyed saffron with the fumes of our lyddite shells.' The destroyer took off 220 survivors. One man, a young German officer who had been directing the removal of the wounded, refused to go. Keyes addressed him personally, saying that he had 'done splendidly, we must clear out, he must come at once, there was nothing more he could do'. The lean, twinkling-eyed British commodore held out his hand. The German stiffened, saluted, and said, 'Thank you, no.' There was a happy postscript to this charmingly soppy episode: a few moments later, when the cruiser rolled over and sank – her starboard propeller narrowly missing *Lurcher*, going full speed astern – the young man accepted rescue from the water.

Eight German light cruisers were now closing on the scene, once more threatening the British with superior firepower. Fortunately for the forces of Tyrwhitt, Goodenough and Keyes, their enemies' movements were uncoordinated. Each German ship in turn attempted sporadic lunges, then dashed away when threatened by heavier metal. Around 12.30 p.m. the battered *Arethusa* once more became a target for German cruiser fire.

Tyrwhitt, on her bridge, said afterwards: 'I really was beginning to feel a bit blue.' The British were momentarily alarmed to see the shape of a big ship looming out of the haze to westward. Then, to their boundless relief and noisily-expressed delight, *Lion* and the rest of the battlecruisers were identified. Thousands of men aboard the British light cruisers and destroyers watched exultantly as Beatty led his column of 30,000-ton monsters at full speed past them, each throwing up a fine bow wave, black funnel-smoke streaming behind, wakes boiling.

Now it became the battlecruisers' engagement. Beatty's crews were keyed to the highest pitch. 'As we approached,' wrote Chatfield, at his post with the admiral on *Lion*'s bridge, 'everyone was at action stations, the guns loaded, the range-finders manned, the control alert, the signalmen's binoculars and telescopes scanning the misty horizon … One could scarcely see two miles. Suddenly the report of guns was heard … [and] on our port bow, we saw … the flash … through the mist. Were they friendly or hostile? No shell could be seen falling. Beatty stood by the compass, his glasses scanning the scene. At length we made out the hulk of a cruiser [*Mainz*] … Her funnel had fallen and her foremast had been shot away, a fire raged on her upper deck … "Leave her to them," said Beatty. "Don't fire!"'

The admiral sought instead to engage the undamaged German light cruisers, and a few moments later his ships' vast turrets traversed, the guns elevated, and amid successive thundering detonations they began to hurl charges across the Bight. Of the enemy ships in sight, *Strassburg* made a successful escape, but *Köln* with her tiny 4-inch guns made pathetic efforts to return fire as 12- and 13.5-inch shells landed with pulverising effect. A minute or two of such devastation reduced her upperworks to flame and tangled steel. A few moments later *Ariadne* suffered the same fate, and still Beatty's column raced on. But the admiral knew time was running out: the moment the tide permitted, German battleships would be out. After forty minutes in the Bight, with the enemy coastline close at hand, at 1.10 p.m. he made a signal to all British forces: 'Retire.' As they swung westwards, *Lion* fired two more salvos to finish off *Köln*, which promptly disappeared stern-first beneath the waves. It was two days before the Germans chanced on a lone survivor from the cruiser; in the interval, a junior admiral and more than five hundred men had perished.

At 2.25 p.m., with the British an hour gone, Ingenohl's big ships at last arrived on the scene, made a cautious sweep, then returned to port, as did the Grand Fleet, which had cruised two hundred miles north of the engagement. Aboard *Lion*, a throng of ecstatic sailors clustered beneath the bridge to cheer their adored admiral. *Arethusa* was towed home at six knots. On 30 August the battlecruisers and light cruisers reached Scapa Flow, to be received with a welcoming roar from men lining the decks and upperworks of every ship of the Grand Fleet.

Three German light cruisers and a destroyer had been sunk, three more cruisers damaged. On the British side, *Arethusa* and three destroyers were badly damaged, but all had returned afloat. Only thirty-five men had been killed, an amazingly small 'butcher's bill' alongside the Germans' 712. Churchill, euphoric, boarded Tyrwhitt's flagship at Sheerness to distribute laurels; he later called Heligoland Bight 'a brilliant episode'. The public were thrilled, and Beatty became hero of the hour. The admiral was 'disgusted' to receive no message of appreciation from the Admiralty, but wrote to Ethel about the Germans with the condescension of a man of his time: 'Poor devils, they fought their ships like men and went down with colours flying like seamen against overwhelming odds ... Whatever their faults, they are gallant.'

The action was immensely serviceable to the British government in the midst of the retreat from Mons, a time of acute national tension about events in France. At the Admiralty Norman Macleod wrote: 'This little battle has had a very cheering effect as showing morale of navy & unlikelihood of invasion.' Asquith expressed delight that 'Winston's little scheme ... has come off very well ... some set-off to our sad losses on land.' In the mood of self-congratulation that followed, few of the questions were asked that should have been: about the shambolic British planning and lack of a clear command chain; failures of communication and indifferent gunnery. Not only were shells poorly aimed, but many which achieved hits failed to explode, or to inflict significant damage: fuses were unreliable and often caused premature detonation. British submarines deployed in the Bight achieved nothing. Had not Jellicoe, on his own initiative, dispatched Beatty to support the raid, Tyrwhitt's and Keyes's force could have been badly mauled by the enemy's light cruisers. A moment's bad luck might have cost a battlecruiser. The Commander-in-Chief believed that the risks of this daring gamble exceeded the rewards.

Yet there were larger, psychological forces in play which were, and remain, underrated by critics of the Heligoland Bight action. Its impact on the High Seas Fleet went far beyond the trifling material losses. German sailors recognised that they had suffered a humiliation. British ships had steamed and skirmished with impunity within a few miles of the coast of the Fatherland. Hundreds of thousands of civilians ashore had heard the gunfire, and trembled. Admiral Tirpitz raged, not least because his son Wolfgang was a lieutenant in the lost *Mainz*. He spoke in extravagant terms to Albert Hopman: 'We disgraced ourselves. I knew that I had to sacrifice my son. But this is dreadful. We came under fire, and in consequence saw the end of our fleet.' Tirpitz refused to be comforted by Hopman's reminder that the British had recovered German survivors: his son might be among them. He persuaded himself the young officer must be dead. Yet next day, the British sent word that they indeed held young Tirpitz as a prisoner.

The Heligoland operation emphasised the Royal Navy's moral dominance over its enemies, which would persist until 1918. The Kaiser was confirmed in his respect for British seapower, and ordered that thenceforward the High Seas Fleet must operate with the utmost circumspection; its big ships could take the offensive only with his personal consent. This was an important British strategic achievement, which went far to justify the operation. On 9 September, the Grand Fleet attempted another coat-trailing foray off Heligoland – and the Germans absolutely declined to respond. Frustrating as was this passivity to sailors eager for battle, it emphasised British naval mastery.

Yet the Heligoland fight also displayed the unfitness of the Admiralty to direct a modern war at sea. A *Quarterly* reviewer in 1860 described the institution as 'intellectually becalmed in the smoke of Trafalgar', and in considerable measure this remained true half a century later. It was dominated by old men of small imagination. Though the First Sea Lord, Prince Louis of Battenberg, enjoyed respect and was unjustly traduced in the press because of his German background, he was unequal to his role. Scornful critics nicknamed him 'Quite Concur' because of the frequency with which he scribbled these acquiescent words on correspondence. The naval war staff was more of a research department than a machine for planning and directing operations. Its structure assumed that admirals at sea would make the decisions once the fleet sailed. But it soon became clear that, in the new era of wireless, the temptation for the Admiralty to intervene was irresistible, while both the institution and its personnel were ill-equipped to do so. 'Brains were at a discount both in the Navy and the Admiralty,' wrote Beatty's staff officer Filson Young. He shared his chief's contempt for the Sea Lords and their staffs: 'The spirit informing the whole was a narrow and lifeless spirit, expressing itself everywhere in the policy that the means were more important than the end.'

Fortunately for the allied cause, however, the Admiralty was not exclusively officered by slow seadogs. One department of the highest importance – intelligence – fell into the best possible hands. From November 1914 Room 40 was directed by Captain Reginald 'Blinker' Hall – the nickname derived from a habit of constantly blinking his eyes. Hall had been a rising star at sea, most recently commanding a battlecruiser, when poor health caused him to be relegated to a shore job. He had gained some experience of amateur intelligence work in1908 by borrowing a yacht from the Duke of Westminster in which he sailed down the German fleet anchorage at Kiel enumerating and photographing its ships while masquerading as a holidaymaker. Now, turned professional, this physically insignificant figure became a vital force, one of the intelligence wizards that Britain occasionally throws up.

An eyewitness described his 'incisive way of talking', adding that 'it was his face and eyes that caught one's attention. A majestic nose over a rather tight-lipped mouth and a firm, cleft chin made one feel instinctively that this was not a man with whom one could take liberties. He looked rather like a peregrine falcon, an impression reinforced by his penetrating eyes, darting around the assembled company.' Another acquaintance described Hall as 'half Machiavelli, half schoolboy'. The latter portion of his character was displayed by his response, in a story he liked to tell himself, when a judge gave a convicted German spy a light sentence, on the grounds that the man was only passing on factory locations to Germany. Hall, intensely irritated, allegedly caused German intelligence to be informed that the judge's home was 'an important factory site'.

Room 40's task was critically assisted by the capture at sea of three German naval codebooks. On 11 August an Australian naval officer seized at pistol point the codebook of the German steamship *Hobart*, off Melbourne, though as a result of dilatoriness this prize did not reach London until the end of October. The Russians passed on another codebook, captured when the cruiser *Magdeburg* ran aground off the Estonian coast in the Baltic on 25 August; this got to the Admiralty on 13 October. Finally, on 30 November a British trawler off the Texel retrieved the codebook of a German destroyer sunk there on 17 October. By December 1914, with the aid of a group of brilliant German-speaking academics recruited for the purpose, Hall's team thus held the secrets of all three principal enemy naval codes – known as VB, HVB and SKM. Later, it would crack others.

Those were days in which wireless still seemed a miracle to men born before its inception. Aboard Beatty's flagship *Lion* at Scapa Flow, one night in its radio room an officer donned headphones and listened entranced to Morse chatter across the airwaves: 'We heard the Russian commander-in-chief in the Baltic; we heard Madrid; we heard the German Commander-in-Chief, from his fastness across the North Sea; and it amused me to turn the wavelength back and forward between the German and British commanders – the two voices that mean so infinitely much to us all – to contrast their tones, and to imagine what they were saying.'

Thanks to Room 40, the British high command soon knew many of the answers to the German end of that puzzle. A growing volume of messages intercepted by a chain of Admiralty radio receiving stations along the east coast were decrypted, translated and read within a few hours. The navy grudgingly forgave civilian translators for their ignorance of nautical parlance, which resulted in the Operations Department being passed a decrypt which asserted – for instance – 'the [German] 2nd Battle Squadron will run out at 2 p.m. and return to harbour athwartwise at 4 p.m.'. Because the High Seas Fleet operated from Wilhelmshaven, where many orders were issued on paper or by telephone, 'Blinker' Hall could not be confident of anticipating every German motion. But, because of the technical excellence of their transmitters, Ingenohl's ships communicated by wireless more than did the Royal Navy. Moreover, one of the first British actions as a belligerent had been to sever Germany's submarine telegraph cable links with the rest of the world. This obliged Berlin to use wireless for much sensitive international traffic, while naval signals often gave the Grand Fleet several hours' warning that the enemy was putting to sea.

In the months following Heligoland Bight, however, the fortunes of the struggle tilted to and fro, in a fashion that frequently embarrassed the Royal Navy. On 22 September U9 was able to sink three old British cruisers performing pointless 'picket duty' off the Dutch coast. *Hogue*, *Aboukir* and *Cressy* were idling along on a steady course, their captains oblivious of any submarine threat. When the first ship was hit, and then the second, incredibly each cruiser in succession stopped to rescue survivors; 1,400 men thus perished. Many sailors of the High Seas Fleet expressed envy of U9's commander, who went home in triumph. Lt. Knobloch of *Rostock* wrote wistfully in his diary: 'It must be a heart-warming feeling to re-enter harbour after such an achievement.' More exalted officers felt the same way. Ernst Weizsäcker wrote proudly of U9's success, in sharp contrast to the surface fleet's inertia: 'One feels happy to be a naval officer today.'

On 27 October, the new British dreadnought *Audacious* was lost to a mine off the north coast of Ireland. For months afterwards the Admiralty made itself ridiculous by declining to admit the sinking even in naval orders, though hundreds of American passengers aboard the passing liner *Olympic* had witnessed it, and German schoolchildren enjoyed a celebratory holiday. Meanwhile commerce raiders, most famously the *Emden*, achieved some embarrassing successes on the far side of the world, in the Pacific and Indian Oceans. There was a dismaying episode on the evening of 1 November, when Rear-Admiral Sir Christopher Cradock's antiquated cruiser squadron was destroyed by Admiral von Spee at Coronel, off the coast of Chile.

'Kit' Cradock had once published a little book entitled *Whispers from the Fleet*, in which he warned that 'the headstrong unthinking naval "dasher" is bound to come to grief'. Yet he himself chose to play precisely that role: he led his squadron beyond reach of support from the 12-inch guns of the pre-dreadnought battleship *Canopus*, which had been placed under his command. *Canopus*'s captain was informed by his engineering officer that technical problems made it necessary to reduce the ship's speed to twelve knots. Thirty-six hours later, it was found that the man concerned had suffered a nervous breakdown – there was no real need for the reduction of speed, which had opened a three-hundred-mile gap between the battleship and the rest of the squadron: *Canopus* could have fought at Coronel.

But this revelation came too late to save Cradock. Though his old armoured cruisers *Good Hope* and *Monmouth* had been mobilised with reservist crews and his only efficient ship was the light cruiser *Glasgow*, he declined a chance to cut and run in the face of overwhelming odds. A loyal courtier, he had been knighted for 'personal services' to the King; like every officer in the navy, he had observed the obloquy heaped upon Admiral Ernest Troubridge in August, for rejecting a chance to fight *Goeben* and *Breslau* in the Mediterranean at the outbreak of war. Though his own force was relatively much weaker than that of Troubridge, Cradock engaged the enemy and was promptly dispatched along with 1,600 British sailors and their ships. Asquith wrote testily to Venetia Stanley: 'I am afraid the poor man has gone to the bottom: otherwise he richly deserves to be court-martialled.'

Coronel, though strategically unimportant, was a blow to British prestige, and rattled an already nervous government. Jellicoe is often criticised as a plodder whose caution later denied the Royal Navy a big victory at

Jutland. Yet the commander-in-chief's prudence, unexciting though it was, contrasted favourably with Cradock's suicidal gesture, Beatty's impulsiveness, and the tactical stupidity which caused *Hogue* and its sister cruisers to be sunk by U9. The problem persisted, however, that in London the government was becoming desperate for some conspicuous British successes. Asquith, with the accustomed flippancy which emphasised his unfitness as a director of war, wrote to Venetia Stanley on 4 November, after Coronel: 'I told Winston ... it is time he bagged something, & broke some crockery.'

In truth, of course, the First Lord was the last man who needed encouragement to take risks: he had just made one extraordinarily perilous decision. In October Prince Louis of Battenberg was hounded from office, and Churchill sought to remedy the lack of grip at the Admiralty by installing as his successor former First Sea Lord Admiral Lord Fisher. One of the wild, brilliant spirits whom Churchill loved – he described 'Jacky' Fisher as 'a veritable volcano of knowledge and of inspiration' – the begetter of the *Dreadnought* was now seventy-three. His admirers justly point out that during his second tenure as First Sea Lord he displayed better judgement and more consistency on operational matters than his intemperate correspondence suggests. But Churchill and Fisher soon fell out, and embarked on a struggle for dominance which contributed to neither the efficiency nor the happiness of the Admiralty.

Fortunately for British prestige, Cradock's defeat at Coronel was erased on 8 December: two battlecruisers commanded by Sir Doveton Sturdee, detached from Beatty's squadron for the purpose, destroyed Spee's ships when he rashly attempted a raid on the Falklands Islands, to secure coal, instead of obeying orders to make for home. Old *Canopus* played a belated part here: it was deliberately beached in Port Stanley harbour and its fire-control equipment was moved onto a hill above the town: this enabled the ageing battleship to fire the first shots of the action. The British were fortunate that Spee made no attempt to close the range and attack with torpedoes as Sturdee's ships left Stanley, probably the Germans' only chance of averting destruction.

Back in England, everybody was too pleased about the victory to take much heed of the prodigious quantity of ammunition the British were obliged to fire – 1,174 12-inch shells over a period of five hours – to sink much weaker opponents. Sturdee's ships achieved only one hit per gun every seventy-five minutes, which augured ill for a fleet encounter in the North Sea. The German press dismissed Spee's lost squadron as old vessels of no strategic importance, which distressed the Kaiser's sailors. 'I think it is mean to depict those brave ships as inferior … and worthless, after they gave of their best,' wrote aggrieved naval cadet Walter Stitzinger of SMS *Lothringen*. The lesson both sides brought home from Coronel and the Falklands was that to engage a much superior enemy constituted not courage, but reckless folly. Moreover, Jellicoe's caution was intensified by accumulating evidence about the lethality of mines and submarines: ill-luck or a bad misjudgement could transform the navies' balance of strength alarmingly quickly. And soon, indeed, the Grand Fleet experienced – all unknowing – the most dangerous moment of its war.

The Germans hankered to assuage the bitterness of Heligoland Bight. Attempts by four destroyers to mine the Thames estuary resulted in all being sunk before they had even started laying a field. Another minelaying operation was planned, off Yarmouth, and Hipper gained the Kaiser's consent to take his battlecruisers in support. On 3 November the German ships staged a brief, futile bombardment of the English east coast town's beach. They fired without effect on some small craft, and escaped home without being engaged. The Admiralty was unable to believe that an assault on harmless little Yarmouth was the sole purpose of the sortie. The Sea Lords sent no ships to chase Hipper, because they thought his movement must be a feint, to distract their attention from some more serious threat. In any event, the raiders got home unscathed, save that an old cruiser, *Yorck*, hit a German mine while approaching Wilhelmshaven, and sank with the loss of 235 lives.

But the limp British response to Yarmouth encouraged Ingenohl to repeat the operation on a grander scale. On 14 December, Hall's Room 40 warned the Admiralty that Hipper's battlecruisers would come out the following day. The codebreakers had no inkling that, in truth, the entire High Seas Fleet intended to put to sea. In London, a decision was made to dispatch Beatty, reinforced by a squadron of battleships and attendant light cruisers and destroyers, to await the Germans at Dogger Bank, in the midst of the North Sea, and to cut off their escape home. The British did not know Hipper's exact target, but they chose to allow the Germans to strike unimpeded, because this would give them a much better chance of trapping Hipper's battlecruisers on the way home – when his objective had been revealed – than on the outbound passage, when he might be headed anywhere along three hundred miles of shoreline. The objective of sinking the enemy's battlecruisers outweighed any consideration of deflecting the enemy from British hearths and homes.

Jellicoe, when informed, was once more deeply troubled by the prospect of seeing the Grand Fleet divided; he wished to bring out his entire force. This was vetoed by the Admiralty, anxious to nurse the big ships, whose engines were wearing out alarmingly quickly under the strain of frequent sea-keeping. The dreadnoughts of Beatty and Rear-Admiral Sir George Warrender sailed in appalling weather conditions, which caused some of the destroyer and light cruiser escorts to be sent home. The six British battleships and four battlecruisers – two of the latter squadron had not yet returned from the Falklands – would be lightly supported at Dogger Bank. Yet bearing down upon them was the entire High Seas Fleet, with its eighteen dreadnoughts, eight pre-dreadnoughts, nine cruisers and fifty-four destroyers. The scene was set for fulfilment of Jellicoe's nightmare: an overwhelmingly powerful German force was approaching a detachment of the Grand Fleet which it had firepower enough to destroy, thus eliminating British superiority in capital ships.

Hipper was initially unenthusiastic about undertaking the bombardment of British towns, which he considered both strategically irrelevant and at odds with the gentlemanly code of his profession. He wrote in his diary on 29 November that if Germany was to risk her precious big ships, she should do so against the Royal Navy. Shore bombardment represented a footling gesture, not a serious operation of war. He was also apprehensive about the peril posed by British minefields. 'To founder without battle and honour would be a sorry end of my career,' he reflected, with a self-pity worthy of Beatty.

At 8.05 on the misty morning of 16 December, at the Yorkshire seaside resort of Scarborough, coastguard officer Arthur Dean looked out to sea and saw two battlecruisers. Six hundred yards from the town's castle they began firing steadily towards the shore as they steamed across South Bay, before reversing course and repeating the exercise. Elderly widows, with whom the town was well-endowed, were reading their letters over genteel breakfast tables in the Grand Hotel when it received a series of direct hits, devastating the interior. The gable end of the town hall was wrecked, along with shopfronts and boarding-house bedrooms on St Nicholas Cliff, and a row of cottages in Stalby Road. A magistrate named John Hall was dressing when a shell obliterated his bedroom and himself. Twenty miles away at Whitby, similar murderous scenes were played out by two other German cruisers: one shell demolished the west bay of the ancient abbey, another reduced to rubble the little houses of Esk Terrace. At nearby Hartlepool, during thirty minutes of firing German warships wrecked Lloyds bank and caused a gasworks to explode. Then Hipper's ships turned away for home.

Meanwhile at Dogger Bank, at intervals through the night and into the day, the rival fleets' destroyers glimpsed each other and exchanged fire as best they could in the heavy seas. As at Heligoland Bight, German gunnery proved superior: British destroyers were hit several times, while Ingenohl's ships remained unscathed. Beatty and Warrender strove to divine the significance of enemy movements, until a vital signal came, reporting that Scarborough was under bombardment. It was now up to the admirals at sea to select appropriate interception courses. Warrender signalled Jellicoe, copied to the battlecruisers: 'Scarborough being shelled; I am proceeding towards Hull.' Beatty, ever the dashing cavalier, messaged back: 'Are you? I am going to Scarborough.' But even as the big ships ploughed westwards, late in the morning visibility deteriorated dramatically. British and German vessels of all shapes and sizes were reduced to groping and firing intermittently in thick mist, befuddled about their adversaries' movements.

And where, meanwhile, were Ingenohl and the might of the High Seas Fleet? At 5.45 that morning, hearing that his destroyers had clashed with the British, the German admiral convinced himself that the entire Grand Fleet must be at hand. Surprise was gone. Ingenohl was at sea solely to support Hipper's raid, and had no mandate from the Kaiser to fight a big battle. He promptly turned for home, oblivious that he thus missed Beatty and Warrender and threw away the German navy's finest strategic opportunity of the war.

Through the late morning and early afternoon, rival light forces played tip and run in the fog, spasmodically glimpsing each other and exchanging fire, while the British big ships remained mystified about the whereabouts of Hipper. In his later report, Warrender expressed exasperation: 'they came out of one rainstorm and disappeared into another'. Beatty made a sudden decision to turn east, hoping to better his chances of cutting off Hipper from home. This was a misjudgement. Had he maintained his westerly track, within the hour he would have met the German battle-cruisers, though it is far from assured that he would have welcomed the outcome of such an encounter. Beatty might have prevailed, but – given the subsequent fate of his squadron at Jutland, where it lost two ships and suffered heavy damage to two more – he might also have suffered a disaster. As it was, on 16 December he missed Hipper, who scuttled back to Wilhelmshaven unscathed. Both fleets reached their home ports without absolute loss of a ship, though two British destroyers were dockyard cases. To the chagrin of the Royal Navy, the last chance of a great sea battle in 1914 was gone.

Midshipman Charles Daniel of HMS *Orion* noted that morning that if the fleet let the Germans get away, its reputation would 'probably be as mud in the eyes of the British public'. Five days later, when the worst had indeed happened, the young man added ruefully: 'The missing of those German cruisers will not be forgotten by us, and the disappointment becomes worse when one thinks what a splendid show it would have been to have sunk [them].' The British had not identified Hipper's exact target, but they knew he was coming, and made no attempt to head him off from the coast, sacrificing the lives of 107 men, women and children in Scarborough, Whitby and Hartlepool, while more than five hundred other civilians were wounded. The Royal Navy thereafter failed to intercept an enemy whose intentions Room 40 had disclosed, even after making contact with some of his squadrons. It was an inglorious day, if characteristic of war at sea in the pre-radar era.

The gravest weakness of the Royal Navy, brilliantly analysed by Andrew Gordon, was its officers' rigidity of thought and subservience to higher authority: captains waited upon the orders of their admiral, and if these were lacking or confused – as Beatty's often were – subordinates never dared to think or act for themselves. On twentieth-century warships, the atmosphere of oppressive masculinity suggested a floating boarding school, and in the Royal Navy even prefects – ships' captains – were fearful of adopting any course of action without their headmaster's consent. On two occasions during the Scarborough raid, chances were missed because captains waited in vain for a lead from their superiors; on one occasion, when a destroyer flotilla leader swung into a wild turn away because the ship's rudder had been jammed by a German shell, his entire command followed suit.

But what had the Germans supposed they were doing, in bombarding the coastal towns? Here was an exercise in terrorism with no military purpose, designed to demoralise the British people by demonstrating their vulnerability to German 'frightfulness'. Instead, however, it served to fuel popular hatred of the enemy and strengthen the nation's will to fight. If on 4 August British people had felt no great animus towards the Kaiser's subjects, by the year's end German deeds and allied propaganda had stirred real passion in many breasts. Twenty-two-year-old James Colvill, an officer on *Lancaster*, wrote after Hipper's ships had done their worst on 18

December: 'May we have a chance of paying them back in their own coin to the last pfennig, but not by slaughtering non-combatants, when we get into Germany. I would like to see a dozen German towns – beginning with Essen & finishing with Berlin – burned to the ground & utterly sacked, in one word – "Louvained".'

The Royal Navy suffered criticism for the Scarborough raid, which would have been much fiercer had the public known that Britain's coastline was wittingly exposed. Naval officers urged that even if Scapa Flow remained the only plausible anchorage for the Grand Fleet, the battlecruisers, at least, should be moved further south, where they could intervene quickly against another German sortie. Beatty's ships were eventually redeployed in the Firth of Forth.

But it was widely recognised that the conduct of the High Seas Fleet, its futile ravaging of seaside resorts, represented weakness, not strength. It was because Ingenohl and Hipper dared not go head to head with the Grand Fleet that they were reduced instead to bombarding boardinghouses. In part also, the Scarborough raid reflected the fact that the war was growing nastier. Many people on both sides were shedding inhibitions and chivalrous anxieties with which they had taken up arms five months earlier. Naval officer Walter Freiherr von Keyserlinck, commanding SMS *Lothringen*, wrote to his uncle on 29 December, demanding an unrestricted U-boat campaign against British commerce: 'Unless war is made something real for the Englishman in his own country, this robber and murderer will not recognise what it means for other people. Since the times of [Dutch admiral] de Ruyter [in the seventeenth century] nobody has exploded a single bomb on [England's] doorstep.'

Even before the Scarborough raid, most naval officers on both sides acknowledged that they might have a long wait before the rival fleets met. Staff officer Ernst Weizsäcker decided that Germany should have concentrated her naval building programme on cruisers and small craft, rather than vastly expensive dreadnoughts Reinhold Knobloch agreed: 'Our inactivity causes us to question the usefulness of surface warships. Many [German sailors now] believe that only submarines, aircraft and mines count.' Walther Zaeschmar, a gunnery officer on *Helgoland*, wrote in his diary in October: 'Apparently there is no war being waged at all.' A month later, he had become even gloomier: 'In the North Sea nothing happens any more. Only the U-boats are operating on a permanent war footing.' The High Seas Fleet adopted a routine which became gloomily familiar: ships served two days on forward picket duty in the outer Jade Roads; then four more closer inshore; followed by eight in harbour. Every officer afloat lamented the crushing monotony of such a rotation, but it would characterise the experience of the German fleet for four years, with only the briefest interludes of action.

'From the point of view of the ordinary naval officer,' wrote Filson Young across the North Sea, 'the real trouble about the war, the thing that robbed it of joy and excitement, was the continued absence of the enemy. Hardly anyone in the Fleet had seen a German since war had been declared, and only a few a German ship … The enemy began to grow unreal, chimerical … Once he appeared as four tiny wedges of smoke, like hurrying hedgehogs visible on the far horizon of a cold grey sea – wedges of which there were presently visible only three. This meant that a great ship, with the population of a large village, after being seared and poured into a shambles, had quenched itself, a white-hot hell of agony, in the pale winter sea.'

Roger Keyes wrote to his wife in October: 'I would give anything to be a soldier until the fleet comes out.' His view strengthened the following month: 'I am very sick of inaction! I think next time I come into the world I shall be a soldier – it was stupid of me not to have thought of it before making up one's mind to go into the Navy. History is plain enough on the subject. Soldiers fight almost every day of a war. Sailors about once a year at the most if they are lucky. The worst of it is one has to make up one's mind for the Navy so young, one probably doesn't know enough about history, and those six volumes of James' naval history … which I lived on about that time were misleading, they are crowded with fights big and small but spread over 30 or 40 years.'

By the war's end the Royal Navy had grown to a strength of 437,000 officers and men, while 32,287 of its sailors had perished. Such casualties were far from negligible, but represented a much slighter proportion of loss than combatants of the army and the RAF – as the RFC became – experienced. This helps to explain the zeal for the fray that persisted in British naval bosoms long after it had vanished from those of most soldiers: if the sailors' war was not without risks and hardships, it could not be compared with the horrors of service on the Western Front. In the years that followed the Scarborough raid, at long intervals there were further North Sea surface clashes, most importantly at Jutland in May 1916. The Grand Fleet, which became Beatty's command after Jellicoe's transfer to the Admiralty in December 1916, was denied the epic triumph in battle for which the sailors yearned.

But whatever the Royal Navy's limitations and failures, it made a critical contribution to allied victory in the First World War. At the end of 1914 Churchill noted with just satisfaction that since August, 809,000 men, 203,000 horses and 250,000 tons of stores had been transported to France without loss. Through the years that followed the navy preserved its battlefleet in being; secured free movement around the world for British commerce and British forces; defeated – albeit belatedly and after some shocking bungling which placed Britain at greater risk of starvation than ever in World War II – the 1917 U-boat campaign; and sustained a blockade of Germany that became formidably effective after April 1917.

Critics of the pre-war 'naval race' between Britain and Germany have often argued that British dreadnought-building helped to precipitate war, yet ultimately proved irrelevant to its outcome. Neither proposition seems true. There is no reason to suppose that any of the continental powers would have behaved differently in 1914 had the Royal Navy been only half its size. And while the Grand Fleet was unable to make a direct contribution towards victory, in the absence of superiority at sea Britain would have been acutely vulnerable. Commander the Hon. Reginald Plunkett, one of Beatty's battlecruiser officers, wrote in the service magazine *Naval Review* towards the end of 1914: 'the British navy has achieved, practically without fighting, all that a Navy has ever been expected to perform'. Though there was vainglory in this statement, almost every German seaman agreed.

12

Three Armies in Poland

In the first months of the war, even as the Austrians suffered humiliation in Serbia, far worse things befell them in Galicia, the region that straddled south-western Poland and the north-eastern province of Austria-Hungary. There, Conrad Hötzendorf presided over a disaster that rent the threadbare fabric of the Hapsburg Empire. To be sure, Russian commanders competed with his incompetence; but by the year's end, Conrad had shown himself the campaign's supreme bungler, having contrived the deaths of 150,000 of Franz Joseph's subjects for no advantage whatsoever.

Both before and after hostilities began, the Austrian chief of staff failed to coordinate plans with Moltke: recriminations between the two nations were the order of the day. In Vienna in the second week of August, Count Berchtold, begetter of the war, wailed to Alexander Pallavicini – father of the officer of the same name who served in Serbia: 'everything is the Germans' fault'. Pallavicini observed that few of his fellow countrymen could for long suppress their lingering bitterness about defeat at Prussian hands in 1866: 'Despite our great danger, and especially in the highest circles, the old hostility persists, and in Berlin they know that very well.'

Conrad, ignoring the fact that the Germans intended to mount only a holding operation in the east until France was disposed of, embarked upon a massively ambitious envelopment in Poland. To achieve this, in August he committed thirty-one divisions against the Russians' forty-five infantry and eighteen cavalry formations. The Tsar's armies were able to deploy rapidly in southern Poland, partly because they set troops in motion before full mobilisation was ordered, and partly because they had lavished French cash on upgrading rail track. Austrian movements were sluggish by comparison: Conrad had planned on dispatching an initial 11,000 trains, but instead could activate only 1,942, which crawled across the Empire at 10 mph, half the speed of German ones. Troop trains halted for six hours a day for their occupants to be fed. Incompetence transcended parody: the stationmaster at Podborze in Austrian Silesia suffered a breakdown, reversed all the signals causing some formations to be delayed for hours, then shot himself during the ensuing investigation.

The four Hapsburg armies dispatched to Galicia were decanted from rail wagons far behind the front and obliged to complete their deployments on foot, covering twenty miles each day between 19 and 26 August. Some men viewed the forthcoming campaign with the same naïveté as their leaders. Lt. Edler von Hoefft led a fighting patrol forward of the Austrian army, which glimpsed Cossacks two kilometres away, then allowed them to close to 1,200 metres before loosing a fusillade. One Russian fell, to the Austrians' exultation. 'Of course everybody claimed to have hit him,' wrote Hoefft. 'My riflemen said: "Wasn't it great, the way he rolled over?"'

Forty-four-year-old Dr Richard von Stenitzer, who had abandoned a fashionable Vienna practice to become an army medical officer, arrived at the front with only a small valise because 'it is said that the campaign could only last a few months'. But staff officer Alexander Pallavicini – Berchtold's acquaintance – was gloomy from the start: 'This is a sad "success" for our diplomacy, which always calculated on [fighting] only Serbia.' He resorted to French in his diary: 'Now, the words are *ordre*, *contreordre*, *désordre*.' When Lt. Col. Theodor Ritter von Zeynek said farewell to his wife in Vienna before joining an army staff in Galicia, he felt as if he was 'jumping into a thick cloudbank'. Poland, western salient of the Tsarist Empire, became one of the war's most exotic battlefields. John Reed painted a vivid portrait of the diversity of its native inhabitants, now overrun by soldiers from every corner of Nicholas II's possessions – 'the dramatic pageant of races', as the American journalist called it:

There were subdued, gentle Moldavian peasants all in white linen, with wide-brimmed, low-crowned hats and long, curling hair falling on their shoulders … Russian *mujiks* in blouses and peaked caps clumped along with heavy boots – bearded giants with blank, simple faces, and hale, flat-faced Russian women dressed in ghastly combinations of coloured kerchiefs and shirts … Here and there the twisted, calculating face of a Russian pope, with his long hair, and a great crucifix dancing on the front of his robe. Cossacks of the Don, without distinctive uniform excepting a broad red stripe down their trousers, silver-inlaid sabre with the guardless hilt, and tufted love-lock over the left eye; pockmarked Tartars, descendants of the Golden Horde who stormed Holy Moscow – the strong men of the army – marked by a narrow red stripe; Turcomans in enormous white or black bearskins, caftans of faded violet or blue, boots with pointed toes turned up – splendid with gold chains, belts, daggers and yataghans, and always Jews, Jews, Jews.

This was the teeming society, at the interface of a multitude of races and rival loyalties, upon which three armies descended in August 1914. Even while Austrian Lt. Constantin Schneider was still on Hapsburg territory it seemed to him that not only the landscape but the demeanour of every soldier changed when his regiment's train approached the Carpathian mountains: 'The high command had marked a line on the map to denote the beginning of the theatre of war, and even nature wore another aspect. The peaceful world ended, the lush fields where hardworking farmhands gathered the harvest were abandoned, the gay city life was left behind … Told that the train might stop, we roused ourselves from poetic dreams and became … dashing heroes, loading our pistols and awaiting the coming of morning armed to the teeth.'

Once through the Carpathian passes, Franz Joseph's army entered the frontier region, studded with huge city-fortresses – Lemberg, Przemyśl, Cracow; thereafter, the Austrians advanced towards the Russians on foot. Constantin Schneider's division was accompanied by six hundred baggage carts. He deplored the stupidity of their untrained civilian drivers, who refused to keep to the left side of the road assigned to them: 'We were constantly distracted by wrangles which caused halts, difficulty, reproaches.' On both sides of the Polish border, roads were poor and railways few. Conrad's supply columns, which purported to be joining a twentieth-century war, moved no faster than those of the nineteenth.

The Austrians advanced to meet the Russians on two fronts: one a hundred miles south of Warsaw, beyond the San river, the other eastwards, straddling the Dniester. In the latter sector, the Austrians were outnumbered three to one. But when Nikolai Ruzsky, the Russian commander, suffered sharp losses in the first clashes after venturing warily into Hapsburg Galicia, he fell back inside Poland. Meanwhile Russian army commanders received irrational and indeed contradictory orders from rivals for authority: army headquarters – the Stavka – presided over by Grand Duke Nicholas and his staff; St Petersburg; and Gen. Nicholas Ivanov, the Front commander. The generals in the field resolved the confusion about who was in charge by doing whatever seemed best to each on the day, heedless of what courses their neighbours might be pursuing.

Senior officers indulged mutual animosities without inhibition or embarrassment. If the tension between Samsonov and Rennenkampf was most notorious, in Galicia Col. Guliewicz, an aristocratic Pole and court favourite serving as chief of staff to Ninth Army, refused to speak to Gen. Lechitsky, his Siberian commander, whom he despised as an incorrigible vulgarian, because the latter declined to allow Guliewicz's wife to live at their headquarters.

Ruzsky, a chronic pessimist, faced an Austrian army, but was meanwhile obsessed by fears that the Germans further north might descend on Warsaw, then advance towards St Petersburg. He thus favoured withdrawing his own command to the river Niemen. Some of the forts and bridges of Warsaw were blown up in gloomy anticipation of such an outcome. Meanwhile, 350,000 Russians advanced south-west from Lublin onto Austrian soil, where Conrad had deployed a similar number of his own troops, both sides looting and burning indiscriminately. Here was territory new to the conflict, where the population had not yet adjusted to its cruel demands. At Opole, only the altar and cross survived from a church that was still burning, while bricks from its bell-tower littered the surrounding fields, scored with abandoned Austrian trenches. By contrast, a mile or two onwards, advancing Russian troops passed families in their Sunday best walking to church as usual, while children cavorted and splashed in a village pond. In the Austrian camp Constantin Schneider gazed curiously upon Galicia's onion-dome churches and strange place-names, reflecting, 'the Orient had to be like this. For sure, we had ventured far from Europe.'

Staff officer Edler Hoefft faced his first Russian barrage on 15 August. The peasant cottage where he was billeted received a direct hit, 'horses reared up, people ran and I was sure some poor devils had copped it'. Yet when the shelling stopped, he was amazed to discover that only one man had been wounded, hit in the knee. He wrote: 'It must be that God makes miracles, because otherwise no human beings would survive.' They learned the lesson of all battlefields, that while shellfire might be dangerous, it did not result in universal annihilation, as from a distance appeared inevitable.

Allied military attachés posted to the South-Western Front were greeted on arrival by Russian commanders and staff officers with the kisses so distasteful to Britain's Maj. Gen. Alfred Knox. They found their hosts drinking sweet lemonade without much enthusiasm: Ivanov had banned alcohol from his mess for the duration, an innovation which seemed to

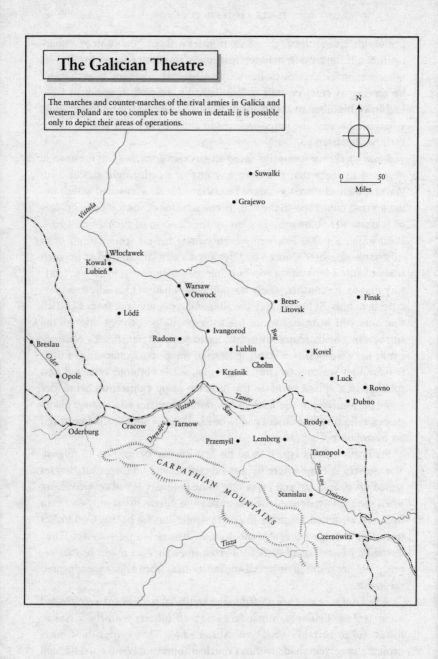

The Galician Theatre

The marches and counter-marches of the rival armies in Galicia and western Poland are too complex to be shown in detail: it is possible only to depict their areas of operations.

N

0   50
Miles

Suwalki

Grajewo

Vistula

Włocławek
Kowal
Lubień

Warsaw
Otwock

Brest-
Litovsk

Pinsk

Lódź

Ivangorod

Radom

Lublin

Kovel

Breslau

Oder

Opole

Cholm

Kraśnik

Luck

Rovno

Dubno

Tanev

San

Vistula

Brody

Oderburg

Cracow

Dunajec

Tarnow

Przemyśl

Lemberg

Tarnopol

CARPATHIAN MOUNTAINS

Złota Lipa

Stanislau

Dniester

Tisza

Czernowitz

assist neither morale nor efficiency. But the general was popular among his soldiers, with whom he chatted constantly. A huge gunner said that he had left at home a wife and five children. His genial commander assured him that he would see them again. The man responded sombrely: 'They say it is a wide road that leads to the war and only a narrow path that leads home again.'

The morning of 19 August found Ivanov watching his army advance through a torrential downpour. At halts, men unwrapped their filthy footrags, laying them out to dry when the rain stopped. A few younger soldiers sang the sort of songs the army favoured:

> I remember when I was a young girl
> During the army manoeuvres
> To my village came a young officer
> With soldiers and he said to me
> Give me some water to drink
> When he finished drinking,
> He stooped from his horse
> And kissed me.
> All night he was in my dreams.

But an eyewitness noted that 'the expression of most of the men was one of dull, unreasoning misery'. Alfred Knox also observed that many of the army's horses, newly requisitioned from farms and stables, were too small for such heavy labour as dragging guns, and too fresh to be easily handled by men inexperienced in animal management. A horse in the Russian army was officially entitled to a daily ration of 14¾lb of oats, 15lb of hay, 4lb of straw – a third more than the peacetime allocation, in recognition of the fact that the poor brutes were being worked so hard. In reality, however, horses were even less likely than men to be decently fed, and they foundered by thousands in consequence.

On 23 August Yanushkevich, the Front chief of staff, declared buoyantly to Ivanov: 'the Austrian forces ranged against us are weaker than those we war-gamed against'. Yet in the next three days, carelessly deployed Russian formations met the enemy with flanks exposed – and received a mauling. Ivanov's men headed smartly back up the road by which they had advanced, to new positions at Kraśnik. Next day, Austrian Edler Hoefft and a comrade found themselves in a churchyard which had been occupied by Russian troops caught in an artillery concentration. Many of the dead lay unburied: 'the air was poisoned and a man had to hold his breath ... Everywhere thick walls had fallen in and huge craters overlapped each other. The victims lay around, in one place seven heaped together. One lacked an abdomen, another had lost his head excepting a lower jaw. A third lacked shoulders and hips. It was worse than gruesome. Wenze took photographs of everything while I quit the place, holding my nose.'

On the Austrian side, among the first to die in Galicia was Gen. Alexander von-Brosch Aarenau, one of the senior officers who had been most eager for war. On 21 August, disdaining reconnaissance, he led a dense formation of *Kaiserjäger* troops into an attack on the Russians, which precipitated a slaughter in which he became merely the most notable of many casualties. Austrian soldiers complained that their grey uniforms, which blended well into mountain terrain, rendered them conspicuous on the flatlands of Galicia. The Russians, by contrast, clad in brown, were scarcely visible on ploughland until they moved.

Franz Joseph's army experienced chronic language difficulties. On several occasions men of a division recruited from Bohemia opened fire on comrades of a neighbouring formation, supposing them to be the enemy – which was understandable, since they spoke only Serbo-Croat. Constantin Schneider led a reconnaissance patrol towards the Russians, in the course of which he met a troop of Hapsburg hussars with whom he was desperate to exchange information. Unfortunately, however, not one of the horsemen spoke or understood the German of Schneider's Tyroleans. On the night of 28 August, a cavalry regiment approached the lines of an Austrian division. 'Cossacks!' screamed one man, a cry that was taken up by a hundred voices, and followed by a furious fusillade towards the enemy, invisible in the darkness. Next morning, Schneider explored the ground before the formation's positions, and was appalled by what he found: 'The ravine was filled with corpses ... men of our hussar regiment, shot not by the enemy but by our own infantry. The grotesquery of it almost made me scream.' Once again, the disaster was caused by a failure of communications: the German-speaking infantrymen thought the hussars' unfamiliar shouts were Russian.

Misery descended upon the region's civilian inhabitants, for whom neither side cared a fig; thatched wooden peasant huts were torched without discrimination. 'You see only the stone foundations of houses, and the stoves left in their midst,' wrote Edler Hoefft. 'Chimneys line the roads like ghostly gravestones. Every tree is scorched from the awful fires, its leaves withered.' The Russians destroyed railway stations and bridges as they retreated, while felling trees and digging ditches across roads to delay the Austrians' passage. A sudden outbreak of rifle fire near a big manor house at Suwałki caused a servant to drop the soup tureen which he was carrying into the dining room for his noble master's lunch. Soon, owners and servants alike were forced to flee. Behind the front in Lublin, war correspondent Sergei Kondurashkin was surprised to find himself hailed by the driver of a peasant cart, accompanied by his wife. The man turned out to be an acquaintance who was a landowner and a former member of the State Council; the Austrians had burned his country mansion. The refugee squire gestured hopelessly to the back of the cart, containing a basket and a chair: 'This is all we've got left. We're looking for shelter.'

The horrors that befell the Jewish people in the Second World War are well known to posterity. There is much less recognition of Jewish sufferings in 1914, mostly at the hands of Russians. Hundreds of Jews perished in Galicia, and many more lost everything they possessed. A pathological suspicion developed among Russians of merchants in general, and Jews in particular. John Reed described Poland's Jews as 'bowed, thin men in rusty derbies and greasy long coats, with stringy beards and crafty desperate eyes, cringing from police, soldiers and priests and staring at the peasants – a hunted people, made hateful by extortion and abuse'.

In October, residents of a Warsaw apartment block reported that a conspiracy was being hatched by Jews gathering in the building, who planned to 'dismember' them. Police who were called found that, instead, the hapless 'conspirators' were discussing possible routes to pass through the front to the relative safety of German territory. Alfred Knox wrote on 14 October: 'It is said that a Jew was caught carrying a German officer in a sack across the bridge at Ivangorod. Both were hung.' During a pogrom in captured Lemberg in November, twenty Jews were killed by Cossacks. In December, sixty-four Warsaw Jews were arrested and detained as alleged members of a conspiracy to raise prices through speculation: all their goods were confiscated.

Progressively worse things befell Eastern Europe's Jews for the rest of the war, and a host of other innocents suffered equally grievously. In Hapsburg territory, minorities roused chronic suspicion. In the fortress city of Przemyśl an Austrian army edict worthy of the Third Reich was issued, proclaiming that 'only extreme ruthlessness and harshness will … choke off potential dissident activity among the inhabitants'. Ruthenes were widely believed to be Russian sympathisers. On 16 September, a group of forty-five detained by military police were being led through the streets of the city when they were attacked by a mob shouting 'Hang the traitors!' Some Hungarian Landwehr troops, hearing the clamour, seized the detainees in Bocianstrasse and hacked all but four to death with their sabres.

The Russians' initial withdrawal made Conrad over-confident. As he pushed forward in their wake into Polish territory, his advance outran its supply lines, and familiar Hapsburg chaos set in. Columns of horse artillery forged ahead of the infantry. Order and counter-order caused some units to march in circles. In dramatic contrast to the almost continuous fronts in France, amid the vast empty spaces of the East units became lost, sometimes for days; the whereabouts of the enemy became matter for speculation. Nightfall often came without rations reaching weary troops. Staff officer Theodor Ritter Zeynek deplored *kinder-krankheiten* – 'teething troubles' – in the cavalry which cost heavy losses: foolish horsemen disported themselves in the face of the enemy with the sort of carelessness their grandfathers had shown in the mid-nineteenth century. Few aircraft were available to either side, and lack of reconnais-sance caused another series of chance clashes between 28 and 30 August, which cost Ivanov's armies the loss of a hundred guns and 20,000 men captured.

One of these was Ivan Kuznetsov. He and his comrades, not to mention their officers, had become utterly bewildered by the manner in which they were marched and counter-marched across the frontier zone. At the end of August, they retreated to a place where they found a large contingent of conscripted civilians digging trenches. The troops occupied these through the hours of darkness, then at dawn were ordered to abandon them and fall back. Yet as they approached a village, a colonel galloped up and shouted that they must return to the trenches.

Chaos descended: 'soldiers from all the companies and platoons got mixed up. Officers were shouting for their own men.' They straggled back to the trenches, a rabble rather than an ordered regiment, just in time to be outflanked by an Austrian advance. Hundreds of Russian soldiers milled, yelled, fired rifles wildly as they searched for their companies, mostly in vain. A shell exploded beside Kuznetsov, hurling him into the air and stunning him into unconsciousness. He awoke to find that silence had descended – and that he was a prisoner. His captors addressed him in Polish: '*Dobje pane bude, dobje!*' Kuznetsov wrote: 'I didn't understand then, but later I learned, that this meant "You will be fine, mister, you will be fine!'" Hundreds of his compatriots, however, were not. As Kuznetsov was assisted onto a cart to be taken to the rear, he saw dead and wounded men lying everywhere.

In the Austrian lines Conrad crowed, claiming a great victory. But the Russians were bringing forward reinforcements, and their supply line was now shorter than that of the Austrians. Even as Conrad's northern armies launched their advance into Russian Poland, south of Lemberg between the 26th and 28th they also attacked the much larger Russian army on the river Złota Lipa; this time, it was the Austrians' turn to suffer a defeat as costly as that which Ivanov's army had incurred further north. Near Chochłów, at a divisional staff meeting a comrade of Constantin Schneider pointed to a cloud overhead. The officer suggested fancifully that its shape resembled a back view of Bismarck's head. 'It was as if he, the creator of the Triple Alliance who had always opposed war with Russia, was now turning his back on us.' On the 29th and 30th, in the south the Austrians attacked again – and were badly beaten. Franz Joseph's regiments advanced in masses with little artillery support, and were rewarded with crippling losses.

Yet Conrad the fantasist persuaded himself that apparent success in the north made defeat in the south unimportant. He conceived a complex plan to allow the Russians in the southern sector to advance further, then swing his northern armies to attack their flank. He became especially excited by news of Tannenberg, which reached him at this time: anything Germans could do, Austrians must match. Through the first week of September, both sides' forces blundered across Galicia, their men exhausted by interminable marching even before they began to fight. Ruzsky occupied the abandoned Austrian fortress of Lemberg on the 3rd, but then during the days that followed was worsted in several brushes with the enemy.

Conrad's most serious folly was to ignore the fact that the Russians were heavily reinforcing in the north, while he prepared his intended Napoleonic masterstroke in the south. By 1 September, some thirty-five Russian divisions faced twenty Austrian ones. These bore down upon Conrad's positions south of Lublin with irresistible force, and even found sufficient spare troops to make a lunge towards a corps of German reservists deployed east of the Vistula, screening the Kaiser's territories. This force fell back in disarray across the river, having lost 8,000 men – it deserves notice that the Russians, in the first two years of the war, captured more German prisoners than the British and French armies put together.

Though the humiliation of defeat at Tannenberg, and soon also at the Masurian Lakes, lay heavy upon the Russian army, in Poland in September its fortunes suddenly soared.

A few miles behind the front, the city of Lublin was in a fever of excitement. Crowds clustered outside the cathedral to examine artillery pieces captured from the Austrians, their shields – one inscribed *Ultima Ratio Regis*, the other *Pro Gloria Patriae* – pockmarked with bullet-holes. A young Russian gunner proudly showed off to ignorant civilians how they worked, giving himself imaginary orders, loading make-believe shells, pulling the trigger lanyard and shouting 'Fire!' Clouds of dust raised by thousands of tramping boots swirled above the streets. At the railway station soldiers lay curled in huddles, sleeping with their rifles beside them and their caps tipped over their eyes. 'Even at two or three in the morning,' wrote an eyewitness, 'the city is unable to quiet itself, streets thronged with people excited and anxious after the victory.' He watched a crowd of Austrian prisoners being escorted through the streets, most gazing fixedly at their feet rather than at their surroundings, unwilling to meet the eyes of local people.

Overwhelming Russian pressure on the enemy's flanks began to tell: in action after action, Conrad's exhausted formations were worsted and obliged to fall back. The mood in the Austrian camp was profoundly gloomy: a soldier, Pàl Kelemen, watched from nearby Halicz as fugitives fled the fortress of Lemberg:

> The population was pouring out of the city in long columns. On carts, on foot, horseback. Everyone making shift to save himself. All of them carrying away what they can, and exhaustion, dust, sweat, panic on every face, terrible dejection, pain and suffering. Their eyes are frightened, their movements craven: ghastly terror oppresses them. As if the dust cloud they stirred up had bound itself to them and could waft them away. I lie sleepless by the roadside and watch the infernal kaleidoscope. There are even military wagons muddled into it, while across the fields march routed infantry, lost cavalry. Not a man of them still carries his full equipment. The exhausted throng pours through the valley. They are running back to Stanislau.

The fall of Lemberg, fourth largest city in the Hapsburg Empire, represented a serious humiliation, and Austrian troubles persisted through the days that followed: many guns were lost, including some simply abandoned by crews to speed their own flight. On the night of the 8th, Conrad's officers, contemplating their filthy, exhausted and dispirited men, recognised that the army was beaten. Next day, Russian forces advanced on them from north, east and west. The Austrians' only avenue of escape lay southwards, and they took it. 'With a stab of awareness, a painful sense of failure, our column crossed the border once more, its dreams of victory shattered,' wrote Constantin Schneider.

Desperate days followed. Rüdiger Freiherr Stillfried von Rathenitz was an eighteen-year-old platoon commander in a *Feldjäger* battalion, ordered to launch a counter-attack near Magierów at dawn on 10 September. His men lost patience with lying at a forest edge under fierce Russian artillery fire, waiting for the order to advance. Somebody shouted '*Vorwärts!*' – 'Come on!' The Austrians sprang to their feet and ran forward across open ground under the barrage, Rathenitz following them and struggling in vain to curb their exuberance: 'I wanted to check this mad dash, but my shouting went unheeded – no orders could be given.' Absurdly, as the men ran, some held their spades protectively in front of their faces. Then they took cover again, and began to dig in. Rathenitz himself had barely started scraping when he felt a slap in his right foot, followed by a fierce pain in the upper leg. He knew he had been hit.

He was obliged to lie in the open for the next fifteen hours, until darkness fell, because no stretcher-bearer would brave the fire sweeping the area. He was solaced by the company of a soldier who helped him to dig in: 'At midday it got unbearably hot; we were dreadfully tormented by thirst.' His comrade found a piece of stale bread which they shared, before rolling a cigarette from toilet paper and pipe tobacco. At 9.30 that evening, at last they were carried to the rear. After a ghastly journey on a cart, among a column of such vehicles whose passengers sustained 'ceaseless moans and groaning', he reached Przemyśl. From there he was taken by train to Vienna, where he remained hospitalised for weeks.

On 11 September Conrad ordered a general retreat. Constantin Schneider was sent to ride through the dark night to beg help from the neighbouring division to plug a dangerous gap in the line. On his way, he met a shattered battalion that had lost 90 per cent of its strength, whose commander was grateful to be told where he was. When Schneider delivered his appeal for succour, the divisional commander dismissed it at once, shrugging that he was himself too short of men to spare any reinforcements. The staff officer's long ride had been in vain. Schneider returned to his own headquarters oppressed by the peril facing the army.

The Tsar's generals continued to pour in reinforcements, while Conrad's numbers shrank and his men wilted under the strain of constant marching. By 9 September the Russians were pushing forward relentlessly, threatening the Austrians with absolute disaster. Conrad appealed to the Germans for assistance. The Kaiser, with his forces in the midst of their crisis retreat from the Marne, responded that nothing could immediately be done.

The Russians' successes owed much more to Austrian blundering than to their own generalship or prowess, but Conrad's humiliation was incontestable. This seemed the less palatable in contrast to German triumphs elsewhere. Alexander Pallavicini described the sour response to news of Tannenberg among his comrades of the army staff. They grumbled: 'Always the Prussians and not us.' Pallavicini responded that 'this should not matter, so long as the victories are there'. The others still dissented, but he stuck to his guns, venturing boldly: 'It would be better to put everything under German command.' This was not well received. 'I do not make myself popular by saying such things.' He added two days later: 'The Germans' success seems ever greater. They must have a secret formula – *die müssen ein geheimes Kraut haben*. In our circumstances this is hard to take, but one should not forget that we face the bulk and cream of the Russian army.' The Tsar's subjects in Galicia's frontier areas rejoiced as the invaders were driven back. Stanislav Kunitsky, a landowner, had sent his children away to Lublin when the Austrians overran his estate, then spent thirty-six hours hiding in the cellar of his mansion with his wife while battle raged around them. Once liberated – for a time – by Cossacks, he invited their officers to a feast dominated by 'a fabulous cabbage soup' and a giant carp from his pond. While the Kunitsky garden remained scarred with shell craters, the table was adorned with autumn asters.

Millions of peasant soldiers' ignorance of technology yielded moments of comedy. A Russian explained to a correspondent how he won a medal: 'Well sir, I was on the road and saw an automobile coming towards me … driven by a man in a German hat. I stepped aside and started shooting. I hit the vehicle and it stopped. I ran forward and shot the fellow who was in it. I thought then of taking it to headquarters. I got into the driver's seat and tried to make it move, but I couldn't. The vehicle was puffing, but it wouldn't go. Then I saw a peasant with a cart. I made him unharness it, and [use his horse to] pull away the automobile.' Soldiers gaped at the first primitive Russian armoured cars, deployed in action near Łódź. One man contemplating a steel-plated monster observed gravely: 'a serious thing'. A correspondent wrote of the cars: 'They are welcome guests, everywhere invited to make a long stay.'

British military attaché Alfred Knox, who was following the Russian advance, one night witnessed the interrogation of some Austrian PoWs. He was fascinated by their captors' lingering attachment to chivalry: 'It was an unforgettable scene, the room crowded with officers, a single flickering candle, and the prisoners. Only NCOs and a few of the men are questioned ... the Russian theory being that the officer is a man of honour and must not be insulted by being pressed to give information against his own country.' In the same spirit later, when the Russians were obliged to withdraw behind the Dunajec river, an Austrian divisional staff took over a castle at Radłów previously occupied by a Russian corps commander. The new occupants were undisturbed by gunfire, because the Russian general promised the castle's owner, Count Henryk Dolański, that in recognition of his own month's tenancy, he would spare it from the attentions of his artillery.

The Austrian line of retreat was strewn with abandoned weapons, vehicles and equipment, together with the usual dead and dying horses. Stragglers crowded into the fortress of Przemyśl, where the garrison was strengthening the fortifications in readiness for another siege. On 12 September, traffic in Przemyśl ground to a halt amid the chaos. By the 17th, the Russians had moved within artillery range, and began firing into the city. Fears grew in Vienna that the enemy might break through to the Danube: 30,000 workers were dispatched to build defences, though in some sectors the only available artillery dated from 1875 and even 1861.

There was a striking contrast between the condition of officers and men in the Austrian ranks. Inside Przemyśl, Dr Richard Stenitzer wrote in his diary on 24 September: 'We pass the time by playing cards, eating and sleeping! In the evening we had a feast in Lieutenant Karara's dugout with several wines and champagne.' He described himself, without irony, as having little work save the care of cholera cases, some of whom later carried the disease to Vienna. Yet during the same period, the war diary of an infantry regiment recorded its ghastly three-week retreat, with the men utterly exhausted, and an order issued: 'Keep marching heedless of stragglers and without halts.' The unit was obliged to cover painful extra miles to bypass Przemyśl, to avoid worsening its chaos of broken units and wrecked vehicles.

The city was very late in starting to stock provisions against a siege. Almost half its 714 guns were nineteenth-century black-powder pieces; when these were fired, many stockpiled shells were found to be duds.

Hasty preparations for defence were made, including construction of new outworks, erection of a million yards of barbed wire, clearance of fields of fire. But nearby trees remained unfelled, so that when the Russians closed in, they were able to exploit the woodland to screen their advance. It was all very Hapsburg: the Austrians had always been determined to hold Przemyśl, but their accustomed lethargy precluded the adoption of active steps to achieve this until the enemy was at the gates. The fortress was besieged for the first time from 26 September to 10 October, when it fell to the Russians, whose occupation lasted several weeks before they were obliged once more to fall back.

Under the stress of defeats, Conrad's discordant, multi-ethnic army became ever more fragmented. Units recruited from the east proved especially unreliable. The 19th *Landsturm* Infantry, for instance, was composed of so-called Ruthenes, mostly Ukrainian. The regiment collapsed during one of the August battles, its men throwing away their weapons and equipment as they fled. In September, the rump of this regiment was expelled from Przemyśl's garrison, deemed too unreliable to defend a sector.

Ludwig Wittgenstein was among the crew of the Austrian picket boat *Goplana* on the Vistula, who abandoned their vessel in the face of the headlong enemy advance. 'The Russians are right at our heels,' he wrote in his diary. '... Haven't slept for 30 hours.' Next day, the crew reboarded the boat, but only in order to retire to Cracow by way of the Dunajec river. Behind Przemyśl, Austrian discipline and morale revived a little as Conrad's troops fell back across their own territory, having broken contact with the enemy. Constantin Schneider noted: 'Men's behaviour improves from one day to the next. They shoulder their weapons according to orders and don't drag them along the ground or carry them like sportsmen. Marauding along the roadside has stopped, and even horses are not herded mindlessly together.'

By mid-September the Austrians had retreated to the rivers east of Cracow, having lost more than 350,000 men. The Russians had suffered a quarter of a million casualties, but could draw upon much deeper reserves of manpower. Among vast quantities of war matériel left behind by the Austrians were a thousand rail locomotives and 15,000 wagons. They were woefully short of tractors and horses, so that some 120mm gun batteries now relied on oxen for mobility. Yet Constantin Schneider observed wonderingly that the campaign had demonstrated an undreamt-of technological revolution in war-making, 'more profound than in the entire period between Napoleon and Moltke'.

Conrad's only course now was to dig in where he stood, and await German assistance. From France, Henry Wilson wrote to his wife Cessie on 19 September: 'the campaign [in the west] will be over in the spring, that is to say if the Russians do moderately well, and I know of no reason why they shouldn't'. His remarks emphasised persistent British and French faith in Russian might, even after the disasters at Tannenberg and the Masurian Lakes, the scale of which was imperfectly grasped in London and Paris. In the conflict of 1914–18, as later in that of 1941–45, it was a source of dismay and frustration to the Western allies that the Russians were obsessively secretive about their operations, and especially about their defeats. Britain's *New Statesman* on 17 October acknowledged the shroud of mystery enfolding events in the east, as far as the outside world was concerned. It conceded that 'the battle which is now in progress may last a very long time, possibly even for weeks … We shall be wise to discount for the present any news of "great victories", from whichever side it comes.'

In the Hapsburg camp, Conrad confessed dryly to his staff that if the Archduke Franz Ferdinand were still alive, he would have had the architect of this appalling military disaster – himself – taken out and shot. 'The Austrians' predicament looks pretty bad,' German colonel Max Hoffmann wrote in his diary on 26 September, 'which shows the dire consequences of neglecting to spend any money on the army for 20 years.' Around a third of Conrad's formations were shattered. But the laggardly Russian pursuit spared the Austrians from conclusive catastrophe. Ivanov elected for a pause, to enable his armies to regroup and resupply, and to fortify Lemberg against a counter-attack.

It was characteristic of the war on the Eastern Front that logistics halted each side's advances in turn. The Russian and Austrian commissariats were alike feeble, and the descent of autumn rain churned unmetalled roads into quagmires. The Russians had much larger armies in Galicia than they could properly supply, in a region of few railways. Everything was short save men: soldiers wandered battlefields with sacks, collecting shoes from dead horses. Sergei Kondurashkin heard a soldier under fire shout to all and sundry from a peasant cottage, 'Come and eat! I've boiled some potatoes, and God knows when our proper rations will turn up.' A trickle of men risked the Austrian shelling to make a dash for the cottage to share the bounty.

The wretched lot of the Tsar's soldiers was only slightly alleviated by deliveries of comforts sent from St Petersburg – cigarettes, bagels and

cakes in small pink bags adorned with lace. In some units it became necessary to provide with rifles only men in the forward trenches. Those in the
second line had to wait for weapons to become available when their
comrades were killed: Vasily Mishnin, a former furniture salesman from
central Russia, recoiled in horror when handed a rifle matted with dried
blood. Inside Lublin post office in mid-October rose a mountain of mail
sacks, thirty-two tons of them, letters for hundreds of thousands of
soldiers desperate for news from home. They could not be delivered
because the chief postal officer lacked carts to take them forward.

At Austrian headquarters, Alexander Pallavicini sought to look on the
bright side, consoling himself with the thought that the army had escaped
terminal disaster: 'No news except of small encounters along the front ...
Looking at the different war theatres there is no reason to get depressed:
the French, British and indeed Russians have suffered considerable
setbacks, not to mention Belgium. And for the present we have halted *die
Russische Dampfwalze* – the Russian steamroller. But because nowhere has
anything happened to our decisive advantage, this killing and destruction
will last for a long time before the angel of peace descends.'

If death was equally terrible in every theatre, the plight of wounded
men was even worse in eastern conditions than in the west. Rocking,
creaking country carts pulled by broken-down horses crept from the
battlefield towards the rear, laden with broken and often dying men, prostrate on beds of bloody straw; of the three customarily carried in each
vehicle, it was unusual for two to reach dressing stations alive; fewer still
survived further. Alexei Ksyunin listened to a Russian casualty conversing
entirely amicably to a Hapsburg prisoner, also wounded, on the same cart.

'Hungarian?'

'No – Slovak.'

'Have a lot of you surrendered?'

'Oh yes, a lot, and a lot are killed ... We had fun in the first days, but
after that not at all. There was no food ... Bread had run out and tins as
well, they only gave us coffee twice.'

The Slovak told the Russian that he had left a wife and two children in
the Carpathians. In the usual placatory fashion of prisoners, he praised the
Russians and called them a kind, good people.

'Tell me, sirs, what have we been fighting for? I don't know why they
sent us to fight our own people.'

Lublin hospital presented a ghastly spectacle – more than 2,500
wounded crammed into three hundred bedspaces. Men lay on floors, in

halls and corridors and kitchens, many of them untended because medical supplies were temporarily exhausted, as were doctors and nurses. One man shrieked an agonised protest about a passer-by: 'Take him away! He is stepping on us, putting his boots on us!' A soldier hit in the head, now stone-blind, groped down a corridor, touching the wall. Another man with a head wound clung to a stove, his eyes bleary and lifeless, until an officer passed. Reflexively, he struggled to his feet to salute.

A warehouse by Lublin station became an overflow for casualties denied space in the hospital. Polish nurses stepped gingerly among the prostrate, bloody, groaning throng, distributing cigarettes. A Russian gestured to his Austrian neighbour and said to a girl, 'Give him one. He's one of us. Speaks our language. He could be a Ukrainian.' The anecdote is credible, because in Galicia more than any other theatre of war, the subjects of the two warring emperors felt a bond of kinship in their shared predicament, shackled to a conflict beyond their comprehension or sympathy, under the orders of rival gold-braided buffoons. At a hospital in Warsaw, correspondent Sergei Kondurashkin asked a wounded soldier why so many of the inmates had been hit in the arms. The man replied with bitter sarcasm: because those hit in the head had been obliged to remain on the battlefield. The journalist wrote: 'One hears dozens of stories but they are all the same, just as the soldiers themselves are the same, and the circumstances in which thousands and tens of thousands of men have found themselves in battle.'

As Aleksei Tolstoy travelled from Moscow towards the front, at first he marvelled at the continuing normalcy of rural life behind the war zone, observing from his train: 'There were the same idle people at the stations, the unaltered tranquillity of villages and farmsteads … a peasant driving his oxen along the railway, herds raising clouds of dust at sunset …' But much bleaker sights and sounds shattered this idyllic view as he approached the battlefield. Southbound rail traffic, including Tolstoy's own train, was constantly interrupted to allow the passage in the opposite direction of Russian wounded being taken to Moscow, in open wagons exposed to the elements. Tolstoy noticed that many were wearing Austrian blue serge tunics and boots – of better quality than anything issued by the Tsar's army.

Almost every soldier taken prisoner experiences a surge of shock and confusion, the realisation that this is a life-changing moment, together with the onset of bottomless uncertainty about the future. Ivan Kuznetsov described his sentiments as he found himself in Austrian hands: 'I thought of my village Lipyagi, my parents, my young wife and child. They are going to have a hard time without me. What is going to happen to me?' Many PoWs died on both sides of the Eastern Front. Russian prisoners transported across Hungary in freight cars were attacked at wayside stations by local people throwing stones and banging sticks against the cars' sides to show their hostility.

Several thousand Russian prisoners were held in appalling conditions at a camp near the Hungarian town of Estergom, where many died from starvation. Ivan Kuznetsov recorded:

We awoke to see dead men lying here and there, who had to be buried at once. Several times ... we assembled to demand food ... approaching the guards and shouting: *'Khleba! Khle – ba!'* [Bread! Bread!] The guards hit us with their rifle butts and drove us back into the barracks ... Some fifteen corpses remained lying on the ground. Sometimes bosses would come to the camp and give us a strict warning, and for a few days we got more bread and they made potato soup for us. But then the food went downhill again. Prisoners stuck together in regional groups, me with others from the Penza area ... Two were relations ... Our greatcoats had been taken away, so we slept on the ground wearing our tunics and trousers. They gave us 200–300 grams of bread every three or four days. Food was cooked once a day, boiled water with a little wheat flour and red ground pepper added, one bucket for every twenty men. Autumn came with its cold, damp and mud. We started digging ourselves into the earth like moles. The soil was sandy, soft, so we were able to dig a hole quickly, and then to make a niche so that several men could lie there. There were three men in our group, and we crawled into the hole and lay there under the arching sandy ceiling. We got up in the morning all covered in sand, shook it off ourselves, washed and walked around the camp all day, and in the night we got back into the hole. It became even colder in October, and our improvised bunkers collapsed.

On the other side, the Austrian army's miseries continued without respite. 'You want to dig in because of the shellfire,' wrote Edler Hoefft, 'but it is no fun amidst huge pools of water. Then came such a torrential downpour that I was soaked below the waist, my boots squelching at every step. Entrenching becomes much too tiring if you do not stay long in one place, and thus I ducked it, rather apathetically.' In those cold autumn Polish days, cranes flew over the battlefields wailing mournfully, while many villages were abandoned by their inhabitants, indiscriminately fearful of the passage of either army. Marching men, horses and carts, spilling over from the narrow roads, carved new thoroughfares across fields of potatoes, beet, carrots.

Sergei Kondurashkin wrote: 'One saw groups of refugees from villages near the Vistula in the empty fields and in the valleys. They have taken all that they could carry on their shoulders and trudge with their families. They don't know where they are going. They sit down in a cold, wet valley to rest and consider what to do next. They try to warm their children. One man chews a dry breadcrust between jaws stiff with cold and misery. It takes him a long time to swallow it and reply to the question I put to him: "How is it in Annopol?" "Oh, sir, like death! The Rushinovitz house was destroyed yesterday. A shell hit it and the house collapsed. The owner was wounded and his wife killed. A soldier was also killed. Maevich, Burak, two cows, Anton Petz, Godzhikovsky were all killed. Almost everyone else has left. Those who haven't will go today."' Both sides conducted relentless searches for enemy agents, most of whom existed only in their imaginations, but nonetheless costing many innocent civilians their lives. In Przemyśl, Richard Stenitzer described often hearing firing at 6 a.m. on the fortress's rifle range, 'where alleged spies are shot'. Constantin Schneider recoiled from the incessant witch-hunts, describing how military police entered a village 'from which shots had been allegedly heard, and recklessly shot all suspicious-looking people'.

Russian troops continued to skirmish inside the border of East Prussia, and their paranoia about suspected *francs-tireurs* prompted spasms of savagery. The small town of Domnau was burnt by the invaders after they were fired on by German troops, and deluded themselves they had been attacked by townspeople. The same happened in Aschwangen, where forty people were executed after shots were fired at passing Russian cars. But a post-war German official account notes with scrupulous fairness: 'With only few exceptions, Russian officers attempted to prevent acts of violence.' In most communities the Russians conducted themselves with moderation, and sought to ensure that local civilians were fed. Indeed, the 1914 Russian invasion of East Prussia – in striking contrast to that which took place thirty years later – was generally characterised by humanity and restraint.

The most notable German grievance was that during the Russians' later retreat, they removed some civilians as hostages – the number is disputed, but may have been in the thousands – and held them for the rest of the war. The Russians reoccupied some East Prussian border communities from which they had retreated after defeat at the Masurian Lakes, one of them Popowen. The activities of looters, predatory patrols and casual arsonists finally persuaded the Sczuka family that they must leave their home there and flee westward, into German-held territory. On 14 September, escorted by a Russian soldier, they walked to the local head-quarters at Grajewo to seek the necessary permission. At first they were warmly received and presented with small jars of honey. But then the Russians told them they must be detained overnight. The following even-ing, they learned that they were to be transported deep into Russia – one family among several hundreds swept away to become hostages. They remained until 1918 in Siberia, latterly held in a prisoner-of-war camp, and then amid the chaos of Russia's civil war were unable to return to their homeland for two years thereafter.

Further south, Alexei Ksyunin visited Austrian prisoners, of whom an apparently endless procession marched through Lublin: 'First there were files of Slovaks in bluish uniforms, then they were replaced by Hungarians in dark-blue jackets. One glimpsed PoWs as soon as one woke up and looked out of the window. Going out of town one saw once again a long column of them. Back in the hotel at nightfall, once again there were the silhouettes of Austrians, like dark spots.' Both sides' spirits had fallen low. Searching for a likely billet one evening, Constantin Schneider's unit chanced upon an abandoned country mansion. Smashing locks, they entered the dining room to find dirty glasses and plates on the table, where the house's owners had sat with Russian officers a few hours earlier. The soldiers looted everything worth taking, then wrecked the furniture. 'In enemy country, moral restraints cease to exist,' wrote Schneider uncom-fortably. Yet, on the following day when the unit came under heavy Russian artillery fire, their colonel refused to allow the destruction of a giant wooden cross that was providing the enemy with an obvious aiming-point, on grounds of religious scruple.

While in the west in September 1914 the rival fronts congealed, a process completed in October, in the immense expanses of the east a war of movement continued. In a world of few roads and fewer railways, large forces moved only as fast as could a marching man. When rain and mud descended, that pace became slow indeed. Distances were so vast that neither side could maintain continuous lines, as in France and Flanders – the front was almost twice the length. Densities of troops were about a third of those in the west.

The Hapsburg army was now recognised by both sides as the sick man of the conflict, requiring constant German assistance merely to keep his feet. The Russians were committed to simultaneous efforts to finish off the Austrians, and to reverse the outcome of their disastrous August campaign in East Prussia. If intelligence was indifferent in the west, it was worse in Galicia. Each side misinterpreted the other's actions, or responded sluggishly to its initiatives. Russian commanders maintained incessant rivalries with each other. In mid-September in the south, Ivanov sought to keep pressing the retreating Austrians, aiming to take Przemyśl then Cracow, and afterwards push for Budapest.

Meanwhile on the other side, the Germans now saw no choice save to respond to Conrad's plight. Falkenhayn and the Kaiser were appalled at the prospect of a wholesale Austrian collapse. They rushed eastwards reinforcements of four corps, which enabled Hindenburg and Ludendorff to ride to the rescue of their allies. This new Ninth Army deployed on the eastern border of Germany north of Cracow, where it immediately threatened the Russians' right flank. The Russian response, at the end of September, was to concentrate thirty divisions against Hindenburg. With this force, commanded by Ivanov, they hoped not merely to defeat Ninth Army, but also to launch an invasion of Germany from the middle Vistula towards the upper Oder. The Vistula initiative prompted a renewed clash of Russian commanders' egos. Ruzsky, nettled by perceived slights from his superiors, determined to pursue his own offensive into East Prussia – yet another reckless diversion of effort. Twenty-five Russian divisions embarked on this operation, while thirty more remained pinned down in Galicia, facing the Austrians.

At the beginning of October, Ivanov decided to regroup forces for his invasion. This required withdrawing them across the San, then moving them up the east bank of the Vistula to safe crossing points. During this three-week manoeuvre, the Russians marched interminably, and fought not at all. On 9 October, when the Germans captured the Russian order of battle from a fallen officer, they realised that their own eighteen exhausted divisions now faced sixty, and that they had no chance of a decisive victory. The Germans and Austrians thus confined themselves to following up the Russian columns. Ludendorff trumpeted a victory, merely because his own forces went forward while those of the enemy went back.

Ivanov, in the best Tsarist style, contrived to inflict grievous damage on his own army even without fighting anybody. On the interminable marches, horses died in thousands for want of fodder; men suffered terribly in relentless rain. When at last the troops reached their designated Vistula crossing points, they lacked supplies and adequate bridging equipment. They were obliged to halt, and for days merely gaze upon the mighty flow. By the time they began to cross on 11 October, the Germans and Austrians were ready for them: Ivanov's men who reached the western bank remained penned in small bridgeheads. A pontoon bridge broke loose in a flood and drifted downstream to the suburbs of Warsaw, where it remained. By mid-October it was plain that the Vistula crossing, and thus Ivanov's invasion of Germany, was going nowhere.

The border zones of Russian Poland lapsed into anarchy as the armies ebbed and flowed across the region. Russian officials prudently retired to Warsaw. Gendarmes changed into civilian clothes to escape unwelcome attention from either side. At Otwock railway station just one such officer remained, fortified with liberal infusions of vodka, to extract a one-rouble personal 'tax' from every passing passenger. In the city of Włocławek, which the Germans occupied for three weeks, order was maintained among the population by local firemen carrying sabres. When the Germans retreated, the firemen carried on as policemen, as they did in Lubień and Kowal. The Russian army had never trained its officers to assume any civic responsibilities, and thus where local government broke down, civilians suffered chronic misrule.

A Tsarist officer, Mikhail Lemke, wrote wearily from general headquarters about his commanders' indifference to the plight of their fellow citizens: 'they go on blindly, lacking the slightest inkling about the life of the country'. A vigorous black market evolved not merely in food and alcohol, but also in uniforms, boots, overcoats and even weapons, most of these garnered by traders scavenging battlefields. Men routinely sold personal equipment – even their precious winter clothing – to buy food.

If all soldiers in all wars find their knowledge largely restricted to events within their own line of sight, the remoteness of Galicia and Poland imposed a special isolation and ignorance. War correspondent Sergei Kondurashkin walked into a big country house near the Vistula, now the headquarters of a cavalry regiment, to be greeted by a barrage of familiar questions from officers desperate for tidings from foreign fields: 'How are things in France?' 'What is Rumania doing?' 'Turkey?' 'Where have the Germans got to?' Kondurashkin wrote: 'I had not imagined that I was privy to so much interesting information. I tried to recall details of all the developments in the world, possibilities, opinions and conversations.'

It was now the turn of the Germans to make their own move. They advanced into Poland in appalling weather, along roads deep in mud. Even as Ninth Army marched, Ludendorff's nerve weakened. He concluded that his forces were too small to have a real chance of taking Warsaw, and on 20 October ordered a withdrawal. Once again, both sides had overreached themselves. A few thousand more men had perished, for no significant advantage to either.

The Polish city of Łódź had difficulty deciding whether it was at war or at peace. The cafés were thronged with both civilian and military customers, undeterred by spasmodic incoming shells. One of these hit the best hotel, the Victoria, entering through the roof, smashing through a top-floor ceiling and floor, then departing through a side wall, mercifully without inflicting casualties. Alexei Ksyunin was gossiping with a fellow war correspondent, Vladimir Nemirovich-Danchenko, founder of the Moscow Art Theatre, when a shell fragment shattered the glass top of the next table to their own. The rest of the clientele remained unmoved by such a trifle; they were soon listening to an intrepid aviator describing how his plane had come down in no man's land, forcing him to spend several hours in a swamp under shellfire before darkness enabled him to creep back to the Russian lines.

The city was thronged with beggars, many of them former factory workers deprived of their livelihoods by the general shutdown of industry. Ksyunin wrote: 'one gets chased by half-mad women with wild eyes, trying to snatch at one's sleeve. Hungry kids in rags follow passers-by, their clogs clattering.' Perversely, the best hotels still offered a semblance of luxury, though their rooms were icy cold because there was no fuel to heat them. Delicious food was served in some restaurants – but without bread. The trams continued to run. Crowds hung around shuttered food stores: after bread ran out, there was a brief run on spaghetti. Once that was gone, most people subsisted on potatoes. In the distance, the crump of explosions and the rattle of small arms provided constant orchestration. When darkness fell, the sky was lit by a red glow, and periodic concussions persisted. Around the clock, a steady stream of wounded men shuffled through the streets. All but the most grievous cases were ordered to make their own way towards the rail station, from which occasional evacuation trains still departed.

But the Kaiser's armies in Poland achieved no new triumph to match those of East Prussia: through the autumn and early winter of 1914, their repeated attempts to break the Russian front and take Łódź failed miserably. Both sides suffered appalling losses. Among the wounded Germans to fall into Russian hands was a former bookkeeper, lamenting alike his pain and his separation from home, wife and children. He was briefly tended by an exotic nurse – thirty-six-year-old Canadian-born opera singer Laura de Turczynowicz, who had married a Polish count and now lived in a big manor house at Suwalki. The stricken enemy soldier told her sorrowfully: 'The great lords have quarrelled, and we must pay for it with our blood, our wives and children.' Countess de Turczynowticz heard later that the German died before reaching an ambulance train to the rear. Most of his comrades on both sides would have agreed that his judgement on the struggle was hard to gainsay.

13

'Did You Ever Dance With Him?'

As early as 16 September, when the war was only six weeks old, André Gide reflected upon 'the impossibility of keeping oneself in a state of tension (which is after all artificial) as soon as nothing in the immediate surroundings motivates it. X goes back to reading, to playing Bach, and even to preferring the fugues with a joyful rhythm.' He recorded the expostulations at a railway station of an enraged woman, confronting staff who pleaded military imperatives to justify train delays: 'I am beginning to have enough of your war!'

Citizens of all the belligerent nations learned to live with a new, sombre and restrictive normality, which would persist for more than four years. *The Economist* deplored the draconian powers conceded to government by Britain's emergency regulations, some of which continued to be used and abused by ministers for decades after peace came. Germany imposed an order prohibiting the speaking of English in public places, which was matched by a German-language ban in St Petersburg. Defiance on the telephone invited a fine of 3,000 roubles, while people reckless enough to engage in German conversation face to face were notionally liable to deportation to Siberia. But such edicts were matched by a characteristically Russian carelessness about enforcement: moneyed Germans continued to live comfortably enough in the Tsar's capital, where on 14 November they held a banquet at which the Kaiser's health was drunk.

In every country many people strove to 'do their bit'; but others stayed at home, some with good reason. Marcel Proust was physically quite unfit for military service, and anyway concluded that in uniform he would be an inconvenience. 'I ask myself,' he said to a friend, 'what chaos I might not introduce into the services.' People fortunate enough to be spared from attendance on the battlefield addressed domestic concerns. In late

September, the vineyard-owners of Bordeaux reported a fine start to the grape harvest, and speculated that 1914 claret might match the magnificence of 1870, a precedent few Frenchmen welcomed. In Austria there was a winter fashion for *Kriegsblusen* and *Kriegshüte* – 'war blouses' and 'war hats'. Wearing such garments, unbecoming as they appeared, was thought patriotic, a gesture of solidarity with soldiers at the front. As prosperous households curtailed menus, more because of a shortage of kitchen staff than – as yet – a shortage of food, *The Lady* advised its genteel British readers: 'The second course – pudding – is especially looked forward to by the younger members of the family. If the dinner is to be reduced to two courses, the choice by them would fall on meat and pudding, or fish and pudding, and would not be in favour of fish and meat with the pudding left out.'

Many businessmen treated the war as an exasperating intrusion. The letterboxes of Europe filled with bad-tempered correspondence between commercial men and industrialists deploring shipments delayed and sales cancelled. The boss of a small company near Ulm wrote in August complaining of the 'unfortunate irruption of war'. On the 20th, German motor manufacturer Wilhelm Maybach wrote to his son Karl, lamenting the poor quality of a technical drawing the young man had produced: 'even if the war often distracts our thoughts, it provides no excuse for allowing such a serious matter as an [engine] transmission to suffer'. The British became obsessed by fears that spies were passing their secrets to Germany by carrier pigeon. This alleged menace caused the prosecution and imprisonment of several enemy aliens. For instance, Anton Lambert of Hermit Row, Plaistow, in East London, was given six months' hard labour for having twenty-four pigeons in his possession without a licence; the birds received a capital sentence.

Soaring prices, especially of food and notably in Germany, became a chronic blight which bore heavily upon the poor. Soup kitchens were established in many cities, to feed those who had suddenly lost their livelihoods. In France, a moratorium on rents was imposed. Each family whose breadwinner had gone to the army was paid an allowance of 1.25 francs a day, plus 50 centimes for each child below sixteen. In a society in which the 1911 average daily wage varied between 3.72 francs in the Vendée and 7.24 francs in Paris, some families found themselves better off with a man in the army. The government recognised this, but considered the price worth paying, to sustain morale. The British were less generous: after two months of war, at a time when a judge received a salary of £5,000 a year and the permanent under-secretary at the Foreign Office was paid £2,500, the cabinet voted on war widows' pensions. Churchill suggested a figure of 7s.6d. a week; others proposed 6s.6d. Lloyd George, the chancellor, argued for five shillings, and this lower figure was accepted.

Hardship and suffering on the home front were most unequally distributed. The poor, and especially those dependent on consumer industries, such as the furniture-makers of Shoreditch and the piano-builders of Islington, underwent severe hardship. Many families resorted to pawn-brokers in order to feed themselves; the better-off sold furniture and bicycles. Music halls were badly hit, accelerating the trend for their conversion into cinemas. Meanwhile the more affluent complained bitterly about the shortage of servants, but had no difficulties in securing nourishment: the menu for the 9 November Lord Mayor's Banquet in London featured turtle soup, fillets of sole, mutton cutlets, baron of beef, casserole of pheasant, smoked tongue, charlotte russe and meringues.

In the autumn, the government was dismayed by reports of indigence and alcoholism at the bottom end of society. One report stated: 'the excessive drinking among women continues, and there is said to be a great deal of begging'. The War Office asked police to keep an eye on the welfare – and implicitly also, the chastity – of absent soldiers' wives, a role they were understandably reluctant to accept. By Christmas, conditions were somewhat improved. Army spouses were being paid separation allowances, and employment was picking up. With more money about, the jewellery trade, which had slumped in the autumn, began to revive. Women started to take on men's jobs, a trend that would grow apace. Where in 1914 there were only a thousand woman railway clerks, four years later there would be 14,000.

Shipowners, millers, corn and sugar merchants prospered. Many factories were converting production lines to manufacture weapons, ammunition or military equipment, some of it esoteric, such as wooden saddle-trees shaped by former cabinet-makers. Kitchener stunned Sir Edward Grey by demanding that the Foreign Office source and supply 10,000 live goats a month to meet the ritual dietary requirements of Indian troops in France. Though the goats were not forthcoming, an acceptable substitute was found. But the general pace of economic mobilisation was sluggish, and in 1915 the shell shortage exposed by the Northcliffe press would reveal its inadequacy.

Some British trades unionists, who had been persuaded to suspend shop-floor hostilities in August for the sake of national solidarity, were losing patience with their truce. They saw their employers garnering handsome profits from the conflict, and found no reason why they should not do likewise. The *Shop Assistant* on 12 December denounced 'that spurious patriotism' which regarded any 'militant attitude [from] which friction would arise between employer and employee' as betrayal of country. Almost three million working days would be lost to industrial disputes in 1915, 2.4 million in 1916, more than five million in 1917, rising to close to six million in 1918. These figures, in years of acute national peril, emphasise the depth and bitterness of Britain's social divisions. Workplace recalcitrance struck a persistently discordant note in the British war effort, albeit less violently and dramatically manifested than were similar sentiments in Russia, Germany and Austria-Hungary in 1917–18.

The word '*Durchhalten*' – 'holding out' – was much used in Vienna newspapers, though an increasing number of people asked what they were holding out *for*. Austrian women were advised that vigorous chewing of food released more nutrients; the virtues of blackberry tea were extolled, and householders were urged to trim and peel vegetables as little as possible before cooking. Most commodities remained readily available, but bread supplies soon became erratic. Food rationing was introduced to Germany and Austria in 1915, to France only in 1917 and to Britain in the following year. But shortages and price inflation were endemic much earlier: French people complained bitterly about the poor quality of their bread.

Many people around the world debated how they might make a profit from the war, including several national governments. Turkey joined the Central Powers on 29 October, having extracted what seemed a handsome price from Germany in both cash and military aid. Turkey's rulers saw an opportunity to end the Ottoman Empire's diplomatic isolation: they were rash enough to believe that Germany would assist Constantinople's ambition to regain mastery of the Balkans. On the other side of the world the British wobbled about the merits of Japan entering the allied camp, and became thoroughly sceptical when it was pointed out that Tokyo's interest was driven solely by its imperialistic ambitions. But the Foreign Office's change of heart came too late: on 23 September Japan declared war on the Central Powers. It thus became one of four combatants – the others were Italy, Bulgaria and Romania – to join the struggle for territorial gains. With modest British help, Japanese troops promptly attacked and captured the German enclave of Tsingtao on the Chinese coast, displaying a tactical ingenuity their Western allies might profitably have emulated.

The Marquis of San Giuliano, Italian ambassador in London, told his French counterpart without embarrassment in October 1914 that three factors influenced the Italian debate about entering the war: morality, advantage and readiness. The Italian army was still unprepared to take the field, and the Rome government invited tenders from the belligerents to discover which would pay best for Italy's support. Sir Francis Bertie wrote contemptuously: 'The Italians imagine themselves to be much superior to the ancient Romans and destined to be the great Mediterranean power and the possessors of Tunis, Malta, Egypt and the Turkish islands.' In the following year Italy joined the allies, in return for agreed territorial gains, a transaction that reflected discredit on both contracting parties, and colossal folly by the Rome government.

Some neutral countries, the United States, Holland and Norway prominent among them, were already profiting mightily from the freedom to exploit commercial markets perforce neglected by the belligerents. By 1918 several Norwegian shipping fortunes would be made, though half the country's merchant fleet was eventually sunk by U-boats. In the United States, at the outbreak of war President Woodrow Wilson called on Americans to remain neutral in heart as well as law, but after some initial government alarm about the potential of the war to damage the US economy, they quickly realised that instead it opened prodigious industrial and trading opportunities, especially after the August opening of the Panama Canal.

At a personal level, war profiteering became a Europe-wide phenomenon, and an Austrian was responsible for one of its more imaginative manifestations. Otto Zeilinger, burdened with a languishing scythe-manufacturing business at Knittelfeld, conceived the idea of converting the premises into a commercial prisoner-of-war camp. On 6 September he wrote to the authorities proposing a deal running until July 1915, which was as long as even this optimistic entrepreneur expected the war to last. There was tough haggling about prices: Zeilinger eventually accepted a rental of 25 crowns for every square metre of barrack space. He was entrusted with several hundred Russians as free labour to build huts, and by December was playing host to 20,000, with an additional contract to feed them.

At a humbler level, in France it proved necessary to place *laitiers* – milk-sellers – under police supervision, when it was found that 58 per cent of milk sold was being diluted with water from public fountains. In a dexterous coupling of social service and commercial opportunism, advertisements in French, addressed to Belgian refugees, began to appear in *The Times*, most offering furnished houses to rent: '*maisons meublées à louer*'. The newspaper announced: 'in view of the large number of French and Belgian subjects in England, advertisements will be translated, free of charge, by *The Times* staff, on request'. Among other visible manifestations of the new world, from October London streetlamps were painted over, for fear of an air attack such as had already befallen several European cities. Londoners of all classes found the blackout bewildering and indeed distressing, especially when the winter passed without German intrusions.

Middle-class civilians, by contrast, considered a display of optimism a patriotic duty. 'Life in London appears to be not merely normal, but even unusually gay,' wrote a journalist in the week before Christmas. Some embryo soldiers acknowledged the same imperative. A recruit to Kitchener's New Armies, training in conditions of acute discomfort and maladministration in southern England, nonetheless wrote almost euphorically in the *New Statesman* about his early experiences in khaki:

> I have been too exhilarated to think. I have certainly never in my life experienced more continuous cheerfulness and – in the truest sense of the word – more happiness than in these three months. The sense of physical fitness; the exhilaration of a collective regimental life; the constant opportunities for the formation of new friendships with men of widely varying experiences; the congeniality of a life which is communistic in just the aspect in which communism is convenient and stimulating … and last and least the humorous aspects of one's own and one's comrades' activities all combine to expel the baneful elements of existence. I may possibly live to think differently; but at the present moment, assuming this war had to come, I feel nothing but gratitude to the gods for sending it in my time. Whatever war itself may be like, preparing to fight in time of war is the greatest game and the finest work in the world.

Such sentiments were widely shared, until the writer and his comrades reached the Western Front in 1915.

Meanwhile, across the Channel, early in December the French government returned to Paris from its unheroic exile in Bordeaux, which had done lasting injury to the prestige of President Poincaré. Social tensions, in abeyance during the autumn crisis, were resurfacing. The middle class, many of whom lived on income from property, were increasingly resentful of the enforced moratorium on rent collection. A cartoon by Harmann-Paul depicted a bourgeois kneeling before the prime minister and saying, 'Take my son for four, five, six years, if you like, but spare, oh! spare my income.' The rich seemed in no mood to take pity on the poor. A French national fund for the relief of distress collected only £200,000 – a fraction of the amounts raised by such appeals in other countries – of which the Rothschilds contributed £40,000. Paris was cautiously returning to life, with some dressmakers in the Rue de Paix reopening their shops and several theatres giving matinees. But public transport shut down at 10 p.m., and many wealthy Parisians who had fled in August found it more congenial to linger in south or south-west France, out of earshot of gunfire, rather than return to a drab wartime capital.

Some of the rich found their fortunes severely injured by wartime inflation, but businessmen with access to military contracts prospered mightily. In September the French war minister invited industrialists to a meeting in Bordeaux at which he informed them that a shell crisis was looming: within a month, stocks of 75mm ammunition would be down to two rounds a gun. A crash programme was introduced, setting a target of 100,000 shells per day that was only achieved a year later; production of explosives rose in the same period from forty-one tons a day to 255 tons. Specialist workers were hastily recalled from the army to assist in manufacturing war matériel, wearing a red armband adorned with a grenade to show that they were not shirkers. This did not prevent some industrialists from exploiting exemptions to bring home their own unskilled friends and loved ones. Fortunes were soon being made, as household-goods makers turned to producing mess tins, water bottles, spades as well as bombs and shells.

After the first weeks, when many French factories closed for lack of buyers for their wares, the war created feverish new demands which persisted for four years. In Isère, an iron foundry at Renage found itself working around the clock to fulfil government contracts for 10,000 spades and pickaxes a week. A Grenoble engineering factory employed five hundred men making metal trench shelters. Another works in the city was contracted to produce a thousand 75mm shells a day by Christmas 1914, which became 9,000 by 1918; its workforce swelled from eight hundred to 2,750. A local paper manufactory turned to shell filling, doubling its pre-war workforce. There was huge demand for canvas, explosives, leather, canteens, writing paper and pencils, ammunition components, canned food. Supplying such products enriched industrialists in every belligerent nation.

Chain letters containing prayers circulated, which recipients were urged to pass on to nine others. Churches in every country reported improved trade, though there was little evidence of increased godliness. War made many genteel people, soldiers and civilians alike, who had never in their lives used obscene language in the presence of others, suddenly find themselves in circumstances which caused them to say 'fuck'. To the dismay of respectable citizens, actions spoke louder than words. Extra-marital sex became an urgent preoccupation of those facing death or enduring separation. As A.E. Housman put it: 'I 'listed at home for a lancer/Oh, who would not sleep with the brave?' In Freiburg, in the first eight months of war venereal-disease figures more than doubled, and court convictions for prostitution soared; the experience of most cities was similar.

Some civilians, especially academics, strove to keep open lines of communication with their peers in enemy countries: this was thought a civilised gesture, emphasising the universality of European culture. In October 1914 Maynard Keynes sent a letter to Ludwig Wittgenstein via neutral Norway, asking the Austrian about the possibility that he might provide a scholarship for a Cambridge logician after the war. Wittgenstein, who was rich, had earlier shown himself a generous benefactor, but now he was crewing a Vistula picket boat. He reacted crossly to receiving a mere business proposal from an old friend 'at such a time as this'.

Premature death became a prevailing theme: in every belligerent nation, people grew accustomed to receiving news of a stream of loved ones and friends killed. Sir Edward Grey wrote to a colleague about his soldier brother Charlie, whose arm had just been amputated – 'we hope to get him home alive', as indeed they did – and a nephew badly wounded: 'It is a load of private grief to carry, but others have grief as heavy and heavier.' The family of schoolteacher Gertrud Schädla in Verden, near Bremen, found themselves unable to face reading the casualty lists published in newspapers – 'we do not feel strong enough'. They were dismayed by news of the Marne – 'we had to retreat a little bit in France'. Then, in October, far worse tidings came: young Ludwig Schädla was among the fallen. The family's letters to him were returned by the army, marked tersely 'Died 4.9'. Gertrud anguished over his fate: 'Was it an attack on his regiment, or perhaps a shot while he stood alone on guard on a dark night? So many perish – many, many more of our enemies than of our own. Alack, I feel bad for them all.'

Two days later, on 12 October, her brother Gottfried's mail was also sent home, marked 'wounded, whereabouts unknown'. They learned that he too had died, aged twenty-one, eight days after being admitted to a field hospital near Reims: 'So we have even lost our youngest, our *Sonnenschein* – "Sunshine"! Death, you are bitter! Wherewith shall we find solace?' She sought to console herself with the reflection that her brothers were with God. 'Lord, keep our beloved boys with you. Their struggle came to an end, they grasped victors' laurels, and we will not wish them back.'

Families yearned, often in vain, for crumbs of news about the fate of fallen loved ones. A dead French soldier's wrist identity tag was customarily dispatched to his next of kin with the laconic words 'Perished on the field of honour'. This practice was known as 'receiving the medal'. One woman with five children who gave birth to twins soon after her husband departed for the front 'received the medal' the same night. It became fashionable to send out mourning cards, such as one for Léon-Pierre-Marie Challamel, pupil at the seminary of Saint-Sulpice, '*mort pour la France, le 24 Septembre 1914 au combat de Crécy (Somme) à l'âge de 22 ans*'. In Verden, Magdalene Fischer, girlfriend of Ludwig Schädla who had perished in France, visited the town photographer in hopes of finding a last picture of him in uniform. Instead, she found only a group shot in which her young man was scarcely visible. Then she discovered that Ludwig's company commander, Lt. Gatzenmeyer, was lying wounded in a local hospital. He offered some crumbs of information, true or invented, about her lover's last days. These were more than many families received.

Because soldiering had been a familiar peacetime occupation for the sons of the British upper classes, losses in France bore heavily upon them. A 19 September fatal casualty list included the names of such gilded young men as Percy Wyndham, Lord Guernsey, Rivvy Grenfell. Asquith enquired about the latter of Venetia Stanley: 'Did you ever dance with him?' She must have done. There was hardly a 'roll of honour' published that winter which did not mention names familiar to every former debutante. Whatever else was said about the war, it could not be suggested that the British ruling class was skimping its share of the blood price: sixty members of the aristocracy died in France and Flanders between 23 August and 31 December; thereafter the combat mortality rate among the peerage steadied at six a month. A long succession of men who had achieved celebrity in their own gilded little world now secured brief obituaries. Lionel Tennyson wrote on 14 October: 'Poor Willy Macneil of the

16th Lancers who used to ride Foolhardy in the Grand National was killed quite close to us here this morning.'

In every country, schools were conscripted to promote enthusiasm for the struggle. Albert Sarraut, France's minister of public instruction, wrote in a circular to heads: 'It is my wish that on the opening day of the term, in every town and every class, the teacher's very first words should raise up all the hearts to the nation, and ... honour the sacred struggle in which our forces are engaged ... Every one of our schools has sent soldiers into the line of fire – teachers or pupils – and every one, I know well, already bears the proud grief of its deaths.' André Gide recoiled from such language: 'A new rubber stamp is being created, a new conventional psychology of the patriot, without which it is impossible to be respectable. The tone used by the journalists to speak of Germany is nauseating. They are all getting on the bandwagon. Each is afraid of being late, of seeming a less "good Frenchman" than the others.'

French schools were urged to set pupils such essay subjects as 'The Regiment Departs', 'Letter From an Unknown Big Brother Who is Fighting for Us', 'Arrival of a Trainload of Wounded Men', 'The Germans Have Killed a Small Boy Aged Seven Whom They Found Playing in a field with a Toy Gun' and 'The Germans Have Invaded Your Town – Describe Your Feelings'. Geography, headmasters were told, should be based upon an operational map of the war zones, updated daily. Wounded men who returned to teach were deemed to have a specially useful role to play, though this may not have turned out to be that which the Education Ministry intended. German-language lessons were dropped in favour of English, and in the history syllabus there was a new emphasis on Latin and Greek heroes.

German *Abitur* certificate exams posed such questions as 'If life is a struggle, what are our weapons?'; 'What motivates every German fit for military service to respond to the Fatherland's call to arms?' One Berlin school invited essays on the theme 'the war as an educational force'. In every nation, children were recruited to conduct street collections of metal that might be forged into munitions. Elfriede Kuhr in Schneidmühl was fascinated by the notion that pots and pans she wrung out of her sceptical family could be transformed into bullets. Elfriede's grandmother complained crossly that all these school collections would be the ruin of her.

Children's games became strongly influenced by the war. The English toy firm Britain's manufactured a wide range of model soldiers of the warring nations. In Hamburg, four-year-old Ingeborg Treplin declared her kiddiecar to be a troop transport. When her mother took all three Treplin girls to Hamburg's Hermann Tietz department store, they found its floor dominated by a vast toy battlefield, adorned with a fortress, French and German soldiers, burning houses and an aeroplane above. Anna Treplin wrote, 'the children were awed'. The trade magazine of the toy-manufacturing industry, *Deutsche Spielwarenzeitung*, sought to claim for its fraternity an important role. Toys, it asserted, were no mere luxury products; rather, they 'inculcated the progress of the war in children's minds, instilling national feeling, honesty, and patriotism'.

Though every nation's children were wooed into the war effort, the commitment of the British public schools was exceptional. In *Death of a Hero*, Richard Aldington penned a portrait of a typical product of the system – the sort who officered Kitchener's New Armies – which was entirely cynical but not wholly unjust:

> He accepted and obeyed every English middle-class prejudice and taboo. What the English middle classes thought and did was right, and what anybody else thought and did was wrong. He was contemptuous of all foreigners. He appeared to have read nothing but Kipling, Jeffrey Farnol, Elinor Glyn, and the daily newspapers. He disapproved of Elinor Glyn as too 'advanced'. He didn't care about Shakespeare, had never heard of the Russian ballets, but liked to 'see a good show'. He thought *Chu Chin Chow* [a popular musical] was the greatest play ever produced ... He thought Americans were a sort of inferior Colonials, regrettably divorced from that finest of all institutions, the British Empire ... He was exasperatingly stupid, but he was honest, he was kindly, he was conscientious, he could obey orders and command obedience in others, he took pains to look after his men. He could be implicitly relied upon to lead a hopeless attack, and to maintain a desperate defence to the very end. There were thousands and tens of thousands like him.

R.C. Sherriff, a wartime officer who later became famous as author of the 'trench play' *Journey's End*, asserted that public schoolboys led men in France not through military skill, for no such accomplishment was needed, but rather by personal example, 'from their reserves of patience and good humour and endurance'. Both the virtues and the vices of the English public-school system were conspicuous on the battlefields of 1914, and its standard-bearers at home responded with an orgy of sentimentality which rendered even some patriots queasy. The first teacher killed was Lt. A.J.N Williamson of Highgate, whose passing prompted an editorial in *The Times Educational Supplement* on 22 September: 'Everybody recognises the fact that the spirit of discipline and sportsmanship inculcated in our schools is bearing rich and glorious fruit on the stern fields of duty, and everyone knows that many of the most stirring and heroic deeds chronicled in the war redound to the credit of young officers whose schooldays ended but a few months ago.' The October issue of the *Eton College Chronicle* commemorated with a poem the death of Lt. A.H. Blacklock of the Argyll & Sutherland Highlanders, who had doffed his tailcoat only the previous summer:

> At the head of your Highland men,
> Charging the terrible wood,
> With only one thought in your dear old head,
> To die as a soldier should.

By November 1914 Eton had lost sixty-five of its former pupils, Wellington thirty-eight, Charterhouse and Harrow twenty-one each, Rugby twenty. This toll did nothing to stem martial ardour among such schools' leavers. Lord Cranborne, heir to the Marquess of Salisbury, invited his two friends Oliver Lyttelton and Arthur Penn to stay at Hatfield, the family palace, until the army was ready to accept their services. They passed much of the time shooting, which prompted laughter about another sort of gunfire they would soon experience. A determination to view the play as a comedy persisted through a later spell in France: when Penn was invalided home after being shot in both legs, he added an entry to his gamebook: 'Beat – Cour de l'Avoue, Bag – Self.'

In a sixth-form debate at Westminster, the motion 'It will be disastrous to the world when Arbitration takes the place of War' was carried by eleven votes to seven, though interestingly another motion – 'The Kaiser is responsible for the present War' – was defeated by ten votes to six. Schoolmasters shepherded their former pupils towards the battlefield with a ruthlessness suggesting that they supposed themselves dispatching a cricket eleven to play in the Great Game. On 2 September Dr A.A. David, headmaster of Rugby, wrote to *The Times* emphasising the moral benefits of volunteering: 'here is a splendid opportunity of giving a lead to young men of all classes. Here also is a supreme test of school spirit and character … To parents we would recommend a mother's advice to a hesitating son

... "My boy, I don't want you to go, but if I were you, I should."' So extravagant was the sentimentality with which the war was promoted in its early months that in due time, as its human cost soared, a lasting revulsion emerged among some of the audience, who felt that they had been duped. The genuine merits of the allied cause became profoundly tarnished by the baroque language and spurious religiosity with which it was marketed, especially in the eyes of the generation that would do most of the dying that made victory belatedly possible.

Deepening shadows over their own prospects of survival caused some men to abandon thoughts of early marriage, but persuaded others to seize the moment. The daughter of a friend of parliamentary lawyer Hugh Godley was married on 23 August, and became a widow when her new husband was killed just four days later. A twenty-four-year-old gunner officer named John Peake Knight, DSO, had been engaged to a Miss Olive Knight of Brighton since 1913. In August 1914 they agreed to delay a wedding until the end of the war, but the approach of winter in the trenches caused them to change their minds. Knight was granted a brief leave. The loving couple were joined at St John's church, Bromley, the groom clad in khaki, as had become fashionable, rather than displaying the glories of full dress uniform. A reception was held at his parents' house, nearby Sundridge Park; within days, John Knight was back with his battery in France, where he was killed in 1916. Many newspaper accounts reported weddings without receptions or perhaps even consummations, such as that of Miss Joan Jameson to Mr John Farrell of the Leinster Regiment: 'The honeymoon was to have been spent in Scotland, but the bridegroom had to rejoin his regiment.'

Amid millions of separations, letters assumed a critical significance in the lives of divided families. Some men wrote home every day they were not in action, and many wives put pen to paper at least as often. Most Europeans were now literate: during the entire 1870 war, the Prussian army in the field received half a million letters and parcels. By contrast, in 1914 that figure rose to 9.9 million pieces dispatched each day to the German army, with 6.8 million coming back. The mere fact of receiving a communication from a loved one was cause for emotion: 'I received such a long and lovely letter from my husband,' wrote Austrian schoolteacher Itha J on 19 October. 'How much we women depend on our beloved spouses!'

But most writers both at home and in the field found it hard to describe events, and especially to avow passion, in a fashion remotely capable of matching the emotional needs of the recipients. Itha J again: 'I write a daily letter to my beloved husband. I recount everything that saddens and moves me. Yesterday I had one letter from him, and today two. He writes in a factual, interesting way about his daily doings. At the end, there is always a little [word of] tenderness! I would like less objective description and more tenderness. But he can't help himself – he must wring every tender word out of his rough heart.' Some French peasants, transformed into *poilus*, wrote home to give their womenfolk minute instructions about their farms. One soldier, from Saint-Alban in the Tarn, expressed anxiety about a mare in the stable, and demanded accusingly of his wife: 'You say that you are not behind [with the tillage] but you do not tell me [how many] sacks of oats and corn you have sown.' A woman in Lot-et-Garonne sent a present of pâté to her husband's commanding officer, hoping desperately that this might persuade him to spare her man from utmost peril.

'It was a polite convention at home, to which men on leave conformed,' wrote gunner officer Rolfe Scott-James, the author's grandfather, 'to respect their supposed disinclination to talk about the war. The real disinclination was that of the people at home to listen. I do not mean that the overseas serviceman was in any degree better or worse than his fellow-countryman at home – only that the latter had turned into one kind of animal, the former into another. If the truth be told, they were not really even in sympathy.'

Some privileged people found it hard to treat the war with the gravity it assuredly demanded. After a visit to France in October, Violet Asquith wrote to her father the prime minister, describing in tones of teasing gaiety her cross-examination of an old woman refugee 'in hope of atrocities': '*Les allemands se sont mal conduits dans votre village?*'

'*Très mal – ils ont tout ravagé etc.*'

'*Ils étaient cruels?*'

'*Très cruels – ils ont tué un cochon!*'

The questioner expressed relief about 'the death of a pig having loomed so large in the category of horrors!' She was too crass to know how large such a tragedy might loom in the economy of a French peasant family.

Contemporary issues of the society magazine *The Lady* likewise emphasise the naïveté that persisted in British polite society. On 15 October a correspondent lamented the privations thrust upon the rural upper classes by losing so many husbands and hunt servants to the army. Under the headline 'Sportswomen and the War', her letter reported crossly: 'Troubles at the kennels are unending, for at present no one has got the work in hand.

Though Evelyn is down there morning, noon and night, she has not sufficient confidence in her own judgement to keep the men in order. The feeding is a constant bother, for the man who now reigns as feeder is a dirty,
slovenly creature who only follows our directions when he is forced to.'

Quite early in the war, there were signs of a trend which became
progressively more pronounced – a decline of social deference, to the
dismay of its former beneficiaries. An Englishman who met an old friend
from Oxford days lamented: 'Ten years ago, when I came into a crowded
bus, a working man would rise and touch his cap and give me his seat. I
am sorry to see that spirit dying out.' Racial distinctions, however,
remained as sharp as ever. The *Clarion* on 10 October deplored a report
that a British general had dined in the same hotel dining room as an
Indian prince in uniform without addressing a word to him. On the
following night in the same hotel's smoking room, an eyewitness saw a
group of officers likewise ignoring the 'dusky potentate'. A *Clarion*
columnist wrote angrily: 'If an Indian Prince is not fit to speak to, why
does our King accept his services?'

This was a good question, but not one which the arbiters of British
society chose to answer. If pressed, many of them would have asserted that
the war was being fought to preserve the standards and decencies of traditional Britain. Almost all the belligerents, indeed, supposed themselves to
be upholding conservative social values. Middle-class volunteers for the
army raised strong objections, in Leo Amery's words, to 'being put down
in the barracks next to a couple of lousy and swearing hooligans'. Cyril
Asquith, the prime minister's younger son who later served as an officer
in France, described war service contemptuously as 'fighting barbarians in
the company of bores and bounders'. Though shared peril caused some
blurring of class distinctions at the front, many middle-class men – and
women – found it hard to adjust to being thrust into enforced intimacy
with their social inferiors: 'Never did I expect it would fall to my lot to
sleep a whole night under heavy shell fire in a room with common soldiers
and all of us lying on straw,' wrote nurse Elsie Knocker in a Belgian barn.
When she accompanied a group of wounded men back to England, they
were all obliged to doss down for the night in a Dover hostel, after being
refused admission to a local hospital. At Euston station, she had difficulty
persuading the authorities to allow her casualties to be laid out in the
ladies' waiting room until their train came.

A few fortunate folk found themselves, by contrast, in environments
more comfortable than those to which they were accustomed at home.

Austrian peasant Karl Auberhofer, a thirty-four-year-old father of seven mobilised with the *Landsturm*, was billeted in a luxury hotel in the Tyrol. He marvelled: 'One can just sit down at a table and be served by a waitress as if one was a nobleman – one doesn't have to think about anything.' As Auberhofer was fortunate enough to escape front-line service, he decided that military duty was much preferable to hard labour on his farm. He and his comrades passed their days and nights drinking and gambling with an abandon unthinkable at home. Duty obliged him only to spend two hours a day guarding a railway line, so 'church parades are our hardest work apart from eating'.

The Lady addressed with sublime condescension the issue of continental refugees in England: 'English life and ways must seem strange to the many Belgians and French staying here. One thing that the womenfolk sadly miss is the bargaining which is the accompaniment of almost every purchase they make in their respective countries. The fixed price which is the joy of most Englishwomen they regard as a dull arrangement.' The magazine's social gossip column picked up the same theme: 'Among the many who are offering hospitality to the Belgians who have suffered so greatly from the war are Lord and Lady Exeter, who have the Belgian Countess Villers and her five children as their guests at Burghley House, their historic place in the Midlands. Lady Exeter, who has the pretty name of Myra, is very attractive, with fair hair and dark eyes. Turquoises become her, and she owns some beautiful ornaments in these stones.'

The Lady strove to help women address unexpected social problems thrown up by the war. In its 'Daily Difficulty' column of 10 December, it raised the dilemma facing a cat-owning woman who houses a dog for an officer setting forth for the front. When the dog starts killing her cats, what should she do? *The Lady* asserted that she had a responsibility to ensure the dog was properly quartered, but might reasonably seek another home for it. The magazine also reported delicate problems of etiquette facing wives returning from the colonies. It urged that they should not have calling cards printed with their temporary addresses, but instead merely strike through their permanent address on existing cards. They should recognise that established residents of a given community would not call on a newcomer unless introduced by a mutual acquaintance. To facilitate this process, *The Lady* suggested that newcomers from abroad should post notice of their arrival in a reputable newspaper. The nearest the magazine came to addressing the travails of British menfolk on the continent was in an article on logistics: 'the task of feeding an army of hard-worked men on a modern battlefield is a truly wonderful achievement – "housekeeping" you may term it, upon a colossal scale. Because we have command of the sea, however, provisioning our Expeditionary Force becomes a fairly easy matter.' It is unsurprising that many people at home remained blissfully ignorant of the horrors unfolding in France, if they relied on *The Lady* for enlightenment – and serious newspapers offered little more substantial fare.

Some innocents allowed lingering wisps of humanitarian sentiment to cross the fronts. In Schneidemühl little Elfriede Kuhr wrote in her diary: 'Sailors whose vessels sink in naval battles must be terribly frightened, because no ship will stop to rescue them. When all those people drowned after the *Titanic* hit an iceberg, the whole world recoiled in horror. Now, ships sink every day and nobody asks what happens to the crews.' The little girl and her friend Gretel embraced a personal mission: to tidy and decorate the graves of Russian PoWs who died in the local camp near Schneidemühl, far from their homes.

PoW compounds became popular tourist attractions in rural areas, where foreign visitors of any kind had a curiosity value. The authorities became exasperated by the peasant practice of taking a Sunday family stroll to peer at the inmates through the wire; in Münster an order was published banning all civilians from approaching within six hundred metres of a camp. In German cities, crowds – mostly women – assembled around trains bearing prisoners on their way to PoW camps. Some patriots were shocked by displays of sympathy for the foreigners' plight: a journalist accused those who indulged in such feelings of succumbing to 'a degenerate desire for erotic adventure', and the government threatened to publish the names of these shameless creatures. When it emerged that four nurses at Thionville had become engaged to French PoWs, the German Red Cross was informed by the government that its volunteers would no longer be permitted to visit the compounds.

Any display of sympathy for the enemy became increasingly unacceptable. In Carinthia a Slovenian Catholic priest was imprisoned as a Serbophile for telling his flock: 'Let us pray for the Emperor and Austria but also for the Serbs to see the light.' Dr Eugen Lampe wrote gleefully from Hapsburg Ljubljana about news of British defeats: 'Everyone wishes ill to the British. Bernatorič, whose Jewish establishment called itself "The English Clothing Warehouse", announces that he has renamed it "The Ljubljana Clothing Warehouse".' An English acquaintance of Ethel Cooper, who lived in Leipzig, had a baby by a German man who was killed in France. The authorities refused either to support the child or to allow the woman, as an enemy alien, to take a job. The Oxford classicist Gilbert Murray initially opposed the war, but before long was writing: 'I find that I desperately desire to hear of German dreadnoughts sunk in the North Sea ... When I see that 20,000 Germans have been killed in such-and-such an engagement and next day that it was only 2,000, I am sorry.'

Louis Barthas found himself among soldiers escorting German prisoners on a train across southern France. Newspapers had incited local people to show their feelings towards such 'monsters with human features', and at every station furious crowds appeared – women spitting, men brandishing knives and rocks. The same people pressed on the French guards wine and grapes which, as soon as the train moved off, they shared with their charges: 'this gesture of camaraderie makes up for the odious displays against the unarmed enemy'. Those who had seen the dreadful realities of war recoiled from displays of chauvinism. A Paris music-hall performer who sang a song suggesting that German troops ran away, and that most of their shells were duds, received an icy reception from an audience which included soldiers on leave. More popular French ditties suggested that the real German crime was submission to despotism: one, 'Le Repas manqué', concerned a supposed invitation to the Kaiser to have dinner in Paris; the chorus went 'Nous f'rons des crêpes et t'en mang'ras!' – 'We'll make the pancakes and you'll eat them!'

Many women across Europe felt a profound sense of frustration that while their menfolk were winning laurels on the battlefield and receiving popular adulation, their own role was confined to knitting socks and writing letters. 'We here, far inland, see scarcely anything of the hardships of war,' wrote Gertrud Schädla in December, 'beyond worrying about our beloved fighting men.' Gertrud and her mother spent much of the winter sewing clothes and collecting charity contributions for refugees from East Prussia. Knitting for soldiers became a universal preoccupation, almost a sacred duty, for Europe's women. Yet the fruits of their labours were sometimes cynically received. Egon Kisch catalogued a consignment which reached his Austrian unit in Serbia in November: 'warm underwear – of course only knitted nonsense – neatly-embroidered gloves, wristlets with a heart stitched in red, mittens to fit baby elephants, kneepads for storks and similar stuff that the lasses knitted during jolly parties to assuage their boredom or satisfy their pretensions'. Corporal Kisch was grudgingly grateful, but would have preferred cigarettes.

Some women enjoyed first-aid classes, which brought them together. But Graz schoolteacher Itha J wrote on 16 September: 'Every day there is a weight upon me. What is it? I believe it is a gnawing discontent that during these great times I can do nothing beyond baby-sitting.' In Britain, even *The Lady* bewailed the limitations on the contributions women might make: 'Soon all the committees will be formed, the needlework in hand, members of the Red Cross Society ready for the word of command, the chosen nurses away to their places – every woman in the land doing all that is possible for her to do in the way of special work. Yet in spite of everything there will still be in all our hearts a sensation of yearning to do more.'

Mrs Mayne was the wife of a British soldier stationed in Ireland. She herself worked in an East London hostel, coping with a throng of German, Belgian and Scandinavian women caught far from home. The war inflicted on her a profound sense of loneliness and isolation from her husband, while her brothers trained to become soldiers: 'almost a feeling of suffocation overwhelmed me'. She watched flag-sellers, shoppers and ambulances coming and going in a frenzy of activity. 'It was all a maze and yet secretly in my heart there was a feeling of pride [in Britain at war] – which now I think was wrong.' She accepted a post as theatre sister at a British hospital in Belgium, and set off after posting her wedding ring to her husband Gerald for safekeeping. Unfortunately, in the emotionalism of her departure she forgot to enclose an explanatory covering note, causing bewilderment and distress to the ring's recipient.

At the end of September, a German girl named Helene Schweida made a courageous but naïve attempt to visit the army in France, to see her beloved boyfriend Wilhelm Kaisen. Her progress was arrested by an officer in western Germany who turned her smartly homewards, declaring loftily that only men could approach the theatre of operations. 'Once again, I forgot that I am a mere woman,' she wrote bitterly. Yet already, in a fashion that gained momentum with every day of the war, women proved their indispensability as substitutes for men in many roles. Toulouse, along with other French cities, acquired its first women postal deliverers, firefighters and even tram conductors, dubbed the '*Ponsinettes*' because the Toulouse transport company was owned by a M. Pons. Women who took work in armament factories were called '*munitionettes*'.

British ambulance driver Dorothie Feilding wrote home from Belgium on 17 October, lamenting her lot: 'Everything has been chaos & I have had to run the whole damn show. I wish there was a man with a head in charge.

As soon as I get back I shall settle down & marry a big strong man who will bully me. I'm sick of trying to run other people.' But it is plain that this cry of dismay reflected only momentary exhaustion: for the most part, Feilding, a twenty-five-year-old daughter of the Earl of Denbigh, revelled in the excitements and opportunities her role offered.

At the outset she had been fearful that her volunteer unit would not be permitted to play an active role: 'Alas I don't think we women will be allowed to do much actual fieldwork. We will have to be behind most of the time if not all.' But she soon found herself exulting in her experiences: 'There's going to be heaps to do, it's topping being up near things & so jolly interesting.' On the night of 8 October, she helped to carry two British casualties three miles back from the trenches. She was unwilling to expose herself, however, to aid fallen enemies: 'I don't mind running risks for our men or the French but I'm blithered if I'm going to have holes put in me by a bally Teuton while I pick up their men.'

Women in all the warring nations would soon follow pioneers such as herself, assuming unprecedented authority and responsibility. But some traditional gender roles were slow to change: behind the front in Belgium, nurse Mrs Elizabeth 'Elsie' Knocker, a twenty-nine-year-old doctor's daughter from Exeter, wrote in her diary on 29 September: 'Sewed a button on the general's coat – he was charming to me.'

In every country, at first at least, the war increased the symbolic importance of the monarchs in whose names it was supposedly being fought. Austrian newspapers reported with slavish deference a visit by Franz Joseph to the military hospital established in Vienna's Augartenpalais. Young aristocrat Rüdiger Rathenitz was one of those who met the Emperor: 'Archduchess Maria Josefa introduced me and he asked about my wound and my unit. The monarch, whom I last saw in 1909 at St Pölten – when I was a pupil in the military school there – was now more stooped than on that occasion, and remained comparatively silent. I was warned … to respond very loudly to his questions. I had brought a Russian haversack, some badges and bullets as souvenirs from the battlefield, and I showed these items to the Emperor … who seemed quite interested.'

Die Neue Zeitung duly told Franz Joseph's subjects: 'The kind manner in which the Supreme Warlord greeted his officers prompted a captain whose right arm had been amputated humbly to beg the privilege of continuing to serve in the army. The sovereign was visibly moved, and gave the loyal officer his promise. In the huge hall in which the monarch stayed for nearly an hour, he spoke to all of the 102 soldiers in their national languages … which visibly infused his soldiers with happiness.' Graz schoolteacher Itha J transcribed this newspaper account almost verbatim into her diary, adding her own characteristically sentimental comment: 'These poor ordinary men will have been infinitely delighted that the Emperor spoke to them. And how many others – even the wounded – will feel jealous of those who received this mercy! – Life is unfair. One is lucky, others are not.'

The monarchs of Europe were not notable for intellect, and some were slow to grasp the vast significance of the course on which Europe was embarked. Douglas Haig wrote on 11 August after lunching with George V: 'The King seemed anxious, but he did not give me the impression that he fully realised the grave issues for our country as well as for his own house, which were about to be put to the test; nor did he really comprehend the uncertainty of the results of all wars between great nations, no matter how well prepared one may think one is.' That winter, Haig met his monarch again after he had inspected troops at Saint-Omer, and noticed no great accession of wisdom: 'The King seemed very cheery but inclined to think that all our troops are by nature brave and is ignorant of all the efforts which Commanders must make to keep up the "morale" of their men in war, and of all the training which is necessary in peace in order to enable a company for instance to go forward as an organized unit in the face of almost certain death.' The King was at pains to explain away the war roles of his many relatives in the opposing camp. He told Asquith that – for instance – his cousin Prince Albert of Schleswig-Holstein was 'not really fighting on the side of the Germans', but merely running a PoW camp.

One night in October Austrian aristocrat Alexander Pallavicini sat next at dinner to the Archduke Karl, who had succeeded Franz Ferdinand as heir-apparent to the Hapsburg throne. Pallavicini recoiled in dismay from his neighbour's ignorance: 'It is unbelievable how "out of the picture" he is, because he has so little contact with soldiers. I completely lost my composure when he confidently asserted that the Russians were finished, the war as good as over. He brushed aside all doubts, stood by his statement.' When Pallavicini said that the war would be decided on the Western Front, where Austria-Hungary must support Germany, the future Emperor's response emphasised his bovine stupidity: 'France does not matter to us. We must march against Italy.'

Germany's ruler, by contrast, already revealed disenchantment with the adventure he had done much to promote. On 25 September, Admiral Albert Hopman sat next to the Kaiser at dinner, and was impressed by a war-weariness that was already in evidence. Wilhelm spoke of 'the awful slaughter of humanity' – '*furchtbare Menschenschlächterei*'. It was a little late to indulge such a spasm of sensitivity. Hopman observed bitterly to Admiral Tirpitz: 'for the last 25 years we have lived with a playful, unreasoning absolutism that found fulfilment in empty appearances and a vain craving for status which the nation indulged for too long. The majority of the people did not want that. But absolutist governance was responsible for our failure to produce statesmen, and instead only bureaucrats and lackeys.' This was a profound and important statement of how Germany stumbled into precipitating a war, written by an intimate observer of its governance.

As autumn deepened into winter, although the allies were deeply troubled about how they might win the conflict, they became less fearful that they might lose it, as they mobilised their strength increasingly effectively. On the other side, however, in many breasts a worm of apprehension grew. Ludwig Wittgenstein wrote on 25 October: 'I feel ever more strongly the awful tragedy of our – the German race's – predicament. It seems to me as good as certain that we cannot prevail against England. The English – the best race in the world – can't lose. But we can lose and will lose, if not this year then next. The idea that our race should be beaten distresses me terribly because I am completely and utterly German!'

The strident bellicosity of some warriors and their families had ebbed. On 26 September, Austrian schoolteacher Itha J wrote in her diary: 'Today I visited Dr K and his wife. I was uplifted by the strength of this clever man's faith. He is convinced that Germany and Austria will prevail, because justice is on their side – If only I could steadfastly believe as much!' On 10 October Elfriede Kuhr was astonished to hear her grandmother say, 'Every mother ought to go to the Kaiser and say: "Peace now!"' The old lady, experiencing the fourth Prussian war of her lifetime, now recoiled in horror at the prospect of almost unlimited bloodshed.

But a November political intelligence report from a workers' neighbourhood in Berlin's Moabit district declared that while local socialists might not be enthused about the struggle, they remained committed to it. Freiburg's veteran lord mayor Otto Winterer told a meeting of a thousand of his most prominent fellow citizens in St Paul's Hall on 28 September: 'We are a unified people of brothers, unified as well in answering the question: who bears the blame for starting this war? … All classes stand together, from the princes to the workers.' Kurt Alexander, editor of the liberal Jewish publication *K.C.-Blätter*, wrote in September, noting that many Germans accused Jews of not pulling their weight in the war effort: 'Therefore it is our holy duty to do more than anyone else. Each Jew must attempt to become a hero, whether in battle or in his [civil] occupation is unimportant. The deeds of each Jew must be worth so much that they are written into the history of the German people with golden letters.' There were as yet only a handful of dissenters, such as Krupp manager Wilhelm Muehlon, a visionary who dreamt of a Europe without frontiers and arbitrated by a common government, who deplored his own country's warmaking. Muehlon wrote in his diary: 'Prussia is today only capable of promoting deeper hatred among European peoples and elevating this to pure obsession.'

On 24 October Britain's *New Statesman* addressed the question being asked with renewed vigour, in intellectual circles at least: 'Why did we go to war?' It spoke of widespread opposition to Britain's alliance with autocratic Russia, 'and distrust of anything that is supported by the reactionary elements in this country'. Suggestions had been made that the war was deliberately started by reactionary forces to avoid social reform, a war of militarist aggression, and 'that we are fighting without any real reason simply and solely to please the diplomatists and arms manufacturers'. Rejecting such conspiracist views, the *Statesman* concluded temperately: 'We know that the mass of the German people did not want war, and those who may be expected to know … are almost unanimous in declaring their conviction that the Kaiser did not want war.' Britain's cabinet, Parliament and people 'consented to war for the sake of Belgium, and no matter what private desires – doubtless numerous and diverse – happen to have been gratified by the national decision, it is none the less true that it was on Belgium's account that that decision was reached'. The last statement was certainly valid.

Lloyd George made a significant contribution to the war effort through a speech, one of the most powerful of his career, delivered on 19 September at London's Queen's Hall. In it, he promulgated a doctrine that became a popular article of faith: that Britain was now engaged in a war to end wars, a crusade 'for the emancipation of Europe from the thraldom of a military caste … The people will gain more from this struggle in all lands than they comprehend at the present moment … The great flood of luxury and sloth which had submerged the land is receding and a new Britain is appearing.' His words made a profound inspirational impact, but would later reap a bitter harvest. When Lloyd George's vision, that the war would secure both a national moral regeneration and a radical political settlement, went conspicuously unfulfilled in 1918, the disillusionment of the British people was very great. Many recoiled in anger not merely from the trench experience – which was inevitable – but also from the false bill of goods sold to them by Lloyd George and his political kin. The Chancellor, who became Britain's prime minister in December 1916, could justly argue that other nations' politicians peddled similar falsehoods, but he would have done better to try to explain the truth to the British people back in 1914: that they, like the French, must pay a terrible price in blood and treasure for a victory from which they could aspire to no measurable advantage save acquisition of a few new colonies of questionable value; but that such a sacrifice must be borne, to avert much worse things if Germany triumphed.

God continued to be passionately invoked in both causes. The Archbishop of York declared fervently in October: 'every man who respects his conscience must stand to his place until the war is ended. There can be no peace until this German spirit of militarism is crushed.' In the same spirit, though for the opposing cause, Germany's churches were packed for every service. The pastor of Bremen's Unser Lieben Frauen church addressed the men of the city's reserve battalion in a farewell sermon before their entrainment for the front: 'It is a hard task that you are called upon to undertake, but one that is essential to your people's salvation. Even amid death and destruction you can become wonderful evangelists for idealism if you keep your consciences clear, even in the face of the enemy. The path you must take is so dark that none of you can be assured of returning home.' On that point at least, the pastor displayed prescience.

2 NEWS AND ABUSE

On 5 September Britain's prime minister wrote with his accustomed levity to the First Lord of the Admiralty: 'My dear Winston, The papers are complaining, not without reason, that we keep them on a starvation diet. I think the time has come for you to … let them have thro' the [Press] Bureau an "appreciation" of the events of the week; with such a seasoning of condiments as your well-skilled hand can supply. For all that the public knows, they might as well be living in the days of the prophet Isaiah, whose idea of battle was "confused noise & garments rolled in blood".'

A German priest observed: 'If before the war the newspaper was the friend of the house, now it is its ruler, for it determines the content of almost every conversation among family and friends.' The consequence of the public addiction to news, in the new age of the mass-circulation press, was that every government strove ruthlessly to manipulate presentation, through the written and spoken word, songs and the newly invented newsreel – by 1918 the French army had produced more than six hundred movies for public consumption. In several Paris music halls, including the Moulin Rouge, cinema performances supplanted live shows.

All the belligerents recognised the importance of American support, and embarked upon a vigorous contest to secure this. *The Times* editorialised smugly in August: 'it is with profound satisfaction that the British people have taken note that the cause in which they are fighting has the sympathy, the virtually unqualified sympathy, of their American kinsmen'. In truth, matters were more complicated. An Indiana editor wrote with a disdain widely echoed across the continent: 'We never appreciated so keenly as now the foresight exercised by our forefathers in emigrating from Europe.' President Woodrow Wilson, unfailingly moralistic, believed that the German and Austro-Hungarian systems of government required radical change, while declining to attribute sole responsibility for the war to the Germans. US industrialists identified, privately at least, a strong interest in an outcome that weakened global competition from Germany. Their country from the outset leaned towards the Entente, and some important Americans offered endorsements, notable among them ex-president Theodore Roosevelt. He emphasised the rights of small nations, especially Belgium, although until the 1915 sinking of the *Lusitania* he favoured armed neutrality rather than American belligerence. But the Central Powers also commanded significant support, especially in German ethnic communities. A German information bureau opened in the United States on 14 August, and the allies followed suit soon afterwards.

In France on 19 September, in the wake of battlefield crisis censorship was drastically tightened: editorial comment was banned that made 'intemperate attacks on the government or on the army high command', as were 'articles encouraging the termination or suspension of hostilities'. Early in October Clemenceau's newspaper *l'Homme libre* was shut down for a week, as a penalty for its exposure of the scandalous neglect of treatment for wounded soldiers. Ministers urged all titles to stop printing casualty lists. In Germany curbs on newspaper comment became rigorously enforced only in 1915, but after a Berlin central censorship office was established in October 1914, all discussion of military setbacks or defeats was officially banned, as were criticism of high policy, discussion of war aims, and dissent about the merits of the struggle.

At this early phase of the war, in all countries there was widespread support for ruthless news management. The writer Hilaire Belloc urged that bad tidings as well as military secrets should be suppressed: 'It is ... wise to keep the mass of people in ignorance of disaster that may be immediately repaired, or of follies or even vices in government which may be repressed before they become dangerous.' Belloc later wrote to G.K. Chesterton: 'It is sometimes necessary to lie damnably in the interests of the nation.' But the relationship between Britain's government and press was poisoned by the draconian manner in which censorship was implemented in the first months of war, and by suppression even of items of news about events at the front that were well known to the enemy.

All the belligerents sought to mobilise their sharpest and most elegant pens to make the case for their causes. Anatole France denounced not merely the Kaiser's regime, but also German culture, history and even wine. The composer Camille Saint-Saëns railed against Wagner. Some writers professed to have discovered that killing was virtuous. In an essay on war and literature, published in the early autumn of 1914, Edmund Gosse characterised war as a 'great scavenger of thought'. He likened the red stream of blood to a fluid the function of which was to 'clean out the stagnant pools and clotted channels of intellect'. Sir Arthur Conan Doyle, creator of Sherlock Holmes, argued in the pamphlet 'To Arms!': 'Happy the man who can die with the thought that in this greatest crisis of all he had served his country to the uttermost.'

On 18 October, fifty-four literary panjandrums jointly put their names to an article in the *New York Times* headed 'Famous British Authors Defend England's War'. Facsimile signatures of the named writers were printed at the foot of the piece. One of them, Arnold Bennett, produced more than three hundred propaganda articles in the course of the war. He confided in a letter to his American publisher that he had penned his first pamphlet – 'Liberty: A Statement of the British Case', published in October 1914 – because he feared that 'pacifist and financial influences' in Britain and the US might 'force a peace too soon' – before German militarism was decisively smashed. When a writer in the *New Statesman* questioned the credentials of novelists to pontificate about the issues of peace and war, Bennett responded somewhat pompously: 'As war is pre-eminently an affair of human nature, a triumph of instinct over reason, it seems to me not improper that serious novelists (who are supposed to know a little about human nature ...) should be permitted to express themselves concerning the phenomenon of a nation at war without being insulted.'

More pragmatically, Bennett found the government shilling useful; he and Ford Madox Ford were among writers who accepted substantial cheques for their services from the government propaganda bureau established at Wellington House.

In Germany, an academic noted in September that forty-three of the nation's sixty-nine history professors were labouring on articles about the war. Rudolf Eucken, a philosophy professor at Jena and a Nobel laureate, made thirty-six propaganda speeches in 1914. Berlin philosopher Alois Riehl exulted in print that 'our first victory ... has been the victory over ourselves. Never was a people so united as in those early, unforgettable August days ... Each of us felt that we lived for the whole and that the whole lived in all of us.' Among the most notorious betrayals of academic integrity was the so-called 'Manifesto of the Intellectuals of Germany', signed in October by ninety-three names headed by Ulrich von Wilamowitz-Moellendorff, protesting at the 'lies and calumnies' of the allies, who were 'endeavouring to stain the honour of Germany in her hard struggle for existence – a struggle which has been forced upon her'.

The violence of competing rhetoric and printed broadsides intensified rapidly. The destruction of Louvain and the bombardment of Reims cathedral became formidable weapons in promoting the allies' case that they were defending civilised values against Germanic barbarism. In France especially, where before the war divisions between Catholics and secularists ran deep, revulsion towards all things German proved a unifying force. In Britain, Wellington House published a report compiled by Lord Bryce's 'Committee to Investigate Alleged German Outrages' in Belgium and France, a document magisterial in language but sensationalist in content.

Several French writers claimed to identify significant physical distinctions between their own people and those of the Kaiser. A distinguished historian, Augustin Cochin, asserted in apparent earnest that there was a uniquely German smell – 'very strong and impossible to get rid of' – as well as an explicitly German species of flea, allegedly larger than those that afflicted French soldiers. It was such excesses as this that caused thoughtful and rational people to recoil in disgust from propaganda. As the war advanced and its horrors increased, some went further, succumbing to cynicism about the merits of all purported evidence and arguments in support of their own national causes.

Those who suppose the modern media uniquely prone to hyperbole, fantasy and deceit should consider the madness of rumour and invention that overtook the world's press in 1914. The *Daily Mail* published a detailed account of an entirely fictional naval victory. 'If damaging rumours start,' wrote Dr Eugen Lampe in Ljubljana early in September 1914, 'they spread at immense speed. If two people meet on the street, they ask each other: Any news? Nobody knows anything. But there are people who always choose to believe and broadcast the worst. For a week, the atmosphere has been extremely tense. Families, whose husbands and sons are in the army, mourn, pray and tremble. They fight to get at newspapers. Then they whisper: there are none of our casualties on the list of wounded. They do not want to tell us! There are so many that they cannot record all of them!'

Few of the journalists called upon to write about the war had any knowledge of military matters, and their ignorance showed. The introduction of trench warfare was at first greeted in the French press as a cowardly innovation by the Germans, who were mocked as 'moles'. Many papers talked up the enemy's weakness, flagging morale and food shortages. Austrian cities were said to be pleading with the Italians to save them from looming famine, while Germany was allegedly struggling in vain to recruit Italians to replace mobilised factory workers. Late in September *The Times* produced a wildly exaggerated calculation, based on the casualty lists, showing that the BEF had lost 40 per cent of its officers in a month of fighting. Ludwig Wittgenstein, aboard a Vistula picket boat, wrote on 25 October: 'Yesterday evening a silly report came that Paris had fallen. At first I was delighted, until I realised the story could not be true. These fantasy reports are always a bad sign. If there was genuine good news, such nonsenses would not be necessary.' Five days later, he eagerly scanned a German newspaper, and feared the worst after recognising the vacuity of its content: 'No good news – which means the same as bad news!'

Meanwhile in France, on 19 August *l'Eclaireur* of Nice announced a fictitious clash between the Royal Navy and the High Seas Fleet in the North Sea, in which the British had allegedly lost sixteen dreadnoughts including *Iron Duke*, *Lion* and *Superb*. French newspapers were especially enthusiastic about publishing reports concerning the German Crown Prince, an army commander in the field. On 5 August he was the victim of an assassination attempt in Berlin; on the 15th seriously wounded on the French front and removed to hospital; on the 24th subject to another assassination attempt; on 4 September he committed suicide, though he was resurrected on 18 October to be wounded again; on the 20th his wife was watching over his death bed; but on 3 November he was certified insane. None of these stories contained the smallest element of truth.

L'Action française informed the public that the Maggi dairies and Kub shop chains were in reality intelligence centres manned by Prussian officers who had become naturalised Frenchmen in anticipation of war; radio transmitters were concealed in every dairy, and Maggi milk was infused with poison. These reports caused mobs to storm the premises of these perfectly innocent, though foreign-owned, businesses. Among the most preposterous myths to be widely broadcast was that of '*turpinite*', a new super-explosive supposedly invented by the chemist Eugène Turpin, which would effortlessly extinguish German troops in their trenches. The French satirical magazine *Le Canard enchaîné* was founded at around this time, as a reaction to the deceits perpetrated in the traditional press.

Some of the shortcomings of newspapers were no fault of their own, but instead the consequence of governments' refusal to provide facts or allow correspondents to visit the front. In Britain Col. Repington complained that censorship was being abused 'as a cloak to cover all political, naval and military mistakes'. It was undoubtedly true that the system was exploited to sustain public morale much more than to conceal operational secrets from the enemy. In France, after the Marne the General Staff began to provide a thin dripfeed of information to the press, but the damage was already done: a credibility gap had opened which was never entirely closed. French journalists – and, before long, their readers – became chronically sceptical about all official pronouncements.

French soldiers in the field referred contemptuously to the '*bourrage de crâne*', literally 'skull-stuffing', but properly 'bullshit', which made up the content of the newspapers that reached them. Maurice Barrès of *l'Echo de Paris* became notorious for his enthusiasm for the war, which prompted the impassioned pacifist Romain Rolland to dub him 'the nightingale of carnage'. *Poilus*, rejecting the conventional press, turned instead to trench newspapers which soldiers wrote and copied for each other, or to Swiss titles when obtainable. Philosopher Alain Emile-Auguste Chartier, now a soldier, wrote on 25 November: 'The *Journal de Genève* is eagerly seized upon here and officers make cuttings from it; the military reports are admirable and everyone agrees that our papers seem ridiculous by comparison.'

Soldier-historian Louis Debidour agreed: 'All of us find intolerable the kind of literature produced by journalists about the trenches, the ingenuity of our men, the general air of enthusiasm, the forced gaiety displayed by the troops, the picturesque layout of the trenches etc. All that is pure invention. The troops are no more than calm and collected; they are resigned to putting the best possible face on dreadful misery caused by the cold and the awful weather.' German newspapers did the same. Frankfurt's *Oder-Zeitung* included a feature entitled 'Our Brandenburgers on the Aisne'. Its author, a war correspondent, applauded soldiers' ability to establish cosiness – '*Gemütlichkeit*' – in the trenches, and their capacity for seeing the funny side of things. Dugouts were described as 'comfortably furnished', while camps in the forward areas were said to resemble those on the old American frontier depicted in James Fenimore Cooper's *Leatherstocking Tales*. The war was presented as a stimulating challenge for young men.

All the peoples of Europe showed themselves susceptible to the most implausible fantasies. On 29 September a writer named Arthur Machen penned a short story for the London *Evening News* in which he described how the men of the BEF at Mons had seen visions of St George at the head of Bowmen of old England, who delivered a shower of arrows which caused 10,000 Germans to fall dead without a mark on them. Though Machen's piece was explicitly billed as fiction, huge numbers of people decided that it described a real happening. Meanwhile on the other side, Austrians warmed to the legend of a twelve-year-old child named Rosa Zenoch, who allegedly carried water to the wounded on the battlefield of Lemberg, at the cost of herself being maimed by shrapnel. The girl indeed lost a leg, and wound up in a Vienna hospital where Franz Joseph himself presented her with a locket and agreed to buy her a prosthetic limb. The story of 'the little angel of Lemberg' became a staple of Austrian children's literature. Not to be outdone, *The Lady* recommended a new English book entitled *Belgian Playmates* by Nellie Pollock: 'an extremely nice and timely little story for children, a tale of the present war, with the scene set partly in England and partly in Belgium'.

It is unsurprising that the soldiers of the rival armies felt a far stronger sense of community with each other than with their peoples at home, whom all the belligerent governments sought to quarantine from any real knowledge of what was being done in their name on the battlefield.

The Germans learned more about Britain's war effort from social gossip transmitted through neutrals than they did from either allied newspapers or their own spies. Their first agent dispatched from Berlin was a reserve officer named Carl Lody, who made himself somewhat conspicuous by speaking English with an American accent. He was arrested on 2 October following the interception of incriminating letters he had dispatched to neutral Stockholm. A public court-martial at Westminster Guildhall sentenced him to death, and Lody was duly shot in the moat of the Tower of London. 'I suppose you will not shake hands with a spy?' the condemned man said to the assistant provost-marshal. 'No,' responded that officer, 'but I will shake hands with a brave man.' Vernon Kell, director of MI5, respected Lody, and deplored the decision to shoot him. Other German agents were rounded up after a Belgian refugee in neutral Holland wrote to the War Office revealing the name – Frans Leibacher – and Rotterdam address to which they were addressing correspondence.

Fortunately for Berlin, however, other sources of information about British military activity were readily accessible. To the despair of commanders in the field, the 'Upper Ten' – the higher echelons of British society – were chronically indiscreet. The most sensitive operational intelligence was served at the tables of grand hostesses, from whence it often found its way into newspapers in neutral countries, and thus to the enemy. 'To know anything one had to go out to lunch, and I am bound to say that at such houses as … Lady Paget's and Mrs J.J. Astor's the information was generally up to date and accurate,' wrote the journalist Filson Young. 'The well-fed oracle from the War Office, carefully waiting until the servants had left the room, with a peach and a glass of port before him and his "Well, I can soon tell the little *I* know," remains a type of those days.' Censorship or no censorship, British military security remained poor throughout the war, as did the quality of information provided to the public by their shackled press. It was a notable feature of the 1914–18 war that by its ending the credibility of governments had been grievously damaged by clumsy and indeed oppressive news-management policies. The deceits peddled to every belligerent society by its rulers contributed vastly to the disillusionment that followed.

14

Open Country, Open Sky

1 CHURCHILL'S ADVENTURE

On 2 September, between Switzerland and Verdun the rival belligerents confronted each other in almost continuous lines. A week later, the front had stabilised along a further sixty miles, between Verdun and Mailly. But there remained 170 miles of open country between the Aisne and the Channel, untraversed and unravaged by the warring armies. The French and British were struggling to find sufficient men to defend their positions. To the north and west, Falkenhayn saw opportunities to achieve before winter the envelopment which had eluded the Kaiser's armies in August. He doubted that an absolute German victory was still attainable, but even if he failed to turn the allied flank, seizure of the Channel ports as far west as Calais would create an overwhelmingly powerful strategic position from which to negotiate a peace.

As the French and British armies redeployed to meet this threat – a remarkable feat of staffwork and logistics – their commanders enjoyed a similar surge of optimism. They supposed that a fast-moving campaign, unlike the profitless pounding on the Chemin des Dames, was still possible in northern France and the unoccupied region of Belgium. September and October witnessed the last awful convulsions of the 1914 campaign on the Western Front. In deteriorating autumn weather, the rival armies engaged in a struggle commonly described as 'the Race to the Sea', though both sides were less interested in the Channel coast than in seeking to get around behind each other. Sir John French elected to move the BEF to the allied left flank, partly to simplify his communications with England, but also under the delusion that his little army and its strong cavalry contingent might there exploit exhilarating possibilities. Instead, the British, French and Belgians found themselves locked first in a series of encounter battles, then in a headlong battering process that persisted through some of the most terrible weeks of the war, as the allies clung precariously to their line in the face of massive German assaults.

On assuming command, Falkenhayn's first move, against his own better judgement, was to allow Bülow's army to make a further attempt to break through on the Soissons–Reims front. After that assault failed on 16 September, he threw everything into reinforcing his right wing. On the French side, and with the same hopes of getting around Kluck, Manoury advanced cautiously up the Oise, where on the 17th his troops clashed with the Germans, and were checked. Joffre began rushing men further north to form a new army commanded by Castelnau, the seventy-three-year-old stalwart who had shown himself 'the rock' on the Couronné de Nancy. But his men were reservists, neither energetic nor well-trained, and Falkenhayn was able to shift forces to meet them, forming his own new army led by Crown Prince Rupprecht of Bavaria. The Germans' problem was that the east–west railway systems of occupied Belgium, Luxembourg and occupied France were ill-adapted for moving large numbers of men northwards from the southern end of the front. The Belgian tracks had been heavily sabotaged by King Albert's retreating countrymen, who also removed most rolling stock to France. In October the rail network was still operating imperfectly, even after the Germans had committed 26,000 labourers to clear blocked tunnels and repair broken track.

Between September and November, the Germans repeatedly pushed reinforcements towards the coast – but never quite sufficient or fast enough to achieve decisive results. The French used their trains better, and the difference proved critical. On the evening of 23 September, Rupprecht's Sixth Army advanced up the Oise. Joffre at GQG was slow to grasp the significance of this movement, but Castelnau's men were able to check it. French troops also stopped another thrust further south on the 26th, inflicting heavy losses. Here, yet again, Falkenhayn's generals sent forward masses of men to suffer the same fate as had Joffre's back in August, when it was their turn to attack. But the north was the real focus of attention: in the bosoms of many men of four nations, there still glowed competing hopes for a historic triumph. France's roads were crowded with cavalry and vehicles moving up towards Amiens, Arras, Lens, Lille, while trains shuttled infantry formations to local detraining points.

In the German lines likewise, on 6 October gunner Herbert Sulzbach watched in awe as column after column of cavalry clattered past his battery on their way towards the front: 'Dragoons from Darmstadt, mounted chasseurs from Trier, regiments from Metz, Karlsruhe, Bruchsal, Mulhouse and Cassel: they look terrific with their lances, and you feel that something very big is going to happen … and you are suffused with hope and excitement. I saw quite a number of people I knew among the men moving past. How strange that people should meet on this gigantic front, pretty well on the field of battle.' Sulzbach was almost equally excited to find his own chin starting to boast stubble, to hear himself swearing and grumbling like an old soldier: 'it is something wonderful to be one of the millions who are able to join in the fighting'.

The Kaiser visited the front at Chauny, and sought to assuage scepticism among soldiers whom he met. 'You'll be home at Christmas,' he said repeatedly. 'I shall be letting you go home soon.' There were matching hopes in Paris, where the euphoria of the Marne persisted. At the British embassy Sir Francis Bertie wrote on 1 October: 'If Joffre be victorious and succeeds in obtaining Alsace-Lorraine for France, he may do anything he may please.' Yet even before such civilian hopes were uttered, the French commander-in-chief had been obliged to abandon his ambitions of outflanking the Germans. Though he continued to rush formations forward, Joffre saw that these could do no more than hold a line, frustrate the enemy's grand design. Prince Rupprecht's men were advancing on Lille and threatening Arras, which by the evening of 4 October faced encirclement. In response to this threat, Joffre appointed Gen. Ferdinand Foch as his deputy, with responsibility for the entire northern area of operations. In this role, through the weeks that followed Foch's contribution was to sustain an iron determination. He told his subordinates there could be no retreat: their men must die where they stood. Maud'huy, now commanding Tenth Army under Foch's leadership, repulsed a major German push against Arras. By nightfall on 6 October, the line was stable. Falkenhayn shifted his attention.

The French were acutely aware that the fate of the north of their country and the rump of Belgium was not in their hands alone: British and Belgian troops would play critical roles. Since the last week of September, even as Prince Rupprecht's army attacked the French east of Arras, his formations had also been sweeping across Belgium, where the local population and the Belgian army fell back in its path. From Ghent, the unhappy Madame Jeanne van Bleyenberghe wrote to a friend: 'We heard the guns many times and you cannot imagine how dreadful it feels to hear the noise – to think that every time so many men are killed … You must have heard in your papers of the sufferings of our people, how old men, women and children were killed, whole villages and towns set on fire.'

On the 30th British volunteer nurse Gladys Winterbottom found herself skirting broken bodies as she drove into Waelham to pick up a casualty. 'By the bridge was one of the nice little sentries – dead. We started to cross under terrific fire … but just then 12 terrified soldiers ran drunkenly across, clutching hold of the bridge railings to pull themselves along. Their commandant had been killed and they fled for their lives. We found no wounded, so I took all the 12 men up with me in the Fiat … The men were quite hysterical and almost embraced me in their relief. I was too racked to go under heavy fire again.'

Falkenhayn decreed that the nuisance of Antwerp should be snuffed out. The Germans had been bothered by two Belgian sorties from the fortress – the first at the time of Le Cateau, the second during the Aisne fighting; they were determined now to remove the lingering threat to their communications. OHL dispatched a reserve corps, reinforced with massive artillery support, to batter the city, where most of the Belgian army was concentrated. Moltke travelled there in person, cherishing threadbare hopes of recovering some fragment of his shattered prestige. Joffre rejected Belgian pleas for aid, for Antwerp had no place in his grand strategic plan – in its isolation, he judged the perimeter indefensible. He sent only a few Zouaves, territorials and marines to cover the retreat of the city's garrison down the coast into France, an outcome the C-in-C considered inevitable.

The British, however, had more ambitious ideas. They had much emotional capital invested in King Albert's country. John Galsworthy demanded in the *Daily Mail*: 'What are we going to do for Belgium – for this most gallant of little countries, ground, because of sheer loyalty, under an iron heel? For this most innocent of sufferers from God's own Armageddon?' The novelist's emotional outburst reflected public opinion. Though Belgium had been invaded, much of the country was still unoccupied. Surely British arms could avert its absolute enslavement? Many people, some of them ministers and generals, were instinctively attracted by the notion of fighting a battle close to home, within reach of the Royal Navy. Here was a chance to conduct independent operations without being bothered by Joffre and his fellow countrymen.

Sir John French, with unerring lack of judgement, dallied with the possibility of taking the entire BEF to Antwerp, where he had wanted to be ever since August. Had this plan been implemented, his army would almost certainly have suffered German encirclement, and perhaps destruction, before it could be evacuated. In the end, it was merely agreed with the French that the BEF should redeploy from the Aisne to the left flank.

On the night of 1 October, their divisions began the extended process of withdrawal from the Chemin des Dames. And even as this began, they launched a local adventure at Antwerp. Though the notion of taking the whole army there had been abandoned, some bold British spirits still saw scope for buccaneering.

In the Admiralty files in those days, civil servant Norman Macleod chanced upon a pre-war strategic memorandum written by the First Lord, which he described as 'wonderful'. In 1911 Churchill had described a clash between the Entente and the Central Powers in which 'he foresaw that [the] French wd have to remain on defensive on NE frontiers and possibly have to give ground before German advance through Belgium and possibly even Paris would be in danger – questioned whether French people cd play the waiting game necessary – Britain wd send 290,000 men to help … after 40th day tide would turn'. Macleod qualified his admiration, however: 'this paper is almost the only evidence of real talent I have seen on Churchill's part – the Naval Division scheme has shown his weaknesses – his mind works quickly, he is fertile in suggestions and he is a tremendous worker, but he lacks balance and consistency, does not work well in harness. I cannot imagine him conceiving a great scheme and carrying it through steadily. He begins no end of things, threatens heads of depts with dire penalties if his plans are not carried out – then falters & delays giving a decision and drops the scheme.'

These criticisms appear prescient, in the light of the bizarre enterprise which the First Lord now sponsored. The 'Naval Division scheme' to which Macleod referred was a characteristically piratical stroke by Churchill. He assembled a hotchpotch of Royal Marines and surplus naval personnel from which he aspired to create his own private army, having persuaded himself that Antwerp offered a chance to fulfil his dream of a British amphibious operation. On every possible count this was imprudent, indeed reckless. Antwerp was untenable as the continental beachhead he envisaged; it could have been supplied up the Scheldt only by breaching Dutch neutrality. The First Lord nonetheless had himself appointed Britain's plenipotentiary to the beleaguered fortress, and set forth with the only British force available – his Naval Division.

The Belgian army deployed around Antwerp was hard-pressed. A month earlier, the French newspaper *Le Matin* had asserted that the city was 'virtually impregnable'. In truth, however, nothing had been done since 1900 to modernise its protective forts, as vulnerable to modern artillery as those of Liège. Among the garrison were grenadiers Edouard and

Charles Beer, two of four sons of a prosperous Brussels family. They had hastened to the Belgian colours seven weeks earlier in expectation of glory, and were crestfallen to be sent to Antwerp, where they merely wielded spades day after day. Now, the German assault engulfed them. Their fort on the outskirts of the city came under heavy fire until one shell struck a magazine, precipitating a huge explosion. Edouard Beer wrote in his diary:

> We needed all our courage. What a ghastly sight! Bodies without heads or faces, detached limbs, chests laid open, groans and shrieks agonising to the ears. Most were without their dogtags, and so unidentifiable. Thirty-seven bodies lay there, while just four survived wounded, two of them seriously.
>
> The stretcher-bearers refused to come forward, so our commandant asked for volunteers to take the two worst cases to the farm. Charles and I and two others came forward. The commandant shook our hands and said, 'Bon courage, mes enfants.' As we crossed the open ground, shells fell all around us, sometimes very close. The wounded man groaned terribly at every step, and every twenty paces or so we had to stop because the blanket in which we were carrying him slipped in our muddy fingers.

At last they reached the main positions, surrendered their burdens, and made their way back to the fort, where they were greeted by comrades astonished to see them alive.

A formal siege of Antwerp's sixty-mile perimeter began on 28 September, though the road west, running along the Dutch–Belgian frontier, remained open. Large tracts of surrounding countryside had been flooded, to deny them to the enemy, but the consequence was that defenders outside the forts could not entrench themselves in the waterlogged ground. By the night of Wednesday the 30th, the bombardment had become continuous. Edouard Beer wrote: 'the spectacle is terrifying; in front of us as well as behind, we see the flashes of the guns; to the north, south and west alike, there are only fires. The whole centre of the village of Havre Sainte Cutheune is blazing like a torch, including the church bell tower.' Next morning, in the face of the shelling, his unit abandoned their positions; that evening, however, they took advantage of thick fog to reoccupy them. A few days later Beer recorded: 'Our third night without rest ... Four more men died in today's shelling, bringing to twenty the number killed in this stretch of trench ... Oh! The rage of impotence. To see comrades fall at one's side, others wounded, and to be unable to avenge them! To see men lost to machine-gun fire who cannot even perish fighting! This period of intense bombardment is intensely dispiriting.'

The men of Churchill's Royal Naval Division were clad in sea-going rig, scantily equipped and almost wholly untrained for land war. He had already dispatched them on brief and abortive sorties that caught his fancy, first to Ostend, then to Dunkirk and thence to Lille. Now the First Lord abandoned his post at the Admiralty and hastened to Antwerp personally to rally the defence, touring the city in an open Rolls-Royce. One of his entourage, Ordinary Seaman Henry Stevens, described the experience: 'To me it appeared that Mr Churchill dominated the proceedings and ... that he was by no means satisfied with the position ... He appeared on occasions to criticise the siting and construction of trenches by the Belgian army ... He put forward his ideas forcefully, waving his stick and thumping the ground with it. After obviously pungent remarks, he would walk away a few steps and stare towards the enemy's direction. On other occasions he would stride away without another word, get into the car and wait impatiently ... At one line of trenches he found the line very thinly held and asked where "the bloody men were".'

It is hard to exaggerate the absurdity of throwing a small, scratch British force into a battle almost no one thought winnable, given the Belgians' weakness and the city's remoteness at the north-western extremity of allied territory. Royal Marine Captain Maurice Festing described the bitterness his men felt about abandoning Lille, whose inhabitants had hailed them as deliverers, in order to hasten to Antwerp at Churchill's behest. He wrote in his diary on 4 October: 'Our exodus is a very painful recollection to me, and I hope I may never again be called upon to carry out so humiliating and unpleasant a withdrawal.'

The Marines who quit the city were disconcerted, as they tramped north, to meet Belgian guns moving the other way, which suggested that the allied commitment to the defence of Antwerp was less than wholehearted. Festing and his comrades were further bewildered about what they were supposed to achieve, 2,500 strong without their own artillery or logistical support, and furthermore extremely hungry. They were astonished suddenly to encounter the First Lord in the flesh, his chubby person attired in a flowing boat cloak and naval cap. 'He inspected our men on the march and promised them every luxury in the way of foodstuffs. He seemed excited.' The Marines arrived in Antwerp to be joined by the other brigade of the ragtag Naval Division, and were led to positions where they soon found themselves under shellfire, directed by German observers in captive balloons. Churchill had laid hands on some Rolls-Royce armoured cars and an armoured train, both manned by bluejackets attired for sea duty, which now saw a little action. Orders arrived to hold to the last man. Maurice Festing wrote: 'the delivery of this message irritated me immensely, for it struck me it would be so much better not to say such a thing about holding onto a perfectly ridiculous and futile position'.

The pre-war Admiralty had earmarked the Marines exclusively for service aboard warships. Before mobilisation, 'military training in the Corps had sunk to a very low ebb and become little more than farcical … [Now it] found itself without plans, equipment or training for such an emergency.' More than a few men committed to the operation were relatively elderly reservists. Festing was appalled, on their first night in Antwerp, to inspect the battalion at its posts and find every man fast asleep, without sentries. Next day, 7 October, they were first ordered to withdraw, then, after marching some distance, told to reoccupy their former line. Festing was appointed brigade-major, in which role his first order was to lower a large Red Cross flag flying over British headquarters, appropriately located in a former lunatic asylum. Next day, his brigadier collapsed with a nervous breakdown.

Meanwhile, the situation on the Belgian perimeter became ever more desperate. Edouard Beer wrote on the 7th: 'Evening soon comes, and with it new orders: we must exploit the fog to retake trenches beyond the village; they must be reoccupied "at any cost", says the general, even if we lose half our strength on the way. The column marches forward in double file, observing absolute silence as we advance into the night. Soon, before us, looms a great red glare; it is blazing Wacherbe; only ruins are left; here and there a burning house still stands; the animals abandoned by the inhabitants wander at will, seeking sustenance; we pass on, grimly impressed, our footsteps echoing on the *pavé*, where great craters mark the detonation of shells.'

Churchill later wrote contemptuously of low-grade German reserve formations which 'wormed and waddled their way' into the Belgian fortress, but it was apparent that the allied line could not hold: Antwerp was doomed. The Royal Marines received their orders to withdraw from Col. Jack Seeley, the former British secretary for war who had betaken himself to the battlefield – in Festing's exasperated words, 'one of those wandering politician-soldiers' – temporarily attached to the RN Divisional staff. Chaos followed, as British units trickled piecemeal back from the line, and out of the city: '… I don't think I have ever felt more angry with any man than I did with Col. Seeley at that moment. He was, I knew, a great friend of Mr Winston Churchill's and I sincerely cursed the day when fate had placed the unfortunate brigade in the hands of two professional politicians and amateur soldiers.'

Once it was plain the British were pulling out, and that the city must fall, the brigade-major, his ailing brigadier and staff crowded aboard their only automobile, some standing on the running boards. In darkness pierced by the flames of burning buildings, they chugged falteringly out of the city with two wheels running on rims after tyre-bursts. Festing wrote: 'the devil himself was holding high holiday in Antwerp that night of 8 October: It was a real inferno.' It proved necessary to beg the dubious city guards to open the Malines gate, to enable the British to make their escape.

Eighty thousand Belgian troops, who also retired from Antwerp, later fought some gallant actions against overwhelming forces of Germans, as Falkenhayn tightened his grip on the country. Among the participants in the retreat was a small group of British nurses and ambulance-drivers who had attached themselves to the Belgian army. On the afternoon of 9 October one of these, 'Elsie' Knocker, was in the village of Melle, north of Ghent. She wrote: 'the Germans suddenly advanced up the street with fixed bayonets & we had to scoot under heavy fire'. Then she heard that many casualties were lying in a nearby turnip field. Driven to the scene, she found scores of dead and wounded Germans lying among French *fusiliers-marins*. Knocker and Tom, her cockney driver, filled their ambulance. He then drove his passengers away to safety, leaving her to tend three Germans and a Belgian with a smashed shoulder.

She wrote in her diary: 'Everywhere there was a deathly silence, not a sound, and I did not realise until I saw the ambulance disappear down the road how utterly alone I was. Sitting in a turnip field surrounded by 200 dead and the four sitting cases. Thoughts went through my head: "Would Tom get cut off and not be able to get back?" "Would the Germans advance over the field and try to retake Melle?" I suddenly heard a voice a little distance away say "*Schwester, sprechen sie Deutsch?*" I replied, "*Ja.*" The sitting case who had spoken then said "Take a greatcoat and cap from one of the dead and come and sit with us" … He told me the Germans were only just the other side of the field and might shoot if they saw [my] khaki uniform.'

At last, in failing light she saw the ambulance making its way back towards her, and an hour later she was safe at her hospital. Nothing more vividly emphasises the stultifying boredom of peacetime existence for middle-class women of that era than Elsie Knocker's later euphoric comment on her experience: 'it was a wonderful & grand day & I would not have missed it'. She retained her sense of excitement and romance through the years ahead, not diminished by marrying a Belgian airman and becoming Baroness de T'Serclaes.

A week later and some miles to the west, the prime minister's daughter revealed something of the same enthusiasm for adventure amid carnage. Violet Asquith, who had crossed to France to engage in a few days' privileged war tourism, severely rebuked civilians in Bailleul, three miles behind the front, whom she saw taunting German PoWs: '*Il ne faut pas se moquer des prisonniers.*' The French were unimpressed: '*Eh, dame! Il faut bien! Que voulez-vous? Les allemands c'est un sale peuple – des brigands – des barbares – ils ont tout pillé – tout ravagé.*' It is easy to see why the French, whose country was being devastated by German invaders, resented the intervention of an Englishwoman who embraced all that she saw with the enthusiasm of a joyrider: 'Darling father,' she wrote home to the prime minister, 'everything that has ever or can ever happen to me pales & shrivels before the thrilling interest of this expedition.'

Antwerp surrendered on the afternoon of 10 October, though most of the garrison and British contingent made good their escape down the coast to join the rest of the allied forces on the narrow strip of Belgian soil now remaining in King Albert's hands. The monarch himself proudly insisted on remaining at La Panne for the rest of the war. The Royal Naval Division was evacuated through Ostend, where the newly formed British 7th Division was landing, although more than a thousand bluejackets ended up as either German prisoners or Dutch internees. The 7th Division was originally intended to strengthen the garrison of Antwerp, but fortunately – although to Churchill's fury – wiser counsels prevailed.

The First Lord wrote to Sir John French on 26 October: 'Antwerp was a bitter blow to me and some aspects have given a handle to my enemies.' Later, licking his political wounds in a mood of rueful self-pity, he observed: 'Looking back with after-knowledge and increasing years, I seem to have been too ready to undertake tasks which were hazardous or even forlorn.' He never acknowledged Antwerp for the fiasco it was. Maurice Festing wrote in disgust, 'one would have thought a limit would have been placed upon Mr Winston Churchill's appetite for daredevil pranks and

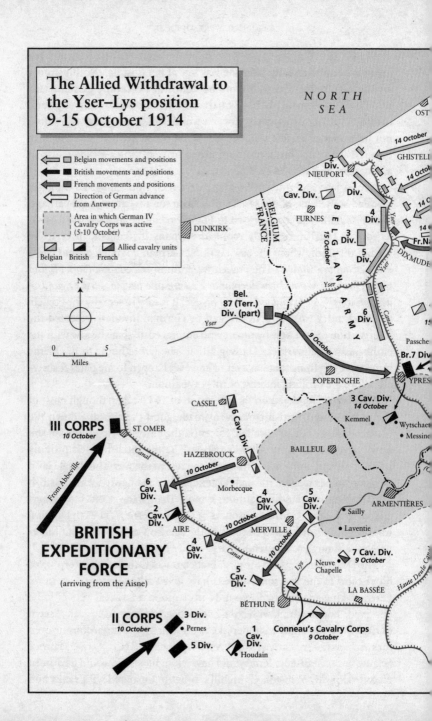

The Allied Withdrawal to the Yser–Lys position 9-15 October 1914

Belgian movements and positions
British movements and positions
French movements and positions
Direction of German advance from Antwerp
Area in which German IV Cavalry Corps was active (5-10 October)
Belgian British French Allied cavalry units

NORTH SEA

N

0   5
Miles

OST

14 October
GHISTELI

2 Div.
NIEUPORT

2 Cav. Div.

FURNES

1 Div.

4 Div.

Yser

14 October

14 O

14 N

Fr. N.

DIXMUDE

B E L G I U M
FRANCE

DUNKIRK

3 Div.
15 October

5 Div.

B E L G I A N   A R M Y

Bel. 87 (Terr.) Div. (part)

Yser

Yser

6 Div.

Canal

9 October

15

Passche

POPERINGHE

Br.7 Div

YPRES

III CORPS
10 October

ST OMER

Canal

3 Cav. Div.
14 October

CASSEL

6 Cav. Div.

Kemmel

Wytschae

Messine

HAZEBROUCK

BAILLEUL

From Abbeville

10 October

6 Cav. Div.

Morbecque

BRITISH EXPEDITIONARY FORCE
(arriving from the Aisne)

2 Cav. Div.

AIRE

4 Cav. Div.

4 Cav. Div.

10 October

5 Cav. Div.

MERVILLE

Canal

Lys

10 October

5 Cav. Div.

ARMENTIÈRES

Sailly

Laventie

7 Cav. Div.
9 October

Neuve Chapelle

Haute Deule Canal

LA BASSÉE

BÉTHUNE

II CORPS
10 October

3 Div.
• Pernes

5 Div.

1 Cav. Div.
• Houdain

Conneau's Cavalry Corps
9 October

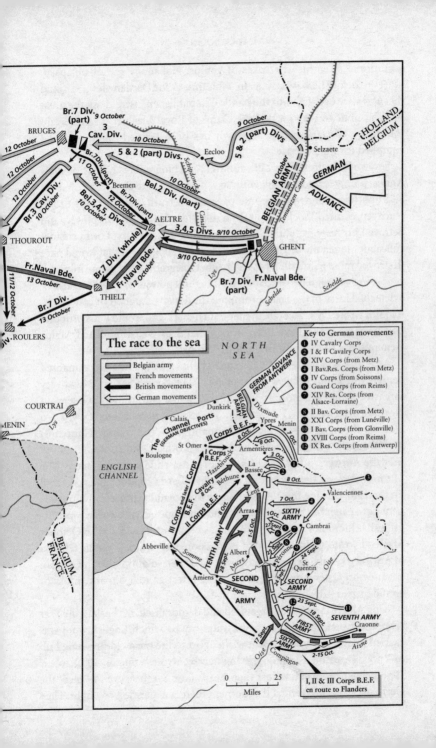

Top map labels:

Br.7 Div. (part) 9 October

3 Cav. Div.

BRUGES
12 October
12 October

Br.7Div.(part) 10 October

5 & 2 (part) Divs.

Eecloo

9 October

5 & 2 (part) Divs

Selzaete

HOLLAND
BELGIUM

GERMAN
ADVANCE

8 October

BELGIAN ARMY

11 October

Schipdonck

Canal

Beemen
Br.7Div.(part)

10 October

Bel.2 Div. (part)

Br.3 Cav. Div.
12 October
10 October

Bel.3,4,5. Divs.
10 October
12 October

THOUROUT

AELTRE

3,4,5 Divs. 9/10 October

GHENT

Temeuzeen Canal

Br.7 Div. (whole)

Fr.Naval Bde.

9/10 October

Lys

Br.7 Div. (part) Fr.Naval Bde.

Schelde

Fr.Naval Bde.
13 October

Br.7 Div.
13 October

THIELT

Fr.Naval Bde.
12 October

Schelde

11/12 October

ROULERS

Bottom map:

The race to the sea

- Belgian army
- French movements
- British movements
- German movements

NORTH SEA

Key to German movements

1 IV Cavalry Corps
2 I & II Cavalry Corps
3 XIV Corps (from Metz)
4 I Bav.Res. Corps (from Metz)
5 IV Corps (from Soissons)
6 Guard Corps (from Reims)
7 XIV Res. Corps (from Alsace-Lorraine)
8 II Bav. Corps (from Metz)
9 XXI Corps (from Lunéville)
10 I Bav. Corps (from Glonville)
11 XVIII Corps (from Reims)
12 IX Res. Corps (from Antwerp)

COURTRAI

MENIN

Lys

GERMAN ADVANCE FROM ANTWERP

BELGIAN ARMY

Dunkirk
Calais
Ports
The Channel (GERMAN OBJECTIVES)

St Omer

Boulogne

ENGLISH CHANNEL

Dixmude
Ypres
Menin

8 Oct.

III Corps B.E.F.
8 Oct.
7 Oct.

I Corps B.E.F.

Armentières
3 Oct.

Hazebrouck

La Bassée

BELGIUM
FRANCE

B.E.F. Cavalry 8 Oct.
and later I Corps

Béthune

Lens

8 Oct.

Valenciennes

7 Oct.

III Corps and later I Corps

II Corps B.E.F.
8 Oct.

Arras

1-5 Oct.

SIXTH ARMY
10 Oct.

27 Sept.

Cambrai

Abbeville

Somme

TENTH ARMY

28 Sept.

Albert

Ancre

Péronne

24 Sept.

St Quentin

Oise

Amiens

SECOND ARMY

22 Sept.

24 Sept.

SECOND ARMY

23 Sept.

18 Oct.

SEVENTH ARMY

Craonne

FIRST ARMY

17 Sept.

Oise

SIXTH ARMY

2-15 Oct.

Arsne

Compiègne

0   25
Miles

I, II & III Corps B.E.F.
en route to Flanders

sensational attempts at strokes of genius. Not many months elapsed, however, before he was busy again – this time at the Dardanelles ... Should this narrative ever fall into the hands of a publisher, I would ask the great British public to see to it that the Corps of Royal Marines is never again told to go to war on land unless it has been trained, organized and equipped for the purpose.'

Some of Winston Churchill's admirers and biographers have treated his Antwerp intervention indulgently, as a picaresque adventure, a colourful addition to a wondrous lifetime pageant. In truth, however, what took place represented shocking folly by a minister who abused his powers and betrayed his responsibilities. It is astonishing that the First Lord's cabinet colleagues so readily forgave him for a lapse of judgement that would have destroyed most men's careers. A 3 October telegram to the prime minister, proposing to resign his office in return for 'full powers of a commander of a detached force in the field', prompted the derisive laughter of colleagues. Asquith wrote: 'W is an ex-lieutenant of Hussars, and would if his proposal had been accepted have been in command of 2 distinguished Major Generals, not to mention Brigadiers, Colonels & c.'

Asquith's wider view of Churchill's behaviour at Antwerp remained benign, but senior officers were appalled. The Fourth Sea Lord 'was very sarcastic about Winston as a strategist', wrote Admiralty civil servant Norman Macleod on 12 October. The King's private secretary, Lord Stamfordham, observed not unreasonably that 'our friend [Churchill] must be quite off his head!' Another naval officer said contemptuously that the Antwerp affair 'read like a story in a child's picture book'. The *Morning Post* was fiercely critical of the First Lord's conduct in an editorial on the 13th, causing the *New Statesman* to applaud the fact that 'a prominent newspaper has broken through the self-imposed rule whereby practically all criticism of the Government has been suppressed'. On 16 October Macleod wrote again: 'Feeling of depression everywhere – public felt loss of Antwerp keenly, especially as reports had been so optimistic ... German advance on Ostend and Warsaw ... had effect as well – marked loss of confidence in Adm[iralt]y.'

King Albert's troops, disorganised and demoralised, fell back to the Yser river and canal, the old medieval waterway by which English wool was carried inland from the sea below Nieuport to the great clothmaking hub of Ypres. Dorothie Feilding, serving nearby, wrote home on 10 October: 'The Belgian troops have lost their heads now & refuse even to meet the Germans. They just retreat the moment there is a question of a fight. They are utterly worn out at having had to stand the brunt of it all these months & now are in a state of funk & run like hares. But it does one good to see all these British soldiers about & you know you won't go under with them about.' Madame Jeanne van Bleyberghe, whose husband was serving with the Belgian army, wrote from Ghent to a friend in England on 11 October: 'we all admire England so much, it really is a grand and generous nation. When your soldiers pass in the street, everybody cheers.'

But the British Army would not be seen again in Ghent for many a long day, as the tide of war washed past the city, leaving the Germans in occupation. The 7th Division, whose men Dorothie Feilding met, marched from their Belgian disembarkation ports towards positions north of Ypres. A Royal Welch Fusilier officer met Col. George Malcolm of the London Scottish, one of the newly-come units, who professed regret about arriving at the war 'too late to have a look in'. Malcolm's apprehension was unjustified. There would be enough war for all comers, and certainly so for himself. The 7th Division marched towards a junction with the rest of the BEF, which was meanwhile approaching from the south. They met on a battlefield that would become, during the months that followed, the graveyard of the old British Army.

2 'INVENTIONS OF THE DEVIL'

New technologies created many opportunities and difficulties for the soldiers of 1914; foremost among them were the consequences of man's achievement of powered flight. On 25 August, staff at a Bavarian corps headquarters east of Nancy saw an aeroplane circling overhead which eventually dropped a brilliant light. While contemplating the significance of this apparently harmless firework, the Bavarians found themselves under French shellfire – their position had been marked by an air-dropped flare.

A modern writer, Christian Kehrt, suggests that the new-found vulnerability of the sky to man's invasion roused in many breasts the same lust for dominance as the wildernesses of Africa. During the previous century, soldiers' ventures into the skies had been limited to sporadic use of observation balloons, tethered to cables. These had their value, and continued to do so throughout the First World War, but their range of vision was limited, and they could be hoisted only behind a combatant's own front. Powered flight represented a stunning advance. In 1903 the Wright brothers had ended mankind's millennia of earthbound bondage with their first successful take-off. In just eleven intervening years before war came, aircraft capabilities advanced at astounding speed. German test pilot Ernst Canter noted in his logbook that while in 1910 he flew at a height of eighty feet, two years later he was ascending to almost 5,000. In 1908 one pilot in five died – a corpse for every thousand miles flown. By 1912, the accidental death rate had fallen to one for every fifty-one pilots – a fatality per 103,000 miles.

German generals were initially more impressed by airships than by aeroplanes, and rejected a 1907 commercial approach from the Wrights. But some pundits quickly predicted that heavier-than-air machines would prove more efficacious than Zeppelins: Wilhelm Hesse argued that they would 'soon outstrip all existing mechanical transportation by their speed and freedom from the ground'. In 1909 Germany began to address the new science more seriously, stimulated by knowledge that France was then training forty-one military pilots to its own ten. Dr Walther Huth of the Albatros company paid for his own chauffeur to learn to fly, who thereafter became a military instructor.

The following year France's Gen. Joseph Manoury, who would command Sixth Army at the Marne, took to the air during manoeuvres, and was profoundly impressed by seeing for himself what flight must do to war. After the German army's 1912 exercises, Falkenhayn reflected upon a range of technological innovations of which aircraft were among the foremost: 'When these inventions of the devil work, then what they achieve is more than amazing; when they do not work, then they achieve less than nothing.' The Kaiser formally accorded Germany's air corps parity with his other services in March 1914, when he ordered the Protestant Church to include fliers in its regular prayer for the armed forces.

The British were slow starters: in 1909 the War Office temporarily closed down army flying experiments, claiming that their cost of £2,500 – this at a time when the Germans had already spent £400,000 and the French little less – was unaffordable. But in 1912 the Royal Flying Corps was formed, and at the following year's manoeuvres Lt. Gen. Sir James Grierson told King George: 'I think, sir, that these aeroplanes are going to spoil war. When they come over I can only tell my men to cover their heads with hay and make a noise like a mushroom!' Grierson was nonetheless an imaginative early convert to the new technology, exploiting air reconnaissance to win an exercise. Senior officers of every army realised that power to view the earth from the sky, reaching far behind enemy lines, changed the rules, rendering concentrations vulnerable to bombardment and every manoeuvre susceptible to enemy counterstroke. In past wars, before a battle commanders liked to position themselves on hilltops with a view. Now, such exposure could be fatal: German staff regulations emphasised the importance of avoiding locating headquarters near landmarks.

But air reconnaissance had its limitations, of which the most obvious was the weather: low cloud and serious rain grounded planes. Even if pilots became airborne and observed troop movements, they had much to learn about interpreting the significance of what they saw. Moreover, they could not be assured that generals would display the imagination to heed their reports – French at Mons and Kluck at the Marne were only two obvious examples of commanders who failed to draw appropriate conclusions from air intelligence received. Finally, aircraft were chronically scarce, especially on the Eastern Front. The Germans started with 254 trained pilots and 246 aircraft, half Taubes and the rest Albatroses and Aviatiks, but only a modest proportion were serviceable at any one time. The same was true of France's *Aviation Militaire*, which had two hundred machines and five hundred trained pilots, soon reinforced by civilian volunteers. The aircraft – mostly Caudrons and Morane-Saulniers – were organised in *escadrilles* – squadrons – of either six two-seaters or four single-seaters. The French air corps' erratic commanding officer first mobilised his fliers on his own initiative at the beginning of July – a month before war – then decided that any conflict would be brief, and in August closed down flying schools and sent all instructors to the front. More rational policies were adopted after a new general was appointed.

The British went to war with 197 pilots and 113 serviceable operational aircraft, mostly Farmans and BE2a biplanes. Churchill had also created a separate Royal Naval Air Service. The army initially deluded itself that replacement pilots could be found by inviting gentleman fliers to secure their own Aero Club certificates of competence, themselves paying the necessary £75, before enlisting for service. 'Members of the RFC who own their own aeroplanes should be encouraged to bring them to the Central Flying School when they undergo their training there,' said a War Office instruction. In the autumn of 1914, however, an RFC flight-training programme was hastily introduced, which before the war's end had killed more pilots than enemy action. The first Flying Corps battlefield casualty was Sgt-Maj. Jillings, hit in the leg by a rifle bullet while flying over Belgium on 22 August.

Meanwhile, the Austrians owned just forty-eight planes and the Belgians twelve. The Russians had an impressive paper strength of two hundred aircraft of sixteen types, and displayed notable design flair. But such was their organisational incompetence that serviceability was chronically low. The French, alone among the belligerents, had gained previous practical experience of using aircraft for military purposes, during their 1913 colonial campaign in Morocco. French biplanes flew at speeds of between 50 and 70 mph, and required between thirty and sixty minutes to reach an altitude of 6,000 feet, depending on conditions; Blériot and Taube monoplanes were somewhat faster and nimbler.

At first, the unfamiliarity of aircraft caused innocents on the ground merely to marvel when they appeared in the sky. In Belgium, Britain's Sister Mayne thought Taubes looked like 'beautiful little birds'. But soon soldiers and civilians alike understood that flying machines posed a direct threat to their welfare, and contrived their destruction when they could. Late on the afternoon of 6 August, the citizens of Freiburg were shocked by the spectacle of two French aircraft flying above their city, having sailed serenely over the Kaiser's frontier and his armies. Some affronted citizens fired sporting guns skywards, as did those soldiers on guard duty who had been issued with ammunition. Frankfurt's militia likewise opened a brisk fusillade at clouds in which, so they were told, French aircraft were hiding.

Austrian Dr Richard Stenitzer, besieged in Przemyśl, took exception to the intrusions of airborne Russians: 'It is a strange unpleasant feeling if an aeroplane appears above oneself high in the skies. You get the impression it tracks you personally although it is not able to distinguish individuals because of its height of 2,000 metres.' Though planes of different nationalities were soon marked with distinguishing symbols – a German cross, a tricolour cockade and suchlike – these were usually invisible from the ground. French soldier François Mayer wrote: 'when any aircraft passes overhead, we bury our heads like ostriches'. On 27 October at Ypres, every rifleman in the Black Watch emptied his magazine at an overhead aircraft, then cheered wildly when it burst into flames and tumbled to earth; better-informed witnesses found this 'a dreadful sight, as we … realized it was British'. Austrian Lt. Constantin Schneider described the sensation created by the appearance of the first aircraft over his division in Galicia: there was a barrage of musketry which officers had difficulty in suppressing, even when they saw that it was one of their own. Three Austrian planes were brought down by friendly fire in the first days of the campaign.

The public became fascinated by the new art of aerial warfare. Herbert Asquith, displaying the wonder of a Victorian, referred to the revolutionary machines as hyphenated 'aero-planes'. Pilots, initially armed only with revolvers or rifles, became national heroes: their voyages into the sky empowered them to rise above the squalor of the battlefield figuratively as well as literally. They appeared to resurrect the glories of personal endeavour in a repugnant new era of industrialised slaughter. Twenty-seven-year-old Pyotr Nesterov, a famous Russian pioneer aviator and the first man to loop the loop, was at the controls of a Morane-Saulnier monoplane over Poland on 25 August when he encountered an Austrian Albatros BII biplane, flown by pilot Fritz Malina and observer Baron Friedrich von Rosenthal. Having emptied his revolver at them without effect, Nesterov resorted to ramming, which brought down the enemy plane. Unfortunately his own Morane was severely damaged in the collision, and followed the German machine down; next day Nesterov died of his injuries. His funeral, in Kiev cathedral, became a major public occasion: the coffin was adorned with his leather helmet and the catafalque was almost submerged in flowers, some brought from the field in which his plane had come down. Nesterov's conduct reflected the suicidally undisciplined ethos of the Russian air service, which had by far the worst accident rate of any combatant, because of its insistence on sending almost untrained pilots into the air.

Maurice Baring, an RFC staff officer, waxed lyrical at the beauties of autumn at a French airfield among young British fliers, despite the incongruities of the ground headquarters in which he served: 'I remember the clicking of the typewriters in our little improvised office, and a soldier singing "Abide With Me" at the top of his voice in the kitchen. And the beauty of the Henry Farmans sailing through the clear evening, "the evening hush broken by homing wings", and the moonlight rising over the stubble of the aerodrome, and a few camp fires glowing in the mist amid the noise of the men singing songs of home.'

A significant consequence of the war's early campaigns was to cause every nation's commanders to recognise the importance and potential of their air arms. Joffre, impressed by the contribution of aerial reconnaissance to his victory on the Marne, demanded an expansion of the *Aviation Militaire* to sixty-five squadrons. By October French orders had been placed for 2,300 aircraft and 3,400 engines, and other nations were thinking equally ambitiously. Kitchener was told of a plan to give the RFC thirty squadrons, and growled laconically, 'Make it sixty!' All the air forces had too many different types of aircraft, which created severe difficulties for training, maintenance and spares. The French were the first to categorise their squadrons explicitly into fighter, bomber and reconnaissance types.

As early as September, the RFC began to experiment with taking primitive radio sets into the air, to signal to the artillery.

Soldiers, increasingly conscious of their own predicament as prisoners of an unlovely ground environment, readily succumbed to enthusiasm for the exploits of their comrades in the sky. Everything to do with aircraft seemed worthy of awe: on 17 September Belgian Charles Stein's entire battalion was given the afternoon off, in the manner of a successful school football team, for shooting down a German plane of which the crew were made prisoners. Capt. Robert Harker of the BEF wrote with unashamed wonder in November: 'I have had some talks with men and officers in the Flying Corps here and it is most interesting. One of them told me that he had been fired on for half an hour at a time and felt like a driven pheasant – he says that [guns aimed at] aeroplanes can shoot up very high and accurately. He says one minute you may be watching a great battle and within an hour be having a good meal in some peaceful place right away as aeroplanes can move about so quickly.'

Caroll Dana Winslow, an American who trained as a pilot at the French flight school at Pau, identified three categories of airman: gentlemen; pre-war aviators and mechanics with specialist qualifications; and civilian chauffeurs and mechanics, admitted to the aristocracy of the air because they were thought to have relevant expertise. Almost all the best pilots were aged between twenty and thirty; those younger were dangerously immature, while older men proved too cautious, their reflexes slowing. Every nation found itself struggling hastily to train riggers, fitters and mechanics to service and repair machines constructed of canvas, wire and plywood. Many French ground crews were recruited from Indochina – these were known as 'les Annamites'.

All fliers were volunteers, and a growing number of army officers offered their services: some to escape from the trenches; others because as cavalrymen they now had little fighting to do; others again because wounds had incapacitated them for ground duties. All soon learned that flying was no less perilous than soldiering: far more airmen perished in accidents than from enemy action. Twelve-year-old Elfriede Kuhr witnessed two crashes a day at her local training airfield at Schneidemühl, and wrote fatalistically in her diary about the pilots: 'When they make their first solo flight they are often nervous, and then an accident happens.'

Fliers had a one-in-four chance of surviving a crash, and none were equipped with parachutes. Everything had to be learned by experience: the perils posed at low altitude by telegraph wires and the cables of captive observation balloons; the case for unbuckling seat straps before a crash, because the risk of breaking one's neck on being thrown clear seemed less than that of being crushed by the engine in a wreck; the menace of clouds, which could hide hostile machines. Gas-filled airships were soon restricted to night operations in the immediate battle zone, because of their vulnerability to both sides' ground fire – French troops repeatedly shot down their own dirigibles. Airships proved useful in the dark, because neither side had yet accepted the necessity to black out military installations behind the front.

One November morning in Hamburg, little Ingeborg Treplin announced, 'When I grow up I'll march far away to war!' Her mother asked, 'Well, what would you do there?' 'Shoot sailors and Zeppelins.' Frau Treplin was 'a little bit shocked', and pleaded in favour of sparing Zeppelins. 'Yes, not our Zeppelins' – the child had seen one over Hamburg a few days earlier – 'but if it comes from France then it will drop bombs on my head.' Her mother exclaimed, 'What such a small child picks up!' Her husband answered that letter by saying: 'the war should not last long enough for our daughters to grow up … to shoot Zeppelins. The reason we are now over here is to finish this conflict in such a way that none of our daughters have to experience war again!'

Unfortunately for Dr Treplin's hopes, energetic efforts were already under way to advance the primitive art of aerial bombardment, which made possible assaults on targets in an enemy's country far beyond any battlefield. There had been several pre-war experiments – France's Michelin Aero Club held a bombing competition. Rudolf Martin, an early German evangelist for bombardment from the air, argued in 1908 that Zeppelins and aircraft could destroy Britain's island security, and 'soften it up' for an invasion: eighty Zeppelins, he pointed out, could be built for the same cost as a single dreadnought. Germany's industrial capacity made it possible to build 100,000 aircraft, each of which could carry two infantrymen to England by night in no more than half an hour. Martin believed that a great German air fleet could become a decisive strategic deterrent to his nation's enemies. Like many prophets, he correctly grasped the importance of the new technology, but underrated – by more than a generation – the time-lag before it would attain maturity, along with the destructive power to fulfil his battlefield expectations.

Germany started aerial bombing trials in 1910, though two years later a report described results as 'very bad', even from a height as low as three hundred feet. In 1914 a secret bomber squadron was created, under the cover-name of *Brieftaubenabteilung Ostende* – the 'Ostend carrier-pigeon unit'. This was disbanded because it proved unable to hit anything, but the experience of war dramatically accelerated the development of both aircraft and bombing techniques. On 18 September, an RFC officer named Maj. Musgrove conducted the first British experiment on dropping a bomb from his aircraft. 'It exploded,' noted an observer laconically, 'but not exactly where nor how it was expected to.' Three weeks later a German plane dropped the inaugural bomb to land on an RFC field – without effect. In December the Russians formed a squadron of Ilya Muromets, the world's first four-engined bombers, which regularly if ineffectually attacked German and Austrian positions.

By the winter of 1914, all the belligerents save the British had staged at least modest raids on each other's accessible cities; the battlefield use of aircraft to spot targets for artillery was also being urgently explored. During the ensuing four years, radio-controlled aerial direction of gunnery would become one of the most important tactical innovations of the conflict. The Germans helped their enemies to celebrate Christmas Eve by mounting the first air attack on British soil – a biplane dropped a small bomb on Dover. This did no harm, but the auguries were plain: a new kind of campaign against civilian populations had become possible, and no moral scruples would impede its prosecution as soon as means permitted. Next day – Christmas – the Royal Naval Air Service launched a seaplane raid against reported new Zeppelin sheds near Cuxhaven. The raid was wholly abortive, and three aircraft had to be abandoned at sea on their return to the fleet. But Erskine Childers, who flew as an observer in one machine, wrote exultantly: 'We are fortunate to have witnessed this remarkable event which is but a foretaste of a complete revolution in warfare.' In 1914–18, what airmen could see beneath them of the enemy's movements proved much more important than the destruction they could inflict. But little more than a decade after man's first powered flight, the blitz era was already at hand.

15

Ypres: 'Something that was Completely Hopeless'

In Belgium in mid-October, even as King Albert's soldiers were falling back from Antwerp, further west allied and German forces surged and milled in open country, hampered by chronic uncertainty about each other's movements. Joffre had been uneasy about accepting Sir John French's demand to move his contingent to the allied left flank: if a new strategic crisis erupted, proximity to the sea might encourage the British to scuttle home, as their C-in-C had been eager to do in August. But there was little chance they would achieve any big advance on the Aisne, whereas in the north-east their strong cavalry could make itself useful. It would be much easier to supply the BEF from England through the Channel ports. Thus, Joffre acceded to the shift of front. Britain's continental army spent the second week of October in transit towards Flanders. The infantry travelled by train, while the cavalry enjoyed a leisurely week-long ride through Picardy in balmy autumn weather, halting in hospitable French villages. Those who survived the year afterwards recalled this as a last brush with relative comfort and happiness before the shades closed in upon them.

On the 13th, the Germans marched into Lille, singing '*Die Wacht am Rhein*' accompanied by their regimental bands, and bewildered to find trams clattering along the streets beside their columns. Joffre afterwards nursed a grievance about losing the great industrial city: he claimed that if the railway system had not been committed to shifting the British to suit their own convenience, French reinforcements might have reached and held Lille. This is implausible, however, and the BEF arrived in the north just in time to play a critical role, though its C-in-C had no inkling about the nature of this. Experiencing one of his spasms of optimism, Sir John persuaded himself that the Germans were weak in north-west Belgium. He thought that the three corps he now mustered might make a rapid advance, capturing Bruges then pushing for Ghent.

As well as delusions, there was a new epidemic of rumours. One of French's divisional commanders, Charles Monro, who might have been expected to know better, asserted confidently: 'large Russian reinforcements are on their way and have already landed in the north of England'. A junior officer, Lionel Tennyson, was somewhat more cautious, writing after a glimpse of a newspaper on 11 October: 'we heard Antwerp had fallen but that the French and Russians were still gaining victories, a thing we have heard now so often that we are rather beginning to disbelieve it'. But the ebullience displayed by the BEF's C-in-C was also in evidence among journalists who frequented the Café Napolitain in Paris, a favourite rendezvous for gossip. A *New Statesman* correspondent reported from its terrace: 'A month ago everyone was grave and preoccupied; today everyone was gay. There [is] victory in the air. I trust we are not giving way to premature optimism, but we cannot help thinking that things are going very well indeed.'

In reality, more than five German corps were concentrating north of the Lys, in the path of the BEF. Falkenhayn was assembling yet another new army, the Fourth, commanded by the Duke of Württemberg, to attack on Prince Rupprecht's right. Many of its units were composed of reservists, scantily trained and officered by 'dug-outs' – over-age veterans. In October, one such regiment lost its CO and all three battalion commanders to infirmity rather than wounds. Some of the middle-aged men were past campaigning, while few of their young soldiers had any understanding of it. All the formations were poorly equipped: several found themselves issued with uniforms and accoutrements dating back to 1871, while lacking spades and field kitchens. To the despair of artillerymen, few gunners had any notion about how to manage the horses in their teams. But here, nonetheless, was an enormous mass of men, bearing down upon the allies.

The new offensive in Belgium began in earnest on 18 October, when Württemberg's army fell upon the Belgians near the Channel coast. German tactical follies matched earlier French ones. An account of one attack on the 20th described the death of Capt. Hans Graf von Wintzingerode, who advanced mounted on a charger: 'holding his sword aloft, he urged his men forward repeatedly'. Wintzingerode suffered an almost inevitable fate, being hit by several bullets. He was then abandoned between the lines in cold, heavy rain. After six days and nights he was found and brought in, only to expire at an aid post.

On the morning of 23 October, Charles Stein and his fellow Belgian grenadiers glimpsed Germans crawling forward. The defenders silently took up firing positions, and waited. When the attackers were three hundred yards away, 'they all jumped up like one man and ran towards us, crying like babies that have toothache. But at the same moment our machine-guns and rifles began to sing, and we saw with great pleasure that many Germans were falling down, and the others were running away as fast as they could.' Peter Kollwitz, the artist's son who back in August had returned so gaily from a Norwegian holiday to serve the Fatherland, was among those killed near Dixmude that day.

But the attackers gained ground: by the 24th, they had got across the Yser. Belgian soldier Edouard Beer, a veteran of Antwerp, watched an exodus of refugees from the town of Malines, 'the whole population fleeing before the barbarians. A tragic cortège of unhappy people carrying in their carts a few sticks of furniture – precious memories – saved from the devastation! A column of mothers clutching their babies in their arms to protect them from the cold, while their other children clung to them. A column of old people, often infirm, whom only terror of the enemy had given strength to move. And as for us, faithful soldiers of the community, we are often obliged to deny these people access to the roads on which they might pursue their journeys to Calvary! Sometimes it is very hard to do one's duty.'

The British Army adopted towards its Belgian comrades a posture of unwavering contempt, but until the last week of October some Belgian units sustained an effective resistance: German accounts give little hint of the feebleness Sir John French's men thought endemic among Albert's soldiers. There were fierce close-quarter firefights amid the network of dykes and waterways, with the attackers obliged to improvise engineer bridges that were frequently destroyed. The Belgians staged repeated counter-attacks. Near the coast, the Germans suffered considerably from the fire of the Royal Navy's shallow-draft monitors, cruising offshore. On 27 October, one German commander reported almost hysterically, 'the attacking spirit of the battalion is completely broken'. The cold, rain and mud oppressed both sides. The pervasive theme was of slow German progress, at heavy cost.

The morale of Albert's men declined as they retreated and their losses mounted: 'The incessant stream of broken men came in and out,' wrote British nursing sister Mrs Mayne, who received Belgian casualties at Furnes hospital. 'The yards were littered with blood-soaked stretchers against which one stumbled in the dark, getting one's hands all sticky.' On the 27th, Pte. Stein wrote in stilted English: 'We are feeling very tired to stay in the trenches.' Two days later, during bitter fighting, 'a very gentle ladybird came and rested on my left hand. I took her and laid it in a piece of paper and so in my pocket. The ladybird that brought me luck is now in possession of my best girlfriend and I hope and wish it will always bring her heaps of luck as it did me.' He spoke too soon. Shortly afterwards, he and his comrades laughed with relief when a shell landed in front of their trench and exploded harmlessly. Then, seconds later, they suffered a direct hit: 'I must have been a very long time senseless because it was nearly dark when I opened my eyes; I tried to get up but I was not able to move and felt awful pain in the back.' Stein spent months in British hospitals, undergoing a series of operations.

On 26 October, the Belgian field commander proposed another retreat, which King Albert vetoed. But it had become plain that drastic measures were needed to check the German coastal offensive. If Belgium's soldiers could not throw back the enemy, nature must be enlisted to do so. On 27 October the sluice gates at Nieuport were opened at high tide, starting a process of inundating the surrounding farmland with sea water. On the 31st, the Germans made a last assault before the rising floods obliged them to withdraw. Thereafter, the allied left flank was secured: 'As soon as a spadeful of earth was lifted, the hole filled with water,' wrote a German soldier ruefully. When rations belatedly reached some of his comrades in front of Dixmude, many were too ill with stomach troubles – probably caused by drinking the polluted water – to be able to eat. Belgian troops redeployed behind breastworks on the waterlogged ground west of the inundations.

Between King Albert's men and the British, French marines fought hard to hold Dixmude. Dorothie Feilding wrote:

> Our cars were going day and night, the last 2 miles into Dixmude was down a dead straight open road, raked by shell as soon as anything living showed down it. Many is the race we have had down there with our scout cars with stretchers laid on ... The towns & villages & farms were burning. The glare helped you see at night but sometimes it looked like hell, with the flames curling & leaping up in the darkness & the crash as the houses fell in had something awful about it. Driving through the streets of Dixmude one night, it was so hot, with the houses on each side burning, I just had to drive through as quick as I could & hope. How the tyres didn't get cut to blazes by glass or burnt by embers oftener than they did I cannot understand ... when you had got your wounded away from the

lines, there was nowhere to take them. The numbers made it possible for the hospital at Furnes only to take in the practically dying men. All the rest had to go on by trains & what trains ... cattle-trucks with a little dirty straw & no light or water or any doctoring to speak of. As soon as a train was full it would be shunted out, but perhaps only to remain on the sidings for many hours. It took as a rule 3 or 4 days before the men got to a hospital at Calais some mere 40 miles back. You can imagine the poor souls by the time they reached the base. Men with fractured legs racked by the jolting, without a stretcher to lie on, or a rug to cover them & shivering with cold in their mud & rain & blood-soaked uniform.

Dixmude was lost to the Germans, but the town cost them many lives. Feilding later became the first woman to be awarded Britain's Military Medal, as well as a French Croix de Guerre. British soldiers further south were scornfully dismissive of their allied neighbours' showing. Grenadier Wilfrid Abel-Smith wrote: 'The Belgians have never done any good, I am told. They will not stand the shelling – no more will any but highly trained and disciplined troops. The French and Belgians who are not far from us are most unreliable.' This was monstrously chauvinistic: these formations had put up a better fight than their allies recognised. Many British troops would soon flinch and indeed flee in the face of persistent shelling. A German NCO wrote ruefully but respectfully about the fighting for Dixmude: 'the Frenchman has shown himself to be a thoroughly courageous chap'.

Inland from the Belgian and French positions, on the ground where the BEF began to deploy in October, between the 6th and the 14th a mass of German cavalry swirled and eddied, seeking to shield the advance of their Fourth Army from allied scrutiny. Marwitz's horsemen entered Ypres – the only occasion in the war that they did so – and began to look for billets. A German officer wrote: 'The people were quite friendly towards me, but expressed neither sympathy nor antipathy towards the German advance. Their every third expression was "poor Belgium".' The cavalrymen were quickly obliged to quit the town, but the ensuing German onslaught became the most terrible British experience of 1914, and marked a decisive transformation of the struggle.

Sir John French's men detrained after their journey from the Aisne in territory still unscarred by war, where civilians and soldiers were going about their business almost carelessly. A French officer was amazed to encounter British soldiers shopping in Béthune, and local people happy to serve them. He shrugged, 'that is the soul of France for you. I was struck by the phlegmatic attitude of the English, and the unthinking manner in which they approach danger. I watched one company dispatched to the front line moving with slow steps, pipes in their mouths and officers carrying walking sticks, as though setting off for a game of golf. We heard that shortly afterwards they suffered a direct hit and lost several men.'

Joffre would have liked his allies to display less phlegm, more urgency. During the first ten weeks of the war – and what an eternity of experience that span embraced – The British Army had suffered far less than the French. Some BEF units recalled cruel days on the Chemin des Dames, but the sight of green and uninjured Flanders countryside lifted spirits, creating a feeling of a fresh beginning. This did not, however, instill any sense of haste in the advance. Signals officer Alexander Johnston deplored its sluggishness, writing on 13 October: 'It has been a most disappointing day: here we are, a whole Division, held up by a few Jaegers & horse artillery practically all day. As far as I can see, everyone is expecting the unit on their right or left to do the hard work. We have been doing practically nothing because we are waiting for the action of the 8th Inf Brigade on our left.'

Meanwhile the 7th Division, landed from England a fortnight earlier, had endured much frustrating footslogging, hither and thither around Belgium, with scarcely a glimpse of a German. Impatient for action and ahead of the rest of the BEF, on 14 October its regiments entered Ypres – 'Wipers', as men immediately dubbed the place. Wilfrid Abel-Smith, who brought his Grenadiers the same way a few days later, described it as 'rather a nice old town with narrow, cobble-stoned streets, and some fine buildings … there seemed to be a tremendous lot of priests and nuns … It seems so odd to be fighting in this sort of country – we have always associated war with the tropics in the past.'

Henry Wilson, with his curious combination of flippancy and insight, observed some months earlier that few British soldiers paid much attention to 'a funny little country like Belgium, though most of them may be buried there before they are much older'. The men of the BEF had no sense of impending doom. Though Sir John French knew that allied formations were in heavy action towards the sea, he assured his officers that they were pushing into empty country where they would meet few enemies. The 7th Division marched out of Ypres on 15 October to form a line a few miles to the east, anticipating a rapid further advance as soon as the rest of the BEF came up.

Gunner Charlie Burrows wrote on the 16th: 'We are getting fed up with all this waiting and are anxious to get in action. Weather dull and cold. Heard that the enemy advance guard was falling back a few miles ahead and had set fire to a village.' A few prisoners were taken: one Bavarian being escorted through Hazebrouck complained bitterly to a British officer that he had been abused by French civilians. 'Allied prisoners, when they get to Germany,' he said, 'are given cakes and even chocolate – yet we are stoned. *Das ist unmenschlich.*' But his captive tribe had cause to acknowledge privileges: their war was over, and they were alive.

On Sunday the 18th, 7th Division was ordered to march towards Menin, and skirmished a little with German pickets and patrols. Next morning, the RFC's pilots reconnoitred eastward, and returned with momentous news: huge columns of Germans, vastly outnumbering the British infantry and screening cavalry, would be upon them within hours. The advance was hastily countermanded; units retraced their steps and bivouacked that night on a low ridge overlooking Ypres. Here was the beginning – there were still yawning voids on both flanks – of what became known to history as the Ypres salient, a fortuitous protrusion from the allied line where, in the years ahead, more than 200,000 British soldiers would find their graves.

That October day, of course, the men supposed themselves to be merely experiencing a halt in farmland pleasantly untouched by the war. Early on Tuesday the 20th, throngs of local civilians began hastening westwards, some driving livestock before them. The British were kept waiting, but not for long. Within hours the first big German assault, supported by intense artillery fire, fell on 7th Division. Most of the attackers were ill-trained – some even wholly untrained – reservists. They had been delivered by rail to Menin, then sent forward on foot. As one regiment advanced on the British, its commander cried to his men: 'Throw the lying rabble back into the sea!'

Across shallow folds in the Belgian fields, then still broken by hedges, farmyards, stretches of woodland, and grazed by livestock, the Germans trudged towards the thin lines of British soldiers, who occupied shallow trenches or merely lay prone in grass, roots or stubble. These defenders, unlike the rest of the BEF, had never before seen masses of enemy infantry: they found Württemberg's Pickelhaubed soldiers an awesome sight. As Smith-Dorrien's men had done earlier at Mons and Le Cateau, they opened a crackling fusillade. The legend of the British 'mad minute' has been exaggerated. The intensity of rifle fire ebbed and surged from one

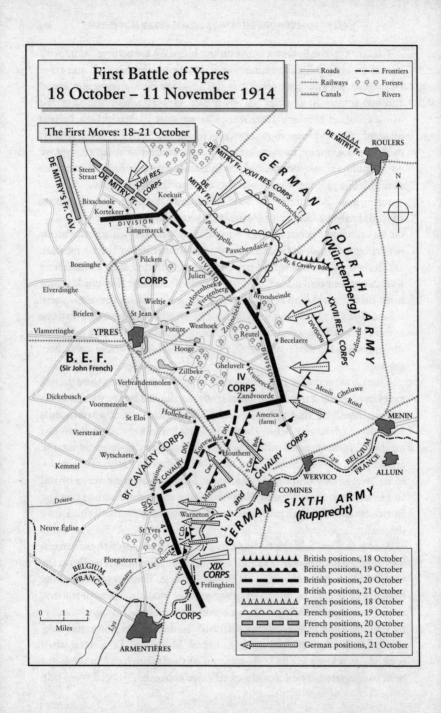

First Battle of Ypres
18 October – 11 November 1914

Roads		Frontiers	
Railways		Forests	
Canals		Rivers	

The First Moves: 18–21 October

ROULERS

DE MITRY Fr.

GERMAN

DE MITRY Fr. XXVI RES. CORPS

DE MITRY Fr. XXIII RES. CORPS

Steen Straat

Koekuit

Westroosebek

F O U R T H   A R M Y (Württemberg)

DE MITRY'S Fr. CAV.

Bixschoole
Kortekeer

1 DIVISION
Langemarck

Poelcapelle

Passchendaele

Br. 6 Cavalry Bde

Boesinghe

Pilcken

2 DIVISION

St Julien

Elverdinghe

I CORPS

Wieltje

Verlorenhoek
Frezenberg

Broodseinde

Brielen

St Jean

Zonnebeke

7 DIVISION

XXVII RES. CORPS

Reutel

Becelaere

Dadizeele

Vlamertinghe

YPRES

Potijze

Westhoek

Hooge

B.E.F.
(Sir John French)

Zillebeke

Gheluvelt
Kruiseecke

IV CORPS

Zandvoorde

Menin   Gheluwe   Road

MENIN

Dickebusch

Verbrandenmolen

Voormezeele

St Eloi

Hollebeke

America (farm)

Vierstraat

Br. CAVALRY CORPS

Kortewilde

Houthem

5 Can Bde

IV. and V CAVALRY CORPS

Lys

BELGIUM
FRANCE

ALLUIN

Kemmel

Wytschaete

Messines
CAVALRY DIV.

Cav.

2   Messines
CAV. DIV.

WERVICO

COMINES

GERMAN SIXTH ARMY (Rupprecht)

Douve

Warneton

Neuve Église

St Yves

4 DIV

Ploegsteert

Le Gheer

XIX CORPS

Frélinghien

BELGIUM
FRANCE

Warnave

III CORPS

0	1	2
Miles		

Lys

ARMENTIÈRES

N

British positions, 18 October
British positions, 19 October
British positions, 20 October
British positions, 21 October
French positions, 18 October
French positions, 19 October
French positions, 20 October
French positions, 21 October
German positions, 21 October

period of the battle to the next: ammunition conservation was a vital consideration, and there seemed an infinite embarrassment of targets.

The men of 7th Division had to learn their business under a storm of incoming bullets and shells. Some officers confused idiocy with courage: Lt. Col. Walter Loring of 2nd Warwicks rode up the Menin road at the head of his battalion on an enormous white horse. He cursed when a bullet struck his heel, and after having the wound dressed insisted on remounting. The horse was soon killed, and Loring took another, which also fell. The colonel was eventually killed on the 24th, hobbling among his men, urging them on with one foot in a carpet slipper. He was the first of three brothers to die in the opening year of the conflict.

The village of Passchendaele was lost, and remained in enemy hands for three years. Orders reached the forward positions to dig in. Men asked: with what? Many had lost or rashly discarded their entrenching tools, and none had heavy spades. They scraped as best they could, some with bare hands. The 21st proved another day of savage action and losses. The first troops arriving from the Aisne began to move into the line, one unit after another arriving just in time to meet new waves of Germans, who were soon attacking by night as well as by day, on an ever broader front. But the Kaiser's soldiers lost heavily on both the 20th and the 21st, and felt anything but invincible. Marwitz, commanding the cavalry, wrote on the 22nd, after studying the British positions: 'The entire countryside here is one mass of small enclosed fields and hedges reinforced with wire. How are we meant to attack through that? The enemy exploits its potential skilfully, firing from inside houses and trenches which they have dug extremely rapidly.'

A German corporal who took part in the initial assault on Langemarck, north of Ypres, wrote wearily afterwards: 'Who that day or during the days that followed had any idea about what was happening or what either we or the enemy intended? ... Quite suddenly bursts of shrapnel spread death and destruction on our positions. What I saw and experienced ... was amongst the sort of images that the wildest imagination can dream up. What was left of our division? ... In every piece of meadow, behind every hedge, were bands of men, some large, some small, but what were they doing? What could they do?' Early that afternoon of the 21st, one battered German regiment broke and ran after all its officers had become casualties. By nightfall every house in the village of Poelkapelle was crowded with wounded brought back from the shambles at Langemarck. When the attack was renewed next day, the outcome was identical.

For decades afterwards, German nationalists sought to evoke a supposed 'Spirit of Langemarck', signifying exemplary courage in the face of adversity. This was a myth, which masked the fact that the German attacks of 21–23 October were exercises in futility, matching anything the French had done in the Battles of the Frontiers. 'A bloody day indeed,' Bavarian Capt. Ottmar Rutz wrote ruefully of the 21st, listing his close friends among officers killed leading attacks down the road to Ypres. British firing continued into the night: 'It seemed as though nobody was meant to quit this place alive.' Next morning, with great difficulty food was brought forward to give the Germans who had been detailed to renew the assault their first hot meal for two days – and the last many ever ate. Falkenhayn's Fourth Army complained that positions won at heavy cost by day were lost again during the night.

Though Ypres and Sir Douglas Haig's I Corps became the principal focus of German assaults, French and British troops further south in front of Armentières and behind La Bassée fought their own bitter battles throughout the last fortnight of October. GHQ was slow to comprehend the scale of the German effort, and still dispatched battalions into the line with orders to assume that they themselves would shortly be doing the attacking. They learned differently. 'Everywhere we advance we find Germans in front of us,' wrote Grenadier George Jeffreys. Wilfrid Abel-Smith fulminated on 22 October: 'It is all rot saying we have nothing in front of us. There are heaps of Germans, and, as an army, they are very good, and their gunners are perfect ... No doubt we will kill heaps of Germans but there are always heaps more ...'

Many British soldiers' clothing was in tatters after their travails since August. Some wore civilian trousers; veteran Welch Fusilier Frank Richards affected a knotted handkerchief in place of his long-lost service cap. He did not care: 'we looked a ragtime lot, but in good spirits and ready for anything that turned up'. Just east of Fromelles, his unit unbuckled its entrenching tools: 'Little did we think ... that we were digging our future homes,' Richards wrote. Two Indian divisions joined the right of the BEF's line on 22 October. The reinforcement was desperately needed, and the first Indian soldier to win a VC was a Baluchi, Sepoy Khudadad Khan, who gained his medal manning a machine-gun in Hollebeke.

It was widely suggested, however, that the Indian corps was ill-suited to continental campaigning. Frank Richards, who had served for years in the subcontinent, wrote later with a ranker's contempt: 'native infantry were no good in France. Some writers in the papers wrote at the time that they couldn't stand the cold weather; but the truth was that they suffered from cold feet, and a few enemy shells exploding around their trenches were enough to demoralize the majority.' Indian cavalry corps commander Lt. Gen. Mike Rimington declared scornfully that his men were 'only fit to feed pigs'. This was grossly unjust: Indian troops taught the rest of the BEF the art of patrolling. But there was a core of truth in the view that it was brutal, even in the British Empire's hour of need, to expose mercenaries from the far side of the world to the appalling cultural shock of the struggle in Flanders.

The Germans attacked by night as well as by day, and many actions were fought out by the light of blazing buildings. One group approached the Grenadiers in darkness on 21 October, crying out almost believably, 'We are the Coldstream!' But the Grenadiers glimpsed spiked helmets silhouetted against the skyline, and shot them down mercilessly. An officer wrote: 'it is too much like shooting a flock of sheep, poor things. They have discipline, and do what they are told, but their attacks at night in this wood developed into the poor devils wandering rather aimlessly about under our terrific rifle fire.' Livestock roamed untended, and some men milked cows between bombardments. In one attack, the Germans drove cattle ahead of their troops: beasts and men were slaughtered together.

The war diary of 2nd Oxf & Bucks recorded on 22 October: 'they came on in thick lines, and our firing was steady and the light sufficiently good to enable a fair aim to be taken'; the foremost Germans fell within twenty-five yards of the battalion's positions. Though British shrapnel inflicted some damage, artillery ammunition was short on both sides: rifles and machine-guns were responsible for most of the killing. In one notorious assault at Langemarck, fifteen hundred young Germans were killed and six hundred prisoners taken. Human fortitude was tested to the limit by the tumult of Ypres. Extreme penalties, or at least the threat of them, were periodically invoked to hold men to their duty. Pte. Edward Tanner of the Wiltshires was shot by a firing squad on 29 October, having been apprehended behind the lines in civilian clothes. L/Sgt. William Walton deserted from the King's Royal Rifle Corps near Ypres, and was duly executed on his recapture, after remaining on the run for several months. Lionel Tennyson threatened to shoot the next man of his who returned prematurely from a listening patrol in no man's land. It was now that this last phrase – used in medieval times to describe a patch of unowned ground north of London's city walls where executions were carried out – first entered soldiers' vernacular, denoting the space between rival trenches, which might vary from fifty yards to two hundred according to the vagaries of the terrain.

Each side's accounts of hardship, misery, terror, despair and sacrifice marched in step during the successive clashes at Ypres. It was a delusion shared by almost every man that the BEF alone confronted the enemy's might. Something of the same feeling reached back to Britain. Churchill wrote of his own deep gloom in those weeks: 'the sense of grappling with and being overpowered by a monster of appalling and apparently inexhaustible strength on land ... oppressed my mind'. In November there was a new invasion scare at home, which briefly infected Kitchener and Churchill, and reinforced their illusions about the limitless resources at the Kaiser's disposal.

It was true that the British sector in Flanders was the focus of a huge effort by Falkenhayn, but the French suffered plentiful tribulations of their own, and made a critical contribution to holding the line. German interrogators reported French prisoners complaining about the allegedly poor showing of their British neighbours, in a fashion that mirrored their allies' ruderies about themselves. South of the BEF's frontage, Foch's men counter-attacked again and again, maintaining pressure on the enemy. Sgt. Paul Cocho, thirty-five-year-old owner of a Breton grocery shop and the father of four young children, went into action for the first time in Flanders, and was stunned by the experience: 'I did not imagine that war would be like this ... I have seen in our regiment so much chaos and so little proper leadership; I have seen wounded poorly cared for ... For the first two days we had to make do with small pieces of dried bread as food, though we were hardly hungry amid so much profoundly emotional experience. We had wine to drink at first because some resourceful chaps went and pillaged the cellars of wrecked houses, then later we had only cold coffee.' Cocho described his experiences as a prolonged nightmare, from which he was awakened only by being evacuated sick at the end of November.

On 23 October French infantry launched a desperate attempt to retake Passchendaele. Among the foremost of the attackers was their commander, Gen. Moussy, who urged them on, saying, '*Allons, allons, mes enfants. En avant! En avant!*' His men replied, '*Bien, mon général!*' But ever more often in the face of the enemy's fire they dropped back to seek cover, and the advance lost momentum. Moussy tried a joke: '*Il faut absolument arriver a Passchendaele ce soir, ou pas de souper, pas de souper!*' Whether or not the survivors got supper, the French failed to get Passchendaele. The British felt that Moussy himself behaved more like a company commander than a general, but more than a few of their own leaders emulated him. Whatever claims were made about 'château generalship' later in the war, at First Ypres senior officers on both sides exposed themselves freely, and perished in proportion.

A contest in pain and sacrifice was unfolding. German soldier Paul Hub wrote home on 23 October: 'Maria, this sort of war is so unspeakably miserable. If only you saw a line of stretcher-bearers with their burdens, you'd know what I mean. I haven't had a chance to shoot at all yet. We have to deal with an unseen enemy.' Blast cost Hub the permanent loss of his hearing, and many of his comrades suffered worse fates. After being badly shot in the chest north of Ypres, a German NCO named Knauth wrote later that he was surprised to find himself thinking with relief, 'Well, you will be spending Christmas at home.' And still Falkenhayn's offensive, and his men's sufferings, continued. Sgt. Gustav Sack described his unit's meagre rations in a letter to his wife Paula, written near Péronne on 26 October. At 7 a.m. they drank coffee or tea, indistinguishable from each other in texture. Late at night they received field-kitchen soup and ration bread. Instead of a continuous trench, men occupied foxholes in which they slept on straw. As for the war, 'everything is quite, quite different and more insane than you could suppose possible … You don't see anything, although the wicked enemy' – this was his heavy humour – 'is only 3–400m away, but you hear plenty.' He added in another letter: 'I am freezing! Tonight I am on outpost duty from seven to seven – the moon high, cotton-wool clouds, nice sunrise, partridges everywhere, everything very picturesque – but cold, cold, cold and hungry!'

Every British soldier now knew that the cessation of an enemy artillery bombardment signalled the onset of an infantry assault. Capt. Henry Dillon wrote to his parents of meeting a night attack on 24 October: 'A great grey mass of humanity was charging, running for all God would let them straight on to us not 50 yards off – about as far as the summer-house to the coach-house … As I fired my rifle the rest all went off almost simultaneously. One saw the great mass of Germans quiver. In reality some fell, some fell over them, and others came on. I have never shot so much in such a short time … My right hand is one huge bruise from banging the bolt up and down … The firing died down and out of the darkness a great moan came. People with their arms and legs off trying to crawl away; others who could not move gasping out their last moments with the cold night wind biting into their broken bodies and the lurid red glare of a farmhouse showing up clumps of grey devils killed by the men on my left further down. A weird, awful scene; some of them would raise themselves on one arm or crawl a little distance.'

Dillon was one of few men on either side who had sufficient emotion to spare to give a thought to those remote masters of mankind who had unleashed the slaughter: 'Well, I suppose if there is a God, Emperor Bill will have to come to book some day. When one thinks of the misery of those wounded and later on wives, mothers and friends, and to think that this great battle where there may have been half a million on either side is only on a front of about 25 miles, and that this sort of thing is now going on on a front of nearly 400. To think that this man could have saved it all!'

The British were not defending a continuous line; there were wide gaps where the Germans were able to infiltrate and gain ground, just as they had done on a much smaller scale at Mons. This was still predominantly a battalion battlefield, where many units fought independently. Most went into action already depleted by losses on the Aisne, reduced from a thousand men to six hundred or less. By November, their numbers would shrink far more grievously. Much of the British artillery was sited behind the line, on lower ground, and thus handicapped by the fact that its officers could not see the Germans over the skyline, and the guns were anyway very short of shells. More seriously, the BEF had little barbed wire. The keys to effective defence in twentieth-century warfare were obstacles covered by fire. Here, there were few obstacles, and thus the principal impediments to attackers were bullets or shells, and never enough of either.

The British christened a large plantation of Scots pine just north of the Menin road Polygon Wood, because of its shape on the map. In its midst, unexpectedly, was a Belgian cavalry riding school, where some exuberant young British officers put their horses over the jumps even as shells fell nearby. On 24 October it became the scene of a long, bitter series of dispersed actions, in which groups of men in tens, twenties, fifties fought Germans as and when they met them. Some British troops who kept firing until the enemy overran their positions then made the mistake of throwing down their arms and raising their hands, only to be bayoneted, not unreasonably. Amid such a slaughter, why should surrenders have been accepted on demand?

But the German assault now lost momentum, and the British strove to use the breathing space to retake lost ground. The 2nd Worcesters had just been pulled back out of the line for rest. 'Every man ... was exhausted and unshaven,' said one of them, Pte. John Cole, 'and we were relieved to get back into reserve. But ... we'd only just arrived when the words came that we were urgently needed to stop another German attack ... We were absolutely fed up to the teeth.' The Worcesters' commanding officer was thirty-six-year-old Maj. Edward Hankey, who had taken over when his colonel was promoted. Now, Hankey led the battalion in a series of bayonet charges to regain Polygon Wood. These cost heavy losses in desperate scrums, but saved the British line. That night a Royal Engineer wrote: 'what awful sights in the wood! The dead are lying in groups everywhere. Our brigade had charged through here three times during the day.' One German unit lost 70 per cent of its fighting strength among the pines. The regiment that had led the enemy assault was reduced from fifty-seven officers and 2,629 men at dawn to six officers and 748 men at nightfall. There was plenty of bloodshed elsewhere also: on 20–21 October the Germans suffered huge losses further south, around Ploegstreet Wood.

On the 25th, Capt. Ottmar Rutz watched heavy artillery wreak havoc among British Guards battalions at Kruiseke, south-east of Ypres: 'The effect was shocking; they could not withstand it. They leapt up out of their trenches with our machine-guns taking them in their sights. Now was the moment of revenge!' Rutz reported the enemy throwing away weapons even before his own infantrymen launched their assault. The Germans sprang down into British trenches and took many prisoners among defenders who had hung on through the barrage. Alexander Johnston recorded that day: 'The reason the Germans got into the 2nd Irish Rifles' trenches is that the men were so tired they were all asleep.' By the day's end, that battalion had only four officers left alive. Counter-attacks during the night failed to restore the line. Next morning, more British troops abandoned their positions, which were promptly seized by dismounted German cavalrymen, many still wearing their spurs. The victors fell eagerly upon captured stores and especially cigarettes.

Throughout history, armies had been accustomed to fight battles that most often lasted a single day, occasionally two or three, but thereafter petered out. Now, however, the allies and Germans explored a terrible new universe of continuous engagement. They accustomed themselves to killing and being killed for weeks on end, with no more than a few hours' interruption. The bombastic CO of the Gordon Highlanders urged his men to ensure that each accounted for forty Germans before New Year's

Day. When the regiment's Sgt. Arthur Robinson was dying of wounds on 24 October, he apologised for having failed to fulfil his quota.

Some who perished were teenagers in their first hours of battle; others were veterans. Among those who fell on the 26th was Pte. William Macpherson. A Leith man, he had served three years with the Royal Scots in South Africa, then a further eight as a Hampshire policeman before re-enlisting in the Scots Guards. The record describes him as 'husband of Alice Macpherson, of 19 Windsor Road, Boscombe, Bournemouth'. Lt. John Brooke of the Gordons, thirty years old and a former Sandhurst sword of honour winner, won a VC before his death in the second of two attacks on German positions south-east of Ypres on the 29th. That day's fighting around Gheluvelt reduced 1st Grenadiers to four officers and a hundred men.

The last days of October witnessed some of the most ferocious German attacks, and the most desperate British resistance. On Monday the 26th Douglas Haig wrote in his diary: 'By 4 p.m. the bulk of the 7th Division had retired from the salient. Most units in disorder … I rode out about 3 p.m. to see what was going on, and was astounded at the terror-stricken men coming back. Still, there were some units in the division which stuck to their trenches.' On the 29th, seven German divisions were committed to the attacks on Ypres. One officer, Capt. Obermann, had spent much of the previous night crawling across no man's land, reconnoitring British positions on the Menin road. During an advance through fog early on the following morning, he was mortally wounded by machine-gun fire from a Scottish unit. Obermann died in the arms of his adjutant, becoming his battalion's second commander to die in Flanders. One of Obermann's corporals eventually led a dash to silence the British machine-gun, which was manned by a tough old veteran who kept shooting until the attackers overran his position and killed him. Thereafter the Germans, many of them volunteers from Munich, reported British troops abandoning their positions and running for the rear, where they encountered their dismayed corps commander. Haig deplored the fashion in which some units had been posted on forward slopes, in full view of the enemy, and paid the price.

But the day became a dreadful experience for the Germans also. Sun slowly dispersed the fog as they pushed forward, enabling British gunners to get a clear sight of them. One attacking officer's eye was caught by farm ponds glistening in the brilliant light. He watched a succession of poplar trees totter and then collapse under shellfire: the natural beauties of the countryside were being progressively obliterated. As the defenders' bombardment intensified, many Germans sought cover. A Prussian officer demanded crossly, 'Why aren't the Bavarians getting forward? Why are they lying down out there?' Reluctantly, the attackers rose and moved forward again, into renewed fire. 'Off we went,' wrote a German officer later, 'but where to? For most of those involved it was to their deaths ... only five men of my platoon are still alive ... The British had dug themselves in well in a tobacco field on top of a broad hill and they fought desperately.' German artillery repeatedly fired short, causing casualties in their own ranks. It is striking to notice that on both the Eastern and Western Fronts, German gunnery was often careless, causing heavy 'friendly fire' losses. That day of the 29th one Bavarian regiment lost 349 men killed, with numbers of wounded in proportion.

All armies, and especially the British, were morbidly sensitive to the supposed dishonour of losing a position. In the three weeks of Ypres, their line bulged and bent repeatedly amid successive attacks and counter-attacks. Ground was won, lost and retaken, sometimes several times in successive days. There was savage close-quarter fighting in which men used swords, bayonets, clubbed rifles, pistols. As in most subsequent battles of the twentieth century, units under bombardment often abandoned their positions in varying degrees of disorder. It was asking too much of even brave and disciplined troops to remain in trenches under a storm of shrapnel and high explosive that was killing and maiming comrades all around them. If staying in a given place promised certain death, rational men moved somewhere else, to the dismay of their generals. Lost trenches had to be recaptured – or not, as the case might be – in counter-attacks launched sometimes within minutes, more often within an hour or two, by which time the Germans had probably sited their own Maxims in them.

Some battalions showed themselves exceptionally staunch, while others became notorious for the readiness with which they fled. On 21 October Alexander Johnston observed contemptuously of the 2nd South Lancs: 'They really are an awful lot ... one cannot rely on them for anything, and today is the 4th time during the War that they have bolted.' On the 29th, amid heavy shelling he wrote: 'It was rather sad to learn that a few of the 1st Wilts and a lot of the 2nd South Lancs were found a little later, very out of breath and with no equipment on ... 2 miles back nearly. The shelling of course was unpleasant but did not last long and I'm afraid it shows what a state the nerves of the men have got into.' The Bedfords, Northumberland Fusiliers and Cheshires were among other units deemed less than reliable.

Capt. Ernest Hamilton, an early chronicler of the BEF, wrote apologetically in the introduction to a book on the battle which he published in 1916: 'It must be clearly understood that the mention from time to time of certain battalions as having been driven from their trenches does not in the smallest degree suggest inefficiency' – a euphemism for cowardice – 'on the part of such battalions. It is probable that every battalion in the British Force has at some time or another during the past twelve months been forced to abandon its trenches ... owing to insupportable shellfire ... It may happen that lost trenches may be retaken by a battalion which is inferior in all military essentials to the battalion that was driven out.'

British leadership was often poor above battalion level. Many men in the line were not merely frightened and exhausted, but also felt painfully isolated in their predicament. Alexander Johnston fumed: 'I think it is just wicked the way certain members of the Brigade HQ never move out of the "dugout" all day for danger of meeting a stray bullet, and even duck and flinch when shells burst quite 200 yards away! while they send all sorts of messages that things have got to be done, and are sometimes rather ungenerous about poor fellows in front who are getting nearly all the hammering and all the discomfort. Even an occasional visit once every other day or so by someone in authority and just an occasional word of encouragement, I am sure would help these poor fellows to stick it out.'

Johnston added two days later: 'I am sure the staff are not really in touch with the situation, and can have no true idea of the state of the men, nor do I think sufficient efforts are really made by the Brigadier to convince them or to open their eyes as to the true state of affairs. It cannot be their intention to break the men's hearts as they are currently doing.' This was an early manifestation of what would become a major issue of the war, once static warfare evolved. To exercise command effectively, senior officers needed to position themselves with their staffs at the hub of a network of telephone lines, necessarily some distance behind the front. But the price of doing so was to open a profound psychological as well as physical divide between their own circumstances and those of the men whom they commanded. Though some staff officers did not trouble to conceal their gratitude for escaping duty in the line, few generals were cowards. It was merely beyond their limited imagination to understand that soldiers undergoing such a sustained nightmare as that of Ypres needed human contact and emotional support such as some senior officers, prisoners of decades of stiff military social convention, were entirely unaccustomed to provide. What is remarkable is not how many British units broke at various moments of First Ypres, but how many held their ground.

In the last days of October a new German force was formed, for the explicit purpose of achieving a breakthrough south of the town. It comprised six divisions under Gen. Max von Fabeck. But when Army Group Fabeck, as it was dubbed, first advanced to attack on 30 October, its infantrymen were dismayed by the feebleness of the preparatory bombardment. Falkenhayn's guns were running desperately short of ammunition. Elsewhere along the Western Front, artillery was rationed to two or three rounds a day, to divert shells to the Ypres sector; but still there were not enough to deliver a heavy bombardment. The assault troops started the operation weary, after making a series of night marches to reach the front. Hollebeke was their first objective, and a senior officer issued a stern warning about the high command's high expectations: 'During recent days, several promising opportunities have been wasted because entire corps have allowed themselves to be held up by vastly inferior forces ... attacks are not being pressed home with the utter disregard for danger that each attack demands which aims at a decisive result.'

On the morning of the 30th, 2nd Royal Welch Fusiliers near Fromelles awoke to a breakfast of three biscuits apiece with a spoonful of jam, an issue of a tin of bully beef between four men, and a rum ration of a tablespoon and a half. Frank Richards's company commander, whom the old soldier disliked but respected, walked the length of the trench with his sword in one hand, pistol in the other, repeating to each greatcoated section in turn on their firesteps that this would be a fight to the last man. The four hundred men of their sister battalion, 1st Royal Welch at Zandvoorde château, met the Germans with a storm of fire, and held up their advance until they were overrun, almost all killed or captured, around noon. The dismounted Household Cavalry in the neighbouring village were attacked after a ninety-minute preliminary barrage and driven back, leaving behind their dead, who included the Royal Horse Guards' machine-gun officer, Lord Worsley. By mid-morning the Germans held the Zandvoorde ridge. A British battalion was lost attempting to retake the position; most of its men were taken prisoner, and only eighty-six survivors rallied at nightfall.

But the attackers had also suffered grievously, not only in the struggle for Zandvoorde, but also in assaults elsewhere. On the same day, the 30th, the Germans made another futile push against Langemarck, without benefit of artillery support. Under heavy fire, men of one unit watched in dismay as their only surviving officer, Lt. Zitzewitz, stood beside a tree peering at the British lines through a telescope. They implored him to take cover, but he ignored their warnings until a shell landed nearby and he collapsed: a splinter had made a small, fatal wound in his chest. When darkness came, the attack had made no significant progress. North of Langemarck an 'officer deputy' named Franke wrote that the worst part of nights in the line was being forced to listen to the hopeless cries of wounded men, invisible in beet fields in no man's land: 'German, over here!', 'Help me!', 'Medical Orderlies!', 'Help!'. The attackers sustained pressure on Langemarck during early November, using troops shifted from the coastal sector, where the floods blocked movement. They got nowhere.

Further south, at a meeting of German unit commanders on the evening of the 30th, the senior officer present announced that battalions would resume their assault next day. This caused one CO to interrupt forcefully, saying, 'Excuse me, *Herr Oberst*. The word "battalion" has been mentioned. We in the centre no longer have a battalion. The men have been in battle now for forty-eight hours and they have had no sleep for three nights.' He then outraged his superior officer by saying it was impossible to renew the assault. The colonel exploded: 'Do you say impossible? There is no such thing as impossible! We are all soldiers and must accept the risk of death!' The high command was implacable. The attack must be renewed on 31 October.

Württemberger Paul Hub, one of the men at the centre of the salient near Gheluvelt, scribbled to his wife that day: 'My dear Maria I feel so terrible I'd really rather not write to you … Every day spent here makes it clearer to me how beautiful home is – what a throng of feelings that word "home" brings out in me. I have lived through such horror recently, no words can describe it, the tragedy all around. Every day the fighting gets fiercer and there is still no end in sight. Our blood is flowing in torrents … All around me the most gruesome devastation. Dead and wounded soldiers, dead and dying animals, horse cadavers, burnt-out houses, churned-up fields, vehicles, clothes, weapons … I didn't think war would be like this … There are only a few of us left to tackle the English.'

The 'English', heavily outnumbered, felt that all the difficulties were on their side. But on 31 October the Germans endured another bitter struggle to secure limited objectives: this day, indeed, became one of the bloodiest and – for the British – most dangerous of the battle. Messines was a village with a church, a mill and a limehouse, customarily occupied by some 1,400 inhabitants, but now defended by the dismounted 9th Lancers and 11th Hussars. Having loopholed every house, they made the attackers suffer terribly for every yard gained. Fabeck's men lacked sufficient fire-power systematically to flatten the village and its occupants: most houses had to be stormed one by one. Nonetheless there were too few British troops in Messines to stem the tide. In one place, the Germans brought forward a field gun battery which shelled the British from a range of two hundred yards, driving some to surrender. Thereafter, gunner sergeant William Edgington wrote: 'A perfect hurricane of bullets from 4 Maxims swept the opposite side of the street, added to which the glare of buildings that had been fired by German incendiary shells and also their fireballs made up a scene that was simply indescribable.' Eventually the surviving defenders were obliged to fall back, conceding important higher ground to the Germans.

One of the units which joined the action on 31 October was the London Scottish, a smart Territorial battalion with a drill hall in Buckingham Gate, beside the Palace. Before reaching Ypres, the unit had spent six dreary weeks providing labour in the rear areas, partly because the BEF's commanders doubted the fighting skills of 'Terriers'. Now, in crisis, they were rushed forward in commandeered double-decker London buses – perhaps the very same that had carried them to their City offices a few months earlier. Arrived at corps headquarters, their colonel was told the unit would be getting 1st Coldstream's transport. He asked, did not the Coldstream need this? No, they did not. They were almost all dead.

The battalion's first action, at Wytschaete – 'Whitesheet', as the British dubbed the village – was a disaster. The men were issued with ammunition which did not fit their rifles, and executed a counter-attack on Messines Ridge at ghastly cost: 394 casualties including 190 dead. They clung on all day under fire, and when their left was turned launched a bayonet charge to try to clear the ground, though that task proved too much for them. L/Cpl. Edward Organ saw the London Scottish come back: 'They weren't an organized force at all ... because they'd been cut to pieces. The Germans mowed them down.' The action may have been wonderful in its courage, but the Territorials lacked the experience of war – and the serviceable weapons – to make much of their terrible initiation.

At Gheluvelt, the prevailing story of the day was of German pressure becoming irresistible: Rupprecht's losses were appalling, but weight of numbers eventually buckled the British line. In one trench the attackers took two hundred prisoners, who were being marched to the rear when British shells began to fall upon them, wreaking havoc. By 12.30 the King's Royal Rifle Corps, the Queen's and the Loyal North Lancashires had been driven from Gheluvelt and some British 60-pounders had been captured. All the batteries in the area were obliged to pull back in desperate haste. 'We got the guns out just as the enemy come over the hill in full view, and away we go,' said gunner Charlie Burrows later. 'How we get out of it is a mystery. Shells are bursting all over the place. My off-horse is wounded and nearly drops down with exhaustion but we go on – we have to – along the Menin road. I never expected to get out of that alive. We go back a mile and stop in a field. We lost an officer, 2 NCOs and one gunner and several drivers wounded.' Six guns had to be abandoned. Gheluvelt fell.

The Oxfordshire Hussars, a Yeomanry unit to which Winston Churchill had lately belonged, had been acting as the C-in-C's headquarters regiment, but now trotted thirty miles to Messines, dismounted after a long, wet overnight ride, and were immediately ordered into the line. 'We had no idea what was going on,' recalled Edward Organ, 'but we could tell that things were pretty hot … You could see farms and houses burning, and shells falling around us. We were well down this ridge, sheltered you might say, but sometimes streams of bullets came zipping over our heads – like bees swarming. We were all nervous – well, frightened I suppose – and when you get frightened someone starts a song and you all yell it out … We were singing "Ragtime Cowboy Joe", and I never hear it but I think of us lying there and those guns banging away … I never knew a day of noise like that first time.'

The Worcesters had saved the British line with their counter-attack a week earlier. The same battered battalion was now once again summoned to restore the centre at Gheluvelt. They were fed stew and a rum ration, then at 2 p.m. set off from their billets for the start line, burdened with cotton bandoliers of extra ammunition. One of their officers noted that as they trudged forward, they encountered a stream of men from other units making for the rear. Haig later described to King George V the 'crowds of fugitives who came back down the Menin road … having thrown [away] everything they could, including their rifles and packs, in order to escape, with a look of absolute terror on their faces, such as I have never before seen on any human being's face'. Some groups of British soldiers waved flags and reversed rifles, then approached enemy positions hands in the air – and were fortunate enough to have their surrenders accepted.

Against this tide, the old county regiment charged under heavy artillery fire, gained a thousand yards and reached Gheluvelt château, where they found a handful of South Wales Borderers still holding out. Maj. Hankey blew his hunting horn triumphantly. The Worcesters chased some lingering Germans away through the shrubbery, dug in, and thereafter repelled every assault with rifle fire. But the generals in the rear only learned of Hankey's success after a grim period of suspense in which they feared the worst. Sir John French agreed with Haig that it was likely the BEF would be obliged to fall back west of Ypres, abandoning the town. The corps commander at one stage rode forward to see for himself the state of the battlefield, and was appalled by the chaos he encountered, the broken units in flight. His staff noticed him tugging at his moustache, an unfailing indication that his customary imperturbability was under stress. The C-in-C later described that afternoon as the BEF's worst crisis of the war, and he may well have been right.

Further south, Allenby's dismounted cavalry clung on, but beyond them the French were suffering even heavier losses than the British. At 2.30 Haig was informed by 1st Division's commander that his formation was 'broken': one of its battalions, the Queen's, had lost 624 men and was reduced to a strength of thirty-two, mostly cooks and transport personnel. The 7th Division was in equally desperate straits. Soon after that conversation, shells falling on 1st Division's headquarters at Hooge killed or wounded its commander and most of his staff. Sir John French succumbed to despair, and was just leaving Haig's headquarters when an ADC ran out with news that the Worcesters had retrieved the position. At 3 p.m. Brigadier Charles FitzClarence reported, 'My line holds.' By nightfall it was plain that the Germans had been stopped.

The Worcesters had won a breathing space, which enabled 7th Division to rally its stragglers and fugitives and redeploy. The battalion had advanced 370 strong, and lost a quarter of its strength that day. For years, a local memorial to the dead listed those who fell 'fighting gloriously against a murderous enemy'; in more temperate modern times, the wording on the stone has been changed to read 'fighting gloriously against a determined enemy'. The Germans were less impressed by the Worcesters' action than were the British, being satisfied that they continued to hold Gheluvelt village. But they had been denied the absolute breakthrough they sought and the British grievously feared. The Germans considered that vigorous counter-attacks by French troops further south were the critical factor in frustrating their advance on 31 October. This is debatable. It is seldom that a single unit alters the course of an army's battle, but the Worcesters may have done so at Ypres. What is for sure is that on that day Foch achieved a moral ascendancy over Falkenhayn, whose will cracked, with decisive consequences for German fortunes.

The British spent the ensuing night alternately digging and repelling new German attacks, including an assault on the London Scottish: 'they made no attempt to rush us', in the words of Private Herbert de Hamel, 'they advanced at a steady walk, falling as they came. Flashes spat out along their line. There was no sound – no shouts or cries, only the crackling of rifle shots. The bullets were cutting through the hedge in front of us and slapped into the bank behind us and all the while as we tried to fire back, our new rifles jammed and stuck, it might be after one shot or after five … But after a while there were no more Germans walking towards us.' The battalion attempted a charge across ground lit by the flames from burning buildings, but was driven back. Paul Maze, a liaison officer, described an encounter with survivors next morning: 'His kilt in rags, looking utterly exhausted, a sergeant of the London Scottish was forming up his men who stood like sailors being photographed on a shore within sight of their wreck.' One of the casualties was a City shipping clerk, Pte. Ronald Colman, a Territorial since 1909, who was hit in the ankle by shrapnel and lamed, probably saving his life by removing him from the war. His wound did not prevent him from later becoming a Hollywood star, as also, by a remarkable fluke, did his comrades in the same regiment Basil Rathbone, Herbert Marshall and Claude Rains.

That day, Sunday, 1 November, George Jeffreys met Sir Thomas Capper, 7th Division's commander. The major said, 'I'm afraid your division has had a bad time, sir.' The general answered, 'Yes, so bad that there's no division left, so that I'm a curiosity – a divisional commander without a division.' Jeffreys, bemused, wrote: 'He seemed to treat it almost as a joke.' Capper's formation had lost four-fifths of its strength in the three weeks since first it went into action. Attrition was almost equally fearsome throughout the BEF. Of Sir John French's eighty-four infantry battalions, seventy-five now mustered fewer than three hundred men; eighteen were reduced to less than one hundred.

Foch, alarmed by the British C-in-C's visible exhaustion and demoralisation, sent two French divisions, supported by Conneau's cavalry, to take

At home, in every country women were dramatically empowered to fill the places of millions of absent men – here, a Suffolk girl stands proudly at the handle of a Lowestoft tram.

Russian soldiers in bivouac: such men became the revolutionaries of 1917, if they survived so long.

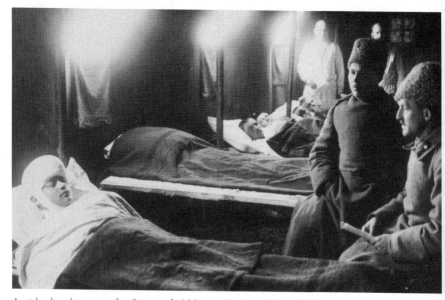

An idealised image of a Russian field hospital. Casualties of all the armies received grossly inadequate care, and often none at all, in the early months of the conflict.

The face of the Western Front, winter 1914: trenches, machine-guns, mud and wire. Except for a posed shot such as this one, no soldier of any army willingly exposed himself above a parapet.

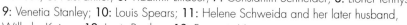

WITNESSES OF CATASTROPHE

1: Dorothie Feilding; **2:** Edouard Cœurdevey; **3:** Jacques Rivière; **4:** Lt. Col. Richard Hentsch; **5:** Paul Lintier; **6:** Vladimir Littauer; **7:** Constantin Schneider; **8:** Lionel Tennyson; **9:** Venetia Stanley; **10:** Louis Spears; **11:** Helene Schweida and her later husband, Wilhelm Kaisen; **12:** Louis Barthas; **13:** François Mayer.

The war created untold civilian misery, inflicting separation, hunger, destitution and the loss of loved ones upon societies across Europe. Here, one family among millions of French, Belgian, Russian, Polish, Serb, East Prussian and Galician refugees flees a battlefield, while behind them gunners approach it.

British soldiers in Belgium during the winter of 1914 contemplate an environment that would remain essentially unaltered for four years, unless exchanged for a permanent resting place in local earth.

over part of Allenby's line. Any reinforcement was welcome, but the French horsemen were still as unsuitably attired as when the war started. A British nursing sister watched them clatter and jangle forward: 'serious-faced men ... making a fine show in their bright uniforms and shining breastplates – it was a sad but wonderful sight'. Kitchener, conscious of allied dismay about Sir John French's mental condition, at this time offered to replace him with Sir Ian Hamilton. However, Joffre and his generals – in many ways surprisingly – decided against precipitating such a leap into the unknown.

Along the rest of the allied line there was limited understanding of the gravity of the allied predicament in Belgium. Charles de Gaulle, back with his regiment in Champagne after his August wound had healed, wrote in his diary on 1 November: 'The news from the north is still good. But how slowly it goes, upon my word! Sauternes and champagne for lunch. Very cheerful. Some guests. We drank to the offensive. The Germans could be heard singing in their trenches. Hymns, no doubt. What strange people!'

That same day, the Germans renewed their attacks around Ypres supported by heavy shellfire, much of it directed against positions held by the British cavalry. Bavarian volunteer Ludwig Engstler wrote to his family describing his own role: 'I have headed this letter "All Souls Day". My God, the words "All Souls" conceal a tremendous amount.' He described breaking through to Wytschaete, where from every cellar and house British fire swept the German ranks. 'There were too few of us. There were no officers in sight and we just had to pull back ... It was a saddened platoon which turned its back on this place of death. "Are you still alive?" asked one of the few who remained.' The allies eventually lost Wytschaete as well as Messines, and their line was again bulging dangerously inwards, but the Germans knew that decisive success still eluded them. Col. Klotz, a gunner, wrote after the 1 November fighting: 'The enemy had everywhere been ejected from their positions, but at the cost of huge casualties on our side. There had been no breakthrough.'

Next day brought no lull. George Jeffreys wrote of meeting a night attack on 2 November: 'We could see the Germans very close now (there was a slight moon): they were coming on very slowly and seemed to stagger back before our rifle fire, but always came on a few paces. With them was a drummer, who was beating his drum all the time and now, like the others, taking cover behind the trees. I never saw him fall and I believe our men didn't shoot at him. The attack gradually died away before our fire, but they got too close to be pleasant.' On 3 November a German corps commander issued an order of the day, noting that his men had captured some forty officers and 2,000 other ranks in three days: 'It is clear that the British surrender if they are subjected to energetic attack. I direct, therefore, that attacks are to be pressed home with bugle calls and with the regimental bands playing. Regimental musicians who play during assaults will be awarded Iron Crosses.' A German soldier described that day's attempt to break the French line north of Langemarck: 'The Frenchies were on high alert ... during our first bounds forward we did not come under enemy fire ... Then, all of a sudden, absolutely murderous fire was opened. The following morning we were relieved. At roll call it was brought home to us that this attack had torn great gaps in our ranks ... The company was more or less wiped out.'

By nightfall on the 3rd, at the headquarters of Army Group Fabeck all hopes of a breakthrough had been abandoned. Its men had suffered 17,500 casualties in three days, and artillery ammunition was almost exhausted. Lt.-Col. Fritz von Lossberg, Fabeck's chief of staff, wrote: 'The events of 3 November demonstrated ... that there was no way of forcing an operational success in Flanders.' But he added that Falkenhayn and the Kaiser continued to resist recognition of this reality. Lossberg himself believed that the right course, in the light of failure on 1–3 November as during the preceding weeks, would have been to shut down major operations on the Western Front and divert forces to the East, where a decisive victory over the Russians might be attainable.

Conditions in both sides' trenches were deteriorating rapidly, compounding the miseries inflicted by enemy action. Bernard Gordon-Lennox noted on 4 November: 'It came on to rain just about nightfall and poured in torrents: altogether a most disagreeable ending to a most disagreeable day. Our trenches are all in the wet clay and marshy ground, which makes things even more disagreeable than they might be, but there is a certain amount of satisfaction in knowing things are equally if not more disagreeable for the Dutchmen.' Gordon-Lennox added wearily: 'I suppose one gets inured to seeing all one's best friends taken away from one and can only think one is lucky enough to be here oneself – for the present.' Sure enough, he himself was killed by a shell six days later.

Wilfrid Abel-Smith wrote: 'When I think of poor Bernard's utter weariness some days ago (I left him in his trench in the early morning, and wished I could take his place, he was so done) ... I think of him now at peace, away from all this noise and misery, and though it must be terrible for her [Gordon-Lennox's wife], poor thing, it can't be bad for him, and must comfort her to know he can rest at last.' Irreligious later generations are tempted to dismiss as empty clichés the phrases inscribed on stone in so many of the war's cemeteries: 'He has found eternal rest'; 'He has gained eternal peace'. But such words had a profound meaning for a host of men who experienced the horrors of Flanders.

On 5 November, Falkenhayn orchestrated a new wave of almost suicidal onslaughts at the northern and southern ends of the Ypres salient, which continued with few intermissions through the week that followed. Men on both sides somehow endured them, chiefly because they found it unthinkable that such carnage and wretchedness could go on much longer. Lt. Richardson of the Royal Welch Fusiliers wrote: 'I am getting awfully bored by the trenches and am feeling fearfully tired. I hope we won't be in them much longer. I wish they would order an advance.' For a few days, the British front was merely subjected to artillery harassing fire. Then on the 6th Falkenhayn's infantry renewed their assaults on Klein Zillebeke, southeast of Ypres. Under the usual storm of defensive fire, some Germans cracked. A volunteer described how the unit he had just joined suddenly broke and ran under heavy fire near Gheluvelt: 'Everyone flooded to the rear, bent over and pushing through the scrub for about two hundred metres ... We thought it terrible that our first experience of battle was to turn our backs on the enemy.' He described the days that followed as 'hell on earth', under constant fire with no medical support for the wounded.

But the allies had their own crises on the 6th. French troops and the Irish Guards – 'very shaky even before today', in the words of 'Ma' Jeffreys – also broke, leaving the British right flank in the air. The Household Cavalry found themselves galloping forward and dismounting to face the Germans amid a throng of fleeing Frenchmen. Maj. Hugh Dawnay, a staff officer, led the Life Guards in a bayonet charge: he himself was killed, but the line was saved. There was now scarcely a unit of the BEF at anything like full strength: 2nd Grenadiers, for instance, had lost at Ypres twenty officers and eight hundred other ranks; the Irish Guards were reduced to three officers and 150 men; 1st Coldstream were down to a hundred.

Haig was disgusted by what he deemed the feeble performance of some units, recording in his diary on 7 November: 'The Lincolns, Northumberland Fusiliers and the Bedfords leave their trenches on account of a little shellfire. Several pass Divisional Headquarters while I am there. I order [all] men to be tried by [court martial] who have funked in this way, and the [abandoned] trenches to be re-occupied at once.' At a brigade headquarters, Alexander Johnston was as shocked and disgusted as the general: 'Suddenly a great flood of men came pouring back on our HQ ... most of them seemed to have even chucked their rifles away and many had not even their equipment on. They were full of the usual stories "we were ordered to retire" "everybody is retiring" "we have been sent back for ammunition" "the Germans are in the trenches" etc. etc. It makes one feel almost ill to see so many Englishmen being such cowards ... I had to threaten to shoot some of the men before I could get them to go on ... [We] were continually routing out men hiding in holes and corners.'

Next day, 3rd Division's commander said 'he could not get his men to charge to retake the old line of trenches'. The following week the colonel of the London Scottish sent a note to corps pleading that his unit 'was not in a fit state to take the field – the men are thoroughly broken. What is urgently required for the Battalion is a period of rest behind the guns. Without the required rest it might be disastrous for the battalion.' Haig commented caustically: 'It struck me that the Colonel (Malcolm by name) wanted the rest more than his men.' Barely a month earlier, this same George Malcolm had expressed alarm lest his unit might have arrived in Belgium too late to join in the war.

Haig's remarks seem to modern generations cruelly unsympathetic about men driven to the limits of endurance by their experiences. But it is the business of generals to harden their hearts. If the allied line was to hold at Ypres, the casualties and sufferings must somehow be borne. There was no tactical alternative save dogged resistance; no room for charity towards the weak nor compassion for the afflicted. Haig himself had performed poorly during the retreat from Mons, and won no plaudits during the advance to the Aisne. But his peers profoundly admired his steely calm and resolution through the three weeks of Ypres, and they seem right to have done so. He was a man of his time in cool reserve, a Roman in his ability to preside over carnage without spoiling his lunch, if duty seemed to require this – as, for the next four years, he believed that it did. Few people found much to love in I Corps' commander. But he displayed high competence at a time when many others, especially Sir John French, conspicuously lacked this. Without Haig, the British line at Ypres would probably have broken.

The Germans' attacks were flagging now, their commanders thrashing and flailing. During an advance down the Menin road on the evening of 7 November, the regimental band of the 143rd Infantry played the '*Yorckscher*

Marsch' and '*Deutschland über alles*'. The operation was a disaster for the musicians: Oboist Waldmeyer was killed, Oboist Wilebinsky wounded along with Sergeant Barth. The latter hastily downed the contents of the bandmaster's brandy flask before being taken to the rear. After that action, the band was ordered to surrender its instruments and take up new duties as stretcher-bearers. It was a symbolic moment.

As the German Grenadier Guards advanced towards their start line on the 9th, they saw by the roadside a senior officer in the uniform of the 1st Dragoon Guards, surrounded by his staff. It was Theobald Bethmann Hollweg: Germany's Chancellor had come to witness in person the evolution of events he had contributed so much to bring about. He told the regiment's colonel flatulently: '*Herr Oberst*, that is the way I have always wanted it: to be present at a time and place where I can really give the lads *die letzte Ölung*' – 'the old oil' was an antique phrase, referring to the days when gladiators about to enter the arena were greased, to make it more difficult for their opponents to get a grip on them. But it did not escape the Chancellor's listeners that the phrase also had a second meaning – as the death rite of the Lutheran Church. Bethmann witnessed no German triumph that day – only more dying.

Once again the fighting briefly slackened. Capt. Eben Pike, a British Grenadier, wrote on 9 November: 'We hold on here like grim Death,' and he himself was killed a few days later. Wilfrid Abel-Smith wrote: 'I can't bear seeing my friends go day after day, and when Eben was hit, my heart sank, but I must face the difficulties and hope for the best. If I didn't put my trust in God, I couldn't have held out as long as I have.' Some men on both sides were despairing. On 9 November Lt. Baehreke of the German Grenadiers was interrogating a British prisoner when suddenly the hedge in front of them parted to reveal a Zouave who shouted in French, 'Don't shoot! I am the father of a large family with many children!' He then grabbed and drained one of the Germans' water-bottles, prompting an outburst of laughter that broke the tension. That same day Lt. von Schauroth, a regimental adjutant, wrote: 'Reports from the front line indicated that an assault in the prevailing conditions offered no prospect of success. All attempts to convince higher authority of the hopelessness of a frontal assault through the morass of Flanders clay, in the face of complete lack of clarity regarding enemy, ground or even our own positions, failed totally … Hundreds of our finest men gave their lives for something which was completely hopeless.'

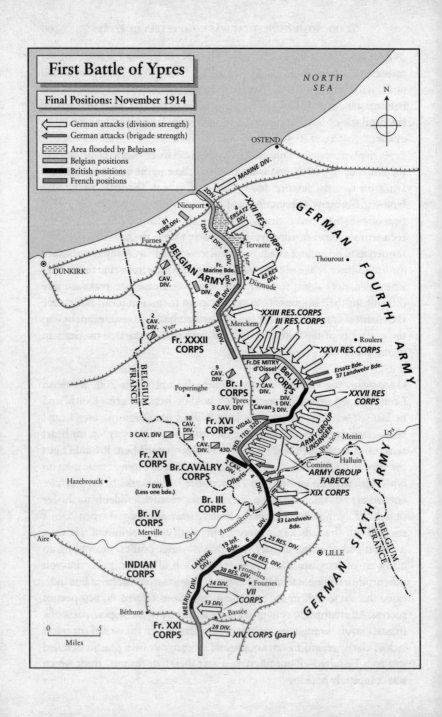

First Battle of Ypres

Final Positions: November 1914

← German attacks (division strength)
← German attacks (brigade strength)
▨ Area flooded by Belgians
▨ Belgian positions
■ British positions
▨ French positions

NORTH
SEA

N

OSTEND

MARINE DIV.

2 DIV.

GERMAN FOURTH ARMY

Nieuport

81 TERR. DIV.

4 ERSATZ DIV.

XXII RES. CORPS

1 DIV. 3 DIV. 4 DIV.

Tervaete

Furnes

BELGIAN ARMY

Fr. Marine Bde.

5 DIV.

Yser

Thourout

DUNKIRK

CAV. DIV.

6 DIV.

89 TERR. DIV.

83 RES. DIV.

Dixmude

2 CAV. DIV.

Yser

38 DIV.

Merckem

XXIII RES. CORPS
III RES. CORPS

Roulers

Fr. XXXII CORPS

BELGIUM
FRANCE

9 CAV. DIV.

Poperinghe

Br. I CORPS

Fr. DE MITRY d'Oissel

XXVI RES. CORPS

Ersatz Bde.
37 Landwehr Bde.

Bel. IX CORPS

7 CAV. DIV.

1 DIV.

XXVII RES CORPS

10 CAV. DIV.

Ypres

3 CAV. DIV

Cavan

3 DIV.

3 CAV. DIV

Fr. XVI CORPS

VIDAL

1 CAV. DIV.

43 D.

39 D. 17 D. 32 D.

ARMY GROUP LINSINGEN

Menin

Lys

Fr. XVI CORPS

Br. CAVALRY CORPS

Ollern

2 CAV. DIV.

Wervicq

Comines

Halluin

Hazebrouck

7 DIV.
(Less one bde.)

4 DIV.

ARMY GROUP FABECK

XIX CORPS

Br. III CORPS

Br. IV CORPS

Merville

Lys

Armentières

33 Landwehr Bde.

Aire

INDIAN CORPS

19 Inf. Bde.

6 DIV.

25 RES. DIV.

LILLE

LAHORE DIV.

48 RES. DIV.

GERMAN SIXTH ARMY

BELGIUM
FRANCE

38 RES. DIV.

Fromelles

Fournes

14 DIV.

VII CORPS

MEERUT DIV.

13 DIV.

La Bassée

Béthune

0   5

Miles

28 DIV.

Fr. XXI CORPS

XIV CORPS (part)

At the insistence of German commanders, on 10 November a doomed attack took place in the French sector. Next day, there was another big push against the British: two brigades of the Prussian Guard were launched down both sides of the Menin road towards Ypres. In the dim light of early morning, the defenders were almost disbelieving at the spectacle of dense formations of enemy once more approaching in numbers which suggested that Prince Rupprecht's strength was inexhaustible. Through the hours of strife that followed, the Germans pushed forward again and again, piercing the defences in several places. One British soldier scribbled tersely in his diary: 'Everybody in a panic, running away and leaving rifles equip[ment] and everything.' Once again the front was restored by counter-attacks: the Oxf & Bucks, who had played a prominent part in the September fighting at Cour de Soupir, won a critical little victory at Nonne Bosschen Wood. Among the fatal casualties that day was the Guards Brigade commander Charles FitzClarence, who by common consent had been one of the heroes of the defence. On the other side, on 11 November one German Guards regiment suffered eight hundred casualties, including seven officers killed. The attackers were stopped less than three miles from Ypres.

Cpl. William Holbrook of the Royal Fusiliers described black-comic experiences while his platoon was pinned down for some hours in no man's land. A German officer suddenly crawled out of the bushes and said in perfect English, 'I am wounded.' Holbrook's subaltern responded irritably, 'You shouldn't make these bloody attacks, then you wouldn't get wounded!' which earned a laugh from the Fusiliers. But the British lieutenant was killed by a stray bullet minutes later, and his men found themselves leaderless as well as lost. Holbrook cut a shrapnel ball out of the knee of a mate, who then crawled away in search of safety. He himself was sitting in a shell crater in failing light when he heard a nearby twig break, and saw a German's head appear. The man was groaning, and badly wounded, murmuring '*Wasser, Wasser!*' Holbrook gave him a drink from his bottle, and was appalled to see the water instantly ooze from the man's side, mingled with blood. Then the German held up three fingers and said wretchedly, '*Kleine Kinder*' – 'Small children' – before expiring in the early hours of the morning. Holbrook exploited the remaining darkness to make good an escape to the British line.

That night, the medieval Cloth Hall of Ypres burned. Quartermaster-Sergeant Gordon Fisher, a Territorial of the Hertfordshires fresh to the war, was being driven by bus towards the battlefield. He gazed in awe upon the darkness broken by brilliant illuminations and thought, 'Doesn't it look pretty! Just like fireworks.' Only slowly did he grasp the horror of the spectacle he was witnessing. Thirty-one-year-old machine-gunner Lt. John Dimmer was that rare creature, an officer who had risen from the ranks. At Ypres on 12 November his Maxim was firing on the advancing Prussian Guard when it jammed on a sodden ammunition belt. Dimmer repaired the gun with an adjustable spanner, and resumed firing. An enemy bullet hit his jaw, and the gun jammed again. While remedying the stoppage he was shot again, this time in the right shoulder, and received three shrapnel fragments in the same place. He nonetheless continued firing until, when the nearest Germans were fifty yards away, they turned and ran. Dimmer was hit again in the face and almost blinded by his own blood, but he lived to receive a VC. He later also won a Military Cross, only to be killed commanding a battalion in January 1918, three months after getting married. At Ypres, by many such local actions as his did the dwindling units of the BEF cling to their positions.

On the British left, the French fought their own terrific battle to hold the line between Zonnebeke and Bixschoote. Langemarck remained under incessant pressure. That day of 12 November, one of the war's most notorious official bulletins appeared in many of Germany's towns and cities, reporting that 'west of Langemarck young regiments, singing "*Deutschland, Deutschland über alles*", attacked the entrenched line of the English position and took it'. In reality the allies held the line in that sector. Elsewhere on the British front, if there was indeed some singing, by nightfall the attackers had little to celebrate: yet again, they had failed to break through.

On the 16th and 17th the Germans staged further local assaults, and poured more shells onto the town of Ypres. 2nd Grenadiers' war diary recorded: 'Attacks repeated with great strength. Battalion fired 24,000 rounds S[mall] A[rms] ammunition.' But the Germans were now as weary as the allies. Alexander Johnston wrote on 16 November of the exhaustion and demoralisation of many British units, but then added: 'fortunately I think the German infantry in front of us have very little kick left in them'. He was right. The weather made movement in any direction difficult. Ambulance driver Dorothie Feilding lamented on the 17th: 'This wet is hell for the poor Tommies in the trenches. It's awful to see the state they are in from it & it takes the heart out of a man to be frozen & soaked & never able to dry.'

With the onset of successive days of high winds and snow blizzards, the battle of Ypres faded away, leaving both sides to hold their blood-soaked positions. The most significant territorial outcome was that the Germans had gained the high ground along the Messines ridge, and held it until June 1917. But they had suffered 80,000 casualties around Ypres, many regiments losing two-thirds of their strength or even more. A German wrote home: 'I have been living through days that defy imagination. I should never have thought men could stand it ... Our 1st battalion, which has fought with unparalleled bravery, is reduced from 1200 men to 194. God grant that I may see you again soon and that this horror may soon be over.' The writer was fortunate enough to be taken prisoner soon afterwards.

The First Battle of Ypres was an undoubted allied victory: the Germans had poured forth blood in the winter's final attempt to achieve a strategic breakthrough on the Western Front, and they had failed. The French, British and Belgian armies conducted a dogged defensive battle in which they were just able to hold a line against heavy odds. Churchill referred afterwards to 'ever-glorious Ypres'. He was right about the importance of success, but the inventory of misery and tragedy was so large for victors and vanquished alike that few men afterwards felt minded to celebrate the battle. The British profited from the fact that most of their soldiers were veteran professionals, fighting against ill-trained reservists – Germany's generals always afterwards blamed Falkenhayn for failing to commit better troops. British leaders displayed no great tactical genius, merely a willingness of their men to stand and die in such a fashion as had characterised the British redcoat for centuries. But the price of Ypres was the destruction of the old army. Losses were 54,105, bringing total casualties between August and the end of November to 89,964 – more than the strength of the BEF's first seven divisions to take the field. Henceforward, the British in Belgium and France could only aspire to hold their positions until they received large reinforcements from the Empire, and from Kitchener's New Armies training at home.

Cpl. George Matheson of the Cameron Highlanders wrote to his family: 'Out of the 1,100 officers and men that came out at the start we have Major Yeadon and about 80 men left. I believe you have plenty of soldiers at home. Well, we could do with a few here.' The civilian public was slow to grasp the scale of the struggle that had taken place. On 21 November the *New Statesman* reported with bloodless complacency: 'Apart from gallant incidents – notably the repulse of the Prussian Guard by British infantry – there is nothing to record in the Western theatre of the war since last week. The movements of the line of contact between the opposing forces have been so slight as to be appreciable only upon a very large-scale map … More and more the struggle in this region is seen as a simple test of relative endurance.'

Though the BEF's losses seemed very terrible to the public at home, the French sacrifice was tenfold. Among commanders, it was Foch whose energy, intuition and genuinely inspirational leadership made the decisive contribution to allied success in holding the line at Ypres, with some help from Haig. The fighting strength of the Belgian army was halved. During the space of those ghastly weeks between 18 October and 12 November, not only did tens of thousands of men perish, but so too did many hopes. To be sure, the generals did not despair: it was not merely their right, but their duty, to continue to strive for victory. But the men confronting each other in the trenches, not only at Ypres but along hundreds of miles of the line stretching across plains, valleys and hills to the Swiss border, saw the truth. Both armies possessed unbounded power to inflict loss and grief upon each other; but as long as each had men and guns, the defence could be reinforced faster than attackers could exploit local success.

Wilfrid Abel-Smith wrote presciently on 28 October: 'The noise of the guns and shells has become positively boring. Of course, one is semi-conscious of danger – but the feeling of boredom is uppermost. One would like to get away for a few days from the never-ceasing din. I can't see how these battles are to end. It becomes a question of stalemate. With a line of this length you can't get ahead anywhere (or else you get in a dangerous position) and you can't get on because there are no flanks, and you cannot therefore get round them. As soon as you outflank, an aeroplane gives away the show, and the enemy meets it, and vice versa with us, so it is a never-ending business. You get to within a few hundred yards of each other and dig, and there you stop, sniping all day and shooting all night.' Here was a vision of the strategic future which appalled both sides' commanders, who would strive for almost four years until their deadly embrace was belatedly broken in the spring of 1918.

16

'War Becomes the Scourge of Mankind'

The Germans on the Eastern Front, in the glow of self-congratulation that followed Tannenberg, were exasperated by the inability of their allies to keep up. 'Here everything is in good shape,' wrote Max Hoffmann, Hindenburg's chief of operations, at Kielce in Poland on 8 October, 'except the Austrians! If only those wretches – "*Kerle*" – would get moving! They have allowed the success we brought them to slip out of their hands.' Franz Joseph's soldiers were indeed exhausted and low-spirited. 'We have been too long without rest,' cavalry commander Count Viktor Dankl wrote on 15 October. 'Every man's nerves have been exposed to so much that there is nothing to be done with them any more … We set forth full of proud hopes, but now find our spirit broken.' Dankl added nine days later: 'The men will not attack any more, we are short of officers and those who remain are shy. It's over and done with. We have descended to the level of the Russians: the men will only defend positions and empty their weapons into the brown.'

At Conrad's headquarters Alexander Pallavicini marvelled at the remoteness from battlefield reality of commanders and staff officers sitting at comfortable desks beside their telephones, 'wasting much paper and ink. Such an institution resembles some international bank except that less of [our] paperwork is probably useful. There are many men here who … have still not heard a shot fired. Yet people say this is how things have to be.' Across the Hapsburg Empire, a growing number of Franz Joseph's subjects recoiled in disgust from the horrors for which such gilded warriors were responsible. Slovenian priest Tomo Župan recalled Conrad's pleas before the conflict began: 'God grant us a war.' Now, wrote Župan, not only might the chief of staff's demented vision bring down the Hapsburg monarchy, but it had already undone European mankind. He castigated Conrad in his diary: 'you have destroyed so many flourishing and hopeful lives. Are you in a position to compensate the family of even a single dead man who would never willingly have chosen to sacrifice him in exchange for all the world's billions?' Another priest, Ivan Vrhovnik, wrote on 18 October: 'Many more men left Ljubljana for the front today. The enthusiasm which characterised the first call to arms against the enemy has entirely disappeared; [the newly departing troops] assuage the pain of separation with drink; their faces reveal their despair.'

The reinforcements were right to fear the worst. Conrad retained a boundless capacity for promoting disaster. In mid-October he committed his Galician army to yet another eastward advance. On the 14th, when troops began to cross the San river, they suffered dreadfully from both sides' artillery fire, so that one assault unit sent back a message, 'For God's sake, tell the batteries to shell the Russians, not us!' Constantin Schneider wailed: 'our heavy howitzers have already killed a hundred of our own men!' There were no pontoons, because Russian shellfire destroyed most of the horses bringing forward bridge sections, and thus only boats were available to ferry troops.

Schneider's divisional commander conceived the idea that the presence of a band playing on the Austrian shore might raise morale. The union of the sounds of shellfire, military music and human anguish convinced many men that they were descending into madness. Most of the assault boats were destroyed by Russian fire. When the survivors were brought back at dawn on the 16th, 'they walked with shaky steps', in Schneider's words, 'hollow-eyed, haggard men, who until three days ago had been full of lust for life. They had now become so numbed that they were speechless, unable to describe their experiences.'

In the confused fighting that followed during the last week of October, the Austrians again suffered appalling casualties. Rampant defeatism swept the army. In Przemyśl, threatened with a new Russian assault, starving soldiers begged in the streets, offering absurd sums of useless money for bread or potatoes. On 3 November, the garrison was invited to dispatch last letters home before an encircling ring again closed on the fortress. Next day the civilian inhabitants, useless mouths, were ordered to leave. Among crowds of frantic people thronging the station, one woman forced her way into a carriage with two of her children, then as the train pulled out was appalled to glimpse through the window her three-year-old son, abandoned alone on the platform.

A Polish widow, Helena Jabiońska, secured a ride out on a cart, and on 8 November reached the village of Olszan. She found its burned-out ruins smouldering, the surviving inhabitants sitting amid their miserable possessions, shivering uncontrollably. 'They are ghosts, not people,' wrote Jabiońska. 'This place is worse than a desert. There is nothing to make a fire with: all the trees have been chopped down, and even the stumps have been burned.' Worst of all, the Russians were already beyond them. The fugitives had no choice save to return to Przemyśl, whose five-month siege thereafter became the longest of the war, a nightmare alike for its 127,000 garrison and 18,000 trapped citizens.

The Austrian field army was once more falling back. Faced with a crippling ammunition shortage, Conrad's artillery was rationed to four rounds a day, even when the infantry were hard-pressed. If nobody gained a big victory in the October fighting, the Central Powers certainly had the worst of it. Cholera spread rapidly through Galicia, causing 3,632 Austrian deaths in a month. At first the War Ministry in Vienna declined to authorise vaccination, and hospitals were too crowded with wounded men to admit cholera cases. Before vaccine was belatedly provided, Austrian troops retreating into Germany's upper Silesia spread disease among civilians there. As a further consequence of the surge of epidemics, many men and even officers faked symptoms in order to secure a passage to the rear; rigorous examinations had to be introduced, to curb the haemorrhage of malingerers.

On the other side, Alexei Tolstoy was in Kiev one night when a great Russian victory was announced. The news roused special enthusiasm among the substantial number of defectors from the Hapsburg cause who were now in the Tsar's service. 'Czech officers were strutting about the hall of my hotel, stroking their red moustaches and dragging their sabres across the floor. Other Czechs were shouting and singing upstairs, celebrating. There are ladies among the Czech volunteers, whom our porters call "the lady reservists".' But the city as a whole was not much impressed: the citizenry had grown cautious about tales of alleged successes which afterwards turned sour. Only around two on the following afternoon did a crowd with processional banners gather for a church service in the square in front of the ancient cathedral. They cheered, sang a hymn and for a long time kept tossing caps and lambswool hats into the air.

'Here, as everywhere,' wrote Tolstoy, 'it is the common people who really respond to the war. For example, women selling bread rolls and apples go to meet the hospital trains and give away half their wares to wounded soldiers. Once, I saw a woman approach an officer whom I knew. She looked pityingly straight into his face, asked his name and promised to remember him in her prayers.' Here, the writer identified a critical weakness of Russia's war effort: the cynicism with which much of its ruling class treated the struggle, striving to spare themselves from its burdens and sacrifices. Moreover, many of the Tsar's subjects nursed ethnic or religious grievances overlaid upon the general misery of campaigning. A Muslim conscript complained that while his Christian comrades-in-arms had their priests, he and his kind were denied such solace, 'notwithstanding the fact that more than half the soldiers [in my unit] are Muslim, who die without mullahs, and are buried together with Russians in a single grave'.

But no man serving on either side in the Eastern campaign was content with its progress. In the German camp, Max Hoffmann was among those much troubled by failure sufficiently to concentrate force to achieve a decision on either front. 'I would have liked to see us settle accounts conclusively with either France or Russia first,' he wrote in his diary at Radom on 21 October. 'If they had given us just two or three more corps I would have guaranteed that we should achieve that here. As it is, however, we must muddle along against vastly superior numbers.' This complaint, which Ludendorff himself was to make with ever-increasing vehemence in Berlin, would become a German theme tune of the Eastern war: a little more, just give us a little more, and a triumph beckons. The Kaiser's generals were almost certainly wrong: there was no prospect of victory until the Tsar's armies had been battered, depleted, drained by years of attrition. But Russia's human resources were by no means infinite, as their enemies sometimes supposed: for most of 1914–15, because of the shortcomings of the Tsar's mobilisation, the rival forces were not hopelessly unequal – around eighty-four Austrian and German divisions against ninety-nine Russian. Meanwhile, indecision prevailed. In the northern sector of the front, late October found rival armies confronting each other, as Lt. Harald von der Marwitz put it, in 'waterlogged trenches where we have one foot on German soil, the other in Russia'. His unit was deployed between the stone frontier markers dividing East Prussia from the Tsar's empire, and was going nowhere in a hurry.

In western Europe, however, naïveté persisted about the allies' prospects: every Russian advance caused hopes to soar. On 7 November the *New Statesman* thrilled to reports that 'we may have only two or three weeks to wait before the main Russian armies are on German soil ... We have the certain knowledge that Germany is beaten in the East, and cannot hold her own against Russia with her present forces in that quarter.' The *Illustrated London News*, in a display of credulous loyalty to Britain's ally, carried a full-page portrait of Grand Duke Nicholas, which claimed that he was 'executing unflinchingly plans which are covering Russian arms with glory'. The Grand Duke's soldiers would have considered such praise extravagant: Nicholas himself was a mere figurehead, and the Russians were incapable of exploiting their autumn advantage in Galicia. The supply chain almost collapsed, and staff cars had to be commandeered to ferry forward crates of biscuit to feed the troops. An acute shell shortage developed, and St Petersburg issued a stream of contradictory directives.

On the other side, Falkenhayn dispatched a message to Conrad, explaining why it was difficult to shift more troops to the Eastern Front. This was carried by, of all people, Col. Richard Hentsch, the same who had been Moltke's intermediary in the critical decisions of the Marne. Hentsch's commission – he arrived at the Austrian headquarters in Galicia on 10 November – is significant, because it seems to confirm that he was considered to have correctly executed Moltke's orders back in September on the Marne. The colonel would scarcely have been given such a job if he was deemed responsible for inflicting disaster on German arms. Now, he told Conrad that the Austrians were on their own.

But Hentsch should have called upon Hindenburg before addressing the Austrians. The German commander-in-chief and his chief of staff reached different conclusions. On 11 November they learned from an intercepted wireless message that the Stavka planned to renew the Russian invasion of Germany. Ludendorff, with or without further reinforcements from Falkenhayn, determined to pre-empt the enemy's offensive with a thrust of his own. He launched a massive attack on the northern flank of Ivanov's armies, precipitating what became known as the Battle of Łódź.

The Russians were as usual oblivious of the impending blow; their northernmost army commander, Rennenkampf, was probing towards East Prussia rather than guarding his flank to the west. The corps in the immediate path of the offensive collapsed with huge losses. Ruzsky, in overall command of the front, was slow to grasp the scale of the German offensive. By 18 November Łódź was almost encircled, the Russians contained within a perimeter approximately sixteen miles by eight. On the 19th, an almost hysterical galloper reached Fifth Army's Gen. Phleve as he rode forward with his staff. 'Your Excellency!' the young officer cried out breathlessly, 'The Second Army is surrounded and will be forced to surrender!' Phleve gazed stonily at the messenger for a few seconds from under

his thick eyebrows, then said: 'Have you come, Little Father, to play a tragedy or to make a report? If you have a report to make, make it to the chief
of staff, but remember – no play-acting, or I place you under arrest.'
Having heard the news, both Phleve and his fellow army commander
acted on their own initiative, diverting forces from the planned invasion
of Germany to save Second Army's bacon. They turned back towards Łódź
with a most un-Russian celerity, miraculously arriving before the
Germans. In an almost accidental fashion, which was characteristic of the
campaign, seven Russian corps drifted into the path of the enemy's
vanguards approaching the city. Ludendorff had overreached himself, and
indeed blundered: a quarter of a million of his own men faced more than
double that number of Russians.

During the week of fighting that followed, the German offensive ran
out of steam and ammunition. The Russians were much stronger, and
occupied terrain favouring the defence. Three German divisions were cut
off in the wooded hills east of the city, and on 22 November the Stavka
ordered sixty trains to be ready to remove an expected 50,000 prisoners to
PoW camps. On the evening of the 23rd, the German corps commander
Freiherr von Scheffer-Boyadel radioed his army headquarters to say that
he would attempt a breakthrough that night, otherwise 'XXV Reserve
Corps will cease to exist tomorrow'. Desperate fighting followed, and next
morning at 0750 Scheffer radioed again: 'No reserves left. Situation grave,'
followed ten minutes later by 'desperately short of ammunition and
rations. Immediate assistance … requested.' In response August
Mackensen, Ninth Army's commander, dispatched two corps to the aid of
Scheffer, whose men were able to cut their way out, bringing with them
16,000 Russian prisoners. On the evening of the 24th the forces met at
Bshesiny, and the Russians were denied their coup. But Ludendorff's
offensive had been a failure, for all his boasts to the contrary. While the
undoubted superior of his Russian opponents in military skill, as were
most of his subordinates, Hindenburg's chief of staff was nowhere near
the mastermind he considered himself.

Ruzsky, though tactically successful in driving back Mackensen, was
now running short of everything. A single Russian division had expended
2.15 million small-arms rounds in just three November days. Russia
started the war with 5,000 guns and reserves of five million shells. By the
end of 1914, the Tsar's factories were producing 35,000 rounds a month
– but the armies at the front were sometimes using 45,000 a day. On 1
December, only 300,000 shells remained in the dumps. Beyond

ammunition, the army lacked rifles and even boots, of which Ruzsky demanded half a million pairs. Carts scoured the battlefield, removing shoes from dead horses that were needed for live ones. The iron-hard ground assisted the movement of supplies, but repulsed the entrenching tools of both sides. In the deep snow, almost every wounded man froze to death before he could be evacuated. Even without the intervention of shells and bullets, some men expired from the sheer overnight cold in their trenches. Aircraft made only short flights, because pilots swiftly became incapable of moving their hands to operate the controls, though the Germans maintained nuisance bombing raids on Warsaw. Both sides experienced a steady stream of desertions. Even though the German attack had been stopped in its tracks, the Russian invasion of Germany was plainly not going to happen. Ludendorff told his masters that he had won another great victory. In truth, he had merely mauled some Russian formations, but his prestige stood sufficiently high to persuade Falkenhayn to send him four more corps from the West.

Further south, among the Austrians, after four months of hardship, defeat and deplorable leadership, morale remained low. The Hapsburg Empire's generals waltzed better than they fought, and lacked the slightest awareness of what man-management meant. When Constantin Schneider reported to his corps commander in Cracow on 29 November, after so long in the field he was traumatised to find himself once more in civilisa-tion: 'it seemed as if military life stopped at the edge of the city. One felt wafted by magic away from the war. The streets were brilliantly lit up ... A wholly new life that had become alien to me suddenly pulsed all around, so that I seemed translated from a dream into reality. Here were people who did not wear uniforms, pursuing tranquil activities: women in fash-ionable clothes; officers wearing peacetime black caps and garrison uniforms. It was strange to reflect that just two hours earlier Russian shrapnel was falling around me, in the midst of a dead zone of devastation that extended for many kilometres beyond the suburbs of this living, vital city.' Schneider found corps headquarters established in a grand hotel. Himself filthy and wearing a threadbare uniform, he was embarrassed to mingle with washed, polished, impeccably dressed staff officers. From them he heard momentous tidings: German reinforcements had arrived, and were even then detraining. 'This news gave everyone new hope, that victory was possible.'

In truth, the fresh forces sufficed only to prevent an absolute Austrian collapse, assisted by disarray in the Russian camp. There was renewed squabbling between the Tsar's generals: in the south, Ivanov wanted to launch a new attack against the Austrians, but this could only happen if his neighbour protected his right flank, which Ruzsky had no interest in doing. It was left to the Austrians, instead, to attempt a new offensive early in December. This achieved some initial success, inspiring in Conrad excitement verging upon euphoria, and causing him to announce a victory. Constantin Schneider found the advance almost worse than retreat: 'the defeated ... do not see the victims of war. The victor, obliged to cross the battlefield, catches sight of them and shudders.' He described a symbolic encounter in those days, when he came upon a Russian and an Austrian who lay where they had been striving to bayonet each other, only to be killed by the same shell. As usual, Conrad's brief success came to nothing: he could not follow through. The Russians counter-attacked. As the year approached its end, Austrian forces found themselves once more pushed back onto the lower slopes of the Carpathians.

Both sides were pursuing incoherent strategies. Falkenhayn recognised that the war would be won or lost in the West. On 26 November he wrote to *Ober Ost* – the high command in Poland: 'Any victories gained in the east at the cost of [success on] the Western Front are worthless.' Such strictures did not deter Hindenburg and Ludendorff from maintaining insistent demands for reinforcements, and in the wake of failure at Ypres, for which Falkenhayn was deemed personally responsible, their prestige stood higher than his. Political imperatives exercised stronger influence than military ones, in persuading the Germans to send more troops east. The Central Powers were morbidly anxious that if they seemed to be losing the Eastern campaign, neutral states might throw in their lot with the allies. Berlin and Vienna were fearful that not only Italy might enter the war against them, but Bulgaria and Romania likewise. Even larger loomed the spectral consequences of an absolute Austro-Hungarian defeat. While the commanders of both Tsar Nicholas and Emperor Franz Joseph were incompetent, and their forces ill-equipped for modern war, the Hapsburg armies were in worse case. Russian troops, on their day and especially in defence, fought well; the Austrians hardly ever did. Henceforward, German activism on the Eastern Front was inspired chiefly by anxiety to keep Austria-Hungary in the war.

The Austrian army's miserable showing reflected its institutional contempt for military science, notably including logistics. Conrad's 1913–14 war games – the *Grosse Etappenkriegsspiel* – had supposedly addressed the very issues now at stake on the battlefield: deployment and supply of several army corps in Galicia. But an instructor named Theodor von Siegringen, who argued that logistics would prove a critical operational factor in a region of few roads and railways, was removed as a trouble-maker. Franz Joseph's soldiers suffered infinite hardship and grief in the winter of 1914 because their commanders refused responsibly to address their feeding and welfare. Lt. Aleksandr Trushnovich, a Slovenian, described the miserable rations issued to his soldiers – black bread, meat-less stew, black coffee substitute – 'they were almost starving'. Meanwhile he and his fellow officers 'received more calories than the entire company – wine and cake, also cigarettes and cigars which I gave to the men. Such inequality seemed revolting, in trenches where we were all obviously equals in the face of death.'

The Austrians waged fantasy warfare. A German officer watching their troops straggle forward one day in December damned their march disci-pline as 'clumsy' – '*hanebüchen*' – contrasted with German units in rigor-ous formation. It was a minor curiosity of the campaign that up to forty of Conrad's 'men' in Galicia are thought to have been women. It was not uncommon in pre-war Eastern Europe for women to empower themselves by donning masculine garb and masquerading as men, and some commanding officers tolerated the presence of women in the ranks, even when their sex was revealed. One identified example was that of Polish-Viennese artist Zofia Plewińska, nineteen in 1914, who enlisted under the name of Leszek Pomianowski. She was posted to the front at Lipnica Murowana in December, and thereafter served in action.

In the course of 1914, Constantin Schneider's division, which reached the battlefield 15,000 strong, suffered twice that number of casualties, including 9,000 men missing, most of them taken prisoner. The forma-tion's Christmas strength fell to 4,000. Overall in the first five months of the conflict, Conrad's armies suffered a million casualties. 'War becomes the scourge of mankind,' lamented Lt. Col. Theodor Zeynek, 'not because of the human lives forfeited, but because of the collapse of moral values.' But the 'human lives forfeited' seemed a sufficient cause for mourning to hundreds of thousands of families.

One December day, Aleksandr Trushnovich led a half-company of Austrian reinforcements to take up positions above the Prut river. Before dawn, in the rear areas they were fed and even given some beer. A general harangued them on their glorious role in the forthcoming battle and victory. Then they travelled for some six hours in a column of peasant carts, before taking to their feet. They found themselves traversing dense woodland, in a silence suddenly shattered by shellfire that tore branches, 'as if a giant deer had careered past. Then there was roaring and moaning, and the noises echoed through the vaults of the forest, such a cacophony that one could not hear oneself speak.'

Reaching the edge of the trees, the bewildered soldiers glimpsed ahead the trenches they were to occupy, and dashed to embrace their shelter. But the positions were shallow and unfinished, and the Russian shelling frighteningly accurate. With frenetic energy, men worked to deepen their holes. Trushnovich risked a glance over the parapet at the grey-green ribbon of the Prut river below. Russian soldiers were visible, dashing across it under Austrian fire: 'A Hungarian machine-gunner was firing from a breastwork ten paces from me. Missed. One could see his rounds hitting the water. Earth cascaded over me – a shell had exploded right by the parapet. I felt terribly reluctant to die.'

When the shelling finally ceased, the newly arrived Austrians were bemused to hear a deep murmur from the valley. Somebody said: 'The Russians are praying!' Darkness fell, broken by spasmodic exchanges of fire, flares, false alarms. At dawn, a new Russian barrage began, causing the forest above and below the Austrian line once more to crack and creak as branches broke. Trushnovich's soldiers 'huddled deeper into their foxholes, each one sharing his refuge with his personal God, praying to be spared'. Wounded men moaned, for no one was willing to expose himself to assist them.

As the fire intensified, 'soon one could no longer hear anything above the roaring of the steel Bacchanalia, which drowned out cries for help. Suddenly the Russian batteries fell silent and a chorus of "*Ura!*" rose in the forest on the left. All went quiet, only the echo of human voices resonated … Deep in the forest we could see people whose tunics were the colour of bushes and grass. They were coming closer, dashing from one tree to the next while we advanced to meet them. Now we could clearly see their faces, and even teeth when they shouted "*Ura!*" There was a fog before one's eyes: what if we had to repel a bayonet attack? … They are almost here …

'I saw the Russians rolling forward something on wheels. My God, that's a machine-gun! God save us from this evil! The sound of its fire burst into the discordant shouts of "*Ura!*" and "*Hurra!*", and all around falling men began moaning and screaming in pain. I barely had time to throw myself into a shallow trench. The firing grew more and more ferocious, then suddenly died away as the [Austrian] grey uniforms began running back ...'

But next day the Russians, in their turn, retired a little way. The Austrians descended cautiously to the river: 'The smell of Russian leather and *makhorka* – shag tobacco – was so strong in the trenches that one knew at once who had been occupying them.' A lot of dead lay there, with nearby a scattered heap of letters. Silence descended on the hills for a time, so that the Austrians could hear dogs barking and field kitchens arriving in the Russian lines. They imagined the invisible enemy walking about, eating, drinking. And as they listened, a man said, with a curious affectionate fellow-feeling in his words, 'Can you hear? The Russkies have brought in their kitchens. What are they cooking up there?' Next day, the killing resumed. Trushnovich later deserted to the Russians, in whose ranks he served for years.

On 16 December, after one of the last significant clashes of the year, at Limanowa, Theodor Zeynek rode across the battlefield:

> The scene was fantastic: a maze of trenches stretching in all directions, all full of spent cases, broken rifles, bent bayonets, fragments of wood, decayed straw, groundwater, debris. There were prayer books, Austrian caps, Prussian *Pickelhauben*, Russian caps ... Whole villages were smashed to pieces, telegraph poles cast down, bridges destroyed, groups of moaning and weeping peasants who came forward with their children because they did not know where to go; here was a heap of dead soldiers, there a row of freshly dug graves; many horse carcasses. In the villages, there were endless manifestations of devastation, most of the inhabitants deported or fled, the fields trampled, while in the skies flocks of screaming ravens cried for prey ... Overhead the winter sun shone as brightly as if nothing was amiss with a world of peace and happiness.

The year ended in Galicia, as elsewhere, without decision. The German victory at Tannenberg obscured, for a season, what historian Gerhard Gross has described as 'the strategic defeat of the *Kaiserreich*' in the East in 1914. Whether or not the transfer of two corps from the West at the end of August decisively weakened Moltke's campaign in France, the transcendent reality was that the German armies failed to achieve conclusive success on either front. While Ludendorff was an able and energetic officer, he was certainly not the genius he supposed himself. No more than any other director of war on either side could he overcome fundamental difficulties of resources, logistics, enemy mass and distances. On the Western Front, there were six rifles for every yard of front; in the East, only one for every two yards.

Russia's forces lacked strength, and were too ill-led, to overcome the Germans. Their successes laid bare the rottenness of the Hapsburg Empire's armies, but their own failures imposed critical strains upon those of the Romanovs. Russia's enemies were awed by the capacity of the Tsar's soldiers to endure suffering, but already perceptive Russians recognised the intolerable burden war was imposing upon millions of hapless imperial subjects, swept into its maw with vastly less understanding of or sympathy for the cause than most of their counterparts in the West. The Russian economy was suffering grievously from the consequences of the closure of the Dardanelles to the Empire's shipping: Russian grain could not be exported to the West, nor vital supplies brought in. Nicholas's people were being invited to suffer and die, so far as they themselves could see, not for any grand ideal, but merely because their emperor willed it. A government agent reported peasants saying, 'Is not all the same, what[ever] Tsar we live under?' They suggested that their government should pay Germany's enemies to end the war.

Alexei Tolstoy described an NCO barking orders at peasant reservists, a tiny portion of the nine million conscripted in the war's first year, in a lice-ridden barracks, its walls dripping with tubercular damp: 'Right dress! Everyone at attention! Heels together, toes the width of a rifle butt apart, no gap between your knees! Heads properly straight ... Then everyone can see that you are a soldier willing to give your life for your faith, the Tsar and the Motherland. You – why are you making faces? Keep your head straight!'

The man stared bitterly at the NCO and cried out, 'I can't, I can't, I can't!'

'Why not?!'

'I have muscle damage. I was beaten as a child!'

The NCO gave up, venting his feelings about being obliged to make soldiers of cripples. Another man began to splutter aloud, then others, in Tolstoy's words 'shaking with incessant wet, deep, sobbing coughs'. The sergeant shouted, 'Why are you breeding consumption here? Silence! Keep still! Now, salute: the arm must move as if it was a spring, while the palm of the hand is stiff as a plank. Saluting is serious business!' Yet Tolstoy already sensed a weariness in the soldiers' conduct. These men were 'unable any longer to see any beauty in military service and were merely succumbing to discipline ... They have already been attacked by their first pangs of anxiety, inner doubt: "What is all this about, God help us?"' The writer perceived men recoiling from the 'monstrous dysfunctionality' of their new lives, wrenched out of shape by the war, which displaced millions from their proper and familiar existences. Years of misery and slaughter lay ahead for all the combatants in the East before their rulers faced a decisive reckoning, which took place far from the battlefields.

2 THE SERBS' LAST TRIUMPH

The Serbian front was much the least important in the big picture of the war, but it contributed mightily to the Hapsburg Empire's descent towards collapse. There, as in Galicia and Western Europe, winter weather intensified all the combatants' miseries. Austrian Lt. Roland Wüster recoiled from the sight of dead Serbs whose entrails had been devoured by animals. Alex Pallavicini described difficulties with his automobiles, constantly bogged in mud from which they could be extricated only by horses – a humiliation for twentieth-century technology. Repairs were difficult for lack of parts, and fuel was often in short supply. As for the Serbians, whatever the successes of their army, civilians suffered dreadfully. The assistant head of Belgrade's psychiatric hospital, Dr Šajnović, said despairingly on 2 November: 'If we do not get peace soon, I shall join my patients instead of treating them. I smoke like a lunatic and swill *tinktura energika* [a mixture of *rakija* and cognac], but it does nothing to give me energy any more!' When cigarettes were no longer obtainable, some people resorted to smoking dried leaves.

Gen. Oskar Potiorek had failed disastrously in his August and September offensives. In early November, however, overwhelmingly superior strength enabled him to inflict a severe reverse on the Serbian army. He was honoured by the Kaiser, and a street was renamed for him in Sarajevo. But Potiorek's conceit, incompetence and insensitivity remained undiminished. He sought to sustain his army's Serbian advance into the winter, though his men were exhausted and ill-equipped. A divisional commander protested in vain that 'extreme weather affects the fitness of troops still clad in summer tunics'. Potiorek dismissed as 'bleating' all requests for boots, winter clothing, more ammunition or equipment. When told that some of his men were starving, he responded: 'Making war means going hungry.' An Austrian soldier wrote of gossip in the ranks about the general:

'They say that he shows no interest at all in the course of battles, forgets everything that happened the previous day and issues the most pointless orders.'

On 6 November, Potiorek launched a new offensive, which drove deep into Serbia. Half a million Austrian troops, advancing on three fronts, fell upon half that number of defenders. 'News that the brave Serbian army has been defeated prompted an indescribable panic in the capital,' wrote Dr Slavka Mihajlović. 'The few people who remain here are preparing to flee.' A few days later she added: 'Incredible cold sets in and working conditions at the hospital are unbearable. The food is terrible and supplies are nearly exhausted. Because of constant shelling, all road links to the countryside are cut.' As the Austrians pushed further into Serbia, they were chiefly impressed by its poverty. Peasant homes were neat enough, but pitifully sparsely furnished, with only embroidered blankets and cloth – sewing machines were the only ubiquitous manifestations of technology. On the walls there were a few icons, and cheap coloured prints depicting heroic images of the Balkan war against the Turks. Austrians despised their enemies as barbarians, and briefly also as losers.

Belgrade fell. On 3 December, Austrian troops staged a triumphal parade through the city, and were soon reported to have advanced within forty-five miles of the Serbian army headquarters at Kraguijevatz. Serb ammunition stocks were almost exhausted. Hundreds of thousands of civilian refugees, terrorised by their earlier experience of Austrian occupation, fled for their lives with the retreating army. Serbia's fortunes seemed irretrievable, and Gen. Putnik, the commander-in-chief, urged his country's politicians to open negotiations with Vienna for an armistice. He was astonished when the Pašić government responded by declaring its determination to fight on. The sufferings intensified of both Serbs who clung to their native land and those who fled as refugees. Russian diplomat Nikolai Charykov's wife was appalled by the conditions she found at a hospital in Niš, whence hundreds of wounded Serbs had been evacuated, and lay untended for lack of chloroform, antiseptics, dressings – even warm water to wash wounds.

Yet the victors were in no better case. By mid-November, the woes of the Austrian columns trudging towards their next objective, Draginje-Bosnak, were very great. Rations often failed to reach units because supply wagons bogged down. Men slept in mud. One soldier wrote: 'All those chaps suffering only coughs and colds were in better shape than the poor fellows enduring toothache, or scarcely able to move their legs because of rheumatism. Packs and blankets grew so heavy with the wet that one's shoulders acquired bloody stripes, and men struggled to avoid falling over backwards. Guns kept getting stuck so deep in the mud that their wheels vanished. Even with six oxen and three pairs of horses hitched to the carriage, it sometimes took over an hour's hard labour to get one artillery piece free.'

They met many refugees – old people, women and children attempting to return to villages they had fled a few weeks or months ago – suffering as much from the mud as the Austrians. At the sight of these tragic columns, in the words of Corporal Egon Kisch, 'our own troubles receded. Quite often a villager's cart became irretrievably bogged down or the draught animal collapsed: dead cattle lay on the road and sometimes an overturned carriage, its contents scattered about. The owners stood gazing in bewilderment, and their despair cut into our hearts. But we could not help them.' Roland Wüster wrote despairingly: 'We no longer have any decent boots or clothing; rations are gone and the men exhausted – the consequence of our hasty advance and fierce fighting. Half the baggage animals have saddle sores which stink so horribly that it is intolerable to march behind them.'

But now, almost miraculously, the wheel of fate turned once more. France shipped to Serbia just sufficient ammunition to refill its ally's empty artillery limbers. Putnik regrouped his forces. Somehow he persuaded his filthy, exhausted, threadbare, half-starved troops to join a counter-attack. On 3 December, in a battle at Arandjelovac, the Serbs achieved a startling victory. Advancing in its wake, they were astonished to find the Austrian army crumbling: first the centre of the front gave way, then the flanks. Roland Wüster wrote on 4 December that the retreat of Potiorek's army resembled that of Napoleon's army from Moscow – a chaos of baggage columns, artillery, siege detachments, pioneers, 'with infantry dispersed between them along with scavengers and wounded – everybody struggling to escape from this ill-starred land'. Next day, Wüster himself was hit in the leg. With no help in sight, he crudely bandaged the wound himself, hobbled into a nearby farmstead and lay down. For the next seven hours he struggled in vain to staunch the bleeding. Despairing, the young officer gave a picture of his family to a nearby sentry, and told him how he wished to be buried. The man casually reassured him that his wound did not look too bad, though he added cheerfully that he had not long since buried a comrade with a similar one. 'Nice words of comfort for me,' scrawled Wüster wretchedly.

Next day, as gunfire drew closer, he secured a ride on an unsprung cart that carried him fifteen miles to Valjevo. Every yard of the 5½-hour journey was agony to the wounded man. When he reached the military hospital the doctors declined to treat him, because they were pulling out. Wüster lapsed into hysterical sobbing, and somehow got himself carried to the town's station. He was laid in an open wagon on a train which next morning reached the Bosnian border, and safety. Three days later he arrived at his own home in Linz, emaciated and bearded; his own son did not recognise him. Wüster collapsed into renewed tears as he described his experiences, and suffered for weeks afterwards from nightmares in which he found himself at the mercy of the Serbs.

On 14 December, Austrian eyewitnesses watched in disbelief as the army's pontoon bridge across the Sava swayed and tottered under the weight of throngs of panic-stricken fugitive soldiers struggling across, desperate to reach the Bosnian shore, while exultant scarecrow Serbs sought to shoot them down. That day, the Serb high command announced: 'The enemy is beaten, dispersed, defeated and expelled from our territory once and for all.'

On the 16th a cluster of Austrian infantrymen gathered eagerly around a fortnight-old newspaper which had reached them from Vienna. Lips curled in cynicism when they found that this proclaimed Austria's triumphal occupation of Belgrade. By the time the soldiers saw the old headlines, they had again evacuated the city, amid yet another precipitate Austrian retreat. That day, 16 December, the Serbs once more stood triumphant in the battered and desolate streets of their capital. Gen. Živojin Mišić, who had directed the counter-offensive, became his country's hero of the hour. He telegraphed proudly: 'there remain no Austrian soldiers on Serbian soil except prisoners'.

Alex Pallavicini wrote on 17 December, describing the Austrians' flight to the Danube and Sava bridges: 'Anger and mistrust against the high command seems justified after this experience, because nothing worse conducted than our leadership and supply system is imaginable. Forty thousand pairs of boots had to be burnt in Valjevo because nobody had got around to issuing them. Our forces literally had to march in shreds of leather and their bare feet.' Potiorek's rout left the Serbians in possession of 130 captured guns and 40,000 prisoners, including 270 officers. Dr Johann Bachmann's infantry regiment fell apart during the December retreat. The doctor had to abandon his most serious casualties, because there was no transport to move them. When at last they crossed the Sava,

Bachmann was found unfit for further service, and sent on extended leave. On reaching home, he fell into an unbroken twelve-hour sleep. Thereafter, however, he found that for many weeks repose escaped him: he was haunted by nightmares of Serbia.

As future events would show, the Hapsburg army's defeat was not irreversible, and Serbian resources were being drained to the dregs. But the prestige of Franz Joseph's empire had been brought low by its hated and despised little neighbour. Conrad Hötzendorf conceded the need to adopt the defensive on his southern front for the rest of the winter. Yet even now he made a further botched strategic compromise: the forces that dug into the barren soil, or stood across river barriers confronting the Serbians, were too weak to take the offensive, but much stronger than were necessary to counter an enemy thrust. Conrad's conduct of the early campaigns against his despised Slav enemies had proved as disastrous as those against the Russians. The Austrians had described their invasion of Serbia as a *Strafexpedition* – punishment mission; now the scornful Serbs renamed it the *bestrafte* expedition – the 'punished expedition'. They composed a song of triumph which began: 'The Emperor Nicholas rides a black horse, the Emperor Franz Joseph rides a mule.'

There seemed no end to the shared sufferings of victors and vanquished, soldiers and civilians. If the Austrians behaved barbarously during their 1914 invasions of Serbia, their hapless soldiers paid an almost equally heavy price if they fell into the hands of the enemy. With little food for themselves, the Serbians gave less to their would-be conquerors. The government allowed any citizen to hire an Austrian worker for a pittance, a practice which the PoWs welcomed, because Serb employers fed them better than Serb camp bosses. But disease took a heavy toll: by the end of 1914, one in five of the 60,000 Austrian prisoners in Belgrade's hands was already dead of typhus, and more would follow. By the year's end Austria-Hungary had paid for its hubris towards Serbia with 273,804 casualties out of 450,000 men deployed. Vienna felt obliged belatedly to recognise the incompetence of most of its most senior officers by sacking four out of six army commanders, including Oskar Potiorek.

But the Serb people had little to celebrate. A young man blinded in battle sang a song which began: 'I am sad, for I have lost the sight of the sun and the green fields and the blossoming plum trees.' The Sava valley west of Belgrade had been devastated. Many small towns and villages had been abandoned by their inhabitants, and grass grew in the streets.

Refugees who trickled back westwards with the army looked in horror at the wreckage of their communities. Belgrade was reduced to a city of beggars, cripples, orphans. The country's few roads had been ruined by military traffic. Serbia was linked to the outside world only by a single-track railway to Salonika, along which supplies moved sluggishly, with scant help from neutral Greece. Spotted typhus, dysentery and cholera ravaged whole tracts of the country, and any man wounded on the battlefield was fortunate to survive gangrene.

Serbia's plight became fashionable in Britain: Lady Wimborne, Lady Paget and Sir Thomas Lipton were only the most prominent of those who travelled to join volunteer medical units in the country alongside Countess Trubetskoy, wife of the new Russian minister. But they could do pitifully little for a nation of such poverty and geographical isolation, temporarily victorious to be sure, but shattered and perilously weak. Serbia had already lost 163,557 men, including 69,022 dead. The country would suffer far worse things in the years to come, unredeemed by the joys of any further victories. 62.5 per cent of Serbian males between fifteen and fifty-five would eventually perish in the war; their entire country would be laid waste.

Lt. Djordje Stanojevitch of the Serbian army demanded of American correspondent John Reed, with the furious passion inspired by alcohol: 'What are these French and English doing? Why do they not beat the Germans? What they need there are a few Serbians to show them how to make war. We Serbians know that all that is needed is the willingness to die – and the war would soon be over …!' Others, some of them commanders-in-chief, shared the same belief, with dreadful consequences for the youth of Europe.

17

Mudlife

As winter descended on Europe, Gertrud Schädla contemplated the cold rain in her home town of Verden, near Bremen, and thought of her nation's soldiers at the front, 'who must face not only such weather, but also deadly peril'. Her concern was not misplaced. A pervasive stench, created by unburied corpses, excrement and seven million sets of water-logged clothing and boots, unchanged for weeks, overhung the Western Front from Switzerland to the sea. Along five hundred miles of rival defences, some men occupied precarious mountaintops among the blasted pines of the Vosges, while others sheltered behind breastworks along the Yser canal, where it was impossible to entrench. At the end of First Ypres, the French held 430 miles of front, the Belgians fifteen and the BEF twenty-one – the maximum its modest manpower then allowed. In February 1918, by contrast, the British line would extend to 110 miles.

Almost all major operations from September 1914 to the end of the war took place between Verdun and the Channel coast – the terrain further south was recognised as unprofitable attacking ground. Some of the towns of western Belgium were pretty places, at least until they were ravaged by the battles of October and November. But the intervening farmland was unprepossessing: flat fields broken by a few hedges; willow trees; roadside avenues of poplar and plane; occasional beechwoods. During the first weeks of fighting cattle grazed freely among the combatants – the prevalence of animal manure in the soil contributed to that of gas gangrene among the wounded. Once the autumn rains took hold, on low-lying ground it became impossible for vehicles to move off roads. Where variations in land height were slight, even the most marginal advantage became important: the Germans almost invariably adopted higher positions, because as occupiers they felt no embarrassment about withdrawing where this was tactically advantageous, heedless of considerations of prestige. The allies, by contrast, could cede a few yards of Belgian or French soil only for the most compelling reasons.

When Edouard Cœurdevey was deployed to north-eastern France, he and his comrades were astonished to find themselves posted in deep trenches, which he described as 'something new for us'. This was the future. Millions of men for months occupied almost unchanging positions within close range of the enemy. 'In those early days of trench warfare,' wrote Frank Richards, 'both sides were pretty reckless, and it was no uncommon sight to see a German pop up and make a dart for the village. He did not always get there, and as time went on both sides respected the marksmanship of each other so much that no one dared to show a finger.' Correspondent Ashmead Bartlett wrote in the *Daily Telegraph*: 'Men are not often visible in modern war, because to make any show at all against the infernal machinations of Messrs. Krupp, Schneider, Creusot and Co., they must bury themselves in the earth, and only rise up to shoot if their enemy is sufficiently foolhardy as to show himself.' Robert Harker noted in November that in his sector the two sides' positions were only yards apart, but 'in this kind of fighting one goes for days in the trenches in some parts of the line and never sees a German'.

Colwyn Phillips of the Royal Horse Guards wrote ruefully from Ypres: 'The first thing we learn here is to forget about "Glory"'. In attacks, some German officers took to carrying rifles and knapsacks, to escape the particular attentions of enemy riflemen. Soldiers unscrewed the spikes from their Pickelhaube helmets, which could protrude above trench parapets with deadly consequences. Rigorous discipline became necessary, to avoid exposing even an inch of flesh. Lionel Tennyson of the Rifle Brigade deplored the carelessness of his battalion's neighbours, the Seaforth Highlanders: 'a most extraordinary lot of men: if a shell has not come over for twenty minutes or so, they get out of their trenches and start exposing themselves as if no battle was on. The consequence is that many get killed unnecessarily.'

The British evolved a routine grinding in its monotony, and unremitting in its discomforts. Stand-to was called before dawn, followed by breakfast at seven, lunch at 12.30, tea at four, dinner at seven, sleep by 9.30 p.m. for those spared duty. But this apparently benign regime was interrupted by alarms throughout the hours of daylight and darkness, along with patrols and fatigue duties, so that most men did not remove their clothes, or even their boots, for days on end. They existed on a diet of bully beef, biscuit, bread and jam, supplemented by whatever little luxuries they could obtain from home. The postal services created a wonderfully efficient machine for enabling millions of men on the brink of death to receive British newspapers within a day or two of publication, together with assorted domestic comforts. Officers ordered consignments of cigars, biscuits and suchlike from smart London shops. One Grenadier officer placed an order with Fortnum & Mason for two pounds of coffee each week, though he only survived to drink a month's worth. Some eggs dispatched from Cookstown, Co. Tyrone at 4 p.m. one Tuesday reached Sister Mayne at her Belgian hospital in Furnes by 5 p.m. on Thursday.

Men learned to appreciate occupying positions close to those of the Germans, which spared them from artillery fire: 'thus they cannot "*marmite*" us', observed François Mayer with satisfaction, using the French slang word for enemy shelling, just as a '*pruneau*' – a prune – was a bullet. Guards officer Lord Cavan wrote in December: 'Our chief work of late has been to learn three things. 1st How to make our own charcoal and how to carry it and use it in the trenches when made. 2nd How to throw hand-grenades – curious work for Grenadiers. 3rd How to shoot at aeroplanes, but the trouble here is – birds are scarce and our guns have very long waits between beats.' In some sectors, such as the Chemin des Dames, both sides mounted searchlights, the better to respond to night attacks. Protective wire entanglements grew in depth, though not yet to the fantastic densities of later years. Some British officers clung to a belief that war should be conducted in accordance with a code of honour which they claimed the Germans breached. Robert Harker complained: 'They have all sorts of dirty unsportsmanlike tricks and attack our men disguised in khaki and sometimes kilts and shout out sentences in English saying "don't shoot we are so-and-so" giving the name of some English regiment. They also shout out "Cease fire" in English and give our signals.'

French *poilu* Louis Barthas's unit was first posted to the front late in November, having spent the previous months guarding prisoners and suchlike. He reached Annequin in the Pas de Calais in winter darkness, after travelling from Narbonne in the far south of France. Early next morning on the edge of the town, he was amazed to be familiarly greeted by three spectral figures, caked in mud from head to foot and scarcely identifiable as human. These were *copains* who had left the same barracks only five days earlier. 'They describe lying for hours in the mud without shelter, amid daily rains and poor food.' Soon he and his comrades found themselves manning a waterlogged trench. When darkness fell, sleep eluded them for some hours, tormented as they were by the fears fed by sporadic firing and flares.

Their slumber, when it belatedly came, was interrupted by the clink and thud of picks and shovels. 'What are you doing?' Barthas demanded dozily of the dim figures above him. 'Burying the dead from the last assault,' growled a voice. But many huddled grey lumps of decaying humanity remained unreachable in no man's land, prey for rats and circling crows. Another French soldier described how attacking infantrymen felled by machine-guns lay thereafter for a month in front of his trench, 'lined up as on a manoeuvre. The rain falls on them inexorably and bullets shatter their bleached bones. One evening Jacques, on patrol, saw enormous rats fleeing from under their faded coats. They were fat from human meat. His heart pounding, he crawled towards a dead man. His helmet had rolled away. He was showing a grimacing face, with no flesh; his skull bare, his eyes eaten. A denture had slid onto his rotting shirt, and out of his gaping mouth a foul animal jumped.'

On 18 November, a letter from an unnamed BEF officer was published in the press at home. 'Sitting here, and reading the English papers that arrive, one cannot help feeling that England has not yet succeeded in banishing the spectacular and romantic conceptions of war which no longer bear any relation to the actuality. The papers still give the impression that war is an affair of dash and clash' – the author cited publicity accorded to the experiences of the London Scottish at Ypres. 'This is not what is happening. The bravery of our men, and they are splendidly brave, consists of sitting, often for days and nights, in sodden trenches, with the terrifying noises and earth-shaking concussions of shells ... I read of the Sportsmen's battalion, all athletes [one of the newly formed 'Pals' units]. All very nice, if individual prowess were in question, but it is not. What is wanted is ordinary men, trained in discipline and trained to shoot, and plenty of them – men who can be held in not to shoot until the proper moment, not men who are going to whoop and slash and kill two Germans at one stroke.'

Georges Clemenceau, statesman and journalist, wrote in the same spirit: 'we always represent the soldier grappling with the enemy ... Yet how much more elusive is the courage required by enduring inactivity under a hail of shells. How much harder is the test imposed by passive suffering, which continues relentlessly and devours all physical and psychological resistance.' It was recognised on both sides of the Western Front that there was no prospect of a significant breakthrough before spring. German officer Rudolf Binding wrote grumpily on 22 November, in Flanders: 'As matters stand now, not only here but all along the line, both we and the enemy have so crippled ourselves ... that ... we cannot get the momentum for a thrust ... It may be an incredible achievement to create this endless, unbroken line from the Alps to the sea as a monstrous whole; but it is not my idea of strategy.' Once it was plain that no further big operations were imminent, the BEF granted leave to some officers and men – their first such reprieve since August. In the ensuing scramble for seats on trains, one party of officers rode a locomotive's coal tender to Boulogne.

Commanders also exploited the breathing space to send home some frail spirits who had been found wanting. These included Brigadier R.H. Davies, a New Zealander deemed to have failed on the Aisne, and Lt. Col. Noel Corry of the Grenadiers, whose crime had been to withdraw without orders from Mons on 23 August. George Jeffreys, his second-in-command, thought Corry badly treated, because his decision had been correct. Other cases were more equivocal: Lt. Col. Delme-Radcliffe of the Royal Welch Fusiliers returned to their depot having suffered a nervous breakdown, a term that covered a range of ill-defined conditions. The simple explanation was that some regular officers had shown themselves unfit for the stresses of war. Such people were treated much more generously by the military hierarchy in 1914 than would be humbler soldiers in the years ahead.

As for those who remained in their trenches, even if victory was not immediately attainable, commanders on both sides convinced themselves that activism was essential, to prevent men from sinking into a slough of despond and inertia. They thus initiated a policy of mounting local attacks, the futility of which was apparent to those obliged to execute them. French junior officers complained bitterly about lives sacrificed by generals merely eager to be seen to be doing something – 'de paraître agir'. On the British front, Capt. John Cowan described a typical battle at Givenchy in December: 'One of our companies attacked a German saphead and captured their trench, but were enfiladed by machine-guns and very heavily cut up, only two men returning out of fifty that attacked. Lt. Kerr was killed while trying to get back to our trench. C Coy went to their support and we were not relieved until our trenches were blown up. I ... was up day & night soaking through & no sleep for five nights. It was hard and onerous work as we expected attacks every night.'

Early on the morning of 21 December, Cowan's men were cleaning their rifles when 'a rumbling noise was heard and all the trenches shook.

The parapet and trenches gave way & the ground opened up all around us [a chain of enemy mines had exploded]. Above this were heard the cheers of Germans 10 yds. away, charging with fixed bayonets ... eventually [we] had to retire. Some of my men were smothered alive, others bayoneted.' The Germans had blown ten mines on the Indian corps' front, which caused severe casualties together with alarm and confusion. In the support trench Cowan rallied ten survivors, and alongside forty Gurkhas of the neighbouring battalion delivered a counter-attack: 'Some of us charged without weapons at all – I gave Sergeant Brisbane my revolver as his was useless but he got shot through the head by my side ... By the grace of God the Germans did not face us but turned about ... I picked up a rifle and accounted for seven Germans all hit in the back. I also shot a German officer ... But the Germans began to bomb us, working from traverse to traverse & we finally retired to the reserve line under heavy fire.' Cowan's battalion lost fourteen officers and 516 men, 'which was terrible ... I was lucky to get through: one shot went through the top of my balaclava.'

The consequence of such a drain of losses in routine trench activity – raids, patrols, sniping, surprise barrages and local attacks – was that British commanders became increasingly concerned about manpower. Home bases were scoured to find replacements until Kitchener's new formations were trained and equipped for the campaigns of 1915. But the dross of the old army was unimpressive material: Lionel Tennyson wrote in his diary: 'Sergeant Swinchat arrived with 2nd reinforcement, a most useless NCO. When I threatened to march him up before the Commanding Officer for idleness, he shot himself in the foot and was awarded a court martial.' Swinchat was reduced to the ranks, but escaped imprisonment in the absence of evidence that he had acted deliberately. He probably thought this the best possible outcome for his interests.

Sir Douglas Haig complained to the War Office about the shortcomings of such men: 'I said we wanted patriots who knew the importance of the cause for which we are fighting. The whole German people have been impregnated from youth up with an intense patriotic feeling, so that they die willingly for their country. There are not many of our men who will do this unless well led. Now we are short of officers to lead them. I said send out young Oxford and Cambridge men as officers; they understand the crisis in which the British Empire is involved.' The Germans certainly did not share Haig's view that their own men were happy to die: they saw themselves facing the same problems of motivation and leadership as their adversaries. Rudolf Binding wrote from Ypres: 'There is no doubt that the

English and French troops would already have been beaten by trained troops. But these young fellows we have only just trained are too helpless, particularly when the officers have been killed. Our light infantry battalion, almost all Marburg students … have suffered terribly from enemy shellfire.'

In Britain the *Morning Post* campaigned stridently for conscription, but the *New Statesman* claimed that such a drastic step 'would amount to the sacrifice of nine-tenths of our moral case in this war. It would not only amount to an admission – wholly unjustified – that the heart of the country is not in the war … It would change the basis of our participation. It would no longer be the war of the British people – it would be the war of the British governing classes.' Lord Northcliffe emphasised his determination to address this issue on his own terms. 'I have seen the government,' he told the *Daily Mail*'s assembled executives one evening, 'and they asked me to work up a strong recruiting campaign. I declined point-blank until our men [press correspondents behind the front] are treated properly, and facilities given them to help recruiting by telling about our army. I can get 500,000 men, but I must do it my own way. They would not agree, so I refused point-blank.' Thus, through the winter of 1914 and the year that followed, the army struggled to recruit through the voluntary system the numbers of men needed if the country was to play a major role in the war on the continent.

In response to desperate need, the army lowered its minimum height requirement from five feet eight inches in August to five feet five inches in October, and five feet three inches in November. This was partially successful: 1,186,351 British civilians joined the colours in 1914. But other combatant armies already deployed in the field three or four times that number of troops. Only in 1916 did British forces in France attain mass proportionate to their country's size, and only the introduction of conscription that year allowed them to sustain reinforcements to meet the insatiable demands of the struggle. In any event it is doubtful that a large army could have been armed and equipped earlier: the BEF suffered chronic shortages of warm clothing – the goatskin coats issued that first winter were quite unsuitable – of every kind of weapon and above all of artillery ammunition, until domestic industrial production reached full capacity in the war's third year.

* * *

Also wanting were draught and pack animals. The British took 53,000 horses to France in 1914, and other armies used them in like proportion. The official historians noted: 'The enormous wastage from animal casualties of a modern war was under-estimated.' The BEF's horses and mules suffered an annual mortality rate of 29 per cent, with over 13,000 dead in France and Flanders before New Year 1915 from disease or enemy action. Alexander Johnston reckoned that on the march to the Aisne he passed a dead horse every two hundred yards: 'poor brutes, they have a terrible time of it'. Many such casualties – shot, crippled or ridden to exhaustion – were drawn from the 165,000 hunters and plough horses purchased for the British Army in the first twelve days of war. In September the retreating Germans threw down spiked metal caltrops, or 'crows' feet', to cripple pursuing cavalry. These frequently achieved their purpose, especially when compounded by French housewives' practice of tossing stove ashes onto rural tracks without removing nails and other old iron.

Many horses fell victim to incompetent or brutal handling. Vets catalogued examples of mistreatment by ignorant riders and grooms: artillery drivers 'chucking' horses in the mouth; cavalry wantonly neglecting to feed or water their mounts; men galloping horses on paved roads without urgent need; riders ignoring saddlesores. Cavalry remount depots were formed at Ormskirk, Swaythling and Shirehampton, and beside each was a veterinary hospital capable of tending a thousand four-legged patients. Army stables at Pitt Corner camp near Winchester at one time held more than 3,000 sick and injured animals.

Meanwhile heavy plough horses, conscripted against expert advice, proved quite unsuitable for the artillery role for which they were earmarked. The official historians noted: 'Veterinary officers ... foresaw their weakness for military purposes, and anticipated the heavy loss which would ensue if they were indiscriminately employed in war ... because of great susceptibility to disease, large food and watering requirements, and inability to stand forced marches.' Heavy horses perished in thousands in France, partly because of the extreme vulnerability of their feet to wet weather. Both the French and the British made huge foreign purchases of replacements, but the right sort of animal was identified only after harsh experience. Many Canadian remounts died on the Atlantic passage, or soon after arriving in Britain. It was found that the most suitable stock were tough American country beasts from areas like the Dakotas, rather than barn-reared horses. By the war's end, the British Army's animal strength rose to 450,000; an estimated total of two million hapless horses and mules served on both sides of the Western Front. The Royal Army Veterinary Corps, which mustered just 360 personnel in 1914, numbered 28,000 four years later.

If healthy and unwounded men, as well as animals, found trench life terrible enough, those who became casualties suffered appallingly. German Alois Löwenstein gazed pityingly upon some typical battlefield victims: 'Among a bunch of corpses lay three wounded Frenchmen. One man had both legs shattered; the second's stomach was torn open; the third had tried to shoot himself until one of our chaps took away his revolver. He fired twice at his own head to escape pain, but aimed clumsily, a little too high. The skullcap was uplifted and he moaned in a fashion to melt the heart. Another man lay apparently dead, but with one leg still twitching like that of a partridge that is unable to die. Awful!'

During the preceding half-century, the treatment of war wounded had advanced less than many other branches of science. In the absence of antibiotics, gangrene remained a massive killer, its contribution increased by the days of delay many men endured before their wounds were properly treated. Patients often deluded themselves that they were recovering because their pain receded. In truth, however, they had merely acquired the numbness and pallor that signified imminent death. Survival required extraordinary luck. René Cassin was shot in the stomach – almost always a fatal occurrence – near Saint-Mihiel on 12 October. The French army's medical services decreed that he could be treated only by his own regiment's doctors, who were four hundred miles away. He endured a ten-day journey to reach them, followed by an operation performed without anaesthetic. The experience made him a lifelong crusader for wounded veterans and human rights.

When Edouard Cœurdevey entered a French field hospital to pay a last visit to a friend who was dying there, he found eighty men lying on straw in a sugar factory, still dressed in their mud-soaked uniforms. The hospital's sole bed was reserved for a man identified as close to expiry. In October a railway points failure dispatched an ambulance train carrying five hundred wounded along a track which led to a blown bridge across the Marne. Only two of the train's fifteen carriages – by chance, those that carried German casualties – escaped a headlong descent into the river. Not every nurse was a sister of mercy. Captain Plieux de Diusse was shocked to see one woman striding down a line of railway wagons laden with groaning men. At each open door she demanded perfunctorily whether anyone needed a doctor, but when a victim begged aid for his comrade whose stomach wound had reopened, unleashing the stench of gas gangrene, the nurse ignored him and marched on. De Diusse eventually found an overworked doctor, told him of the case, then fled the scene: 'I have had enough of these horrors, and leave them to it,' he wrote.

Louis Maufrais, an army medical orderly, described his own pathetic efforts to treat a wounded man: 'his face, with a broken jaw, is no more than a bloody mess. Having removed some fragments from his mouth we managed to lower a tube into the oesophagus through which we pass a sort of enema, some water and then some coffee.' Maufrais's aid post often lacked sufficient water even to wash the mud from his own hands before he dressed a wound. He and his comrades had nothing to offer patients suffering shock, as were most, and blood transfusions were impossible in such an unhygienic environment. He depicted one post at which he served: 'to the left of the entrance two corpses are lying in the sun covered with a fragment of tent canvas; behind them is a tall heap of equipment, rifles, bayonets, blood-soaked linen. The interior is lit only by a few candles and two lamps. Gradually my eyes discern the wounded lying on the ground, almost on top of each other. There is a smell of living matter, blood, vomit; the only sounds [are] ceaseless cries. The most difficult challenge is to place a foot between one boy's legs and a knee under the armpit of another in order to attend to a third.'

Maufrais was also required to bury the dead, 'often stinking appallingly, in a state of total putrefaction, their faces black, swollen and crawling with maggots. One needed a strong stomach to undress them and remove their identity tags.' In the first months of the war, officers were interred separately from their men, but as casualties mounted the French army issued orders that only those holding the rank of captain and above should qualify for such a privilege. The French government, in response to a public clamour, eventually allowed families to choose to take home their dead loved ones, but this became a contentious issue when many proved unable to afford the cost of moving the bodies. The British and Germans, meanwhile, buried almost all their private soldiers in common graves close to where they fell.

The battlefield had not yet been ironed by explosives into a featureless mudscape – this required the labour of many more months and thousands of heavy guns. In 1914 some buildings still survived, together with battered hedges and woods, but day by day their numbers were depleted. A German regimental commander near Poelkapelle, one Maj. Grimm, described how some of his men made themselves wonderfully comfortable in a farmhouse, where he himself had his first shave for days. But then their haven became the target of an artillery concentration which killed most of the occupants.

As men grew accustomed to living and exchanging fire month after month in unchanging settings, local landmarks achieved notoriety. The Rifle Brigade fought a fierce battle for a position near Messines known as 'the Birdcage', because it was so heavily wired. At Le Bassée, 'the Leave Train' was a derelict chain of wagons, filled with concrete by the Germans and used to some effect by their snipers. There, a fortunate British soldier might 'cop a Blighty one' – suffer a light wound that earned him a ride home, hence the name. There was much slaughter at a position in the Vosges known to Germans as 'HWK' – *Hartsmannsweilerkopf* – while the French called it '*Vieille Amande*', 'Old Almond'. The Kaiser's soldiers devoted immense effort and accepted heavy casualties to gain possession of this hilltop, because it commanded the road to Mulhouse.

In 1914 the armies lacked almost every necessity for positional warfare. Telephones were in short supply, but signallers could not expose themselves to flash Morse signals or use semaphore flags, as they had been accustomed to do in colonial campaigns. Instead, commanders were often obliged to send written messages, at mortal risk to the runners who carried them. Rifles fouled with mud and powder residue could not be properly cleaned, because of a lack of oil and cotton waste. As a result they often jammed, a problem compounded by poor-quality ammunition, supplied by shoddy manufacturers. When some Royal Welch soldiers killed a pig at an abandoned farm, they used its fat to grease their weapons. Sanitary arrangements were primitive: men urinated into bully-beef tins, which were then tossed as far as possible over the parapet. It was likewise necessary to defecate in the shelter of a trench. Until routines for removing waste were introduced, this too was merely thrown into no man's land. When engineers laid a single strand of protective barbed wire across the Royal Welch's front, one of Frank Richards's mates said contemptuously that a giraffe could walk under it. But for weeks, there was no more British wire to be had.

The Germans took much more trouble to make themselves comfortable than did the British, French or Belgians. They not only entrenched deeply, but also added homely touches to their dugouts. Lt. Adolf Spemann admired the shelving, skylights and recesses with which his men adorned their quarters. Neatly painted entrance signs identified such residences as 'Villa Sorgenfrei' – Carefree House. Another bunker was lined with dud French projectiles, and christened 'Palais des Obus' – Shell Palace. The Germans ate better than the French, too: Louis Barthas's unit subsisted for weeks upon cold coffee, a chunk of dried meat and some mudstained bread, distributed daily at dawn. Private enterprise supplemented this meagre diet, for those willing and able to pay: each night, one of Barthas's comrades risked court-martial to slip out of the line and walk to Béthune, where he fulfilled food orders for half the company, returning before daybreak heavily burdened.

Professional soldiers, including the highest, now viewed the struggle as a contest of rival wills, in which it was essential that their side should prevail by displaying a superior tolerance of suffering and loss. On 7 December, Charles de Gaulle wrote to his mother: 'What is this conflict but a war of extermination? A struggle of this kind, which in its range, significance and fury goes beyond anything that Europe has ever known, cannot be waged without enormous sacrifices. It has to be won. The winner will be the side that desires it most ardently.' De Gaulle recoiled in disgust from the spirit of co-existence that developed in many parts of the line. After digging a trench towards the Germans to frustrate a matching enemy sap, he urged his battalion commander that they should use it to bring down fire. The major strongly dissented: 'Don't start anything like this in our sector. You will cause fireworks. Leave the enemy in peace at the Bonnet Persan, since he leaves us in peace in our part of the world!' De Gaulle wrote sourly: 'Trench warfare has a serious drawback: it exaggerates this feeling in everyone – if I leave the enemy alone he will not bother me ... It is lamentable.'

Yet units which confronted each other for weeks on end disagreed with the earnest young French officer. They pursued accommodations to make existence fractionally less intolerable. In woods north of Pont à Mousson lay the spring of Père Hilarion, from which both the French and the Germans drew water. North of Ypres, after heavy rain British and Germans alike sometimes perched on their parapets because trenches were flooded and field drains wrecked by shelling. Amid common misery, neither showed much enthusiasm for starting a firefight. Early in December, a German surgeon reported that his neighbouring infantry regiment had a regular half-hour evening truce with the French, during which the dead were brought in for burial, and the combatants exchanged newspapers. Eventually, however, the French abandoned this easy relationship:

'obviously they were cross about our latest victories against the Russians'. More likely, some senior officer intervened. Gen. d'Urbal wrote warning his *confrère* Gen. Grossetti: 'Please note that men who stay too long in the same sector become familiar with their neighbours opposite. This results in conversations and sometimes visits which often lead to unfortunate consequences.'

A new mood was sweeping the warring nations, which owed nothing to the romantic delusions and enthusiasms of August. When Louis Barthas left Narbonne for the front in November, he contrasted the lack of ceremony, the absence of cheers and kisses, attending his unit's departure with late-summer's parades of enthusiasm. It seemed to him symbolic that whereas four months earlier women had crowded the station platform pressing fruit, jam, wine on soldiers, now they sold these commodities to them for cash. Minor wounds had become objects of desire. After Sgt. Wilhelm Kaisen's brother was shot in the left hand, Kaisen told his family jealously: 'he really hit the jackpot'. François Mayer suffered severe lacerations when he threw himself to the ground under shellfire and landed on a heap of broken glass. His injuries secured him a precious few days out of the line. 'I am desolated to abandon my *copains*, but have promised to return to them within the week.' Behind the line, he overcame his initial embarrassment about being fussed over by sympathetic civilians: 'Everywhere I am evasive about admitting the nature of my wound and give the impression it was made by a bullet. The fruits of my half-lie are several quarts of coffee and glasses of rum, given free.'

Young German gunner Herbert Sulzbach met some French prisoners, and was bewildered to hear most profess relief that they were on their way to Germany with whole skins, the war behind them. It was the same in the French lines: a German prisoner told Edouard Cœurdevey: 'We are much better off here than fighting.' When some of the man's comrades reproached him, Cœurdevey asked if they thought France was to blame for the war. Neither France nor Germany, they said: 'it is Russia that is responsible. We soldiers fight because we have to.' There were still a few aspirant heroes, however, who derived a flagellatory delight from their predicament, or at least from pretending that they did. Julian Grenfell, idolised by his peers for reasons mystifying to posterity, wrote in October: 'I adore war … It is like a big picnic without the objectlessness of a picnic. It is all the best fun … It just suits my stolid health and stolid nerves and barbaric disposition. The fighting-excitement vitalizes everything, every sight and action. One loves one's fellow-man so much more when one is bent on killing him.'

Far more soldiers, however, loathed every moment of their ordeal, of which the infantry bore the overwhelming burden. They also resented the fact that behind the lines, hundreds of thousands of support troops lived in relative comfort, able to sleep, wash, enjoy wholesome food with little danger of violent interruption. A German soldier said sourly: 'The war is like a cinema. The action's at the front and the best seats are at the back.' Gunner Wilhelm Hillern-Flinsch wrote: 'In the rear they are living exactly as in peacetime and indeed do not notice the war. Infantry and pioneers bear the brunt of it all, as I see it. They wear funeral shrouds day and night.' Alois Löwenstein wrote home to his daughter Agnes, expressing dismay about his own privileged role as a driver, not much in harm's way: 'Some soldiers conduct lightning: it strikes them again and again. Your adored father, however, is located far from any thunderbolts, which sometimes makes me feel ashamed of myself. I can't help my position: I would like to face the thunderstorm if I was allowed to.'

If Löwenstein was sincere, he was unusual. As 'Ma' Jeffreys led his men forward to take another turn in the line, he described an encounter at Merville with an unnamed fellow Grenadier officer. Jeffreys demanded, 'When are you coming back to the regiment?' His acquaintance answered, 'Good God, you don't think I'd be such a fool as to do that! I've got a good job.' Jeffreys wrote bitterly: 'He's an arch-shirker and brazen-faced about it into the bargain. He's a draft-conducting officer on the railway, or something of the sort.'

Les biffins – 'the scavengers', as French infantry sardonically called themselves – felt increasing contempt towards the long 'tail' of men who wore the same uniform as themselves, but shared few of their risks. One officer happened upon some marines on the road, travelling in vehicles rather than footslogging. He asked their commander if they had taken any losses, and received a shrug: 'very few', which seemed to mean none. The army officer wrote: 'I look at my poor troopers, marching up the road on their way to be pulverised in waterlogged trenches. No, decidedly in this war there is no equality in the sufferings endured by the different combatants at the front.' A party of French officers, back from the line for a few days, were eating in a hotel at Houdain, where a corps headquarters was stationed. One of the *biffins* recoiled in disgust from the cries of 'Waiter! Another Chartreuse!' uttered by staff officers obviously accustomed to dine every night in such easy circumstances.

Edouard Cœurdevey expressed bitterness at the everyday sight of officers in glittering cars hastening past long columns of wounded men who were obliged to trudge on foot to the nearest aid station – a matter of twelve miles on one occasion: 'These gentlemen pass without one car stopping to pick up the most exhausted [casualties]. The major mustn't be late for his roast!' Alois Löwenstein described the same contempt of *Frontsoldaten*, facing shot and shell, towards the staff: 'They are posted many km behind the front and man desks, telephones and ticker tapes. The horses of ordnance officers grow fat.'

Every intelligent man in the line was in some degree afflicted by fear, but some succumbed more visibly than others. 'It is curious to see the eyes of a frightened man,' wrote François Mayer. 'They are mad with anguish and terror. These nasty shells are not worth the fear they inspire. Unless they achieve a direct hit, they are harmless. One hears their whistle a long way off, then counts to ten before the moment of their detonation.' Ambulance driver Dorothie Feilding wrote scornfully about the inadequacies of some men under fire, notably a volunteer named Johnyson, in civilian life a land agent: 'It's odd how the mere sound of [a shell] crumples men up. It was that way with Johnyson from Dunchurch – the moment there was a "black maria" [German shell] in sight he got in a sort of faint & utterly collapsed & one of the other chauffeurs the same way.'

Beyond psychological burdens, there were plenty of physical ones. As winter tightened its grip, many of even the fittest young men began to suffer from rheumatism and trench foot, caused by living around the clock in sodden boots and socks, often wading to the knee or above in filthy water. Sick lists soared. Bronchial infections became commonplace, and sometimes fatal. Lice were no mere nuisance, but carriers of disease. 'My darling, today is our seventh in the trenches,' Sgt. Gustav Sack wrote from Hardecourt on 5 November. 'We look like pigs in the proper meaning of the word, a layer of mud a centimetre thick – no exaggeration – sticks to greatcoats, tunics and trousers … If the disgusting newspapers say: "slowly gaining ground" that means we advance 50–60m[etres] towards the enemy by digging for two nights!' Sack was a journalist, but he described himself recoiling from almost everything he read in German newspapers about the nobility of the war and the trench experience. He felt that he could never put pen to paper to describe what he had experienced in France: 'all those who go around talking about "writing something great after witnessing war" are talking rubbish'.

On 24 December George Jeffreys wrote, on the morning after relieving a unit in the line during darkness: 'I went round early. The water up to my waist in some places. Daylight showed our trenches to be very badly sited as well as full of water and mud … The country quite flat and featureless, and intersected with dykes … the Germans can overlook us … It took me over two hours getting along the line, wading a good bit of the way.' Robert Harker was in the same condition: 'It's extraordinary out here at this game, we lose all accounts of time both the day of the week and date, it all seems to be reckoned by the way we go into the trenches and then come out for rest … The mud … is extraordinary. It has a lot of clay and mineral matter in it and it goes into a thick paste like bird-lime with tremendous suction in which feet stick. Five men in another section got stuck and bogged in a communication trench up to the firing line and it was 7 hours before 3 of them were got out … by kneeling on faggots out of a hedge and scraping the mud away from their legs and feet with our hands … The mud sticks on to one's clothes, overcoat, trousers and equipment in half-inches of depth and we have almost double the weight to carry, it is almost impossible to keep one's rifle in working order as it all gets coated and clogged.' Harker endured several more months of this purgatory before death delivered him.

François Mayer began the autumn by writing cheerfully home to his wife: 'We are happy, very well fed. Of course there are plenty of moaners – *grognards* – but I would say that men's morale is generally better than it was at the start of this thing. Some violent socialists have passionately rediscovered patriotism.' Only a few men had started to mutter about deserting, he said, though some Prussians in the opposing trenches did so, coming forward with raised hands and crying out, '*Vive la France! C'est atroce!*' Interrogation revealed complaints of poor rations and ill-treatment by their officers. But as weeks went by and the weather worsened, Mayer's spirits flagged along with those of millions of others. On 31 October he took part in an attack in which most of his company fell before the survivors were ordered to retreat: 'It was then that our luck ran out. Scurrying back, all three of my *copains* were hit: Chabrier fell shot in the head; Dufour was wounded and died a few hours later; Blanc received three bullets in his haversack.'

Mayer found himself prey to a growing sense of futility, intensified by each new operation in which he participated. 'Yesterday we made a feint attack to draw German reserves into our area,' he wrote from Rosières, south-east of Amiens, on 29 November, 'and thus assist a real attack near

Quesnoy-en-Sarterre. It was unenjoyable from my viewpoint. After our guns had put down several salvos on the enemy, he opened an intense fire after which ten men led by a sergeant advanced about sixty metres from our lines. This provoked a rain of incoming shrapnel. After about an hour, our ten men returned, but the enemy bombardment continued until evening. What was it all for? I don't know. In the company, one man was killed and two wounded, for meagre results.' Col. Wilfrid Abel-Smith was appalled to read Lord Kitchener's prediction that the war would be protracted, observing disbelievingly, 'It is impossible to believe that the world can stand such a thing for two years.'

All the armies found it necessary to employ sanctions to maintain discipline. When at last Frank Richards's unit secured a respite from the line, its commanding officer exploited this to inflict extra route marches – delayed imposition of punishments given to all those, including officers, who had straggled – dropped out and fallen behind – during the retreat from Mons. Even a man who had taken part in a bayonet charge with another unit had to march, cursing profusely. In rest billets, the same martinet administered No. 1 Field Punishment to soldiers found guilty of disciplinary offences. Instead of being lashed to a wagon wheel – the usual procedure – the men were tied to railings outside a factory in Houplines. Local women gathered around, some to sympathise, others to mock. One man said he didn't mind doing field punishment, 'but he didn't want a bloody lot of frog-eating bastards gaping at him'.

Every nation imposed some capital sentences for battlefield flight or desertion, though the Germans executed far fewer of their own men than did the allies. Lucien Laby witnessed the shooting of a Frenchman from a cyclists' regiment, convicted of abandoning his post in the face of the enemy: 'He dies courageously, unbuttoning his tunic and saying, "My dear comrades, aim at my breast not my head."' The victim refused a blindfold and shouted at the last, 'Long live France! Long live Alsace!' Edouard Beer described a hideously botched Belgian execution: two condemned men were lashed to posts, and at the order a ten-strong firing squad unleashed a volley. One victim fell, but when the doctor examined the other he found him still alive, and muttered to the officer in command, who in turn told off a corporal to deliver a *coup de grâce*. After a shot, the doctor checked the man again – and found him still clinging to life. This time the officer seized the corporal's rifle and himself ended the wretched victim's sufferings. Beer wrote: 'The officers retired, the men cut down the corpses. All were profoundly impressed. I heard one say, "Ah! I'd rather have my head blown off by a German shell than be ignominiously carved up by an incompetent brute.'"

Boredom and immobility prompted trench-dwellers to pursue whatever diversions they could contrive within the confines of unit positions. Frank Richards wrote: 'A pukka old soldier's Bible was his pack of cards.' He and his mates played incessant games of Kitty Nap, Pontoon, Brag and Crown & Anchor. Sgt. Alf Brisley spent a week carving the regimental crest of the Hampshire Regiment into the chalk face of a quarry below the Chemin des Dames – French and German soldiers later made their own artistic contributions alongside his own. Edouard Cœurdevey marvelled at the spectacle of a dozen men engrossed in a makeshift game of bagatelle, professing indifference to spasmodic shells landing in the vicinity. At last a near-miss caused them to raise their heads, and one exclaimed irritably, 'Those imbeciles are trying to wreck our game.'

Static warfare created a market for new skills. A well-known French painter named Guirand de Scévola, serving as an army telephonist, conceived the notion of camouflaging artillery with material designed explicitly to blend in with local terrain features – rocks, grass, trees. After the Marne he secured the support of Poincaré and Joffre for implementing his ideas. 'I used the same methods as the cubists,' he wrote later. He mobilised the assistance of fellow painters: Forain, Dunoyer de Segonzac, Albert Laurens, Abel Truchet, Devambez, Boussingault, Dufresne, Camoin, Jaulmes, Braque and Roger de la Fresnayne, together with the sculptors Despiau, Bouchard, Landowski. Camouflage became ubiquitous. André Mare taught the technique to the British, and kept notebooks in which he depicted his own masterpieces in watercolour: observation posts sited in artificial trees and faked ruins.

'We no longer take heed of the dead – we care only for the living,' wrote François Mayer on 28 November. 'That is what debases this human sacrifice. No one has seen anything who has not seen war, eaten beside corpses on which the crows are preying, laughing and chatting with our comrades as we do so. It is utterly terrifying.' Edouard Cœurdevey also noted this callousness: he came upon a German sitting upright against his rucksack, who had bled to death slowly enough to put a groundsheet over his head against the rain. 'He had also had time to take from his overcoat a photograph of his young wife and two chubby little daughters.' Cœurdevey was shocked that his own compatriots not merely declined to bother burying the German, but mocked his condition by drawing moustaches on the figures in the photograph that his dead hands clutched. A French sergeant wrote to his wife in December: 'during the pause at the front the stretcher-bearers went past carrying a dead man a few metres from us and while some looked to see who it was, others remained calmly playing cards as if nothing had happened'.

Sgt. Gustav Sack gazed out from his trench at Hardecourt on a vista of French corpses, a fortnight unburied, whose only merit was that night patrols could scavenge rations from their haversacks. 'One opens the tins half-carelessly, half-shaking with disgust, then eats. *Dulce et decorum est pro patria mori*. Dreadful, very dreadful. If only one could get drunk, mindlessly drunk!' Trench walls, dug with such hard labour, collapsed in the relentless wet. When it rained long enough, dugout roofs likewise fell in, 'so we can wallow like pigs'. Thoughtful men expressed unremitting revulsion at all that they saw around them. German gunner Lt. Adolf Spemann wrote from the Somme front on 1 November:

> In this beautiful autumn light, the view across the plain is really pleasant, despite its uniformity. But everything is messed up, the landscape seamed for miles by ribbons of trenches and dugouts; one thinks of it as a single trench line stretching from Dunkirk to Verdun. The whole plain looks dead and empty ... a few cows graze the fields; over there on enemy territory, you can see peasants ploughing and an occasional vehicle.
>
> Tomorrow Thiepval church steeple is to be demolished. It is a long-standing aiming-point for French gunners, and thus endangers the whole position. Steeples are favoured observation posts, and thus special artillery targets. Charges are being laid in Pozières tower, too, to be detonated immediately in the event of an enemy barrage. Amid all the devastation before our eyes, we give hourly thanks that we brought this war into the enemy's territory. If this was our homeland, how would those beasts treat it?

Alois Löwenstein echoed Spemann's thoughts: 'Poor inhabitants! I always think: thank goodness the war is not being fought in our country.' The German military authorities contemplated the vast destruction already evident in France and Belgium, and recognised that when the war ended there would be a row about who was to blame. In December, OHL gave orders that occupied towns and buildings should be photographed, to show them intact. If they were later destroyed, Germany could prove that the allies were responsible.

Sigmund Freud, though a civilian, recognised the unprecedented savagery of the conflict: 'It is not only more bloody and more murderous than any previous wars but also more cruel, more relentless, more pitiless ... It discards all the parameters to which we defer in times of peace and which we called the rights of man. It does not recognise the privileges of the wounded man or of the doctor and it does not distinguish between non-combatants and the fighting part of the population.' The International Committee of the Red Cross, based in Geneva, had a staff of just sixteen in September 1914, when the first list of French prisoners held in Germany was issued, which the ICRC was responsible for passing on to Paris. Thereafter, the organisation's staff swelled with its responsibilities, to two hundred in October and 1,200 soon afterwards.

The ICRC became responsible for arranging visits by neutral monitors to all the belligerents' prison camps. These inspectors reported that the Germans, French and British were fulfilling their humanitarian commitments to military PoWs – as the Austrians and Russians did not. In German camps, the French and Russian inmates cohabited quite amiably, giving each other language lessons and discussing their respective cultures. André Warnod, a French PoW, wrote somewhat idealistically that the shared experience 'achieves a fine sort of internationalism from which the Germans are excluded and in which we feel one single heart beat and pulsate'. Alois Löwenstein reported home that wounded French prisoners were more popular than English ones because they showed their appreciation to their German nurses. By contrast the English, he claimed, were 'rude and ungrateful'.

Civilians behind the lines endured varying gradations of hardship at the hands of the armies. For most of the war, artillery fire provided background orchestration for the townspeople and villagers of south-western Germany and eastern France. Many innocents were shot as alleged spies. Local people often asserted that their own army displayed as much contempt for property as did the enemy. Belgian Pte. Charles Stein had an altercation with a farmer, one of his fellow countrymen, who complained bitterly about soldiers stealing straw to sleep on. Stein suggested that if the Germans were in their place, they would give him a much harder time. Not so, said the farmer doggedly, 'we had Germans here before you came and they were good people who paid for everything they took'.

In enemy-occupied eastern France, however, two million civilians were subjected to a relentlessly harsh regime, which caused them to refer to the land beyond the lines as 'Free France'. The Germans imposed their own time zone, one or two hours ahead of Paris according to the season. A few bold spirits contrived to escape westwards because, as a citizen of Fontaine au Pire wrote, 'living at Fontaine was no longer France – we were living by German time'. Passes were required for all travel, public gatherings were banned. The occupiers devised a range of extortionate financial levies. Yves Congar, a boy living in Sedan, had to see his family's dog killed to escape a German tax on pets.

The occupiers ignored the provisions of the Hague Convention and conscripted tens of thousands of civilians for forced labour. One old man of seventy-four was obliged to sweep the streets of Lille in all weathers, 'scarcely fed, exposed to both sides' shellfire. He patiently endured a harsh form of slavery.' A priest likewise described how all age groups and both sexes were set to work, 'the children to mind their animals and pick apples, while young girls had to sweep the streets, the stables, houses occupied by Germans; others to work in the fields or stitch machine-gun belts. Meanwhile the young men were set to digging graves in which to bury the many dead brought back from the front.'

Not all the occupiers behaved brutally to their unwilling French hosts. At Cannectancourt in October, medical officer Lorenz Treplin organised a boys' race in the village which attracted a crowd of both soldiers and civilians – the winner was awarded a prize of peppermint candy. When a tearful woman came to protest about soldiers removing her cow, saying that she had to nurture both a one-year-old baby and a ninety-year-old grandfather, Treplin wrote: 'After I convinced myself that both alleged milk-consumers were real, we returned the cow to her on the understanding that she would provide us with several litres of milk daily. With that, all parties were satisfied.' During the long winter lulls between offensives, the medical officer opened his surgery to local people, who rewarded him with pears.

Maurice Delmotte, an elderly farmer in Fontaine, described how at first German officers billeted in French homes would eat with their weapons handy. But as both unwilling hosts and lodgers grew to understand that the war might last a long time, most families contrived accommodations with 'their' Germans. Paul Hub, a soldier billeted in the Belgian village of Pipaix, wrote to his wife Maria asking for a pocket French-German dictionary: 'The people are very friendly and kind to us.' Paul Kessler was stationed in Lille, where he worked in the army postal service. He recoiled in dismay from the harsh tone adopted in a German–French phrasebook issued to occupying troops. Men entering billets were invited to address their involuntary hosts with such lines as: 'Show me to my room immediately' ... 'This cruddy hole? How dare you!' ... 'Open all the doors immediately' ... 'I shall hold you liable for ...' The phrasebook had been compiled in Berlin long ago, for the enlightenment of soldiers serving with victorious occupation forces. Kessler found himself perusing the 33rd edition, issued in 1913. He wrote to his wife Elise: 'Great – you can be happy if you do not belong to the other side. I have never adopted such a tone ... It is possible to be both friendly and vigilant.'

Georg Bantlin, a twenty-six-year-old staff surgeon who was also his regiment's billeting officer, found himself wrestling with the problem of accommodating in the small Belgian town of Ronquières (pop. 7,000) two headquarters staffs, an infantry regiment, two ammunition trains, an artillery detachment, and two medical companies – in all, almost 5,000 men and seven hundred horses. Ordinary soldiers slept on straw, laid on the floor of almost every living space. Only officers were allocated beds, and ate in a local château. Bantlin wrote home: 'We eat in the magnificent dining room overlooking gorgeous gardens ... Carefully-prepared dinners and superb wines eaten off a nobleman's service taste a little different from field-kitchen soup eaten with tin spoons off tin plates. We make rather a sharp contrast to our surroundings: nailed boots tread on beautiful Persian carpets. Our weather-worn uniforms clash strangely with silk-upholstered armchairs, Flemish leather wallpapers and old Gobelin tapestries.'

Posters in the streets of every occupied community assured the inhabitants that they had nothing to fear so long as they respected German regulations; contrarily, if these were breached they would be shot. Initial attempts were made to persuade men voluntarily to enlist for labour service, which in 1916 became compulsory and brutally harsh. Local roll calls were held twice weekly in every community. Some Germans behaved entirely correctly to their French and Belgian hosts, and were usually repaid in kind. Others, however, seized whatever property took their fancy. One soldier wrote to a friend of an experience east of Laon: 'We take from the French population all their lead, tin, copper, cork, oil, candlesticks, kitchen pots ... which are sent off to Germany. I had a good haul the other day with one of my comrades. In a walled-up room we found fifteen copper musical instruments, a new bicycle, 150 pairs of sheets, some towels and six beaten-copper candlesticks. You can imagine the fuss made by the old hag who owned them. I just laughed. The commandant was very pleased.'

Paranoia, not merely about *francs-tireurs*, but also about duplicitous pigeons bearing messages to the French lines, infected the entire German army. Adolf Spemann in Lorraine noted in his diary that fulfilling an order to shoot down all passing pigeons 'has become quite a popular sport'. 'A flock took wing in the village behind us and flew straight and fast towards the west. These poor minxes now cop it, too, but that's better than Germans [dying].' The occupiers inflicted savage communal punishments on communities they believed guilty of harbouring *francs-tireurs*. On 19 October Lt. Hans Rensch, a Leipziger serving in a rail-construction company, drove through the village of Orchies, which had been put to the torch ten days earlier: 'It is a heap of ruins. I saw a sobbing woman with her small child standing in front of the remains of her house. It's such a shame and misery. I nearly broke down as I saw some twenty women and children digging around in the ruins of their homes. But what's the use? If the population acts bestially against wounded [Germans allegedly attacked by *francs-tireurs*] the whole locality has to be burnt. The guilty ones are hard to find, the 99% who are innocents must suffer. A nameless misery has come upon the French people. And what will [this place be like] in winter?' Rensch's scruples did not extend to property, however: when a friend from home offered to send some comforts for his men, the lieutenant dismissed the idea, saying that they were already spoilt for good things, for the French were obliged to supply them with anything they wanted. 'We never find ourselves short of clothing or food. Our men "discover" those things France does not hand over. Our fellows have a flair for that. They ferret out the loveliest stuff even in wrecked villages.'

One day early in December, the regiment of Louis Barthas, the former barrel-maker from Aude, exulted on receiving orders for their relief, with departure at 4 a.m. for rest billets in Mazingharbe. But lips curled in cynicism when, as they marched joyfully to the rear, they halted four miles from Mazingharbe and were issued with two days' rations. They understood that they were to fight once more. Their officers told them they would attack at dawn. Barthas wrote bitterly: 'So this was to be our rest; yes – eternal rest for some ... But why this ridiculous comedy, this hateful trickery. What do they fear, a mutiny perhaps? They value us so highly that they think us capable of some small gesture of protest as we are led to the abattoir. We were not citizens but a herd of beasts of burden.' Their bitterness intensified when they learned that their own assault was designed merely as a diversion, to cover a British attack on La Bassée and a French operation against Arras. 'Oh *Patrie*, what crimes are committed in your name!' lamented Barthas.

Carnage followed: the regiment became pinned down by fire as it advanced across a field of sugar beet, 'providing mere target practice for the Germans'. Barthas found himself struggling vainly to staunch the wounds of a comrade whose cheeks, tongue and entire jaw had been torn open by shrapnel. After a night spent carrying the wounded to the rear in the absence of stretcher-bearers, Barthas's unit renewed their assault next morning. Their officer, Lt. Rodière, became wildly excited and apparently drunk. He strutted along their trench under a barrage waving a German bayonet and promising to 'skewer the Boche with his own steel'. A few minutes later he was dead, hit as he peered incautiously over the parapet.

In several French units there were the first spasms not of mutiny, but of resistance to such mindless follies. 'Some reservists,' wrote François Mayer, 'have lost the habit of discipline, and indicate to their leaders that they don't care to advance under fire under their command – some speak of going to join another company, properly run.' As Louis Barthas gazed upon the horrors before him, he thought savagely about 'all those pictures of battle which adorn the walls of our museums or illustrate the pages of our history books, in which commanders are depicted on plumed horses, amid waving flags, bugles, drums, cannon sounding, illuminated by heroic frenzy and intoxication. Where are our great commanders and even our lesser ones today? Holed up in some dugout with their ears to a telephone.'

Robert Scott-Mcfie had left the British Army as a sergeant in 1907 after seven years' service, then at the age of forty-six re-enlisted in the Liverpool Scottish on the outbreak of war, and went to France in November. His company's early experiences of the trenches were as ghastly as most. 'We are none of us particularly well,' he wrote to his father on 23 December, 'and the whole battalion is weakened by an epidemic of diarrhoea which has been going on for several weeks.' Marching forward along broken and waterlogged roads, 'a pitiable number of men dropped out, unable to keep up … my first misfortune was to fall into a deep ditch full of water, right up to the waist. A little later I tumbled on my face in the deep slime, and with a heavy pack on the back … had some difficulty extricating myself.' On reaching the line, the battalion immediately became engaged in a brisk firefight which cost a stream of casualties. Beyond the losses, wrote Scott-Mcfie gloomily, nobody seemed to care 'that all our clothes are soaked, that we shall not have an opportunity of drying them for weeks, that half

our equipment is lost, our rifles clogged with mud, etc … There will not
be much left of the Liverpool Scottish soon … It is amazing to me that I
am among the survivors considering my age.'

German soldier Kresten Andresen wrote, after seeing a town in Picardy
looted by his comrades: 'How brutal and ruthless war is! The finest values
are trampled underfoot – Christianity, morality, home and hearth. And
yet, in our time, there is so much talk about Civilisation. One is inclined
to lose faith in civilisation and [other] values when they are not shown
more respect than this.' Rudolf Binding described the scene of desolation
in Flanders, then reflected despairingly: 'everything becomes senseless, a
lunacy, a horrible bad joke of peoples and their history, an endless reproach
to mankind, a negation of all civilisation, killing all belief in the capacity
of mankind and men for progress, a desecration of what is holy, so that
one feels that all human beings are doomed in this war'.

Neither side had a monopoly of brutality. On 5 October Lucien Laby
was in charge of an escort taking fourteen German prisoners to the rear,
when their little column was suddenly beset by Senegalese troops determined to cut off the Germans' ears. After a violent scuffle, the colonial
soldiers were driven back. One big Senegalese saluted Laby and said wistfully, 'O my lieutenant – you might have let me cut off two ears … just two
ears!' A French army chaplain, while applauding the terror that such colonial infantry inspired among the Germans, deplored the difficulties of
dealing with their wounded as patients at his hospital: 'the blacks from
North Africa are almost as civilised as their Berber or Arab compatriots …
[but] there are others from West Africa and the French Congo … who are
very primitive indeed'. Few Moroccans, Tunisians, Algerians and the like
even spoke the language of their colonial masters. A wounded Sudanese
resisted being undressed, and when being treated 'roared like a wild animal
and bit the nurse's hand badly … taken next day to the operating theatre
for the draining of the wound, he looked curiously at the tube of ether and
put it to his nose himself'.

A sense of shared victimhood was evolving among men of all the
warring armies which progressively grew to transcend, in the minds of
more than a few, commitment to a national cause. British officer Wilbert
Spencer described an encounter with German prisoners: 'An awfully nice
lot of fellows. I was awfully popular, having simply crowds round me
listening to my excellent German pronunciation. I had long talks with all
and promised to go over to Berlin after the war to drink a bottle of Lager
with them. They said they wished I could come oftener. They of course

were rather dirty after fighting and travelling but were really a gentlemanly lot on the whole.' The socialist anti-militarist Jean Petit wrote in a later narrative of his own life as a PoW of the Germans: 'French, Belgians, Russians, English all sleep jumbled up together. It is a new Tower of Babel. Each nation has its good and bad points; some are good, honest and clean, others are aggressive, rapacious and disgusting. They were our enemies once and today they are our allies. Neither they nor we know why. We are but toys or puppets.'

Alois Löwenstein wrote home in November, reflecting on the fact that his unit had occupied the same positions for four weeks, then added presciently: 'Curious. We thought we had come for four days. Will the whole war last for four years because we reckoned on four months?' A sinking sense of the enormity and intractability of their predicament suffused millions of men of the rival armies, sunk into their unlovely earthen homes.

18

Silent Night, Holy Night

The approach of Christmas 1914 prompted profound reflection among the peoples of Europe, both at home and on foreign fields. If they had ever doubted the gravity of the course to which their governments had committed them, they did so no longer. In Vienna, Sigmund Freud, who in July had greeted the struggle with enthusiasm, now wrote with revulsion of 'these wretched times, this war, which impoverishes as much in spirit as in material goods'. Richard Meinertzhagen, an officer serving with British forces in East Africa, was confused by an amiable truce meeting with the Germans at Tanga: 'It seemed so odd that I should be having a meal today with people whom I was trying to kill yesterday. It seemed so wrong and made me wonder whether this really was war or whether we had all made a ghastly mistake.' Helene Schweida wrote from Bremen to her boyfriend serving on the Western Front: 'Everybody's mood today is deeply depressed. Even the otherwise happy expectations of the children have been dampened a little.' Each nation's civilians dispatched vast quantities of seasonal gifts to its soldiers: the city of Frankfurt's contributions alone filled fifty rail wagons.

Sobriety characterised year-end press comment. The *Daily Mail*'s editorialist wrote: 'the Allies in the west have spent the latter half of 1914 in meeting and beating off the German onslaught upon the capital of France. Their task in 1915 is to clear the whole of France of the enemy and to regain Belgium ... Their attainment by repeated and incessant attacks when all the military conditions favour the defence will in itself demand from us, as from the Belgians and the French, an enormous effort.' If such assertions represented a tiptoe towards realism, they fell short of recognition of the view now privately adopted by some senior soldiers, Falkenhayn prominent among them, that forcing an outcome on the battlefield might take years, if it was achievable at all.

To sustain popular support for the war on the German home front, a parade of optimism was deemed essential. The Berlin newspaper *Vossische*

Zeitung claimed that it was clear why the German people were bound to win: 'Stronger nerves! ... Stronger nerves in this unprecedented world war will guarantee victory, conferring an advantage in a situation in which the odds are otherwise even.' Tsar Nicholas had predicted at the outset that it would be very hard to stop a conflict once it began, and this was emphasised by the progressive escalation of all the belligerents' war aims. A new slogan became popular in Germany, '*Siegfrieden*' – 'Peace through victory'. This must be a peace dictated by the winners, rather than brokered by negotiation, and the same spirit was evident across much of Europe. Every national leadership wanted the killing – and the vast expenditures – to stop, but only when sufficient gains had been secured to justify the sacrifices of 1914.

Britain and France committed themselves to the destruction of 'Prussian militarism', which meant ensuring that post-war Germany would lack the industrial and military means to start another war. They rejected an early attempt at mediation by America's President Woodrow Wilson, arguing not unreasonably that any outcome which failed to shackle or cripple the *Kaiserreich* merely promised a renewal of the conflict at German convenience. This seems entirely rational, but caused the allies more questionably to conclude that in order to be able to dictate appropriate terms to Berlin, total victory was necessary, followed by punitive economic measures, which were explicitly intended to secure their commercial advantage in the post-war world. President Poincaré favoured the creation of an occupied buffer zone between the Moselle and Rhine. On 21 December Théophile Delcassé, the foreign minister, telegraphed to the Russian government, emphasising France's commitment: 'The French army will not limit its effort even to the frontier of Alsace-Lorraine, but will keep marching ... until a day when the allied governments can obtain for their nations all legitimate reparations, and institute a new dispensation in Europe which guarantees the peace of the world for many years.'

The converse of this was, of course, that Germans viewed the struggle in existential terms. The words '*sein oder nichtsein*' – 'to be or not to be' – were constantly on people's lips. They anticipated, correctly, that defeat must presage the abasement of their nation. If the war had not begun as a struggle between Western European democracy and Central European conservatism, it had at least partly assumed such a character. The Germans had no initial programme for world domination, but the fact of war caused their leaders both to recognise the dire consequences of defeat and to frame increasingly ambitious schemes to be implemented in the event of victory. Bethmann Hollweg remained committed to securing political control of Europe by economic means, with only limited territorial acquisitions. But many of his foremost compatriots, especially industrialists and bankers, rejected his notions of a mere European customs union, and were insistently enthusiastic about annexations. Falkenhayn in particular, though he had no designs on the Russian Empire, became a 'maximalist' on Western issues, with far-reaching designs for permanent conquest.

By the September Declaration of London, the allies had committed themselves not only to forswear separate peace deals, but also to secure common consent for any specific peace condition one party might aspire to impose. Mutual Anglo-French suspicions persisted about rival aspirations for extending post-war empires. There was consternation in Paris when a rumour reached ministers that the British were negotiating for the Japanese to dispatch forces to the Western Front in return for being granted Indochina, jewel of the French colonial empire. It was true that the Western allies were eager to bring a Japanese army to Europe, and that Tokyo rejected this notion in the absence of large incentives; but neither a satisfactory bribe nor any Japanese troops were forthcoming. In November the allies began to consider the distribution of the spoils of the Ottoman Empire once its owners had been beaten on the battlefield, an issue that would precipitate increasingly tortuous Anglo–French negotiations in 1915–16. The French were bent on having Syria. Beyond Britain's own shopping list, Asquith agreed to meet Russia's principal demand, that the Tsar should take Constantinople and the Dardanelles.

All the belligerents wrestled for moral high ground. The *Daily Mail* in the last days of the year contrasted the barbarity of the German naval bombardment of Scarborough with the alleged decency of a British Christmas air attack on naval targets at Cuxhaven (though this had failed to hit anything at all): 'There are some people who still pretend that, war being essentially inhuman, the more or less of ruthlessness and cruelty injected into its conduct does not matter. The contrast between Cuxhaven and Scarborough is the best answer to their trivial case. It is a contrast which shows that the inevitable miseries of war can, on the one hand, be restrained and limited, without any loss of military advantage, when it is waged by gentlemen and sportsmen, and on the other hand can be indefinitely extended, when it is waged by Germans.'

The atrocities in Belgium and northern France make this claim seem marginally less absurd than does the language in which it was advanced.

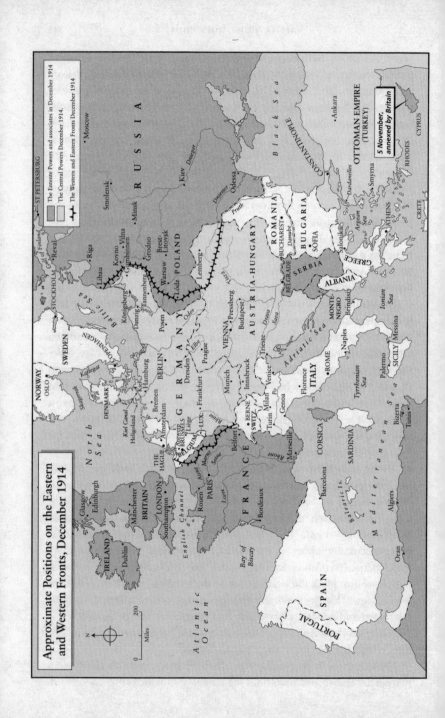

Approximate Positions on the Eastern and Western Fronts, December 1914

ST PETERSBURG

The Entente Powers and associates in December 1914

The Central Powers December 1914.

The Western and Eastern Fronts December 1914

5 November, annexed by Britain

OTTOMAN EMPIRE (TURKEY)

N

0   200

Miles

Atlantic Ocean

IRELAND
Dublin

BRITAIN
Glasgow
Edinburgh
Manchester
LONDON
Southampton

English Channel

NORWAY
OSLO

SWEDEN

Skagerrak

Kattegat

DENMARK
Kiel Canal
Heligoland

STOCKHOLM

Baltic Sea

North Sea

THE HAGUE
Amsterdam
BELGIUM
BRUSSELS
LUX.
Liège

Bremen
Hamburg
Kiel
BERLIN
Dresden
Prague
Frankfurt
Munich
Innsbruck

GERMANY

Elbe
Oder
Rhine

Königsberg
Danzig
Tannenberg
Posen

COPENHAGEN

Libau
Riga
Reval
Gulf of Finland

Kovno
Vilna
Gumbinnen
Grodno
Warsaw
Brest-Litovsk
Łódź
Lemberg

POLAND

Minsk

Smolensk

Kiev
Dnieper

Moscow

RUSSIA

St Petersburg

Belfort
PARIS
Rouen
Aisne
Marne
Seine
Loire
Bordeaux
Marseille

FRANCE

Bay of Biscay

Rhône

BERNE
SWITZ.
Turin
Milan
Genoa
Venice
Trieste
Florence
ROME
Naples
Palermo
Messina

ITALY

CORSICA

SARDINIA

SICILY

Tyrrhenian Sea

Adriatic Sea

Po

VIENNA
Pressberg
Budapest

AUSTRIA-HUNGARY

Drau
Save

Dniester
Pruth

ROMANIA
BUCHAREST
Danube

BELGRADE
SERBIA

MONTE-
NEGRO
Brindisi

ALBANIA

BULGARIA
SOFIA

Salonika
GREECE
ATHENS

Ionian Sea

Black Sea

Odessa

CONSTANTINOPLE
Dardanelles

Ankara

Smyrna

Aegean Sea

CRETE

RHODES

CYPRUS

SPAIN

PORTUGAL

Barcelona
Balearic Is.

Algiers
Oran

Tunis
Bizerta

Tunis

Mediterranean Sea

Although the Western allies made moral compromises, and like all belligerents in every war were guilty of local lapses of conduct, they behaved
significantly better than did the Central Powers. In the East the Russians'
persecution of Jews, in 1914 and especially during their 1915 long retreat,
constitute a deep blot upon their record. But no major massacres of civilians were ever laid at the door of the British, French or Italians to match
those repeatedly committed by the Germans, Austrians and Turks. The
Germans later became responsible for recruiting large numbers of Belgian
and French men in occupied regions as slave labour, under atrocious
conditions. The Central Powers claimed that the allied economic blockade
inflicted such privations on their peoples that this too constituted a war
crime. It is certainly true that the legality of the blockade, especially as
rigorously enforced from 1917 onwards, was disputable. Nevertheless,
blockade seems to belong to a different moral order of conduct from the
deliberate murder of civilians.

The dominant realities at the year's end were the failure of either side
to achieve a strategic breakthrough in East or West, and the commitments
of both to renew offensives as soon as weather conditions and ammunition supplies permitted. While every military leadership was chastened by
its experiences of 1914, none was ready to acknowledge outright failure,
though Falkenhayn's personal views will be discussed below. A modest
number of ordinary citizens, almost all socialists of varied hues and
nationalities, believed that no purpose, honourable or otherwise, could
justify the cost. The peacemakers argued that it was preferable to abandon
the struggle, whatever the political consequences of doing so, than to
persist with the destruction of European manhood, wealth and culture.
This view commands widespread popular support in the twenty-first
century, but ignores huge practical and moral obstacles.

Machiavelli observed that 'wars begin when you will, but do not end
when you please'. Could any responsible allied government have negotiated with Germany and Austria such a peace as the Kaiser, together with
his generals and ministers, sought and continued to seek? Nations which
have paid the huge moral, political and financial price for entering a
conflict are seldom interested in quitting it as long as they think they
might win. Bethmann Hollweg in 1917 became a belated convert to a
compromise peace, but was obliged to resign when Ludendorff's alternative view prevailed, that Germany must continue to strive for victory. It is
important to recognise that beyond territorial war aims at the expense of
the allies, German leaders were acutely sensitive to their enemy within. A

key factor in Berlin's original decision to fight had been a desire to crush the perceived domestic socialist menace, by achieving a conspicuous triumph over Germany's foreign foes. Any outcome that threatened to concede political ascendancy to the socialists – which meant anything less than a clear victory – was unacceptable.

In France and Britain, while many people yearned with increasing fervour for peace, few would have supported a settlement that rewarded the Central Powers – and why should they have been expected to do so? The arguments for resisting German dominance of the continent were no less strong in December than in August, even if the cost had risen steeply. Hundreds of thousands of families had already lost loved ones. It is incontrovertible that the First World War was a catastrophe for Europe. It remains hard to see, however, by what means its statesmen could have extracted themselves from the struggle once it began, in advance of a decision on the battlefield.

It seems mistaken to suppose that, if Britain had unilaterally held aloof or withdrawn, almost certainly making possible the victory of the Central Powers, the consequences would have been benign, even for the narrow self-interest of the subjects of King George V. The 'poets' view', that the alleged merits of the allied cause became meaningless amid the horrors of the struggle and the brutish incompetence of many commanders, has been allowed drastically to distort modern perceptions. Many British veterans in their lifetimes deplored the supposition that Wilfred Owen or Siegfried Sassoon spoke for their generation. One such revisionist was Henry Mellersh, who declared that he wholeheartedly rejected the notion 'that the war was one vast, useless, futile tragedy, worthy to be remembered only as a pitiable mistake'. Instead, wrote the old soldier in 1978, 'I and my like entered the war expecting an heroic adventure and believing implicitly in the rightness of our cause; we ended greatly disillusioned as to the nature of the adventure but still believing that our cause was right and we had not fought in vain.'

Whether or not a modern reader endorses Mellersh's view, it was far more widely held by his contemporaries than the 'futility' vision of Owen, Sassoon and their kind, none of whom ever outlined a credible diplomatic process whereby the nightmare they so vividly depicted might be ended. Almost every sane combatant recoiled from the miseries of the battlefield, voicing the revulsion articulated by so many soldiers in these pages. But their sentiments should not be misread as indicating that such writers consequently wished to acquiesce in the triumph of their enemies.

How best to avert this? As winter deepened, each belligerent war leadership contemplated the future. A bitter debate raged within the British government about whether to tighten the absurdly loose blockade upon Germany. Lord Fisher and the Admiralty were eager to mine the North Sea, to stem the huge flow of commodities including coal, food and American cotton, which was a key component for explosives manufacture, But Grey and the Foreign Office stubbornly resisted a dispute with the USA, which claimed that sustaining its cotton exports – for instance – was essential to its own economy. The Foreign Secretary and several other ministers also rejected tough policies towards Holland, through which huge quantities of supplies reached Germany. It would be deeply embarrassing, they argued, to act harshly against one neutral nation, having gone to war in support of the sanctity of its neighbour.

Some influential voices argued for abandoning the blockade, on the grounds that it was ineffectual as well as diplomatically damaging. Ministers were dismayed to discover that American consular officials in Europe were actively assisting the passage of freight to Germany in collusion with shippers, while neutral Italy was supplying the Central Powers with grain and rubber. Grey, whom the war had rendered profoundly melancholy and increasingly erratic, produced a bizarre personal suggestion: to allow luxury goods into Germany so that it wasted its foreign exchange on buying them. There were additional fears in Whitehall that a ruthless blockade would precipitate the collapse of the entire global financial system, with especially disastrous consequences for Britain. In consequence of all these arguments and doubts, in October the British almost abandoned their blockade. This was an extraordinary development, since before 1914 the Admiralty had expended much energy on planning economic warfare as Britain's principal weapon against Germany. In December, British ships were discharging food at Rotterdam, of which a substantial proportion found its way into the stomachs of Britain's enemies. Only in 1917, when the United States entered the war, did the allied blockade belatedly become a critical instrument in forcing Germany to its knees.

Meanwhile, in the British government's debate about its strategy, John Horne and Alan Kramer have written that by 1916 'war as a military process threatened to dwarf the moral and political significance of its outbreak'. This was already true at Christmas 1914. Any romantic ideal professed by soldiers in August was dead, displaced by huge and bewildering new realities. A eulogy for the old way was pronounced by Winston Churchill, who wrote with characteristic wit and only mild self-parody: 'It is a shame that War should have flung aside [cavalry charges] in its greedy, base, opportunist march, and should turn instead to chemists in spectacles and chauffeurs pulling the levers of aeroplanes or machine-guns ... [Politicians] let war pass out of the hands of the experts and properly-trained persons who knew about it, and reduced it to a mere disgusting matter of Men, Money and Machinery.' These last words reflected the sincere nostalgia of many senior soldiers, though their civilian compatriots might have riposted that the professionals' conduct of operations in 1914 was scarcely an endorsement of their claims to ownership of the conflict.

The BEF now deployed 270,000 soldiers, organised as a cavalry corps under Allenby and two armies, one commanded by Haig, the other by Smith-Dorrien. Since August it had lost 16,200 officers and men killed, 47,707 wounded, 16,746 missing or taken prisoner. Forty-seven heirs to noble titles had perished, many of them among 150 dead Old Etonians, 15 per cent of the school's final wartime loss. These casualty figures seemed terrible enough to the British people, but remained small by comparison with those of the other belligerents, reflecting the country's relatively modest 1914 contribution to the war. Later, of course, everything changed: by the time of the armistice, and as a consequence of conscription, almost six million men – a quarter of Britain's adult male population – had passed through the ranks of the army, and about one in eight had perished.

On 20 December Sir John French paid a brief visit to Walmer, on the Kent coast, to meet Asquith and Kitchener. The prime minister and his cabinet colleagues found it irksome to be obliged so largely to entrust the courses of the government and the fortunes of the nation to its generals, alien beings, but who else was there with any understanding of military affairs? Asquith was also increasingly exasperated by the public indiscretions of senior officers, optimists and doomsayers alike. He wrote: 'The authorities should ... clap a padlock on the tongues of all fighting men – whether Generals or Admirals.'

Kitchener was incorrigibly remote from his fellow men, and few found his company congenial: young Cyril Asquith contemplated the field-marshal's ruddy, densely-veined features, and observed with disdain that 'his cheeks resemble a map of the Polish railway system'. However, the victor of Omdurman, though a limited human being who had once proposed to dispatch the skull of the long-dead Dervish leader the Mahdi from Khartoum to London for public exhibition, was no fool – and a great deal more sensible than the BEF's commander-in-chief. Cyril Asquith's sister Violet, who was also staying at Walmer, told her friend Rupert Brooke that Sir John French was 'amazingly optimistic about things, much more so than either Father or K[itchener]. [The C-in-C] detected great signs of "strain" in the Germans – says he has taken practically nothing but professors prisoners for the last 3 weeks! ... He thought it quite on the cards a sudden collapse might take place & the whole thing might be over in April or May without anyone getting anywhere sensational – like Berlin!'

Here was further evidence of French's threadbare judgement, founded in a conviction that the spring offensives planned by the Western allies could yield a decisive outcome. It was astonishing that the BEF's commander had not been sacked for his deplorable conduct since August, especially before and during the Marne battle. He wrote in November about France's commanders in unpardonable terms for an allied C-in-C in the field: 'au fond they are a low lot, and one always has to remember the class these French generals mostly come from'. But he kept his job because the government was confused about how to fight the war. Many of its members, including Churchill, still harboured delusions that Sir John was a competent commander, let down by pusillanimous allies. Even Kitchener had felt compelled to praise French to the House of Lords in September for displaying leadership, 'calm courage' and 'consummate skill', a travesty of the truth. Sir John's egregious misconduct – for his tenure of command in 1914 amounted to nothing less – did not alter the course of history, because forces far larger than the BEF determined outcomes. But his continuance as C-in-C through 1915 was a misfortune for those whom he led. His successor Haig, unsympathetic human being though he appears to modern generations, and by no means one of history's great commanders, was an abler manager of armies.

Asquith himself inclined towards optimism, inspired more by events on the Eastern than the Western Front. He confided to Venetia Stanley after the Walmer weekend: 'There seems to be some solid reason for thinking that Austria wd. like to make peace on her own account.' His mind sometimes wandered strangely. He told Stanley that one winter night he dreamed he had been supplanted at Downing Street by Herbert Samuel, about whom he quoted Prince Hal: 'A Jew, an 'Ebrew Jew!' Lacking energy and instincts for warmaking, Asquith nonetheless clung to office until December 1916. An apologist might best say that the French, Russian, German, Austrian and Italian governments displayed no greater wisdom than Britain's Liberal administration during the first years of the conflict.

Elsewhere in the cabinet, Churchill displayed unflagging enthusiasm for the fray, but now feared a stalemate on the Western Front which would leave millions of fighting men 'chewing barbed wire'. The prime minister wrote on 5 December: '[Winston's] volatile mind is at present set on Turkey & Bulgaria, & he wants to organise a heroic adventure against Gallipoli and the Dardanelles: to wh[ich] I am altogether opposed.' Churchill himself was increasingly bored and frustrated by his role at the Admiralty, and yearned for a military command. He argued after the war that it was a great mistake no Anglo-French strategy conference was held in the winter of 1914, and was probably right. Inter-allied cooperation was organised piecemeal, with initial emphasis more on how to fund the war than on how to fight it. Britain's allies took the view that, since its manpower contribution was relatively small, it could at least pay a lion's share of the bills – as indeed it did, especially through loans to France. Meanwhile, however, nothing was done to resolve the serious problems created by divided command. Only in the desperate circumstances of the March 1918 German offensive did the British do what they should have done forty-four months earlier, placing their armies under a French supreme commander, Foch.

Britain's most brilliant orator and most popular Liberal politician shared Churchill's belief that the Western Front was stalemated. Lloyd George already harboured a private scepticism about allied generalship which would mature into contempt, writing to Asquith: 'I am uneasy about the prospects of the War unless the Government takes some decisive measures to grip the situation. I can see no signs anywhere that our military leaders and guides are considering any plans for extricating us from our present unsatisfactory position. Had I not been a witness of their deplorable lack of prevision I should not have thought it possible that men so responsibly placed could have so little forethought.'

The Chancellor favoured opening a Balkan front: contributing men and resources to support operations by the Serbs, Greeks and Romanians, and seeking to strike at the Turks through Syria. His view that a more imaginative military leadership could have found a way to avoid heavy casualties and achieve an early victory over the Central Powers was almost certainly mistaken, but he passionately adhered to it for the rest of his life. Churchill in lesser measure shared his opinion, writing after the war: 'Battles are won by slaughter and manoeuvre. The greater the general, the more he contributes in manoeuvre, the less he demands in slaughter.' He himself retained into the Second World War a delusion that if sufficiently ingenious military means were employed, victory might be secured at modest cost. But in twentieth-century conflicts between powerful industrial states, he was wrong.

In *The General*, C.S. Forester's brilliantly contemptuous 1936 portrait of a British wartime officer, the novelist likened the commanders of World War I to savages, striving to extract a screw from a piece of timber by main force, assisted by ever more fulcrums and levers. It was such a pity, wrote Forester, that they failed to grasp the fact that had they instead twisted the screw, it might have been withdrawn with a fraction of the effort. This view of wartime generalship, which was essentially also that of Churchill and Lloyd George, has commanded widespread favour ever since. But what if, as most scholars of the conflict today believe, it was impossible to 'turn the screw', to identify any credible means for breaking the stalemate?

The attempt to defeat Turkey through an assault on the Dardanelles was probably a chimera, with little prospect of achieving its objectives even had the Gallipoli campaign been better conducted. Britain certainly had to engage the Turks to protect its vital imperial interests, for instance on the Suez Canal, but it is very questionable that the 1915 allied operations could have contrived a Turkish surrender, even had they secured the gateway to the Black Sea. Russia would have benefited importantly from freedom to ship exports abroad, especially grain. But it remains implausible that the Tsarist regime could have been saved, the war won on the Eastern Front, by dispatching arms through the Straits. Russia's institutional military incompetence represented a huge handicap. Moreover, in 1915–16 the Western allies were chronically short of munitions to supply their own armies, far less to re-equip Russia's forces on a scale sufficient to alter history, though some powerful voices in London favoured allowing Russian soldiers to fight with British-made arms, as a cynical alternative to the enlargement of the British Army on the Western Front and consequent 'butcher's bill'. Anglo-French operations against Turkey, and the subsequent pillage of the defeated Ottoman Empire, exerted a profound influence on the destinies of the Middle East, but very little upon the outcome of the conflict.

The Western Front was the cockpit of the war, and in such clashes as those of 1914–18, it was almost inevitable that a vast amount of dying had to be done before a decisive outcome became attainable. The same was true in 1939–45: much-diminished Western allied losses reflected not better leadership than that of the earlier conflict, but the fact that the second time around, the Russians bore the overwhelming burden of necessary sacrifice. On the only occasion that a large Anglo-American army went head to head with the Wehrmacht on a limited front, in Normandy in 1944, some infantry rates of loss were briefly comparable with those of 1916, until the German line was broken and Eisenhower's armies could exploit their terrific mobile capability, such as did not exist in World War I.

Among the commanders of 1914, Joffre, especially, merits extreme censure for his Plan XVII assaults. But had France's C-in-C lacked his elephantine stubbornness – or strength of purpose, if you will – the subsequent successful Marne counter-offensive would not have taken place. In the winter of 1914, following his supremely important triumph in the battle of wills with Moltke outside Paris, Joffre's standing as director of France's war effort was unchallenged. Ypres, in October, showed that Falkenhayn had no more successful formula than his allied counterparts for conducting attacks. Germany's army was institutionally superior to those of its enemies, but none of the Kaiser's generals displayed genius: even Ludendorff, a master tactician, proved a dismal strategist.

Allied commanders from September 1914 onwards laboured under the fundamental handicap that in order to regain occupied Belgium and eastern France they were obliged to attack, while the Germans could exercise at will their privilege of adopting the defensive, yielding ground when it seemed advantageous to do so. Winning Britain's share of the war on the battlefield became in 1916–18 the responsibility of Sir Douglas Haig, who succeeded Sir John French as commander-in-chief. Haig's thinking was powerfully influenced by his experience at Ypres in October 1914. Recalling how close the Germans had come to breaking through, he deduced that determination and persistence – superiority of will – could yield decisive results to an attacker who displayed such qualities. But at no time before 1918 does it today seem plausible that any of the rival successive offensives on the Western Front could have proved a war-winner. Only with the exhaustion of Germany, American entry into the war and a remarkable improvement in the operational methods of the British Army – for which Haig can claim significant credit – did victory become attainable.

There was never a credible shortcut. As George Orwell wisely observed a generation later, the only way swiftly to end a war is to lose it. The Western Front's generals' reputations would stand higher today had they exercised greater economy with lives and less conspicuous callousness about the loss of them, but it is hard to see how they could have broken the stalemate. Until 1918, the fundamental options before the Western allies were those of acquiescing in German hegemony on the continent, or of continuing to bear the ghastly cost of resisting this. It was, and remains, a huge delusion to suppose that a third path existed.

France would pay dearly for becoming the foremost theatre of war. The nation eventually mobilised the largest number of soldiers of any belligerent – eight million – and suffered the most grievous proportionate losses of all the great powers – 1.3 million dead from metropolitan France, or 16.5 per cent of those conscripted. By comparison, Germany lost 15.4 per cent, Britain 12.5 per cent, Austria-Hungary 12.2 per cent, Russia 11.5 per cent and Italy 10.3 per cent. French deaths amounted to 3.4 per cent of its entire population, a proportion exceeded only by Serbia and Turkey – the latter's toll was inflated by the self-inflicted horror of more than a million Armenians massacred by their Turkish compatriots. A further three million French soldiers were wounded: 40 per cent of all conscripts became casualties of one kind or another, including one in five officers. But in December 1914, while Frenchmen acknowledged the misery of their predicament as readily as their counterparts in every other nation, they retained deep reserves of will and commitment, which revealed exhaustion only with the mutinies of 1917.

In the Hapsburg Empire, many of Franz Joseph's subjects recognised the war as a disaster; the Russians cherished hopes that Hungary might make a separate peace. By December the Austrians, having suffered a million casualties including 189,000 dead fighting the Russians, mustered only 303,000 combatants on the Galician front. Conrad urged Berlin that a great victory was still attainable if Germany contributed more troops, but also gave a dire warning that his nation's war effort could collapse by spring if these were not forthcoming. The Russians, in their turn, believed that one more big heave in Galicia could complete Austria's defeat, although there was rival support in the Stavka for a new offensive into East Prussia. While Russians were dismayed by their losses, and there was widespread despondency about the conflict throughout the Tsar's empire, no articulate faction save that of the revolutionaries was yet pressing for peace at any price.

That winter, by far the most serious dissension at the summit of any national leadership took place in Germany. The Kaiser complained that he was excluded from strategic decision-making. 'The General Staff tells me nothing and doesn't ask me anything either,' he asserted petulantly on 6

November. 'If they are under the impression in Germany that I am leading the army, then they are very much mistaken.' But Wilhelm retained one important power: that of appointing and dismissing the chief of staff who issued orders in his name, as commander-in-chief. This critically influenced strife between the Kaiser's generals which persisted for the rest of the war.

Germany's officer corps would spend the next quarter of a century seeking scapegoats for the army's historic failure to deliver victory in 1914. Moltke was obviously the foremost candidate, but Falkenhayn's prestige was severely damaged by the losses incurred during his unsuccessful October offensive on the Belgian front. In the last four months of the year Germany suffered 800,000 casualties, including 18,000 officers; 116,000 of these men were killed. The chief of staff wrote of the Kaiser: 'His Majesty is in a very depressed mood. Is of the opinion that the attack on Ypres has failed and come to grief, and with it the campaign ... It is a moral defeat of the first class.' Moreover, Falkenhayn's own confidence in the Central Powers' ability to prevail over the Entente was severely shaken.

His drastic solution was to seek a separate peace with the Russians, imposing cash reparations but no territorial forfeits. He believed that if German forces in the East could be shifted to the Western Front, the French would soon crack. He saw Britain as Germany's 'arch-enemy', sharing the view expressed by the *Vossische Zeitung*: 'The driving force of the world war is England. That is today plainly proved and everywhere recognised. Millions of innocent people [suffer in the cause of] mercantilism – *Krämergeist* – the enrichment of London's merchants and their disdainful lust for mammon. War is simply business for England, a commercial competition designed to destroy its rival, in this case Germany, by means of warfare.'

On 18 November, Falkenhayn presented to Bethmann Hollweg his proposal for closing down the Eastern Front. The chancellor was appalled. In contradiction of the chief of staff, he himself had always regarded Russia as the irreconcilable menace to German interests. Rejecting any outcome of the struggle that left Russian power unbroken, he drew Falkenhayn's attention to the allies' September pact, whereby each renounced a separate peace. He was also alarmed by Conrad's warnings that without fresh German aid, Austria-Hungary might collapse. Early in December, Bethmann paid a visit to Hindenburg's headquarters, where he discussed all these matters with Ludendorff. The bleak, driven, highly-strung general was obsessed with the belief that with more forces he could defeat Russia, thus making possible victory in the West. He despised Falkenhayn, and did not even consult or inform him when lending several German divisions to Conrad in January 1915. Ludendorff was hereafter committed to securing the chief of staff's dismissal.

Bethmann returned to Berlin bursting with confidence in the 'Easterners'. Major Hans von Haeften, Ludendorff's liaison officer at the Chancellery, lobbied energetically for Falkenhayn's sacking and replacement by the victor of Tannenberg. Bethmann concurred, but such a step was vetoed by the Kaiser, who asserted passionately that he would never appoint such 'a dubious character' as Ludendorff, 'devoured by personal ambition'. To circumvent Wilhelm, former chancellor Prince Bülow and Grand-Admiral Tirpitz discussed the possibility that he might be declared insane and replaced by his son as regent, with Hindenburg as *Reichsverweser* – imperial administrator. Hindenburg and Ludendorff even for a time favoured recalling Moltke as chief of staff, and their puppet.

Though such conversations came to nothing, they reflected the desperate mood prevailing in Berlin's corridors of power, five months after the German government had enthusiastically embraced European war. If there was stalemate at the front, thereafter there was also stalemate among Germany's leaders. Bethmann became a bitter critic of Falkenhayn – 'a gambler ... an execrable person' – and an enthusiastic supporter of the Easterners' demands for more troops, their insistence that in Poland they could win the war for Germany. More than that, the chancellor was personally responsible for quashing the proposal that the Central Powers should accept the unattainability of victory, and seek peace at least in the East. It was ironic that, while the allies supposed Germany in the grip of Prussian militarism, it was Bethmann the politician who rejected any negotiated compromise in the winter of 1914.

Meanwhile Falkenhayn's personal authority, unbuttressed by any major victory such as Hindenburg and Ludendorff had won, was sufficiently weakened that he had the worst of all worlds. Clever enough to recognise that he bore responsibility for achieving the impossible, he nonetheless kept his post through 1915–16. The chief of staff was obliged to accede to Ludendorff's demands for troop reinforcements at the expense of the Western Front, while enjoying the barren satisfaction of seeing his own judgement vindicated, that these forces would achieve nothing decisive. The Germans defeated the Russians again and again, securing huge swathes of territory and eventually a victory recognised at the February 1918 Treaty of Brest-Litovsk, signed by the Bolsheviks.

Russia suffered a total of 6.5 million casualties in the war – probably the highest total loss of any belligerent, though the statistics are unreliable. But Ludendorff proved mistaken in his belief that defeating the armies of the Tsar could determine the outcome of the entire global conflict. Falkenhayn was right, that Eastern victories were of illusory significance amidst the vastness of Russia. He himself was sacked late in 1916, after his failure to take Verdun. Hindenburg became chief of staff, with Ludendorff wielding real power as First Quartermaster-General. But the Bolshevik revolutionaries, rather than the Hohenzollern Empire, proved the beneficiaries of the disaster that befell Romanov arms.

As Christmas approached, Pope Benedict XV issued a public appeal for a suspension of hostilities over the sacred Christian holiday. Such an idea was quickly rejected by governments and commanders, but their soldiers proved more amenable. The spontaneous truces of 1914 – for there were many on all fronts save the Serb one – have seized the imagination of posterity, as symbolising the futility of a conflict in which there was no real animosity or purpose. Such a conclusion is quite unjustified, because they represented nothing unusual. Interludes of fraternisation have occurred in many wars over many centuries, without doing anything to deter soldiers from killing each other afterwards. The spasms of sentimentality and self-pity displayed in December 1914, nearly all initiated by Germans, reflected only the fact that at Christmas almost every adherent of a Christian culture yearned to be at home with loved ones, while now instead millions found themselves huddled shivering in the snow and filth of alien killing fields. The emotionalism generated by such circumstances caused some men to make brief gestures of humanity before resuming the routines of barbarism willed by their national leaderships.

On 24 December a Bavarian soldier named Carl Mühlegg walked nine miles to Comines, where he purchased a small pine tree before returning to his unit in the line. He then played Father Christmas, inviting his company commander to light the tree candles and wish peace to comrades, to the German people and the world. After midnight in Mühlegg's sector, German and French soldiers met in no man's land. Belgians likewise clambered out of their positions near Dixmude and spoke across the Yser canal to Germans whom they persuaded to post cards to their families in occupied territory. Some German officers appeared, and asked to see a Belgian field chaplain. The invaders then offered him a communion vessel found by their men during the battle for Dixmude, which was placed in a burlap bag attached to a rope tossed across the waterway. The Belgians pulled it to their own bank with suitable expressions of gratitude.

On Christmas Day in Galicia, Austrian troops were ordered not to fire unless provoked, and the Russians displayed the same restraint. Some of the besiegers of Przemyśl deposited three Christmas trees in no man's land with a polite accompanying note addressed to the enemy: 'We wish you, the heroes of Przemyśl, a Merry Christmas and hope that we can come to a peaceful agreement as soon as possible.' In no man's land, soldiers met and exchanged Austrian tobacco and schnapps for Russian bread and meat. When the Tsar's soldiers held their own seasonal festivities a few days later, Hapsburg troops reciprocated.

Along several sectors of the Western Front, a singing competition developed between rival trenches. The German 2nd Guards Division, for instance, sang '*Stille Nacht*' and '*O du Fröhliche*', and hoisted a Christmas tree on their parapet. When the French had made their own choral contribution, the Germans answered with '*Vom Himmel hoch*'. Then the contest became more nationalistic: the French bellowed the *Marseillaise*, the Germans '*Wacht am Rhein*' and '*Deutschland über alles*' before giving three cheers for the Kaiser.

Alexander Johnston wrote laconically: 'my first and I hope my last Xmas on active service'. Near Ypres, Wilbert Spencer 'saw about 9 or 10 lights along the German lines. These I said were Xmas trees and I happened to be right ... On Xmas day we heard the words "Happy Xmas" being called out, whereupon we wrote up on a board "*Glückliches Weihnachten*" and stuck it up. There was no firing, so by degrees each side began gradually showing more of themselves and then two of them came half-way over and called out for an officer. I went and found out that they were willing to have an armistice for 4 hours and carry our dead men half-way for us to bury – a few days previous we had had an attack with many losses. This I arranged and then – well you could never imagine such a thing. Both sides came out and met in the middle, shook hands, wished each other the compliments of the season and had a chat.'

Men of the French 99th Infantry Regiment, which had similar experiences, were affronted to find the truce shattered by heavy German fire on New Year's Day. The following morning a Bavarian lieutenant came over to explain apologetically that his superiors had taken fright about the malign impact of fraternisation on the serious business of winning the war. A German regimental report described another such incident near Biaches, in the Somme sector. Some French infantry waved to the opposing Bavarians, and a French colonel suggested that a German officer should advance to meet him. 'Reserve Lieutenant Vogel, a company commander in the 15th Infantry, walked over. The officers met between the lines. The lieutenant-colonel proposed a truce because of the holiday. Lt. Vogel refused. The lieutenant-colonel then asked at least to bury the body of a fallen Frenchman who had been lying for a long time between the lines. Vogel agreed to this suggestion. The corpse was buried by two French and two German soldiers.' The report regretted the failure of attempts to prevent fraternisation, but assured formation headquarters that several officers and men had been punished for this breach of discipline.

Twenty-year-old Gervais Morillon wrote to his parents: 'The Boches waved a white flag and shouted "*Kamarades, Kamarades, rendez-vous.*" When we didn't move they came towards us unarmed, led by an officer. Although we are not clean they are disgustingly filthy. I am telling you this but don't speak of it to anyone. We must not mention it even to other soldiers.' Morillon was killed in 1915. Elsewhere twenty-five-year-old Gustave Berthier wrote: 'On Christmas day the Boches made a sign showing they wished to speak to us. They said they didn't want to shoot … They were tired of making war, they were married like me, they didn't have any differences with the French but with the English.' Berthier perished in June 1917.

But goodwill was by no means universal. Yves Congar, the ten-year-old French boy living at Sedan who had welcomed the outbreak of war as a fine excitement, now experienced Christmas in German-occupied territory. He wrote in his diary that night: 'We hope that next year will be better than the one we've just had. It is very cold. Dad is being held hostage overnight. There is no midnight mass … Foreign feet trample the old road and everything is silent and gloomy … It is the rule of the strongest. It is invasion and ruin; it is the cry of the hungry who don't even have a crust of bread; it is the resentment against the race that pilfers, burns and holds us prisoners; our country is no longer our home, when our cabbages, leeks and all other goods are in the hands of those thieves.'

The British 2nd Grenadiers lost three men killed, two missing and nineteen wounded on Christmas Day; one further man was hospitalised with frostbite, as were a further twenty-two next morning. On 28 December the battalion's war diary recorded: 'wet and mud awful. Terrible night. Thunder, hail and rain terrific, very high wind, some sniping.' In François Mayer's sector, the Germans in trenches eighty yards distant cried out

'*Français kaputt!*' and suchlike. At midnight on New Year's Eve, they delivered a volley of fire, to which the French replied with a chorus of the *Marseillaise*. Mayer wrote: 'It was moving to hear all those soldiers throwing their warlike voices back at the bullets which were whistling past. When we fell silent, they cried "Long live the Kaiser!"' Rival commanders took care that the Christmas truces were never repeated on the same scale in later war years, but proved unable to prevent many informal local understandings – sustained periods of 'live and let live' by both sides – which became an enduring feature of the conflict on all fronts.

When the war was over, Austrian Lt. Constantin Schneider looked back on his experiences and remarked upon a phenomenon characteristic of most conflicts, but especially that one, after a man's phase of initiation had passed: 'Nothing new happened to me; everything seemed a repetition of sensations experienced before. The war had become a weary business.' Similarly Seaman Richard Stumpf, serving with the German High Seas Fleet, wrote in his diary just after Christmas 1914: 'Nothing happens that deserves notice. Shall I describe each day's duties? Such a record would be identical, day after day.'

On Christmas Eve a French writer named J.J. Chastenet observed in *Le Droit du peuple* that France's churches had been fuller since August than at any time since the middle of the previous century: 'people pray out of fear. As more and more people become accustomed to this war … we shall see fewer people return and things will return to normal.' Chastenet was right. While the first funerals of local war dead attracted attendance by entire village populations, once such events became familiar, congregations dwindled. Earlier in the year, many French rural communities accepted refugees from Belgium and north-west France. By Christmas there were three million such people – a huge burden upon those housing and feeding them. A growing number of towns and villages turned their backs on the outsiders, denouncing them as locusts – dirty or immoral, verminous or unfit for agricultural work.

Back in August local *maires* had solemnly donned their black coats, medals and sashes of office to visit families and announce tragic bereavements. Five months later, many such dignitaries delegated this task to the local teacher. One such, a woman named Marie Plissonier in the Isère village of Lavadens, assumed the former duties of the postman, departed to war, because she seemed the most sympathetic person to deliver ill tidings, such as so often came. She said: 'People reacted differently, of course. Some received the news hysterically, but most reacted with a kind of numbed shock, as if they had expected it in some way.' Thirty of Lavadens' four hundred conscripted soldiers eventually perished, and over a hundred more were wounded. At the village hall Mme Plissonier also presided over regular teach-ins, at which she explained the progress of the war with the aid of maps and newspapers. Initially these sessions were well attended. Later, however, as the fronts congealed, audiences dwindled and even vanished. One day became much like the last, for civilians at home just as for such men as Constantin Schneider on the battlefield.

By the end of 1914, the war had ceased to seem interesting or rewarding to any but a tiny proportion of its participants; it represented instead a profoundly distasteful duty, borne with varying degrees of stoicism. On the Eastern Front, most Hapsburg and Russian soldiers would have been happy to embrace peace on any terms, though their rulers willed otherwise. Among soldiers in the West, however, for all their dismay about their personal circumstances, few were yet ready to despair of victory or to bow to their enemies' demands. For a further forty-six months of struggle they displayed a remarkable willingness to suffer, to obey, and if necessary to perish. It seems a conceit on the part of later generations to assert that in doing so, they exhibited oxlike stupidity. To argue that the Western allies should have accepted German hegemony as a fair price for deliverance from the mudscape of Flanders seems as simplistic and questionable a proposition now as it did at the time to most of those who fought for Britain, France and Belgium. And that was what abandoning the war implied. Not until 1918, after suffering defeat on the battlefield, was Germany ready to abandon its brutal occupation of Belgium and eastern France, to forswear its claims to mastery.

Serbia paid a dreadful price for defying Austria in 1914: in the following year the country was overrun by the Central Powers, the remains of its army forced into exile. Yet much later, after losing possession of their country, adherence to the allied cause enabled the Serbs to achieve one of history's most notable Pyrrhic victories when peace came: they secured their grand ambition, the creation of Yugoslavia, embracing much of the eastern Hapsburg Empire, a state which endured for more than seventy years. Romania too, though it suffered heavily for its 1916 entry into the war on the allied side, gained due rewards at the peace – more lands than it later proved capable of keeping. The Italians embarked on hostilities in 1915 explicitly in pursuit of territorial booty. In 1918 they too received their share of Hapsburg territory, including the port of Trieste, but these lands cost them 460,000 dead. Russian, Hapsburg and German Poles joined together to proclaim themselves an independent state on 7 October 1918, though they had to fight the Russian Bolsheviks until 1921 to hold their borders. On 28 October 1918 a Czechoslovak republic was declared in Prague, and on 1 November Hungary announced its independence from Austria. Finland, Estonia, Latvia and Lithuania also declared themselves independent states.

The United States gained immense economic benefits from selling weapons and goods to the Western allies, and to a lesser degree to Germany, in the first thirty-three months of the struggle. Its entry into the war in April 1917 exercised a critical moral and industrial though marginal military influence on the outcome. The allies were suitably heartened, the Central Powers appropriately dismayed. The American accession of strength more than compensated for the Russians' retirement from the conflict in March 1918. Japan became the only belligerent to emerge from the struggle with exactly the prizes it sought on joining the allies in 1914, acquired at negligible cost in blood and cash. The Japanese thus had better reason than any other people to celebrate their participation. Among the vanquished, the war cost the Hapsburg Empire 1.5 million military dead, Germany two million, Turkey 770,000. The Wilhelmine Empire became a republic with the fall of the Hohenzollern dynasty, as did Austria with the passing of the Hapsburgs. The British Empire lost more than a million dead, over 800,000 of them from the United Kingdom; the Russian and French empires around 1.7 million apiece. The Bolshevik revolution extinguished the Romanovs, leaving Britain's George V as the only major imperial monarch in Europe.

Posterity has puzzled endlessly over how the leaderships of the world's greatest powers, mostly composed of men no more stupid or wicked than their modern counterparts, could first have allowed the war to happen, then continued it for four more years. It seems mistaken to brand the 1914 rulers of Europe, and especially those of Austria and Germany, as sleepwalkers, because that suggests unconsciousness of their own actions. It is more appropriate to call them deniers, who preferred to persist with supremely dangerous policies and strategies rather than accept the consequences of admitting the prospective implausibility, and retrospective failure, of these. The most important immediate cause of the First World War was that Germany chose to support an Austrian invasion of Serbia, believing that the Central Powers could win any wider conflict such action might unleash. The Tsar, his ministers and generals may justly be branded foolish, even reckless, for dooming their own precarious polity by going to war for Serbia, but they reacted to an Austrian initiative, for which moral opprobrium must rest in Vienna. A critical force in precipitating disaster was the institutional hubris of the German army, embodied in the inadequate person of Moltke. A yearning for a decisive outcome in place of successive inconclusive crises suffused the conduct of Vienna and Berlin – and in lesser degree, also that of St Petersburg and Paris.

Yet despite, or perhaps because of, the vast effort lavished upon wartime propaganda, within a decade of the armistice the British body politic which took the nation to war conspicuously lost the confidence of many of those who fought it. Soldiers, especially, recoiled from what they saw as the moral debility of the society to which they returned. Some extended this alienation to the cause for which the struggle had been conducted. The author's grandfather, former gunner officer Rolfe Scott-James, reported an old comrade saying in 1923: 'Some of us can't help thinking that we fought the war for nothing.' Scott-James added: 'There was none of the rage of despair in the speaker's voice. His slight shrug of the shoulder simply expressed his sense of disillusion.' At that time, this was still a minority opinion, in comparison to the faith of Henry Mellersh and his kind, cited above. But in the decades that followed, ever more people embraced the view that the enemies against whom Britain and its allies took up arms had not been worth fighting, as were the Nazis a generation later. These contrasting views were surely powerfully influenced by the fact that the soldiers of 1918 returned from France to a dismayingly unreformed society, which offered them only the most barren fruits of victory, while those of 1945 came home to a Labour government committed to creating the Welfare State. In the twenty-first century, most British people remain extravagantly triumphalist about their nation's role in the Second World War, while seeming extravagantly eager to dismiss the arguments for resisting German aggression in 1914.

The case still seems overwhelmingly strong that Germany bore principal blame. Even if it did not conspire to bring war about, it declined to exercise its power to prevent the outbreak by restraining Austria. Even if Berlin did not seek to contrive a general European conflagration, it was willing for one, because it believed that it could win. The greatest mistake of the German leaders was to view their grand ambitions through the prism of warriors, supposing that power could be secured and increased only through battle, and grossly underrating their country's economic and industrial might. The Kaiser, Bethmann Hollweg and Moltke attempted a stroke of Bismarckian ruthlessness and magnificence, such as Bismarck himself would surely never have made.

Once the struggle had begun, it seems mistaken to suppose, as do so many people in the twenty-first century, that it did not matter which side won. The allies imposed a clumsy peace settlement at Versailles in 1919, but if the Germans had instead been dictating the terms as victors, European freedom, justice and democracy would have paid a dreadful forfeit. Germany adopted territorial war aims in the course of the First World War which were not much less ambitious than those favoured by its ruler in the Second. It thus seems wrong to describe the undoubted European tragedy of 1914–18 as also futile, a view overwhelmingly driven in the eyes of posterity by the human cost of the military experience. If the *Kaiserreich* did not deserve to triumph, those who fought and died in the ultimately successful struggle to prevent such an outcome did not perish for nothing, save insofar as all sacrifice in all wars is just cause for lamentation.

Acknowledgements

I must acknowledge many debts for this book, the first to Clive Harris and Mike Sheil, splendid battlefield guides who in April 2012 conducted me on a tour of the 1914 Western Front from the snowclad ridges of the Vosges to the old floodplains behind the Belgian coast. Christoph Nübel did outstanding work on German and Austrian sources, and will plainly become an important scholar; Pavlina Bobić provided material from Serbia and Slovenia; Serena Sissons trawled French sources; Dr Lyuba Vinogradovna, as for my last four books, produced a mass of Russian accounts. I learned much from the October 2011 conference organised by the German Historical Institute in London under the title 'New Perspectives on the Fischer Controversy'. Josh Sanborn passed on some of his important writings on Russian experiences in 1914. John Röhl generously gave me access to relevant draft passages of his forthcoming book on the Kaiser in the war.

Jack Sheldon shared his unpublished monograph on Le Cateau, and also read and commented upon my draft chapters about the British Expeditionary Force's experience. Gary Sheffield did likewise for my entire manuscript, which reflected extraordinary generosity with his time. My old newspaper colleague Don Berry cast over the text the eye of a layman who is also a splendid critic. I owe gratitude to those who provided me with copies of unpublished contemporary correspondence, including James Illingworth for the papers of his grandfather Percy, Liberal chief whip in 1914; Anthony Gray for the MS of his grandfather Robert Emmet; John Festing for that of his great-uncle Maurice. As for my earlier books, for this one also Professor Sir Michael Howard OM, CH, MC has been throughout a peerless tutor and critic, though he bears no responsibility for either my judgements or my errors. Professor Nicholas Rodger and Matthew Seligmann read and commented upon the draft of the naval chapter, much to the advantage of the final text. Professor Mark Cornwall gave some guidance on Serbian sources. It seems prudent to reiterate my usual caution about all large numbers quoted in my text above, and for that matter in any other historical study: they have been extracted from the best available sources, but must be regarded as indicative rather than precise.

I should also acknowledge thanks which are none the less sincere because common to all my books, to the British National Archive, the Imperial War Museum and the London Library for the invaluable assistance of their splendid staffs. Many collections in Europe likewise made possible the studies and translations of my researchers in France, Russia, Germany, Austria, Serbia and Slovenia. Michael Sissons and Peter Matson have been my London and New York agents for more than three decades, and I value their guidance and advice as much as ever. Arabella Pike and Robert Lacey at HarperCollins in London and Andrew Miller at Knopf in New York supported the project from its inception and have much improved my words during its gestation. My secretary Rachel Lawrence has been assisting my labours for most of the past thirty years, and her energy and commitment never cease to earn my gratitude. My wife Penny endured the writing of this book, like so many others before it, with a fortitude and sympathy that would command the respect of a war veteran.

Notes and References

The following abbreviations are employed in the references below: NA –
British National Archive at Kew; IWM – Imperial War Museum document
collections; ASA – Austrian State Archives (Österreichisches Staatsarchiv,
Kriegsarchiv – OeStA/KA); AS – Arhiv Srbije (Serbian National Archive);
ASC1938 – the British Army staff college study pack on the Battle of Le
Cateau dated 1938, which includes important 1930–33 correspondence
with military eyewitnesses; GW – correspondence with veterans preserved
in the author's files from BBC TV's 1964 *Great War* series; SB – Staatsarchiv
Bremen; NUK – Slovenian State Archive, Ljubljana; GHAC – German
Historical Association October 2011 conference: *New Perspectives on the
Fischer Controversy*. I have omitted references for quotations from the
principals' speeches and statements long in the public record or domain.

xix 'As commandant' Jeffrey, Keith *Field Marshal Sir Henry Wilson: A Political Soldier* OUP
   2006 p.80
xix 'We are readying' Gide, André *Journals 1914–27* trans. Justin O'Brien Secker & Warburg
   1948 p.48
xix 'You soldiers ought' Knox, Sir Alfred *With the Russian Army* Hutchinson 1921 Vol. I p.45

Introduction
xxi 'No part of the Great War' Spears, Edward *Liaison 1914* p.vii
xxiii 'a creative activity' Brenda Horsfield *The Listener* 20.1.72
xxiv 'The war of 1914 was' McMeekin, Sean *The Russian Origins of the First World War*
   Belknap 2011 p.5
xxv 'When an ocean liner' Spears p.9

Prologue
xxxiii 'Excellency!' Morton, Frederic *Thunder at Twilight* NY 1989 p.92
xxxiv 'Never have I' Steed, Wickham *The Hapsburg Monarchy* Constable 1913 p.282
xxxv 'a menace to democracy' Đurič, Silvija and Stevanović, Vidosav (eds) *Golgota i vaskrs
   Srbije, 1914–1915* Beograd 1990 3rd edn p.242 diary of Jovan Žujović
xxxviii 'My dear Dr Sunarić' Dedijer, Vladimir *The Road to Sarajevo* MacGibbon & Kee 1967
   p.10
xl 'He received it with' Dirr, P. (ed.) *Bayerische Dokumente zum Kriegsausbruch und zum
   Versailler Schuldspruch*, Munich, Berlin 1922 pp.114–15

xl 'a dreadful act' Hopman, Albert *Das ereignisreiche Leben eines 'Wilhelminers'. Tagebücher, Briefe, Aufzeichnungen 1901 bis 1920* ed. Epkenhans, Michael Munich Oldenbourg 2004 p.380

xl 'a characteristic bit' Ransome p.166

xli 'Princip is better-looking' Mihaly, Jo ... *da gibt's ein Wiedersehn! Kriegstagebuch eines Mädchens 1914–1918* Freiburg F.H. Kerle 1982 p.26 5.8.14

xli 'there is no sense of grief' Mitrovic, Andrej *Serbia's Great War* Hurst 2007 p.13

Chapter 1 – 'A Feeling that Events are in the Air'

1 CHANGE AND DECAY

1 'What will happen' Churchill, Winston *The Great War* George Newnes 1933–34

1 'The sardonic objectivity' Pound, Reginald *The Lost Generation* Constable 1964 p.12

3 'whether civilization is' Masterman, Charles *The Condition of England* London 1909 p.74

3 'There is a feeling that' Lang, Carl von *Die Lage auf dem Balkan* in: *Danzer's Armee-Zeitung 19* (1914) No 1/2 pp.10–11

4 'Scarcely anything' Churchill, *My Early Life* p.67

4 'we obtain a sum of' BNA FO371/1374 Russell dispatch

4 'Early in 1914, the British' Seligmann *Naval Intelligence* p.535

5 'Durch Kampf zum Sieg' Hirschfeld *Kriegserfahrungen. Studien zur Sozial – und Mentalitätsgeschichte des Ersten Weltkriegs* Essen Klartext 1997 pp.330–1

5 'He was an extreme' Clark, Christopher *The Sleepwalkers* Allen Lane 2012 p.182

6 'He is vanity itself' Hopman p.368

6 'I stood in front of a castle' ibid. p.378

6 'Bismarck ... left a system' Steinberg, Jonathan *Bismarck: A Life* OUP 2011 p.458

6 'He left a nation' ibid. p.479

7 'other large European maritime' Seligmann *Naval Intelligence* p.528

7 'the two white nations' ibid. p.545

8 'rather trying guests' *H.H. Asquith Letters to Venetia Stanley* ed. Michael and Eleanor Brock OUP 1982 14.6.14 p.86

9 'we will not leave Austria' Rohl, John C. *The Kaiser and His Court* CUP 1994 p.175

10 'a system of institutionalised escapism' Stone, Norman *The Eastern Front* Hodder & Stoughton 1975 p.71

10 'It was less a legislature than' Morton p.19

11 'The combination of stateliness' Steed p.202

12 'create for me a new' Lieven, D.C.B. *Russia and the Origins of the First World War* NY St Martin's 1983 p.46

12 'the Straits must become' ibid. p.128

12 'Russia was perfectly' McMeekin p.32

13 'this vast country' *The Lady* 27.8.14

14 'We shall not let' Lieven p.65

15 'Russian youth, unfortunately' ibid. p.15

15 'we are a great, powerless' ibid. p.23

15 'we have become a' ibid. p.21

15 'we saw much martial' Knox p.37

16 'France's Gen. Joseph Joffre' Joffre, Joseph Jacques Césaire *The Memoirs of Marshal Joffre* trans. Col T Bentley Mott Bles 1931 p.59

16 'some of the characteristics' Lieven p.113

16 'without ceasing to' NV 1/14.6.08 p.3

16 'Serbia is, practically' Lieven p.41

17 'shows the activity' ibid. p.42

17 'Within little more' Vivian, Herbert *Servia: The Poor Man's Paradise* Longmans 1897 p.vi

17 'there lies an' ibid. p.236

18 'I am so fond' Reed, John *The War in Eastern Europe* London Eveleigh Nash 1916 p.53

18 'All sorts of people' ibid. p.3

19 'In Paris in June' Becker *Guerre* p.47

20 'The influence of the Church' ibid. p.21

20 'most people had' Minaudier, Jean-Pierre *Population et Société de 1850 à 1914* Lycée La Bruyère, Versailles 2004 p.4

20 'the 1907 census' ibid. p.7

20 'when one in ten' ibid. p.2

21 'Poincaré presented' Becker *Guerre* pp.52–3

21 'The new financier' Dangerfield, George *The Strange Death of Liberal England* Constable 1935 p.211

21 'The English world' Montague, C.E. *Rough Justice* Chatto & Windus 1926 p.49

22 'Everyone seems to have' Dangerfield p.242

23 'we soldiers beat' Wilson, Henry diary 23.3.14

24 'a Roman reserve' Jenkins, Roy *Asquith* Collins 1964 p.52

24 'He was ingenious' Dangerfield p.17

24 'government by a cabinet' ibid. p.49

24 'an intelligent fanatic' ibid. p.79

25 'Very few prime ministers' ibid. p.322

25 'the country is menaced' ibid. p.281

2 BATTLE PLANS

27 'This man could be' Mombauer, Annika *Helmuth von Moltke and the Origins of the First World War* CUP 2000 p.50

27 'Austria's fate will not' Herwig *War* p.45

29 'dark, small' Churchill *World Crisis* Vol. I p.154

29 'Such an ancient' Zeynek, Theodor Ritter von *Ein Offizier im Generalstabskorps erinnert sich*. Broucek, Peter (ed.) Vienna, Cologne, Weimar 2009 p.47

30 'In proportion to' Bihl, Wolfdieter *Der Erste Weltkrieg 1914–1918. Chronik – Daten – Fakten* Wien Böhlau 2010 pp.61–2

30 'he does not draw' Rohl pp.162–3

31 'Three other sources' see ibid. passim

32 'Germany has no reason' Wilson, Keith (ed.) *Decisions for War 1914* UCL Press 1995 p.44

34 'they proposed to make' Becker *Guerre* p.55

34 'England is embracing' Lloyd George, David *War Memoirs* Vol. I Ivor Nicholson & Watson 1933 p.30

35 'Both powers are scarcely' Lieven p.48

35 'Do you trust' Recouly p.104

35 'You are all wrong' Lloyd George Vol. I p.1

35 'It's not the Germans' Sitwell, Osbert *Great Morning* Macmillan 1948 p.297

36 'there was still no' Jeffrey p.97

36 'you have over' Clark p.213

36 'enthusiastic planning' ibid. p.211

36 'Winston Churchill wrote' *My Early Life* p.66

37 'Grey's most recent biographer' Waterhouse, Michael *Edwardian Requiem* Biteback 2013 passim

37 'During the eight years' Lloyd George Vol. I p.46

38 'At a dinner party' ibid. p.48

38 'Sir Edward Grey belongs' ibid. p.97

38 'the grasp of the situation' Henry Wilson diary 9.8.11

38 'a Junker from his' Holroyd, Michael *Bernard Shaw* Chatto & Windus 1997 p.450

39 'our funny little army' Henry Wilson diary 22.11.13

39 'the best & most patriotic' Jeffrey p.76

39 'inconceivable stupidity' ibid. p.80
40 'with a sense of' ibid. p.84
40 'that poisonous' Asquith to Stanley 20.12.14

Chapter 2 – The Descent to War
1 THE AUSTRIANS THREATEN

41 'Joven Avakumović' Avakumović, Joven D. Memoari Izdavačka knjižarnica Zorana
     Stojanovića Sremski Karlovci-Novi Sad 2008 p.587
41 'I noticed especially' ibid. p.589
41 'Down with Serbia' Dirr p.120
42 'leap through fire' Dinić Jovan, 'Stupanje u đački bataljon' in Đurič and Stevanović p.261
42 'We decided on war' Keith Wilson p.13
43 'the man who caused the war' ibid. p.14
43 'if we really saw' Thompson, Wayne C. In the Eye of the Storm University of Iowa Press 1980
     p.74
44 'if war should come' ibid. p.78
44 'In my opinion' Hopman 6.7.14 p.383
44 'personally, I do not' ibid. p.385
45 'However the Serbs' Keith Wilson p.15
45 'No one today can' Mombauer pp.213–14
45 'real success cannot' Kronenbitter pp.485–6
46 'war is not the worst' Mombauer p.122
48 'as if in competition' quoted Verhey, Jeffrey The Spirit of 1914 CUP 2000 p.14
48 'Today, the balance is' Wetterleuchten in Danzer's Armee-Zeitung 19 1914 No 5/6,
     pp.9–10
49 'sailing under the illusion' Poincaré, Raymond Comment fut déclarée la Guerre de 1914
     Flammarion 1939 passim
50 'I can't believe' Paléologue, Maurice An Ambassador's Memoirs trans. F.A. Holt NY George
     H. Doran 1925 p.3
50 'I shall long remember' ibid. p.4
50 'It was Poincaré' ibid. p.3
51 'whenever we have taken' Clark p.209
51 'a sad wobbler' ibid. p.266
52 'Monsieur le Président' Paléologue p.7
53 'Between 14 and 25 July' Hayne pp.272–3

2 THE RUSSIANS REACT

54 'The situation is very' Đurič and Stevanović p.48
55 'What will Russia do?' Strandmann.p.300
55 'Raymond Recouly' Recouly p.94
55 'Everybody's selling everything' ibid. p.95
55 'nobody could think' Krafft-Krivanec, Johanna Niedergeschrieben für euch. Ein
     Kriegstagebuch aus kulturanthropologischer Perspektive Vienna Passagen Verlag 2005 p.47
     10.8.14
56 'We are astounded' Mihajlović 25.7.14 in Đurič and Stevanović p.26
57 'public opinion would not' Lieven p.143
58 'how her family' Emigholz, Bjorn (ed.) Die Tagebücher der Gertrud Schädla 1914–1918
     Verden 2000
59 'In the intervening period' Lloyd George Vol. I p.53
60 'the parishes of Fermanagh and Tyrone' Churchill Vol. I p.193
61 'Russia is trying' Asquith letter to VS 24.7.14 p.125
62 'Sir Ernest Cassell' Thomson, George Malcolm Lord Castlerosse Weidenfeld & Nicolson
     1973 p.35

62 'People are relieved' Gide p.45 27.7.14

63 'Jovan Žujović' AS Jovan Žujović, enota 81.MS diary p.244

64 'in the evening' Riezler diary 25.7.14

64 *'Monsieur le Ministre'* Joffre p.115 24.7.14

64 'That night, French intelligence' ibid. p.116

64 'Today the fate of France' Keith Wilson p.158

65 'On the 26th also' *Russky Invalid* No. 164

65 'Next day all Germans' ibid. No. 163, 27.7.14, Sunday Section 'The Public Life'

65 'The officers' mess silver' Littauer, Vladimir *Russkie gusary* [The Russian Hussars] Moscow 2006 p.126

65 'we noticed mobilisation' McMeekin p.67

66 'Once completed, a message' GW files, private information to the author 1964

66 'War – those letters embrace' SB S 7 97/2-2 Kaisen MS

66 'In spite of your "liberty' Seligmann *Naval Intelligence* p.538

67 *'Vorwärts'* p.15

67 'a wave of the highest' Chickering pp.59–60

67 'unthinkable, horrible' Verhey p.20

67 'you have your information' Recouly p.23

68 'It seems incredible' Bertie, Francis *The Diary of Viscount Bertie of Thame, 1914–1918* ed. Lady Algernon Gordon Lennox Hodder & Stoughton 1924

68 'not impossible that' Keith Wilson p.16

68 'its form was so very' Stojadinović, Milan M. *Ni rat ni pakt* Otokar Kerošvani, Rijeka 1970 p.71

69 'Lord, great merciful' Štrandman, Vasilij N (Basil de Strandman) *Balkanske uspomene* [Balkan Memoirs]. Knjiga I., Deo 1–2, Žagor Belgrade 2009 p.329

69 'The main preoccupation' Joffre p.120

70 *'Mort aux Boches!'* Wencke, Meteling *Ehre, Einheit, Ordnung. Preußische und französische Städte und ihre Regimenter im Krieg, 1870/71 und 1914–19* Baden-Baden Nomos 2010 p.321 Derenne diary 29.7.14

70 'We are getting ready' Gide p.48 28.7.14

71 'Late that night' Clarke, Tom *My Northcliffe Diary* Gollancz 1931 p.60

71 'Paul Cambon said later' Recouly p.45

72 'My darling One' Soames, Mary *Speaking for Themselves* p.96

72 'There is no record' SSA Belgrade 80-7-356-7

72 '30 July will be proclaimed' McMeekin p.73

73 'our prestige in the Slav world' Lieven p.147

73 'You commit a serious error' ibid. p.86

73 'They were just like' Littauer p.127

73 'After a last' Knox p.39

74 'The military measures which' Geiss, Immanuel *July 1914* Batsford 1967 p.132

3 THE GERMANS MARCH

75 'the press and its' Hesse p.2

75 'Moltke told me' Mombauer p.118

76 'We must appear as' Keith Wilson p.39

76 'The Kaiser absolutely' ibid. p.199

77 'There is something crude' Asquith to VS 30.7.14 p.136

77 'Who rules in Berlin' Mombauer p.205

78 'Things are hanging' Bertie diary 30.7.14

79 'It was like a funeral' Flood, P.J. *France 1914–18: Public Opinion and the War Effort* Macmillan 1990 p.10

79 'As soon as the diplomats' Recouly p.110

79 'Henri de Rothschild' ibid. p.111

80 'Only on 3 August' Reichsarchiv (ed.) *Der Weltkrieg 1914–1918, Vol. I* Berlin Mittler 1925 pp.104–5

81 'I want to wage' Mombauer p.223

81 'Played in the garden' Longerich, Peter *Heinrich Himmler: A Life* OUP 2011 p.19

81 'It was a warm, sunny' Verhey p.59

81 'The mood is brilliant' Keith Wilson p.39

81 'it is dreadful' Mombauer 14.6.15

81 'Gottlieb Jagow' Keith Wilson p.28

82 'We were reconciled' Wolff diary 17.2.15

82 'most people were' Verhey p.58

82 'We were half happy' Schädla diary 1.8.14

82 'Now all our fears' ibid. 19.8.14

83 'In a highly nervous state' Bertie diary 31.7.14

83 'like all Parisian drivers' Rioux, Jean-Pierre *La Dernière journée de paix* p.66

83 'just at the moment' ibid. p.68

83 'As I came out' Recouly p.114

84 'Mobilisation is not war' ibid. p.116

84 'no one believed him' ibid.

84 'The populace is very calm' Bertie diary 1.8.14

84 'everything seemed strange' Wharton, Edith *A Backward Glance* NY Appleton-Century 1934 p.336

4 THE BRITISH DECIDE

85 'a civilised people' Jay, John *Freud: A Life* Little Books 2006 p.347

85 'one feels bitter' Stumpf, Richard *Erinnerungen aus dem deutsch-englischen Seekriege auf S.M.S. Helgoland*, in: *Die Ursachen des Deutschen Zusammenbruches im Jahre 1918*, 4th Series, Vol. X, 2, Berlin Deutsche Verlagsgesellschaft für Politik und Geschichte 1928 p.11 2.8.14

85 'no one who was not in Paris' Guard, William J. *The Soul of Paris: Two Months in the French Capital During the War of 1914* Sun Co. 1914 p.12

86 'At a dinner on 31 July' Baring, Maurice *Flying Corps Headquarters 1914–18* Buchan & Enright 1985 p.6

87 'or rather, lack of it' Recouly p.51

87 '*The Economist* warned' *Economist* 1.8.14

87 'I can honestly say' Asquith to VS 1.8.14 p.139

88 'this was the decision' Recouly p.55

88 'Lloyd George sent back' Keith Wilson p.179

88 'At 3 p.m. on 2 August' Recouly p.130

88 'Let us go to mass' ibid. p.128

89 'small countries, such as Belgium' Albert, King of the Belgians *Le Roi Albert à travers de ses lettres inédites 1882–1916* ed. Thielemans and Vandevoude Brussels 1982 p.85

89 'The response was very' Recouly p.137

89 'Oh, the poor fools' Gibson, Hugh *A Journal from Our Legation* NY 1917 p.43

90 'British and French soldiers' see Keith Wilson p.155

91 'the nightmare of' *l'Express* 24.7.14

91 'looked very pale and anxious' IWM 05/63/1 papers of N Macleod

92 'Felt very unhappy' ibid.

92 'Capt. Maurice Festing' Festing MS p.4

93 'Grey's speech ... was splendid' Bertie diary 4.8.14

93 'We were extraordinarily' Recouly p.25

94 'Are you going to go' Clark pp.63–4

94 '*L'Angleterre se dégage!*' Strong p.21

95 'an extraordinary change' IWM 05/63/1 papers of N Macleod

95 'Commence hostilities' Festing MS p.11
96 'What a real piece of luck' Herwig *War* p.31
97 'Am I surrounded by dolts?' Andrew, Christopher *The Defence of the Realm: The Authorized History of MI5* Allen Lane 2005 p.52
97 'Well it's come!' Holroyd p.448 4.8.14
98 'he was glad that the *Anglichanka*' Knox p.xxxv
98 'Now you will give thanks' Šuklje, Fran *Iz mojih spominov II* Ljubljana 1995
98 'On the night of 4 August' Baring p.9
100 'Isabel Hull' Hull, Isabel V. *Absolute Destruction* pp.91–1000
100 'The aim of the war' Soutou, Georges-Henri p.22
100 'Georges-Henri Soutou' ibid. p.22 and passim
101 'it is well understood' ibid. p.30

Chapter 3 – 'The Superb Spectacle of the World Bursting Into Flames'

1 MIGRATIONS

103 'Maurice Hankey' BNA CAB15/5
104 'because it is a Serb custom' Tadija Pejović, '*Dvadesetšesti juli 1914*' in Đurić and Stevanović pp.31–2
104 'Only ignorance can' Oman, J. *The War and its Issues* CUP 1915 p.91
105 'I am sorry' Krafft-Krivanec, Johnanna *Niedergeschrieben für euch. Ein Kriegstagebuch aus kulturanthropologischer Perspektive* Vienna Passagen Verlag 2005 pp.59–60
105 '*Omnium Gallorum fortissimi*' IWM 91/3/1 Edouard Beer MS
105 'The omnipotent state' Kondurashkin, S.S. *Vsled za voinoi* [In the Footsteps of War] Petrograd 1915 p.9
105 'OK boys' Sanborn *Mobilization* p.272
106 'The schoolmaster shouted' Prévost, Alain *Paysan français Ephraim Grenadou* Éditions du Seuil 1966 p.76
106 'it seemed that suddenly' Flood p.7
106 'God gave me strength' ibid. p.12
107 'Papa must go' ibid. p.13
107 'People smiled' Gide p.51
107 'all along the valley' ibid. p.34
107 'Captain the Hon. Lionel Tennyson' IWM 76/21/1 Ms Tennyson
108 'Early casualty lists' Überegger, Oswald (ed.) *Heimatfronten. Dokumente zur Erfahrungsgeschichte der Tiroler Kriegsgesellschaft im Ersten Weltkrieg* Innsbruck UP Wagner 2006 pp.24–5
108 'The call-up of doctors' ibid. pp.405–6
108 'The same was said' Schneider, Constantin *Die Kriegserinnerungen 1914–1919* ed. Oskar Dohle Vienna Böhlau 2003 pp.22–3
108 'Geoffrey Clarke' *The Times* letters 5.8.14
109 'Don't worry too much' GW files G. Galpin letter to the author 7.5.64
109 'talking excitedly about' Egremont, Max *Forgotten Land: Journeys Among the Ghosts of East Prussia* Picador 2011 p.75
109 'Where the devil' Recouly p.36

2 PASSIONS

110 'We have never lost' Mihaly p.15 2.8.14
110 'We eat white rolls' ibid. p.16 2.8.14
112 'The mock warfare' Clarke p.64
113 '[The people of Britain] feel and know' *The Times* 6.8.14
114 '*Norddeutsche Allgemeine Zeitung*' NAZ 22.8.14
114 'In Paris knitwear shops' Rioux pp.63–4
114 'Bernard Shaw found himself' Holroyd p.449

115 'Shaw remained impenitent' ibid. p.453
115 'Many German restaurants' *Berliner Geschichtswerkstatt* p.161
115 'In Münster, a notably' Nubel p.80
116 'In Belgrade several men' Slavka Mihajlovic 17.9.14 in Đurič and Stevanović p.140
116 'there will be a good many' Bertie diary 7.8.14
116 'During the last' *The Times* 22.8.14
116 'Asta Nielsen' Verhey p.84
116 'Austrian soldiers in Mostar' ASA MS Matija Malešić, War Diary 1914 p.44
116 'Animals!' *Stahl und Steckrüben. Beiträge und Quellen zur Geschichte Niedersachsens im Ersten Weltkrieg (1914–1918)* Vol. I Hamelin Niemeyer 1993 p.75 3.8.14
117 'one was delighted' Kondurashkin p.8
117 'When two days' newspapers' ibid. p.10
117 'To be sure, some clashes' *Stahl und Steckrüben* p.117 19.8.14
117 'This 1905 work' Gudehus-Schomerus
118 'the grandeur of the times' Krafft-Krivanec p.59
118 'war, war, the *Volk* has arisen' Thompson p.96
118 'Gertrud Bäumer' Verhey p.128
118 'feeling of confidence' IWM 05/63/1 papers of N Macleod
119 '*The Economist* asserted' *The Economist* 8.8.14
119 'A.P. Herbert' Turner, E.S. *Dear Old Blighty* Michael Joseph 1980 p.26
120 'England was innocent' Tomalin, Claire *Thomas Hardy* Penguin 2006 p.332
120 'I've often known' Wallace, Stuart *War and the Image of Germany* John Donald 1988 p.74
120 'who worked themselves' Emmet MS, family collection, lent to the author
121 'The haste with which' *Berliner Geschichtswerkstatt* pp.165–6
121 'issued an abrupt' Bonham-Carter, Violet *Champion Redoubtable: The Diaries and Letters of Violet Bonham-Carter 1914–45* ed. Mark Pottle Weidenfeld & Nicolson 1998 p.7
121 'a stronghold of penury' Playne, Caroline *Society At War* Allen & Unwin 1931 p.100
121 'Gustav Mayer' Niedhart, Gottfried (ed.) *Gustav Mayer. Als deutsch-jüdischer Historiker in Krieg und Revolution 1914–1920. Tagebücher, Aufzeichnungen, Briefe*, Munich Oldenbourg 2009 pp.314–15
122 'In the German countryside' Verhey p.92
122 'This war ought to' IWM 07/63/1 GCF Harcourt-Vernon papers 6.8.14
122 'By 8 p.m. on 5 August' Mallinson, Allan *The Times* 10.9.2011
123 'Hello, pastor' Verhey p.75
123 'We have to learn' Palmer, Svetlana and Wallis, Sarah (eds) *The War in Words* Simon & Schuster 2003 p.44
123 'It was an undignified' Muggeridge, Kitty and Adam, Ruth *Beatrice Webb* Secker & Warburg 1967 p.206
124 'This is the greatest fight' Holroyd p.447
124 'The Catholic Archbishop of Freiburg' Chickering *Urban Life* p.73
124 '*Germania delenda*' Ransome, Arthur *Autobiography* Cape 1976 p.169
124 'Long live the Tsar' ibid. p.273
124 'a fruitless venture' Neiburg, Michael *Dance of the Furies: Europe and the Outbreak of World War 1* Belknap 2011 p.132
124 'There isn't nowadays' Lieven p.21
124 'Reservists are producing' Sanborn, Joshua *The Mobilization of 1914* p.275
125 'Will I be able to' Wittgenstein, Ludwig *Geheime Tagebücher 1914–1916* Vienna Turia & Kant 1991 p.13
125 'Dispatched to serve' ibid. p.17 15.8.14
125 'Please keep my washing' Palmer and Wallis p.19
126 'The plan of invasion' Boyle, Andrew *The Riddle of Erskine Childers* Hutchinson 1977 p.198
126 'The atmosphere on board' ibid. p.201

3 DEPARTURES

127 'loud staccato voice' Lloyd George p.83
127 'walk through them' ibid. p.63
127 'my inability to stomach' Palmer and Wallis p.20
128 'What a cosmopolitan' ibid. p.21
128 'The Times published' The Times 22.8.14
128 'The young females' GW files Lt. Col. G.B. Hamley to the author 16.5.64
128 'Nineteen?' GW files Stephen Lang to the author 1964
131 'What is this' Clarke p.65
131 'I trembled at the' Haig, Douglas War Diaries and Letters ed. Gary Sheffield and John Bourne Weidenfeld & Nicolson 2005 p.54
133 'I know that French' ibid. p.56
134 'Quick, Monsieur l'Abbé' Painter, George Marcel Proust Pimlico 1996 p.217
134 'Within the echoing' ibid. p.217
135 'Suddenly a cheer' Chickering Urban Life p.67
135 'Behind the army' Hirschfeld, Gerhard et al. (eds) Kriegserfahrungen. Studien zur Sozial- und Mentalitätsgeschichte des Ersten Weltkriegs, Essen Klartext 1997 p.41
135 'Leb wohl!' Mihaly pp.24–5 4.8.14
135 'Women bade them' Kondurashkin p.13
135 'As the horses and men' Littauer p.129
135 'They would simply' ibid. p.128
136 'Among the Irish Guards' officers' Thomson p.83
136 'We'll die hearty!' Strong p.128
136 'At 5 a.m. on 3 August' Stein MS IWM 86/30/1
136 'Jože Cvelbar' NUK/R, J. Cvelbar, Ms 1774
136 'Goodbye, my rooms' Lacouture, Jean De Gaulle: The Rebel 1890–1944 Collins Harvill 1990 p.29
136 'unknown adventure' ibid. p.26
137 'If there is any justice' Mombauer p.233
137 'I can only think about' Palmer and Wallis p.53
137 'so small and thin' Farmborough, Florence Nurse at the Russian Front: A Diary 1914–18 London 1977 p.17

Chapter 4 – Disaster on the Drina

138 'The sound of gunfire' Đurić and Stevanović pp.35, 37
138 'The war that Austria-Hungary' ibid. p.45 et seq.
139 'is dear to every Serbian' Vivian p.198
139 'More than America' Kronenbitter pp.484–5
139 'Perhaps for the first time' Jay p.346
140 'to play with absolutely' Herwig War p.52
140 'Commanders neglected' Kronenbitter p.87
141 'waging war means' ibid. p.107
141 'not to be despised' The Times 27.7.14
142 'We are all peasants' Reed p.47
142 'Živan Živanović' Živanović in Đurić and Stevanović p.50
142 'These are to bury' ibid. p.32
143 'Once ensconced' Strandman p.323
143 'We were still oblivious' Stojadinović p.72
143 'Many seized what' Milutinović, Sveta Kako se u Beogradu živelo prvim danima svetskog rata p.39
143 'I felt how much the Old' Đurić and Stevanović p.52
143 'As soon as the gunfire' ibid. pp.121–2
145 'Jovan Žujović' Žujović diary p.246

145 'On Monday we marched' ASA MS Matija Malešič War Diary 1914
145 'If we go on like' ASA B 1600/6: Alexander Koloman Maria Pallavicini *The Serbian Campaign 1914* 6.8.14
145 'If this story is true' Kisch p.31 10.8.14
146 'big, buzzing flies' ibid. p.33
146 '*Herrgott!*' ibid. pp.34–5 12.8.1
146 'The whole horizon' ASA Pallavicini, Alexander *Markgraf Pallavicini B 1600*
146 'Though the enemy was' Kisch p.40 14.8.14
146 'Alex Pallavicini reported' ASA B1600/6 AKM Pallavicini 14/15.8.14
147 'apparently contented' Kisch p.36
147 'our moral and numerical' Gumz, Jonathan *The Resurrection and Collapse of Empire in Habsburg Serbia 1914–18* CUP 2009 p.46
147 'On 16 August, for instance' Kisch p.46
148 'An hour later' ASA Pallavicini MS diary B 1600/6
148 'Hangmen presented' Holzer, Anton *Das Lächeln der Henker. Der unbekannte Krieg gegen die Zivilbevölkerung 1914–1918* Darmstadt Primus 2008 p.101
148 'I met a column' ASA B 1600/6: Alexander Koloman Maria Pallavicini MS diary, 'The Serbian Campaign 1914'
149 'Lütgendorf without further' Holzer pp.133–7, 141–4
149 'the population, among them' Gumz p.47
150 'such a way of fighting' ASA Pallavicini MS 18.8.14
150 'resembling a strongly-struck' ASA B609 Bachmann MS
150 'The Austrian commissariat' Kisch p.50 16.8.14
150 'as if they wanted' ibid. pp.41–2
150 'I looked wistfully' ibid. p.43
150 'Hirtenberger Patronen-' ibid. pp.127–8 19.9.14
152 'amid horrendous heat' ASA Matija Malešič, War Diary 1914
152 'The army is beaten' Kisch pp.59–61
152 'The road is strewn' ASA B1600/6 AKM Pallavicini
153 'The army is beaten' Mitrovic p.69
153 'We feel heartache' Krafft-Krivanec p.63 17.8.14
153 'Wonderful!' ibid. pp.75–6
153 'thirty Serb battalions' ibid. pp.77–8 23.8.14
153 'One said that 8,000' ibid. p.84
153 'our generals are inept' Kisch p.64 20.8.14
154 'This represented 71 per cent' ibid. pp.69–70
154 '[our men] suffer terribly' Lampe p.51
154 'The heart stops' Krafft-Krivanec p.85 24.8.14
154 'The impression made' Lampe p.50
154 'Everyone lapsed from' Kisch pp.77–9 29.8.14
154 'Austrian officers responded' ibid. p.79 29.8.14
154 'is indeed the best' ibid. pp.92–3
155 'welcomed Serbian troops' Đurič and Stevanović pp.250–1
155 'Sir E. Grey presents' SSA, Belgrade 10-7-419
155 'Every unit was provided' Kisch p.73
155 'Water doesn't feel' ibid. p.94 7.9.14
155 'Of Kisch's platoon' ibid. pp.98–9
156 'How hungry I am' ASA MS Matija Malešič, War Diary 1914
157 'Our Serbs fight' Mitrovic p.75
157 'Such an order' ASA B 609 Bachmann MS
157 'because they too can' ibid.
158 'first came a strong guard' ibid. 15.10

Chapter 5 – Death with Flags and Trumpets
1 THE EXECUTION OF PLAN XVII

159 'The dust clung' Lintier, Paul *My Seventy-Five: The Journal of a French Gunner* Peter Davies 1929 p.28

160 'It is critical that' Herwig, Holger *The First World War: Germany and Austria-Hungary 1914–18* Arnold 1997 p.35

161 'As line after line' Herwig, Holger *The Marne* Random House 2009 p.111

162 'Next day schoolchildren' Kuhr, Elfriede *There We'll Meet Again: The First World War Diary of a Young German Girl* Gloucester 1998 p.31 7.8.14

162 'stupor and tranquillity' Gudenhus-Schomerus pp.53–4

162 'But then I shan't' ibid. p.61 20.8.14

162 'You cannot think' IWM 99/41/1 MS Letters Madame Jeanne van Bleyenberghe

163 'When the local burgomaster' Horne, John and Kramer, Alan *German Atrocities 1914: A History of Denial* Yale 2001 passim

163 'It doesn't matter' ibid. p.17

163 'Graf Harry Kessler' Kessler, Harry Graf *Das Tagebuch Vol. V 1914–1916* ed. Günter Riederer and Ulrich Ott Cotta Stuttgart 2008 p.87

164 'Ruthless destruction' Schwarte, Max (ed.), *Technik des Kriegswesens* Leipzig Berlin B.G. Teubner 1913 p.115

165 'That's what happened' Blond, Georges *La Marne* Presses de la Cité 1962 p.23

165 'Pte. Charles Stein' IWM papers of C Stein 86/30/1

165 'A company of German reservists' Mahnke, Dietrich *Kriegstaten und Schicksale des Res.-Inf.-Regiments 75 1914/18* Bremen 1932 p.17

166 'They really look like' Gudenhus-Schomerus p.66 28.8.14

167 'This difference in visibility' Miguel, Pierre *L'Année 14* pp.104–5

167 'They told me that' Herwig *Marne* p.78

168 'in an indescribable disorder' Miguel p.110

168 'In the evening news spread' Krafft-Krivanec p.183

168 'For so long' SB S7 Kaisen Collection, 97/2–3

169 'Millions of men' Rivière, Jacques *Carnets 1914–1918* ed. Isabelle and Alain Rivière, Pub. Fayard 1974 p.16

169 'Lucien Laby' Laby, Lucien *Les Carnets de l'aspirant Laby, médecin dans les tranchées 28 juillet 1914 – 14 juillet 1919*, Editions Bayard 2001 p.19

171 'lay siege to Strasbourg' Delabeye, B. (Lt) *Avant la ligne Maginot. Admirable résistance de la 1ère armée à la frontière des Vosges. Héroïque sacrifice de l'infanterie française* Montpellier, Causse, Graille & Castelnau, 1939 pp.114–15

172 'A countess' Strong p.49

175 'a sublime chaos' Clayton, Anthony *Paths of Glory: The French Army 1914–1916* p.24

177 'something struck my knee' Lacouture p.30

178 'I can still hear' Blond p.20

179 'Frenchmen must look' Bertie diary 5.11.14

179 'The battle was lost' Lintier p.60

180 'Mown down' ibid. p.25

182 'Exhausting week' Cœurdevey, Edouard *Carnets de guerre 1914–1918: Un témoin lucide* Plon 2008 23.8.14

182 '5 a.m. movement order' ibid.

182 'theatrical and a great error' Bertie diary 10.9.14

182 'The Mulhouse business' Gide diary 4.9.14

183 'There can be no talk' Herwig *War* p.89

183 'Jacques Rivière's regiment' Rivière pp.20, 30, 31, 46

183 'It was finished' ibid. pp.33, 39

183 'From that comes' ibid. p.42

183 'With us, the army' ibid. 8.9.14 p.80

184 'Even before the fight' Jones, Heather et al. (eds) *Untold War: New Perspectives in First World War Studies* Leiden 2008 p.29

184 'Lieutenant, will we' Herwig Marne p.100

185 'What good things' IWM 09/65/1 Papers of Sir James Stubblefield

186 'We civilians know' SB 7, 97/2–17

186 'decked itself out' Chickering *Urban Life* p.431

186 'An elderly dowager' Strong p.100

186 'I think that the French' Bertie diary 16.8.14

186 'There is much more' ibid. 31.8.14

186 'We soldiers were usually' Flood p.51

187 'Louis Barthas' Barthas pp.19–20

187 'Self-evidently' ibid. p.88

2 'GERMAN BEASTLINESS'

187 'Our cavalry patrols' Horne and Kramer p.96

188 'all soldiers are comrades' Rivière p.35

188 'It is utter rot' Wolz, Nicolas *Das lange Warten. Kriegserfahrungen deutscher und britischer Seeoffiziere 1914 bis 1918* Schöningh Paderborn 2008 pp.354–5

189 'An American in Paris' Gide 15.11.14

189 'We fought the Guard Corps' IWM HET/1 P229 Trevor papers

189 'It seems to be universally' *New Statesman* 10.10.14

189 'the clamour of' Holroyd p.447

190 'We can state' Horne and Kramer p.419

191 'Our soldiers have been' ibid. p.36

191 'Decidedly, I do not like' Knoch, Peter (ed.) *Menschen im Krieg 1914–1918*, Ludwigsburg Pädagogische Hochschule 1987 p.78

192 'Harry Graf Kessler' Kessler 22.8.14

192 'We pushed on' ibid. p.47

193 'Russian atrocities have' ibid. p.80

3 LANREZAC ENCOUNTERS SCHLIEFFEN

198 'As if at manoeuvres' Spears p.134

198 'they were like eager children' ibid. p.135

198 '[a] most dangerous person' Jackson, Julian *The Fall of France* OUP 2003 p.91

Chapter 6 – The British Fight

1 MONS

201 'Last mile ½ battalion' IWM 07/63/1Harcourt-Vernon MS

202 'No longer was it' Harding Davis, Richard *With the Allies* Duckworth 1915 p.22

202 'These French people' Craster J.M. (ed.) *Fifteen Rounds a Minute* Macmillan 1976 p.23

203 'All day men have been' IWM 07/63/1

203 'When he personally' GW interview transcript

208 'There was no hatred' Bridges, Sir Tom *Alarms and Excursions* Longman 1938 p.73

208 'I said to this' BBC Home Service radio broadcast 23.8.54

209 'Funny to notice' IWM 07/63/1 Harcourt-Vernon MS

209 'They were in solid' Terraine, John *Mons* Batsford 1960 p.91

210 'God! How their artillery' Ascoli p.92

210 'The men were digging' IWM 89/7/1 Wollocombe papers

211 'it was too late' ibid.

211 'Our faithful gunners' ibid.

211 'A very trying day' IWM 88/52/1 Edgington papers

211 'masses of grey-clad' Sheffield *The Chief* p.72

211 'if Sgt. —' IWM 89/7/1 Wollocombe MS

212 'You are the only' Wencke p.224
213 'the spirit of victory' Zuber p.132
213 'Gentlemen, please' ibid. p.136
214 'even had time to think' IWM 89/7/1 Wollocombe MS
216 'Our troops advance' Longerich p.20 24.8.14
216 'a long and trying march' Craster p.37
216 'most disheartening' ibid. p.39
216 'I have never been' Harris, Simon *History of the 43rd and 52nd (Ox and Bucks) Light Infantry in the Great War 1914–18* Simon Harris 2012 p.22
217 'The whole way back' Rose narrative, Journal of the Wiltshire Regiment
217 'But who will feed' Spears p.319
217 'It makes you cry' IWM 99/41/1 Madame Jeanne van Bleyenberghe correspondence
217 'their guard does not' Haig p.65
218 'I like most others' Craster pp.44–6
219 'D.H. had ... been' ASC1938

2 LE CATEAU: 'WHERE THE FUN COMES IN, I DON'T KNOW'
219 'That evening their colonel' ASC1938 Bird Narrative
221 'You needn't bother' ASC 1938 Edmonds letter 11.5.33
222 'Don't call a' ibid.
223 'everyone spoke in' Spears p.228
223 'The sense of doom' ibid. p.230
223 'It was perhaps' ibid. p.233
224 'to me it was a period' ASC1938 Murray letter of 18.12.30
224 '[the airmen's] maps were black' Baring p.25
224 'A sun-baked drowsy' Spears p.235
225 'Salisbury Plain' Ascoli p.97
225 'At the outset' Priestley, R.E. *The Signal Service in the European War of 1914–18* W. and J. Mackay 1921 p.33
226 'On your feet!' Cave and Sheldon *Le Cateau* p.40
226 'An hour later' ASC1938 Bird narrative
226 '[He] was most anxious' ASC1938 Arthur Hildebrand letter of 21.12.30
227 'It is impossible to miss' IWM HET/1 P229 Trevor papers
227 'I did not think' Ascoli p.100
227 'We could see a [British]' Cave and Cowley p.52
228 'too terrible for words' IWM HET/1 P229 Trevor papers
228 'Capt. R.G. Beaumont' ASC1938 Bird narrative
229 'we sat there talking' IWM 89/7/1 Wollocombe papers
229 'At the same time' Cave and Sheldon p.76
230 'I have lost my' ibid. p.106
230 'what we want to do' ASC 1938 Bird narrative
231 'which left me pretty well' Ascoli p.105
231 'About 2.30 the situation' IWM HET/1 P229 Trevor letter of 2.9.14
233 'however, we retired' IWM HET/1 P229 Trevor letter of 14.9.14
233 'It was a wonderful sight' Terraine p.152
233 'I must warn you' ASC1938 Bird narrative
235 'Our losses had been' Cave and Sheldon p.80
235 'In the British centre' ASC1938 Major C.M. Usher Narrative
236 'The British had withdrawn' Cave and Sheldon p.100
236 'but the British also' ibid. p.163
237 'No news of II Corps' ASC1938 Edmonds letter 11.5.33
238 'I fancy Haig' ibid.

Chapter 7 – The Retreat

239 'marched to St. Quentin' IWM 88/52/1 Edgington diary
240 'behaving in a scandalous' Babington, Anthony *For the Sake of Example* Leo Cooper 1983
      p.6
242 'Marches are much slower' IWM 07/63/1 Harcourt-Vernon MS
242 'The chief' Clarke p.67
242 'They were acting' BNA WO95/1347
243 'We had to wait' H. Goatham taped interview transcript, GW files
243 'despite the fact that' Macarthur, Brian *For King and Country* Little, Brown 2008 p.21
245 '*Les anglais sont*' Baring p.28
245 'quite calm, approachable' ASC1938 HS Jeudwine letter
245 'it was the old story' Craster p.50
246 'In six weeks' Reichsarchiv (ed.), *Der Weltkrieg 1914–1918*, Vol. I Berlin Mittler 1925 p.440
248 'One is already beginning' Thompson p.98
248 'We Germans have' ibid. p.106
249 'the French considered' Spears p.250
249 'He manipulated his units' ibid. p.269
250 'A French officer gleefully' ibid. pp.339–40
252 'I stand bad news' Smith, Leonard et al. *France and the Great War 1914–1918* trans. Helen
      McPhail CUP 2003 p.41
254 'It is one of the worst' Harris p.44
255 'The Germans did not' Craster p.56
255 'Do you know that' Thomson p.45
255 'If ever a German' ibid.
256 'They've got their cavalry' Craster p.57
256 'The departure was a' Terraine p.193
256 'We didn't know where' Ascoli p.140
257 'the damned French army' ASC1938 Harper letter 8.9.14
257 'which all seems to point' IWM 88/51/1 Edgington diary

Chapter 8 – Tannenberg: 'Alas, How Many Thousands Lie There Bleeding!'

259 'Russian society had not' Kondurashkin p.8
260 'Think of me' Knox p.46
260 'you soldiers ought' ibid. p.45
261 'big, red-bearded' ibid. p.103
261 'The yellow and purple' Ksyunin A. *Narod na voine (iz zapisok voennogo korrespondenta)*
      [People at War: From the Notes of a War Correspondent] Petrograd 1916 p.69
261 'a hundred half-savage' Reed p.186
263 'When a Russian officer' Ksyunin p.5
263 'The Belobeevsky infantry' Sanborn, Josh *Daily Life in Russian Poland* p.49
263 'soldiers knew that' ibid. p.50
263 'in the guise of buying' Sanborn, Josh *Unsettling the Russian Empire* p.304
263 'with the goal' ibid. p.305
264 'After occupying Kalitz' Sanborn *Poland* p.52
264 'Where can we' Palmer and Wallis p.36
264 'Across its vast' See Koenigswald, Harald von *Stirb und Werde. Aus Briefen und
      Kriegstagebuchblättern des Leutnant Bernhard von der Marwitz*, Breslau Korn Verlag 1931
      pp.29–33
265 'Nikolai Gumilev' Gumilev, Nikolai *Zapiski Kavalerista* [Diaries of a Cavalryman]
      Moscow 2007 p.23
265 'Johann Sczuka' Borck/Sczuka p.17
265 'On their wanderings' ibid. p.18
265 'Capt. Lazarev' Littauer p.136

266 'But it is only' Kondurashkin p.41
266 'the soldiers were relieved' Littauer p.137
266 'We didn't know' ibid. p.129
269 'a cavalryman is used' ibid. p.138
269 'Vladimir Littauer' ibid. p.144
269 'Two Hussar squadrons' ibid.
269 'He rebuked' Borck/Sczuka p.21
271 'savagely mauled' Pohlmann p.282
272 'not a stone' Mihaly pp.32, 55
272 'This town is completely' Kessler p.106
272 'Prittwitz's staff' Reichsarchiv (ed.) *Der Weltkrieg 1914–1918* Vol. II Berlin Mittler 1925
    p.321
276 'Where do you' Knox p.59
278 'Officials at the post office' Reichsarchiv p.324
280 'The position is very' Knox p.87
280 'he did not know' ibid. p.74
281 'I had never imagined' Nowak, Karl Friedrich (ed.) *Die Aufzeichnungen des Generalmajor
    Max Hoffman* Vol. 1 Berlin Verlag für Kulturpolitik 1930 p.54 9.9.14
281 'To gain this critical' Reichsarchiv Vol. II p.243
281 'The Kaiser, with his' Herwig *Marne* p.xvi
282 'Our hearts are full' Schädla diary 31.8.14
282 'The Emperor trusted' Knox p.82
282 'that it does not matter' ibid. p.80
283 'Passing through Johannisberg' Reed p.119
283 'An elderly couple' Borck/Sczuka pp.26–7
283 'Loyal Germans all' ibid. p.23

Chapter 9 – The Hour of Joffre

1 PARIS AT BAY
286 'More than 50,000 people' Guard p.9
286 'The Parc de Belleville' ibid. p.66
287 'It was considered' ibid. p.39
287 'The five hundred men' Bertie diary 16.8.145
287 'Many domestic titles' ibid. pp.10, 12, 15, 21, 45
287 'I wonder he doesn't' Painter p.224
287 'From what mad optimism' Gide 25.8.14
287 'The Germans seem sure' Bertie diary 30.8.14
288 'Bertie complained' ibid. 3.9.14
288 'it is sad to see' quoted Englund, Peter *The Beauty and the Sorrow* Bloomsbury 2011 p.73
288 'evidently a very' Lloyd George p.154
288 'Gallieni had retired' Gallieni, Joseph *Mémoires du Maréchal Gallieni: Défense de Paris, 25
    Aout–11 Septembre 1914* Paris Payot 1928
289 'One afternoon a crowd' Strong p.128

2 SIR JOHN DESPAIRS
290 'Ah, Napoleon' Lloyd George Vol. I p.156
292 'showed little interest' Spears p.312
293 'Our people have done' Asquith to VS 27.8.14 p.215
293 'The Belgians ... are really' Asquith to VS 25.8.14 p.195
294 'It is extraordinary' Bonham-Carter p.216
295 'If [the] French cannot' IWM papers of N. Macleod 05/63/1
295 'our men had done' ibid.
295 'Published first British' Clarke p.68

296 'One proclaimed himself' Guard p.107
297 'Norman Macleod' IWM 05/63/1 3.9.14 Macleod papers

3 SEEDS OF HOPE
300 'Uncertainty about British' Terraine p.216
300 'On the night of 31 August' Spears p.316
300 'The great towering cuirassiers' ibid.
302 'Gen. Joseph de Maistre' ibid. p.319
302 'They looked like ghosts' ibid. p.318
302 'The mayor of a hamlet' Lintier p.43
303 'Above all they have' Hirschfeld letter of 12.9.14 p.180
304 'I was seized by' Sulzbach p.26
306 'One of our lorries' IWM 06/61/1 Hacker diary 22.8.14
307 'I wonder if that' Harcourt-Vernon MS IWM 07/63/1
307 'On 3 September, Gallieni' Gallieni p.68
307 'his head reminded me' Spears p.384
308 'He refuses a blindfold' Allard, Capitaine Jules *Journal d'un gendarme 1914–1916*
        Présentation d'Arlette Farge Bayard Éditions 2010 p.60
308 'Joffre spent' Spears p.394
308 'The French are most' Haig p.68
308 'we could hold a position' ibid.
309 'his black uniform' Spears p.401
310 'Unshaved, and scarcely' Bloem, Walter *The Advance From Mons 1914* Peter Davies 1930
        p.101
310 'Charles Péguy' Smith et al. p.41
311 'Here was a vivid' Painter p.222
311 'At once he began' Spears p.414

Chapter 10 – The Nemesis of Moltke
1 THE MARNE
318 'a small active man' Haig p.104
319 'Lt. Paul Tuffnau' Palmer and Wallis p.26
322 'It was extraordinary' Flood p.51
322 'we passed Jimmy Rothschild's' Tennyson IWM 76/21/1
322 'Orders to the provost-marshal' Corns and Hughes-Wilson p.119
322 'The most exciting thing' Baring p.54
324 'Have all taxis' Blond p.172
325 'ploughing its way' Lintier p.71
325 'Never mind' Blond p.186
326 'At the attack on Etrepilly' ibid. p.193
328 'Our pursuit could not' Bridges p.94
332 'everyone much more' William Edgington IWM 88/52/1
332 'It's a precious slow' Craster p.76
332 'heavy defeat' Sheffield p.83
332 'his nerve is wonderful' Tennyson MS IWM 76/21/1
335 'What's that?' Lintier p.156
336 'This could not be' Herwig *The Marne* pp.302–3
336 'rumours have reached' IWM 76/21/1 Tennyson MS 17.9.14
336 'My God, how could' ibid. p.302
337 'The nervousness' Mombauer p.264
338 'The army blamed' Strachan p.262
338 'Following a report' *Stahl und Steckrüben* pp.365–6
338 'This much is certain' Gudenhus-Schomerus p.87 23.9.14

338 'Gertrud Schädla' Schädla diary 3.9.14
341 'The general news' Grey to Percy Illingworth 14.9.14 Illingworth papers
341 'The enemy will not' Lacouture p.31
341 'This would be' Cœurdevey pp.35–6
341 'The whole situation' Hopman 15.9.14 p.43
341 'incredible folly' ibid. 17.9.14 p.439
342 'we have experienced' Desfontaines p.133
342 'The massive, historic' Reichsarchiv Vol. IV p.270
342 'The army was not defeated' Ludendorff *Das Marne-Drama* Munich 1934 p.1
342 'What a question' Givray, Jacques (*Capitaine Plieux de Diusse*) *Journal d'un Officier de Liaison (La Marne -: – La Somme -: – L'Yser)* Paris Jouve 1917 p.86

2 'STALEMATE IN OUR FAVOUR'
345 'Everything is going well' Harris p.50
345 'I am deeply thankful' Spears p.469
346 'As a man I do not' IWM 76/21/1 Tennyson MS
347 'The advance proceeded' Kendall, Paul *Aisne 1914: The Dawn of Trench Warfare* Spellmount 2012 p.342
347 'We had an awful' ibid. p.99
348 'It is a terrible place' ibid. p.152
348 'We stop a lot of' IWM 07/63/1 Harcourt-Vernon MS
349 'I tried to sleep' Craster p.89
350 'Meanwhile the bodies' ibid. p.90
350 'A week ago … we' Harris p.63
350 'We were subject to' Craster p.94
350 'The men are splendid' ibid. p.96
351 'Major Zeppelin' Knoch p.78
351 'in this war the last' Guard p.125
351 'it was impossible to rely' Haig p.70
351 'On the 20th he' ibid. p.72
352 'Had we but known' Kendall p.344
352 'Troops are beginning' IWM T.H. Cubbon
352 'I have seen attacks' SB S7, 97/2–3 Kaisen collection
353 'Fancy a thousand' *New York Times* 13.9.14
353 'one does not take' Reimann, Aribert *Der große Krieg der Sprachen. Untersuchungen zur historischen Semantik in Deutschland und England zur Zeit des Ersten Weltkrieges*, Essen Klartext 2000 p.181 4.10.14
353 'it is terrible' Gudenhus-Schomerus p.89 21.9.14
353 'We are so benumbed' Kresten Andresen quoted Englund p.30
354 'On 16 September, Sir John' IWM 07/63/1 Harcourt-Vernon MS
354 'I think the battle' Royal Archives GV Q832/72
355 'This trench- and siege-warfare' Herwig *The Marne* p.216
355 'One day very like' Craster p.103
355 'It beats me' Guest to Percy Illingworth 21.9.14 Illingworth papers

Chapter 11 – 'Poor Devils, They Fought Their Ships Like Men'

356 'The living spaces' Hipper diary 7.9.14, Wolz p.203
357 'Very great excitement' ibid. p.99
357 'If it comes off' ibid.
357 'One profound' Young, Filson *With the Battlecruisers* Cassell 1921 p.121
357 'The German "High Seas Fleet"' Wolz p.344
358 'Following the outbreak' Seligmann *New Weapons for New Targets* p.328
358 'Boredom feeds depression' Stumpf p.14 13.8.14

358 'Everywhere people express' ibid. p.15
359 'On 9 August, a German' ibid. p.13
360 'This ... was a salutary' Wolz diary p.115 21.8.14
360 'Morale slides because' ibid. p.100
360 'The naval mind was' Young p.54
361 'It does not make us' Knobloch diary p.328 22.8.14
361 'She [the *Emden*] is undoubtedly' Wolz p.357 24.10.14
361 'The Navy are very bad' Shelden, Michael *Young Titan* Simon & Schuster 2013 p.300
361 'At Coblenz on 18 August' Hopman p.411
362 'It was quite clear' Young p.84
362 'If he does that' ibid. p.85
362 'They Want to Starve' Healey, Maureen *Vienna and the Fall of the Hapsburg Empire: Total War and Everyday Life in World War I* CUP 2004 p.38
363 'They control the oceans' Wolz p.345 25.8.14
363 'If we were to risk' ibid. p.100
363 'The dark shapes' Young p.126
364 'I would have preferred' Wolz p.121
365 'The least informed' Young p.120
366 'In the clear seawater' Palmer and Wallis p.234
366 'young, distinguished-looking' Young p.6
366 'the most publicised' Gordon, Andrew *The Rules of the Game: Jutland and British Naval Command* John Murray 1996 p.27
368 'I see no reason' Seligmann *Naval Intelligence* p.517
369 'I always had a feeling' Wolz p.332 22.10.14
370 'Every salvo they' Bywater, Hector *Cruisers in Battle* p.56
370 'A most extraordinary' King-Hall, Stephen *A North Sea Diary 1914–1918* pp.54–5
371 'She had settled' Bywater p.57
372 'As we approached' Chatfield, Lord Ernle *The Navy and Defence: An Autobiography* Heinemann 1942 p.125
373 'a brilliant episode' Churchill *Great War* Vol. I p.306
373 'This little battle' IWM Macleod Papers
373 'Winston's little scheme' Asquith to VS 28.8.14 p.203
374 'We disgraced ourselves' Hopman diary 29.8.14 pp.419–20
374 'Yet next day' ibid. p.421 30.8.14
374 'Brains were at' Young p.10
374 'The spirit informing' ibid. p.47
376 'We heard the Russian' ibid. p.68
376 'It must be a heartwarming' Wolz p.326
376 'One feels happy' ibid. p.416 23.9.14
377 'I am afraid' Asquith to VS 4.11.14 p.309
378 'I told Winston' ibid.
378 'a veritable volcano' Churchill Vol. I p.77
379 'I think it is mean' Wolz p.417
380 'To founder without' ibid. p.420
382 'The missing of those' ibid. p.429
382 'The gravest weakness' Andrew Gordon passim
383 'May we have a chance' Wolz pp.356–7
383 'Unless war is made' ibid. p.349
383 'Ernst Weizsäcker' ibid. p.324 28.10.14
383 'Our inactivity causes' ibid. p.450
383 'In the North Sea nothing' ibid. p.101 21.11.14
384 'From the point of view' Young p.157
384 'Once he appeared' ibid. p.161

384 'I would give anything' Wolz p.318 Keyes letter 9.10.14
385 'the British navy has' *Naval Review* 14.10.14

Chapter 12 – Three Armies in Poland
386 'everything is' ASA B1600/7 Pallavicini diary 12.8.14
387 'Of course everybody' ASA B1492 von Hoefft MS
387 'it is said that' Stenitzer, Richard von *Belagerung und Gefangenschaft. Von Przemyśl bis Russisch-Turkestan. Das Kriegstagebuch des Dr Richard Ritter von Stenitzer 1914–1917* ed. Albert Petho Graz Ares 2010 p.23
387 'jumping into a thick' Zeynek p.183
387 'There were subdued' Reed p.123
388 'The high command had' Schneider pp.30–1
388 'Constantin Schneider's division' ibid. pp.60–1 29.8.14
388 'We were constantly' ibid. p.35
389 'Guliewicz, an aristocratic' Stone p.58
389 'By contrast, a mile' Ksyunin p.17
389 'the Orient had to' Schneider p.69 30.8.14
389 'It must be that God' OS B1492 von Hoefft MS
391 'A huge gunner' Knox p.50
391 'A few younger soldiers' Reed p.164
391 'the expression of most' Knox p.51
392 'the air was poisoned' ASA B1492 von Hoefft MS
392 'On the Austrian side' Kronenbitter p.522
392 'The Russians, by contrast' Schneider p.201
392 'On several occasions men' Schindler, John *Disaster on the Drina: The Austro-Hungarian Army in Bosnia* in War in History 9 (2002) p.169
392 'Constantin Schneider' Schneider p.46
392 'The ravine was' ibid. pp.56–8
392 'You see only' ASA B1492 Hoefft MS
393 'This is all we've' Kondurashkin p.40
393 'bowed, thin men' ibid.
393 'Police who were called' ibid. p.51
393 'It is said that a Jew' Knox p.145
393 'On 16 September, a group' Stenitzer pp.158–9
394 'Theodor Ritter Zeynek' Zeynek p.185
394 'He and his comrades' Kuznetsov, Ivan (ed.) *Petrov Pobeg Iz Plenov* Penza 1998 pp.67–8
395 'It was as if he' Schneider p.62
396 'Even at two or three' Kondurashkin p.31
397 'With a stab of awareness' ibid. pp.89–90
397 'I wanted to check' ASA B863/1 Rathenitz MS
397 'When Schneider delivered' ibid. pp.99–100
398 'this should not matter' ANA B 1600/7 Pallavicini diary
398 'a fabulous cabbage soup' Ksyunin p.18
398 'Well sir, I was' ibid. p.68
399 'It was an unforgettable' Knox p.115
399 'The new occupants' Schneider pp.231–2 14.12.14
399 'We pass the time' Stenitzer p.40
399 'Keep marching heedless' Biwald p.344
399 'The city was very' Forstner, Franz *Przemyśl. Österreich-Ungarns bedeutendste Festung* Vienna ÖBV Pädagogischer 1997 pp.146, 148
400 'In September, the rump' ibid. p.151
400 'The Russians are right' Wittgenstein p.21

400 'Men's behaviour improves' Schneider p.108
401 'the campaign [in the west]' Jeffrey p.138
401 'The Austrians' predicament' Hoffman p.55
401 'Come and eat' Kondurashkin p.67
402 'In some units it became' Reed p.154
402 'Vasily Mishnin' Palmer and Wallis p.37
402 'No news except' ASA B1600/7: Pallavicini MS
402 'Tell me, sirs' Kysunin p.6
403 'Take him away!' ibid. p.7
403 'Give him one' ibid. p.9
403 'One hears dozens' Kondurashkin p.25
403 'There were the same' ibid. p.370
404 'I thought of my village' Kuznetsov p.68
404 'We awoke to see' ibid. p.69
404 'You want to dig in' ASA B1492 von Hoefft MS
405 'One saw groups' Kondurashkin pp.60–1
405 'where alleged spies' Stenitzer p.25 22.8.14
405 'from which shots had' Schneider pp.72–3
405 'With only few exceptions' Reichsarchiv (ed.) Der Weltkrieg 1914–1918 Vol. II Berlin Mittler 1925 pp.325–7
405 'The most notable' see Borck, Karin and Kölm, Lothar (eds) Gefangen in Sibirien. Tagebuch eines ostpreußischen Mädchens 1914–1920 Osnabrück Fibre 2001 p.8
406 'On 14 September, escorted' Sczuka pp.27–30
406 'In enemy country' ibid. p.77
406 'Yet, on the following' ibid. pp.84–5 6.9.14
408 'At Otwock railway station' Sanborn Poland p.45
408 'they go on blindly' ibid. p.48
408 'How are things' Kondurashkin p.63
409 'Alexei Ksyunin' Ksyunin p.62
409 'All but the most' ibid. p.64

Chapter 13 – 'Did You Ever Dance With Him?'
1 HOME FRONTS

411 'the impossibility of keeping' Gide p.80
412 'In Austria there was' Krafft-Krivanec p.147 12.10.14
412 'The government recognised' Becker, Jean-Jacques The Great War and the French People trans. Arnold Pomerans 1985 p.13
414 'The word "Durchhalten"' Healey p.34
414 'Austrian women were' ibid. p.38
415 'The Marquis of San Giuliano' Bertie diary 26.10.14
415 'The Italians imagine' ibid. 11.10.14
415 'Otto Zeilinger' Brenner, Stefan Das Kriegsgefangenenlager in Knittelfeld: Eine Untersuchung der Akten des Kriegsarchivs Wien von den ersten Bemühungen Otto Zeilingers zur Errichtung des Lagers Knittelfeld bis zur Umwandlung des Kriegsgefangenenlagers in ein Militärspital MA thesis Graz 2011 pp.45–85
415 'It proved necessary' La Vie quotidienne à Nice en Août 1914 d'après l'Eclaireur de Nice
416 'I have been too exhilarated' NS 5.12.14
417 'A crash programme' Becker p.23
417 'Specialist workers were' ibid. pp.26 –7
418 'In Freiburg' Chickering Urban Life p.358
418 'Maynard Keynes' Wittgenstein p.27 5.10.14
418 'It is a load of private' Grey to Percy Illingworth 20.9.14, Illingworth Papers
418 'we do not feel' Schädla diary 19.9.14

418 'we had to retreat' ibid. 23.9.14
418 'Was it an attack' ibid. 6.10.14
419 'So we have even' ibid. 22.10.14
419 'Did you ever dance' Asquith to VS 19.9.14 p.247
419 'Poor Willy Macneil' IWM Tennyson MS
420 'It is my wish' Horne, John (ed.) *State, Society and Mobilization in Europe during the First World War* CUP 1997 p.41
420 'The Germans Have Killed' Flood pp.87–8
420 'the war as an educational' *Berliner Geschichtswerkstatt* p.183
420 'Elfriede Kuhr' Mihaly pp.71, 94
421 'the children were awed' Gudenhus-Schomerus p.130 4.11.14
421 'The trade magazine' Hirschfeld p.325 10.9.14
421 'from their reserves' Macarthur p.69
423 'Most Europeans were now' Herwig *Marne* p.101
424 'I write a daily letter' ibid. pp.157–8 8.8.14
424 'You say that you' *www.ladepeche.fr*: 1914–18. *Scènes de vie quotidienne à l'arrière* 2.11.08 Sabine Bernèd
424 'in hope of atrocities' Asquith p.13
425 'Ten years ago' Gleason, A. *What the Workers Want* London 1920 p.250
425 'Never did I expect' IWM P404 Baroness de T'Serclaes Vol. III
425 'At Euston station' ibid.
426 'One can just sit down' Wisthaler, Sigrid (ed.) *Karl Außerhofer: Das Kriegstagebuch eines Soldaten im Ersten Weltkrieg* Innsbruck UP 2010
426 'church parades are' ibid. p.102 3.11.14
426 'English life and ways' *The Lady* 3.12.14
426 'Among the many' ibid. 29.10.14
426 'the task of feeding' ibid. 22.10.14
427 'Sailors whose vessels' Mihaly p.99 8.11.14
427 'The little girl and her friend' ibid. p.88
427 'a degenerate desire' Verhey p.82
427 'Let us pray' Ambrožič, Matjaz *Dnevniški zapiski dr. Evgena Lampeta (1898–1917)* Ljubljana 2007 p.56
427 'Everyone wishes ill' ibid. p.51
427 'An English acquaintance' Cooper, C.E. *Behind the Lines: One Woman's War* Norman & Hobbes 1982 pp.21–2
428 'I find that I' Murray, Gilbert *Faith, War and Policy* OUP 1918 p.9
428 'We here, far inland' Schädla diary 12.12.14
429 'Every day there is' Krafft-Krivanec pp.125–6
429 'Soon all the committees' *The Lady* 20.8.14
429 'Once again, I forgot' SB 7, 97/2–17
429 'Everything has been' Feilding, Lady Dorothie *Lady Under Fire on the Western Front* ed. Hallam, Andrew and Nicola Pen & Sword 2010 p.13
430 'Alas I don't think' ibid. p.9
430 'I don't mind' ibid. p.12
430 'Archduchess Maria Josefa' ASA diary of Rüdiger Freiherr Stillfried von Rathenitz B 863/1 RS (1894–1972) 19.9.14
430 'The kind manner' *Die Neue Zeitung* no.259 20.89.14
431 'The King seemed anxious' Haig p.56
431 'The King seemed very cheery' ibid. p.83 4.12.14
431 'not really fighting' Asquith to VS 24.10.14 p.285
431 'It is unbelievable' ASA Pallavicini 9.10.14
432 'the awful slaughter' Hopman diary p.446 25.9.14
432 'for the last 25' ibid. p.441 18.9.14

432 'Today I visited' Krafft-Krivanec p.180
432 'a November political intelligence' *Berliner Geschichtswerkstatt* p.124
432 'We are a unified people' Chickering p.438
433 'Therefore it is our' Horne p.94
433 'Prussia is today' Muehlon p.192
434 'every man who' *Daily Chronicle* 12.10.14
434 'It is a hard task' *Abschiedsfeier für das Ersatzbataillon des Inf.-Rgts. 75*, Bremen 1914

2 NEWS AND ABUSE
434 'If before the war' Verhey p.111
435 'it is with profound' *The Times* 8.8.14
435 'We never appreciated' Leuchtenberg, William *The Perils of Prosperity 1914–32* Chicago University Press 1958 p.14
435 'intemperate attacks' Becker *The Great War and the French People* p.53
435 'Ministers urged' ibid. pp.67–8
436 'It is ... wise' Belloc, Hilaire *The Two Maps of Europe* Pearson 1915 p.102
436 'pacifist and financial' Bennett, Arnold *The Letters of Arnold Bennett* ed. James Hepburn OUP 1968 2: 351
436 'As war is pre-eminently' *New Statesman* 1.9.14
437 'he and Ford Madox Ford' Buitenhuis, p.72
437 'our first victory' Verhey p.130
437 'very strong and' Becker *Guerre* p.58
438 'If damaging rumours' Ambrožič, Matjaž *Dnevniški zapiski dr. Evgena Lampeta (1898–1917)* Ljubljana 2007 p.54
438 'The introduction of trench' Becker p.66
438 'Austrian cities were said' ibid. p.57
438 'Yesterday evening a silly' Wittgenstein pp.33–4
438 'No good news' ibid. p.36 30.10.14
439 'These reports caused' Kupferman, Fred *14–18: Mourir pour la patrie: Rumeurs, bobards et propagande* Editions du Seuil 1992 pp.212–13
439 'French journalists' ibid. p.67
439 'the nightingale of' Becker *The Great War and the French People* p.162
439 '*Poilus*, rejecting' ibid. pp.57–8
440 'Our Brandenburgers' *Oder-Zeitung* 14.11.14
440 'The war was presented' Becker p.43
440 'The story of "the little' Healey p.230
440 'an extremely nice' *The Lady* 3.12.14
441 'To know anything' Young p.32

Chapter 14 – Open Country, Open Sky

1 CHURCHILL'S ADVENTURE
443 'Dragoons from Darmstadt' Sulzbach p.32
444 'it is something' ibid. p.33
444 'If Joffre be victorious' Bertie diary 1.10.14
444 'We heard the guns' IWM 99/41/1 Van Bleyenberghe letters 24.9.14
445 'What are we going' *Daily Mail* 31.8.14
446 'Among the garrison' IWM 91/3/1 Beer MS
447 'We needed all our' ibid.
447 'Our third night' ibid.
448 'Our exodus is' Festing MS p.55
448 'He inspected' ibid. p.62
449 'the delivery of this' ibid. p.69
449 'military training in' ibid. p.10

449 'Next day, his brigadier' ibid. p.74
449 'Evening soon comes' Beer MS IWM 91/3/1
450 'I don't think I have' Festing MS p.84
450 'the devil himself' ibid. p.85
450 'the Germans suddenly' IWM P404 Baroness de T'Serclaes MS
451 'Il ne faut pas' Bonham Carter p.12 18.10.14
451 'Darling father' ibid. p.11
451 'Antwerp was a' Churchill Great War p.336
451 'Looking back' ibid. p.292
451 'one would have thought' Festing MS p.95
454 'Should this narrative' ibid. p.2
454 'W is an ex-lieutenant' Asquith letter to VS 5.10.14 p.263
454 'Norman Macleod' IWM 05/63/1 Macleod papers
454 'our friend [Churchill]' Gilbert, Martin Winston S. Churchill Vol. III p.120
454 'read like a story' IWM 05/63/1 Macleod papers
454 'Feeling of depression' ibid.
454 'The Belgian troops have' Feilding p.10 letter of 10.10.14
455 'we all admire' IWM 99/41/1 Van Bleyenberghe MS
455 'too late to have' Dunn p.69

2 'INVENTIONS OF THE DEVIL'
455 'While contemplating' Gebsattel pp.22–3
456 'soon outstrip' Hesse p.20
456 'When these inventions' Strachan p.233
456 'I think, sir' Bridges p.80
457 'German staff regulations' Bayerisches Hauptstaatsarchiv, Abt. IV Kriegsarchiv Bavarian
     Central Archive, Munich, IV. Dept. War Archive HS3180
457 'Members of the RFC' Winter, Denis First of the Few Penguin 1982 p.18
458 'The French, alone' Clayton p.233
458 'French biplanes flew at' Rougevin-Baville, Col. J. Revue historique de l'armée Ministère des
     armées 1964: L'aéronautique militaire française, les débuts de la guerre aérienne 1914 p.6
458 'beautiful little birds' Mayne MS IWM 81/26/1
458 'It is a strange' Stenitzer p.56 2.12.14
458 'when any aircraft' IWM 80/35/1 Mayer MS
458 'a dreadful sight' Craster p.118
458 'Three Austrian planes' ibid. p.59 29.8.14
459 'I remember the clicking' Baring p.50
460 'Charles Stein's' IWM 86/30/1 Stein papers
460 'I have had some' Goebel, Stefan The Great War and Medieval Memory: War,
     Remembrance and Medievalism in Britain and Germany, 1914–1940 CUP 2007 p.70
460 'Caroll Dana Winslow' Winslow, Carroll Dana With the French Flying Corps Charles
     Scribner's Sons 1917 p.19
460 'When they make' Palmer and Wallis p.36
461 'When I grow up' Gudehus-Schomerus p.157 24.11.14
461 'the war should not' ibid. p.170 30.11.44
461 'Rudolf Martin' Martin, Rudolf Stehen wir vor einem Weltkrieg? Leipzig Engelmann 1908
461 'Germany started aerial' Kehrt pp.192–3
462 'It exploded but not' Baring p.44
462 'We are fortunate' Boyle p.209

Chapter 15 – Ypres: 'Something that was Completely Hopeless'

464 'we heard Antwerp' IWM Tennyson MS
464 'A month ago everyone' *New Statesman* 10.10.14
465 'they all jumped up' IWM 86/30/1 C. Stein papers
465 'the whole population fleeing' IWM 91/3/1 Beer MS
465 'The incessant stream of' IWM 82/26/1
466 'Our cars were going' Feilding p.20
467 'The Belgians have never' Craster p.106
468 'that is the soul' Givray pp.191–3 12.10.14
468 'rather a nice' Craster pp.108, 111
469 'We are getting' Macdonald, Lynn *1914* Michael Joseph 1987 p.357
469 'Allied prisoners, when they' Baring p.54
472 'Everywhere we advance' Craster p.107
472 'It is all rot' ibid. p.111
472 'we looked a ragtime' Richards, Frank *Old Soldiers Never Die* Mott 1983 p.31
472 'Little did we think' ibid. p.34
472 'native infantry were no' ibid. p.39
473 'We are the Coldstream!' BNA WO95/1342
473 'it is too much like' Craster p.132
473 'they came on in' BNA WO95/1348
473 'Lionel Tennyson' IWM Tennyson MS p.121
474 'Churchill wrote of' Churchill *Great War* Vol. I p.378
474 'I did not imagine' Cocho, Paul *Mes Carnets de guerre et de prisonnier 1914–1919* Presses Universitaires de Rennes 2010 pp.8, 19
474 '*Il faut absolument*' Craster p.113
475 'Maria, this sort' Palmer and Wallis p.29
475 'Sgt. Gustav Sack' Hirschfeld p.29
475 'everything is quite' ibid. p.30
475 'I am freezing!' ibid. p.31 2.11.14
475 'A great grey mass' Macarthur p.43
477 'Every man … was exhausted' Macdonald p.368
477 'what awful sights' ibid. p.370
478 'By 4 p.m. the bulk' Haig p.75
480 'It must be clearly' Hamilton, Ernest *The First Seven Divisions* Hurst & Blackett 1916, p.83
482 'My dear Maria' Palmer and Wallis p.33
483 'A perfect hurricane' IWM88/52/1 Edgington diary
483 'They weren't an organized' Macdonald p.398
484 'We got the guns out' ibid. p.389
484 'We had no idea' ibid. pp.396–7
484 'crowds of fugitives' Haig p.83 4.12.14
486 'they made no attempt' Macdonald p.399
486 'His kilt in rags' Maze, Paul *A Frenchman in Khaki* Heinemann 1934 p.75
486 'I'm afraid your division' Craster p.125
487 'serious-faced men' IWM 82/26/1 Mayne MS
487 'The news from' Lacouture p.32
487 'We could see' Craster p.127
488 'It came on' ibid. p.128
488 'I suppose one' ibid. p.129
488 'When I think' ibid. p.140
489 'very shaky even' ibid. p.131
489 'The Lincolns, Northumberland' Haig p.78
490 'It struck me that' ibid. p.81
491 'We hold on' Craster p.134

493 'Everybody in a panic' IWM T.H. Cubbon diary
493 'Cpl. William Holbrook' Macdonald p.418
494 'Doesn't it look' ibid. p.420
494 'Attacks repeated with' BNA WO95/1342
494 'This wet is hell' Feilding p.32
495 'Churchill referred afterwards' Churchill *Great War* Vol. I p.325
495 'Out of the 1,100' Macdonald p.421
496 'The noise of the guns' Craster p.119

Chapter 16 – 'War Becomes the Scourge of Mankind'

1 POLAND
497 'Here everything is' Hoffman p.57 8.10.14
497 'We have been too long' Groß, Gerhard P. (ed.) *Die vergessene Front. Der Osten 1914/15.*
    Ereignis, Wirkung, Nachwirkung Paderborn Schöningh 2006
497 'Tomo Župan' Dr Tomo Župan NUK/R, Ms 1390, m. 29, Spominji XXVII
498 'Many more men' NUK/R, Ivan Vrhovnik, Ms 1207, m.74
498 'For God's sake' Schneider pp.138–40
498 'they walked with shaky' ibid. pp.144–5
499 'Faced with a crippling' ibid. p.154
499 'At first the War Ministry' Biwald pp.534–5
499 'As a further consequence' ibid. pp.261–2
499 'Czech officers were' Tolstoy, A. *In Volyn* p.371
500 'notwithstanding the fact' Sanborn *Mobilization* p.288
500 'I would have liked' Hoffman diary p.58
500 'waterlogged trenches' Koenigswald p.26 26.10.14
501 'Your Excellency!' Knox p.205
502 'On the evening of the 23rd' Reichsarchiv Vol. II pp.152–226
503 'it seemed as if' Schneider pp.210–11
503 'This news gave' ibid. p.212
504 'the defeated ... do not see' ibid. p.200 20.11.14
504 'Any victories gained' Hoffman diary p.58
505 'a minor curiosity' Cole, Laurence, Hämmerle, Christa and Scheutz, Martin (eds) *Glanz –*
    Gewalt – Gehorsam. Militär und Gesellschaft in der Habsburgermonarchie (1800 bis 1918)
    Essen Klartext 2011 pp.55–76, citing Angelique Leszczawski-Schwerk
505 'In the course of 1914' Schneider p.239
505 'War becomes the scourge' Zeynek p.192
507 'The scene was fantastic' ibid. p.202
507 'the strategic defeat' Groß p.55
508 'A government agent' Figes, Orlando *A People's Tragedy* Cape 1996 p.258
508 'Right dress!' Tolstoy p.377

2 THE SERBS' LAST TRIUMPH
509 'If we do not get' Slavka Mihajlović 17.11.14 in Đurič and Stevanović p.141
509 'Making war means' Kronenbitter p.107
510 'They say that he' Kisch p.185 6.11.14
510 'News that the brave' Mihajlović 6.11.14 in Đurič and Stevanović p.149
510 'Incredible cold' ibid. p.151 16.11.14
510 'On the walls' Kisch pp.174–5
510 'All those chaps' ibid. pp.195–7 13.11.14
511 'our own troubles' ibid. p.198
511 'We no longer have' ASA B729 Wüster MS
511 'with infantry dispersed' ibid. 4.12.14
512 'By the time the soldiers' Kisch p.239 16.12.14

512 'Anger and mistrust' ASA B1600/7 Alex Pallavicini MS
512 'The doctor had to' ASA Bachmann MS
513 'I am sad' Reed p.86
514 'What are these French' ibid. p.49

Chapter 17 – Mudlife

515 'who must face' Schädla diary 1.11.14
516 'In those early' Richards p.41
516 'in this kind' Reimann p.180 letter of 26.11.14
516 'a most extraordinary' IWM Tennyson MS 2.10.14
517 'Some eggs' IWM Mayne MS 81/26/1
517 'thus they cannot' IWM Mayer MS 80/35/1
517 'Our chief work' Craster p.161
517 'They have all sorts' Robert P. Harker 6.11.14, Reimann p.240
517 'They describe lying' Barthas pp.43, 45
518 'infantrymen felled by' Naegelen R. Les Suppliciés Paris 1927 p.89
519 'As matters stand' Binding, Rudolf A Fatalist at War p.69
519 'One of our companies' Cowan letters, private collection
520 'Sergeant Swinchat' IWM Tennyson MS 25.9.14
520 'I said we wanted' Haig p.83
521 'would amount to the sacrifice' New Statesman 14.11.14
521 'I have seen the government' Clarke pp.70–1
522 'The enormous wastage' Blenkinsop, Maj.-Gen. Sir L.J. et al. History of the Great War: Veterinary Services HMSO 1925 p.71
522 'The BEF's horses and mules' ibid. p.510
522 'Vets catalogued examples' ibid. p.703
522 'Veterinary officers … foresaw' ibid. p.64
523 'Among a bunch' ibid. p.175
523 'René Cassin' Winter p.63
525 'that a giraffe' Richards p.45
525 'Lt. Adolf Spemann' HStA Stuttgart, M 660/041 No 2 Spemann diary 6.11.14
526 'What is this conflict' Lacouture p.32
526 'The French abandoned' Gudenhus-Schomerus p.173 3.12.14
527 'Please note that' Barluet, Alain Les Fraternisations de Noël pp.171–2
527 'Louis Barthas' Barthas p.40
527 'he really hit' SB S7, 97/2–3 Kaisen collection
528 'The war is like a cinema' Ziemann, Benjamin War Experiences in Rural Germany 1914–23 OUP 2007 p.44
528 'In the rear they are' BA-MA PH 3/542 Hillern-Flinsch diary pp.70–1
528 'Some soldiers conduct' Hirschfeld Kriegserfahrungen. Studien zur Sozial- und Mentalitätsgeschichte des Ersten Weltkriegs, Essen Klartext 1997 p.180
528 'When are you' Craster p.165 22.12.14
528 'I look at my poor' Delvert, A. Histoire d'une compagnie Berger-Leverault 1918 p.164
528 'One of the biffins' Givray pp.213–14
529 'These gentlemen pass' Cœurdevey p.45
529 'They are posted' Hirschfeld p.185 letter of 12.9.14
529 'It is curious' IWM Mayer MS 80/35/1
529 'It's odd how' Feilding p.23
529 'My darling, today' Hirschfeld p.32
529 'all those who go' ibid. p.34 17.11.14
530 'I went round' Craster p.166
530 'It's extraordinary' Robert P. Harker Reimann p.261
530 'We are happy' IWM Mayer MS 80/35/1

530 'It was then that' ibid.
531 'It is impossible to believe' Craster p.161
531 'but he didn't want' ibid. p.53
531 'He dies courageously' Laby 7.12.14
531 'The officers retired' IWM 91/3/1 Beer MS 20.9.14
532 'A pukka old' Richards p.29
532 'André Mare' Meyer, Jacques *La Vie quotidienne des soldats pendant la Grande Guerre* Hachette 1966 pp.64–5
532 'We no longer take' IWM Mayer MS 80/35/1
532 'He had also had' Cœurdevey p.78
533 'during the pause' Audoin-Rouzeau, Stéphane *L'Enfer c'est la boue!* p.141
533 'so we can wallow' Hirschfeld p.34 31.12.14
533 'In this beautiful' HStA Stuttgart, M 660/0414
533 'Poor inhabitants!' ibid. p.175 Löwenstein letter of 4.10.14
534 'It is not only' Becker, Annette *Oubliés de la Grand Guerre: Humanitaire et culture de guerre* Hachette Littératures Editions Noèsis 1998 pp.155–8
534 'The International Committee' ibid. pp.181–9
534 'rude and ungrateful' Hirschfeld p.181 letter of 24.9.14
534 'we had Germans here' IWM 86/30/1 C. Stein papers
535 'living at Fontaine' Delmotte, Maurice *Vie quotidienne en France occupée: Journaux de Maurice Delmotte 1914–1918* ed. Nathalie Philippe L'Harmattan 2007 p.38
535 'scarcely fed' Becker, Annette p.57
535 'After I convinced' Gudenhus-Schomerus pp.116–17 18.10.14
535 'The people are very' Palmer and Wallis p.29
536 'Great – you can be happy' Hirschfeld pp.37–8 26.11.14
536 'We eat in the magnificent' Gerhard Hirschfeld, Gerd Krumeich and Irina Renz (eds) *Die Deutschen an der Somme 1914–1918. Krieg, Besatzung, Verbrannte Erde.* Essen Klartext 2006 pp.22–3 14.10.14
536 'We take from the French' Yerta, Gabrielle and Marguerite *Six Women and the Invasion* Macmillan 1917, republished as an e-book by Gutenberg p.2
537 'has become quite' HStA Stuttgart, M 660/041 No 2 Spemann diary 14.10.14
537 'So this was to be' Barthas p.66
538 'After a night' ibid. p.72
538 'Some reservists have' IWM Mayer MS 80/35/1
538 'all those pictures' Barthas pp.76–7
538 'We are none of us' Tapert, Annette *Despatches from the Heart* Hamish Hamilton 1984 p.16
539 'How brutal' Englund p.64
539 'everything becomes senseless' Binding p.87
539 'O my lieutenant' Laby diary 5.10.14
539 'roared like a wild' Capes p.40
539 'An awfully nice lot' Wilbert Spencer quoted Wolz p.185

Chapter 18 – Silent Night, Holy Night

541 'these wretched times' Jay p.311
541 'Richard Meinertzhagen' Meinertzhagen, Richard *Army Diary 1899–1926* Oliver & Boyd 1960 p.98
541 'Everybody's mood' SB 7 97/2–17HS 26.12.14
542 'The French army will not' Soutou p.114
543 'Falkenhayn in particular' ibid. p.50 and passim
546 'I and my like' Mellersh, Henry *Schoolboy into War* London 1978 p.16
547 'war as a military process' Horne and Kramer p.317
547 'It is a shame' Churchill, Winston *My Early Life* Eland Books 2000 pp.64, 66

548 'The authorities should' Asquith to VS 26.12.14 p.340
548 'his cheeks resemble' *Geoffrey Madan's Notebooks* p.41
549 'amazingly optimistic' Bonham-Carter p.17
549 'Even Kitchener' Lords speech 18.9.14 quoted Magnus, Philip *Kitchener: Portrait of an Imperialist* Penguin 1968 p.355
549 'A Jew, an 'Ebrew Jew' Asquith to VS 3.11.14 p.306
550 'volatile mind' ibid. 5.12.14 p.327
550 'I am uneasy about' Lloyd George Vol. I p.356
550 'Battles are won' Churchill *Great War* Vol. I p.498
556 'After midnight' Arand, Tobias (ed.) *Die 'Urkatastrophe' als Erinnerung – Geschichtskultur des Ersten Weltkriegs* Münster ZfL-Verlag 2006 p.32
557 'We wish you' ibid. p.77
558 'The Boches waved' Guéno, Jean-Pierre (ed.) *Paroles de Poilus: Lettres et carnets du front 1914–1918* Librio & Radio France 1998 p.78
558 'We hope that next year' Palmer and Wallis p.59
558 'wet and mud awful' BNA WO95/1342
559 'It was moving' IWM Mayer MS 80/35/1
559 'Nothing new happened' Schneider p.215
559 'Nothing happens that deserves' Stumpf p.33
559 'People reacted differently' Flood p.91

Bibliography

Papers, Journals, Documents and Internet Sources

Abschiedsfeier für das Ersatzbataillon des Inf.-Rgts. 75, Bremen 1914

Audoin-Rouzeau, Stéphane and Becker, Annette *14–18: Understanding the Great War* Hill & Wang 2002

Becker, Jean-Jacques *La Guerre était-elle inevitable?* pp.41–3

—*Les Innovations stratégiques* pp.86–7

—*La Bataille de la Marne, ou le fin des illusions* pp.123, 125–6

Blume, Wilhelm von *Inwiefern haben sich die Bedingungen des Erfolges im Kriege seit 1871 verändert?* [How have the conditions required for success in war altered since 1871?] Vierteljahrshefte für Truppenführung und Heereskunde 5 1908

—*Der Einfluß des heutigen Verkehrs- und Nachrichtenmittel auf die Kriegsführung* [The impact of modern transportation and communication media on warfare] in *Beihefte zum Militär-Wochenblatt* 1910

—*Kriegserfahrung* (War experience), in *Militär-Wochenblatt* 1908 No. 26 pp.583–90

Brenner, Stefan *Das Kriegsgefangenenlager in Knittelfeld: Eine Untersuchung der Akten des Kriegsarchivs Wien von den ersten Bemühungen Otto Zeilingers zur Errichtung des Lagers Knittelfeld bis zur Umwandlung des Kriegsgefangenenlagers in ein Militärspital* MA thesis Graz 2011

Castle, Terry *Our First View of the End of the World: The US Chronicle of Higher Education* 5.11.04

Chiari, Bernard and Gerhard P. Groß (eds) *Am Rande Europas? Der Balkan – Raum und Bevölkerung als Wirkungsfelder militärischer Gewalt*, Munich Oldenbourg 2009 pp.121–36

Cowan, John Manuscript letters from France copied to the author by a descendant

Emmet, Major Robert *An American in the British Army during World War I*, unpublished MS by courtesy of Anthony Gray

Evans. R.J.W. *Communicating Empire: The Hapsburgs and Their Critics 1700–1919* Transactions of the RHS 2008

Festing, Maurice an unpublished account of his experiences as a Royal Marine officer at Antwerp, MS courtesy of John Festing

Förster, Stig *Der deutsche Generalstab und die Illusion des kurzen Krieges, 1871–1914. Metakritik eines Mythos* in *Militärgeschichtliche Mitteilungen* 54 (1995), pp.61–95

House, Dr. Simon Unpublished doctoral thesis for the Department of War Studies, KCL, on the Ardennes battles of 22 August 1914

Howard, Michael *Encounter* January 1964

Illingworth, Percy private papers of the Liberal chief whip in the possession of James Illingworth

Morgan, Kenneth O. *England, Britain and the Audit of War* Transactions of the RHS 2006

Mourir pour la patrie Editions de Seuil 1992

Pallavicini, Alexander *Markgraf Pallavicini B 1600* [two collections of diaries in the Austrian State Archives]

Russky Invalid No. 163 27.7.14, Sunday Section 'The Public Life'

Sanborn, Josh 'Unsettling the Russian Empire' in *The Journal of Modern History* June 2005 pp.295–309

—*Daily Life in Russian Poland*, Festschrift pp.44–55

—'The Mobilization of 1914 and the Question of the Russian Nation: A Re-examination' *Slavic Review* Vol. LIX No. 2 Summer 2000

Schmitt, Bernadotte *The Fashion and Future of History: Historical Studies and Addresses* Cleveland Press of Western Reserve University 1960 pp.129–50

Seligmann, Matthew '"A Barometer of National Confidence": A British Assessment of the Role of Insecurity in the Formulation of German Military Policy before the First World War' *English Historical Review* Vol. CXVII No. 471 April 2002 pp.333–55

—'New Weapons for New Targets' *International History Review* Vol. XXX No. 2 June 2008 pp.303–31

—'Switching Horses: The Admiralty's Recognition of the Threat from Germany 1900–1905' *International History Review* Vol. XXX No. 2 June 2008 pp.239–58

—'The Mobilization of 1914 and The Question of the Russian Nation: A Re-examination' *Slavic Review* Vol. LIX No. 2 Summer 2000 pp.272–89

Stengers, Jean *Le Rôle de l'opinion publique dans la genèse d'une guerre: 1870 et 1914* (Internet)

Trachtenberg, Marc *The Coming of the First World War: A Reassessment in History and Strategy* Princeton 1991 pp.47–99

Überegger, Oswald *Man mache diese Leute, wenn sie halbwegs verdächtig erscheinen, nieder. Militärische Normübertretungen, Guerillakrieg und ziviler Widerstand an der Balkanfront 1914* in Rougevin-Baville, Col. J *Revue historique de l'armée Ministère des armées* 1964: *L'aéronautique militaire française, les débuts de la guerre aérienne 1914*

Ueber Angriff und Verteidigung befestigter Stellungen (On attacking and defending fortified emplacements), in *Militär-Wochenblatt* 1909 No. 18

La Vie quotidienne à Nice en août 1914 d'après l'Eclaireur de Nice (Internet)

Books

Adam, H. Pearl *Paris Sees it Through: A Diary 1914–1919* Hodder & Stoughton 1919

Albert, King of the Belgians *Le Roi Albert à travers de ses lettres inédites 1882–1916* ed. Thielemans and Vandevoude Brussels 1982

Albertini, Luigi *The Origins of the War of 1914* OUP 1953

Allard, Capitaine Jules *Journal d'un gendarme 1914–1916* Présentation d'Arlette Farge Bayard Éditions 2010

Ambrožič, Matjaž *Dnevniški zapiski dr. Evgena Lampeta (1898–1917)* Ljubljana 2007

Andrew, Christopher *The Defence of the Realm: The Authorized History of MI5* Allen Lane 2005

Angelow, Jürgen (ed.) *Der Erste Weltkrieg auf dem Balkan* Perspektiven der Forschung, Berlin 2011

Anglesey, The Marquis of *A History of the British Cavalry* Vol. VII Leo Cooper 1996

Arand, Tobias (ed.) *Die 'Urkatastrophe' als Erinnerung – Geschichtskultur des Ersten Weltkriegs* Münster ZfL-Verlag 2006

Ascoli, David *The Mons Star* Harrap 1981

Asquith, Violet *Champion Redoubtable: The Diaries and Letters of Violet Bonham-Carter 1914–45* ed. Mark Pottle Weidenfeld & Nicolson 1998

Audoin-Rouzeau, Stéphane *L'Enfer c'est la boue!* Paris Seuil 1992

Avakumović, Joven D. Memoari Izdavačka knjižarnica Zorana Stojanovića Sremski Karlovci-Novi Sad 2008

Babington, Anthony *For the Sake of Example* Leo Cooper 1983

Baker-Carr, C.D. *From Chauffeur to Brigadier* Benn 1930

Ball, Simon *The Guardsmen* HarperCollins 2004

Barbusse, Henri *Le Feu* Flammarion 1917

Baring, Maurice *Flying Corps Headquarters 1914–18* Buchan & Enright 1985

Barluet, Alain *Les fraternisations de Noël*

Barthas, Louis *Les Carnets de guerre de Louis Barthas, tonnelier, 1914–1918* La Decouverte/ Poche 2003

Basedow, Heinow von *Reiseeindrücke aus dem militärischen Rußland*, in: *Beihefte zum Militär-Wochenblatt* 1910

Becker, Annette *Oubliés de la Grande Guerre: Humanitaire et culture de guerre* Hachette Littératures Editions Noêsis 1998

Becker, Jean-Jacques *La Guerre était-elle inévitable?*

—*La France en guerre, 1914–1918: La Grande Mutation* Paris 1985

Beesly, Patrick *Room 40: British Naval Intelligence 1914–18* Hamish Hamilton 1982

Belloc, Hilaire *The Two Maps of Europe* Pearson 1915

Bennett, Arnold *The Letters of Arnold Bennett* ed. James Hepburn OUP 1968

Berliner Geschichtswerkstatt (ed.) *August 1914: Ein Volk zieht in den Krieg*, Berlin Nishen 1989

Bernhardi, Gen. Friedrich von *Germany and the Next War* Edward Arnold 1914

Bertie, Francis *The Diary of Sir Francis Bertie of Thame, 1914–1918* ed. Lady Algernon Gordon Lennox Hodder & Stoughton 1924

Bihl, Wolfdieter *Der Erste Weltkrieg 1914–1918. Chronik – Daten – Fakten* Vienna Böhlau 2010

Binding, Rudolf *A Fatalist at War* Allen & Unwin 1929

Biwald, Brigitte *Von Helden und Krüppeln. Das österreichisch-ungarische Militärsanitätswesen im Ersten Weltkrieg* Vols I, II Vienna ÖBV & Hpt 2002

Blenkinsop, Maj-Gen Sir L.J. et al. *History of the Great War: Veterinary Services* HMSO 1925

Bloem, Walter *The Advance from Mons 1914* Peter Davies 1930

Blond, Georges *La Marne* Presses de la Cité 1962

Borck, Karin and Kölm, Lothar (eds) *Gefangen in Sibirien. Tagebuch eines ostpreußischen Mädchens 1914–1920* Osnabrück Fibre 2001

Boyle, Andrew *The Riddle of Erskine Childers* Hutchinson 1977

Bridges, Sir Tom *Alarms and Excursions* Longman 1938

Buitenhuis, Peter *The Great War of Words* Batsford 1989

Bywater, Hector *Cruisers in Battle* Constable 1939

Capes, Harriet M. *Diary of a French Army Chaplain* Abbé Felix Klein trans. from *La Guerre vue d'une ambulance* Andrew Melrose 1915

Cave, Nigel and Sheldon, Jack *Le Cateau 26 August 1914* Pen & Sword 2008

Charykov, N.V. *Glimpses of High Politics* Allen & Unwin 1931

Chatfield, Lord Ernle *The Navy and Defence: An Autobiography* Heinemann 1942

Chickering, Roger *The Great War and Urban Life in Germany* CUP 2007

—*Imperial Germany and the Great War* CUP 1998

Churchill, Winston S. *The World Crisis* Vol. I Thornton Butterworth 1923

—*My Early Life* Eland 2000

Clark, Christopher *The Sleepwalkers* Penguin 2012

Clarke, Tom *My Northcliffe Diary* Gollancz 1931

Clayton, Anthony *Paths of Glory: The French Army 1914–1918* Cassell 2003

Cocho, Paul *Mes Carnets de guerre et de prisonnier 1914–1919* Presses Universitaires de Rennes 2010

Cœurdevey, Edouard *Carnets de guerre 1914–1918: Un Témoin lucide* Plon 2008

Cole, Laurence, Hämmerle, Christa and Scheutz, Martin (eds) *Glanz – Gewalt – Gehorsam. Militär und Gesellschaft in der Habsburgermonarchie (1800 bis 1918)* Essen Klartext 2011

Cooper, C.E. *Behind the Lines: One Woman's War* Norman & Hobbes 1982

Corday, Michel *The Paris Front: An Unpublished Diary 1914–18* NY 1934

Corns, Cathryn and Hughes-Wilson, John *Blindfold and Alone: British Military Executions in the Great War* Cassell 2001

Cornwall, Mark *The Hapsburg Elite and the South Slav Question*

—*A Living Anachronism? European Diplomacy and the Hapsburg Monarchy* ed. L. Nobelt and T.G. Otte Vienna Böhlau 2010

Craster J.M. (ed.) *Fifteen Rounds a Minute* Macmillan 1976

Dangerfield, George *The Strange Death of Liberal England* Constable 1935

Dedijer, Vladimir *The Road to Sarajevo* MacGibbon & Kee 1967

Delabeye, B (Lt) *Avant la ligne Maginot. Admirable résistance de la 1ère armée à la frontière des Vosges. Héroïque sacrifice de l'infanterie française* Montpellier Causse Graille and Castelnau 1939

Delmotte, Maurice *Vie quotidienne en France occupée: Journaux de Maurice Delmotte 1914–1918* ed. Philippe, Nathalie L'Harmattan 2007

Delvert, A. *Histoire d'une compagnie* Berger-Leverault 1918

Dirr, P. (ed.) *Bayerische Dokumente zum Kriegsausbruch und zum Versailler Schuldspruch* Munich and Berlin 1922

Druène, Lt.-Col. B. *Revue Historique de l'armée 1964. Numéro 3: De la guerre de mouvement à la guerre de tranchées*

Dunn, Captain J.C. *The War the Infantry Knew* Jane's 1987

Đurič, Silvija and Stevanović, Vidosav (eds) *Golgota i vaskrs Srbije, 1914–1915* Beograd 1990 3rd edn

Egremont, Max *Forgotten Land: Journeys Among the Ghosts of East Prussia* Picador 2011

Emigholz, Björn (ed.) *Die Tagebücher der Gertrud Schädla 1914–1918* Verden 2000

Englund, Peter *The Beauty and the Sorrow* Bloomsbury 2011

Farmborough, Florence *Nurse at the Russian Front: A Diary 1914–18* London 1977

Feilding, Lady Dorothie *Lady Under Fire on the Western Front* ed. Hallam, Andrew and Nicola Pen & Sword 2010

Ferguson, Niall *The Pity of War* Penguin 2003

Flood, P.J. *France 1914–18: Public Opinion and the War Effort* Macmillan 1990

Forstner, Franz *Przemyśl. Österreich-Ungarns bedeutendste Festung* Vienna ÖBV Pädagogischer 2nd edn 1997

French, Field Marshal Viscount *1914* Houghton Mifflin 1914

Freud, Sigmund *Letters 1873–1939* Hogarth Press 1961

Gallieni, Joseph *Mémoires du Maréchal Gallieni: Défense de Paris, 25 août–11 septembre 1914* Payot Paris 1928

Gebsattel, Ludwig von *Schlachten des Weltkrieges, Vol. VI Von Nancy bis zum Camp des Romains 1914* Stalling 2nd edn 1928

—*Vol. X Ypern 1914*

Geiss, Immanuel *July 1914* Batsford 1967

Gibson, Hugh *A Journal from Our Legation* NY 1917

Gide, André *Journals 1914–27* trans. Justin O'Brien Secker & Warburg 1948

Gilbert, Martin *Winston S. Churchill* Vol. III Heinemann 1971

Givray, Jacques (Capitaine Plieux de Diusse) *Journal d'un Officier de Liaison (la Marne: la Somme: l'Yser)* Paris Jouvé 1917

Gleason, A. *What the Workers Want* London 1920

Goebel, Stefan *The Great War and Medieval Memory: War, Remembrance and Medievalism in Britain and Germany, 1914–1940* CUP 2007

Gordon, Andrew *The Rules of the Game: Jutland and British Naval Command* John Murray 1996

Grdina, Igor *Slovenci med tradicijo in perspektivo. Politični mozaik 1860–1918* Ljubljana 2003

Grigg, John *Lloyd George: From Peace to War 1912–16* Methuen 1985

Groß, Gerhard P. (ed.) *Die Vergessene Front. Der Osten 1914/15 Ereignis Wirkung Nachwirkung* Paderborn Schöningh 2006

Guard, William J. *The Soul of Paris: Two Months in the French Capital During the War of 1914* Sun Printing & Publishing 1914

Gudehus-Schomerus, Heilwig et al. (eds) *'Einmal muß doch das wirkliche Leben wieder kommen!' Die Kriegsbriefe von Anna und Lorenz Treplin 1914–1918* Paderborn Schöningh 2010

Gueno, Jean-Pierre (ed.) *Paroles de Poilus: Lettres et carnets du front 1914–1918* Librio & Radio France 1998

Gumilev, Nikolai *Zapiski Kavalerista* [Diaries of a Cavalryman] Moscow 2007

Gumz, Jonathan *The Resurrection and Collapse of Empire in Habsburg Serbia 1914–18* CUP 2009

Haig, Douglas *War Diaries and Letters* ed. Sheffield, Gary and Bourne, John Weidenfeld & Nicolson 2005

Hamilton, Ernest *The First Seven Divisions* Hurst & Blackett 1916

Harding Davis, Richard *With the Allies* Duckworth 1915

Harel, Ambroise *Mémoires d'un poilu Breton* Odilon Ouest France 2003

Harris, Simon *History of the 43rd and 52nd (Ox and Bucks) Light Infantry in the Great War 1914–18* Simon Harris 2012

Hayne, M.B. *The French Foreign Office and the Origins of the First World War 1898–1914* OUP 1993

Healey, Maureen *Vienna and the Fall of the Hapsburg Empire: Total War and Everyday Life in World War I* CUP 2004

Herwig, Holger *The First World War: Germany and Austria-Hungary 1914–18* Edward Arnold 1997

—*The Marne* Random House 2009

Hirschfeld, Gerhard, Krumeich, Gerd and Renz, Irina (eds) *Keiner fühlt sich hier mehr als Mensch. Erlebnis und Wirkung des Ersten Weltkrieges* Essen 1993

—*Kriegserfahrungen. Studien zur Sozial – und Mentalitätsgeschichte des Ersten Weltkriegs* Essen Klartext 1997

—*Die Deutschen an der Somme 1914–1918. Krieg, Besatzung, Verbrannte Erde* Essen Klartext 2006

—*Enzyklopädie Erster Weltkrieg* Paderborn Schöningh 2009

Holmes, Richard *Tommy: The British Soldier on the Western Front 1914–18* HarperCollins 2004

Holroyd, Michael *Bernard Shaw* Chatto & Windus 1997

Holzer, Anton *Das Lächeln der Henker. Der unbekannte Krieg gegen die Zivilbevölkerung 1914–1918* Darmstadt Primus 2008

Hopman, Albert *Das ereignisreiche Leben eines 'Wilhelminers'. Tagebücher, Briefe, Aufzeichnungen 1901 bis 1920* ed. Epkenhans, Michael Munich Oldenbourg 2004

Horne, John (ed.) *State, Society and Mobilization in Europe During the First World War* CUP 1997

Horne, John and Kramer, Alan *German Atrocities 1914: A History of Denial* Yale 2001

Hull, Isabel *Absolute Destruction: Military Culture and the Practices of War in Imperial Germany* Cornell 2003

Huot, Louis and Voivenel, Paul *La Psychologie du soldat* Renaissance du Livre 1918

Jackson, Julian *The Fall of France* OUP 2003

Jay, John *Freud: A Life* Little Books 2006

Jeffrey, Keith *Field Marshal Sir Henry Wilson: A Political Soldier* OUP 2006

Jenkins, Roy *Asquith* Collins 1964

Joffre, Joseph Jacques Césaire *The Memoirs of Marshal Joffre* trans. Col. T. Bentley Mott Bles 1931

Johnston, Alexander *The Great War Diaries of Brigadier Alexander Johnston* ed. Edwin Astill Pen & Sword 2007

Joll, James *The Origins of the First World War* London 1984

Jones, Heather et al. (eds) *Untold War: New Perspectives in First World War Studies* Leiden 2008

Kehrt, Christian *Moderne Krieger. Die Technikerfahrungen deutscher Militärpiloten 1910–1945* Paderborn Schöningh 2010

Kelemen, Pal *Hussar's Picture Book, from the Diary of a Hungarian Cavalry Officer in World War I* Bloomington 1972

Kendall, Paul *Aisne 1914: The Dawn of Trench Warfare* Spellmount 2012

Kennedy, David M. *Over Here: The First World War and American Society* OUP 1980

Kessler, Harry Graf *Das Tagebuch. Vol. V: 1914–1916* ed. Günter Riederer and Ulrich Ott Stuttgart Cotta 2008

King-Hall, Stephen *A North Sea Diary 1914–1918* NY 2012

Kisch, Egon Erwin *'Schreib das auf, Kisch!' Das Kriegstagebuch von Egon Erwin Kisch* Berlin Reiss 1930

Knoch, Peter (ed.) *Menschen im Krieg 1914–1918*, Ludwigsburg Pädagogische Hochschule 1987

Knox, Sir Alfred *With the Russian Army* Vol. I Hutchinson 1921

Koenigswald, Harald Von *Stirb und Werde. Aus Briefen und Kriegstagebuchblättern des Leutnants Bernhard von der Marwitz* Breslau Korn Verlag 1931

Kondurashkin, S.S. *Vsled za voinoi* [In the Footsteps of War] Petrograd 1915

Krafft-Krivanec, Johnanna *Niedergeschrieben für euch. Ein Kriegstagebuch aus kulturanthropologischer Perspektive* Vienna Passagen Verlag 2005

Kronenbitter, Gunther *Krieg im Frieden. Die Führung der k.u.k. Armee und die Großmachtpolitik Österreich-Ungarns 1906–1914* Munich Oldenbourg 2003

Ksyunin A. *Narod na voine (iz zapisok voennogo korrespondenta)* [People at War (From the Notes of a War Correspondent)] Petrograd, 1916

Kupferman, Fred *14–18: Mourir pour la patrie. Rumeurs, bobards et propagande* Editions du Seuil 1992

Kuznetsov, Ivan (ed.) *Petrov Pobeg Iz Plena* Penza 1998

Laby, Lucien *Les Carnets de l'aspirant Laby, médecin dans les tranchées 28 juillet 1914–14 juillet 1919* Editions Bayard 2001

Lacouture, Jean *De Gaulle: The Rebel 1890–1944* Collins Harvill 1990

Ladurner-Parthanes, Matthias *Kriegstagebuch eines Kaiserjägers* Bozen Athesia 1996

Lambert, Nicholas A. *Planning Armageddon: British Economic Warfare and the First World War* Harvard University Press 2012

Lang, Carl von *Die Lage auf dem Balkan* in *Danzer's Armee-Zeitung 19* (1914) No. 1

Lasswell, Harold D. *Propaganda Technique in the World War* Knopf 1927

Lieven, D.C.B. *Russia and the Origins of the First World War* NY St Martin's 1983

Lintier, Paul *My Seventy-Five: The Journal of a French Gunner* Peter Davies 1929

Lipp, Anne *Meinungslenkung im Krieg. Kriegserfahrungen deutscher Soldaten und ihre Deutung 1914–1918* Göttingen Vandenhoek & Ruprecht 2003

Littauer, Vladimir *Russkie gusary* [The Russian Hussars] Moscow 2006

Lloyd George, David *War Memoirs* Ivor Nicholson & Watson 1933

Lobanov-Rostovsky, Andrei *The Grinding Mill: Reminiscences of War and Revolution in Russia* NY 1935

Longerich, Peter *Heinrich Himmler: A Life* OUP 2011

Ludendorff, Gen. Erich *Das Marne-Drama* Munich 1934

Macarthur, Brian *For King and Country* Little, Brown 2008

Macdonald, Lynn *1914* Michael Joseph 1987

McMeekin, Sean *The Russian Origins of the First World War* Belknap 2011

Madan, Geoffrey *Geoffrey Madan's Notebooks* OUP 1985

Mahnke, Dietrich *Kriegstaten und Schicksale des Res.-Inf.-Regiments 75 1914/18* Bremen 1932

Martin, Rudolf *Stehen wir vor einem Weltkrieg?* Leipzig Engelmann 1908

Masterman, Charles *The Condition of England* London 1909

Maufrais, Louis *J'étais médecin dans les tranchées août 1914-juillet 1919* ed. Martine Veillet Robert Laffont 2008

Maze, Paul *A Frenchman in Khaki* Heinemann 1934

Meinertzhagen, Richard *Army Diary 1899–1926* Oliver & Boyd 1960

Mellersh, H.E.L. *Schoolboy into War* Kimber 1978

Meštrović, Ivan *Spomini* Ljubljana 1971

Meteling, Wencke *Ehre, Einheit, Ordnung. Preußische und französische Städte und ihre Regimenter im Krieg, 1870/71 und 1914–19* Baden-Baden Nomos 2010

Meyer, Jacques *La Vie quotidienne des soldats pendant la Grande Guerre* Hachette 1966

Mihaly, Jo … *da gibt's ein Wiedersehn! Kriegstagebuch eines Mädchens 1914–1918* Freiburg F.H. Kerle 1982

Minaudier, Jean-Pierre *Population et société de 1850 à 1914* Versailles Lycée La Bruyère 2004

Miquel, Pierre *L'Année 14*

Mitrovic, Andrej *Serbia's Great War* Hurst 2007

Mombauer, Annika *Helmuth von Moltke and the Origins of the First World War* CUP 2000

Mommsen, Wolfgang J. *Der Topos vom unvermeidlichen Krieg. Außenpolitik und öffentliche Meinung im Deutschen Reich im letzten Jahrzehnt vor 1914* in Dülffer, Jost and Holl, Karl (eds) *Bereit zum Krieg. Kriegsmentalität im wilhelminischen Deutschland 1890–1914* Göttingen Vandenhoek & Ruprecht 1986

Montague, C.E. *Rough Justice* Chatto & Windus 1926

Morton, Frederick *Thunder at Twilight* Peter Owen 1991

Muehlon, Wilhelm *Ein Fremder im eigenen Land. Erinnerungen und Tagebuchaufzeichnungen eines Krupp-Direktors 1908–1914* ed.Wolfgang Benz Bremen Donat 1989

Muggeridge, Kitty and Adam, Ruth *Beatrice Webb* Secker & Warburg 1967

Murray, Gilbert *Faith, War and Policy* OUP 1918

Naegelen, R. *Les Suppliciés* Paris 1927

Neiberg, Michael *Dance of the Furies: Europe and the Outbreak of World War 1* Belknap 2011

Niedhart, Gottfried (ed.) *Gustav Mayer. Als deutsch-jüdischer Historiker in Krieg und Revolution 1914–1920. Tagebücher, Aufzeichnungen, Briefe* Munich Oldenbourg 2009

Nogales, Rafael de *Four Years Beneath the Crescent* London 2003

Nowak, Karl Friedrich (ed.) *Die Aufzeichnungen des Generalmajor Max Hoffmann* Vol. I Berlin Verlag für Kulturpolitik 1930

Nübel, Christoph *Die Mobilisierung der Kriegsgesellschaft. Propaganda und Alltag im Ersten Weltkrieg in Münster* Münster 2008

Oman, J. *The War and its Issues* CUP 1915

Painter, George *Marcel Proust* Pimlico 1996

Paléologue, Maurice *An Ambassador's Memoirs* trans. F.A. Holt NY George H. Doran 1925

Palmer, Svetlana and Wallis, Sarah (eds) *The War in Words* Simon & Schuster 2003

Playne, Caroline *Society at War* Allen & Unwin 1931

Poincaré, Raymond *Comment fut déclarée la Guerre de 1914* Flammarion 1939

Ponsonby, Arthur *Falsehood in Wartime* London 1928

Pound, Reginald *The Lost Generation* Constable 1964

Prévost, Alain *Paysan français Ephraim Grenadou* Éditions du Seuil 1966

Priestley, R.E. *The Signal Service in the European War of 1914–18* W. & J. Mackay 1921

Ransome, Arthur *Autobiography* Cape 1976

Recouly, Raymond *Les Heures tragiques d'Avant-Guerre* Paris 1922

Reed, John *The War in Eastern Europe* Eveleigh Nash 1916

Reichsarchiv (ed.) *Der Weltkrieg 1914–1918* Vol. I Berlin Mittler 1925

Reimann, Aribert *Der große Krieg der Sprachen. Untersuchungen zur historischen Semantik in Deutschland und England zur Zeit des Ersten Weltkrieges* Essen Klartext 2000

Reinschedl, Manfred *Die Aufrüstung der Habsburgermonarchie von 1880 bis 1914 im internationalen Vergleich. Der Anteil Österreich-Ungarns am Wettrüsten vor dem Ersten Weltkrieg* Frankfurt 2001

Richards, Frank *Old Soldiers Never Die* Mott 1983

Rioux, Jean-Pierre *La Dernière journée de paix*

Ritter, Gerhard *The Sword and the Sceptre: The Problem of Militarism in Germany* 4 vols Allen Lane 1970–73

Rivière, Jacques *Carnets 1914–1918* ed. Isabelle and Alain Rivière Fayard 1974

Rohl, John C. *The Kaiser and His Court* CUP 1994

—*Wilhelm II: Into the Abyss of War and Exile* CUP 2013

Rougevin-Baville, Col. J. *Revue historique de l'armée. Ministère des armées 1964: L'Aéronautique militaire française, les débuts de la guerre aérienne 1914*

Sanders, M.L. and Taylor, Philip M. *British Propaganda During the First World War 1914–18* Macmillan 1982

Schindler, John 'Disaster on the Drina: The Austro-Hungarian Army in Bosnia' in *War in History 9* 2002

Schmitt, Bernadotte *The Fashion and Future of History: Historical Studies and Addresses* Cleveland Press of Western Reserve University 1960

Schneider, Constantin *Die Kriegserinnerungen 1914–1919* ed. Oskar Dohle Vienna Böhlau 2003

Schwarte, Max (ed.) *Technik des Kriegswesens*, Leipzig and Berlin B.G. Teubner 1913

Seligmann, Matthew *The Royal Navy and the German Threat 1901–1914* OUP 2012

—*Naval Intelligence from Germany* Navy Records Society 2007

Sheldon, Jack *The German Army at Ypres 1914* Pen & Sword 2010

Showalter, Dennis *Tannenberg: Clash of Empires* Archon 1991

Sitwell, Osbert *The Scarlet Tree* Macmillan 1947

Smith, Douglas *Former People* Macmillan 2012

Smith, Leonard et al. *France and the Great War 1914–1918* trans. Helen McPhail CUP 2003

Soames, Mary *Speaking for Themselves* Doubleday 1998

Soutou, Georges-Henri *L'Or et le sang: Les buts de guerre économique de la première guerre mondiale* Paris Fayard 1989

Spears, Edward *Liaison 1914* Stein & Day 1968

Stahl und Steckrüben. Beiträge und Quellen zur Geschichte Niedersachsens im Ersten Weltkrieg (1914–1918) Vols I, II Hamelin Niemeyer 1993

Steed, Wickham *The Hapsburg Monarchy* Constable 1913

Steffen, Gustaf F. *Krieg und Kultur. Sozialpsychologische Dokumente und Beobachtungen vom Weltkrieg 1914* Jena 1915

Steinberg, Jonathan *Bismarck: A Life* OUP 2011

Stojadinović, Milan *Ni rat ni pakt* Otokar Kerošvani Rijeka 1970

Stone, Norman *The Eastern Front* Hodder & Stoughton 1975

Strachan, Hew *The First World War Vol I: To Arms* OUP 2001

Štrandman, Vasily N (Basil de Strandman) *Balkanske uspomene* [Balkan Memoirs] Knjiga I., Deo 1–2, Žagor Beograd 2009

Strong, Rowland *Diary of an English Resident in France* Eveleigh Nash 1915

Stumpf, Richard *Erinnerungen aus dem deutsch-englischen Seekriege auf S.M.S. Helgoland*, in: *Die Ursachen des Deutschen Zusammenbruches im Jahre 1918* 4th Series Vol. X 2 Berlin Deutsche Verlagsgesellschaft für Politik und Geschichte 1928

Šuklje, Fran *Iz mojih spominov II* Ljubljana 1995

Sulzbach, Herbert *With the German Guns* Warne 1981

Tapert, Annette *Despatches from the Heart* Hamish Hamilton 1984

Terraine, John *Mons* Batsford 1960

Thiel, Jens *Anwerbung, Deportation und Zwangsarbeit im Ersten Weltkrieg* Essen Klartext 2007

Thompson, John A. *Reformers and War* CUP 1987

Thompson, Wayne C. *In the Eye of the Storm* University of Iowa Press 1980

Thomson, George Malcolm *Lord Castlerosse* Weidenfeld & Nicolson 1973

Tolstoy, Alexei *Pisma s Puti* [Travel Reports] Russkie Vedomosti 1914

Tomalin, Claire *Thomas Hardy* Penguin 2006

Trushnovich, Aleksandr *Vospominaniya kornilovtsa* [Memoirs of a Kornilov Man] *1914–1934* Moscow and Frankfurt 2004

Tuffrau, Paul *Quatre années sur le front: Carnets d'un combatant* Paris Imago 1998

Turczynowitcz, Laura de G. *When the Prussians Came to Poland* NY 1916

Turner, E.S. *Dear Old Blighty* Michael Joseph 1980

Turner, L.C.F. *Origins of the First World War* Edward Arnold 1970

Überegger, Oswald *Heimatfronten. Dokumente zur Erfahrungsgeschichte der Tiroler Kriegsgesellschaft im Ersten Weltkrieg* Innsbruck UP Wagner 2006

Verhey, Jeffrey *The Spirit of 1914* CUP 2000

Viard, Albert *Lettres à Léa 1914–18* Editions de l'Aube 1998

Waites, Bernard *A Class Society at War: England 1914–18* Berg 1977

Wallace, Stuart *War and the Image of Germany* John Donald 1988

Waterhouse, Michael *Edwardian Requiem: A Life of Sir Edward Grey* Biteback 2013

Wharton, Edith *A Backward Glance* NY Appleton-Century 1934

Williamson, Samuel *Austria-Hungary and the Origins of the First World War* Macmillan 1991

—*The Politics of Grand Strategy* Harvard 1970

Wilson, Keith (ed.) *Decisions for War 1914* UCL Press 1995

Wilson, Trevor *The Myriad Faces of War* Blackwell 1986

Winslow, Carroll Dana *With the French Flying Corps* Charles Scribner's Sons 1917

Winter, Denis *First of the Few* Penguin 1982

Winter, Jay *Remembering War* Yale 2006

Winter, Jay and Robert, Jean-Louis (eds) *Capital Cities at War* CUP 1997

Wisthaler, Sigrid (ed.) *Karl Außerhofer: Das Kriegstagebuch eines Soldaten im Ersten Weltkrieg* Innsbruck UP 2010

Wittgenstein, Ludwig *Geheime Tagebücher 1914–1916* Vienna Turia & Kant 2nd edn 1991

Wolff, Theodor *Diaries 1914–19* Vol. I Boldt Verlag Boppert/Rhine 1984

Wolmar, Christian *Engines of War: How Wars Were Won and Lost on the Railways* Atlantic 2010

Wolz, Nicolas *Das lange Warten. Kriegserfahrungen deutscher und britischer Seeoffiziere 1914 bis 1918* Paderborn Schöningh 2008

Yerta, Gabrielle and Marguerite *Six Women and the Invasion* Macmillan 1917 republished as an e-book by Gutenberg

Young, Filson *With the Battlecruisers* Cassell 1921

Zeynek, Theodor Ritter von *Ein Offizier im Generalstabskorps* ed. Broucek, Peter Vienna 2009

Ziemann, Bejamin *War Experiences in Rural Germany 1914–23* OUP 2007

Index

NOTE: Ranks and titles are generally those applying at the time

Aarschot, Belgium, 191
Abel-Smith, Col. Wilfrid, 350, 467–8, 472, 488, 491, 496, 531
Aberhofer, Karl, 426
Action française, l' (newspaper), 430
Admiralty: inadequacy, 374; intelligence department (Room 40), 375–6, 379, 382; Churchill and Fisher at, 378
agents (intelligence), 440–1
aircraft: in warfare, 455–61
airships (Zeppelins): bombing raids, 161; in East Prussia, 280; Germans employ, 456; vulnerability, 461
Aisne, river, 339, 345–8, 351–5, 463
Albert I, King of the Belgians, 89–91, 94, 189, 195, 451, 466
Albert, Prince of Schleswig-Holstein, 431
Albertini, Luigi: *The Origins of the War of 1914*, xxiv
Albrecht, Duke, 336
Aldington, Richard: *Death of a Hero*, 421
Alexander, King of Serbia: murdered, xxxv, 17
Alexander, Prince Regent of Serbia, xxxiv, 18, 55
Alexander, Kurt, 432
Allard, Jules, 308
Allenby, Maj. Gen. Edmund: and Gladys Winterbottom, 129; at Mons, 204, 213; at Le Cateau, 221–2; French seek help from, 292; at First Ypres, 485, 487; commands cavalry corps, 548
Allenstein, 278, 280
Alsace and Lorraine: Bismarck annexes, 19; French campaign and defeat in, 165–7, 169, 172–7, 182; conscripts in German army,

166; French attack (August 1914), 246, 303; German need to attack, 314; and French war aims, 542
Amade, Gen. Albert d', 213, 222, 303
Amery, Leo, 435
Andenne, Belgium, 187, 191
Andresen, Kresten, 353, 539
anti-Semitism: in Vienna, 10; and Dreyfus case, 19
Antwerp: Belgians fall back on, 194; Belgians sortie from, 328; Falkenhayn threatens, 445–6; Churchill's plans for, 446, 448–51, 454; siege, 447–9; Royal Marines withdraw from, 449–50; falls, 450–1
Apis *see* Dimitrijević, Col. Dragutin
Ardennes, 181, 195, 199
Arenau, Gen. Alexander Brosch, 392
Armentières, 472
armies: organisation, xxix
Army Bill (Germany, 1913), 31, 57
Arras, 444
Aschwangen, East Prussia, 405
Asquith, Cyril, 548–9
Asquith, Herbert Henry (*later* 1st Earl of Oxford and Asquith): on Lichnowskys, 8; and domestic unrest, 23, 25; background and character, 24; on British intervention in war, 36; neglects foreign affairs, 37, 59, 101; on Anglo-French agreement, 38; and Venetia Stanley, 59, 61, 72, 87, 95, 293, 419, 549; on Irish problem, 60; on Serbian crisis, 61; indifference to prospect of outbreak of war, 72; on Bethmann's diplomatic blunder over Belgium, 77; indecision over declaring war, 85–6, 101; and German invasion of Belgium, 90–1; cheered by crowds, 95; attitude to European situation, 101; and military advisers, 126; chairs War Council, 131; told of German atrocities in Belgium,

Asquith, Herbert Henry – *cont.*
    188; on Battle of Mons, 293; qualities,
    293–4; denounces *Times'* report on British
    retreat, 297; insists on BEF participation at
    Marne, 340; and Heligoland Bight action,
    373; on Cradock's defeat at Coronel, 377;
    on death of Rivvy Grenfell, 419; and
    George V's complacency, 431; asks
    Churchill to publicise progress, 434;
    Churchill requests field command from,
    454; on aerial warfare, 458; and Russian
    claims on Dardanelles and Constantinople,
    543; Sir John French meets at Walmer, 548;
    optimism, 549; retains office until 1916,
    549
Asquith, Margot (*later* Countess of Oxford
    and Asquith), 23–4
Asquith, Violet (*later* Bonham Carter), 121,
    293–4, 424, 451, 549
Astor, Mrs John Jacob, 443
Aubrey, John, xxiii
Audregnies, 215
August Victoria, Empress of Germany, 76
Austria-Hungary: casualties, xxii, 153–4, 554,
    561; annexes Bosnia-Herzegovina, xxxiii–
    xxxiv, 14–15; potential dissolution, 9; in
    Triple Alliance, 9; rural society, 10;
    militancy towards Serbia, 11, 17, 29–30,
    41–2; subject minorities, 11, 30; battle
    plans, 28–9; army backwardness and
    composition, 29–30; Germany promises to
    support, 30; ultimatum to Serbia, 45, 49,
    51, 54–5, 58, 60–1; becomes republic, 51;
    invasion of Serbia, 54, 561; Serbia replies
    to, 62; mobilises, 63, 72, 107–8; declares
    war on Serbia, 68; bombards Belgrade, 73,
    77; Russia declares war on, 81; attacks
    Serbia, 138; patriotism, 139; conduct of
    war in Serbia, 145–53, 510–13; repressive
    measures in Serbia, 147–9, 157; withdraws
    from Serbia, 152–3; second invasion of
    Serbia (September 1914), 155–7; Russia
    concentrates on, 259; campaign in Poland/
    Galicia, 386–407, 497–9; language
    confusion, 392; commissariat and logistical
    weaknesses, 401; industrial disputes, 414;
    living conditions, 414; aircraft, 457;
    military incompetence, 504–5; prisoners in
    Serbia, 513
Austrian army: condition, 140; low morale,
    503–5; casualties, 505; women in, 505
Austrian army formations and units: 19th
    Landsturm Infantry regiment, 400

authors: propaganda and patriotic writings,
    436
Avakumović, Joven, 41
Awdry, Lt., 243

Bachmann, Dr Johann, 150, 157, 512–13
Baehreke, Lt., 491
Baekeland, Leo, 2
Bailly, 292
Baker-Carr, Maj. Christopher, 256
Balfour, Arthur James, 24
Balkan Wars (1912 and 1913), 16
Balkans: unrest, 7, 19; Russian status in,
    15–16
Ballin, Albert, 82
balloons, observation, 455
Bantlin, Georg, 536
Bar-sur-Aube, 309
Baranovichi, Belorussia, 259–60
Barclay, G.H., 16
Baring, Maurice, 98, 459
Bark, Peter, 56
Barnard, Bob, 256
Barrès, Maurice, 341–2, 439
Barth, Sgt., 491
Barthas, Louis, 187, 428, 517–18, 526, 527,
    537–8
Bartlett, Ashmead, 516
Basedow, Heino von, 270
Basily, Nikolai de, 73
Bassée, La, 472, 537
Battenberg, Admiral Prince Louis of, 71, 374
Bäumer, Gertrud, 118
Bavay, 216
Beatty, Vice-Admiral Sir David: character,
    357, 378; and Heligoland action, 364–6,
    369, 372–3; at Scarborough raid, 380–1;
    succeeds Jellicoe as commander of Grand
    Fleet, 384
Beatty, Ethel, Lady (*née* Field), 366, 373
Beauchamp, William Lygon, 7th Earl, 91, 93
Beaumont, Capt. R.G., 228
Bebel, August, 47
Becker, Capt., 191
Beer, Charles, 446–7
Beer, Edouard, 105, 446–7, 495, 531
Behr, Ferdinand, xxxix
Belgium: Germany demands right to pass
    through, 76; under threat, 78, 88–9;
    Germany invades, 90–2, 94–5, 97, 102; early
    battles, 160–4, 179–81; German reprisals
    and atrocities in, 162–3, 181, 187–93, 213,
    444, 543; French advance in, 177; troop

movements, 178; German advance through, 195, 198, 201–2; civilian refugees, 217; refugees' life in England, 426; as cause of war, 433; railway system, 443; Rupprecht advances over, 444; troops demoralised, 454–5; aircraft, 457; renewed German offensive (October 1914), 464–7

Belgrade: Austria proposes to annex, 63; Austrians bombard, 73; Kaiser proposes limited occupation of, 77; shelled, 138, 143, 145; vulnerability, 142; falls to Austrians, 510, 512

Belloc, Hilaire, 436

Benedict XV, Pope, 556

Bennett, Arnold, 436–7

Berchtold, Count Leopold: visits Franz Ferdinand, xxxii–xxxiii ; considers rapprochement with Russia, 7; on Franz Ferdinand's death as excuse for war, 29; advocates action against Serbia, 42–4, 48–9, 68; ultimatum to Serbia, 54; reports Serbs firing on Austrian steamers, 63; on German interference, 77; blames Germans for military reverses, 386

Berchtold, Countess Nandine, xxxii

Berlin: anti-war demonstrations, 71; British embassy attacked, 98; anti-foreigner actions, 116

Bernhardi, Gen. Friedrich von: Germany and the Next War, 48

Berthier, Gustave, 558

Bertie, Sir Francis, 35, 68, 78, 83–4, 93, 182, 186, 200, 287–8, 415, 444

Bethmann Hollweg, Theobald: seeks improved relations with Britain, 7; powers, 26; and prospect of war, 28, 31, 77; promises support for Austria, 30; fears encirclement, 34; and Austrian delay over Serbia, 43–4; character, 46–7; sees Russia as threat, 46; and popular demonstrations against war, 59; warns Russia against mobilisation, 73; Kaiser's relations with, 76; proposal to Grey requesting neutrality for assuring respect for Belgian and French territorial rights, 76–7; on seeing Germany as victim, 76; urges Austria to accept diplomatic mediation, 77; overruled by Moltke, 78–9, 81; Bülow blames for war, 82; on declaration of war, 95; on invasion of Belgium, 95; loses stature at outbreak of war, 97; lists demands (9 September 1914), 100; welcomes outbreak of war, 118; anticipates early victory, 248; at front, 491;

war aims, 543; hopes for compromise peace, 545; and Falkenhayn's plan for separate peace in East, 554; criticises Falkenhayn, 555; rejects compromise negotiations, 555; responsibility for war, 563

Biddulph, Col. Henry, 332

Bidou, Henri, 287

Bilinski, Léon, Ritter von, 42

Binding, Rudolf, 519–20, 539

Birch, 'Curly', 222

Bird, Col. Wilkinson, 219, 226, 230, 233–5

'Birdcage, The' (near Messines), 525

Bismarck, Prince Otto von, 6, 31, 90

Bixschoote, 494

Black Hand, the (Ujedinjenje ili Smrt; movement), xxxiv–xxxv, xxxvii, 139

Black Sea: domination of, 34; Russian access to, 53

Blacklock, Lt. A.H., 422

Blewitt, Capt. Guy, 216

Bleyenberghe, Jeanne van, 162, 217, 444

Bloch, Marc, 252

Bloem, Capt. Walter, 209, 212–13, 310

Blunt, Wilfrid Scawen, 25

Bonham Carter, Maurice, 293

Bonneau, Gen. Louis, 167

Bordeaux: French government moves to, 287

Bosnia-Herzegovina: annexed by Austria, xxxiii–xxxiv, 14–15; Austrian troops in, 147; fighting in, 155; Serbs withdraw from, 157; assassins and conspirators tried, 158

Botha, Louis, 96

Bottomley, Horatio, 294

Bouchard, Henri, 532

Bouillot, Georges, 291

Bourg-et-Comin, 347

Boussingault, Jean-Louis, 532

Bradbury, Capt. Edward, VC, 253

Bradford, Col. Sir Evelyn, 332

Braque, Georges, 532

Breinlinger, Sgt. Otto, 183

Brest-Litovsk, Treaty of (1918), 555

Bridges, Elizabeth, 114

Bridges, Maj. Tom, 206, 208, 215, 240, 328

Brisbane, Sgt., 520

Brisley, Sgt. Alf, 532

Britain: industrial decline, 3–4; naval rivalry with Germany, 7–8; economic and social changes, 21–3; strikes and unrest, 22–3, 413–14; preparations for war, 34, 36; agreement with France, 38; support for Austria in Serb crisis, 58, 61; presumed

Britain: – *cont.*
  non-intervention in war, 67–8, 85;
  indecision over entering war, 85–8;
  guarantees Belgian neutrality, 89;
  Commons debate on entering war, 92–3;
  mobilisation, 92, 95; declares war, 95; entry
  into war, 99; and European balance of
  power, 101–2; lacks universal military
  service, 107; professional army and
  reservists, 107; patriotism and
  reconciliation, 112; profiteering, 114; anti-
  German hysteria, 116; supposed invasion
  threat, 117; popular reaction to outbreak of
  war, 118–20; hesitates over early military
  operations, 129–30; role on Western Front,
  201; citizens volunteer to aid France, 287;
  believes France unwilling to fight, 293;
  casualties, 295, 553; press denied access to
  army, 295–7; deserters shot, 322; war
  widows' pensions, 412–13; women's role in,
  413; public school ethos, 421–2; decline in
  social deference, 425; disillusionment with
  war, 433–4; use of aircraft, 457; war aims,
  542–3; and prospective peace settlement,
  546; leadership weaknesses, 550; *see also*
  Royal Air Force; Royal Marines; Royal
  Naval Air Service; Royal Navy
Britain's (toy manufacturer), 420
British Army: Field Service Regulations, 26;
  weakness, 36–7, 39; reorganised by
  Kitchener, 127; recruitment and
  conscription, 128–9, 521; officers, 206;
  social composition, 208; command
  weakness, 216; demoralised, 252, 257;
  unpreparedness for war, 300; at Marne,
  321; aristocratic deaths, 419; phlegmatism,
  467–8; attacked at Ypres, 469; leadership
  weaknesses, 480; unheroic behaviour,
  489–90; officers returned from front, 519;
  equipment shortages, 521–2; horses, 522–3
BRITISH ARMY FORMATIONS AND
UNITS
Corps: I, 204, 213, 216, 221, 242, 332; II, 204,
  211, 214–16, 219–21, 226–7, 231, 236–7,
  241, 245, 258, 291; III, 332
Divisions: 1st, 485; 3rd, 351, 490; 4th, 221,
  234; 5th, 221, 233–4; 7th, 451, 455, 468–9,
  471, 478, 485–6; Royal Naval, 446, 448, 451
Brigades: Guards, 254–6; 11th Infantry, 346
Regiments: Argyll & Sutherland Highlanders,
  228, 233; Bedfords, 347, 480, 489;
  Berkshires, 243; Cameron Highlanders,
  348, 495; Cheshires, 480; Coldstream
  Guards, 216–18, 348–9, 483, 489;
  Connaught Rangers, 242, 348–9;
  Cornwalls, 228; Dragoon Guards, 215, 254,
  347; Dublin Fusiliers, 240; East Surreys,
  228; Gordon Highlanders, 235, 447;
  Grenadier Guards, 216–14, 218, 242, 355,
  348–50, 473, 448, 489, 494, 558;
  Hampshires, 229, 346; Hertfordshire, 493;
  Household Cavalry, 481, 489; Hussars, 256,
  483; Irish Guards, 242, 245, 349, 489; King's
  Own, 228–9; King's Royal Rifle Corps,
  473,484; Lancers (9th), 215, 483; Life
  Guards, 481, 489; Lincolnshire, 489;
  Liverpool Scottish, 538; London Scottish,
  455, 483, 486, 490, 518; Loyal North
  Lancashires, 351, 484; Middlesex, 204–5,
  209, 211, 213, 230, 254; Norfolks, 225;
  Northumberland Fusiliers, 212, 480, 489;
  Oxford and Bucks Light Infantry, 216, 243,
  345, 350, 473, 493; Oxfordshire Hussars,
  484; Queen's, 484, 485; Rifle Brigade, 346,
  516, 525; Royal Fusiliers, 204, 209–10, 254,
  493; Royal Horse Guards, 516; Royal Irish
  Dragoon Guards, 203, 213; Royal Irish
  Rifles, 207, 219, 230, 233–4, 477; Royal
  Munster Fusiliers, 242–3; Royal Welch
  Fusiliers, 245, 256, 455, 472, 481, 489, 525;
  Scots Greys, 256; Scots Guards, 348;
  Seaforth Highlanders, 516; Sherwood
  Foresters, 115; Somerset, 346; South
  Lancashire, 479; South Wales Borderers,
  485; Suffolk, 225–6, 228, 231, 233;
  Warwicks, 240, 471; West Surrey, 347; West
  Yorkshire, 351; Wiltshire, 241, 473, 479;
  Worcestershire, 476, 484–6; Yorkshire Light
  Infantry, 225–6, 228, 231, 233, 235
Other: Royal Army Veterinary Corps, 523;
  Royal Engineers, 225; Royal Horse Artillery,
  252–4
British Empire: power, 15; not consulted over
  declaring war, 95; casualties, 561
British Expeditionary Force (BEF): initial
  deployment, 37, 39; strength, 40, 548;
  convoyed to France, 97, 132; Northcliffe
  opposes, 131; Sir John French commands,
  132; approaches French-Belgian border,
  177; numbers, 195, 201; opposes German
  advance, 194; at Battle of Mons, 199, 201;
  welcomed in France, 202; equipment, 206;
  separated from French, 214; withdraws
  from Mons, 214, 238–9; stragglers and
  deserters, 239–40; retires southward, 242–4,
  246, 248, 256, 291, 298; morale falls, 245;

Germans overtake on Marne, 252; casualties, 257, 548; limited press reports on, 296–7; defeatism, 297; Joffre requests support from, 303; support in Joffre's offensive, 306; deployment before Battle of Marne, 309; tardy advance to Marne, 321–2, 324, 328–30; crosses Marne, 332; slow pursuit of Germans at Marne, 337, 340, 345, 353; shifted to allies' left flank, 442, 445, 463, 467; in Flanders, 468; shortage of barbed wire, 476; losses at Ypres, 495; extent of front, 515

Brooke, Lt. John, VC, 478

Brosch Aarenau, Alexander von, 139

Brownlow, Capt. Jimmy, 332

Bruges, 463

Brussels, 202

Bryce, James, Viscount, 437

Buchanan, Sir George, 52, 56, 65

Bulgaria, 504

Bülow, Bernhard, Prince von, 28, 82, 555

Bülow, Gen. Karl von, 198, 199, 202, 204, 246–51, 310, 318, 326–31, 337–9, 341, 443

burial of dead, 52

Burián, Count István, 63

Burns, John, 93

Burrows, Gunner Charlie, 469, 484

Burton, Stephen, 255

Čabrinović, Nedeljko, xxxv–xxxvi, xxxix–xl

Cadorna, Count Luigi, 108

Caillaux, Henriette, 49–50, 69, 348

Caillaux, Joseph, 33

Calmette, Gaston, 49, 69

Cambon, Jules, 64, 69, 93, 109

Cambon, Paul, 36–7, 71, 87–8

Camoin, Charles, 532

camouflage, 532

Campbell, Lt. Col. David, 215, 332

Canard enchaîné, Le (magazine), 439

Canter, Ernst, 456

Capper, Gen. Sir Thomas, 486

Carson, Sir Edward (later Baron), 24

Cassell, Sir Ernest, 62, 113

Cassin, René, 523

Castelnau, sous-lieutenant Charles de Curières de, 175–6

Castelnau, Gen. Edouard de, 172, 174–6, 182, 248, 290–1, 315–16, 328, 443

Castlerosse, Valentine Browne, Viscount, 62, 136, 255

Cateau, Le, 219–22, 224–38, 240, 252

cavalry: susceptibility to modern weapons,

151; weapons and battle tactics, 164–5

Cavan, Hugh Frederick Vaughan, 4th Earl of, 517

Cecil, Lt. George, 255

censorship, 435, 439

Cer, Mount (Serbia), 151

Challamel, Léon-Pierre-Marie, 419

Chamberlain, Neville, 294

Chambrey, Lorraine, 174

Chapron, M. (of Vitry-le-François), 170

Charleroi, 178, 195

Charrier, Col. Paul, 242–3

Chartier, Alain Emile-Auguste, 439

Charykov, Mrs Nikolai, 510

Chassigne, Coudurier de, 94

Chastenet, J.J., 559

Château-Thierry, 252

Chatfield, Capt. Alfred Ernle, RN, 369

Chaulet, Col., 319

Chemin des Dames, Le, 343, 345, 347–8, 350–1, 354, 442, 446, 517

Chesterton, G.K., 436

Childers, Erskine, 125–6, 462; The Riddle of the Sands, 117, 126

children: subjected to patriotic propaganda, 420–1

Childs, 'Fido', 222

Chotek, Sophie (Franz Ferdinand's morganatic wife), xxxi, xxxiii, xxxvi, xxxviii

Christmas 1914, 541, 556–9

Churchill, Clementine (later Lady), 72

Churchill (Sir) Winston: on opening of Great War, xxi–xxii; conversation with Harcourt, 1; on change and impermanence, 4; as Home Secretary, 22; as First Lord of Admiralty, 23; attacked in Commons library, 24; and British intervention in war, 36; on insignificance of British Army, 36; on hearing of Austrian ultimatum, 60; and fleet mobilisation, 71; on inevitability of war, 72; urges support for Entente partners, 85; on British decision to enter war, 93, 102; eagerness for battle, 95, 97; and intelligence services, 97; and escape of Goeben and Breslau, 110; commandeers Turkish warships, 114; recruits Childers, 126; weeps at Wilson's departure for France, 136; befriends Spears, 198; character, 294; on Jellicoe's responsibilities, 357; on navy's role, 360–1; wishes to land army on German coast, 360–1; supports Keyes's submarine plan, 364; favours

Churchill, Winston: – *cont.*
  Beatty, 366; congratulates Heligoland Bight
    action, 373; appoints Fisher to replace
    Battenberg, 378; on successful transport to
    France of men and equipment, 385;
    Asquith asks to publicise progress, 434;
    Macleod on qualities, 446; and defence of
    Antwerp, 448–51, 454; gloom during Ypres
    battle, 474; on Ypres victory, 495; on
    modern war, 548; regard for Sir John
    French, 549; Gallipoli plan, 550; on losses
    in combat, 550–1
ciphers: broken, 313
civilians: life behind lines, 534–6
Clark, Christopher, 5
Clarke, Geoffrey, 108
Clarke, Tom, 94, 112
Clemenceau, Georges, 20, 435, 518
Cobb, Irving S., 192–3
Coblenz: German HQ established in, 185
Cochin, Augustin, 437
Cocho, Sgt. Paul, 474
Cœurdevey, Edouard, 182, 301–2, 341, 343,
  516, 523, 527, 529, 532
Cole, Pte. John, 477
Colman, Pte. Ronald, 486
Colvill, James, 382
Committee of Imperial Defence (British), 36
Committee to Investigate Alleged German
  Outrages (Bryce Report), 437
communications, 313–14; *see also* radio
  communications
Compiègne, 251
Congar, Yves, 137, 535, 558
Conneau, Gen. Louis-Napoléon, 165, 486
Conrad, Joseph, xxxiii
Conrad von Hötzendorf, Franz, Baron: detests
  Russia, xxix; and grand strategy, 27, 140,
  259; character, 29, 78; urges aggressive
  action against Serbia, 45, 48; and German
  advice, 77; deploys Slav minorities against
  Serbs, 108; attacks Serbs, 138, 140; conduct
  of war, 141; repressive measures in Serbia,
  148–9; and Mount Cer defeat, 151; diverts
  troops to Galicia, 152; army defeat in
  Serbia, 158; strategy and campaign in
  Galicia, 386, 388, 394–8, 400–1, 407, 498–9,
  553; in Poland, 497–8; denied German
  troop support, 501; pre-war manoeuvres
  and war games, 504–5; casualties, 505;
  renews campaign in Serbia, 513; warns of
  prospective Austro-Hungarian collapse, 554
Constantinople: Young Turks coup (1908), 11

Cooper, Ethel, 427
Corday, Michel, 118, 288
Coronel, Battle of (1914), 377–9
Corry, Lt. Col. Noel, 519
Cossacks, 261
Cotton Powder Company, 72
Cowan, Capt. John, 519–20
Cracow, 400, 503
Cradock, Rear-Admiral Sir Christopher,
  377–8
Craig, Capt. James, 24
Cranborne, Robert Gascoyne-Cecil (*later* 5th
  Marquess of Salisbury), 422
Croix d'Isère, La (French newspaper), 107,
  112
Crowe, Sir Eyre, 37, 64
Cude, Robert, 127–8
Cunliffe, Walter (*later* Sir), 62
Curie, Marie, 2
Curnock, George, 242
Curragh Mutiny (1914), 23
Cuxhaven, 543
Cvelbar, Jože, 136
Czechs: in Austro-Hungarian army, 150–1;
  defectors to Russian service, 499

Daily Chronicle, 86–7
Daily Mail, 71, 86, 295, 438, 541, 543
Daily News, 86–7
Dangerfield, George: *The Strange Death of
  Liberal England*, 21, 24–5
Daniel, Midshipman Charles, 382
Danilov, Gen. Yuri, 51, 65
Dankl, Count Viktor, 497
Dardanelles: control of, 11–12, 53; Churchill's
  plan for, 454, 550; closed, 508
Davenport, Lt. Jimmy, 347
David, A.A., 422
Davier, Lt. von, 230
Davies, Brig. R.H., 519
Davignon, Jean, 88
Davis, Richard Harding, 202
Davison, Emily Wilding, 25
Dawnay, Maj. Hugh, 489
Dean, Arthur, 380
Dease, Lt. Maurice, VC, 212
Debidour, Louis, 439
Debout, Sgt., 177
Delabeye, Cpl. Bernard, 171
Delcassé, Théophile, 14
Dellmensingen, Gen. *see* Krafft von
  Dellmensingen, Gen. Konrad
Delme-Radcliffe, Lt. Col., 519

Delmotte, Maurice, 535

Denore, Cpl. Bernard, 243

Derby, Edward George Villiers Stanley, 17th Earl of, 113

Derenne, Louis, 70

Deschanel, Paul, 182

deserters: executed, 307–8, 322, 473, 531

Desfontaines, Col., 342

Despiau, Charles, 532

Devambez, André, 532

Deventer, Jacobus, 96

Dillon, Capt. (Irish Rifles), 226

Dillon, Capt. Harry, 254, 292, 345, 475–6

Dillon, John, 25, 60

Dimitrijević, Col. Dragutin ('Apis'), xxxiv–xxxv, 18, 54, 99, 138

Dimmer, Lt. John, VC, MC, 494

Dinant, Belgium, 177

Dinić, Jovan, 42

discipline, 531

disease and epidemics, 499

Dixmude, Belgium, 466–7, 556

Djordje, Prince of Serbia, 18

Dohna, Gen. Count, 281

Dolański, Count Henryk, 399

Domnau, East Prussia, 405

Dorrell, Battery-Sgt.-Maj. George Thomas, VC, 253–4

Dover: bombed, 462

Doyle, Sir Arthur Conan, 48, 188, 436

Draga, Queen of Serbia: murdered, xxxv, 17

Draginje-Bosnak, Serbia, 510

Dreyfus case, 19

Drina, river, 145–6, 152–3, 156–7

Dubail, Gen. Yvon, 167

Dufresne, Charles, 532

Dunoyer de Segonzac, André, 532

Dupierreux, Father, 191–2

East Prussia: civilians killed, 192–3, 405; German deployment in, 247, 259; campaign in, 264–72, 405, 500; Hindenburg and Ludendorff in, 273–4; German victories in, 280–4; Russians reoccupy parts, 406

Echo de Paris, l' (newspaper), 439

Economist, The (journal), 60, 87, 119, 411

Edgington, Sgt. William, 211, 239, 257, 332, 483

Edmonds, Col. James (later Sir), 218, 221–2, 237–8, 251

Edward VII, King of Great Britain: funeral, xxxii

Einem, Gen. Karl von: on strategic difficulties, 27; commands at siege of Liège, 162; at Marne, 330, 336–7

Einstein, Albert, 2

Eisenhower, Gen. Dwight D., 552

Elcho, Hugo Charteris, Lord, 121

Elkington, Col. John, 240

Emmet, Robert, 120–1

Emmich, Gen. Otto von, 160–1

Engstler, Ludwig, 487

entertainment, 435

Ernst, Karl, 97

Esher, Reginald Baliol Brett, 2nd Viscount, 40

Estienne, Col., 318

Estonia: independence, 561

Eton College, 548

Eton College Chronicle, 422

Eucken, Rudolf, 437

Evelegh, Capt. Rosslyn, 350

Evening News (London newspaper), 44, 440

Exeter, William Brownlow, 5th Marquess and Myra, Marchioness of, 426

Express, l' (Belgian newspaper), 90

Fabeck, Gen. Max von, 481, 483

Fairholme, Col., 38

Falkenhayn, Erich von: takes leave before outbreak of war, 44; on decision to fight, 76–7; bellicosity, 80; welcomes outbreak of war, 118; early actions, 160; warns Moltke of French strength, 247; appointed chief of staff, 338, 342; character and qualities, 342–3; strategy, 343, 442–3; questions Tirpitz on naval inaction, 361–2; and attack on Ypres, 388–9, 472, 486, 495, 552; and Conrad's plight in Galicia, 407; threatens Antwerp, 445, 450; on use of aircraft, 456; assembles new army (4th), 464; assault in Flanders, 474–5, 481, 554; and troop numbers on Eastern Front, 501; belittles campaign in East, 504; predicts long war, 541; war aims, 543; view of campaign, 545; advocates separate peace in East, 554; blames Britain for war, 554; reputation suffers, 554; Ludendorff opposes, 555; dismissed (1916), 556

Falkland Islands, Battle of the (1914), 378

Farnborough, Florence, 137

Farrell, John, 423

Fashoda incident (1898), 35

Feilding, Lady Dorothie, 429–30, 454, 466–7, 494, 529

Ferron, Gen. Henri de, 236

Festing, Capt. Maurice, RM, 92, 448–51
Feunette, Lt. Paul, 181
Finland: independence, 561
Firle, Lt. Rudolph, 360
Firth of Forth: battle cruisers moved to, 383
Fischer, Fritz, 31; *Germany's War Aims in the First World War*, xxiv
Fischer, Magdalene, 419
Fisher, Quartermaster-Sgt. Gordon, 493
Fisher, Admiral John Arbuthnot, 1st Baron, 378
FitzClarence, Brig. Charles, 485, 493
Fitzgerald, Lord Desmond, 242
Fitzgerald, Lord Gerald, 347
Flack, Gen. Paul, 336
Flanders: BEF moves to, 463, 468; actions in, 474; landscape, 515; *see also* Belgium
Fleetwood-Wilson, Guy, 92
Foch, Marshal Ferdinand: modesty, 20; pre-war warning of German strategy, 171; and offensive in Alsace-Lorraine, 174–6; son and son-in-law killed, 181; commands Ninth Army, 310; at Marne, 312, 320–1, 326–8, 330, 335, 339; appointed deputy by Joffre, 444; counter-attacks in Flanders, 474; sends force to cover Allenby's lines at Ypres, 486; success at Ypres, 496; appointed supreme commander in 1918, 550
Fontaine au Pire, France, 535
food rationing, 414
Forain, Jean-Louis, 532
Ford, Ford Madox, 437
Forester, C.S.: *The General*, 551
Forgách, Janós, Count, 43
France: casualties, xxi, 182, 199, 496, 553, 561; economic status, 4; attitude to England, 7; British commitment to protect, 8; advances loans to Russia, 15; revival and conditions after 1870 defeat by Prussia, 19–20; low birthrate, 20–1; compulsory military service, 21; and German grand strategy, 26–7; strategic plan ('Plan XVII'), 32–3, 129, 164, 175; in Triple Entente, 32; preparations for war, 33–4; alliance with Russia, 35; agreement with Britain, 38; warns Austria over ultimatum to Serbia, 51; popular reaction to forthcoming war, 70; promises support to Russia, 74; and German threat, 79; Germany invades (3 August 1914), 80, 85, 137; mobilises, 80, 83–4, 106–7; public reaction to mobilisation, 83; spirit of patriotism, 111–12; armies deploy, 159; cavalry, 164–5;

news shortage, 185–6, 287; government moves to Bordeaux, 287; government reshuffled (August 1914), 289; British believe unwilling to fight, 293, 297; denies press access to armies, 295; German advance in, 299–300; pillaging in, 301; railway system, 303, 443; communications systems, 314; conditions and restriction on home front, 416–17; armaments and matériel manufacture, 417; school propaganda, 420; use of aircraft (*Aviation Militaire*), 457–9; sends supplies to Serbia, 511; war aims, 542–3; suspicion of British colonial ambitions, 543; and prospective peace settlement, 546
France, Anatole, 436
Franchet d'Espèrey, Gen. Louis, 213–14, 250, 307–9, 312, 318, 320, 325–7, 330, 334, 337, 339–40, 345
Franco-Prussian War (1870), 19
François, Gen. Hermann von, 280
Frankfurter Zeitung, 82
Franz Ferdinand, Archduke of Austria: character and qualities, xxxi–xxxiii; visit to Bosnia, xxxiv; assassination in Sarajevo, xxxvi–xxxix, 29, 41–2, 98; funeral, xli; Wilhelm writes to on Haldane's comment, 8
Franz Joseph, Emperor of Austria-Hungary: resents Franz Ferdinand, xxi; and annexation of Bosnia-Herzegovina, xxxiv; attends Franz Ferdinand's funeral, xli; reign, 9–11; on retribution against Serbia, 43; rashness, 58; signs mobilisation order, 63; declares war on Serbia, 68; rejects renaming of regiments, 114; symbolic role, 430; visits Rosa Zenoch, 440
French, Field-Marshal Sir John: resigns over Curragh Mutiny, 23; seeks guidance from Riddell over military intentions, 88; advocates independent British campaign, 131; commands BEF, 132, 241; arrives in France, 200; informed of French retreat, 203; and Battle of Mons, 205; accepts strength of German army, 214; despises French allies, 214, 292, 306, 549; concern over Haig's position, 219; loathes Smith-Dorrien, 220, 242; and action at Le Cateau, 221; defeatism, 222, 297–8, 302; non-cooperation with Joffre, 223, 308; disharmony at GHQ, 224; considers flight to sea, 241; and BEF's retirement southwards, 248, 251, 309; refuses Haig's

request to support Lanrezac, 249; informs Joffre of inability to give support, 251; weakness, 251; abandons Dammartin HQ, 256; Kitchener orders to cooperate fully with French allies, 298, 306; and Joffre's offensive, 306; agrees to support Joffre, 309–10; Joffre visits and explains plan, 311–12, 316; slow advance to Marne, 328–9, 332, 340; on favourable stalemate, 354; reinforced by Foch at Ypres, 386; shifts BEF to allies' left flank, 442, 463; considers moving to Antwerp, 445; letter from Churchill on fall of Antwerp, 451; ignores air intelligence, 457; and First Battle of Ypres, 485; meets Asquith and Kitchener at Walmer, 548; unrealistic optimism, 549; Haig succeeds, 552

French army: initial casualty rate, 159; uniforms, 159, 166–7; machine-guns, 170; officer qualities, 171–2; colonial troops, 180, 539; casualties, 181, 199, 496, 553, 561; demoralised, 252; deserters executed, 307–8; resistance to digging trenches, 321; command system, 340; rations and diet, 526; indiscipline and resistance to orders, 538

FRENCH ARMY FORMATIONS AND UNITS

Armies: First, 174; Second, 172, 315; Third, 178, 180, 183, 199, 328; Fourth, 178, 180, 181, 199, 213, 326; Fifth, 28, 164, 177–8, 194–5, 198–9, 203, 213, 222, 248–9, 302, 308, 311, 316, 318, 320, 325, 339, 345; Sixth, 291, 303, 307, 311, 316, 318, 320, 327, 335; Ninth, 310, 312, 320, 326–9; Tenth, 444

Divisions: 7th, 324; 3rd Colonial Infantry, 181

Regiments: 1st Tirailleurs, 198; 2nd Zouaves, 198; 12th Hussars, 179; 99th Infantry, 557; Chasseurs d'Afrique, 181

Fresnayne, Roger de la, 532

Freud, Alexander, 85

Freud, Sigmund, 85, 534, 541

Frewen, Lt. Oswald, RN, 364

Fricke, Lt., 230

'Frontiers, Battles of the' (August 1914), 199

Gaiffier d'Hestroy, Baron de, 78, 88–9

Galicia, 32, 140, 152, 386–407, 498–9, 553; Christmas truce, 557

Gallieni, Gen. Joseph: as military governor in Paris, 171, 288–90; on German advance in northern France, 300; given command of Sixth Army, 303; and Joffre's counter-offensive, 306–7; meets foreign diplomats in Paris, 308; Murray dislikes, 309; and Battle of the Marne, 312; sends troops to Marne, 324; calls at Manoury's HQ, 327

Gallipoli, 550–1

Galpin, George, 109

Galsworthy, John, 445

Gamelin, Maurice, 321

Gardiner, A.G., 86

Gatzenmeyer, Lt., 419

Gaulle, Lt. Charles de, 136, 177, 341, 487, 526

Gemmerich, Belgium, 94

George V, King of Great Britain: calls conference on Irish conflict, 59; Prince Heinrich meets, 85; proclaims mobilisation, 95; contributes to National Relief Fund, 113; letter from Sir John French on Battle of Aisne, 354; unawareness of gravity of war, 431; Haig describes British fugitives to, 484

German army: uniforms, 166–7; soldiers' qualities, 183, 520–1; machinery of command, 184; misconduct towards civilians, 187–94; advance through Belgium, 201–2; campaign in East Prussia, 271; occupies northern France, 299–300; communications and logistical problems, 314, 327; gunnery inadequacies, 479; drums and music in battle, 487–8, 490–1; conditions on Western Front, 525–6; paranoia, 537; institutional superiority, 552

GERMAN ARMY FORMATIONS AND UNITS

Armies: First, 305, 310, 331, 334; Second, 330–1, 340; Third, 213, 310, 330, 336; Fourth, 184, 330, 464, 472; Fifth, 184, 330; Sixth, 172, 443; Seventh, 172, 345; Eighth, 266, 273–5, 278; Ninth, 407, 409, 502

Army Groups: Fabeck, 481, 488

Corps: IV, 226; VII Reserve, 345; XXV Reserve, 502

Divisions: 1st Guards, 336; 2nd Guards, 557; Guards Cavalry, 305

Regiments: 41st Infantry (Prussian), 280; 143rd Infantry, 490; Grenadier Guards, 491; Prussian Guard, 493, 495

German General Staff, 26–7

German navy: prepares for war, 356; inactivity, 358, 361–3, 383; surface raiders, 358, 377; codebooks captured, 375; wireless communications, 376; bombards English coastal towns, 379, 380–2; minelaying, 379;

German navy: – *cont.*
  Ships: *Ariadne*, 372; *Breslau*, 101, 377; *Emden*, 361; *Frauenlob*, 367; *Goeben*, 109–10, 377; *Helgoland*, 383; *Köln*, 372; *Lothringen*, 379, 383; *Magdeburg*, 375; *Mainz*, 370–3; *Rostock*, 360; *Stettin*, 367–8; *Strassburg*, 372; *Yorck*, 379
German South-West Africa, 100
Germany: casualties, xxi, 160, 315, 495, 553–4, 561; as potential British enemy, 3; preparations for war, 4–5, 9, 31, 57; rise to power, 4; naval rivalry with Britain, 7–8; in Triple Alliance, 9; birthrate, 20; and prospective two-front war, 26; promises support for Austria, 30, 43–4, 52; war council (December 1912), 30–1; discounts British intervention in war, 39; supports Austrian action against Serbia, 43, 47, 561; militancy, 46–8; jams French communications, 52, 70; confidence of victory, 54; reaction to Serbia's rejection of ultimatum, 63–4; press comments on impending war, 67; authority in, 75; invades France (3 August 1914), 80, 85, 137; mobilises, 80, 82–3, 103; declares war on Russia, 81; popular reaction to outbreak of war, 82, 114, 116–18, 121, 123–4; British pre-war view of, 87, 104; invades Belgium, 90, 94–5, 102; intelligence services, 97; ambition for supremacy, 99; regime, 100; expectations from war success, 101; *Burgfrieden* (internal truce), 111; fear of encirclement, 111; gifts of food, 113; food prices rise, 114; civilian reactions to battles, 185; fails to win decisive early victory, 303–4; keeps silence over defeats, 338; British economic blockade, 359, 362, 385, 546; industrial disputes, 414; patriotic promotion, 420; socialists' commitment to war, 432; censorship in, 435; propaganda in USA, 435; academics write on war, 437; agents and spies in England, 441; use of aircraft, 456–7, 461–2; and allied war aims, 542; doctrine of *Siegfrieden*, 542; war aims, 542–3, 563; slave labour from Belgium and France, 545; internal socialist threat, 546; dissensions among leaders, 553–5; victory over Russia, 555; becomes republic, 561; responsibility for war, 562
Gheluvelt, Flanders, 483–5, 489
Ghent, Belgium, 455, 463
Gide, André, 62, 70, 107, 169, 182–3, 189, 287, 411, 420

Giers, Aleksandr, 73
Giesl, Baron Wladimir von, 45, 62
Gilkison, Capt. Dugald Stewart, 295
Gilmore, Ginger, 243
Goatham, Horace, 243
Godley, Hugh, 294, 423
Godley, Pte. Sid, VC, 208, 212
Goltz, Field-Marshal Wilhelm von der, 31
Goodenough, Commodore William, 367, 370–1
Gorchakov, Prince, 15
Gordon, Andrew, 382
Gordon, Col. W.E., VC, 235
Gordon-Lennox, Lord Bernard, 202, 216, 350, 488
Goschen, Sir Edward, 95
Gosse, Sir Edmund, 436
Gourdant, Sgt. Paul, 106
Grabež, Trifko, xxxv–xxxvi, xl
Grand Couronné de Nancy, 176, 310, 315–16
Grauthoff, Ferdinand *see* Seestern
Greffulhe, Comte, 134
Grenadou, Ephraim, 106
Grenelle, Julian, 351, 527
Grenfell, Rivvy, 419
Grenoble, 186
Grey, Charles, 418
Grey, Sir Edward: character, 37–8; neglects strengthening forces for future war, 37; assures France of support, 38–9; power as Foreign Secretary, 38–9; prepares for war, 40; reports on Austrian ultimatum to Serbia, 60; hopes for German mediation in Serbian crisis, 64; offers Lichnowsky proposals to end Serbian crisis, 65–6; proposes conference to deter war, 72; and Bethmann's offer over Belgium, 77; letter from Bertie on British support for France, 79; suggests British neutrality in war, 80; advocates supporting Entente partners, 85; Cambon meets, 87; reports mobilisation of French fleet, 88; and German invasion of Belgium, 91; Commons statement on entering war, 92–3, 96; cheered by crowds, 95; blamed for British entry into war, 99, 102; advocates dispatch of troops to France, 131; reports dispatch of rice to Serbs, 155; on Marne victory, 341; and Kitchener's demand for goats for Indian troops, 413; brother and nephew wounded, 418; melancholy 547
Grierson, Lt. Gen. Sir James, 220, 456

Grimm, Maj., 525

Gronau, Gen. Hans von, 316, 318

Gross, Gerhard, 507

Grossetti, Gen., 527

Gruber, Karl, 184

Guernsey, Heneage Grenville Finch-
  Knightley, Lord, 349, 419

Guest, Freddie, 355

Guise, 249–50, 252

Guliewicz, Col., 389

Gumbinnen, East Prussia, 271–3

Gumilev, Nikolai, 265

Günther, Duke of Schleswig-Holstein, 325

Hacker, Lt. Edward, 305

Haeften, Maj. Hans von, 81, 555

Haig, Alexandra, Lady, 132

Haig, Gen. Sir Douglas: drafts Field Service
  Regulations, 26; disagrees with Sir John
  French over deployment, 131; reputation,
  131–2; at Mons, 204, 210–11; HQ at
  Landrecies, 217–18; panic attack at
  Landrecies, 218–19; withdraws, 221;
  retreats from Le Cateau battle, 231, 237–8;
  informed of Joffre's counter-attack, 248–9;
  early weakness, 251; complains of French
  unreliability, 308; on Maud'huy, 318; halts
  advance to Marne, 322; crosses Marne,
  332; on poor performance of some British
  units, 351, 489–90; on George V in war,
  431; and First Battle of Ypres, 472, 478,
  485, 490, 496; on British fugitives along
  Menin road, 484; army command, 548;
  qualities, 549; succeeds Sir John French,
  552

Haldane, Richard Burdon, Viscount: seeks
  improved relations with Germany, 7;
  informs Lichnowsky of British
  commitment to support France, 8, 30; as
  Lord Chancellor, 23–4; army reforms, 36,
  206; urges support for Entente partners, 85;
  and German invasion of Belgium, 91;
  military expertise, 126

Hall, John, 380

Hall, Capt. Reginald ('Blinker'), 375–6

Halsbury, Hardinge Stanley Giffard, 1st Earl
  of, 24

Hamburger Echo, 82

Hamel, Pte. Herbert de, 486

Hamilton, Capt. Ernest, 480

Hamilton, Gen. Hubert, 221

Hamilton, Gen. Sir Ian, 487

Hamley, Bernard, 128

Hankey, Maj. Edward, 477, 485

Hankey, Maurice, 103

Hapsburg Empire *see* Austria-Hungary

Harcourt, Sir William, 2

Harcourt-Vernon, Lt. Guy, 122, 201, 203, 209,
  241, 245, 257, 307, 348

Hardie, Keir, 123

Hardy, Thomas, 120

Harker, Capt. Robert, 460, 516–17, 530

Harper, Geoffrey, 188, 356–7, 369

Harrison, Charles, 245

Hartlepool: bombarded, 380–1

Hartwig, Lyudmila Nikolaevna, 54

Hartwig, Nikolai, xxxv, 17, 54

Hausen, Gen. Max von, 213–14, 250, 310,
  326, 330–1, 336, 338

Havre Sainte Cutheune, Belgium, 447

Hay, Lord Arthur, 349

Heberlein, Wilhelm, 82

Heinrich, Prince of Prussia: racial views, 7;
  calls off visit to Cowes, 62; reports British
  non-intervention to Kaiser, 85

Heligoland: submarine base, 31

Heligoland Bight: naval battle (1914), 363–4,
  366–74

Hell, Col. Emil, 276

Heller, Wolfgang, 45

Henderson, Capt. Wilfred, 7

Hentsch, Lt. Col. Richard, 329–31, 334–5,
  338, 501

Herbert, A.P., 119

Herero people, 100

Hesse, Wilhelm, 456

Highgate, Pte. Thomas, 322

Hillern-Flinsch, Gunner Wilhelm, 528

Himmler, Heinrich, 81, 215

Hindenburg, Field-Marshal Paul von: takes
  command in East Prussia, 273–4, 276;
  Tannenberg and Masurian Lakes victories,
  275–84; supports Austrians in Galicia, 407;
  and proposed Russian invasion of
  Germany, 501; requests reinforcements in
  East, 504; and leadership dissensions, 555;
  appointed Chief of Staff, 556

Hipper, Admiral Franz von, 356, 363, 367–8,
  379–82

Hitler, Adolf, 10

Hobart (German steamship), 375

Hoefft, Lt. Edler von, 387, 389, 391–2, 404

Hoffmann, Lt. Col. Max, 268, 271, 273–5,
  281, 401, 497, 500

Hohenburg, Sophie, xxxii

Hohenzollern family, 6

Holbrook, Cpl. William, 493

Holland: neutrality preserved, 160; profits from neutrality, 415

Hollebeke, Flanders, 481

home front: conditions and restrictions, 411–34

Home Office (British): and War Book, 104

Home Rule (Ireland), 23–4, 60

Homme libre, l' (newspaper), 435

Hopman, Rear-Admiral Albert, xl, 6, 44, 341, 374, 431–2

Hornby, Capt. Charles, 203–4

Horne, John, 190, 192, 547

horses: commandeered for service, 122; lameness, 245; numberless killed, 254, 522; numbers in German army, 305; shortage, 362–3; in Russian army, 391, 407; numbers in British army, 522

Housman, A.E., 418

Howell, Dr, 350

Hoyos, Alexander, Count, 43–5

Hranilović, Col. Oskar von, 147

Hub, Paul, 125, 475, 482, 535

Huggan, Dr, 350

Huguet, Col. Charles, 241, 309

Hull, Lt. Col. Charles, 204–5, 209, 211, 230, 234

Hülsen-Haeseler, Dietrich, Graf von, 5

Humbert, Gen., 321

Hungary: supports invasion of Serbia, 54; Russia hopes for separate peace with, 553; independence (1918), 561

Hunter-Watson, Gen. Aylmer, 332, 346

Huth, Walther, 456

Hutier, Gen. Oskar von, 336

'HWK', Vosges, 525

Illustrated London News, 134, 296, 501

India: support for Britain, 295; troops' diet, 413; performance in France, 472–3

Indochina, 543

Ingenohl, Admiral Friedrich von, 361, 363, 372, 383

International Committee of the Red Cross, 534

Ireland: and Home Rule, 23–4, 60; and British declaration of war, 96; attitude to war, 112

Italy: in Triple Alliance, 9; enters war, 99, 414–15; condition of army, 108; votes for neutrality, 108, 303; as potential threat to France, 236; casualties, 553, 561; territorial gains at war's end, 560

Itha J (Austrian nationalist), 105, 118, 153–4, 168, 424, 432

'It's a Long Way to Tipperary' (song), 242

Ivanov, Gen. Nicholas, 388–9, 391, 394–5, 401, 407–8

Jabiońska, Helena, 499

Jack, Pte., 209

Jagow, Gottlieb von: absent from war council (Dec. 1912), 30; and Moltke's fear of Russian threat, 46; believes in British neutrality, 67; on German wish for war, 82

James, Henry, xxxvii

Jameson, Joan, 423

Japan: joins war, 99; Britain persuades to enter war, 414; supposed British agreement with, 543; gains from war, 561

Jaulmes, Gustave Louis, 532

Jaurès, Jean, 83

Jeffreys, Maj. George ('Ma'), 216, 218, 332, 349–50, 355, 472, 486, 487, 489, 519, 528, 530

Jellicoe, Admiral Sir John (*later* Earl): Childers salutes, 126; command, 357; patrols North Sea, 359; protects fleet from danger, 362; and Heligoland action, 364, 373; prudence, 377–8; and Scarborough raid, 380; transfers to Admiralty, 384

Jerome, Jerome K., 98, 128

Jews: persecuted in Poland, 263–4, 393; patriotism, 433; persecuted by Russians, 545

Jillings, Sgt.-Maj., 457

Joachim Albrecht, Prince of Prussia, 184

Joffre, Gen. Joseph Césaire: on Russian army, 16; modesty, 20; Sir John French declines support to, 21; strategic ideas and movements, 32–4, 171–2, 177–8; discussion with Fairholme, 38; Wilson promises support to, 40; and Serbian rejection of Austrian ultimatum, 64; and political paralysis in Serbian crisis, 69; promises support to Russia, 70; on delay in mobilisation, 83; agrees not to violate Belgian neutrality, 90; leaves for HQ, 94; powers and authority, 111, 184; battle tactics, 160; employs Plan XVII, 164, 252, 340, 552; opposes Germans in Belgium, 165; on withdrawal from Alsace, 168; qualities and appearance, 170–1; and offensive in Alsace-Lorraine, 174–6; early setbacks, 182; and German advance through Belgium, 194–5, 199; on British inertia, 200; withholds information from government, 200; Moltke attempts to envelop, 201; on failed offensive, 215; *Instruction Général No. 2* strengthening left flank, 215, 223, 291; urges Fifth Army to attack, 222; and delay to German advance, 238; told of BEF's failure, 241; counter-attack and Battle of Mortagne, 246; bars ministers from front, 289; Gallieni advises against offensive, 289; keeps nerve, 290–1; redeploys troops from Alsace, 291; Sir John French ordered to cooperate fully with, 298; relations with Sir John French, 303; offensive and victory at Marne, 306, 314, 328–9, 334, 337, 339–40; dismisses generals and orders deserters shot, 307; reputation, 310; visit to Sir John French before Marne, 311–12; and French communications systems, 314; pushes north, 443; holds line against German advance, 444; refuses support to Antwerp, 445; use of aircraft, 459; British move to left flank, 463; declines to endorse removal of Sir John French, 487; achievements, 552

Johnston, Alexander, 230, 234, 324, 345, 468, 477, 479–80, 490, 494, 522, 557

Johnyson (driver), 529

Joiselle, Château de, 325

Journal de Genève, 439

Jutland, Battle of (1916), 384

Kageneck, Lt. Col. Karl von, 140

Kaisen, Sgt. Wilhelm, 66, 168, 185, 352, 428, 527

Karge, Capt., 191

Karl, Archduke (*later* Emperor) of Austria, 431

Karwendel, 57

K.C.-Blatter (journal), 432

Kehrt, Christian, 455

Keleman, Pál, 396

Kell, Vernon, 97, 441

Keppel, Mrs George (Alice), 60

Kerquence, Capt., 179

Kerr, Lt., 519

Kessler, Elise, 536

Kessler, Graf Harry, 163, 192

Kessler, Paul, 535–6

Keyes, Commodore Roger, 363–4, 368, 371, 373, 384

Keynes, John Maynard, Baron, xxii, 418

Keyserlinck, Walter, Freiherr von, 383

Khan, Sepoy Khudadad, VC, 472

Kiderlen-Waechter, Alfred von, 30

Kiel canal, 31, 57

Kiel Regatta (1914), xl, 7

Kielce, Poland, 497

King-Hall, Lt. Stephen, 359, 370

Kisch, Cpl. Egon, 145–7, 150, 152, 154–6, 428, 511

Kitchener, Field-Marshal Horatio Herbert, 1st Earl: recalled to London, 91; as secretary of state for war, 127; New Army, 127, 495, 520; retains troops for home defence, 132; instructions to Sir John French, 133; Lloyd George disparages, 133; strategy, 133–4; appoints Smith-Dorrien to II Corps, 220; Henry Wilson criticises, 224; orders Sir John French to cooperate with French allies, 298, 306, 340; demands goats for Indian troops, 413; and invasion scare, 474; offers to replace Sir John French, 487; predicts long war, 531; Sir John French meets at Walmer, 548; isolation, 549; praises Sir John French, 549

Klein Zillbeke, Ypres, 489

Klopper, Warrant Officer Ernst, 168

Klotz, Col., 487

Kluck, Gen. Alexander von: and Battle of Mons, 202, 203, 208–10, 213–14, 238; at Le Cateau, 226–7, 236–8; incompetence, 241, 251; advance slowed, 246–8; flank exposed, 249; and French counter-attack, 250; directs forces eastwards, 303, 305; Joffre attacks, 306; requests reinforcements, 310; communications problems, 314; march south, 316; counter-attack at Battle of Marne, 319, 321, 324, 326–9, 334, 337, 339; Hentsch visits, 331; blamed for Marne defeat, 338; and withdrawal from Marne, 340–1; ignores air intelligence, 457

Knight, John Peake, 423

Knight, Olive, 423

Knobloch, Lt. Reinhold, 360, 376, 383

Knocker, Elizabeth (*later* Baroness de T'Serclaes; 'Elsie'), 425, 430, 450–1

Knox, Maj.-Gen. Alfred, 260, 270, 280, 282, 389, 391, 393, 399

Kokotović, Oberstleutnant, 148

Kollwitz, Hans, 109

Kollwitz, Käthe, 109

Kollwitz, Peter, 101, 465

Kölnische Zeitung, 193

Kondurashkin, Sergei, 105, 117, 135, 259, 393, 401, 403, 408

Kraewel, Maj. Gen. von, 163

Krafft von Dellmensingen, Gen. Konrad, 76

Kraguijevatz, Serbia, 510

Kramer, Alan, 190, 192, 547

Krivoshein, Alexander, 57

Krobatin, Alexander von, 42

Kruiseke, Flanders, 477

Krupp (industrial company), 7

Ksyunin, Alexei, 261, 402, 406, 409

Kuchernigo, Ivan, 105

Kuhl, Hermann von, 334

Kuhlorn, Lt., 226

Kuhr, Elfriede, xli, 110, 123, 135, 264, 420, 427, 432, 460

Kunitzky, Stanislav, 398

Kuznetsov, Ivan, 394–5, 403–4

Labour Party (British): stop-the-war rallies, 123

Laby, Lucien, 169, 301, 531

Lady, The (magazine), 13, 412, 424, 426–7, 429, 440

Laguiche, Gen. Marquis de, 260

Lambert, Anton, 412

Lambert, Capt. Cecil, RN, 295

Lambert, George, 91

Lamotte, Commandant, 301

Lampe, Dr Eugen, 154, 427, 438

Landowski, Paul, 532

Landrecies, 217–189

Lang, Carl von, 3

Lang, Cosmo Gordon, Archbishop of York, 434

Lang, Stephen, 128

Langemarck, Belgium, 471–3, 482, 488, 494

Langle de Cary, Gen., 182, 310

Langlois, Capt., 15

Lanrezac, Gen. Charles: early actions, 28, 177, 195, 198–9, 203, 213, 222–3, 246, 248–50, 252, 289, 291–2, 300; dismissed, 307

Lansbury, George, 123

Lansdowne, Henry Charles Keith Petty-Fitzmaurice, 5th Marquess of, 14

Lascelles, Henry Charles, Viscount, 62

Latvia: independence, 561

Lauenstein, Otto, 330

Laurens, Albert, 532

Lavadens, Isère, France, 559–60

Law, Andrew Bonar, 24, 88

Lazarev, Capt., 265

Lechitzky, Gen., 389

Leffe, Belgium, 192

Leibacher, Frans, 441

Leipzig, Battle of the Nations (1813), 5

Lemaire, Madeleine, 311

Leman, Gen. Gérard, 161, 164

Le Marchant, Col., 332

Lemberg, Galicia, 395–6

Lemke, Mikhail, 408

letters and mail, 423, 517

Liberal Party (British): government, 23–4

Lichnowsky, Prince Karl Max, 8, 65, 80, 87, 92, 136

Liège, 160–3, 194

Lille, 463

Liman von Sanders, Gen. Otto, 12

Limanova, Galicia, 507

Lintier, Paul, 159, 179–180, 325, 335

Lipton, Sir Thomas, 514

Lithuania: independence, 561

Littauer, Lt. Vladimir, 73, 135

Lloyd George, David (*later* Earl): on Grey, 3; introduces state insurance scheme, 22; in Liberal government, 23; and Bethmann's fear of encirclement, 34; Mansion House speech declaring British support for France (1911), 40; on Bethmann, 46; optimism during Serbian crisis, 49; and British indifference to Serbian crisis, 59; on press influence, 75; reluctance to enter war, 85; sends for Sir John French, 88; accepts case for entering war, 91–2; on averting war, 99; on Kitchener, 127; antipathy to military, 133; on Gallieni, 288; discussion with Castelnau, 290; awards five shillings as war widow's pension, 413; speech on war to end wars, 433–4; scepticism over generals and leadership, 550

Lobanov-Rostovsky, Lt. Andrei, 263

Lody, Carl, 440–5

Łódź, Poland, 409; Battle of (1914), 501–2

Londesborough, Grace Augusta, Countess of, 24

London: defence measures, 117; blackout, 416

London, Declaration of (September 1914), 309, 543

Loring, Lt. Col. Walter, 471

Lossberg, Lt.-Col. Fritz von, 488

Louvain, Belgium, 190–1, 437

Lowe, Charles, 296

Löwenstein-Wertheim-Rosenberg, Lt. Alois, Fürst zu, 113, 303, 523, 528–9, 533–4, 540

Lublin, Galicia, 395–6, 402

Ludendorff, Gen. Erich: in Liège, 160, 162; on behaviour of Russian troops, 193;

transferred to East Prussia, 273–4; campaign in East Prussia, 275; and Tannenberg victory, 278, 280, 282; and Hindenburg's reputation, 281; Wilhelm disdains, 342; supports Austrians in Galicia, 407; advance in Poland, 409; complains of troop shortage on Eastern Front, 500, 504; counters threatened Russian attack, 501–3; performance on Eastern Front, 507; tactical mastery, 552; discusses aims with Bethmann, 554; conflict with Falkenhayn, 555; authority under Hindenburg, 556; miscalculates effect of victory in East, 556

Ludendorff, Margarethe (*earlier* Pernet), 274

Lunéville, 315

Lunn, Lt. Algy, 253

Lusitania (ship), 358, 435

Lütgendorf, Gen. Kasimir, 149

Luxembourg: Germans enter, 88; Germany demands annexation of, 100; French thrust towards, 178; German reprisals in, 190; German HQ established in, 250; railway system, 443

Lyck, East Prussia, 270

Lyncker, Gen. Moriz, Freiherr von, 33

Lys, river, 464

Lyttelton, Edward, 294

Lyttelton, Oliver, 422

MacDonald, Ramsay, 96, 123

MacDonogh, Col. George, 203, 214

Mackenzie, Pte. Charles, 348

McLeod, Commander John, 357

Macleod, Norman, 86, 91, 95, 118, 295, 297, 373, 446, 454

Macneil, Willy, 419

Macpherson, Pte. William, 478

Macready, Capt. John, 352

Macready, Sir Nevil, 256

Machen, Arthur, 440

Machiavelli, Niccolò, 545

machine-guns: in Serbia, 151; use and effectiveness, 169–70, 179

Mackensen, Gen. August von, 271, 502

Mailly, 442

Mainwaring, Col. Arthur, 240

Maistre, Gen. Joseph de, 302

Malcolm, Col. George, 455, 490

Malešič, Matija, 145, 152, 156

Malina, Fritz, 459

Malvy (of French Foreign Office), 79

Manchester Guardian, 60, 86–7

Mangin, Gen. Charles, 180, 320, 325; *La Force noir*, 180

Manoury, Gen. Joseph, 303, 306–7, 309, 311–12, 316, 318, 320–2, 324–5, 327, 334–5, 345, 443

Mare, André, 532

Maria Josefa, Archduchess of Austria, 430

Marne, river, 252; Paris taxis employed as transport, 307, 324–5; First Battle of the (September 1914), 316–42; bridges left intact, 332; Germans withdraw from, 337, 340–2

Marshall, Herbert, 486

Martin, Rudolf, 461

Martos, Gen., 269, 282

Marwitz, Gen. Georg von, 229, 253–4, 324, 467, 471

Marwitz, Lt. Harald von der, 500

Mary, Queen of George V, 113

Masterman, Charles, 3

Masurian Lakes, 268, 276; Battle of (1914), 283, 296, 401

Matheson, Cpl. George, 495

Maubeuge, 134, 214

Maud'huy, Gen. Comte Louis de, 176, 318, 325, 327, 330

Maufrais, Louis, 524

Mauretania (ship), 58

Mavissen, Gustav, 257

Maximilian, Duke of Hohenberg (Franz Ferdinand's son), xxxviii

Mayer, François, 517, 527, 529–30, 532, 558–9

Mayer, Gustav, 121

Mayne, Mrs Gerald, 429, 458, 465, 517

Mayor, François, 458

Maze, Paul, 125, 486

medical services, 301–2, 523–4

Mehmedbašić, Mehmed, xl

Meinertzhagen, Richard, 541

Mellersh, Henry, 546, 562

Menin, 469, 484

Menshikov (Russian journalist), 124

Mesnil-Amelot, Le, 301

Messimy, Adolphe, 64, 69, 215, 288–9

Messines, Flanders, 483–4, 495

Meurthe, river, 315

MI5: organises arrest of German agents, 97

Michelin Aero Club, 461

Mihajlović, Dr Slavka, 56, 143, 510

Millerand, Alexandre, 289

Milutinović, Sveta, 138

Mishnin, Vasily, 402

Mišić, Gen. Živojin, 512

Moltke, Eliza von, 27, 137
Moltke, Gen. Helmuth von: disparages British Army, 8; character, 26, 28; inherits and modifies Schlieffen plan, 26–7, 129, 160, 194, 201, 215; on prospect of war, 28, 30–1, 44; troop deployment, 33–4; sees Russia as threat, 46; view of Bethmann, 47; dismisses Bernhardi as dreamer, 48; on prospective British intervention in war, 67; urges Austria to mobilise, 68; war preparations, 69; and war on two fronts, 70; disregards anti-war protests, 71; on Germany as victim, 75, 81; proposes Austria deploy against Russia, 77; bellicosity, 78–80; Bethmann dislikes, 81; nervous reaction, 81; warns King Albert of Belgian vulnerability, 89; and invasion of Belgium, 90; stature at outbreak of war, 97; subservience to Kaiser, 111; troops move to front, 135; moves to advanced HQ, 137; early actions at Liège, 160–1; anticipates French recovery of Alsace-Lorraine, 166; and campaign in Alsace, 172, 182; delegates authority, 184; assault increases, 187, 195; advance through Belgium, 194, 201–2; praises Le Cateau engagement, 237; advance delayed, 238; alters early plans, 246–7; moves HQ to Luxembourg, 250; loses control, 251, 257; blocking force against Russia, 259; orders to Prittwitz in East Prussia, 268, 271; appoints Hindenburg and Ludendorff to East Prussia, 273–5; and failure to achieve early decisive victory, 304; logistical problems, 305; abandons Schlieffen strategy, 310; communications problems, 314; failings, 315; and Battle of Marne, 320, 328–9, 334–7, 340; delegates to Hentsch, 329–31; demoralised, 330–1; letters to wife, 330; relieved of command, 337, 342; death, 338; and Crown Prince Wilhelm's assault at Vaux-Marie, 339–40; final orders to withdraw and dig in, 342; travels to Antwerp, 445; troops transferred to Eastern Front, 507; Joffre halts before Paris, 552; Hindenburg and Ludendorff consider recalling, 555; and causes of war, 563
Moltke, Gen. Helmuth von, the Elder, 27
Mondement, Château de, 321, 331, 335
Monro, Maj. Gen. Charles, 256, 464
Mons, Battle of (1914): conduct of, 199, 201, 203–12, 214; falls to Germans, 212; British withdraw in order, 213, 239, 295

Montague, C.E.: *Rough Justice*, 21, 120
Montaigne, Michel de, 252
Montenegro: as Serb ally, 141; *see also* Nicholas I, King
Montenuovo, Alfred, Prince, xxxii
Montgomery, Lt. Bernard Law, 228, 240
Montmirail, 330–1
Moore, Arthur, 296–7
Morgan, Kenneth O., xxii
Morhange, 174–7, 316
Morillon, Gervais, 558
Morning Post, 454, 521
Morocco crisis, Second (1912), 133
Morris, Col. George, 245
Mortagne, Battle of (15 Aug. 1914), 246
motor vehicles: unreliability, 305–6
Moussy, Gen., 474–5
Muehlon, Wilhelm, 433
Mugnier, Abbé, 134
Mühlegg, Carl, 556
Mulhouse, 167–8, 172, 183
Müller, Georg Alexander von: informs Kaiser of Franz Ferdinand's murder, xl; on prospect of war, 30–1, 46; on German appearance as victims, 81
Müller, Capt. Karl von, 361
Murray, Maj. Gen. Sir Archibald, 132, 214, 222–4, 251, 309–10
Murray, Gilbert, 428
Musgrove, Maj. (of RFC), 462
Musulin, Alexander, Baron von, 43, 54
Mutzig (fortress), 166

Namaqua people, 100
Namur, 161, 191, 194
Nancy, 174, 176, 183, 291, 304, 315, 328
Napoleon I (Bonaparte), Emperor of the French, 185
National Free Church Council (Britain), 104
National Relief Fund (Britain), 113
Nelson, Sgt. David, VC, 253
Nemirovich-Danchenko, Vladimir, 409
Néry, 252–4, 298
Nesterov, Pyotr, 459
Neue Zeitung, Die, 430
Nevinson, H.W., 104
New Statesman (journal), 189, 401, 416, 433, 436, 454, 464, 495, 500, 521
Nicholas I, King of Montenegro, 57
Nicholas II, Tsar of Russia: distaste for Franz Ferdinand, xxxiii; and assassination of Franz Ferdinand, xxxvi; and Liman's appointment to Constantinople, 12;

qualities, 13; rule, 14; commitment to support Serbia, 46; and Poincaré's state visit, 49–50; disbelieves Wilhelm's wish for war, 50; and Austrian ultimatum to Serbia, 55–6; reluctance for war, 58, 69; agrees to mobilisation, 72–3; and responsibility for war, 74; loses stature at outbreak of war, 97; armed forces, 260; foresees long war, 542

Nicholas, Grand Duke of Russia, 57, 388, 501

Nicolson, Sir Arthur, 36

Nielsen, Asta, 116

Niemeyer, Oskar, 210–11

Nieuport, Belgium, 466

Niš, Serbia, 142, 510

Nivelle, Robert, 326

no man's land: as term, 473–4

Nogat, river, East Prussia, 272

Nopper, W.O. Ernst, 351

Normandy campaign (1944), 552

Northcliffe, Alfred Harmsworth, Viscount, 37–8, 71, 94, 97, 113, 131, 242, 296, 521

Northern Ireland (Ulster): and Irish troubles, 23–5, 59–60; and outbreak of war, 112

Norway: profits from neutrality, 415

Novikov, Gen., 261

Obermann, Capt., 478

Oblak, Valentin, 141

Oder-Zeitung, 440

Odescalchi, Prince, 148

Oh, What a Lovely War (satirical musical), 119

Organ, Edward, 483–4

Orwell, George, 552

Ostrolęka, 280

Ottoman Empire: decline, 9; and German-Russian differences, 9; British build warships for, 34, 114; joins war, 99; hostility to Russia, 110; and allied war aims, 543

Ourcq, river, 316

Paar, Count von, xl

Paču, Laza, 54

Paget, Walburga, Lady, 441, 514

Paléologue, Maurice, 49–50, 52–3, 56

Pallavicini, Alex, 145–8, 152, 509, 512

Pallavicini, Alexander (father of Alex), 386–7, 398, 402, 431, 497

Pals' units, 518

pan-Slavism, xxxiv, 11, 45, 139, 141

Pankhurst, Christabel, 112

Pankhurst, Emmeline, 112

Pankhurst, Sylvia, 112

Parežanin, Vid, 157

Paris: wartime conditions, 111, 116, 286–7, 289, 417; bombed, 287; under threat of capture, 287–8; Gallieni appointed military governor, 288–9; refugees from, 288; defences, 289; taxis commandeered for Marne, 307, 324–5; government returns to from Bordeaux, 416

Parry, Lt. William, RN, 361

Parsons, Guardsman, 349

Pašić, Nikola, xxxv–xxxvi, 54, 62, 68–9, 510

Passchendaele: Germans capture, 471; French attempt to recapture, 474

patriotism: and xenophobia, 427–8

Pau, Gen. Paul-Marie, 172

Péguy, Charles, 310

Pejović, Tadija, 104, 142

Pénelon, Col. Marie-Jean, 183

Penn, Arthur, 422

Percy, Henry Algernon George, Earl, 38

Père Hilarion (spring), 526

Perrin, Henri, 106–7

Pétain, Marshal Philippe: modesty, 20; at Battle of Marne, 318

Petch, Pte. Fred, 231

Peter, Grand Duke of Russia, 57

Peter, King of Serbia, 18, 151

Petit, Jean, 540

Pfeffer, Leo, xxxix

Phillips, Colwyn, 516

Phleve, Gen., 501–2

pigeons: shot, 537

Pike, Capt. Eben, 491

Plewińska, Zofia, 505

Plieux de Diusse, Capt., 165, 342, 523–4

Plissonier, Marie, 559–60

Ploegstreet Wood, Flanders, 477

Plunkett, Commander Reginald, 385

Poelkapelle, 525

Pohl, Admiral Hugo von, 363

Poincaré, Raymond: learns of Franz Ferdinand's murder, xli; advocates support for Russia against Germany, 19; background, 20; introduces compulsory military service, 21; and Russian alliance, 35; state visit to Russia, 49–53, 69; absence criticised, 70; Joffre leaves, 94; calls for national unity, 123; told of defeat in Alsace-Lorraine, 183; Joffre bars from front, 289; takes government to Bordeaux, 416; favours occupied buffer zone between Moselle and Rhine, 542

Poland: in Russian strategy, 32, 65; Jews maltreated by Russians, 194; Russian campaign in, 260–1, 408, 502–7; Russian and German behaviour in, 263–4; Austrian campaign in, 386–9, 497; German advance in, 409; stalemate in, 497; declares independence (1918), 561; war with Soviet Russia, 561

Pollock, Nellie: *Belgian Playmates*, 440

Polygon Wood, Flanders, 476–7

Ponsonby, Arthur, 96; *Falsehood in Wartime*, 189

Popowen, East Prussia, 265, 283

postal service *see* letters and mail

Postovsky, Gen., 276, 280

Potiorek, Gen. Oskar, 42, 140–1, 146, 151, 155–7, 509–10, 512–13

Potocki, Count, xxxvii

Pound, Reginald, 1

Pridham, Lt. Francis, RN, 357

Princip, Gavrilo, xxxi, xxxiv–xli, 99, 158

prisoners of war, 403–4, 406; compounds, 427; monitored by Red Cross, 534; nationalities mix together, 540

Prittwitz und Gaffron, Gen. Maximilian, 266, 268, 271, 273

profiteering, 415

propaganda, 436–7

Protić, Milan, xxxv

Proust, Marcel, 287–8, 411

Prussia: militancy, 46

Prut, river, Poland, 505

Przemyśl, Galicia, 397, 399–400, 405, 407, 458, 498–9, 557

Pucará, Mihajlo, xxxix

punishment, 531

Putnik, Marshal Radomir, 142, 510, 511

puttees, 206

race: in Britain, 425

Race to the Sea (France), 442

radio communications: intercepted, 275; inadequacies, 313, 525; naval use, 376

railways: logistical importance, 303–4, 443

Railways Executive Committee, 133

Rains, Claude, 486

Raleigh, Sir Walter, 120

Ransome, Arthur, xl, 124

Rathbone, Basil, 486

Rathenitz, Rüdiger *see* Stillried von Rathenitz, Rüdiger

Recouly, Raymond, xli, 35, 55, 79, 83

Redl, Col. Alfred, 51

Redlich, Josef, xli, 87

Redmond, John, 24, 60, 112

Reed, John, 387, 393, 514

refugees, 405, 559

Reims, 345, 437

Reininghaus, Virginie von, 29

Remagen: Rhine bridge, 57

Rennenkampf, Gen. Paul, 264, 268–73, 275–6, 278, 283–4, 389, 501

Rensch, Lt. Hans, 537

Repington, Col. Charles à Court, 200, 439

Revigny Gap, 328

Reynolds, George, 231

Rhodes, Cecil, 6–7

Richards, Frank, 472, 481, 516, 531–2

Richardson, Lt. (of R. Welch Fusiliers), 489

Richepin, Jean, 189

Riddell, Sir George, 88, 92

Riehl, Alois, 437

Riezler, Kurt, 43–4, 64, 118, 248

Rimann, Walter, 97

Rimington, Gen. Mike, 514

Rivière, Jacques, 169, 182–4

Roberts, Field-Marshal Frederick Sleigh, 1st Earl, 25, 60, 123

Robertson, Gen. Sir William ('Wully'): skill as quartermaster-general, 214, 242; in flight from Dammartin, 256

Robinson, Sgt. Arthur, 478

Rodière, Lt., 438

Roebbling, Lt., 229–30

Rolland, Romain, 439

Romania, 504, 560

Ronquières, Belgium, 536

Roosevelt, Theodore, xxxii, 435

Rose, Lt. (of Wiltshire), 217

Rosebery, Archibald Philip Primrose, 5th Earl of, 35

Rosen, Baron, 14

Rosenthal, Baron Friedrich von, 459

Rothschild, Edmond de, 84

Rothschild, Henri de, 79

Rothschild family, 417

Round, Lt. A.F.H., 295

Royal Air Force (*formerly* Royal Flying Corps): buys equipment in Paris, 245; casualties, 384; formed (as RFC), 456; radio signalling, 460

Royal Marines: at Antwerp, 448–9, 454

Royal Naval Air Service, 457, 462

Royal Navy: unpreparedness for continental war, 40; mobilised, 71; commitment to Channel and North Sea, 88; allows *Goeben* to escape, 110; and proposed Baltic coast landing, 131; reputation, 356; dominance, 357, 374; and German surface raiders, 358; economic blockade of Germany, 359, 362, 385, 547; inactivity, 360, 384; successfully convoys troops to France, 362, 385; conditions, 365; communications weakness, 366–7, 376; ship losses, 377; gunnery, 378; subordination and lack of initiative, 382; contribution to war, 385; strength and casualties, 384; shells Belgian coast, 465; Ships: *Aboukir*, 376; *Agincourt* (earlier *Sultan Osman I*), 115; *Amphion*, 295; *Arethusa*, 364, 367–8, 371–2; *Audacious*, 377; *Birmingham*, 359–60; *Canopus*, 377–8; *Cressy*, 376; *Dreadnought*, 2, 213; *Endymion*, 356; *Fearless*, 367–8; *Glasgow*, 377; *Good Hope*, 377; *Hogue*, 376–7; *Invincible*, 368–9; *Laertes*, 370; *Lancaster*, 382; *Laurel*, 370; *Liberty*, 370; *Lion*, 365, 369, 372; *Lookout*, 364; *Lurcher*, 364, 368, 371; *Monmouth*, 377; *New Zealand*, 369; *Orion*, 382; *Princess Royal*, 369; *Queen Mary*, 369; *Southampton*, 359, 368, 370; *Weymouth*, 357; Submarines: E–4, 368

Rupprecht, Crown Prince of Bavaria: commands German Sixth and Seventh Armies, 172, 175, 443; awarded Iron Cross, 180; in Battle of Mortagne, 246, 248; drive on Nancy, 304; Moltke supports in westward drive, 314–15; repulsed at Nancy, 316; complains to Moltke, 329; on retreat at Marne, 336; blamed for Marne failure, 338; threatens Arras, 444; losses, 484; and attack on Ypres, 493

Russell, Lt. Col. Alick, 4
Russell, Bertrand, 125
Russell, Charles Edward, 208
Russia: revolution (1905), 3; in Triple Entente, 7, 32; believes in impending conflict with Germany, 11; economic development, 12; ethnic minorities in, 13; upper-class lifestyle, 13; alliance and relations with France, 15, 35; army strength, 15, 129, 500; influence in Balkans, 15–16; internal unrest and dissatisfaction, 15; as rival to Britain in central Asia, 35; prospective landing in Pomerania, 40; and Austria's ultimatum to Serbia, 45, 54–5; French presidential state visit to, 49–53; warns Austria over ultimatum to Serbia, 51; wishes for postponement of war, 53; preparations for war, 56–8, 65–6, 73;

reaction to Serb rejection of Austrian ultimatum, 64–5; on Austrian mobilisation, 72; mobilisation, 72–4, 81, 87, 105; French support for, 74; German hostility to, 78; Germany declares war on, 81; view of England, 97–8; supposed responsibility for war, 102; popular attitudes to war, 124, 500; early troop dispositions, 129; Austrian forces face, 140; atrocities against Polish Jews, 193; defeats by Germany, 280–3, 396, 555; prisoners at Tannenberg, 281; military inadequacies, 284; signs Declaration of London, 309; defeats Austria in Galicia, 386–401; army composition and variety, 387; anti-Semitism, 393, 545; takes German prisoners, 395; casualties, 400, 553, 556, 561; commissariat and logistical weaknesses, 401, 408; wounded and treatment, 402–3; opposes Germans, 407; industrial disputes, 414; aircraft, 457–9, 462; troops rumoured on way to Britain, 464; shell and equipment shortage, 502–3; in Second World War, 551; hopes for separate Hungarian peace, 553; quits war (1918), 561; supports Serbia, 561–2

Russian army: behaviour towards civilians, 193; officers and troops, 260–1; behaviour and ill-discipline, 270; dress and equipment, 270; campaign in East Prussia, 271; fighting qualities, 504; composition and standards, 508

RUSSIAN ARMY FORMATIONS AND UNITS
Armies: First, 268, 273, 283; Second, 268, 281, 501–2; Fifth, 501
Regiments: Sumskoi Hussars, 265–6; 85th Infantry, 280

Russo-Japanese War (1904–5), 3, 13, 15
Ruthenes, 393
Rutz, Capt. Ottmar, 472, 477
Ruzsky, Gen. Nicolai, 388–9, 395, 502–3

Sack, Sgt. Gustav, 475, 529, 533
Saint-Gond marshes, 328
Saint-Mihiel salient, 315
St Petersburg: popular reaction to war, 124
Saint-Quentin, 222–3, 239–41, 249
Saint-Saëns, Camille, 437
Sainte-Geneviève, 315
Šajnović, Dr, 509
Saki: 'The Easter Egg', xxxvii
Sanborn, Josh, 263
Sambre, river, 195

Samsonov, Gen. Aleksandr: command in East Prussia, 268, 270, 273–6, 278, 389; Tannenberg defeat, 280–2, 284; suicide, 282

Samuel, Herbert, 549

San, river, Galicia, 498

San Giuliano, Antonio di, Marquis of, 415

Santoopen, 193

Sarajevo: assassination (1914), xxxi, xxxvii–xxxix

Sarrail, Gen. Maurice, 328, 339

Sarraut, Albert, 420

Sarsfield, Maj. William, 348

Sava, river and valley, 154–6, 512–13

Savinsky, Alexander A., 73

Sazonov, Sergei: as Russian foreign minister, 14; and Russian need for Britain, 35; disbelieves Austrian threat to Serbia, 50; indecisiveness, 51–3; on Austrian ultimatum to Serbia, 56; orders mobilisation, 56–7; promises to support Serbia, 58; wants partial mobilisation, 65; urges general mobilisation, 72–3; and outbreak of war, 97

Scapa Flow, 356, 358, 383

Scarborough: German navy bombards, 380–3, 543

Scévola, Guirand de, 532

Schacht, Lt., 227, 231

Schädla, Gertrud, 5, 58, 82, 282, 338, 418, 428, 515

Schädla, Gottfried ('Friedel'), 338, 419

Schädla, Ludwig, 418

Schauroth, Lt. von, 491

Scheidemühl, East Prussia, 272

Schleswig-Holstein, 336

Schlieffen, Alfred, Graf von: strategic plan, 26–7, 32, 78, 129, 160, 202, 247, 305; fallacy in plan, 314; fears stalemate, 354

Schneider, Lt. Constantin, 388–9, 392, 395, 397, 400, 405–6, 458, 498, 503, 559–60

Schneider, Capt. Fritz, 236

Schratt, Katharina, 9

Schulz, Lt. Hugo, 147

Schwald, Lt. Col., 276

Schweida, Helene, 185, 429, 541

Schweinetz, Lt. Hermann, Graf von, 363

Scott, Charles Prestwich, 98

Scott-James, Rolfe, 424, 562

Scott-Mcfie, Robert, 538

Sczuka, Elizabeth, 283

Sczuka, Johann, 265, 269

Sczuka family, 283, 406

Seely, Col. Jack, 23, 449–50

Seestern (pseud., i.e. Ferdinand Grauthoff): 1906, 117–18

Seilles, Belgium, 192

Senegalese troops, 539

Septmonts, 346

Serbia: ambitions for pan-Slav state, xxxiv; Austria first invades, xli, 54, 138–9, 561; Austrian militancy towards, 11, 17, 29–30, 41; Russian influence in, 16; conditions, 17–18; Austrian ultimatum to, 45, 49, 51, 54–6, 58, 60–1; replies to Austria's ultimatum, 62; mobilises, 63, 104; Austria declares war on, 68; army complicity in Franz Ferdinand murder, 98; defences against Austria, 129; martial qualities, 141–2, 149–50; campaign in, 145–53, 386, 509–13; partisan guerrillas, 146–8; civilians executed, 147–9, 157; casualties, 153, 158, 553; troops occupy Zemun, 154–5; Austria invades for second time (September 1914), 155–7; receives ammunition from France, 511; refugees, 511, 514; laid waste by war, 513–14; treatment of Austrians in war, 513; overrun, 560

Serbian Relief Fund, 113

Serret, Col., 166–7, 172

sexual activity, 418

Shaw, George Bernard: disparages Grey, 38; at outbreak of war, 97; satirical comments, 114–15; disbelieves German atrocities, 189

Shepherd, Capt. Ernest, 353

Sherriff, R.C., 421

sicknesses and illness, 529; see also medical services

Siegener, Lt., 235

Siegringen, Theodor von, 505

signalling and communications, 525; see also radio

Simon, Sir John, 61, 91, 93

Singer, Maj., 347

Slade, Rear-Admiral Sir Edmund, 357, 362

Slavdom: Kaiser's hostility to, 9; and prospective struggle with Germanism, 11; Conrad wishes to destroy, 29

Slavs: distribution, 16; in Austrian army, 140

Slovenia: martial law, 141

Smith, Sgt: at Mons, 212

Smith-Dorrien, Lt. Gen. Sir Horace: at Mons, 204–6, 210, 469; and Haig's panic attack at Landries, 218–19; qualities, 220, 245; stand at Le Cateau, 220–9, 231, 233, 236–7, 252; countermands Wilson's order to abandon equipment, 242; told of Joffre's counterattack, 248; refuses access to press, 296; reluctance to support Joffre, 308; orders witnessing of execution of deserters, 322; army command, 548

Social Democratic Party (German): hostility to militarism, 4; anti-war protests, 59, 66, 71; and Russian mobilisation, 81; agrees to fund war loan, 111

socialism: rise of, 3

'soixante-quinze' (French 75 mm field gun), 179, 183

Sokolov, Cornet, 73

soldiers: reaction to war, 527–33, 538–9

Somme, river, 292

Somme, Battle of the: British casualties, 181

Sordet, Gen. Jean-François, 164, 236

Soupir, 348–50, 493

South Africa: enters war, 96

Soutou, Georges-Henri, 100

Spears, Lt. Edward Louis (later Sir): on widespread effect of war, xxv; on French attack, 198; on secretive conferences, 223; on Lanrezac, 249–50, 300; on German comments on British running away, 254; makes telephone contact with British unit, 292; and Maistre's pessimism, 302; describes Franchet d'Espèrey, 307; on Joffre, 308; on British agreeing to support Joffre, 309; on Joffre's visit to Sir John French, 311–12; on Maud'huy's encounter with deserter, 327; on operations across Aisne, 345; *Liaison 1914*, 198

Spee, Admiral Graf Maximilian von, 377, 378

Spemann, Lt. Adolf, 525, 533

Spencer, Wilbert, 539, 557

Speyer, Gen. Alexei, 259

Spies, Johannes, 366

Squire, Sir John C., 115

Stanley, Venetia, 59, 61, 72, 87, 95, 121, 293, 377, 378, 419, 549

Stanojevitch, Lt. Djordje, 514

Stavka (Russian high command), 168, 259, 388

Steed, Henry Wickham, 11, 97

Stein, Pte. Charles, 136, 165, 460, 464–6, 534

Steinhauer, Gustav, 97

Stenitzer, Dr Richard von, 387, 399, 405, 458

Stevens, Henry, 448

Stiebing, Cpl. Franz, 192

Stillried von Rathenitz, Rüdiger, Freiherr, 397, 430

Stitzinger, Walter, 379

Stojadinović, Milan, 68

Stork, Wilhelm von, 41

Strachan, Sir Hew, 338

Strandman, Vasily, 54–5, 68, 143

Strasbourg, 166, 171

Stumm, Wilhelm von, 2

Stumpf, Richard, 85, 358, 559

Sturdee, Rear Admiral Sir Doveton, 378

Subenbach, Cpl., 229

submarines: prejudices against, 369–70

Sukhomlinov, Vladimir, 14, 57, 268

Šuklje, Fran, 98

Sulzbach, Herbert, 304, 433–4, 527

Sunarić, Dr Josip, xxxviii

Sutherland, George Granville, 5th Duke of, 113

Swinchat, Sgt., 520

Sykes, Sir Mark, 122

Szapáry, Count Friedrich, 52

Szécsen, Count, 109

Tankosić, Maj. Vojin, xxxiv

Tannenberg, Battle of (1914), 275–82, 284, 395–6, 401, 507

Tanner, Pte. Edward, 473

Tappen, Lt. Col. Gerhard, 103, 185, 246, 329, 335–6, 343

Tastenfeld, Baron Schluga von, 33

Tennyson, Capt. Lionel (later Lord), 107, 322, 336, 346, 464, 473, 516, 520

Terraine, John, 299

Tersztyanzky, Gen. Karl, 149

Teschner, Maj. Otto, 167

Thalloczy, Lajos, 58

Thomas, Cpl. Ted, 204

Thurston, Capt. Lionel, 350

Times, The: on servant shortage, 49; opposes Austria's hostility to Serbia, 58, 61, 87; on Ulster question, 59–60; on European balance of power, 85; blames Germans for war, 91; patriotic sentiments, 112; denounces Haldane, 126; publishes letter complaining on age limits on officers, 128; on Joffre's armies, 174; on early actions on Western Front, 186, 292; argues for non-resistance by civilians in invasion, 188; letter from Edward Lyttelton, 294; obituaries of fallen officers, 295; reporting difficulties from front, 296–7; questions German retreat, 351; advertises houses for rent to refugees, 416; on officer casualties, 438

Tirpitz, Grand-Admiral Alfred von: visits Franz Ferdinand, xxxii ; British wariness

Tirpitz, Grand Admiral Alfred von: – *cont.*
of, 8; daughters' education, 8; wishes to
postpone war, 31; on British and German
press freedom, 66; on Bethmann's
statement to Reichstag on outbreak of war,
95; on naval inaction, 361–2; on Heligoland
Bight action, 374; and Kaiser's
disenchantment with war, 432; on
declaring Wilhelm insane, 555
Tirpitz, Lt. Wolfgang, 374
Tisza, Count István, 45, 54
Tolstoy, Aleksei, 403, 499, 508
Tonypandy, S. Wales, 22
Toulouse: women postal workers, 429
Trades Union Congress, 112
trenches and trench warfare, 516, 526, 530,
532
Trentinian, Gen. Edgard de, 178–9
Treplin, Anna, 117, 338, 421, 461
Treplin, Ingeborg, 421, 461
Treplin, Lorenz, 162, 353, 535
Trevor, Maj. Bertie, 189, 227–8, 231, 235
Trieste, 561
Triple Alliance (Germany-Austria-Italy), 7, 9,
32
Triple Entente (Britain-France-Russia), 7, 21,
32
Troubridge, Admiral Ernest, 377
Trouée des Charmes, 246
Troyon, 315
Truchet, Abel, 532
Trushnovich, Lt. Aleksandr, 505–7
Tuchman, Barbara: *August 1914*, xxvi
Tuffnau, Lt. Paul, 319–20
Turkey: enters war, 414; campaign against,
551; casualties, 553, 561
Turpin, Eugène, 439
Tyrwhitt, Commodore Reginald, 363–4,
367–71, 373
Tzynowicz, Laura, Countess de, 410

U-boats: 1917 campaign, 356–7, 359, 385;
increasing use, 383; Individual: U9, 376–7;
U15, 360
Ulster *see* Northern Ireland
United States of America: economic strength,
4; protests at British blockade of Germany,
359, 547; profits from neutrality, 415, 561;
view of war, 435; enters war, 552
Urbal, Gen. d', 527

Vaillant, Edouard, 341
Valjevo, Serbia, 512

Vansittart, Sir Robert, 51
Varešanin, Gen. Marijan, xxxvii
Velino Selo, Serbia, 155
Verdun, 178, 310, 315–16, 335, 442, 515, 556
Versailles Treaty (1919), xxiii, 563
Vickers (company), 7
Victor Emmanuel III, King of Italy, 55, 108
Victoria Cross: awards, 212, 218, 233, 235,
253–4, 472, 478, 494
Vienna: cultural-social life, 10–11
Villers, Countess, 426
Villers-Cotterêts, 254, 256, 298
Virton, Belgium, 178–80
Vistula, river, 271
Vitry-le-François (Joffre's HQ), 170
Viviani, René: on state visit to Russia, 49–50,
52–3, 69; absence criticised, 70; on
mobilisation, 83–4; receives German
declaration of war, 94; on *l'union sacrée*,
112; Bertie describes as nervous, 200;
retains premiership, 289
Vogel, Lt., 558
Vogel, Pte. (of Silesian 105th Regiment), 185
Vosges, 515
Vossische Zeitung, 257, 541–2, 554
Vrhovnik, Ivan, 498

Wagner, Capt., 150
Waldersee, Gen. Count Georg von, on
prospect of war, 32
Waldmeyer (German oboist), 491
Walton, L/Sgt. William, 473
War Book (British), 103–4
War Council (British): appointed, 129; meets,
131–2
War Office (British): and War Book, 104
warfare: technological developments, 2–3;
moral and idealistic considerations, 547–8
Warnod, André, 534
Warrender, Rear-Admiral Sir George, 8, 380–1
Warsaw: bombed, 503
Waterloo, Battle of (1815): centenary, 34
Watson, Capt. Hugh, RN, 367–8
Webb, Beatrice, 123–4
Weber, Max, 6
Wedgwood, Josiah Clement, 96
Weiss, Lt., 148
Weizsäcker, Ernst, 376, 383
Wells, H.G., 48, 188
Wenninger, Gen. Karl, Ritter von, 80, 336
Western Front: 1914 campaign ends, 442;
extent, 515; life on, 516–18, 525; trench
warfare, 516; sorties, 519–20; mined, 520;

wounded and medical services, 523–4; centrality to war, 551; stalemate, 552–3

Weygand, Col. Maxime: as Foch's chief of staff, 320; on French resistance to trenches, 321

Wharton, Edith, 84

Whitby: bombarded, 380–1

Wichura, Gen. George, 335

Wilamowitz-Moellendorff, Ulrich von, 437

Wilde, Oscar, 24

Wildman, Alan, 124

Wilebinsky (German oboist), 491

Wiles, Frederick, 98

Wilhelm II, Kaiser of Germany: visits Franz Ferdinand, xxxii; informed of Franz Ferdinand's assassination, xl; recklessness, xxix; celebrates centenary of Battle of Leipzig, 5; character and lifestyle, 5–7; commitment to naval enlargement, 8; dismisses British concept of balance of power, 8; rule and authority, 26, 75; and prospect of war, 28, 77; calls war council (Dec. 1912), 30–1; and Franz Joseph's retribution against Serbia, 43; annual yachting trip, 44; militancy, 46; ignores anti-war protests, 71; vacillations, 76; advises Austria to limit action, 77; Falkenhayn warns against interference, 78; despises French, 80; signs mobilisation order, 80; presumes British non-intervention, 85; on declaration of war, 94; loses stature at outbreak of war, 97; on incompetence of spy chiefs, 97; regime, 99; addresses Reichstag on outbreak of war, 102; returns British uniforms, 114; on Lorraine fighting, 176; as Supreme Warlord, 184; alleges misconduct by Belgian civilians, 190; moves HQ to Luxembourg, 250; power to appoint and dismiss chief of staff, 338, 554; encourages naval development, 361; acknowledges British naval superiority, 374; and Conrad's plight in Galicia, 407; war-weariness, 431–2; visits front, 444; peace conditions, 545; complains of exclusion by General Staff, 553; resists appointment of Ludendorff as C.in C., 555; responsibility for war, 563

Wilhelm II, King of Württemberg, 136

Wilhelm, Crown Prince of Germany ('Little Willy'): believes in Germany's popularity in England, 6; command in Belgium, 178; awarded Iron Cross, 180; Fifth Army casualties, 184; assault at Vaux-Marie, 339; false news stories on, 438

Williamson, Lt. A.J.N., 422

Wilson, Cessie, Lady, 401

Wilson, Maj. Gen. Sir Henry: and Curragh Mutiny, 23; on lack of commitment to France, 36; unimpressed by Grey and Haldane, 38; on inadequacy of army, 39; promotes military relations with France, 39; qualities, 39–40; advocates sending troops to France, 131–2; as sub-chief of staff, 133; on early British military objective, 134; urges strengthening Belgian defences, 161; on Verdun battle, 178; incompetence at GHQ, 214; instructs II Corps to retreat from Le Cateau, 221; and disharmony at GHQ, 224; orders divisional commanders to abandon equipment, 241; refuses support to Lanrezac, 250; meets Franchet d'Espèrey, 309; persuades Sir John French to support Joffre, 310; hopes for early Russian success, 401; on British attitude to Belgium, 468

Wilson, Woodrow: calls for US neutrality, 415; view of belligerents, 435; mediation offer, 542

Wimborne, Alice Katherine, Viscountess, 514

Winslow, Caroll Dana, 40

Winterbottom, Gladys, 129, 445

Winterer, Otto, 432

Wintzingerode, Capt. Hans, Graf von, 64

wireless see radio

Wittgenstein, Ludwig, 125, 400, 418, 432, 438

Wolff, Theodor, 63–4, 81–2

Wollocombe, Lt. Tom, 205, 210–11, 214, 222, 229, 237

women: emancipation, 3; provoke men to enlist, 128; role in war, 129, 428–30; service wives' pensions and payments, 413; in Austrian army, 505

Worsley, Sackville George, Lord, 481

Wright, Capt. Theodore, VC, 212

Württemberg, Albrecht, Duke of, 184, 464, 469; see also Wilhelm II, King of Württemberg

Wüster, Lt. Roland, 152, 509, 511–12

Wyatt, Guardsman George, VC, 218

Wyndham, Percy, 419

Wytschaete, 483, 487

Yanushkevich, Gen., 391

Yarmouth, 379

Yate, Maj. Cal, VC, 235

Yeadon, Maj., 495
Young, Filson, 357, 360, 366, 374, 384, 431
Young Bosnians, xxxiv–xxxv, xxxvi–xxxviii
Young Turks, 11, 110
Ypres, First Battle of (1914), 467–79, 481–96,
 552
Yser canal, 515
Yugoslavia: proposed, 139; established, 560

Zaeschmar, Walther, 383
Zandvoorde ridge, Flanders, 481–2
Zeilinger, Otto, 415
Zemun, Serbia, 138, 155
Zenoch, Rosa, 440

Zeppelin, Ferdinand, Count, 2
Zeppelin, Maj., 351
Zeppelins see airships
Zerajić, Bogdan, xxxvii
Zeynek, Lt. Col. Theodor, Ritter von, 387,
 394, 505, 507
Zimmermann, Arthur, 43
Zitzewitz, Lt., 482
Živanović, Živan, 54, 138, 142–3
Zlota Lipa, river, 395
Zonnebeke, 494
Zouaves, 320
Zujović, Jovan, 63, 145, 155
Župan, Tomo, 497